Tolley's Inheritance Tax

AF741457

Barcode: 16232
Tolley's Inheritance Tax 2024-25
Taunton > Library

In the preparation of this guide, every effort has been made to offer current, correct and clearly expressed information. However, the information in the text is intended to afford general guidelines only. This publication should not be regarded as offering a complete explanation of the tax matters referred to and is subject to changes in law and practice.

No responsibility for any loss occasioned to any person acting or refraining from action as a result of any material included in or omitted from this publication can be accepted by the authors or publishers. This work does not render legal, accounting or tax advice. Readers are encouraged to consult with professional advisers for advice concerning specific matters before making any decision.

Tolley's Inheritance Tax 2024–25

by

Malcolm Gunn CTA (Fellow)

Tolley®

LexisNexis® UK & Worldwide

United Kingdom	RELX (UK) Limited trading as LexisNexis®, 1–3 Strand, London WC2N 5JR
LNUK Global Partners	LexisNexis® encompasses authoritative legal publishing brands dating back to the 19th century including: Butterworths® in the United Kingdom, Canada and the Asia-Pacific region; Les Editions du Juris Classeur® in France; and Matthew Bender® worldwide. Details of LexisNexis® locations worldwide can be found at www.lexisnexis.com

© 2024 RELX (UK) Ltd.

Published by LexisNexis®
This is a Tolley title®

All rights reserved. No part of this publication may be reproduced in any material form (including photocopying or storing it in any medium by electronic means and whether or not transiently or incidentally to some other use of this publication) without the written permission of the copyright owner except in accordance with the provisions of the Copyright, Designs and Patents Act 1988 or under the terms of a licence issued by the Copyright Licensing Agency, 1 St Katharine's Way, London, E1W 1UN. Applications for the copyright owner's written permission to reproduce any part of this publication should be addressed to the publisher.
Warning: The doing of an unauthorised act in relation to a copyright work may result in both a civil claim for damages and criminal prosecution.

Some of the content in this title is reproduced under Crown copyright, under various different licensing arrangements. These may include Crown copyright and database right material re-used under the Open Government Licence v3.0 and case law licensed under the Open Justice – Licence v1.0 (or any update of such licences). Material derived from the European Institutions is © European Union, 1998-2024 and re-used under the terms of the Commission Decision 2011/833/EU. To the extent that the above licences do not apply, Crown copyright material is reproduced with the permission of the Controller of His Majesty's Stationery Office and the King's Printer for Scotland, while Parliamentary copyright material is reproduced with the permission of the Controller of His Majesty's Stationery Office.

LexisNexis® and the Knowledge Burst logo are registered trademarks of RELX Group plc, used under license. Butterworths® and Tolley® are registered trademarks of RELX (UK) Ltd. Matthew Bender® is a registered trademark of Matthew Bender & Company Inc. Other products and services may be trademarks or registered trademarks of their respective companies.
A CIP Catalogue record for this book is available from the British Library.

ISBN for this volume: 9780754559498

Printed and bound by CPI Group (UK) Ltd, Croydon, CRO 4YY

Visit LexisNexis® UK at www.lexisnexis.co.uk

About This Book

This edition gives the position for the tax year 2024–25 and includes coverage of inheritance tax provisions of **Finance (No 2) Act 2024** and all other relevant material to **1 July 2024** e.g. statutes, statutory instruments, court cases, tribunal decisions, online announcements/guidance, Statements of Practice, concessions, HMRC Manuals and other publications. The text has been updated to cover new developments such as the restriction of agricultural property relief to UK land, the proposed abolition of domicile in relation to liability to IHT, and recent changes to pension provision. Numerous improvements have been made to clarify practical points or cover recent developments, and various examples have been updated and in some cases revised to illustrate current planning techniques. The law and practice back to the introduction of inheritance are also covered in this edition. The chapters are arranged alphabetically. Worked examples are given to explain how IHT rules work in practice

We welcome all comments and suggestions for improvement to this work. You can contact us in this respect by emailing the Editor, Elaine Pugh at elaine.pugh@lexisnexis.co.uk. Any technical queries will be passed on to the author.

Contributors

Malcolm Gunn CTA (Fellow)

Malcolm Gunn is a fellow of the Chartered Institute of Taxation. He has over 50 years of experience in advising on UK tax matters. For 16 years he was editor of the weekly magazine Taxation, and in 2004 he left the magazine to concentrate on tax consultancy and advisory work, with particular focus on capital taxes and tax planning for individuals and family businesses.

Contents

Abbreviations and References

Abbreviations

A-G	Attorney-General.
AIM	Alternative Investment Market.
CA	Court of Appeal.
CCA	Court of Criminal Appeal.
CCAB	Consultative Committee of Accountancy Bodies.
CGT	Capital Gains Tax.
Ch	Chapter.
Ch D	Chancery Division.
CIR	Commissioners of HMRC ('the Board').
Commr(s)	Commissioner(s) (General or Special).
CPA	Civil Partnership Act 2004.
CTO	HMRC Capital Taxes Office.
CTT	Capital Transfer Tax.
CTTA 1984	Capital Transfer Tax Act 1984.
DTR	Double Taxation Relief.
DV	District Valuer.
ESC	HMRC Extra-Statutory Concession.
FA	Finance Act.
F(No 2)A	Finance (No 2) Act.
Fam D	Family Division (formerly Probate, Divorce and Admiralty Division).
FTT	First-tier Tribunal.
HC	House of Commons.
HL	House of Lords.
HMRC	Her Majesty's Revenue and Customs.
HMRCC	Her Majesty's Revenue and Customs Commissioners.

ICTA 1970	Income and Corporation Taxes Act 1970.
ICTA 1988	Income and Corporation Taxes Act 1988.
IHT	Inheritance Tax.
IHTA 1984	Inheritance Tax Act 1984.
IHTM	Inheritance Tax Manual.
IPDI	Immediate Post-Death Interest.
ITA	Income Tax Act 2007.
ITEPA 2003	Income Tax (Earnings and Pensions) Act 2003.
ITTOIA 2005	Income Tax (Trading and Other Income) Act 2005.
NAO	National Audit Office.
NI	Northern Ireland.
PC	Privy Council.
PCm	Personal Contact (HMRC Manual).
PDA	Probate, Divorce and Admiralty Division (now Family Division).
Pt	Part.
QB	Queen's Bench Division.
R	Rex or Regina (i.e. The Crown).
RI	Republic of Ireland (Eire).
s	Section.
Sch	Schedule [4 Sch para 10 = 4th Schedule, paragraph 10].
SC	Supreme Court.
SCS	Scottish Court of Session.
SDLT	Stamp Duty Land Tax.
SI	Statutory Instrument.
SP	HMRC Statement of Practice. (SP 7/87, 15 July 1987 = 7th Statement of Practice in 1987 issued on date shown).
SVD	Shares Valuation Division.
TCGA 1992	Taxation of Chargeable Gains Act 1992.
TSI	Transitional Serial Interest.
UKFTT	UK First-tier Tax Tribunal.
USM	Unlisted Securities Market.
VOA	Valuation Office Agency.

References

(*denotes a series accredited for citation in court).

All ER	*All England Law Reports, (Butterworths, Halsbury House, 35 Chancery Lane, London WC2A 1EL).
AC	*Law Reports, Appeal Cases, (Incorporated Council of Law Reporting for England and Wales, 3 Stone Buildings, Lincoln's Inn, London WC2A 3XN).
ATC	*Annotated Tax Cases (publication discontinued).
BTC	British Tax Cases, CCH Editions Ltd, Telford Road, Bicester, Oxfordshire OX6 0XD.
Ch	*Law Reports, Chancery Division.
EG	Estates Gazette, (The Estates Gazette Ltd., 151 Wardour Street, London W1V 4BN).
ILT	Irish Law Times.
IR	*Irish Reports, (Law Reporting Council, Law Library, Four Courts, Dublin).
KB	*Law Reports, King's Bench Division (1900–1952).
LT	Decisions of the Lands Tribunal, (Lands Tribunal, 48–49 Chancery Lane, London WC2A 1JR).
[Year] QB	*Law Reports, Queen's Bench Division (1891–1901 and 1952 onwards).
QBD	Law Reports, Queen's Bench Division (1875–1890).
Sp C	Special Commissioners' decisions, (The Court Service, 15/19 Bedford Avenue, London WC1B 3AS).
SLT	Scots Law Times.
SCD	*Simon's Special Commissioners' Decisions, (Butterworths, as above).
STC	*Simon's Tax Cases, (Butterworths, as above).
STI	Simon's Tax Intelligence, (Butterworths, as above).
TC	*Official Reports of Tax Cases, (H.M. Stationery Office, as above).
TLR	Times Law Reports.
TR	*Taxation Reports (publication discontinued).
WLR	*Weekly Law Reports, (Incorporated Council of Law Reporting, as above).

The first number in the citation refers to the volume, and the second to the page, so that [1979] 2 All ER 80 means that the report is to be found on page eighty of the second volume of the All England Law Reports for 1979. Where no volume number is given, only one volume was produced in that year. Some series have continuous volume numbers.

The Tax Chamber First-tier Tax Tribunal decisions now replace the previous General Commissioners and citation references have changed to reflect this such as FTT [2009] UKFTT 141(TC), TC00109 showing the tax case year and report number followed by the hearing number in the Tax Tribunal. Earlier cases heard before the General and Special Commissioners are still shown by their original citation reference before the change.

Where legal decisions are very recent and in the lower Courts, it must be remembered that they may be reversed on appeal. But references to the official Tax Cases ('*TC*'), and to the Appeal Cases ('*AC*') may be taken as final.

In English cases, Scottish and N. Irish decisions (unless there is a difference of law between the countries) are generally followed but are not binding, and Republic of Ireland decisions are considered (and vice versa).

Acts of Parliament, Command Papers, 'Hansard' Parliamentary Reports and Statutory Instruments are obtainable from The Stationery Office, (bookshops at 12 Bridge Street, Parliament Square, London SW1A 2JX (tel 0207 219 3890) and elsewhere at http://www.tso.co.uk/contact/bookshops/ **Hansard** (referred to as HC Official Report or HL Official Report) references are to daily issues and do not always correspond to the columns in the bound editions. **N.B.** Statements in Parliament, while useful as indicating the intention of enactments, have no legal authority if the Courts interpret the wording of the Act differently (except in the limited circumstances mentioned in **14.11** DETERMINATIONS AND APPEALS).

1

Introduction and Basic Principles

Simon's Taxes. See **I1.3**, **I1.4**.

Other Sources. Foster, Part A and E1.02.

Inheritance tax — an introduction

[1.1] The aim of this chapter is to provide a brief outline of the principal features and key concepts of inheritance tax. It is intended to illustrate only the basic mechanism of the tax as this is essential for an understanding of the detailed provisions covered in the following chapters. For complete details of any particular topic or area, reference should be made to the appropriate chapter.

Function and scope of tax

[1.2] Inheritance tax is a tax on chargeable transfers made by an *individual* during his life and on the value of his estate on his death. Various exemptions and reliefs are available to lessen the impact of the tax.

The tax is charged on certain events relating to settled property and there is a separate charging structure for settlements without interests in possession. See 40 SETTLEMENTS: DISCRETIONARY TRUSTS AND OTHER TRUSTS OF RELEVANT PROPERTY for new trusts arising on or after 22 March 2006. In addition, certain transfers made by close companies may be attributed to the individual participators. See 11 CLOSE COMPANIES.

Individuals domiciled in the UK are liable to inheritance tax on all chargeable transfers, whether or not the property transferred is situated in the UK. Individuals who are not domiciled or deemed domiciled in the UK are not liable to IHT on transfers of property situated outside the UK, except in relation to certain assets holding UK residential property, but are so liable, with certain exceptions, on chargeable transfers of property in the UK. In certain circumstances, double tax relief may be available. See **16** DOMICILE for the extended IHT meaning of 'domicile', **20** EXCLUDED PROPERTY and **46** SITUS for full details of what property is outside the scope of the tax, and **18** DOUBLE TAXATION RELIEF for situations where DTR may be available.

Starting date and main changes to CTT

[1.3] The revised provisions relating to inheritance tax effectively replaced capital transfer tax for events occurring after 17 March 1986 although the name of the tax was not formally changed until 25 July 1986, the date of Royal Assent to the *Finance Act 1986*. The revised provisions do not affect the tax chargeable on a transfer of value occurring before 18 March 1986. [*FA 1986, Sch 19 para 40*]. However, chargeable transfers made before that date and within the lifetime cumulation period for IHT purposes may affect the tax payable on subsequent transfers.

The main amendments to the CTT provisions in the IHT legislation were:

(a) the removal of liability for tax on certain transfers of value where the transfer occurs at least seven years before the transferor's death;
(b) the reduction in the period during which the values transferred by chargeable transfers are aggregated from ten to seven years;
(c) the increase in the period before death within which tax on chargeable lifetime transfers is recomputed at the higher rates applicable on death from three to seven years (but subject to the introduction of taper relief where the transfer is more than three years before death); and
(d) the re-introduction of legislation for **22** GIFTS WITH RESERVATION similar to the old estate duty provisions.

The *Capital Transfer Tax Act 1984* may be cited as the *Inheritance Tax Act 1984*. Any reference to CTT in the *1984 Act* or any other Act passed before or in the same session as the *FA 1986* or any document executed, made, served or issued on or before the passing of *FA 1986* has effect as a reference to inheritance tax unless relating to a liability to tax arising before 25 July 1986. [*FA 1986, s 100*].

Charge to tax

[1.4] Inheritance tax is charged on the value transferred by a chargeable transfer. [*IHTA 1984, s 1*].

A chargeable transfer is any transfer of value made by an individual other than an **21** EXEMPT TRANSFER. [*IHTA 1984, s 2(1)*]. Accordingly, companies are outside the scope of charge but there are provisions for apportionment of transfers of value to the participators where a close company makes a transfer of value: see **11** CLOSE COMPANIES.

A potentially exempt transfer (PET)

A potentially exempt transfer (PET) is a transfer of value made by an individual after 17 March 1986 but before 22 March 2006 which would otherwise be a chargeable transfer and which is either a gift to another individual or a gift into an accumulation and maintenance trust or a trust for a disabled person. After 21 March 2006 a PET is a transfer of value made by an individual which would otherwise be a chargeable transfer and which is either a gift to another individual (see Example 1 below) or into a trust for a disabled person or into a trust for bereaved minors on the ending of an immediate post-death interest (IPDI). See **39** SETTLEMENTS WITH INTERESTS IN POSSESSION and **43** SETTLEMENTS: TRUSTS FOR BEREAVED MINORS.

With respect to transfers of value made, and other events occurring, after 16 March 1987 but before 22 March 2006, certain gifts by individuals into and out of settlements with interests in possession are also included. From 22 March 2006, however, there are certain transitional rules that ensure that new interests in possession which are created out existing ones before 6 October 2008 (originally 6 April 2008) i.e. TSIs ('transitional serial interests') still will qualify as PETs. See **35** POTENTIALLY EXEMPT TRANSFERS for full details. A potentially exempt transfer made seven years or more before the transferor's death is an exempt transfer and any other potentially exempt transfer is a chargeable transfer. A potentially exempt transfer is assumed to be an exempt transfer during the seven years following the transfer (or, if earlier, until immediately before the transferor's death). [*IHTA 1984, s 3A; FA 1986, Sch 19 para 1; F(No 2)A 1987, s 96; FA 2006, Sch 20 para 9; FA 2010, s 53(2)*].

In summary therefore a PET will, from 22 March 2006, comprise:

- transfers by individuals to other individuals;
- transfers by individuals to certain trusts for the disabled (see **44** SETTLEMENTS: TRUSTS FOR DISABLED PERSONS);
- transfers on or after 22 March 2006 by an individual to a bereaved minor's trust on the coming to an end of an immediate post-death interest (see **43** SETTLEMENTS: TRUSTS FOR BEREAVED MINORS);
- transfers before 22 March 2006 by an individual to an accumulation and maintenance trust (see *Marquess of Linlithgow v HMRC (and related appeals)* [2010] CSIH 19 at **41** SETTLEMENTS: ACCUMULATION AND MAINTENANCE TRUSTS);
- transfers by an individual into an interest in possession trust in which, for transfers on or after 22 March 2006, the beneficiary has a disabled person's interest (see **44** SETTLEMENTS: TRUSTS FOR DISABLED PERSONS); and
- certain transfers on the termination or disposal of an individual's beneficial interest in possession in settled property (these are in restricted circumstances following *FA 2006* and *FA 2010* below and at **28** LIFE ASSURANCE POLICIES AND ANNUITIES; **39** SETTLEMENTS WITH INTERESTS IN POSSESSION).

FA 2010 PET anti-avoidance

Following the *Finance Act 2010* it was clarified that a potential loophole whereby a person makes a settlement which confers an interest in possession on another person was to be blocked from 9 December 2009. That other person, it suggests, pays full value within *IHTA 1984, s 10* (i.e. arm's length price between two unconnected people) for the interest in settled property. In such an event neither person would have made a transfer of value because of *s 10*. The settled property then falls out of the estate of the purchaser of the interest because *IHTA 1984, s 5(1)(1A)* has the effect that an interest in possession (but this does not apply to a disabled person's interest) acquired under a new lifetime settlement made after 21 March 2006 does not for IHT purposes form part of the estate of the person entitled to the interest in possession. The new legislation has the effect of applying to a *s 5(1B)* interest the IHT charging provisions relating to the termination of an interest in possession during the life of the person entitled to it, and prevent such an event from being a potentially exempt transfer.

In summary, this anti-avoidance strategy ensures that the pre-22 March 2006 IHT treatment for settled property subject to an interest in possession also applies to settled property subject to an interest in possession to which a person domiciled in the UK became beneficially entitled on or after 9 December 2009 by virtue of a disposition not intended to confer gratuitous benefit, i.e. *s 10*. See below. [*IHTA 1984, ss 3A, 5 as amended by FA 2010, s 53(2)(3)(10)*].

Transfer of value

A transfer of value is any disposition made by a person (and not just individuals) as a result of which the value of their estate immediately after the disposition is less than it would be but for the disposition; and the amount by which it is less is the value transferred by the transfer. A person is treated as making a notional transfer of value of their whole estate immediately before their death. [*IHTA 1984, ss 3(1), 4(1)*]. A disposition is not a transfer of value if made in an arm's length (or similar) transaction. [*IHTA 1984, s 10*]. (See **48** TRANSFER OF VALUE for extended meanings of 'transfer of value' and 'disposition' and **49** TRANSFERS ON DEATH for provisions relating specifically to such transfers.)

Since the reduction in value in a person's estate includes the payment of the IHT itself where this is paid by the transferor, it is necessary in such cases to gross-up the 'net' value at the appropriate tax rate (see **1.7** below).

Person's estate

A person's estate is the combination of all the property to which *they* are beneficially entitled. However, a person's estate immediately before their death (on which inheritance tax is payable) does not include excluded property. A person beneficially entitled to an interest in possession in settled property created under a lifetime settlement made before 22 March 2006 is treated as beneficially entitled to that property. Trust property held on statutory trusts for a minor child due to intestacy or trusts drawn in similar terms by reason of the parent's will or as a result of the Criminal Injuries Compensation Scheme is a bereaved minors trust and is not part of the child's estate whilst the trust continues even if the child is entitled to the income. Similarly, where a person becomes beneficially entitled to an interest in possession in settled property after 21 March 2006 and the interest is not an immediate post-death interest, a disabled person's interest or a transitional serial interest, the property does not form part of the beneficiary's estate. [*IHTA 1984, ss 5(1)(1A), 49(1), 71A; FA 2006, Sch 20 para 10*]. See *Faulkner (Adams' Trustee) v CIR* [2001] STC SCD 112 Sp C 278. See **19** ESTATE for extensions and qualifications of this basic definition.

Example 1

A wishes to pay for his grandson AA's school fees in respect of attendance at independent school and contracts with the said school (see below) for a one-off payment in the current year to be made of £74,000 in advance which will ensure that the child's education is paid for from the age of 13 to 18 without any increases in school fees over the period. Mr A has only made previous transfers to his son in 2009/10 of £318,000 which equates to a cumulation of £312,000 after using available annual exemptions as at 6 April 2010. Mr A has also agreed with the school that there will not be a refund due to Mr A of the school fees on his death.

This agreement is made between the Governors of [**Select Independent School**] by their duly authorised officer [**A. Bursar**] (hereinafter called 'the school') of the first part; and [**Mr A**].

Whereas it is proposed that [**Mr A**] does make a payment of school fees to the school until [**Mr A's**] grandson [**Master AA**] completes full time education (or as the case may be). Such said fees shall be paid to the school by [**Mr A**] in advance in the sum of £74,000 and the receipt by the school shall be sufficient discharge.

1. In consideration of the payment by [**Mr A**] of the said school fees the school agrees to keep a place open for the child [**Master AA**] until he has completed full time education or cease such education at the agreement of the contracting parties.

Etc.

This is a transfer of value within *IHTA 1984, s 3(1)* since the value of A's estate is diminished by the disposition. However, Master AA does not receive any property from A so the gift is not within *IHTA 1984, s 3A(2)(a)*. But whilst benefiting Master AA is his estate increased? Is therefore the transfer a PET?

Under *IHTA 1984, s 3A(2)(b)*, where property does not becomes comprised in the estate of another person, a transfer may still be treated as a gift to an individual provided two conditions are satisfied. These conditions are that:

(a) property does not become comprised in the estate of another person (not 'individual'), but

(b) the estate of another individual is increased.

The first condition is not satisfied because the cash given does not become directly comprised in the estate of Master AA. The second condition is not satisfied either even though the value of Master AA's estate is effectively increased by the gift. This is because the value transferred is attributable to property that has become comprised in the estate of another person. See also IHTM04058 and IHTM04060.

On the one hand tested against the definition of a PET, the gift is a transfer of value by Mr A which is chargeable but on the other hand it does not satisfy the condition that it is a transfer to an individual and cannot therefore be treated as a PET.

As IHT is based on the 'loss to the donor' principle the 'gift' of the payment to the school of the fees of the grandchild would potentially be immediately chargeable to IHT because the gift is not to an individual. Obviously if there is part (or all) of the Nil rate band available to cover the fees paid directly to the school then no actual tax would be payable. However, on death a chargeable transfer should be taken into account again when applying death rates. Whereas if the cash is given to the child or grandchild, normally to the parents as bare trustees, then it will drop out of account after seven years. In this case though Mr A has already utilised a majority of his Nil rate band and the following calculation has to be made.

Transferor (Mr A) bears tax

		£	£
Value of gift			74,000
Deduct exempt transfers	Note (A)		
Annual exemption 2010/11		3,000	
Annual exemption 2009/10		N/A	
			3,000
			71,000
Tax on £71,000 + £312,000 (per grossing-up table **37.1** 2010.B2). See also **1.7** below.			
0–325,000 = Nil + 1/4 (383,000 – 325,000)			14,500
Mr A's chargeable transfer			£85,500
Tax payable by Mr A			£14,500

Notes to the example

(A) As A has made previous transfers up to the Nil rate band threshold only part i.e. £13,000 (£325,000 – £312,000) to set against the transfer but also he will have only one year of annual exemption available to deduct from the transfer of value.

(B) The transfer of value is £88,500. A's estate is reduced by the gift of £74,000 plus the tax of £14,500 and has proved to an expensive way of funding the fees. With better planning Mr A should have made the school fees contribution before the gift of £318,000 to his son and utilised part of the nil rate band to cover the gift. The gift to the son would be a PET and drop out of account after seven years or, if Mr A died within the seven years, be covered by part of the nil rate band and possibly attract tapering relief on the balance. See **50** TRANSFERS WITHIN SEVEN YEARS OF DEATH.

Amount of tax charge

Rates

[1.5] After 14 March 1988 inheritance tax is charged at a single rate of 40%. After 17 March 1986 and before 15 March 1988 it was charged at progressively steeper rates. Only one table of rates is enacted which is applicable to transfers on death. Chargeable lifetime transfers are charged at one half of those rates, currently 20%, throughout the range of rate bands. Transfers made within seven years of death are charged at the death rates but in the case of chargeable transfers made in that period and more than three years before death, the tax charge is tapered. See **37** RATES OF TAX for tables and **50** TRANSFERS WITHIN SEVEN YEARS BEFORE DEATH for taper relief.

Cumulation

[1.6] Chargeable transfers are cumulated over a seven-year period and the rate of tax on any chargeable transfer will depend on the total value of any other chargeable transfers within the seven-year period ending with the date of the transfer (including, where applicable, chargeable transfers made before 18 March 1986 under the rules relating to Capital Transfer Tax). After seven years transfers drop out of the cumulative total. After 5 April 2009 no tax is payable on the first £325,000 of chargeable transfers as the rate is nil per cent. For the following year 2010–11 to the year 2014–15 the threshold remains at £325,000. See 37 RATES OF TAX for tables. Lower limits applied previously. References are made to the 'nil rate band maximum' which means that calculated in accordance with *IHTA 1984, s 8A(7)* and the Table depending on the date of death as stipulated in *FA 2008, Sch 4 para 10*. [*IHTA 1984, ss 7, 8, Sch 1; FA 1986, Sch 19 para 2; FA 2010, s 8*].

Grossing-up

[1.7] Although inheritance tax is essentially a tax based on the loss to the person giving rather than on the benefit to the person receiving, the tax itself may be paid either by the transferor or the transferee. Where the tax is paid by the transferor, it is part of the diminution in value of his estate and is itself included in the transfer of value. A 'net' transfer has to be grossed-up to arrive at the amount of the chargeable transfer.

Example 2

A transfers £352,000 to a discretionary trust on 1 October 2010. He has made no previous transfers.

(i) Transferor (A) bears tax

		£	£
Value of gift			352,000
Deduct exempt transfers	note (A)		
Annual exemption 2010/11		3,000	
Annual exemption 2009/10		3,000	
			6,000
			346,000
Tax on £346,000 (per grossing-up table 37.1 2010.B2)			
0–346,000 = Nil + 1/4 (346,000 – 325,000)			5,250
A's chargeable transfer			£351,250
Tax payable by A			£5,250

Notes to the example

(A) As A has made no previous transfers he will have two years' annual exemptions available but in cases where *FA 1986, s 102(4)* creates a deemed PET the annual exemption is not available. See http://www.hmrc.gov.uk/manuals/ihtmanual/index.htm. **21.12** EXEMPT TRANSFERS; **22** GIFTS WITH RESERVATION.

(B) The transfer of value is £357,250. A's estate is reduced by the gift of £352,000 plus the tax of £5,250.

(ii) Transferees (trustees) bear tax

	£	£
Value of gift		352,000
Deduct exempt transfers (as in (i))		6,000
A's chargeable transfer		£346,000
Tax on £346,000 (per table **37.1 2010.B1**)		
1–325,000 at 0%		
325,001–346,000 at 20%	4,200	
Tax payable by trustees		£4,200

Note

The transfer of value is £352,000. The value of the gift is the amount of the reduction in A's estate. See 7 CALCULATION OF TAX for more detailed examples.

Reduction of tax rates

[1.8] There were frequent changes in the tax rates following the introduction of capital transfer tax. For IHT purposes (and previously for CTT purposes) the rate bands are indexed in line with the retail prices index and must be increased each year unless otherwise determined by Parliament. [*IHTA 1984, s 8*]. The freezing for 2010–11 onwards of the nil rate band at £325,000 has meant that the retail prices index and the statutory indexing provisions to the RPI have been disallowed for the years to 2017–18. [*IHTA 1984, ss 7, 8, Sch; FA 2005, s 98(6); FA 2006, s 155(5); FA 2010, s 8; FA 2014, Sch 25 para* 2]. Where there has been a rate change, the new rates are used to calculate the tax on any subsequent transfer. In certain cases, because of the cumulative nature of the tax, this may mean that earlier transfers need to be 'revised' before the calculation can be made. This revision does *not* affect the amount of earlier chargeable transfers or the actual tax paid on them.

Example 3

C made a gift to a discretionary trust of £265,000 on 1 February 2004. He had made no previous transfers. He makes a further gift of £150,000 to the discretionary trust on 1 October 2010. In each case he pays any tax due.

Gift on 1 February 2004

	£	£
Value of gift		265,000
Deduct exempt transfers		
Annual exemption 2003/04	3,000	
Annual exemption 2002/03	3,000	
		6,000
		£259,000
Tax on net £254,000 per grossing-up table 37.1 2003.B2		
0–255,000 = Nil + $\frac{1}{4}$ (255,000 – 259,000)		1,000
C's chargeable transfer		£260,000
Tax payable by C		£1,000

Gift on 1 October 2010

		Gross	Tax	Net
	£	£	£	£
Cumulative totals 1.2.2004		260,000	1,000	259,000
Revision for changes of rates (per table 37.1 2010.B1)		260,000	Nil	260,000
Value of gift	150,000			
Deduct annual exemption				
2010/11	(3,000)			
2009/10	(3,000)			
	£144,000	162,500	19,500*	143,000
		£422,500	£19,500	£403,000
*Tax on net £399,000 per grossing-up table 37.1 2010.B2				
0–399,000 = Nil + $\frac{1}{4}$ (403,000 – 325,000)			19,500	
Deduct tax on previous transfer at rates applicable at 1.10.2010			Nil	
Tax payable by C			£19,500	

Although the cumulative totals of tax and 'net' transfers are subject to change every time there is a change of rates, it is important to note that

(a) the figures change for the purpose of calculating the amount of any tax on subsequent transfers only: there is no question of any repayment of tax; and

(b) the chargeable transfer (sometimes called the gross transfer) never alters. See 7 CALCULATION OF TAX for more detailed examples.

Death within seven years of transfer

[1.9] The tax on a chargeable lifetime transfer is initially calculated at one half of the death scale rates currently 20%. Where the transferor then dies within seven years of the transfer, the tax is recomputed at the higher death scale but the tax rates are tapered where the death is more than three years after the gift. If there is a reduction in tax rates between the chargeable lifetime transfer and the date of death, the additional tax, if any, is calculated as if the new table applicable on death had applied to the transfer. The tax payable cannot be reduced below that originally chargeable at half death rates. [*IHTA 1984, s 7, Sch 2 para 2; FA 1986, Sch 19 para 2, para 37*].

Where potentially exempt transfers are made within seven years of death, no tax would have been payable at the time of the transfer. On death, tax is calculated at the full death rates applying at the time of death, subject to the tapering relief.

Where a death occurs after 17 March 1986, the above provisions do not affect the tax chargeable on a chargeable transfer occurring before 18 March 1986. The tax on such a chargeable transfer will only be recomputed at the higher death rates if the transferor dies within three years of the transfer. [*FA 1986, Sch 19 para 40*].

See 50 TRANSFERS WITHIN SEVEN YEARS BEFORE DEATH.

Example 4

C in Example 3 in **1.8** above dies on 1 April 2011. He leaves his entire estate to his wife so no tax is payable on his estate on death (see **21.9** EXEMPT TRANSFERS). No further tax is due on the gift made on 1 February 2004 as the gift was made more than seven years previously so no tax is payable. Further tax is due on the gift to the discretionary trust made on 1 October 2010.

	£
Gift on 1 October 2010	
Chargeable transfer	£162,500
Tax at death rates applicable on 1 April 2011 (table **37.1** 2010.A1)	
325,000 – 422,500 at 40%	39,000
Deduct tax paid by C	19,500
Further tax payable by the trustees of the discretionary trust	£19,500

Interaction with other taxes

[1.10] Inheritance tax is levied separately from any other tax, so that it is possible, for example, for a transfer to suffer both inheritance tax and capital gains tax without any allowance in one for the other. For example, a lifetime gift of a property will be a disposal for capital gains tax purposes and if a benefit is reserved in the asset the value of it will be chargeable to IHT on the death of the donor but without the capital gains tax position being revisited. In general however a chargeable transfer for IHT enables capital gains tax hold over relief to apply. See 8 CAPITAL GAINS TAX.

Key points concerning inheritance tax

[1.11] Points to consider are as follows.

- Where property is owned as a joint tenancy, then that interest passes to the surviving joint tenant on the death of one of the joint owners but it still forms part of the deceased's estate on death for IHT purposes.
- Where a lifetime gift was made within seven years of death and IHT was charged at 20% in *lifetime* then the tax is recomputed at 40% on *death* and any additional tax is in the first instance payable by the transferee.
- Similarly where a PET becomes chargeable on the death of the transferor any extra tax will primarily become the liability of the transferee.
- Insurance cover such as diminishing term assurance may be taken out on the life of the transferor by the transferee to meet any IHT that becomes payable in the event of the transferors' death within seven years.

2

Accounts and Returns

Cross-reference. See also 3 ADMINISTRATION AND COLLECTION.

Other Sources. Foster, Part L; IHT 400 (Notes); IHTM10000.

Introduction to accounts and returns

[2.1] An account or return must be rendered in such form and containing such particulars as the Board may prescribe and an account must be supported by such books, papers and other documents, and verified (whether on oath or otherwise) in such manner as the Board may require. An account delivered to a probate registry i.e. the Probate Service (or the Probate and Matrimonial Office in Northern Ireland) is treated as delivered to the Board. [*IHTA 1984, s 257*]. See also **2.9** below. HMRC are satisfied that an accurate facsimile of an official account or other required document is within the scope of *IHTA 1984, s 257*. The most important criteria to be met are that the substitute document etc. must provide the same information as the official one; be readily recognisable as a substitute of the relevant official form; be in a form approved by HMRC and carry an agreed unique imprint; and bear the reference number of the issued official form it replaces or otherwise the taxpayer's reference. The returns for IHT on death (IHT 400, IHT 404, IHT 421, IHT 430 and IOV2) were revised in November 2012. Application for approval should be made to the Customer Service Manager at the Nottingham office of HMRC Inheritance Tax, (see below) as appropriate. (Inland Revenue Statement of Practice SP 2/93, 13 January 1993).

HMRC are introducing electronic filing of returns via the Government Gateway. Currently personal applicants are eligible to use the service where there is no IHT to pay and the application is for a grant of probate in England and Wales. Directions made under the *Inheritance Tax (Electronic Communications) Regulations 2015, SI 2015 No 1378* require that a copy of the information sent electronically should be retained for 'the specified period' which is the period of five years after the later of the following events: (i) the end of the month in which the relevant death occurred; (ii) the date on which an enquiry into the information is concluded; or (iii) the date the information is delivered by electronic communications.

Other returns on forms IHT 400 and IHT 100 may be submitted via Dropbox for which no special software is required, but contact needs to be made beforehand with HMRC at iht.agents@hmrc.gov.uk (see *Trusts and Estates Newsletter June 2020*).

Applications for an IHT reference number for a chargeable event on a trust or lifetime transfer should be made on form IHT122.

Accounts and returns

[2.2] An account is a document completed by a transferor or other taxable person providing details of a transaction in respect of which inheritance tax may apply.

A return is a document normally submitted by a person other than the transferor about transactions affecting others.

The Board has power to make regulations by statutory instrument to dispense with the delivery of accounts and also to require information where accounts are not delivered. Secondary legislation provides for simplified IHT procedures in cases of minor nil-IHT paying estates and the *Finance Act 2004* extended this to bring in most non-taxpaying estates not already qualifying. This will also include estates which are substantially over the IHT threshold (currently £325,000) but are covered by the inter-spousal exemption or bequests to charitable organisations. See *Excepted estates* at **2.11** below. Under *IHTA 1984, s 256(1)(aa)* regulations will allow personal representatives to complete a short form of return which will meet the minimum requirements for both tax and probate purposes. Once such cases are dealt with under this simplified procedure they may be considered closed to further enquiry allowing the estate to be distributed and avoiding the necessity for a certificate of discharge. Further, *s 256(1A)* may require that the information and documents provided to the probate registry (England and Wales), the sheriff in Scotland and the Probate and Matrimonial Office in Northern Ireland can be passed on to HMRC and treated as if they had been passed originally to the Board of HMRC. The penalty position would be unaffected by this conduit process. See **33** PENALTIES. [*IHTA 1984, s 256* as amended by *FA 2004, s 293*].

See 2.21 below for addresses to which accounts etc. should be delivered.

Printed signature is acceptable

[2.3] It was announced on 9 April 2020 that until further notice, HMRC will accept printed signatures on IHT400 and IHT100 forms in the circumstances where there is a professional agent acting and both:

- The names and other personal details of the LPRs or trustees are shown on the declaration page.
- The account includes a clear and unambiguous statement from the agent to confirm that all the LPRs or trustees have seen the account and have agreed to be bound by the declaration.

The suggested wording for this statement is:

> 'As the agent acting on their behalf, I confirm that all the people whose names appear on the declaration page of this Inheritance Tax Account have both:
>
> - seen the Inheritance Tax Account
> - agreed to be bound by the declaration on (page 14 of the IHT400) or (page 8 of the IHT100).'

Forms

[2.4] The principal forms currently prescribed by the Board for IHT purposes are as follows. The forms should be used for deaths and other transfers after 17 March 1986 (chargeable events after 24 July 1986 for IHT 101). Form IHT 400 must be used where a full account is required. Completed IHT 200 forms will no longer be accepted from 9 June 2009.

IHT 100 **An account of a transfer of value** (for use for lifetime transfers by individuals or the termination (during life or on death) of an interest in possession in settled property, but not by personal representatives intending to obtain a grant of probate from a Probate Registry). Also includes an account of a chargeable event (which arises under the provisions relating to settlements without interests in possession in *IHTA 1984, Pt III, Ch III*). Instruction booklet is IHT 110. This form was updated in December 2005 and includes a worksheet IHT100WS.

IHT 100 has the following event forms:

100(a) – gifts and other transfers of value;
100(b) – termination of interest in possession;
100(c) – assets ceasing to be held on discretionary trusts;
100(d) – non-interest in possession settlements, principal charge;
100(e) – charges on special trusts;
100(f) – cessation of conditional exemption;
100(g) – alternatively secured pension chargeable event.

IHT 100 has the following supplementary sheets:

D31 – domicile outside the United Kingdom;
D32 – stocks and shares;
D33 – debts due to the settlement or trust;
D34 – life assurance and annuities;
D35 – household and personal goods;
D36 – buildings and interests in land;
D37 – agricultural relief;
D38 – business relief, business or partnership interests;
D39 – foreign assets.

IHT 205 — **Return of estate information** for excepted estates.

IHT 400 — **HMRC Account** See form IHT 400 for use in applying for a grant of representation where the deceased died domiciled in the UK, except where the deceased died domiciled in the UK and personal application for a grant is being made by the proposed legal personal representative *and* the net estate chargeable to tax does not exceed the threshold for the imposition of tax at the date of death (taking into account any reliefs claimed) *and* the property to be covered by the grant does not include any settled land.

IHT400 has the following Schedules:

IHT216 – claim to transfer unused IHT nil band;
IHT401 – domicile outside the United Kingdom;
IHT402 – claim to transfer unused nil-rate band;
IHT403 – gifts and other transfers of value;
IHT404 – jointly owned assets;
IHT405 – houses, land and buildings;
IHT406 – bank and building society accounts;
IHT407 – household and personal goods;
IHT408 – household goods donated to charity;
IHT409 – pensions;
IHT410 – life assurance and annuities;
IHT411 – listed stocks and shares;
IHT412 – unlisted stocks and shares and control holdings;
IHT413 – business and partnership interests and assets;
IHT414 – agricultural relief;
IHT415 – interest in another estate;
IHT416 – debts due to the estate;
IHT417 – foreign assets;
IHT418 – assets held in trust;
IHT419 – debts owed by the deceased;
IHT420 – national heritage assets;

IHT421 – probate summary;
IHT423 – direct payment scheme for bank accounts;
IHT430 – reduced rate of inheritance tax;
IHT35 – claim for relief loss on sale of shares;
IHT38 – claim for relief, loss on sale of land.

Instruction booklet is IHT 400 notes.

A grant of representation granted by the High Court in England and Wales in respect of the estate of a person dying domiciled there and noting the domicile will be recognised throughout the UK. This can be achieved by the delivery of a single HMRC Account. If such a grant is obtained when the domicile is in Scotland or NI, the grant is limited to assets in England and Wales and a further grant (requiring a further HMRC Account) may be required. The appropriate form in Scotland is also now IHT 400.

Appointment of Literary Executors: if separate executors are appointed in relation to part of an estate, for example Literary Executors to handle publishing rights and copyrights, separate forms IHT400 are required from each set of executors.

The IHT 400 must be used in all cases unless the gross value of the estate and the gifts within the previous seven years does not exceed £325,000. See **2.10** below. [*SI 2003/1658; SI 2004/2543 as amended*].

C4 **Corrective account** (for use where too much or too little tax has been paid on a previous account). C4–S in Scotland.

Forms relating to other matters are mentioned under the appropriate subject headings elsewhere in this book.

Accounts for lifetime transfer

[2.5] Accounts for lifetime transfer are treated as follows:

(a) Every transferor who is liable for tax on the value transferred by a chargeable transfer; and
(b) every person liable for tax on the value transferred by a potentially exempt transfer (including, in relation to transfers and other events after 16 March 1987, such a transfer made under *IHTA 1984, s 52* as amended by *FA 2006, Sch 20 para 13* on the termination of an interest in possession) which proves to be a chargeable transfer; and
(c) any person within (a) or (b) above who would be so liable if tax were chargeable on that value,

must deliver to the Board an account (see **29** LIFETIME TRANSFERS for Form IHT 100) specifying all property comprised in that transfer to which tax is or would be attributable and its value, unless some other person liable for the tax (other than a joint trustee) has already delivered such an account. [*IHTA 1984, s 216(1)(4)(5); FA 1986, Sch 19 para 29; F(No 2)A 1987, Sch 7 para 4; FA 2006, Sch 22 para 7*].

Potentially exempt transfers

[2.6] There is no requirement to notify the Board on the making of such a transfer nor to deliver an account. In the case of a transfer on or after 17 March 1987 but before 22 March 2006 involving an interest in possession trust, that transfer may also become an exempt transfer if the transferor survives for seven years.

After 21 March 2006 a PET is a transfer of value made by an individual which would otherwise be a chargeable transfer and which is either a gift to another individual or into a trust for a disabled person or into a trust for bereaved minors on the ending of an immediate post-death interest (IPDI). See **35** POTENTIALLY EXEMPT TRANSFERS. There was also no immediate lifetime charge on the termination or disposal of an individual's beneficial interest in possession in trust property before 22 March 2006 where another individual becomes beneficially entitled or that trust property becomes comprised of an accumulation and maintenance settlement or the value of another individual's estate is increased. An account must be submitted where there has been a potentially exempt transfer and the transferor has not survived for seven years. The donee of a potentially exempt transfer is liable to deliver an account if the transferor dies within seven years of the transfer.

Excepted transfers by individuals

[2.7] From 6 April 2007, no account is required to be delivered for 'excepted transfers'. These cover two separate circumstances:

(1) where the value transferred is wholly attributable to cash or quoted stocks and securities, and the cumulative total of all chargeable transfers made by the transferor in the seven years before the transfer does not exceed the IHT nil rate band.

(2) where the value transferred is wholly or partly attributable to property other than cash or quoted stocks and securities, and the chargeable transfer together with the cumulative total of all chargeable transfers made by the transferor in the seven years before the transfer (disregarding business property relief and agricultural property relief) does not exceed 80% of the relevant IHT nil rate band. The value transferred must also not exceed the 'net IHT threshold' being the IHT nil band after deduction of the transferor's cumulative total.

The Board retain the right to call for an account by notice in writing to the individual.

[*Inheritance Tax (Delivery of Accounts) (Excepted Transfers and Terminations) Regulations 2008, SI 2008/605, Reg 4*].

See **2.15** below for time limits and **2.16** for submission of accounts where a transfer was originally treated as 'excepted'.

Gifts with reservation

[2.8] Property given but subject to a reservation where that reservation is retained until the death of the donor or where the reservation ceases within seven years of the death should be the subject of an IHT 100 account return. However, where a reservation ceases before the death of the donor then the donor is treated as having made a potentially exempt transfer of the property at the time the reservation ceases. In addition, the dismantling of pre-owned assets avoidance schemes by way of election on form IHT 500 in respect of any relevant year of assessment will ensure that the property is treated as being comprised in the original donor's estate for these purposes as a gift with reservation but will preclude the income tax charge on the annual taxable value of the pre-owned asset. See **22** GIFTS WITH RESERVATION.

Accounts for transfers on death

[2.9] The **personal representatives** of a deceased person must deliver to the Board an account of all property which formed part of the deceased's estate immediately before his death (other than property which only forms part of his estate by virtue of the provisions relating to **22** GIFTS WITH RESERVATION) and its value unless the estate is an 'excepted estate' (see below).

The information provided by the personal representatives must include details of any chargeable transfers made by the deceased within seven years of his death. The personal representatives may also provide a provisional estimate of the value of an asset included in their account where, despite making all reasonable enquiries to ascertain the value, they cannot establish the exact value. In such cases, the account must contain a statement to that effect and an undertaking to deliver a further account as soon as the value is ascertained. An executor in England and Wales of settled land need only give details of the trust property comprised in the transfer (see IHT 405 below). In the case of pension scheme administrators of alternatively secured pension (ASP) funds who become liable to the payment of IHT by reason of *IHTA 1984, s 151A–D* they are responsible for delivering an account to HMRC of the property expended on dependant's benefits. [*IHTA 1984, ss 216(1)(bca), 272; FA 2006, s 160, Sch 22 paras 7, 10; FA 2008, Sch 28 para 12*]. See also **2.15** below and **34.2** PENSION SCHEMES.

The account must be submitted to HMRC who will then supply a code number to include with application for probate. Any tax due must be paid before a grant of representation can be obtained. Only in very exceptional circumstances can a grant be obtained without payment of the IHT due. Payment can be by cheque, but one of the other methods of payment is preferred: see **32.4**.

The cost of obtaining the grant is £300 for estates valued at more than £5,000 and cheques should be made payable to 'HM Courts and Tribunals Service'. In Scotland, such an account is called an inventory and it must be presented at a local Sheriff Court or the Commissary Office in Edinburgh. The Scottish equivalent of the grant of representation is the confirmation. See **2.21** below for addresses. The Board of HMRC may also give directions restricting assets to be included in accounts to be delivered by personal representatives. See *Robertson v CIR* [2002] STC SCD 182 Sp C 309. [*IHTA 1984, ss 216(1)(3)(3A)(3B)(4), 261; FA 1986, Sch 19 para 29; FA 1999, s 105*]. See also **33.14** PENALTIES.

Under the *Non-Contentious Probate (Amendment) Rules 2018, SI 2018/1137*, it is no longer a requirement that executors swear an oath in order apply for a grant. Instead, a Statement of Truth is now contained in Form PA1.

Where there are no personal representatives because no grant of representation or confirmation has been obtained in the UK within twelve months of the end of the month in which death occurred:

(a) every person in whom *any property* of the estate vests as beneficial owner or otherwise, or who is beneficially entitled to an interest in possession in such property, on or after the deceased's death; and
(b) where property is comprised in a settlement with no person entitled to an interest in possession, every person for whose benefit any of that property, or income from it, is applied, on or after the deceased's death,

must deliver an account to the Board, specifying to the best of his knowledge and belief, the property in which he has an interest (or which is applicable for his benefit) and its value. Any property includes property which is expended on dependants' benefits arising from an alternatively secured pension (ASP) under *IHTA 1984, s 151A* or property paid to a charity within *IHTA 1984, ss 151B(4), 151C(3)(b)*. See **34.2** PENSION SCHEMES. Such an account is not required if the person concerned has satisfied the Board that an account will in due course be delivered by the personal representatives or has already been delivered by some other liable person. [*IHTA 1984, s 216(2)(4)(5)*]. See Form 409.

Gifts with reservation

[2.10] Any person who is liable for tax on the value of property forming part of the deceased's estate by virtue only of the provisions relating to **22** GIFTS WITH RESERVATION (or would be so liable if tax were chargeable on that value) must deliver to the Board an account specifying all property to the value of which the tax is or would be attributable and its value unless some other person liable for the tax (other than a joint trustee) has already delivered such an account. [*IHTA 1984, s 216(1)(4)(5); FA 1986, Sch 19 para 29*].

Excepted estates

[2.11] No account need be delivered for the estate of any person who has died domiciled in the UK on or after 1 September 2006 where:

(i) the estate comprises only property which has passed under the deceased's will or intestacy, or by nomination on death, or entitlement to a single interest in possession settlement, or beneficially by survivorship;
(ii) the total gross value of the estate for tax purposes (inclusive of (iii)–(v) below for deaths before 1 January 2022) does not exceed £325,000 and no IHT is due (£312,000 for deaths before 6 April 2009 and after 5 April

2008; £300,000 for deaths before 6 April 2008 and after 5 April 2007; £285,000 for deaths before 6 April 2007 and after 5 April 2006; £275,000 for deaths before 6 April 2006 but after 5 April 2005). For this purpose, any APR or BPR reliefs within *IHTA 1984, ss 104, 116* must be disregarded;

(iii) not more than £100,000 (£75,000 for deaths before 1 September 2006 but after 5 April 2002) consists of property situated outside the UK and by reason of that person's death an ASP fund provision under *IHTA 1984, ss 151A–D* does not apply; and

(iv) the deceased had made no lifetime gifts chargeable to inheritance tax (including potentially exempt transfers becoming chargeable on death and gifts with reservation where the reservation subsists at death or where the property ceased to be subject to the reservation in the seven years before the donor's death) excepting lifetime transfers made within seven years of the deceased's death consisting of 'specified transfers' i.e. cash, listed shares or securities, an interest over land (and furnishings and chattels enjoyed with the land and transferred at the same time) that did not exceed £250,000 (for deaths before 1 January 2022, £150,000, or £100,000 for deaths before 1 September but after 5 April 2000) after ignoring transfers attracting APR or BPR within *IHTA 1984, ss 104, 116* and by reason of that person's death an ASP fund provision under *IHTA 1984, ss 151A–D* does not apply. For the purposes of this condition, with effect from 1 March 2011 transfers within the normal expenditure out of income exemption and which exceed the available annual £3,000 exempt amount are treated as chargeable transfers;

(v) not more than £250,000 (for deaths before 1 January 2022, £150,000) represents value attributable to property which, immediately before the person's death, was settled property. But for deaths on or after 1 January 2022, if the estate includes trust property passing to the surviving spouse or civil partner, or to charity and the value of the trust property exceeds £1 million, or £250,000 after deduction of spouse or charity exemption, it is necessary to file a full return.

No account need be delivered for the estate of any person who died on or after 6 April 2004 who was domiciled in the UK or treated as domiciled in the UK [*FA 2004, s 293*] where:

(vi) the aggregate gross value of the deceased's estate (inclusive of (iii)–(v) above, as may be the case) is £3,000,000 (for deaths before 1 January 2022, £1,000,000) or less after ignoring transfers attracting APR or BPR within *IHTA 1984, ss 104, 116* and after deducting any specified exemptions (e.g. spousal, charities, etc.) so that the net chargeable estate is less than £325,000. With effect from 1 March 2011 it is also a condition that at least part of the estate passes to the surviving spouse or to charity.

(vii) with effect from 1 March 2011, an estate benefiting from the transferred unused nil rate band of a pre-deceased spouse will have that taken into account for the purposes of the Excepted Estates Regulations. For deaths before 1 January 2022, this applied only where all of the pre-deceased spouse's nil band was unused. For deaths on or after that date, this applies in relation to any available amount of transferable nil rate band.

[*Inheritance Tax (Delivery of Accounts) (Excepted Estates) (Amendment) Regulations 2006, SI 2006/2141; The Inheritance Tax (Delivery of Accounts) (Excepted Estates) (Amendment) Regulations 2011, SI 2011/214)*].

No account need be delivered for the estate of any person who died on or after 6 April 2002 who was never domiciled in the UK or treated as domiciled in the UK [*FA 1986, s 267*] where:

(viii) the value of such a person's estate that is situated in the UK which is attributable to cash or quoted shares or securities that pass by will, or by intestacy, or beneficially by survivorship and does not exceed £150,000. For deaths on or after 1 January 2022, it is also a requirement that the deceased did not hold any indirect interest in UK residential property and had not made gifts in excess of £3,000 in any year during the seven years before death.

For deaths before 1 January 2022 where the estate qualified as an excepted estate, Form IHT 205 was required if an application for probate was being made. This form is not applicable for deaths on or after 2022; instead, the value of the estate is reported as part of the process of applying for probate. This means that an IHT return is no longer required for many estates, i.e. those below the nil rate band threshold as in the first category of excepted estates set out above, or those where the spouse exemption or charitable reliefs reduce the chargeable value below the nil band threshold, as in the second category of excepted estates set out above.

The Board retain the right to call for an account by issuing a notice to the personal representatives within 60 days (35 days for deaths before 1 January 2022) of the issue of the grant of probate. In Scotland, the Board may give notice to the personal representatives within 60 days of the issue of confirmation to the estate that the Registrar, HMRC Inheritance Tax at Edinburgh has required the Commissary Clerk or Sheriff Clerk to transmit to him an inventory of the excepted estate. If no notice is issued, the personal representatives will be automatically discharged from any further tax claims (unless there is fraud or non-disclosure of material facts) and any HMRC charge (see **32.12** PAYMENT OF TAX) is extinguished without formal application. See leaflet 'What to do after a death in Scotland'.

[*IHTA 1984, s 256; SI 1981/880, SI 1981/881, SI 1981/1441; SI 1983/1039, SI 1983/1040, SI 1983/1911; SI 1987/1127, SI 1987/1128, SI 1987/1129; SI 1989/1078, SI 1989/1079, SI 1989/1080; SI 1990/1110, SI 1990/1111, SI 1990/1112; SI 1991/1248, SI 1991/1249, SI 1991/1250; SI 1996/1470, SI 1996/1472,SI 1996/1473; SI 1998/1429, SI 1998/1430, SI 1998/1431; SI 2000/965, SI 2000/966, SI 2000/967; SI 2002/1733; SI 2003/1658; SI 2004/2543*].

See **2.15** below for time limits and **2.16** for submission of accounts where estate originally treated as 'excepted'.

A simpler reporting regime was announced on 17 March 2004 and is now incorporated into *FA 2004, s 293* whereby an IHT account will be required only where there is tax to pay. In most other cases, contact will only be with the Probate Service in England and the Sheriff's Court in Scotland. [*Supreme Court*

Act 1981, s 109(1); Probate and Legacy Duties Act 1808, s 42; Administration of Estates (Northern Ireland) Order 1979, SI 1979/1575 as amended by *FA 2004, s 294(3); The Finance Act 2004, Section 294 (Appointed Day) Order 2004, SI 2004/2571*]. As a result, in a majority of cases, the information on a deceased's estate will be provided once to the Probate Service (or the Sheriff's Court in Scotland) who in turn will provide HMRC with information from which HMRC will determine selected cases for enquiry. This procedure ensures that only the basic information will be provided in such cases and not the full account as in past years. The changes are incorporated in the *Inheritance Tax (Delivery of Accounts) (Excepted Estates) Regulations 2004, SI 2004/2543* as amended by *The Tax and Civil Partnership (No 2) Regulations 2005, SI 2005/3230, Reg 15* ensuring that a new category of qualifying estate where the gross value does not exceed £1 million, subject to a number of provisos, is excluded. See above at (vi). [*IHTA 1984, s 256(3A)* as inserted by *FA 2004, s 293(6)*]. See **2.2** above.

In order to ensure that compliance requirements are met the penalty rules (see **33** PENALTIES for failure to provide accounts, etc.) will apply to the delivery of incorrect information under these simplified reporting arrangements. As a result of this provision will be made to allow the information delivered to the Probate Service and then passed on to HMRC to be treated as having been delivered direct to HMRC as will be the case for the delivery of information via the Scottish Court Service. [*IHTA 1984, s 256(1A)* as inserted by *FA 2004, s 293(3)*]. Contact the Principal Probate Registry on 0207 947 7431/7414.

Many estates are exempt from IHT because most or all of the estate passes to a surviving spouse/civil partner, a UK charity or other exempt bodies. HMRC has identified certain circumstances where a reduced IHT 400 account may be delivered. These circumstances are as follows:

- the deceased was domiciled in the UK at the date of death, and
- most or all of the property passing by will or under intestacy passes to an 'exempt beneficiary' either:
  - (i) absolutely, or through an interest in possession trust, to the surviving spouse/civil partner, who must also be domiciled in the UK, or
  - (ii) so as to immediately become the property of a body listed in *IHTA 1984, Sch 3*, or
  - (iii) so as to immediately become the property of a charity registered in the UK, or held on trusts established in the UK for charitable purposes only, and
- the gross value of the property passing by will or under intestacy to beneficiaries other than exempt beneficiaries together with the value of 'other property chargeable on death' and the chargeable value of any gifts made in the seven years prior to death do not, in total, exceed the IHT threshold.

Other property chargeable on death mentioned above includes:

(a) joint property passing by survivorship to someone other than the deceased's surviving spouse/civil partner (assuming that he or she was domiciled in the UK);

(b) settled property in which the deceased had a life interest, other than settled property which then devolves to the deceased's spouse/civil partner, to a body listed in *IHTA 1984, Sch 3*, or to a charity registered in the UK;
(c) property that the deceased had given away but in which they reserved a benefit that either continued until death or ceased within seven years of death;
(d) property situated outside the UK which does not devolve under the UK will or intestacy.

Where the circumstances above are met, the requirement to deliver an account containing all appropriate property and the value of that property is relaxed. The account must still be delivered on Form IHT 400 and the declaration on p 13 signed.

Accounts by trustees of settlements

[2.12] The **trustees** of a settlement liable for tax on the value transferred by a transfer of value or for tax under provisions relating to **40** SETTLEMENTS: DISCRETIONARY TRUSTS AND OTHER TRUSTS OF RELEVANT PROPERTY (or who would be so liable if tax were chargeable) must deliver an account specifying all property to which tax is or would be attributable and its value, unless some other person liable for the tax (other than as joint trustee) has already delivered such an account. [*IHTA 1984, s 216(1)(4)(5)*]. An account must be rendered to the best of a taxpayer's knowledge and belief. This does not mean that he can be compelled to act as an information gatherer if he does not have information himself. (*Re Clore (decd.) (No 3), CIR v Stype Trustees (Jersey) Ltd and Others* Ch D, [1985] STC 394). (The *Stype* case also held that foreign trustees liable to pay tax are also liable to produce accounts despite difficulties of enforcement.)

Excepted terminations of interests in possession

[2.13] No account need be delivered on a termination of an interest in possession in settled property where:

(i) the transferor has given notice to the trustees of available exemptions under *IHTA 1984, s 57(3)* (annual exemption and gifts in consideration of marriage — see **39.9** SETTLEMENTS WITH INTERESTS IN POSSESSION), and
(ii) the value transferred does not exceed the amount of the exemption specified in the notice. See **2.5** above.

There are two other circumstances where no account is required to be delivered:

(1) where the value transferred by the chargeable transfer concerned is wholly attributable to cash or quoted stocks and securities, and that value together with the cumulative total of all chargeable transfers made by the transferor in the seven years before the transfer does not exceed the IHT nil rate band;
(2) where the value transferred by the chargeable transfer concerned is wholly or partly attributable to property other than cash or quoted stocks and securities, and that value together with the cumulative total

of all chargeable transfers made by the transferor in the seven years before the transfer (disregarding business property relief and agricultural property relief) does not exceed 80% of the relevant IHT nil rate band. The value transferred must also not exceed the 'net IHT threshold' being the IHT nil band after deduction of the transferor's cumulative total.

The Board retain the right to call for an account by written notice to the trustees. If no such notice is issued within six months of the termination, the trustees will automatically be discharged from any claim for tax at the expiration of that period (unless there is fraud or non-disclosure of material facts). [*Inheritance Tax (Delivery of Accounts) (Excepted Transfers and Terminations) Regulations 2008, SI 2008/605, Reg 5*].

See **2.15** below for time limits and **2.16** below for submission of accounts where the termination was originally treated as 'excepted'.

Excepted settlements without interest in possession

[2.14] No account need be delivered in respect of an excepted settlement (i.e. one with no qualifying interest in possession) on an occasion of a chargeable event on or after 6 April 2007 where either of the following applies:

Small settlements of cash

(i) cash is the only property comprised in the settlement;
(ii) after making the settlement, the settlor provided no further property which became comprised in the settlement;
(iii) the trustees of the settlement are resident in the UK throughout the existence of the settlement;
(iv) the gross value of the settled property throughout the existence of the settlement does not exceed £1,000; and
(v) there are no related settlements.

All other settlements

- the settlor must be domiciled in the UK at the time the settlement was set up and remain so domiciled throughout the existence of the settlement until either the occasion of charge or the settlor's earlier death;
- the trustees of the settlement must be resident in the UK throughout the existence of the settlement; and
- there must be no related settlements for IHT purposes (these are other settlements created by the settlor on the same day as the RPT).
- on the relevant event (for example the ten-year anniversary of a RPT or the distribution of assets from a RPT) the value of the notional aggregate chargeable transfer does not exceed 80% of the IHT nil rate band. Similarly, where an IHT charge arises in connection with an age 18–25 trust, that trust will qualify as an excepted settlement where the value of the notional aggregate chargeable transfer under *IHTA 1984, s 71F(8)* does not exceed 80% of the nil rate band. For the purposes of calculating value for the 80% test, any possible IHT reliefs, such as business or agricultural property relief, must be ignored as well as any liabilities of the settlement. See also **40** SETTLEMENTS: DISCRETIONARY TRUSTS AND OTHER TRUSTS OF RELEVANT PROPERTY and **43** TRUSTS FOR BEREAVED MINORS.

The Board retain the right to call for an account by written notice to the trustees of the excepted settlement. If no such notice is issued within six months of the termination, the trustees will automatically be discharged from any claim for tax at the expiration of that period (unless there is fraud or non-disclosure of material facts). [*SI 2002/1732* revoked from 6 April 2007 and replaced by *Inheritance Tax (Delivery of Accounts) (Excepted Settlements) Regulations 2008, SI 2008/606, Reg 5*].

[*Inheritance Tax (Delivery of Accounts) (Excepted Transfers and Terminations) Regulations 2008, SI 2008/606, Reg 4*].

Time limits for delivery of above accounts

[2.15] Table of accounts delivery dates for:

Potentially exempt transfers which prove to be chargeable	— within **twelve months** from the end of the month in which the transferor dies.
Other lifetime transfers and, for chargeable transfers on or before 5 April 2014, by trustees of settlements	— within **twelve months** from the end of the month in which a transfer is made or, if later, within the three months beginning with the date on which the person delivering the account first becomes liable for tax.
For chargeable transfers on or after 6 April 2014 by trustees of settlements	— within **six months** from the end of the month in which the event occurs or, if later, 31 December 2017 where an account is required following the changes to deemed domicile under *F(No 2)A 2017, s 30* or UK residential property interests by *F(No 2)A 2017, Sch 10*.
Gifts with reservation chargeable on death	— within **twelve months** from the end of the month in which the death occurs.
Other transfers on death	— within **twelve months** from the end of the month in which death occurs or, if later, within the three months beginning with the date on which the personal representatives first act or the person liable under **2.9** (a) or (b) above first has reason to believe he is required to deliver an account.
Accounts where charge arises on ending of conditional exemption for works of art, historic buildings, etc. (whether settled property or otherwise) and for trees or underwood	— within **six months** from the end of the month in which the chargeable event occurs.

Alternatively Secured Pension (ASP) schemes on death of the scheme member	— within **twelve months** from the end of the month in which the scheme administrator makes discovery of the scheme member's death where there is a left-over pension amount at the death of the scheme member who was over the age of 75 on death and was traced after their death by the ASP scheme administrator. In such cases the left-over ASP funds are brought within the charge to IHT by *IHTA 1984, s 151A(6)*.

[*IHTA 1984, s 216(6)(6)(ac)(7); FA 1985, Sch 26 para 11; FA 1986, Sch 19 para 29; F(No 2)A 1987, Sch 7 para 4; FA 1999, s 105; FA 2006, Sch 22 para 7(5); FA 2007, Sch 19 para 24; FA 2008, Sch 28 para 12; FA 2009, Sch 56 para 1; FA 2014, Sch 21 para 4*].

See **2.16** below for position where an estate, transfer or termination originally considered 'excepted' is discovered not to be so. See also **33** PENALTIES.

Corrective and supplementary accounts

[2.16] If a person who has delivered any of the accounts under **2.5** to **2.15** above discovers a material defect, he must deliver a further account within six months to remedy the defect. If a person has not delivered an account in the mistaken belief that the transfer was an 'excepted transfer' (see **2.5** above) or the termination an 'excepted termination' (see **2.12** above), an account must be delivered within six months of the discovery. The same time limit applies where an 'excepted estate' (see **2.9** above) or an excepted settlement (see **2.12** above) is later discovered to be no longer excepted. [*IHTA 1984, s 217; SI 1981/880, SI 1981/881, SI 1981/1440, SI 1981/1441* now replaced by *SI 2002/1731; SI 2002/1732; SI 2002/1733* revoked from 6 April 2007 and replaced by *SI 2008/605 and SI 2008/606*].

From 1 May 2014 HMRC confirmed in their Trusts and Estates Newsletter that in certain circumstances they do not require corrective accounts to be submitted as soon as an amendment to figures previously returned is identified, but instead all corrections can be included on one account when it is believed that they are the final amendments to the value of the estate, or 18 months has passed since the date of death, whichever is earlier. Interest remains due on any additional tax in the normal way and additional payments on account can still be made in advance of submitting a corrective account. This practice is now set out at IHTM 31023.

The circumstances when this does not apply are:

- When HMRC have written to the personal representatives to notify them that a compliance check is to be made.
- The deceased's estate on death includes:
  (i) a qualifying interest in possession in settled property, or
  (ii) a gift with reservation of benefit.

- There is an overall change in the value of the estate of more than £50,000, before any exemptions or reliefs are deducted.
- The amendments relate to changes in the value of land or buildings or unlisted shares.
- The amendments relate to a claim for loss on sale of land or shares.
- Assets have been sold on which tax is being paid by instalments.

After 18 months from the date of death, all corrections should be notified as soon as they are known.

For late reporting of transfers, see **7.15** CALCULATION OF TAX.

Clearance certificates

[2.17] On application by the person liable for tax on a transfer of value, or failed potentially exempt transfer, the Board may give a certificate to confirm that all IHT attributable to it has been, or will be, paid. Application is made on Form IHT30. See **32.15** for further details.

Returns by certain persons acting for settlors

[2.18] Where a person (other than a barrister) has been concerned with the making of a settlement in the course of his trade or profession, and knows or has reason to believe (a) that the settlor was domiciled in the UK, and (b) that the trustees of the settlement are not or will not be resident in the UK, he must, within three months of the making of the settlement, make a return to the Board of the names and addresses of the settlor and the trustees of the settlement. This does not apply to any settlement made by will or where a return has already been made by another person or if any account relating to it has been delivered under **2.5** to **2.15** above. For this purpose, trustees of a settlement are not regarded as resident in the UK unless the general administration of the settlement is ordinarily carried on in the UK and the trustees or a majority of them (and where there is more than one class of trustees a majority of each class) are for the time being resident in the UK. [*IHTA 1984, s 218*].

Power to require information and call for documents

Power of the Board to require information

[2.19] The Board may by written notice (which may be combined with an income tax notice) require any person to supply any information they require for IHT purposes within not less than 30 days. Any such notice requires the consent of a Special Commissioner, which he is only to give on being satisfied that in all the circumstances the Board are justified in requiring the information.

A barrister or solicitor need not disclose, without his client's consent, any information subject to professional privilege, except that a solicitor:

(a) may be obliged to disclose the name and address of his client, and

(b) if his client is resident outside the UK and carries on a business abroad which includes the provision of services for persons in the UK relating to:
   (i) the formation of companies or settlements abroad; or
   (ii) the securing of control over, or the management or administration of, companies and settlements,

may be obliged to disclose the names and addresses of persons in the UK for whom the services are provided.

A notice can also require information for the purposes of taxes similar to IHT or chargeable on or by reference to death or gifts *inter vivos* which are contained in the law of another EC member state and to which *EC Directive No 77/799/EEC* of 19 December 1977 (as extended subsequently) applies and any other territory with taxed charged of a character similar to IHT. (Such a notice can be combined with one relating to any tax of another EC member state which is a tax on income or on capital for the purposes of the above EC Directive.) The Board may then disclose the information so obtained to the competent authorities of other EC member states and any other territory which observe rules of confidentiality no less strict than those applying in the UK.

[*FA 1978, s 77; IHTA 1984, s 219; FA 1990, ss 124, 125; FA 2000, s 147(2)*].

Power of the Board to call for documents

The Board may by written notice require any person who has delivered, or is liable to deliver, an IHT account to produce, in not less than 30 days, such documents and accounts as are reasonably required for:

(i) enquiring into the account (including a claim or election);
(ii) determining whether the account is incorrect or incomplete; and
(iii) making a determination for the purposes of a notice under *IHTA 1984, s 221* (see **14** DETERMINATIONS AND APPEALS),

except that a notice cannot oblige a person to produce documents, etc. relating to the conduct of any pending appeal by him.

Copies may be produced instead of originals but, if required in writing, the originals must be produced for inspection.

An appeal to the First-tier Tribunal (FTT) may be brought against any such requirement within 30 days of the issue of the notice. The FTT may then confirm the notice (in which case the person has 30 days to comply) or set it aside. Neither party to the appeal can appeal against the decision of the FTT.

[*IHTA 1984, ss 219A, 219B; FA 1999, s 106; The Transfer of Tribunal Functions and Revenue and Customs Appeals Order 2009, SI 2009/56, Sch 1, paras 112, 113*].

Power of the Special Commissioners to require particulars

On a preliminary or substantive hearing of any proceedings, the Special Commissioners may direct a party to the proceedings, other than HMRC, to deliver particulars, and to make available books, accounts and other documents, relating to the proceedings for inspection and copying by them and officers of the Board. [*SI 1994/1811, Reg 10*].

Penalties

[2.20] See 33 PENALTIES for failure to provide accounts etc. for provision of incorrect information and for failure to remedy errors in accounts etc. Also, see 33.2 PENALTIES.

Addresses

HMRC Inheritance Tax

[2.21]

All correspondence should now be directed to:	Inheritance Tax H M Revenue and Customs BX9 1HT United Kingdom Tel. 0300 123 1072

Grants of representation or confirmation

[2.22]

England and Wales	HMCTS Probate PO Box 12625 Harlow CM20 9QE
Scotland	Application for confirmation is made to the Sheriff Clerk of the Sheriff Court in the area in which the deceased had been domiciled at their death.
Northern Ireland	Probate Office Royal Courts of Justice (Northern Ireland) Chichester Street Belfast BT1 3JF

In Great Britain there are a number of local offices at which applications for grants of representation may be made. The addresses can be obtained from the Principal Probate Registry and the Commissary Office in Edinburgh. In the first instance Form IHT 400 is to be sent to HMRC Nottingham office (see address above). The case will then be allocated to the nominated office.

In England and Wales, solicitors are asked not to send accounts to probate registries unless they have been previously submitted to, and properly receipted by, HMRC for PAYMENT OF TAX (32.4) (Family Division Practice Note 30 November 1989).

Key points concerning accounts and returns

[2.23] Points to consider are as follows.

- IHT400 must be sent to HMRC within twelve months of the date of death but interest will be payable after only six months following the date of death.
- IHT100 is to be completed in cases where there are chargeable lifetime transfers by individuals or where there is a termination during the lifetime of a person entitled to an interest in possession. Where a life interest ends on death, both Forms IHT400 (including IHT418) and IHT100 are required. IHT 418 gives basic information on the trust assets but IHT 100 is required to provide more detail. See SETTLEMENTS WITH INTERESTS IN POSSESSION (**39.1**).
- Supplementary schedules IHT401 to IHT420 should accompany the IHT400 schedule where applicable in respect of assets the deceased was beneficially entitled to on death.
- Corrective or supplementary accounts should be submitted as soon as the personal representatives become aware of the position requiring the corrective account, except as stated at **2.16** above.
- Supporting documentary evidence is required to be submitted with the schedules e.g. IHT405 (houses, land, buildings and interests in land). it is recommended that three independent valuations are obtained with average market value being taken.

3

Administration and Collection

Simon's Taxes. See **Part I11**.

Other Sources. HMRC Customer Guide to Inheritance Tax; Mellows, Chapter 5; Foster, Part L; IHTM 30000, IHTM31000, IHTM38000, IHTM36000.

Administration and collection — management

[3.1] Inheritance tax is 'under the care and management of the Board' (i.e. the Commissioners for Her Majesty's Revenue and Customs, 100 Parliament Street, London SW1A 2BQ). [*IHTA 1984, s 215*]. HMRC deals with the levying of inheritance tax, and accounts and correspondence should be sent to them at the addresses given at **2.21** ACCOUNTS AND RETURNS.

HMRC has produced a Taxpayer's Charter which sets out the principles it endeavours to meet in its dealings with taxpayers. This is available at www.gov.uk/government/publications/hmrc-charter.

Accounts and information

[3.2] Transferors and other taxable persons have a duty to provide the Board with accounts containing information about transfers within a certain time after the transfers. The Board also has power to require any person to furnish them with information for IHT purposes. [*IHTA 1984, ss 216–219, 256, 257, 261*]. See **2** ACCOUNTS AND RETURNS. The Board has powers of inspection for valuation purposes. [*IHTA 1984, s 220*]. See **53.1** VALUATION.

Determinations and appeals

[3.3] When a transfer of value has been made, the Board issues a notice of determination (with a similar function to a notice of assessment for income tax, capital gains tax, etc.) showing the value of the transfer and the tax chargeable.

A person who receives a notice of determination may appeal against it. The appeal will be heard by the First-tier Tax Tribunal, or, in certain circumstances, by the Lands Tribunal or the High Court. [*IHTA 1984, ss 221–225*]. See **14** DETERMINATIONS AND APPEALS.

Payment of tax

[3.4] Tax is generally due six months after the end of the month of the transfer, with an extension to the end of the following April where a chargeable lifetime transfer takes place after 5 April and before 1 October in any year. On the transfer of certain types of property, broadly land, shares and businesses, tax may be paid by instalments. Certain 'pre-eminent' types of property such as works of art, historic buildings etc. may be accepted in lieu of tax.

Where tax is not paid an HMRC charge for the unpaid tax is imposed on the property transferred. However, a person who has paid tax on a transfer or who has confirmed with HMRC that no tax is due, may obtain a certificate of discharge which serves to free the property in question from any HMRC charge. [*IHTA 1984, ss 226–232, 237–239*]. See **32** PAYMENT OF TAX.

Interest and penalties

[3.5] Interest is charged on unpaid tax and paid on any repayment of tax overpaid (currently 3%). [*IHTA 1984, ss 233–236*]. See **25** INTEREST ON TAX. Penalties are charged for various failures to comply with the IHT legislation, for providing incorrect information and for failing to remedy errors. By reason of the *FA 2004* penalties have been increased substantially. [*IHTA 1984, ss 245–253; FA 2004, s 295*]. See **33** PENALTIES and http://www.hmrc.gov.uk/cto/customerguide/page22.htm.

Recovery of tax

[3.6] The Board may issue a notice of determination (see **3.3** above) if it appears that a transfer of value has been made, even if no account or return (see 3.2 above) of the transfer has been made. If tax or interest on tax is unpaid, the Board may take legal proceedings to recover it. If it is discovered that too little tax has been paid, the underpayment is payable with interest. However, where tax is paid and accepted on the view of the law current at the time, the amount of tax due is not affected if it appears subsequently that that view was wrong. The New Disclosure Opportunity (NDO) and Liechtenstein Disclosure Facility (LDF) follow the previous Offshore Disclosure Facility (ODF) on 2007 and can apply for IHT purposes. See **5** ANTI-AVOIDANCE. [*IHTA 1984, ss 240–244, 254, 255*]. See **32** PAYMENT OF TAX.

Limitation of liability

[3.7] The Statute of Limitations does not apply in relation IHT liabilities. Instead the position is governed by *IHTA 1984, s 240.*

Where an account has been delivered and tax paid and accepted by HMRC in full satisfaction of the liability, no further claim can be made in respect of that account more than four years after the tax was paid and accepted, or the last instalment fell due. If, however, there is a loss of tax in these circumstances brought about 'carelessly' by the taxpayer or agent for the taxpayer, the time limit for recovering any additional tax is six years.

Where no account has been delivered, and the loss of tax was not brought about deliberately by the person liable for the tax, or a person acting for them, then the time limit is 20 years. But if the loss of tax has been caused deliberately, there is no time limit at all.

For cases involving either an 'offshore matter' or an 'offshore transfer which makes the lost tax significantly harder to identify', extended collection dates apply where accounts have been delivered to HMRC. For cases where the loss of tax is brought about carelessly, the extended dates apply for chargeable transfers on or after 1 April 2013. In any other case, they apply for chargeable transfers on or after 1 April 2015. An offshore matter is one which relates to foreign situs assets immediately after the time of the relevant chargeable transfer. An offshore transfer is any other case where property was transferred outside the UK after the chargeable transfer but before the date on which an account is delivered to HMRC in relation to it, or before the date of any corrective account. The extended time limit is 12 years instead of the normal four-year time limit in *IHTA 1984, s 240(2)*. However, this will not apply where HMRC has 'relevant overseas information', being information from an overseas tax authority, on the basis of which HMRC could reasonably have been expected to identify the lost tax and bring proceedings within the normal time limits.

Service of documents

[3.8] A notice or other document which is to be served on a person under *IHTA 1984* may be delivered to him or left at his usual or last known place of residence or served by post, addressed to him at that address or his place of business or employment. [*IHTA 1984, s 258*].

Administration and collection: publications

[3.9] A short guide to IHT is published by HMRC at www.gov.uk/inheritance-tax. The HMRC Trusts and Estates Newsletters are available at www.gov.uk/government/publications/hm-revenue-and-customs-trusts-and-estates-newsletters.

4

Agricultural Property

Cross-references. See **6** BUSINESS PROPERTY; **7.6** CALCULATION OF TAX for application of agricultural relief where transfer partly exempt; **22.11** GIFTS WITH RESERVATION where such a gift is of agricultural property or shares in an agricultural company; **30.3** NATIONAL HERITAGE; **32** PAYMENT OF TAX and **54** WOODLANDS.

Simon's Taxes. See I3.159, I7.3, I8.348, I8.349.

Other Sources. Foster, Parts G2–3; Mellows, Parts 5.36–5.50; IHTM24000, IHTM24036.

Introduction to agricultural property

[4.1] Where certain conditions are satisfied, relief from inheritance tax is available on the transfer of agricultural property in the UK. The relief is a percentage reduction of either 100% or 50%, as detailed at **4.4,** in the agricultural value transferred by a transfer of value. Relief is also available on occasions on which tax is chargeable under the provisions relating to **40** SETTLEMENTS: DISCRETIONARY TRUSTS AND OTHER TRUSTS OF RELEVANT PROPERTY. [*IHTA 1984, ss 115(1)(5), 116(1)* as amended by *FA 2009, s 122(3); Interpretation Act 1978, Sch 1*].

Up to 6 April 2024 agricultural relief always applied to agricultural land in the Channel Islands, the Isle of Man, and this dated back to the introduction of capital transfer tax in 1975. Relief was extended to land within an EEA state with effect from 22 April 2009, with provision for retrospective claims back to 2003, as set out at **26.3**. However, relief for land outside the UK is now withdrawn for chargeable events arising on or after 6 April 2024 [*F(No 2)A 2024*], so from that date only, land within the UK may qualify. There remains no restriction for business property relief, and accordingly, where land outside the UK is used for the purposes of a business, including a farming business, BPR may apply: see **6** BUSINESS PROPERTY.

Agricultural relief has priority over business property relief so that where the agricultural value of land qualifies to any extent for agricultural relief, that same value cannot qualify for business property relief. [*IHTA 1984, s 114(1)*]. Thus, if only 50% relief is available, business property relief cannot be claimed on the remaining 50% of the value. The latter relief may, however, apply to any excess value over agricultural relief, where the conditions for business property relief are satisfied, and in a farming business, other farm assets such as machinery, plant and working capital may also qualify for business relief.

The meaning of 'Agricultural Property'

Agricultural property means agricultural land or pasture and includes woodlands and any building used in connection with the intensive rearing of livestock or fish if the woodlands or building is occupied with agricultural land or pasture and the occupation is ancillary to that of the agricultural land or pasture. It also includes such cottages, farm buildings and farmhouses, together with the land occupied with them, as are of a character appropriate to the property. The definition of 'agriculture' in the *Agricultural Holdings Act 1986, s 96(1)* is: '"agriculture" includes horticulture, fruit growing, seed growing whether for fruit or flowers, dairy farming and livestock breeding and keeping, the use of land as grazing land, meadow land, osier land, market gardens and nursery grounds, and the use of land for woodlands where that use is ancillary to the farming of land for other agricultural purposes'. Growing grapes for wine and apples for cider qualifies. Agricultural land which is taken out of production can still qualify for APR (including GAEC land) because *IHTA 1984, s 117* does not require the land to be in production either continuously or at a specific time (though there must be an intention or expectation that the land will be back in production at some time in the future). So, for example, agricultural land set aside to rotational, or even permanent, fallow can still qualify as agricultural property within the definition of *IHTA 1984, s 115(2)* and as occupied for the purposes of agriculture within the meaning of *IHTA 1984, s 117*. See HMRC IHT Manual, para 24064. The breeding and rearing of horses on a stud farm and the grazing of horses in connection with those activities is to be taken to be agriculture and any buildings used in connection with those activities to be farm buildings. See also *Wheatley and another (Executors of Wheatley Deceased) v CIR* [1998] STC SCD 60 Sp C 149 e.g. grazing by draught horses. Livestock, deadstock and farm plant and machinery are not included but these may qualify for **6** BUSINESS PROPERTY RELIEF, as may the value of land in excess of its agricultural value and milk quota where it is valued separately (HMRC Tax Bulletin February 1993 p 51). [*IHTA 1984, s 115(2)(4)*]. From 6 April 1995 land used for short rotation coppice (a cultivation method of producing willow, poplar and elephant grass cuttings for renewable fuel for biomass-fed power stations) will count as agricultural property and qualify for either 100% or 50% relief depending on the circumstances as will buildings used in the cultivation which will be regarded as farm buildings. Other biomass crops such as oilseed rape and wheat for biofuels 'may' constitute qualifying use of the land (IHTM24061). Similarly, farmland and buildings used for the management of the habitat land (see (c) below) counts as agricultural property for the purposes of relief at 100% or 50%. The new provisions apply from 26 November 1996 and apply to land dedicated under the Government's Habitat Schemes. [*SI 1994/1291, SI 1994/1292, SI 1994/1293, SI 1994/2710; SI 1995/134*]. See **4.4** below and Inland Revenue Press Release 27 January 1995. [*IHTA 1984, ss 116, 124C; FA 1995, s 154(2)(3)(5); FA 1997, s 94*]. Land used for agricultural purposes may occasionally be used for other purposes (e.g. an annual point to point horse race) without the relief being jeopardised (IHTM24061).

However, where land is used for purposes outside the scope of basic agricultural activity, the availability of relief may be open to question. HMRC deny relief for growing reeds for thatching on the basis that this does not involve cultivation of a crop; likewise keeping pheasants for sport, and fishing rights for sport, are not considered to be agriculture. However, growing grass for turf appears to be accepted by HMRC as agriculture (IHTM24062). In addition, where derelict land has been restored to previous levels of agricultural production due to the application of manures and calcified seaweed in order to make the grasses more palatable to cattle then even though the process is not considered an 'intensive agricultural purpose' it would constitute agricultural/pasture land and not moorland.

See **2.21** ACCOUNTS AND RETURNS for Helpline numbers and now IHT 400 Notes, page 36 point 5.

Case law — 'agricultural land or pasture'

In *Starke and another (Executors of Brown) v CIR* CA, [1995] STC 689 the property in question comprised a site with an area of just over one hectare containing a farmhouse and an assortment of outbuildings, the site being used as part of a farm devoted to mixed farming, although the remainder of the farm, however, was substantially in the ownership of a farming company. The taxpayer, whilst successful in being granted leave to appeal direct to the High Court, a point of law being involved (see **14.4** DETERMINATIONS AND APPEALS), undertook in the application for leave not to contend that the land in question fell within the concluding part of *IHTA 1984, s 115(2)*, namely 'such cottages, farm buildings and farmhouses, together with the land occupied with them, as are of a character appropriate to the property'. The reason for such an undertaking being given was that the former Inland Revenue did not agree with the taxpayer that the appeal should be to the High Court and would have opposed the taxpayer's application for leave to appeal direct to the High Court if such contention had been made. In addition, because of the differing ownerships of the property in question and the remainder of the farm, such a contention may not have been possible. Consequently, because no contention was made concerning woodlands or buildings used for intensive rearing, the appeal turned on whether the land constituted 'agricultural land or pasture' within the first leg of that provision. The taxpayer contended that the *Interpretation Act 1978, Sch 1* definition of 'land' so as to include 'buildings and other structures' should apply in the expression 'agricultural land'. It was held that it did not apply because *Interpretation Act 1978, s 5* provides that definitions provided by that *Act* only apply 'unless the contrary intention appears' and by giving the expression 'agricultural land or pasture' the more limited and natural meaning for which the former Inland Revenue contended, namely that the primary meaning of 'agricultural property' was 'agricultural land or pasture' which meant 'bare land', i.e. fields or land used either for the cultivation of crops or for the grazing of animals, it was possible to give a sensible meaning to the remainder of the definition by extending the meaning of 'agricultural property' to include species of property which the expression 'agricultural land' did not cover. Because of the taxpayer's undertaking in the application for leave to appeal direct to the High Court, the decision in the case may have to be considered special to its circumstances. In a decision on 19 May 1995 the Court of Appeal dismissed the appeal by the executors.

In *Farmer v CIR* [1999] STC SCD 321 Sp C 216 it was accepted that there was a single composite business comprising of farming and letting of various farm buildings. The Special Commissioners in this case came to the decision that on the application of the 'wholly or mainly' test and taking the business as a whole it consisted mainly of farming. In support of this were the facts that the property was a business property of landed estate with a majority of the land being used for farming. The lettings element was subsidiary to the farming enterprise and was of short duration. In viewing the capital that was employed in the business amounting to about £3.5 million, £1.25 million was attributable to the letting element and the balance to farming. Also, the employees and consultants spent a greater proportion of time on the farming activities and the farm turnover exceeded the letting turnover in six years out of eight but significantly the net profit of the lettings exceeded the net profit from the farming. This last point did not sway the view that the farm was a business rather than an investment because the 'wholly or mainly' test could not be determined solely on the basis of net profits but the character of the business should be looked at as a whole. In addition, it is necessary to consider the overall position over a period of time rather than for a particular period in isolation. (See also *Millington v Secretary of State for the Environment and Another* CA, [1999] TLR 29 June 1999). See also *Harrold and others (executors of Harrold deceased) v CIR* [1996] STC (SCD) 195 Sp C 71 and *Dixon v CIR* [2002] STC SCD 53 Sp C 297.

In an appeal to the Special Commissioners in 2008, a claim for BPR was made for land let under a conacre agreement. A widow (M) inherited 33 acres of farmland on the death of her husband. She did not farm the land herself, but let it to local farmers under an agreement of this type. Her personal representatives contended that the farmland qualified for BPR. The Special Commissioner rejected this contention and dismissed the appeal, holding that although M was carrying on a business on the land, that business consisted mainly of making or holding investments, within *IHTA 1984, s 105(3)*, so that the land was not 'relevant business property'. This decision was upheld by the Northern Ireland Court of Appeal. APR of 100% applies to the ordinary value of farmland

and is unaffected by the decision. *PN McCall & BJA Keenan (Personal Representatives of Mrs E McClean) v HMRC* [2009] STC 990. See Example 1 below and also **6.3** BUSINESS PROPERTY and **55** TAX CASES.

The First-tier Tribunal considered the above decision in *Allen v HMRC* [2016] UKFTT 342 (TC), a case concerning business asset taper relief for capital gains tax purposes. It was concluded that the land sold by the taxpayer, previously let from year to year under a conacre arrangement, was occupied by the taxpayer for the purposes of husbandry. The taxpayer had supplied some fertiliser for the land and gave instructions concerning the management of it as well as cutting the hedges and eradicating poisonous weeds.

HMRC accept that in appropriate cases APR is available for land let under a licence although where nothing more is done than collect rent and maintain boundaries no farming activity is undertaken by the landowner and relief will be refused. As regards conacre arrangements relief depends entirely on the facts of the case: 'Where such arrangements are in place the availability of agricultural relief on the land, and on any "farmhouse" where occupation for agricultural purposes is claimed by reference to the deceased's involvement with the land, is considered in exactly the same way as in the rest of the UK. That is, the availability of agricultural relief is a question of fact and degree to be decided upon the particular facts of each case.' IHT Manual at IHTM24075.

Example 1

D has owned and let 70 acres of land in Northern Ireland since 1980. This land was farmed for arable crops but under the conacre scheme he has, since 1994 let it for periods of 11 months to another local farmer for the growing of rapeseed and wheat. The 70 acres are valued at £1,200 per acre of agricultural land and the value of the farmhouse is £280,000. The land is situated in a newly designated brownfield site under a Regional Development Strategy Plan to be implemented by 2026 which will be valued at £4m. On 1 July 2019, D died and by will bequeaths all the land to his son, E, at a time when its agricultural value has increased to £1,500 per acre but its potential open market value is £57,000 per acre. E continues to run the farm conacre business from the farmhouse which he inherited under the terms of his father's will, the value of which has decreased to £225,000 due to the potential development encroachment.

		£
Valuations for IHT purposes		
70 acres at £1,500 per acre		105,000
Farmhouse		225,000
Development value		3,895,000
Total value		4,225,000
The transfers subject to tax on D's death:		
(i) Agricultural value of land		
70 acres × £1,500	105,000	
Less agricultural property relief at 100%	(105,000)	—
(ii) Farmhouse		225,000

(iii) Value of development land potential not attracting BPR	3,895,000
	4,120,000
Deduct Nil rate band	325,000
Chargeable at 40% on death of D	£3,795,000
	£
IHT payable	1,518,000
Payable by ten-yearly instalments (*IHTA 1984, s 227*) of	151,800

Notes to the example

(A) Conacre is a specifically Irish tradition of letting small parcels of land for a single crop. It is part and parcel of the business of small farming in particular and it is temporary by its very nature as lettings are always limited to 11 months. The rents the lets earn are normally low returns and it is essentially a way of maintaining land for which a farming family has no plans in a particular season.

(B) If the whole or any part of the property concerned is sold, then the related tax still outstanding (with accrued interest if relevant) becomes payable immediately unless (i) the sale precedes the date that the first instalment is due in which case the tax does not become due until that date; or (ii) the sale is by a transferee following a **35** POTENTIALLY EXEMPT TRANSFERS and the transferee dies before the transferor. Where there is a delay between the dates of contract and completion, the sale for the purposes of *IHTA 1984, s 227(4)* is deemed to take place at the completion date.

Where the prudent lotting of an agricultural estate rests on the basis of separate farm lots, the question of sporting rights should be considered as the value may be materially affected by the hypothesis of separate ownership of farms. (VOA IHT manual, section 9, para 9.3). If the whole of one or more of the lots is exempt then it is not necessary to value that lot and if it is only a part that is exempt the valuation should be done on a just and reasonable basis. (VOA IHT manual, section 9, para 9.4).

Farmhouses

[4.2] Whether a farmhouse is to be classed as agricultural property is mainly a question of the purpose of occupation rather than the actual use to which it is put by the owner/occupier. The property must also be of a 'character appropriate' to the land.

As the farmhouse is, in terms of the legislation, a form of agricultural property, the occupation and ownership tests applicable to all such property for the purposes of the relief (see **4.3**) must be satisfied *throughout* the period of two years up to the time of the chargeable event. This gives rise to difficulties in the case of a farmer whose health fails in his or her final years, such that the farmer has to move out of the home into care; see for example *HMRC v Atkinson and Smith* [2011] UKUT 506 (TCC), [2012] STC 289 summarised below. The report of the Office of Tax Simplification issued in July 2019 highlighted this as a matter on which HMRC should review its approach, although without a change in the legislation it is thought that HMRC is unlikely to adopt this recommendation.

HMRC apply the following tests to determine whether a farmhouse is of a character appropriate to the land:

- Is the farmhouse appropriate by reference to its size, layout and content with the farm buildings and the particular area of farmland being farmed?
- Is the farmhouse proportionate in size and nature to the requirements of the agricultural activities conducted on the agricultural land?
- Within the agricultural land does the land predominate so that the farmhouse is ancillary to the land?
- Would a reasonable and informed person regard the property simply as a house with land or as a farmhouse?
- Applying the 'elephant test', would you recognise this as a farmhouse if you saw it?
- How long has the farmhouse and agricultural property been associated and is there a history of agricultural production?
- Considering the relationship between the value of the house and the profitability of the land, would the house attract demand from a commercial farmer who has to earn a living from the land, or is its value significantly out of proportion to the profitability of the land?
- Considering all other relevant factors, including whether any land is let out and on what terms, is the scale of the agricultural operations in context?
- There must be some connection or nexus between 'such cottages, farm buildings and farmhouses, together with the land occupied with them' and the property to which they must be of a character appropriate.

Case law — 'Farmhouse'

In the case of *Higginson's Executors v CIR* [2002] STC SCD 483 Sp C 337 the farmhouse was originally a nineteenth-century hunting lodge with six bedrooms, 63 acres of agricultural land, three acres of formal gardens and 68 acres of woodlands. The Special Commissioner dismissed the appeal, holding that:

> 'for the purposes of *section 115(2)* the unit must be an agricultural unit: that is to say that within the unit, the land must predominate . . . (and) any qualifying cottages, farm buildings or farmhouses must be ancillary to the land.'

However, in view of the price paid for the property, it was clear that

> 'within this particular unit it is the house which predominates, and that what we have here is a house with farmland going with it (and not vice versa).'

Accordingly, the lodge was not a 'farmhouse' for the purposes of *s 115(2)*. In the case of *Lloyds TSB plc (Antrobus' Personal Representatives) v CIR* [2002] STC SCD 468 Sp C 336 however, the farmhouse, Cookhill Priory, comprised of six bedrooms and the farm was 126 acres of freehold land and six and a half acres of tenanted land. It was accepted that the Priory and the land and surrounding buildings (including a chapel) were agricultural property. The Special Commissioner allowed the appeal, finding that the property 'was in a poor state of repair and maintenance'. The result was that, even if the dwelling-house had at one time been a family home of some distinction, it had, both in appearance and in use, become a farmhouse on a working farm. On the evidence, the house was 'a farmhouse with a farm and definitely not a house with land'. It was 'of a character appropriate to the property' for the purposes of *s 115(2)*. However, having lost the case at the Special Commissioners in October 2002, HMRC issued a notice of determination on the basis that the agricultural value of the farmhouse was less than the market value. Subsequently, the case went to the Lands Tribunal where the day-to-day operations were given more focus than the management of the farm when considering the actual business of farming. When considering the operational components of the farming business for the purposes of securing APR the Tribunal stated:

> 'There is, we think, no dispute about the definition when it is expressed in this way. The question is: who is the farmer of the land for the purposes of s 115(2)? In our view it is the person who lives in the farmhouse in order to farm the land on a day-to-day basis. It is likely, although it may not necessarily always be the case, that his principal occupation will consist of farming the land comprised in the farm. We do not think that a house occupied with a farm is a farmhouse simply because the person living there is in overall control of the agricultural business conducted on the land; and in particular we think that the lifestyle of the farmer, the person whose bid for the land is treated as establishing the agricultural value of the land, is not the farmer for the purposes of these provisions.'

It may be a matter of dispute whether the above *dictum* is persuasive enough to influence other cases where the farmhouse under scrutiny for APR incorporates this 'lifestyle buyers' application. The result did secure discount of 30% in the value for APR purposes. See *Lloyds TSB plc (Antrobus' Personal Representatives) v Twiddy (Inland Revenue Capital Taxes)* [2006] 1 EGLR 157, [2006] RVR 138, Land Trib, 53 VALUATION and IHTM24036.

In *Rosser v CIR* [2003] STC 311, SCD a former farmhouse was ostensibly treated as a 'retirement' home and did not qualify as agricultural property whereas a barn within the same curtilage was treated as such due to the fact that is was in general use for farming. The effect of *s 115(2)* was that 'broiler houses' on a farm could only qualify for relief if they had been 'a subsidiary part of the purpose of an overall agricultural activity carried out on the land'. Since they had been let to a separate company, this was not the case. Accordingly, the broiler houses were not 'ancillary' to the farm, within *s 115(2)*, and did not qualify for relief. See *Williams (Williams' Personal Representatives) v HMRC* [2005] STC 782, SCD.

In *Arnander, Lloyd & Villiers (McKenna's Executors)*, a small country estate comprising a large house with six acres of gardens and some domestic outbuildings, and 187 acres of land, most of which was farmland, the Special Commissioner reviewed the evidence in detail and held that three of the outbuildings qualified for relief but that the main house and eight of the outbuildings did not. The house which the couple lived in was not 'the main dwelling from which the agricultural operations over the land were conducted and managed'. See *Arnander (executors of McKenna, decd) v HMRC* [2006] STC 800, [2007] RVR 208, SCD.

In *HMRC v Atkinson and Smith* [2011] UKUT 506 (TCC), [2012] STC 289 decision date 31 October 2011, relief was held not to be available for a bungalow let to a family farming partnership of which the deceased was a member. He had lived in a bungalow on the farm until 2002, when he became ill and moved to a care home where he died in 2006. His bungalow remained uninhabited during his illness, although he occasionally visited it and his possessions remained there. His executors claimed that the bungalow qualified for agricultural property relief as being occupied by the partnership for agricultural purposes up to the date of death. HMRC rejected the claim and the Upper Tax Tribunal upheld HMRC's case on the basis that the partnership had made no use of the bungalow after the deceased moved into care. Accordingly it was not correct to say that it was occupied for the purposes of agriculture after the deceased moved out. See **55** TAX CASES.

In *Hanson v HMRC* [2012] UKFTT 95 a farmhouse owned by a settlement in which the deceased had an interest in possession had been jointly occupied by him and his son up to the date of his death. The son ran his own farming business from the property on land which he owned personally. Originally the business was conducted in partnership with the deceased but on dissolution of the partnership the son continued the business as a sole trader. The trustee of the settlement claimed agricultural property relief in respect of the farmhouse as it was occupied for agricultural purposes. HMRC refused the claim, citing the decision in *Rosser v CIR* (see above) as authority for the proposition that the house and applicable farmland must be in both common occupation and common ownership. The First-tier Tax Tribunal allowed the trustee's appeal on the basis that a test of common occupation of farmhouse and farmland fits the scheme of the IHT legislation best. Relief was therefore due.

In *Golding and Middleton (executors of Golding dec'd) v Revenue and Customs Comrs* [2011] UKFTT 351 (TC) a modest three-bedroom detached property was held to be of a character appropriate to the 16.29 acres of land held with it. HMRC did not argue that the property was outside the definition of farmhouse and the First-tier Tax Tribunal said that they were right to concede this point. The dispute centred on the limited farming activity conducted by the deceased (egg production from approximately 70 free range hens) and the paucity of profit from the sale of eggs, which never exceeded £1,600 in the fours years up to the date of death. However, the Tribunal considered that the level of profit was not of particular interest in deciding the point at issue and that the question was this: was the deceased farming? The Tribunal noted that the deceased was 80 years of age at the time of his death and accordingly it would not be reasonable to expect an extensive farming activity from someone of that age. Otherwise very few farms would qualify for relief. It was held that he was farming as a vocational activity, as is common amongst farmers who may be prepared to forgo luxuries. See now IHTM24053 where HMRC state that 'you should advise taxpayers relying on this case that each case is judged on its own particular facts' and it is unlikely that similar facts will be found in many other cases. HMRC remain of the view that the profit of a farmer is a useful indicator of the activities undertaken in considering whether or not a property is a 'farmhouse'.

In *Charnley and Hodgkinson (as Gill's executors) v HMRC* [2019] UKFTT 650 (TC), a grazing agreement was held to be sufficient to allow both agricultural relief on both the land and the farmhouse, and business relief on the farm machinery. The farm owner, Mr Gill, had entered into an agreement with a third party B under which the latter's animals would be allowed onto Mr Gill's land, who would provide full care for them and only inform B if there was a problem. The evidence was that Mr Gill worked every day around the farm and was said therefore to be farming his own land but using B's stock. The First-tier Tax Tribunal held that the deceased was an active farmer so that reliefs were available in respect of all the farming assets except two properties which were let commercially.

Conditions and rates

Occupation and ownership

[4.3] The agricultural property must have been either:

(a) **occupied** by the transferor for the purposes of agriculture throughout the period of two years ending with the date of transfer, or

(b) **owned** by the transferor for the period of seven years ending with the date of transfer and have been occupied throughout that period either by the transferor or by any third party for the purposes of agriculture. [*IHTA 1984, s 117*]. See *Wheatley (Executors of Wheatley dec'd) v IRC* [1998] STC (SCD) 60.

Where neither of these conditions is satisfied, there will be no relief. Thus for example, if land has been farmed in hand by the owner for his entire lifetime save for the final period of one year when he or she was too ill to continue to work, no relief will be due.

Relief extends to shares and securities if agricultural property forms part of the company's assets and part of the value of the shares or securities can be attributed to the agricultural value of the agricultural property. [*IHTA 1984, s 122*]. See **4.13** below.

After establishing that relief is due, it is then a question of what the rate of relief is.

Rate of relief

[4.4] The rate of relief is a percentage reduction of the value transferred by a transfer of value (including an occasion on which tax is chargeable under the rules on **40** SETTLEMENTS WITHOUT INTERESTS IN POSSESSION). The percentage reduction is made before deduction of the annual exemption and other **21** EXEMPT TRANSFERS and before grossing-up where the transferor pays the tax. Subject to the conditions in **4.3** above, the percentage is 50% unless any of the following apply to allow 100% relief:

(a) **100%** in relation to transfers of value made, and other events occurring, after 9 March 1992 (previously 50%) of the agricultural value of the property transferred if either:

  (i) the transferor immediately before the transfer enjoyed either the right to vacant possession or the right to obtain it within the next twelve months; or

  (ii) the transferor has been beneficially entitled to his interest since before 10 March 1981; and

(1) if he had disposed of it by a transfer of value immediately before that date, he would have been entitled to claim the 50% relief available after 6 April 1976 and before 10 March 1981; and

(2) that relief would not have been restricted by reference to the limits of £250,000 or 1,000 acres (whichever was the more favourable to the taxpayer) applying between those dates (see also Note (A) below); and

(3) the interest did not in the period from 10 March 1981 to the date of transfer, give him the vacant possession rights in (a)(i) above and did not fail to give him those rights because of any act or deliberate omission by him during that period.

(b) **100%** in relation to transfers of value of farmland let for periods exceeding twelve months which is let on or after 1 September 1995 (the commencement date of the *Agricultural Tenancies Act 1995* and *Agricultural Holdings (Scotland) Act 1991, s 12* by right of succession in Scotland). [*IHTA 1984, s 116(2)(c) as inserted by FA 1995, s 155(1)*]. Previously the relief was 50% where let farmland which did not or still does not, under an existing pre-1 September 1995 agreement, entitle the transferor to vacant possession or the right to obtain vacant possession within the next twelve months. A tenancy starting on or after 1 September 1995 by reason of statutory succession to an existing tenancy is not excluded from the full relief. Where land is added after 1995 to an existing AHA tenancy, 100% relief may then apply due to an implied surrender and regrant of the tenancy (see IHTM24241). However, *FA 1996, s 185* enables a tenancy acquired by succession by way of death of the existing tenant to be treated as commencing on the date of death where this is on or after 1 September 1995. A statutory succession would normally take effect from the grant of succession to the new tenancy but this is overridden for the purposes of *IHTA 1984* and the commencement is taken as the date of death of the tenant being succeeded. In the case of a tenant's retirement in favour of a new tenant on or after 1 September 1995 but there is the landowner's death in between the notice of retirement and the succession by the new tenant, the date of the tenancy is deemed to have commenced for these purposes as just before the landowner's death. This has the effect of allowing 100% relief from the date of the death of the landowner whereas under normal rules the relief would only be available from the grant of the new tenancy. [*IHTA 1984, s 116(5A)–(5D)* as inserted by *FA 1996, s 185*].

Example 2

A and B, who are brothers, farm 1,500 acres of arable land under a tenancy agreement with the landowner X. B dies on 26 July 2017 and leaves his share of the tenancy to A's son C. At the beginning of October 2017, A retires and lets his son C have his share of the tenancy as from 1 November 2017 and advises X by notice in writing. Landowner X dies on 16 November 2018. The tenancy agreement and the provisions of B's will are not resolved until 18 January and 28 August 2019 respectively.

In the case of C's succession to B's tenancy, this will be treated as having commenced on B's death notwithstanding X's death later on 16 November 2018. In the case of A's decision to retire in favour of his son C, the tenancy will be treated as having commenced on 16 November 2018 for the purposes of the rate of any agricultural relief on the death of X. In this latter case of retirement, the succession by C to the tenancy of the land let to A can take effect up to 30 months from November 2017. Therefore 100% agricultural property relief applies to the let land on gift or transfer subject to the other qualifying conditions.

Notes to the example

(A) *IHTA 1984, s 116(5A)*, inserted by *FA 1996, s 185*, relates to successions to tenancies in Scotland whereas *s 116(5B)* relates to tenancies other than in Scotland. See also *Agricultural Holdings (Scotland) Act 2003, ss 20, 22* where a short limited duration tenancy or a limited duration tenancy may be bequeathed or transferred by reason of intestacy to a person entitled to succeed to the deceased's intestate estate and the executor shall be entitled so to transfer the interest without the consent of the landlord. This may well have been preceded by a Notice of Interest in Acquiring Land signed by a tenant under the *Agricultural Holdings (Forms) (Scotland) Regulations 2004* but still 100% APR should be available to the landlord in these cases.

(B) *IHTA 1984, s 116(5D)* relates to the situation above where X dies on or after 1 September 1995 following a notice of retirement but before the new tenancy has taken effect and takes place within 30 months of the notice being given (which also includes an assignment or assignation in Scotland).

(C) The notice of retirement must be a notice or other written intimation given by the tenant (joint tenants or tenants in common) to the landowner indicating, under whatever terms, that the person or persons in the notice should become the tenant of the property. This may arise from, say, a three-generation tenancy renewable every five years.

Agricultural Holdings Act tenancies

The *Agricultural Tenancies Act 1995, s 4(1)(g)* affords the opportunity to grant a new tenancy, on or after 1 September 1995, thereby permitting the landlord 100% agricultural property relief and allowing the tenant to remain under the protection of *AHA 1986* (see **4.20** at the conclusion of this chapter).

[IHTA 1984, s 116(1)–(3), (5A)–(5E), (7); F(No 2)A 1992, s 73, Sch 14 paras 4, 8; FA 1995, ss 154(2), 155; FA 1996, s 185].

(c) **100%** in relation to chargeable transfers of value of farmland and related buildings that have been dedicated to wildlife habitats on or after 26 November 1996 which meet the usual ownership criteria. [*FA 1997, s 94* inserting new *IHTA 1984, s 124C*]. Land and any related buildings will be treated as agricultural land and associated farm buildings where the land and buildings are dedicated to the Government's Habitat Schemes under any of the following:
- *Habitat (Water Fringe) Regulations 1994, SI 1994/1291, Reg 3(1)* as amended by *SI 1996/1480* and *SI 1996/3106.*
- *Habitat (Former Set-Aside Land) Regulations 1994, SI 1994/1292* as amended by *SI 1996/1478* and *SI 1996/3107.*
- *Habitat (Salt-Marsh) Regulations 1994, SI 1994/1293* as amended by *SI 1995/2871* and *SI 1995/2891; SI 1996/1479* and *SI 1996/3108.*
- *Habitats (Scotland) Regulations 1994, SI 1994/2710, Reg 3(2)(a)* as amended by *SI 1996/3035.*
- *Habitat Improvement Regulations (Northern Ireland) 1995, SR(NI) 1995/134, Reg 3(1)(a).*

Habitat and stewardship schemes

The relief at (c) above was designed for the habitat schemes listed many of which have closed over the years or been amalgamated with other stewardship schemes. Relief for existing cases may still apply as in Example 3. To update the position, it was announced in the 2024 Budget that relief for land managed under an environmental agreement with, or on behalf of, the UK Government, devolved administrations, public bodies, local authorities, or approved responsible bodies will be available for lifetime transfers and transfers at death on or after 6 April 2025. This will apply where there is an agreement in place for the environmental land management scheme on or after 6 March 2024. It will be a requirement that the land was agricultural land within the conditions for agricultural relief for at least two years immediately prior to the land use change. The existing holding period for agricultural property relief will not be restarted by land use change. The valuation of the qualifying land will be the market value of environmental land subject to the special assumption of a restriction to its existing use. Consistent with the current rules, buildings used in connection with environmental land, including farmhouses, will qualify for relief where that building is occupied with, and that occupation is ancillary to, environmental land. In relation to the farmhouse, it will remain the case that the character appropriate test must be satisfied. The legislation for this extension of agricultural relief was not made available prior to the dissolution of Parliament on 30 May 2024 and it remains to be seen if the proposals will be carried forward under a new government.

Prior to this announcement, land which is taken out of agricultural use and entered into an agri-environment scheme would not qualify for agricultural relief but it may qualify for business property relief, assuming that it forms part of a business which continues to be mainly farming

(IHTM25252). Land used for generating credits to offset carbon and other gases connected to climate change will, in principle, qualify for business property relief in their own right.

Example 3

D has owned and farmed 700 acres of land since 1970. This land has been farmed for arable crops but under the set-aside scheme he has, since 1994 under the *Habitat (Former Set-Aside Land) Regulations 1994*, taken out 200 acres for a period of 20 years to be used for rare nesting owls in accordance with the Government's Habitat Scheme. Also, two former grain storage warehouses, valued at £34,000, have been converted to a hide and an information centre. These have both been let to the Conservation Volunteer Development Society since 1994. The remaining 500 acres continue to be farmed as crops for human consumption. The value of the farmland is £1,500 per acre and the set-aside land is valued at £950 per acre. D dies on 30 September 2019 and leaves all the farmland including set-aside to his son E. The value of the farmhouse is £500,000.

	£
500 acres at £1,500 per acre	750,000
Farmhouse	500,000
200 acres of Habitat land at £950 per acre	190,000
Value of agricultural property	1,440,000
Less amount of agricultural relief @ 100%	(1,440,000)
Chargeable	Nil
	£
Former grain storage warehouse	34,000
Less amount of agricultural relief @ 50%	(17,000)
Total value of farm on which tax is chargeable	17,000

Notes to the example

(A) As the former grain storage warehouses are associated farm buildings within the Habitat Scheme, the owner is entitled to agricultural property relief but because the buildings were rented out on or before 31 August 1995 only 50% relief is due.

(B) The normal conditions for relief in **4.3** above apply to the land in the Habitat Scheme.

Example 4

X has owned, since 1983, 1,000 acres of land. In June 1992, he began to farm the land, utilising 800 acres for that purpose. The remaining 200 acres are used for grazing by horses. On 1 July 2018, X transfers all the land to his son, Y, at a time when its agricultural value was £1,000 per acre and its open market value £1,500 per acre. He had not used his annual exemptions for 2018/19 and 2017/18. X dies on 6 September 2021. Y has continued to run the farm business since the date of the gift.

The value of the gift for inheritance tax purposes before relief is

		£	£
1,000 acres at £1,500 per acre			£1,500,000
The transfer subject to tax is			
(i)	Agricultural value of land		
	800 acres × £1,000	800,000	
	Less agricultural property relief at 100%	(800,000)	—
(ii)	Non-agricultural value of land		
	800 acres × £500		400,000
(iii)	Value of land not used in business		
	200 acres at £1,500 per acre		300,000
			700,000
Deduct annual exemptions (2018/19 and 2017/18)			6,000
Value transferred by PET becoming chargeable on death			£694,000

Notes to the example

(A) Business property relief may be available in respect of the £400,000 excess of the open market value over the agricultural value.

(B) IHT will be charged at 80% of full rates as X died more than three but not more than four years after the gift.

100% relief by concession

Extra-Statutory Concession F17 allows 100% agricultural property relief in place of 50% relief where the transferor's interest in the property either:

(i) carries the right to vacant possession within 24 months of the date of transfer; or

(ii) is, notwithstanding the terms of the tenancy, valued at an amount broadly equivalent to the vacant possession value.

The landlord of tenanted farmland may have a contractual right to serve notice to the tenant to vacate the property within 12 months of the date of transfer but because of the *Agricultural Holdings Act 1986* (and similar legislation in Scotland and Northern Ireland), vacant possession cannot be obtained for a further 12 months after the tenancy agreement is terminated. The same situation arises where there is a tenancy which lasts for more than one and less than two years (*Gladstone v Bower* [1960] 2 QB 384, [1960] 3 All ER 353, CA type of arrangement). In such cases, the concession allows 100% relief under the first limb above.

The second limb of the concession applies where the transferor and the tenant are so closely connected that in practice, the value of the property on the open market is broadly the same as with vacant possession e.g. land let to a company by the transferor who also controls that company. See also *IRC v Gray (Executor of Lady Fox)* [1994] STC 360, [1994] RVR 129, CA.

APR summary — land and buildings

A summary of the above may be detailed as follows:

Summary of situations where 100% relief is due in respect of agricultural property

Circumstance	Qualifying requirements	Relevant legislation applicable
Vacant possession.	Vacant possession of the agricultural property must be held by the transferor including land farmed subject to a licence. See (a)(i) above.	*IHTA 1984, s 116(2)(a).*
Land let subject to a tenancy beginning on or after 1 September 1995.	Applies in respect of all land that is subject to a farm business tenancy. It applies to land let that is subject to a succession tenancy granted on or after 1 September 1995. An extension of the relief applies where either (i) a valid retirement notice for succession has been made after 1 September 1995, or (ii) the tenant has died after that date and the tenancy has become vested or obtained by another person. See (b) above.	*IHTA 1984, s 116(2)(c), (5A)–(5D)* as extended by *FA 1996, s 185(2); Agricultural Holdings Act 1986, s 25.*
Near vacant possession value or short-term loss of vacant possession.	Applies where the transferor's interest in the property does not carry vacant possession but is valued near vacant possession value e.g. land let to a company where the company is controlled by the transferor. See (e) above and **4.14** below. Alternatively, the transferor must have the right to obtain vacant possession within 24 months.	Extra-Statutory Concession F17. *IHTA 1984, s 116(2)(a).*
Pre-1981 'full-time working farmer' provision.	Applies where land has been continuously let to a partnership or company since prior to 10 March 1981 which the transferor has previously farmed in some capacity. See (a)(ii) above.	*IHTA 1984, s 116(2)(b).*
Post-5 April 1995.	Applies where land and buildings used in the cultivation of short-rotation coppice.	*FA 1995, s 154.*
Post-25 November 1996 'dedicated wildlife habitats'.	Applies where land is being used or has been let on or after 26 November 1996 dedicated to wildlife habitats. See (c) above.	*IHTA 1984, s 124C.*

'Agricultural value'

[4.5] Agricultural value is the value of agricultural property on the assumption that it is subject to perpetual covenant prohibiting its use otherwise than as agricultural property. Therefore any development value cannot benefit from agricultural property relief, although it may qualify for business property relief if it is farmed in hand.

Farm cottages occupied by persons employed solely for agricultural purposes in connection with the agricultural property are valued without taking any account of the fact that the cottages are suitable for the residential purposes of persons not so employed. Thus the value of such cottages for IHT purposes will normally be restricted to their agricultural value. *IHTA 1984, s 115(3)* does not require 'exclusive occupation' for agricultural purposes as evidenced in the case of, say, a country manor house which is purchased at a premium (because of the tax shelter relief obtained) where agricultural land adjoining the manor house is also acquired notwithstanding the fact that it is farmed under a contracting agreement. See Taxation Magazine, 3 April 2003 p 14. [*IHTA 1984, ss 115(3), 169*].

Extra-Statutory Concession F16 gives relief to certain farm cottages that would not normally be relieved from IHT on a lifetime or death transfer. The condition that a farm cottage is occupied by persons employed solely for agricultural purposes is also satisfied in respect of chargeable transfers from 13 February 1995 where the cottage is occupied by a retired farm worker or his/her surviving spouse or civil partner if the occupation is either:

(a) protected under the *Rent (Agriculture) Act 1976* or *Housing Act 1988* (or similar legislation in Scotland and Northern Ireland); or
(b) under a lease granted as part of the worker's contract of employment in agriculture which has a similar effect to that of a protected tenancy or licence (e.g. lease granted as terms of employment).

Where the valuation of the land reflects the benefit of milk quota, agricultural relief is given on that value (HMRC Tax Bulletin February 1993 p 51).

If at the date of transfer there are crops growing on the land these are legally part of the land until severed. However, the DV should exclude the value of growing crops from their report unless HMRC specifically requests otherwise and if the DV is aware that the value includes growing crops without a separate figure then the case should be returned to HMRC. (VOA IHT manual, section 9, paras 9.40 and 9.41). The value of permanent or temporary pasture and the value of cultivations or unexhausted manures should be included and where the value of growing crops have been included with the value of the land then HMRC will ask them to state their separate values. (VOA IHT manual, section 9, para 9.41).

Example 5

A has owned and occupied land for the purposes of agriculture for the last three years and transfers it to a discretionary trust in May 2020. He has not used his annual exemption for either the year 2019/20 or 2020/21. The value of the gift for inheritance tax purposes is £400,000 and the agricultural value is agreed at £280,000.

		£	£
Value transferred			400,000
Less relief of 100% on £280,000			280,000
			120,000
Less	Annual exemption 2020/21	3,000	
	Annual exemption 2019/20	3,000	6,000
Net value transferred (subject to grossing-up if tax paid by A)			£114,000

Interest in possession in settled agricultural property

[4.6] A person with an interest in possession is regarded as the beneficial owner of the settled property where it arose before 22 March 2006, or where it is an immediate post-death interest, a transitional serial interest or a disabled person's interest. In such circumstances, a change of beneficial interest will cause a new period of ownership to commence for the purposes of the relief except where the agricultural property is inherited on the death of the spouse, see **4.12**. [*IHTA 1984, s 49(1)*].

Replacements

[4.7] Where agricultural property *occupied* by the transferor on the date of transfer replaced other agricultural property, condition (a) at **4.6** is satisfied if both properties, together with any earlier agricultural property directly or indirectly replaced, were occupied by that person for the purposes of agriculture for periods comprising at least two years within the five years ending with the date of the transfer. Where agricultural property *owned* by the transferor on the date of the transfer replaced other agricultural property, condition (b) is satisfied if the respective properties were both owned by the transferor and occupied (by them or another person) for the purposes of agriculture for at least seven years within the ten years ending with the date of the transfer.

In both cases relief is limited to what it would have been if any one or more of the replacements in the respective periods had not taken place. For this purpose, changes resulting from the formation, alteration or dissolution of a partnership are disregarded. [*IHTA 1984, s 118*].

Occupation by company or partnership

[4.8] Occupation by a company controlled by the transferor is treated as occupation by the transferor. 'Control' is defined by *IHTA 1984, s 269*, and is essentially based on voting control for matters affecting the company as a whole. Voting rights on shares held by the spouse or civil partner are counted, so if together the two have voting control of a company, both will be regarded as being in occupation of land farmed by the company. For further details of the test for control of companies, see **32.8** PAYMENT OF TAX. Occupation by a Scottish partnership is treated as occupation by the partners. [*IHTA 1984, s 119*].

Binding contract for sale

[4.9] Relief will not be given if at the time of the transfer, the transferor has entered into a binding contract for sale of (i) agricultural property (unless the sale is to a company in return for an issue of shares which will give the transferor control of that company); or (ii) shares or securities in agricultural companies (see **4.13** below) except where the sale is made for the purpose of reconstruction or amalgamation. [*IHTA 1984, s 124*].

Further conditions for lifetime transfers

[4.10] Agricultural property relief is only available where any part of the value transferred by a 35 POTENTIALLY EXEMPT TRANSFERS proves to be a chargeable transfer if, in addition to the conditions in **4.3** above, the conditions listed below are also satisfied. Similarly, where a chargeable lifetime transfer, other than a potentially exempt transfer, made within seven years of the transferor's death is reduced under the agricultural property relief provisions, the additional tax chargeable by reason of death must be calculated as if the relief had not been received unless the following additional conditions are satisfied.

Subject to the provisions below for replacement property, the additional conditions are:

(a) that the original property was owned by the 'transferee' throughout the period beginning with the date of the chargeable transfer and ending with the transferor's death or, if earlier, the transferee's death (the 'relevant period') and is not at the time of death subject to a binding contract for sale; and

(b) except in a case falling within (c) below, the original property is agricultural property immediately before the death and has been occupied (by the transferee or another) for the purposes of agriculture throughout the relevant period; and

(c) where the original property consists of shares or securities of a company, that throughout the relevant period the agricultural property in question was owned by the company and occupied (by the company or another) for the purposes of agriculture.

'*Transferee*' means the person whose property the original property became on that chargeable transfer or, where on the transfer the original property became or remained settled property in which no qualifying interest in possession subsists, the trustees of the settlement.

Where any shares owned by the transferee immediately before the death would either be identified with the original property under the provisions of *TCGA 1992, ss 126–136* (reorganisations of share capital, conversion of securities and company reconstructions and amalgamations) *or* were issued to him in consideration of the transfer of agricultural property consisting of the original property (or part), his period of ownership of the original property is treated as including his period of ownership of the shares (in relation to transfers of value made, and other events occurring, before 17 March 1987 the shares were treated as if they were the original property (or part)).

Where part only of the original property satisfies the conditions in (a) to (c) above, proportionate agricultural property relief is given.

Example 6

A is the freehold owner of agricultural land which at current vacant possession value is estimated to be valued at £850,000. On 29 September 1989, he enters into an agricultural tenancy (with more than two years to run) with a farming partnership comprising his two sons and his grandson for a full market rental of £25,000 p.a. The tenanted value is estimated at £500,000.

In July 2010 his grandson is killed in a farming accident and a new letting agreement is made between the two sons and A for a full market rent of £35,000 p.a. on 15 September 2010.

A dies on 1 October 2020 when the tenanted value of the land has risen to £600,000.

	£
Transfer at death (tenanted valuation)	600,000
Deduct agricultural property relief	600,000
IHT payable	Nil

Notes to the example

(A) As the land is let under an agreement on or after 1 September 1995 relief of 100% is available. Only 50% relief would have been available if the existing tenancy had continued. [*IHTA 1984, s 116; FA 1995, s 155; FA 1996, s 185*].

(B) The addition of land to an *AHA 1986* tenancy will have the effect of a surrender and re-grant on or after 1 September 1995 thereby ensuring the landlord receives 100% relief.

Replacement property

[4.11] Where the transferee has disposed of all or part of the original property before the death of the transferor and applied the whole of the consideration received in acquiring a replacement property within the 'allowed period' after the disposal of the original property or part (or has entered into a binding contract to acquire replacement property within that time), then, provided the disposal and acquisition are both made in transactions at arm's length or on terms such as might be expected to be included in such a transaction, the conditions in (a) to (c) above are taken as satisfied if:

(i) the replacement property is owned by the transferee immediately before the transferor's death (or immediately before the transferee's death if earlier) and is not at that time subject to a binding contract; and

(ii) throughout the period beginning with the date of the chargeable transfer and ending with the disposal, the original property was owned by the transferee and occupied (by him or another) for the purposes of agriculture; and

(iii) throughout the period beginning with the date when the transferee acquired the replacement property and ending with the death, the replacement property was owned by the transferee and occupied (by him or another) for the purposes of agriculture; and

(iv) the replacement property is agricultural property immediately before the death.

If the transferor dies before the transferee and all or part of the original property has been disposed of before the transferor's death (or is subject to a binding contract for sale at that time) then if the replacement property is acquired (or a binding contract entered into) after the transferor's death but within the 'allowed period' after the disposal of the original property, or part, conditions (i) and (iii) above do not apply and any reference to a time immediately before the transferor's death is taken as a reference to the time when the replacement property is acquired.

Where any shares owned by the transferee immediately before the death would either be identified with the replacement property under the provisions of *TCGA 1992, ss 126–136* (as above) *or* were issued to him in consideration of the transfer of agricultural property consisting of the replacement property (or part), his period of ownership of the original property is treated as including his period of ownership of the shares.

Where a binding contract for the disposal is entered into at any time before the disposal of the property, the disposal is regarded as taking place at that time.

'Allowed period' means the period of three years or such longer period as the Board may allow. In relation to transfers of value made, and other events occurring, before 30 November 1993, the legislation effectively provided for the allowed period to be twelve months. [*IHTA 1984, ss 124A, 124B; FA 1986, Sch 19 para 22; FA 1987, s 58, Sch 8 para 9; FA 1994, s 247(2)(3)*]. Where agricultural property which is a farming business is replaced shortly before the owner's death by non-agricultural business property the period of ownership of the original property will be relevant for applying the minimum ownership condition to the replacement property. If all the conditions for business property relief (see 6 BUSINESS PROPERTY) are satisfied relief will be available on the replacement business property. (HMRC Tax Bulletin December 1994 p 183).

The availability of APR is ignored for the purposes of determining whether there is a potentially exempt or chargeable transfer in any case. [*IHTA 1984, s 124A(7A)*].

Gifts with reservation of benefit

Where a person makes a lifetime gift of property which qualifies for agricultural property relief, and reserves a benefit in it, the amount of relief available on the death of the donor is determined by treating ownership and any occupation by the donor prior to the gift as ownership and occupation of the donee. So the donee thereby acquires the donor's history of ownership and occupation.

In the case of a gift of shares in a farming company, three conditions apply for agricultural property relief to be available on the death of the donor who reserves a benefit in them:

- at the time of the gift the shares must qualify for either business or agricultural relief;
- the donee must retain ownership of the shares throughout the period between the date of gift and the date of charge; and

- at the time of the charge the shares must remain eligible for relief if the donee were to make a gift of them at that time.

Successions and successive transfers

[4.12] Where property transferred had been inherited on a death, for the purposes of **4.3**(a) and (b) above, the transferor is deemed to have owned it (and, if he subsequently occupies it, to have occupied it) from the date of death. If, however, the deceased was the transferor's spouse or civil partner, the periods are extended to include any period of occupation or ownership of the spouse or civil partner. Therefore, where agricultural land qualifying for relief is inherited by a surviving spouse, that spouse is deemed to have owned it for the time when it was in the ownership of the deceased spouse and to have occupied it for agricultural purposes for the time when it was occupied by the deceased spouse for those purposes [*IHTA 1984, s 120(1); The Tax and Civil Partnership Regulations 2005, SI 2005/3229, Reg 22*]. See also **4.4** above.

Agricultural property which does not satisfy the qualifying periods of ownership or occupation at **4.3**(a) or (b) above can qualify for relief if all the following conditions are satisfied.

(a) All or part of the value transferred by an earlier transfer was eligible for the relief in **4.4** above (or would have been if such relief had been capable of being given at the time of that transfer).

(b) All or part of that property became the property of the subsequent transferor or his spouse or civil partner because of the earlier transfer, and at the time of the subsequent transfer it was occupied for the purposes of agriculture by that person or the personal representative of the earlier transferor.

(c) That property, or any directly or indirectly replacing it, would otherwise have been eligible for relief were it not for **4.3**(a) or (b) above. If the value transferred by the earlier transfer only partly relates to the property or any replacing it, only the same proportion of the value on the later transfer qualifies for relief.

(d) Either the earlier or the subsequent transfer is a transfer on the death of the transferor.

This provision can be broken down into two separate parts. The first is where there is a lifetime transfer qualifying for agricultural relief. Subsequently, the donee dies before they satisfy the minimum period of ownership. It is provided that in such cases, the gift on the death of the donee will qualify for relief assuming the land continues to be occupied for agricultural purposes. The second case is where there is a transfer of agricultural land on the death of an individual and agricultural relief applies. The person inheriting the land then makes a lifetime gift of it before they satisfy the qualifying period of ownership. It is provided that in such cases, the lifetime gift by the donee will nevertheless be eligible for relief assuming the land continues to be occupied for agricultural purposes.

Where the property eligible for relief above replaced the property or part referred to in (c) above, relief is limited to what it would have been if any one or more of the replacements had not taken place. For this purpose, changes resulting from the formation, alteration or dissolution of a partnership are disregarded. [*IHTA 1984, s 121; Tax and Civil Partnership Regulations 2005, SI 2005/3229, Reg 23*].

Shares etc. in agricultural companies

[4.13] The transfer of shares or securities in a company may attract relief if:

(a) agricultural property forms part of the company's assets and part of the value of the shares or securities can be attributable to the agricultural value of the property; and

(b) the shares or securities gave control of the company to the transferor immediately before the transfer. For 'control' see **32.8** PAYMENT OF TAX. If their value is reduced under the rules relating to sales of related property within three years after death (see **53.22** VALUATION) the shares or securities must be sufficient, without any other property, to give control; and

(c) either:
   (i) the agricultural property was occupied by the company for the purposes of agriculture throughout the period of two years ending with the date of the transfer and the shares or securities were owned by the transferor throughout that period; or
   (ii) the agricultural property was owned by the company throughout the period of seven years ending with that date and was throughout that period occupied (by the company or another) for the purposes of agriculture *and* the shares or securities were owned by the transferor throughout that period.

In applying the relief in the above circumstances, it is provided that:

(A) For the purposes of **4.4**(a)(i) and **4.4**(a)(ii)(3) above, the transferor's interest in agricultural property means the company's interest.

(B) For the purposes of (c) above, the company is treated as occupying land at any time when it was occupied by a person who subsequently controls the company.

However, there is no application of the 100% relief for farmland let on or after 1 September 1995 (see **4.4**(b)) so it appears that only 50% relief is available in such cases.

Example 7

AC Ltd is an unquoted agricultural company of which A owns 80% of the shares.

The company owns	£
4,000 acres of land – agricultural value	4M
Other trading assets (net)	2M
Total value of company	£6M
A's shareholding is valued at	£4.5M

All necessary conditions for relief are satisfied.

On the death of A, the position as regards his shareholding would be as follows

	Total Value	Land	Other Assets
	£	£	£
Value of assets of company	£6M	£4M	£2M
Value of shares, split in same proportions	£4.5M	£3M	£1.5M
Agricultural property relief (100% of £3M)	(3.0M)		
Business property relief (100% of £1.5M)	(1.5M)		
Chargeable to IHT	Nil		

Note to the example

(A) The legislation appears to require that both agricultural property relief and business property relief be given, each against its appropriate part of the value. [*IHTA 1984, s 114*]. When some of the land owned by the company is tenanted and attracts only 50% agricultural property relief, the total relief given will be less than would be the case if business property relief at 100% were given on the whole value.

Where the transferred shares etc. replaced other eligible property (i.e. either agricultural property, or shares etc. the value of which is wholly or partly attributable to agricultural property), the conditions regarding the transferor's period of ownership of the shares etc. are treated as satisfied if the transferor owned the shares etc. and the other eligible property which preceded it for at least two of the last five years in the case of (i) above and at least seven of the last ten years in the case of (ii) above.

The provisions relating to replacements of agricultural property at **4.7** above also apply to agricultural shares etc.

Where land farmed by a company is inherited by an individual and he or she subsequently acquires a controlling shareholding in the company, the question arises as to whether two further years must then ensue before 100% agricultural relief will be due. Occupation by the company is treated as occupation by the controlling shareholder, but on its own *IHTA 1984, s 119(1)* does not allow any backdating of occupation. In fact, however, HMRC have confirmed that this point is covered by *IHTA 1984, s 120(1)(a)*. That subsection applies where land is inherited on death and states that the individual is treated as having owned it, *and if he subsequently occupies it*, from the date of death. The occupation referred to can be via the controlling shareholding (IHTM24124) so 100% relief starts two years from the date of death so long as the controlling shareholding is acquired in that period.

[*IHTA 1984, ss 122, 123*].

Liabilities to acquire agricultural property

[4.14] For transfers of value made or treated as made on or after 17 July 2013, it is no longer possible to reduce the value of an asset for IHT purposes by securing a loan on it where the loan is used to acquire or maintain (directly or indirectly) another asset which qualifies for certain IHT reliefs, including agricultural property relief. Instead the loan will be primarily deductible from the asset qualifying for relief. These rules have equal effect for charges on settlements holding relevant property within *IHTA 1984, s 58*.

This rule applies to any liability incurred on or after 6 April 2013. In the case of any such liability incurred in respect of agricultural property, the loan is to be primarily deducted from the value of that property before any applicable reliefs for such property are given. If the liability exceeds the value of the asset concerned, the excess may be deducted from other chargeable assets, first those qualifying for agricultural or business reliefs and thereafter other assets without relief. If the agricultural property is gifted during lifetime, the loan is to be deducted only from the value of that property if the lifetime gift is or becomes a chargeable transfer, so that the liability cannot also be deducted from the estate on death. But if the lifetime gift is a PET and the donor survives for seven years, retaining liability for the loan, it may then be deducted from the estate on death.

A loan is considered by HMRC to indirectly finance an asset where it is initially used to buy asset 1 which is later sold and the proceeds reinvested in asset 2. The loan then indirectly finances asset 2 (see IHTM28018). On this view it is not possible to circumvent the disallowance by first acquiring non-agricultural property with a loan, subsequently selling that property and then acquiring agricultural property with the proceeds.

Where a liability is incurred partly for relievable property, as described above, and partly for other assets not qualifying for the reliefs, any part repayments of a liability are to be attributed first to the proportion of it incurred for the non-relievable property. If a loan is incurred partly in relation to assets within any of (ii), (iii) or (iv) above and partly in relation to assets within (i) above, part repayments are to be attributed primarily to the part relating to the assets within (ii), (iii) or (iv). For HMRC's view on apportionments of liabilities between relievable and non-relievable property, see IHT Manual para 28021. [*IHTA 1984, ss 162A and 162B*].

Grants of agricultural tenancies

[4.15] When agricultural tenancies were governed by the *Agricultural Holdings Act 1986*, or earlier legislation, the statutory security of tenure given to the tenant would have meant that the value of the landlord's interest would be reduced by the grant of the tenancy. It is therefore provided that the grant of a tenancy of agricultural property in the United Kingdom, Channel Islands or Isle of Man for use for agricultural purposes is not a transfer of value if made for full consideration in money or money's worth. Note that due to an oversight, this provision has not been amended in line with the withdrawal of agricultural relief for all land outside the UK. [*IHTA 1984, s 16*]. See also **53.3** VALUATION.

Scottish agricultural leases

Scottish agricultural leases — fixed terms

[4.16] Where on a person's death any part of the value of his estate is attributable to the interest of a tenant in *an unexpired portion of a lease* for a fixed term of agricultural property in Scotland, any value associated with any prospect of renewal of the lease by tacit relocation is left out of account, provided either he had been tenant of that property for at least two years immediately preceding his death or he had become tenant of that property by succession. [*IHTA 1984, s 177(1)(3)*].

Scottish agricultural leases — tacit relocation

[4.17] Where on a person's death any part of the value of his estate is attributable to the value of the interest of a tenant of agricultural property in Scotland *held by virtue of tacit relocation* (i.e. on a year to year basis), and the interest is acquired at his death by a new tenant, the value of that interest is left out of account, provided either he had been tenant of that property for at least two years immediately preceding his death or he had become tenant of that property by succession. The value to be left out of account does not include the value of any rights to compensation in respect of tenant's improvements. [*IHTA 1984, s 177(2)–(4)*]. See also **53.3** VALUATION.

Disasters of national significance

[4.18] The incidence of foot and mouth disease throughout the United Kingdom in the earlier part of 2001 and 2007 had an impact on the farming community resulting in the deferment of payment of tax and interest. See **25.4** INTEREST ON TAX. Now where there is a disaster or emergency interest on unpaid tax, it may be deferred where the Commissioners specify this by Statutory Instrument. [*FA 2008, s 135*]. See also **30.3** NATIONAL HERITAGE.

Will planning for agricultural property

[4.19] A situation may arise where the farmer wishes to leave the farm and agricultural land to his or her surviving spouse or civil partner who will then pass it by will to the children but by doing so would not benefit from the 100% APR as the gift/willed assets would in any case be exempt due to the inter spouse or civil partner exemption. If there are other non-agricultural/business assets that do not attract any relief an option may be to leave the farm and agricultural land to the children and the other assets to the wife as in the example below. The wife may then use the assets to purchase property qualifying for APR. This is in the nature of 'double dip' planning (see **23.16** INHERITANCE TAX PLANNING).

Example 8

Farmer A, who is married to W and has a daughter D, is the freehold owner of a farm and agricultural land which at current vacant possession value is estimated to be valued at £1,850,000. On 29 September 2019, A dies and leaves by his will the farm and agricultural property and his other assets including investments valued at £1.25 million into a two-year discretionary trust. There are specific powers in the will to appoint out before grant. Within the two-year period the Trustees appoint out of the trust £325,000 in cash and the farm to the daughter D. W is appointed £925,000 in cash and investments. After a period D sells a one-half share in the farm to W who pays for it out of part of the assets inherited from her late husband A and then farms in partnership with D. The position is then as follows:

STEP 1	
Daughter (D)	£
Transfer of farm by appointment from trust	1,850,000
Deduct agricultural property relief	1,850,000
IHT payable	Nil
Transfer of cash by appointment from trust	325,000
Deduct nil rate band	325,000
IHT payable	Nil
Wife (W)	£
Transfer of cash/investments by appointment from trust	925,000
Deduct inter-spouse/civil partner exemption	925,000
IHT payable	Nil

STEP 2: sale by the daughter	Assets
D	£
Cash for farm	925,000
One-half share in farm	925,000
Cash from original nil rate band transfer	325,000
Total assets derived from the estate	£2,175,000
W	£
One-half share in farm	925,000
Total derived from the estate	£925,000

Notes to the example

(A) The Stamp Duty Land Tax implications have not been addressed here and this potential charge must be weighed up with the potential saving in IHT, i.e. £240,000 (£1,250,000 – two nil bands of 325,000 × 40%) if the estate had been left entirely to W.

(B) A transfer of the farm to D on the death of W, assuming she will die first and has been farming the land for two years, will once again be covered by APR.

(C) There may be a concern that the daughter may not wish to sell the farm to W but it must be in the daughter's own interests in view of the overall savings in IHT.

(D) In a case where, for example, a deceased's estate has a farm that would qualify for APR which is left to the wife and a share portfolio that would be taxable and is left to the daughter, a deed of variation may be entered into whereby there is an exchange of assets under *IHTA 1984, s 142(1)* i.e. '. . . the making, in respect of another of the dispositions, of a variation . . .' so that the wife receives the share portfolio and the daughter receives the farm, each being exempt. In any other case a transfer, such as the one in the example above, by deed of variation might constitute transfers for any consideration, including consideration less than full consideration, which would be ineffective under *IHTA 1984, s 142(1)(3)*. See also **13.2** and **13.3** DEEDS OF VARIATION AND DISCLAIMER.

Key points concerning agricultural property

[4.20] Points to consider are as follows.

- Most farming businesses are undertaken as a sole trader or in partnership. In the case of a partnership, any assets held outside the partnership by the partners individually but used in the business may be entitled to only 50% BPR and the amount of APR will depend whether or not the conditions for 100% relief are satisfied (see **4.4**). Other business structures may be considered, such as Limited Liability Partnerships and private limited companies, which offer limited liability and flexibility in terms of keeping assets outside of creditor entitlement in cases of business failure. However, those assets would be entitled to BPR at only 50% if held by the business owners outside such limited liability vehicles, although 100% APR may nevertheless be available so long as a farm business tenancy is in place or, in the case of occupation by a company, the landowner has control of the company. BPR will be important if the land has development value and in such cases, a partner holding the land outside the partnership should consider declaring it to be partnership property; the partnership agreement could, if wished, allocate that asset in its entirety to the partner contributing it.
- Landlords whose tenants enjoy security of tenure under the *Agricultural Holdings Act 1986* provisions, should consider taking advantage of an amendment to the *Agricultural Tenancies Act 1995* which came into effect from 19 October 2006. *Agricultural Tenancies Act 1995, s 4(1)(g)* (inserted by *Regulatory Reform (Agricultural Tenancies) (England and Wales) Order 2006, SI 2006/2805*) permits a new tenancy to be granted from 19 October 2006 to an existing *Agricultural Holdings Act 1986* tenant over the same (or substantially the same) land and allows the tenant to enjoy the same security of tenure as before even though a new tenancy is expressly granted. 100% APR relief is available for the new lease in such circumstances, in place of 50% APR for the previous lease. ESC D39 may enable this to be free of capital gains tax liability for the tenant's deemed disposal of the old lease so long as the new lease or tenancy is on identical terms to the previous one except as regards duration and rent payable. There is however no similar concession for stamp duty land tax purposes and a surren-

der and a re-grant will normally incur liability to that tax. The stamp duty land tax position may be improved by an alternative arrangement which is to grant a lease reversionary to the existing lease and then merge the two.

- APR applies to assets within the definition of agricultural property and occupation of such property and is given in priority to BPR, which is given generally where there is an interest in a business. BPR is only given if it is claimed and therefore where APR is not available with regard to a farming activity for live stock, dead-stock, farm equipment, milk quota, single farm payments and bank balances (within reasonable case law boundaries) then as long as they are within a qualifying trading activity BPR will be available to be claimed. See 7 CALCULATION OF TAX.
- Certain areas of diversification a farmer may undertake will not attract entitlement to APR, such as land rented for caravan and tent pitches, car boot sales, etc. as these constitute income from land or property. Sporting rights such as shooting and fishing on the farmer's land would not entitle the farmer to APR. See *Earl of Normanton v Giles* [1980] 1 WLR 28 where occupation by livestock otherwise than to produce food for human consumption, for example, the keeping of birds such as pheasants for sport was held not to be agricultural for the purposes of *Rent (Agriculture) Act 1976, s 1*.
- Certain aspects of a working farm do not attract APR such as farm equipment, e.g. combines, tractors, derelict buildings/redundant buildings, harvested crops or livestock but these will normally be within BPR. Growing crops transferred with the land being transferred will qualify for APR.
- Farm cottages occupied by someone not connected with the farming do not qualify for APR unless the person is (see HMRC Concession F16):
  (i) a retired farm employee;
  (ii) a spouse/civil partner of a deceased farm worker;
  (iii) living in the cottage under a lease granted by reason of their former farming employment contract; or
  (iv) a protected tenant with statutory rights vis *Rent (Agriculture) Act 1976*.
- However, farm cottages not qualifying for APR may qualify for BPR if rents are received from them which support the farm business. See *Farmer (Farmer's Executors) v IRC* [1999] STC (SCD) 321 summarised at **55.1** TAX CASES.

5

Anti-Avoidance

Cross-references. See **11.8** CLOSE COMPANIES; **21.24** EXEMPT TRANSFERS; **22** GIFTS WITH RESERVATION; **27.2** LIABILITY FOR TAX; **28.9** LIFE ASSURANCE POLICIES AND ANNUITIES; **42** SETTLEMENTS: INTERESTS HELD ON PROTECTIVE TRUSTS; **39.11** SETTLEMENTS WITH INTERESTS IN POSSESSION; **40.13** and **40.22** SETTLEMENTS: DISCRETIONARY TRUSTS AND OTHER TRUSTS OF RELEVANT PROPERTY; **53.21** VALUATION.

Simon's Taxes. See **A7.403, A6.1212, I2.104, I2.2, I3.115, I3.7.**

Other Sources. Tolley's Income Tax; IHTM09151 et seq.

Approach of the courts

The *Duke of Westminster* case and Ramsay approach

[5.1] The classical interpretation of the constraints upon the Courts in deciding cases involving tax avoidance schemes is summed up in Lord Tomlin's statement in the *Duke of Westminster v CIR* HL 1935, 19 TC 490 that 'every man is entitled if he can to order his affairs so that the tax attaching . . . is less than it otherwise would be'. The judgment was concerned with the tax consequences of a single transaction, but in *Ramsay*, and subsequently in *Furniss v Dawson*, the House of Lords has set bounds on the ambit within which this principle can be applied in relation to modern sophisticated and increasingly artificial arrangements to avoid tax. With the introduction of the general anti-abuse rule in *FA 2013*, HMRC now consider that the decision in the *Duke of Westminster* case is no longer relevant and it seems likely that the focus of all future counteraction of avoidance schemes will be under this new statutory rule.

Cases on past IHT avoidance arrangements

Countess Fitzwilliam and others v CIR is the first case in which the question of the application of the *Ramsay* principle to transactions entered into with a view to the avoidance of inheritance tax (or, more strictly, its predecessor, capital transfer tax) has arisen. The trustees of a will trust (who included the deceased's widow F and her daughter H) were empowered to appoint within 23 months of the death of the deceased (which occurred in September 1979) the residue of the estate amongst a class of beneficiaries which included F (then aged 81) and H. In order to avoid a heavy charge to tax on an appointment directly to H or, should an appointment be made to F, on her death when it was envisaged she would make H the beneficiary of her own will, a complex five-step scheme was entered into by F, H and the trustees ('the taxpayers'). It was claimed by the taxpayers that the five steps, the first of which took place on 20 December 1979 and the last on 7 February 1980, should be viewed separately with the result that by reason of a number of available reliefs (some of which still have application to inheritance tax) no liability to capital transfer tax arose. The former Inland Revenue issued notices of determination claiming that the five steps constituted a preordained single composite transaction effected to avoid tax and that *Ramsay* applied to permit a charge to tax on the deceased's estate on the basis of appointments directly to F and H.

In the House of Lords the Revenue accepted that step 1 did not form part of such a series but argued that the steps 2 to 5 did. The leading judgment in the House of Lords stated that the correct approach to a consideration of steps 2 to 5 was to ask whether realistically they constituted a single and indivisible whole in which one or more of the steps was simply an element without independent effect and whether it was intellectually possible so to treat them. It was held that both questions should be answered in the negative. The case put by the Revenue did not depend on disregarding for fiscal purposes any one or more of steps 2 to 5 as having been introduced for fiscal purposes only and as having no independent effect, nor on treating the whole of steps 2 to 5 as having no such effect. Each of the four steps had a fiscal effect of giving rise to an income tax charge on F or H for a period of time, and there was a potential capital transfer tax charge should either have died whilst in enjoyment of the income. The fact of preordainment was not sufficient in itself to negative the application of an exemption from liability to tax which the series of transactions was intended to create, unless the series was capable of being construed in a manner inconsistent with the application of the exemption. In the particular circumstances of the case, the series of transactions could not be so construed. Accordingly, the case was one to which the *Ramsay* principle, as extended by *Furniss v Dawson*, did not apply.

In *Hatton*, a scheme to avoid tax, which bore some similarity to that in *Fitzwilliam*, was found by the Special Commissioners and Chancery Division to be preordained and one to which the *Ramsay* principle applied (although it should be noted that the Chancery Division judgment in the case was given prior to the judgments of the Court of Appeal and House of Lords in *Fitzwilliam*).

In the decision by the House of Lords in the *Ingram* case concerning a scheme whereby a lease over a property was retained and the freehold was given away, Lord Hoffmann stated: 'The scope of the Ramsay principle does not arise and I therefore prefer to say nothing about it'. The legislation at *FA 1986, ss102A, 102B and 102C* was introduced to counteract the arrangement.

In another case *Melville v CIR* [2000] STC 628; Ch D [2000] All ER(D) 832; CA [2001] STC 1271 the Court of Appeal held that powers over trusts are potential 'property' for inheritance tax purposes. This had the effect of creating an avoidance of IHT liability when used as part of an avoidance scheme because the holder of the power had effective dominion over the settled property, if he chose to exercise it. A power was different in character from a reversionary interest.

Nevertheless, the holder of a general power of appointment had a valuable right, the value of which had to be taken into account in the holder's estate under *IHTA 1984, s 5(1)* unless excluded by some other provision. See now *IHTA 1984, s 272*, which states that property does not include a settlement power, and *IHTA 1984, s 47A* inserted by *FA 2002, s 119*, which defines a settlement power as any power over, or exercisable (whether directly or indirectly) in relation to, settled property or a settlement. However, for deaths on or before 16 April 2002, *FA 2002, s 119* disapplies charges on those earlier deaths which might have otherwise arisen from the stated side effects of the decision arising out of the *Melville* case.

Targeted legislation

[5.2] Anti-avoidance legislation is intended to counteract transactions designed to avoid taxation but *bona fide* transactions may sometimes be caught also.

In *CIR v Eversden and another (executors of Greenstock deceased)* CA, [2003] STC 822, the strategy was effected by the husband making a gift into trust under which the wife took an initial interest in possession for life or six months, whichever was the shorter. Alternatively, the trustees of the settlement can be given wide powers to terminate the life interest and appoint on varied trusts. Husband and wife are capable of benefiting in a reversionary interest by being added as potential beneficiaries and without the gifts with reservation rules applying. Although the settlor will in these circumstances almost certainly have made a gift, the gifts with reservation rules in *FA 1986, s 102* did not apply as it was excluded by *FA 1986, s 102(5A)* with respect to the inter-spouse/civil partner exemption i.e. *IHTA 1984, s 18*. The settlor and wife were able therefore to reserve whatever benefits over the settled property as required. The exemption by *FA 1986, s 102(5A)* came into play only if the gift in settlement constituted a transfer of value and one which was exempt by virtue of the spousal exemption. The strategy was blocked by *FA 2003, s 185* with effect from 20 June 2003.

IHTA 1984, s 81A counters the use of '*Melville*' type schemes, after *Melville* above, a case on an aspect of an earlier version of the scheme which was superseded by anti-avoidance legislation. See above. The strategy was that the settlor of a settlement retains a valuable reversionary beneficial interest which was taken into account in determining the amount by which the value of his 'estate' is diminished when he makes the settlement, so that the value transferred under *IHTA 1984, s 3* is within the IHT nil rate band even though the actual value of the settled property exceeded it. However, Melville type schemes were adapted as a means of avoiding an immediate IHT charge on settling property by lifetime disposition under the post-21 March 2006 IHT rules.

In order to counteract the use of similar schemes to avoid IHT liability *IHTA 1984, s 81A* was introduced which makes two provisions in relation to any reversionary interest in 'relevant property' which is owned by someone who has acquired that interest for a consideration in money or money's worth, or which is owned by the settlor, the settlor's wife, or the settlor's civil partner. The first is that the falling in of the reversion by reason of the reversioner becoming entitled to an interest in possession in the settled property, is treated as a disposition of a reversionary interest at that time i.e. *IHTA 1984, s 81A(1)*. The second is that a transfer of value of such a reversionary interest, whether before it falls in or at the time when a reversionary interest in possession falls in, is not now a PET, i.e. *IHTA 1984, s 81A(2)*. See **39.11** SETTLEMENTS WITH INTERESTS IN POSSESSION and example below. This anti-avoidance applies on or after 9 December 2009. [*FA 2010, s 52(2)*.]

Example 1

Melvin settles property on trusts under which after a period of trusts for other persons (discretionary or interest in possession) Melvin has a life interest then the retained future life interest is not initially an interest in possession. However, it is a reversionary interest. Therefore for these purposes it would be part of Melvin's estate for IHT and the value of it as a retained interest is taken into account in assessing the value transferred by the transfer of value, which is thus a low value. When the initial period of trusts for other persons come to an end Melvin's interest becomes an interest in possession, the falling into possession of the reversionary interest would not normally cause an IHT charge because it happens automatically. There would in these circumstances be neither a disposal nor any operation effected by any person which might be classed as an associated operation. On becoming an interest in possession the interest ceases to form part of Melvin's estate under the terms of *IHTA 1984, s 5(1)(1A)*, as amended and inserted by *FA 2006*. Therefore once it is an interest in possession Melvin could assign it onto trusts for other beneficiaries without it becoming an occasion of charge. Also, if Melvin decides to give away his reversionary interest while it is still a reversionary interest by making an absolute assignment of it to another individual, it would be a PET. Alternatively, a similar result arises where a person pays someone else full or substantial consideration for making a settlement under which the purchaser has a reversionary interest.

The anti-avoidance consequence is that Melvin is now deemed to have given away his reversionary interest at the earlier date rather than at the later date when it falls in. It will therefore now be an immediately chargeable lifetime transfer and not a PET as above. At that stage then, unless there is another exemption for Melvin to call on, or it does not exceed Melvin's available nil rate band, there is immediately a charge to IHT at 20% of the value of the reversionary interest. Alternatively, if Melvin retains the reversionary interest until it falls in and he becomes entitled to an interest in possession then there is a deemed disposition of the reversionary interest by Melvin and the transfer of value is no longer a PET i.e. new *IHTA 1984, s 81A(2)*. In most cases the value transferred is likely to be the value of the reversionary interest at the time of gift by Melvin and this is likely to be the same as the value of the succeeding interest in possession.

The wide-ranging anti-avoidance provisions of *FA 2010, s 53* ensure that the pre-22 March 2006 IHT regime for settled property subject to an interest in possession now applies to settled property subject to an interest in possession to which a person domiciled in the UK became beneficially entitled on or after 9 December 2009 which is within *IHTA 1984, s 10* (not conferring gratuitous benefit). This new category of interest in possession is now caught within *IHTA 1984, s 5(1B)* inserted by *FA 2010, s 53(3)(b)*. The anti-avoidance relating to interests in possession acquired in transactions not conferring any gratuitous benefit on or after 9 December 2009 is in encapsulated in *FA 2010, s 53* as in the example below. The various IHT charging provisions are applied to *IHTA 1984* throughout by reference to *FA 2010, s 5(1B)* and cross-referenced to this chapter section and the example below and throughout this work. See **39.11** SETTLEMENTS WITH INTERESTS IN POSSESSION. This anti-avoidance applies on or after 9 December 2009. [*FA 2010, s 53(10)*].

Example 2

Whereas the type of scheme at Example 1 above counteracts an avoidance scheme which took advantage of a shortcoming in the *FA 2006* changes to trusts, the *IHTA 1984, s 53* anti-avoidance appears to be proactive legislation. For instance, say Patricia makes a settlement which confers an interest in possession on Bertie for life, and he is well off financially compared to Patricia so pays full value for the interest and therefore it is a commercial transaction to which *IHTA 1984, s 10* applies. Therefore neither of them, because of *IHTA 1984, s 10*, makes a transfer of value. Bertie then ensures that on his death the remainder is passed on to his relative Charlie who also pays a commercial rate for his future interest. When Bertie dies the settlement passes to Charlie and there is no IHT charge because all transactions were to date ordinary commercial transactions per se. Because of this the settled property has fallen out of the estate of Bertie. Patricia's estate did of course increase in value by the amount paid but this could well have been within the nil rate band. This has the subsidiary effect of ensuring that Bertie's estate on death is not encumbered by the life interest and the nil rate band to the extent it has not been depleted and any transferable nil rate band is available to set against the chargeable estate on death whereas it would have been 'apportioned' between the free estate and life interest. However, *FA 2010, s 53* now has the effect that an interest in possession (other than a disabled person's interest which is different) acquired under a new lifetime settlement made after 21 March 2006 now notwithstanding *IHTA 1984, s 10* exclusion does now form part of the estate of the person entitled to the interest in possession. In consequence the pre-22 March 2006 IHT regime for settled property subject to an interest in possession applies to settled property subject to an interest in possession to which a person domiciled in the UK became beneficially entitled on or after 9 December 2009 by virtue of a disposition falling within *FA 2010, s 53(10)*. See **38.2** SETTLEMENTS — GENERAL.

The following anti-avoidance provisions relating to inheritance tax include some which have not been formally so designated but have been selected from the legislation as being broadly of an anti-avoidance nature.

(a) **Associated operations.** See **5.5** below.
(b) **Close companies.** See **11.2** and **11.8** CLOSE COMPANIES.

(c) **Exempt transfers.** See **21.9** for transfers between spouses/civil partners and **21.24** EXEMPT TRANSFERS for abatement of certain exemptions on death.
(d) **Gifts with reservation.** See **22** GIFTS WITH RESERVATION.
(e) **Liability for tax of transferor's spouse/civil partner.** See **27.2** LIABILITY FOR TAX.
(f) **Annuity purchased in conjunction with life policy.** See **28.9** LIFE ASSURANCE POLICIES AND ANNUITIES.
(g) **Protective trusts.** See **42** SETTLEMENTS: INTERESTS HELD ON PROTECTIVE TRUSTS.
(h) **Termination of an interest in possession.** See **39.9–39.11** SETTLEMENTS WITH INTERESTS IN POSSESSION.
(i) **Initial interest of settlor or spouse/civil partner and property moving between settlements.** See **40.19** and **40.22** SETTLEMENTS: DISCRETIONARY TRUSTS AND OTHER TRUSTS OF RELEVANT PROPERTY.
(j) **Related property.** See **53.21** VALUATION.
(k) **Excluded property settlements.** See **20.2** and **20.12** EXCLUDED PROPERTY.
(l) **Funds in alternatively secured pensions.** See **34.2** PENSION SCHEMES.
(m) **Reversionary interests of purchasers or settlors in relevant property.** **39.11** SETTLEMENTS WITH INTERESTS IN POSSESSION.

General anti-avoidance rule

[5.3] With effect from Royal Assent to the *Finance Act 2013*, 17 July 2013, a general anti-abuse rule applies for most tax purposes, including inheritance tax. The rule is designed to counteract tax advantages arising from tax arrangements that are abusive. For these purposes, 'tax arrangements' are widely defined to include any arrangements where it would be reasonable to conclude that the obtaining of a tax advantage was the main purpose or one of the main purposes of the arrangements.

Arrangements are 'abusive' if they 'cannot reasonably be regarded as a reasonable course of action in relation to the relevant tax provisions'. This test requires having regard to all the circumstances, including whether the arrangements are consistent with any principles on which the tax provisions are based, including their policy objectives, whether the arrangements include one or more contrived or abnormal steps, and whether they are intended to exploit any shortcomings in the relevant tax provisions. If however the tax arrangements accord with established practice, and HMRC have indicated its acceptance of that practice, this is an example of something which might indicate that the arrangements are not abusive.

Tax arrangements which are caught by the new rule may be counteracted by an adjustment on a 'just and reasonable' basis.

Where HMRC consider that the general anti-abuse rule applies, the 'designated HMRC officer' must follow the procedural requirements set out in *FA 2013, Sch 41*. This involves giving written notice to the taxpayer specifying the arrangements and the tax advantage which the officer considers to be caught by the general anti-abuse rule, and the counteraction which the officer considers ought to be taken. The taxpayer then has 45 days beginning with the day on which the notice is given (not the day on which it is received) to send written representations in response to the notice. If no representations are made, or if they are made but the officer still considers that the tax advantage should be counteracted, the matter must then be referred to the 'GAAR Advisory Panel'. At the same time as referring the matter to the Panel, the designated HMRC officer must give the taxpayer notice that this reference has been made and the taxpayer then has 21 days from the date on which notice is given to send to the Panel written representations on the latter. These representations must be copied to the HMRC officer. The decision of the Panel is not binding on HMRC, although it will be taken into account in any subsequent appeal to the Tax Tribunals.

Provision is made for consequential relieving adjustments to be made after a counteraction of a tax advantage has become final. A person has 12 months from that date to make a claim for one or more consequential adjustments to be made in respect of any tax to which the general anti-abuse rule applies. Upon receipt of the claim, HMRC must make such of the consequential adjustments claimed as are just and reasonable. For inheritance tax purposes, the claim must be made in writing and the provisions of *IHTA 1984, s 221* apply as if the claim were a claim under that Act.

Guidance from the GAAR Panel

[5.4] HMRC have published guidance on the new general anti-abuse rule which has been approved by the Advisory Panel. See https://assets.publishing.service.gov.uk/government/uploads/system/uploads/attachment_data/file/396179/gaar-part-abc.pdff. The guidance states that the new rule amounts to a rejection of the approach taken by the Courts in cases such as *Duke of Westminster v CIR* (1936) 19 TC 490 to the effect that taxpayers are free to use their ingenuity to reduce their tax bills by any lawful means, however contrived those means might be and however much the tax consequences might diverge from the real economic position. The guidance goes on to state that 'in many circumstances there are different courses of action that a taxpayer can quite properly choose between. The GAAR is carefully constructed to include a number of safeguards that ensure that any reasonable choice of a course of action is kept outside the target area of the GAAR'.

Part D of the guidance was updated on 30 January 2015 and discusses specific tax planning arrangements. Part VI of Part D considers six inheritance tax arrangements and sets out views on whether or not they would be liable to counteraction. The 6 examples are as follows.

Pilot trusts

C wishes to leave his estate in trust for his seven grandchildren. He wants to ensure that the settlements are not subject to IHT after his death. C establishes one settlement per day over a period of seven days, settling £100 on each. He revises his Will so that he leaves a specific legacy of £250,000 free of tax to each settlement.

The GAAR analysis of this arrangement is explained as follows. Because the settlements were created on consecutive days, they are not related settlements and so the rate of tax is calculated without reference to the other settlements, notwithstanding that the substantial addition of funds came about as a result of a single event – C's death.

Do the means of achieving the substantive tax results involve one or more contrived or abnormal steps? Had C's Will established a single settlement for the benefit of all of his grandchildren that trust would have been subject to IHT. And if seven separate settlements had been established by his Will, they would have been related settlements so each would have been taken into account with the other to establish the rate of tax. Establishing the 'pilot' trusts on separate days before death had no purpose other than to put the trusts in a tax-advantaged position. Arguably therefore these are contrived steps.

Do the tax arrangements accord with established practice and has HMRC indicated its acceptance of that practice? The practice was litigated in the case of *Rysaffe Trustee v IRC* [2003] STC 536. HMRC lost the case and did nothing to change the legislation prior to 2013, and so must be taken to have accepted the practice.

The conclusion is therefore that the arrangements accord with established practice accepted by HMRC and are accordingly not regarded as abusive.

Discounted gift schemes

The settlor makes a gift into settlement but retains certain rights in the insurance bond. Typically the rights retained may be in a series of single premium policies maturing on successive anniversaries of the creation of the settlement or to future capital payments if the settlor is alive at the prospective payment date. The arrangement is viewed as a 'carve-out' or 'shearing arrangement' so that provided the rights in the bond retained by the settlor are sufficiently clearly defined he is not taxed on the value of the gifted property.

The GAAR analysis of this arrangement is explained as follows. In *Ingram v CIR* [1999] STC 37, the House of Lords held that there is nothing in principle behind the gifts with reservation provisions that stops the donor carefully dividing up his cake, giving away a slice and retaining the remaining cake. Continued enjoyment of the latter does not amount to a reservation in the former. Arrangements of the type adopted are known as 'shearing' operations. *FA 1986, s 102A–C* were introduced to stop shearing arrangements in relation to certain carve out schemes over land, but no legislative action has been taken in relation to other types of assets to stop such arrangements. The discounted gift scheme can be seen as a classic shearing operation on property other than land.

Are there contrived or abnormal steps? Creating two distinct funds or a carve out may be considered contrived.

Do arrangements accord with established practice? These arrangements accord with established practice as is indicated by a number of technical publications.

Accordingly the arrangements are not within the scope of the GAAR.

Excluded property trust and debt

The trustees of a settlement made by a person not domiciled in the United Kingdom buy a property in the UK. At the ten-year anniversary of the settlement, it will be liable to inheritance tax at a maximum of 6%. Shortly before that time, the trustees borrow funds from a bank and secure the debt on the property. The borrowed money is paid out to the settlor on the understanding that the money will be returned. Shortly after the ten-year anniversary, the settlor resettles the funds back to the trust and the trustees use it to repay the loan.

The GAAR analysis of this arrangement is explained as follows. By charging the UK property with debt and paying the cash out to the settlor abroad, the trustees have tried to avoid the ten-year charge. Even if the taxpayer has found a way to circumvent the specific provisions of *FA 2013, Sch 36*, it is clear (according to the Guidance) that the policy intent expressed there is to prevent a deduction against UK property except where the loan was taken out to acquire the UK property.

Are there contrived or abnormal steps? Borrowing with the intention of removing the cash from charge and then repaying the loan shortly thereafter is not a normal transaction. Borrowing taken out simply to avoid tax may in this context be regarded as a contrived step.

Are the arrangements intended to exploit any shortcomings in the relevant tax provisions? FA 2013 makes it clear that the general intention of the legislation is to grant inheritance tax deductions only in respect of borrowing taken out to acquire the particular property, with only limited exceptions, for example, where the value of the property acquired with the borrowings at the relevant time of charge is less than the amount borrowed (and not artificially devalued) in which case the excess may be set against other property. If the UK property was sold just before the ten-year anniversary, HMRC accept that the sale proceeds (if retained abroad) would not be subject to inheritance tax. In looking at the application of the GAAR it is appropriate to look at the wider context of the transaction before and after the ten-year anniversary and in the light of *FA 2013* to consider the context in which liabilities have been incurred.

Do the tax arrangements accord with established practice which has been accepted by HMRC? HMRC have not indicated its acceptance of this practice and HMRC consider that in the light of *FA 2013* it is clear that liabilities may be deducted only if certain principles are satisfied.

On the facts given, the conclusion is that the arrangements are abusive arrangements to which HMRC would seek to apply the GAAR. Under the proposed counteraction, the liabilities would be ignored in calculating the tax due on the house and the transaction counteracted on this basis.

Use of employee benefit trust

The taxpayer arranges for a private company to be incorporated with substantial share capital. The taxpayer and her advisers are the only employees of the company. The company does not trade but holds the money on deposit. The company establishes an employee benefit trust for the benefit of the employees of the company and their families with existing participators being excluded from benefit under the trust except in relation to distributions taxable as income. The funds in the trust are claimed to be exempt from inheritance tax as being within *IHTA 1984, s 86*. The same result could have been achieved by including the terms of the trust in her Will.

Are the arrangements consistent with any principles on which the relevant tax provisions are based and the policy objectives of those provisions? The arrangement is plainly contrary to the principles behind the legislation which is to give favoured treatment to trusts for employees of a genuine business. In this case, there is no genuine business that is set to continue and no genuine employees.

Are there contrived or abnormal steps? The scheme as a whole is contrived, serving no real purpose other than to allow wealth to pass from S to her children without an IHT charge on her death.

Are the arrangements intended to exploit any shortcomings in the relevant tax provisions? Although the definition of 'connected persons' is extended for IHT purposes by *IHTA 1984, s 270*, the normal interpretation, which breaks a connection with someone who has died, continues to apply. *IHTA 1984, s 28* does not limit the exemption to employee trusts with a minimum number of unrelated employees.

Do the tax arrangements accord with established practice? HMRC have not indicated its acceptance of this practice.

The conclusion is that the arrangements are abusive arrangements to which HMRC would seek to apply the GAAR. The proposed counteraction would be to ignore the fact that the trust qualified as an employee trust and impose an immediate entry charge on the taxpayer in respect of the settlement of the shares on the basis that it is a relevant property settlement and a further charge if she died within seven years.

In a decision dated 2 March 2020, the GAAR panel gave its opinion in a case where an elderly person set up a family investment company and transferred the shares to an EBT claiming this was an exempt transfer for IHT. However, the company had no employees and did not need any and therefore the panel concluded that it was 'contrived and abnormal' to transfer shares to an employee trust if no employees existed. The panel did note, however, that 'it might be possible to make a qualifying gift under s 28 (even just before someone died) where the only or main beneficiaries were employee family members on the basis of an ongoing substantive and active business with employees happening to be family members'.

Acquisition of excluded property settlement interest

A non-UK domiciled settlor settles funds upon trust and the trustees have power to nominate another person who can become entitled to the reversionary interest in it. A UK domiciled individual (D) who wishes to avoid inheritance tax, is nominated as the reversionary beneficiary, this nomination becoming irrevocable after a given period of time. The existing income beneficiary of the trust grants D the option to purchase its income interest for £1 million, exercisable on the payment of a further nominal sum. D transfers his newly acquired reversionary interest to a UK trust for his intended beneficiaries and then exercises the option to acquire the income interest. That interest is now part of D's estate but separate from the reversionary interest and has little or no value for IHT. It therefore escapes inheritance tax on his death.

It is argued that the value of D's estate has been reduced by the £1 million used to purchase the trust interests. At the time of the purchase, D exchanged £1 million for rights that would enable him to access the £1 million in the trust, so there is little or no loss to his estate. As D did not purchase the reversionary interest in the offshore trust, it is not prevented from being excluded property, so no account is taken of the value of the interest when it is transferred into trust, and no charge to IHT arises. The purchased income interest is not an interest in possession for IHT purposes, so the underlying trust assets do not form part of the taxpayer's estate.

Are the substantive results of the arrangements consistent with any principles on which the relevant tax provisions are based? In 2005, Parliament legislated to stop UK domiciliaries from buying interests in possession in excluded property trusts and thereby avoiding inheritance tax in a way similar to that outlined above. Further legislation stopping similar schemes was passed in 2010 and 2012. Therefore even if the taxpayer devises a scheme that is not caught by the specific terms of existing anti-avoidance legislation or he purchases slightly different types of interest or acquires similar interests in a slightly different way this is clearly contrary to the policy and intent of Parliament.

Are contrived or abnormal steps involved? If D had transferred £1 million directly to his heirs, there would have been no immediate charge to tax; but had he failed to survive seven years, it would have been subject to IHT. He would not have been able to benefit from the income. If D had transferred £1 million into trust, there would have been an immediate charge to tax at up to 20% of the value transferred. These could be described as the 'normal steps' that D might take. The steps taken by D are significantly different to these normal steps and can therefore be called abnormal. The scheme is contrived in that it involves a number of steps that must be executed in a particular order and to a specific time frame to gain the tax advantage.

Are the arrangements intended to exploit any shortcomings in the relevant tax provisions? Although it is considered by HMRC that the above arrangement is caught by the *FA 2012* legislation the taxpayer may devise even more complex and contrived variants whereby he acquires a slightly different type of interest in the trust without falling foul of the existing anti-avoidance provisions and thereby exploits shortcomings in the provisions.

Do the tax arrangements accord with established practice? HMRC have not indicated that these arrangements give rise to the claimed tax result. Parliament has repeatedly indicated by passing further anti-avoidance legislation that it is not an acceptable practice.

Accordingly on the facts given, the arrangements are abusive arrangements to which HMRC would seek to apply the GAAR. The likely counteraction would be to adopt the policy approach taken in the legislation and impose an immediate entry charge on D in respect of the purchase of the trust interest and a further charge if he died within seven years.

Mortgage on UK real estate by foreign domiciliary

R is domiciled abroad and wishes to buy a valuable house in the UK for his occupation. He has a number of options:

1. R buys the house in his own name, using his own cash resources to fund the purchase.
2. R settles cash from his own resources into a trust that purchases the house. R is a beneficiary of the trust.
3. R, even if he could have funded the purchase from his existing resources, chooses to borrow from a bank to fund a large part, say 70%, of the purchase price.
4. R (as in 2. above) partially funds the trust. The trustees (as in 3. above) then borrow the remainder of the purchase price from a bank.
5. R deposits foreign investments with a bank thereby enabling the bank to lend a greater amount (say 95%) to fund the purchase of the property. The borrowing is again secured on the property.
6. R having funded a trust to the value of, say, 5%, of the purchase price of the house, agrees to guarantee the trustees' borrowing. This enables R's trust to borrow the remainder of the purchase price from a bank. The borrowing is again secured on the property.
7. R has an existing substantive discretionary trust which he settled many years ago. R is one of the beneficiaries. The trustees have been looking to buy UK property suitable for R and his children to use as each of them visit the UK for a few weeks a year. The trustees could afford to buy the new house using existing resources but instead they accept an offer from R to lend them the purchase price via an offshore company that is wholly owned by R. The loan is interest free and repayable on demand. The company owned by R secures the loan on the house.
8. R settles cash from his overseas resources into a newly established trust which then lends it back to him via an underlying company for the purchase of the house in his own name.
9. R adds cash from his overseas resources to a trust, known as the Loan Trust, where he is settlor and beneficiary. His spouse or other relative sets up another trust, known as the Property Trust, which is funded with, say, £1,000 cash. R adds no funds to the Property Trust. The Loan Trust forms an overseas company into which the cash is transferred and the company lends the cash to the Property Trustees who acquire the UK property that R wishes to occupy. The loan is repayable on demand and may be interest-free, interest-bearing or index-linked. The Property Trustees incur no personal liability as the lender may have recourse to the house only.

The Guidance notes that in options 3 and 4 the borrowing provides a clear inheritance tax advantage compared to options 1 and 2. As R is not domiciled in the UK the cash he retains personally abroad is not subject to inheritance tax and the UK property is devalued by commercial borrowing. The same tax advantage, albeit to a greater extent, is claimed to apply in options 5 to 9. The reservation of benefit rules do not apply to options 1, 3, 5 and 8 because R owns the property. There is a reservation of benefit in options 2, 4, 6 and 7, but the taxpayer argues that this is only on the net value of the property. In option 8, the liability is not, it is claimed, caught by *FA 1986, s 103* as a self-generated liability due to it being funded with excluded property (see *FA 1986, s 103(4)*).

In option 9, there is no charge on the death of R because he has not gifted any property to the Property Trust (so the reservation of benefit provisions do not apply) and he is a beneficiary only of the Loan Trust that holds excluded property. As he has made no gift to the Property Trust, *FA 1986, s 102, Sch 20 para 5(4)* are not in point. If he has made such a gift then it is argued that the UK property is devalued by the loan taken out to acquire it.

HMRC do not accept R's analysis of the legislation and in particular the deductibility of loans against UK property in which he reserves a benefit under options 2, 4, 6 and 7. The GAAR analysis below should be read with this point in mind.

Are the substantive results of the arrangements consistent with any principles on which the relevant tax provisions are based? It is reasonable to conclude that the obtaining of a tax advantage was the main purpose or one of the main purposes of options 7 to 9. This may not be so in relation to options 3 to 6. R might prefer to borrow from a bank to allow him more flexibility to make other investments with his cash or to preserve his liquidity. The intention behind the inheritance tax legislation is to tax UK assets and UK domiciliaries. Options 3 and 4 are an application of the rules whereby IHT is chargeable on the net value of UK assets. The fact that R or his trustees could have funded the purchase using foreign investments is irrelevant: R is not compelled to turn assets which are outside the territorial scope of the tax into assets which are subject to tax, whatever his motivation for the borrowing. R's or the trustees' borrowing is a normal commercial transaction and is not contrived or abnormal. While reservation of benefit may be in point in relation to option 4, the GAAR is not thought to apply to option 3 or option 4.

Options 5 and 6, similarly, represent a commercial decision by R or his trustees. Choosing to borrow a higher amount is similarly neither contrived nor abnormal. R takes the economic consequences of borrowing commercially. It can reasonably be regarded as a reasonable course of action.

In option 7, loans to trusts do occur for all sorts of non-tax reasons and therefore cannot be considered in themselves to be necessarily abnormal or contrived. Even though the loan is tax-motivated and (in some senses) self-generated, it involves a single straightforward step. The position might well be different, however, if the trust were not established for some time already or substantive: for instance if R were the sole or principal beneficiary or able to direct the trustees or revoke the trust. A loan to such a newly created trust might be considered a contrivance. In the above example the loan may not be mainly tax motivated anyway e.g. the trustees may wish to preserve cash for liquidity purposes, but even if it were the arrangement is still not necessarily abusive.

In option 8, the cash goes in a circle back to the settlor via a trust and loan arrangement. The position might be different under the GAAR if the trust had been in existence for some time so the gift was not made in contemplation of a loan back. The settlor sets up a trust as a vehicle to lend to himself. The setting up of the trust and company is done simply to enable a loan to be made back to the settlor and this is a contrived step. *FA 1986, s 103* was designed to stop assets being given away that are then lent back by the donee and it may be thought that option 8 is using a possible loophole in *s 103* to circumvent the intended policy.

In option 9, the combination of a nominal-value settlement specifically set up to own the property coupled with the establishment of a separate loan trust and a corporate vehicle underlying it which is then used to make a loan which is on a non-recourse basis is on these facts set up only to achieve an artificial tax deduction. And, while taken individually, the steps may be considered normal, when taken in combination they may be considered abnormal. However, each case would be taken on its own facts and a situation where, for instance, both trusts were substantial and existing trusts or where the loan was on fully commercial terms or where the property trust was established for a different beneficiary apart from the settlor might be considered differently (see option 7 above).

Do the tax arrangements accord with established practice? Neither of the last two options accord with established practice and HMRC have not indicated acceptance of the interpretation that foreign domiciliaries are not caught by *s 103* as a matter of principle.

The conclusion reached is that options 3 and 4 are straightforward applications of the legislation and would not be caught by the GAAR. Similarly, options 5 and 6 involve commercial arrangements which are neither contrived nor abnormal and HMRC would not seek to invoke the GAAR against them. With option 7, it is possible to see that some might reach a view that the arrangements are not unreasonable. As such these particular facts may well not be caught by the GAAR but it is important to realise that this is a borderline case and each such case would have to be considered on its own facts. Options 8 and 9, on these particular facts, would be caught by GAAR.

Reversionary lease scheme in relation to a residence

Not included in Part D of the guidance are *Ingram* type arrangements. As an example, the taxpayer grants a long lease over his home to his son for no consideration, to take effect in 20 years' time. Under the lease, the son covenants to pay the cost of maintaining the property. The taxpayer is able to continue to occupy the property for the next 20 years as he continues to own the freehold. *FA 1986, s 102A* is considered not to apply where the taxpayer has held the freehold for at least seven years.

HMRC's 11 December 2012 draft guidance document gave the view that the failure of the reservation of benefit rules to cover a situation where an individual creates two different interests in a property is a shortcoming that the scheme is intended to exploit. On the facts given, the arrangements are abusive arrangements to which HMRC would seek to apply the GAAR. However this draft guidance does not appear in the guidance approved by the GAAR Advisory Panel with effect from 15 April 2013 and so it would appear that the panel did not agree HMRC's view. Instead the April 2013 guidance contains a reference to the House of Lords decision in *Ingram v IRC* [2000] 1 AC 293; [1999] 1 All ER 297 in which it was held that there is nothing in principle behind the gifts with reservation provisions that stops the donor carefully dividing up his cake, giving away a slice and retaining the remaining cake.

Associated operations

[5.5] If inheritance tax applied only to each separate transaction, it would be possible to split some transfers of value into several parts, the sum of which was less than the total value actually transferred. To counter this, the separate transactions are treated as 'associated operations' which together comprise one transfer of value. But see *Rysaffe Trustee Co (CI) Ltd v CIR* [2001] STC SCD 225 Sp C 290; [2002] STC 872; CA [2003] EWCA Civ 356.

Definitions

'*Associated operations*' are any two or more operations of any kind by the same person or different persons and whether simultaneous or not:

(a) which affect the same property, or one of which affects some property while the other or others affect property which represents, whether directly or indirectly, that property, or income arising from that property, or any property representing accumulations of any such income, or
(b) where one operation is effected with reference to a second or with a view to enabling the other to be effected or facilitating its being effected, and any further operation having a like relation to any of those two, and so on.

'*Operation*' includes an omission.

Where a transfer of value is made by associated operations carried out at different times it shall be treated as made at the time of the last of them. The transfer of value is reduced by the value transferred by any earlier operations which were also transfers of value by the same transferor, except to the extent that the transfer made by earlier operations, but not the operations as a whole, was covered by the exemption for transfers between spouses/civil partners (see **21.9** EXEMPT TRANSFERS). [*IHTA 1984, s 268(1)(3)*].

In *Reynaud v CIR* [1999] STC (SCD) 185 it was held that there was no associated operation where shares qualifying for business property relief were sold to trustees, after which the shares were subject a buy back by the company.

In *Rysaffe Trustee Co (CI) Ltd* [2003] STC 536 it was held that there were no associated operations where five identical settlements were set up within about one month. The decision in the High Court reported at [2002] STC 872 provides a detailed analysis of when the associated operations might apply and when they will not be in point. Examples given of when these provisions may apply are (i) where a disposition which is effectively by A to C is channelled through B with a view to picking up a saving of inheritance tax in the process, and (ii) where an asset, instead of being transferred to a transferee by a single transfer of the whole asset, is fragmented and transferred in stages, with a view to achieving an overall reduction in the value transferred.

Example 3

H owns a set of four Chippendale chairs valued, as a set, at £6,000. Individually they would be valued at only £1,000, although a pair would be worth £2,500 and three £4,000.

He gives one chair to his son each year over four years, during which time all values increase at 10% p.a. (simple). In the fifth year H dies.

	£	£
Year 1		
Value of four chairs	6,000	
Deduct value of three	4,000	
Value transferred		2,000
Year 2		
Basic computation ignoring the associated operations rule		
Current value of three chairs	4,400	
Deduct value of two	2,750	
Value transferred	£1,650	
Revised to take account of associated operations rule		
Current value of four chairs	6,600	
Deduct value of two	2,750	
	3,850	
Deduct value transferred in Year 1	2,000	
		1,850
Year 3		
Current value of four chairs	7,200	
Deduct value of one	1,200	
	6,000	
Deduct value transferred in Years 1 and 2	3,850	
		2,150
Year 4		
Current value of four chairs	7,800	
Deduct value transferred in Years 1, 2 and 3	6,000	
Value transferred		1,800
Total values transferred		£7,800

The following are *not* associated operations.

(i) The granting of a lease for full consideration with any operation effected more than three years later.

(ii) An operation effected on or after 27 March 1974 with any operation before that date.

[*IHTA 1984, s 268(2)*].

See *CIR v Macpherson and Another*, HL 1988 [1988] STC 362 where, by a majority decision, on the special facts of the case, a commercial agreement (involving custody of paintings), which both facilitated an appointment made the following day and reduced the value of the property so appointed, was regarded as an operation associated with the appointment. See also *Reynaud & Others v CIR* [1999] STC SCD 185 Sp C 196 where the transfer of shares in a company into a discretionary trust and the subsequent purchase by that company of its own shares was not a disposition affected by the associated operations rules. In *HMRC v Parry* [2020] UKSC 35, the Supreme Court applied *dicta* in *CIR v Macpherson and Another* to the effect that an operation is material for this purpose only if it forms part of, and contributes to, a scheme which confers a gratuitous benefit and is intended to do so. For this reason, the multiple settlements created in *Rysaffe Trustee Co (CI) Ltd v IRC* [2003] STC 536 were not together to be regarded as associated operations because each was a discreet transfer of the asset settled into it.

In practice, HMRC will not use the associated operation provisions where a husband shares capital with his wife who 'chooses to make gifts out of the money she has received from her husband', unless it is a blatant case of a husband's gift to his wife made on condition that she should at once use the money to make gifts to others. (Official Report, Standing Committee A 13 February 1975 Col 1596). See also IHTM14833.

Example 4

If in the example above H had wished to give away the chairs over two years instead of four, he might first have given two chairs to his wife (exempt), so that each could give the son one chair each year.

	£	£
Year 1		
(i) Value transferred by husband to son		
Value of two chairs (as half of a set of four linked by the related property rule)	3,000	
Deduct value of one chair (as half of a pair)	1,250	
		1,750
(ii) Value transferred by wife (similar calculation)		1,750
Year 2		
Value transferred by husband, applying the associated operations rule		
Current value of four chairs	6,600	
Deduct value transferred in Year 1 by H and W	3,500	
Value transferred		3,100
Total values transferred		£6,600

Notes to the example

(A) In this case, the total of the values transferred can exceed the value of the assets, although it must be doubtful whether HMRC would seek to apply the full rigours of the section unless the transfer by the wife in Year 1 had fallen within her annual exemptions, or she had survived seven years so that the gift was exempt.

(B) See *IHTA 1984, s 161* for the related property rule, and see also **53.21** VALUATION.

(C) The result above could have been achieved in another way. The first transfer by the husband to his spouse is quantified at £3,000 – the second to the son is quantified at £1,750 as in the example. If through *section 268* one looks at the position as if the transfer of value was made on the last of the operations, the calculation would be:

Value in H's estate before any transfer (i.e. value of 4 chairs at the date of last transfer	£6,600
Value in husband's estate after all transfers	Nil
Value transferred	£6,600
Deduct value of earlier operations:	
Transfer to wife disregarded *s 268(3)*	Nil
Transfer to son	£1,750
Value transferred	£4,850

So the value transferred is £1,750 + £4,850 = £6,600. HMRC would not seek to raise a charge to tax on the actual transfers by the wife to the son.

HMRC may ask the DV for the value effectively transferred by one transfer being the last of a series of associated operations. If any of the earlier operations were themselves transfers of value, other than transfers between spouses/civil partners [*IHTA 1984, s 18*], then the adjustment will be dealt with by HMRC.

Pre-owned assets

[5.6] Further anti-avoidance measures apply from 6 April 2005 which were introduced following a short consultation period (consultation document 'The Tax Treatment of Pre-Owned Assets') to counteract the free continuing use of assets that have been ostensibly gifted. It appears that this anti-avoidance was instigated because of the large amount of tax that has been, and is likely to be, lost through for example the 'double trust' home loan schemes, successful *Eversden* structures (see above) and chattels that are gifted and then rented back under *FA 1986, Sch 20 para 6(1)(a)*. The income tax charge is to be applied in respect of any benefit received in chargeable circumstances in the initial year of assessment or thereafter, but donor(s) will not be chargeable if the scheme is dismantled, or the donor(s) decides to pay a full market rent. This anti-avoidance legislation institutes latent retrospective taxation and applies to existing arrangements that have been in place for many years as well as future arrangements. The income tax charge can apply to assets in circumstances where the user of the asset does not own it but it was purchased with funds provided by him. Tangible assets e.g. a house or land or chattels, and intangible assets such as life assurance policies will come within the income tax charge. In the case of realty the 'appropriate rental value' is the annual rent equal to the annual value. For chattels the chargeable amount is the interest that would be payable for the taxable period at a prescribed rate on an amount equal to the value of the chattel at the valuation date. In the case of intangible assets the chargeable amount is the interest that would be payable for the taxable period at a prescribed rate on an amount equal to the value of the intangible asset at the valuation date. The prescribed rate is currently 3.25% and is related to the official rate of interest as defined in *ITEPA 2003, s 181*. In all three cases apportionment applies where the asset is not wholly within the charge due to retained ownership of part of the asset or in relation to part of the year of assessment by reference to the valuation date. [*FA 2004, Sch 15 paras 4, 7, 9; Charge to Income Tax by Reference to Enjoyment of Property Previously Owned Regulations 2005, SI 2005/724, Regs 2–4*]. See also **53.1** VALUATION. Regulations provide that land and chattels will be valued every five years. In the initial year *FA 2004, Sch 15; Charge to Income Tax by Reference to Enjoyment of Property Previously Owned Regulations 2005, SI 2005/724, Reg 4* applies a valuation will be made and this will apply to the following four succeeding years. In the fifth year *after* the first chargeable year a new valuation will be made on 6 April and this will then apply for that year and the four succeeding years and so on. The actual valuation date for these purposes will be 6 April in the year or if later the commencement of the 'taxable period' when the asset first becomes chargeable. Initially, therefore, the first valuation date may be any date in the tax year from 6 April but subsequent valuation dates after five years have expired will normally be on 6 April. However, no income tax charge will apply where the appropriate amount for any given tax year is not more than £5,000.

In order to provide an escape route from incurring the income tax charge detailed above, taxpayers who have existing schemes that come within the charge may elect for special transitional relief that allows them to avoid the charge to income tax by dismantling the original gift scheme. The timing of the election is not tied to a particular date as it is related to the point at which the individual first came within the charge but the latest date for existing schemes was to be 31 January 2007 for 2005/06. [*FA 2004, Sch 15 paras 21, 22 and 23*]. However, *FA 2007* inserted an amendment to the 2004 legislation so that HMRC may allow a later time limit in particular cases that are deemed appropriate. [*FA 2004, Sch 15 para 23(3); FA 2007, s 66*]. This election (see IHT500 below) will then ensure that the asset is treated as part of the individual's taxable estate for IHT purposes while he continues to enjoy the property in accordance with the gifts with reservation rules. Under the gifts with reservation rules the property would be potentially eligible for IHT reliefs and exemptions providing the necessary requirements for those reliefs and exemptions were met. In the case of a couple who are married or in a civil partnership who jointly own a property and who are both caught by the provisions of *Sch 15*, if they both wish to have it treated as property subject to a reservation, they must both make an election. However, it may still, in certain circumstances, be appropriate for the taxpayer to suffer the income tax charge under existing schemes and avoid the IHT charge. See **22** GIFTS WITH RESERVATION.

In order to prevent avoidance the pre-owned assets income tax charge applies from 5 December 2005 to such situations so that where the former owner of an asset (or a person who contributed to its acquisition) enjoys the asset under the terms of the trust, and the trust property may in due course revert to the settlor (or to the spouse, civil partner or the widow, widower or surviving civil partner of the settlor) where an exemption is applicable under *IHTA 1984, ss 53(3)(4), 54(1)(2)* the income tax charge will apply subject to an election for the property to fall back into their estate for IHT purposes. It applies to all trusts, whenever created, where the property will or could qualify for the reverter to settlor or settlor's spouse/civil partner exemption. [*IHTA 1984, ss 53(3)(4), 54; FA 2004, Sch 15; FA 2006, s 80*].

The method of election recommended by HMRC is that prescribed in the form IHT 500.

Disclosure of Tax Avoidance Schemes

[5.7] *FA 2004, ss 306–319* impose obligations on promoters of certain tax avoidance schemes, and in some cases on persons entering into transactions under such schemes, to disclose those schemes to HMRC. See **5.8** below. The primary legislation provides the framework for these disclosure rules, with the detail provided by regulations made by statutory instrument.

HMRC have published detailed guidance notes on the disclosure rules which may be accessed via the search facility on its website ('DOTAS Guidance'). The legislation is policed by HMRC's Counter Avoidance unit; see www.hmrc.gov.uk/avoidance/index.htm, which includes links to the legislation and the official guidance plus various forms to be used for making disclosures. The address of the unit is HM Revenue & Customs Counter Avoidance, DOTAS Taskforce SO483, Newcastle, NE98 1ZZ.

Simon's Taxes. See A7.2.

Arrangements covered by the rules

[5.8] Initially, the *Tax Avoidance Schemes (Prescribed Descriptions of Arrangements) Regulations 2004* (*SI 2004/1863* as amended by *SI 2004/2429* and revoked by *SI 2006/1543*) applied the disclosure rules only to certain arrangements related to financial products and certain arrangements connected with employment and limited the scope of the rules to income tax, corporation tax and capital gains tax advantages. The rules have been progressively extended and with effect from 6 April 2011 apply to certain inheritance tax arrangements by virtue of the *Tax Inheritance Tax Avoidance Schemes (Prescribed Descriptions of Arrangements) Regulations 2011* (*SI 2011/170*) and *The Inheritance Tax Avoidance Schemes (Information) (Amendment) Regulations 2011 (SI 2011/171)*. They are further extended with effect from 1 April 2018 by the *Inheritance Tax Avoidance Schemes (Prescribed Descriptions of Arrangements) Regulations 2017 (SI 2017/1172)*.

Under the 2011 Regulations arrangements fall with the scope of the disclosure rules if:

(a) as a result of any element of them property becomes relevant property within the meaning of *IHTA 1984, s 58(1)*; and
(b) a main benefit of the arrangements is that an advantage is obtained in respect of the lifetime IHT entry charge on the transfer of value by which the property becomes relevant property.

The regulations contain three exceptions from the new disclosure requirements. These cover arrangements which are the same, or substantially the same as those:

(i) which were first made available for implementation before 6 April 2011; or
(ii) in relation to which the date of any transaction forming part them falls before 6 April 2011: or
(iii) in relation to which a promoter first made a firm approach to another person before 6 April 2011.

In broad terms therefore only schemes to avoid the lifetime IHT entry charge on a transfer into trust were caught and if the scheme itself pre-dates 6 April 2011 it did need not be disclosed. Note also that the hallmarks of tax avoidance schemes in the 2004 Regulations were not applied for these purposes, so disclosure had to be made even though the scheme concerned could not be regarded as commanding a premium fee.

The disclosure rules in relation to IHT were widened by an amendment to the 2004 Regulations having effect from 23 February 2016. IHT arrangements which fall within *Reg* 6 (confidentiality in cases involving a promoter) and *Reg 8* (premium fee) were brought within disclosure requirements from that date. Thus IHT planning is now to be disclosed where the promoter wishes the way in which the tax advantage is achieved is kept confidential from any other promoter, or from HMRC for a period of time to enable repeated or continued use of it. IHT planning is also to be disclosed where it might reasonably be expected that a promoter, or someone connected with a promoter, could obtain a premium fee from a person experienced in receiving services of the type being provided. A *premium fee* is one which is to a significant extent attributable to the IHT advantage or to any extent contingent on obtaining that advantage.

They are extended further with effect from 1 April 2018 as detailed below.

[*Tax Avoidance Schemes (Prescribed Descriptions of Arrangements) (Amendment) Regulations 2016, SI 2016/99*].

Grandfathering

[5.9] HMRC published a list of schemes which it did not require to be disclosed under the above provisions because it was already aware of them. However, a scheme may nevertheless have to be disclosed if it is part of wider arrangements which are outside those which are grandfathered. See below as regards the disclosure requirements effective from 1 April 2018 which contain a different grandfathering rule.

The list of schemes not requiring disclosure was:

(1) **Arrangements that qualify for reliefs/exemptions**: this includes a single step that qualifies for a relief/exemption, where this does not depend on the inclusion of other steps, and also arrangements which qualify for

multiple reliefs/exemptions or more than one application of the same relief, or a single relief/exemption plus further steps in each case where they are covered by the grandfathering rule.

(2) **The purchase of business assets with a view to transferring them into a relevant property trust after 2 years.**

(3) **The purchase of agricultural assets with a view to transferring them into a relevant property trust after the qualify for relief.**

(4) **Pilot trusts:** these do not require disclosure if there is no advantage in relation to the IHT entry charge on creation. Note that an advantage in relation to 10 yearly or exit charges is not disclosable under the Regulations.

(5) **Discounted gift trusts:** most of these are not disclosable because all the trusts are bare trusts but where this is not the case disclosure is not required where the grandfathering provisions apply.

(6) **Excluded property trusts, disabled trusts, employee benefit trusts within *IHTA 1984, s 86* and qualifying interest in possession trusts:** these are not disclosable unless there is an advantage in relation to the relevant property entry charge.

(7) **Transfers on death into relevant property trusts.**

(8) **Changes in the distribution of deceased's estates:** variations, disclaimers etc. of interests in a deceased's estate which are not transfers of value by virtue of *IHTA 1984, s 17* are not disclosable, nor are distributions from property settled by will within *s 144*.

(9) **Transfers within the nil band every seven years.**

(10) **Loan into relevant property trust: this is not disclosable where it is made a single step.**

(11) **Insurance property trusts:** the transfer of death benefits into trust and the payment of premiums on a trust policy are not disclosable, except where part of other arrangements giving an advantage in relation the relevant property entry charge.

(12) **Chargeable transfer followed by potentially exempt transfer:** this is within the grandfathering exemption, except where there are further arrangements giving an advantage with respect to the relevant property entry charge.

(13) **Deferred share schemes:** normally non disclosable unless part of scheme outside the grandfathering provisions.

(14) **Retention of reversionary interest by settlor:** not disclosable if grandfathering rule applies.

(15) **Gifts to companies:** these are chargeable transfers but do no involve relevant property in trust and so are outside the scope of the Regulations.

Extension of disclosure rules from 1 April 2018

[5.10] The disclosure rules are to be widened with effect from 1 April 2018. From that date, IHT planning arrangements will be within the disclosure requirements if it would be reasonable to expect an informed observer to conclude that both conditions 1 and 2 below are met.

Condition 1 is that the main purpose, or one of the main purposes, of the arrangements is to enable a person to obtain one or more of the following advantages in relation to inheritance tax:

(a) the avoidance or reduction of a relevant property entry charge;
(b) the avoidance or reduction of a charge to inheritance tax under *sections 64, 65, 72* (charges on relevant property) or *94* (charges on participators) of *IHTA 1984*;
(c) the avoidance or reduction of a charge to inheritance tax arising from the application of *sections 102, 102ZA, 102A* or *102B* of *Finance Act 1986* (reservation of benefits) in circumstances where there is also no charge under the pre-owned assets legislation;
(d) a reduction in the value of a person's estate without giving rise to a chargeable transfer or potentially exempt transfer.

Condition 2 is that the arrangements involve one or more contrived or abnormal steps without which the tax advantage could not be obtained.

Arrangements are excepted from being prescribed under if they (a) implement a proposal which has been implemented by 'related arrangements'; and (b) are substantially the same as such arrangements. 'Related arrangements' means arrangements which were entered into before 1 April 2018 and at the time they were entered into accorded with established practice of which HMRC had indicated their acceptance.

HMRC guidance lists the following arrangements as being outside the requirement for disclosure:

(a) lifetime gift to spouse or civil partner;
(b) regular gifts out of income;
(c) chargeable transfers to use the nil band every seven years;
(d) lifetime transfer to a bare trust for a minor beneficiary;
(e) deeds of variation, including a variation in favour of an exempt beneficiary;
(f) leaving assets by will to an exempt beneficiary such as the spouse;
(g) a disclaimer where there is an exempt residuary beneficiary;
(h) acquisition of property qualifying for statutory relief or a transfer which is specifically provided for in the legislation;
(i) purchase of shares qualifying for business property relief after two years;
(j) gift of land followed by continued use for full consideration;
(k) gift of share in land used subsequently by donor and donee (note that the acceptable amount of the gifted share is discussed in the guidance and HMRC consider that significantly disproportionate ownership as compared to the use of the property may be disclosable);
(l) transfers of funds by a non-domiciliary to an offshore bank account;
(m) transfer of excluded property into trust by a non-domiciliary;
(n) distribution from trust before ten-year anniversary to reduce the ten-year charge.
(o) products such as gift and loan trusts;
(p) loans to companies or other entities from which the lender cannot benefit.

Examples of potentially notifiable arrangements, according to the guidance, are:

(a) gift into trust of shares qualifying for business property relief which are to be sold back to the settlor;
(b) creation of reversionary lease in circumstances where no pre-owned asset charge arises;
(c) use of employee trust exemption to secure IHT exemption for shares in an investment company;
(d) purchase of gilts by a non-resident person in order to make a gift of them;
(e) setting up several trusts to split value between them, which HMRC consider is not within the established practice exception which does not cover bespoke schemes.

[*The Inheritance Tax Avoidance Schemes (Prescribed Descriptions of Arrangements) Regulations 2017, SI 2017/1172*].

Returns

[5.11] The promoter of arrangements within the disclosure Regulations must make disclosure to HMRC under the provisions of the 2004 Regulations and the applicable time limit is the same as for other direct tax schemes, usually being within 5 days of making the scheme available for implementation. The Scheme Reference Number will then be allocated by HMRC and any person who is a party to arrangements which are notifiable under the Regulations, and who is also required to make a return under *IHTA 1984, s 216* (Delivery of accounts) in respect of them, must disclose the scheme reference number in that return. Where no return under *s 216* is required, disclosure to HMRC must be made on form AAG4 within 12 months of the end of the month in which the first of the relevant transactions is entered into.

Penalties

[5.12] Penalties are chargeable for failures to comply with the duties summarised at **5.11** above and detailed in the primary legislation noted below contained in *FA 2004*:

(a) duty of promoter to notify HMRC of notifiable proposals or arrangements (*FA 2004, s 308(1)(3)*);
(b) duty of taxpayer to notify where the promoter is not UK-resident (*FA 2004, s 309(1)*);
(c) duty of parties to arrangements to notify where there is no promoter (*FA 2004, s 310*);
(d) duty of promoter to notify parties of the scheme reference number (*FA 2004, s 312(2)*);
(e) duty of client to notify other parties to the arrangements concerned and who might be expected gain a tax advantage from them of the reference number (*FA 2004, s 312A(2)*);
(f) (from 1 January 2011) duty of promoter to provide details of clients (*FA 2004, s 313ZA*);
(g) duty of promoter to respond to inquiry (*FA 2004, ss 313A, 313B*);
(h) duty of introducer to give details of persons who have provided information (*FA 2004, s 313C*);

There is an initial penalty of up to £5,000 for any failure to comply with any one of the above duties. However, with effect from 1 January 2011, where the failure relates to (a), (b) or (c) above, the initial penalty is up to £600 for each day during the 'initial period'. The 'initial period' begins with the day after that on which the time limit for complying with the requirement expires and ends with the earlier of the day on which the penalty is determined and the last day before the failure ceases. The actual amount of the daily penalty should be arrived at after taking account of all relevant considerations, including the desirability of providing a deterrent and the amount of fees likely to be received by a promoter or the tax saving sought by the taxpayer. If, after taking account of those considerations, the maximum daily penalty seems inappropriately low, it can be increased to any amount up to £1 million.

Penalties are determined by the First-tier Tribunal. Where HMRC consider that a daily penalty has been determined to run from a date later than it should, they can commence proceedings for a redetermination of the penalty.

A further penalty or penalties of up to £600 applies for each day on which the failure continues after the initial penalty is imposed.

HMRC may appeal to the Tribunal for an order that a specified proposal or arrangements shall be treated as notifiable. There is also a separate power for HMRC to apply to the Tribunal, specifying the promoter, for an order that a specified proposal or arrangements is notifiable. Wherever daily penalties apply, the maximum is increased to £5,000 per day where, in relation to the proposal or arrangements in question, an order has been made by the Tribunal. Where the order is made, the increased maximum only applies to days falling after the period of ten days beginning with the date of the order.

Where an order is made by the Tribunal, doubt as to notifiability is not a reasonable excuse for the purposes of *TMA 1970, s 118(2)* after the expiry of ten days beginning with the date of the order.

Parties to notifiable arrangements who fail to notify HMRC of the scheme reference number etc. are liable to a penalty of £100 in respect of each scheme to which the failure relates. The penalty is increased for a second failure, occurring within three years from the date on which the first failure began, to £500 in respect of each scheme to which the failure relates (whether or not the same as the scheme to which the first failure relates). Any further such failures occurring within three years from the date on which the previous failure began, result in a penalty of £1,000 in respect of each scheme to which the failure relates (whether or not the same as the schemes to which any of the previous failures relates).

The Treasury has the power to amend the above maxima of £600, £5,000, and £1 million by statutory instrument.

A party to notifiable arrangements who fails to give the reference number (for example, by including it in a return) is liable to a penalty of £100 for each scheme (i.e. each set of notifiable arrangements) to which the failure relates. A second such failure within a period of 36 months gives rise to a penalty of £500 per scheme. A third or subsequent failure within 36 months gives rise to a penalty of £1,000 per scheme. The normal penalty regime for incorrect tax returns does not, however, apply in relation to any such failure.

[TMA 1970, s 98C; FA 2004, ss 315, 319; FA 2007, s 108(9); FA 2008, s 116, Sch 38 para 7; FA 2010, Sch 17 paras 10, 11; SI 2004 No 1864, Reg 8B; SI 2007 Nos 3103, 3104; SI 2008 No 1935; SI 2010 No 2743; SI 2010 No 2928, Regs 1, 4; SI 2010 No 3019; SI 2011 No 170; SI 2011 No 171].

Promoters of Tax Avoidance Schemes

[5.13] Legislation to enable HMRC to monitor closely those who are considered to be high risk promoters of tax avoidance schemes was introduced in 2014 and includes those promoting inheritance tax avoidance arrangements. A person is a promoter in respect of a relevant proposal if, at any time, the person is responsible for the design of the proposed arrangements, makes a 'firm approach' to someone with a view to making the proposal available for implementation by that person or another, or makes the relevant proposal available for implementation by others. A conduct notice can be issued by HMRC to such a promoter if the promoter has, within the previous three years triggered a threshold condition. There is an extensive list of threshold conditions including dishonest as a tax agent, non-compliance with DOTAS requirements, disciplinary action by a professional body and receipt of an adverse opinion by the GAAR panel in relation to arrangements promoted by the person concerned. Although the final of these appears out of place as against the other threshold conditions, it is required that HMRC consider first whether the particular threshold condition which has been met is 'significant' for the purposes of these provisions and so an adverse GAAR opinion may not on its own be sufficiently significant.

If a promoter fails to comply with a conduct notice then an authorised officer of HMRC may apply to the Tribunal for approval to give a monitoring notice. The promoter has the opportunity to make representations to the Tribunal including representations about the reasonableness of the conditions in the conduct notice which HMRC consider it to have breached. If the monitoring notice is authorised by the Tribunal, the promoter may be required to publish to its clients, and on the internet or in its marketing material, that it is a monitored promoter. HMRC will issue the monitored promoter with a promoter reference number. Within 30 days of receipt of a monitoring notice, the promoter must notify its clients of the promoter reference number to their clients and they in turn must report the number to HMRC if they expect to obtain a tax advantage from the monitored promoter's relevant arrangements. If the person makes a tax return then the promoter reference number should be included on the return. For inheritance tax notification must be made in accordance with regulations to be made under these provisions. Draft regulations were published in March 2015 but were later withdrawn. A monitored promoter must also provide detailed information and documents in relation to schemes being promoted at the time of the notice.

HMRC may serve a notice requiring the monitored promoter to make returns supplying names and addresses of its clients on a calendar quarterly basis. The first return must contain details about current clients, and thereafter there is an ongoing duty to file returns with details of new clients.

If the monitored promoter is offshore and has failed to provide the information required under these provisions about monitored proposals or monitored arrangements then HMRC may approach an intermediary of it to provide the information.

These provisions are exceedingly harsh on those affected and are backed with penalties for non-compliance which can in certain cases be as high as £1 million. Detailed guidance notes on the legislation were published by HMRC on 12 February 2015 – www.gov.uk/government/publications/promoters-of-tax-avoidance-schemes-guidance.

[*FA 2014, ss 234–283, Schs 34, 35*].

6

Business Property

Cross-references. See **4** AGRICULTURAL PROPERTY; **5.1** ANTI-AVOIDANCE; **7.6** CALCULATION OF TAX for application of business relief where transfers partly exempt; and **22.11** GIFTS WITH RESERVATION where such a gift is of relevant business property.

Simon's Taxes. See **I5.373, I7.1.**

Other Sources. Tolley's Capital Gains Tax; Foster, Part G1; Mellows, Parts 5.24–5.34; HMRC Inheritance Tax Manual; IHTM25000, IHTM18331.

Introduction to business property

[6.1] Where the qualifying conditions are satisfied, relief from inheritance tax is available on a transfer of value which is attributable to the value 'relevant business property'. It is a fallacy therefore to state that the relief only applies to transfers of business property, since the requirement is that the value of the transfer must be attributable to such property. The significance of this distinction was highlighted in the *Nelson Dance case* (see **6.4** RELEVANT BUSINESS PROPERTY) where it was held that relief applied to a gift of an asset used for a business, whilst the business itself was not transferred. The relief is a percentage reduction in the value transferred by the transfer of value (see Table below) and applies to transfers in life and on death and to occasions on which tax is chargeable under the provisions relating to SETTLEMENTS: DISCRETIONARY TRUSTS AND OTHER TRUSTS OF RELEVANT PROPERTY (**40**). The percentage reduction is made before deduction of the annual exemption and other EXEMPT TRANSFERS (**21**) and before grossing-up where the transferor pays the tax. It should be noted that unlike agricultural property relief there is no territorial limitation on undertakings entitled to business property relief and therefore can include businesses situated worldwide. See also Foster on inheritance tax at section G1.11.

Anomalies with business property relief were highlighted in a report of the Office of Tax Simplification issued in July 2019. In particular, the over 50% test for the level of trading activity in a company for it to qualify for relief as a whole (see **6.4**), as compared to a much higher test for certain capital gains tax purposes, should be reviewed according to the authors of the report, as also should the differing treatment of furnished holiday lets for IHT and CGT. More ominously, it was questioned whether the relief for trading companies listed on the Alternative Investment Market achieves any policy objective. The IHT treatment of indirect minority holdings in trading companies was also put forward as a matter for review. It was subsequently announced that no action on any of these points was to be taken although the income tax and capital gains tax reliefs for holiday lets are due to be withdrawn from April 2025; how that will be carried forward on a change of government remains to be seen.

Interaction with other reliefs

Business property relief applies only to the part of a transfer represented by relevant business property (see **6.4** below). The legislation does not make the relief dependent on a claim for it. Agricultural property relief has priority, where it applies, since business property relief is not given on any part of a transfer of value if it qualifies to any extent for the agricultural relief. Hence where the agricultural value of land qualifies for only 50% agricultural relief that same value cannot qualify for business property relief, although any development value in excess of agricultural value may so qualify, assuming the conditions for business property relief are satisfied. [*IHTA 1984, s 114(1)*].

Where woodlands are transferred and capital transfer tax or inheritance tax previously deferred (see **54** WOODLANDS) becomes chargeable, that tax is deducted from the later transfer before business property relief is applied. [*IHTA 1984, s 114(2)*].

Relevant business property after 5 April 1996

In relation to transfers of value made, and other events occurring, **after 5 April 1996** the categories of 'relevant business property' qualifying for business property relief (BPR) are as follows:

(a)	Unincorporated business (**6.4**(a) below)	**100%**
(b)	Unquoted securities which either by themselves or with other such securities or unquoted shares gave the transferor control (**6.4**(b) below)	**100%**
(c)	Any unquoted shares in a company not listed on a recognised stock exchange but including those traded in the USM or the AIM or OFFEX markets (**6.4**(b), (d) below)	**100%**
(d)	Shares or securities giving control of a 'quoted' company (**6.4**(b) below)	**50%**

(e)	Land, buildings, machinery or plant held either (a) by a partner and used for the purposes of a business conducted by the partnership or (b) by a controlling shareholder and used by that company for the purposes of its business or (c) by the trustees of a settlement and used for the purposes of a business carried on by a life tenant of the settlement (but see **6.4**(d) below — HMRC suggest that this relief for settled property applies only to lifetime transfers)	50%

Conditions for business property relief

[6.2] The conditions to be satisfied are that:

(a) the business, whether unincorporated or incorporated into a company in respect of the value of which relief is claimed, is a qualifying business, see **6.3** below; and
(b) the asset must be relevant business property, see above and **6.4** below; and
(c) the asset must have been owned for a minimum period, see **6.8** below.

There are further conditions to be satisfied by lifetime transfers, see **6.11** below.

Definition of qualifying business

[6.3] '*Business*' includes a business carried on in the exercise of a profession or vocation but does not include a business carried on otherwise than for gain which will therefore exclude from the relief most 'hobby' businesses, and in certain cases, loss-making businesses, although temporary periods of loss should not prevent relief nor loss-making in the initial years of a start-up business. [*IHTA 1984, s 103(3)*]. See *C & E Commissioners v Lord Fisher* [1981] STC 238 for Ralph Gibson J's six tests on the factors to be considered in respect of a business carried on for gain. See HMRC Tax Bulletin October 1999, p 699.

Property owners who use land under schemes to generate credits to offset carbon and other gases connected to climate change are considered to be eligible for business property relief. The relevant schemes are the Woodland Carbon Code and the Peatland Carbon Code. (See IHTM25253.)

Example 1

Bill 'the bet' Hill, an Authorised Bookmaker, is an on-course bookmaker with a 'pitch' at Sandown Park racecourse as well as his own independent bookmakers in Wallington, Surrey. He had originally obtained the bookmaking business by inheritance from his father many years previously. The 'pitch' is valued at £98,000 (see point (C) below) and the business in Wallington where he conducts his business other than on race days at Sandown Park is valued at £210,000. Bill also provides a deposit to the National Joint Pitch Council of £25,000, being the security required for a rails bookmaker. Bill dies on 25 December 2020 and leaves the business to his son Alan.

	£
Value of Wallington bookmakers	210,000
Pitch at Sandown Park racecourse	98,000
Deposit held by National Joint Pitch Council	25,000
Total	333,000
Deduct business property relief 100%	(333,000)
IHT payable	Nil

Notes to the example

(A) The business including pitch must meet the statutory requirements of *IHTA 1984, ss 103–114* in order to qualify for 100% BPR.

(B) Under *TCGA 1992, s 274* where the market value of an asset has been 'ascertained' for IHT purposes then that value is also used for CGT purposes to be the market value. In the case of a bookmaker's pitch see HMRC Interpretation RI 210.

Exclusions

A business or interest in a business, or shares or securities of a company, do not qualify if the business (or the business of the company) *consists wholly or mainly* (see below) of dealing in securities, stock or shares, land or buildings or making or holding investments, unless the business is:

(a) wholly that of a 'market maker' (before the Stock Exchange reform, a jobber) or that of a discount house and, in either case, is carried on in the UK; or

(b) wholly or mainly that of a holding company of one or more companies whose business does qualify.

Land holding or dealing businesses

A land holding or dealing business, however, can qualify, provided it includes building construction or land development, and the housing stock of a building business can qualify if regarded as stock in trade.

> '*Mr Lawson:* "As with many, if not all building companies their stock of houses would be regarded as stock in trade—I know that in some cases the houses may rapidly be transferred to a holding company in the Group, but in the company which does the building they will be regarded as stock in trade—will the Chief Secretary assure us that that type of company is not comprised in the category of company that is described as that dealing in land or buildings."'
>
> '*Mr Barnett:* "I can give the hon and learned Gentleman that assurance."'

HC Official Report, 30 June 1976, cols 1268, 1269.

In *DWC Piercy's Executors v HMRC* [2008] STC SCD 858 Sp C 687 a property development company (T) owned some land in Islington on which it had erected some workshops, which it let out. T's major shareholder died in 1999. His executors claimed business property relief. HMRC rejected the claim on the grounds that because T received significant rental income, its business consisted mainly of 'making or holding investments', within *IHTA 1984, s 105(3)*. The executors appealed, contending that it still wished to develop the land in Islington for residential purposes but had been unable to do so because of uncertainty about proposals for a new railway line. The Special Commissioner accepted this evidence and allowed the appeal, finding that the company continued to hold its land as trading stock, and holding that it was not an 'investment company' for the purposes of *s 105*. The Commissioner also held that 'the only type of land-dealing company whose shares fail to qualify for the relief is . . . some sort of dealing or speculative trader that does not actively develop or actually build on land'.

Definition — 'wholly or mainly'

The term '**consists wholly or mainly**' is not simply a quantitative test of 50% or more, but it is a qualitative test determined by 'not the degree or level of activity, but rather the nature of the activities which are carried on' (*HMRC v Personal Representatives of Pawson deceased* [2013] UKUT 50 (TCC)). See *Powell and Halfhide (executor of G E Pearce deceased) v CIR* [1997] STC SCD 181 Sp C 120; *Furness v CIR* [1999] STC SCD 232 Sp C 202. The leading decision is now *Carnwath J in George & Loochin (Stedman's Executors) v CIR* CA [2003] EWCA Civ 1763 [2004] STC 147, where staff time, turnover, gross and net profit on each activity were all taken into account. See **55** TAX CASES.

Case law

In the case of *Hall & Hall (Hall's Executors) v CIR* [1997] STC SCD 126 Sp C 114; the letting of caravans on 45-year leases which comprised 84% of the deceased's income in the form of rent and standing charges resulted in the determination that the business had consisted 'mainly of making or holding investments'.

In contrast, the net profitability of lettings on a farm when compared with that of the less profitable farming business could not be the sole yardstick as to whether the business consisted 'mainly' of holding investments in *Farmer and another (Executors of Farmer deceased) v CIR* [1999] STC SCD 321 Sp C 216. Although the lettings were more profitable than the farm, the overall context of the business, the capital employed, the time spent by the employees and consultants and the levels of turnover supported the conclusion that the business consisted mainly of farming.

In *Weston (Weston's Executor) v CIR* [2000] STC SCD 30 Sp C 222, the business of a company included the purchase and sale of caravans, the sale of caravans for commission on behalf of owners, and the grant of the right to pitch caravans on the caravan park run by the company. The business also included the maintenance and administration of the park, and the supply for a consideration of electricity and bottled gas used by the pitch holders at the park. However looked at in the round, the business was mainly an investment business with ancillary sales, and business property relief was therefore denied.

In *Burkinyoung (executor of Burkinyoung deceased) v CIR* [1995] STC SCD 29 Sp C 3 a business of letting furnished flats on assured shorthold tenancies was held to be wholly one of making and holding investments and so is excluded from relief. Also, in the similar case of *Martin and Horsfall (executors of Moore deceased) v CIR* [1995] STC SCD 5 Sp C 2 the letting of properties as small industrial units was not a business as the units consisted wholly or mainly of the 'making or holding of investments'. In determining these cases, Stephen Oliver QC referred to an income tax decision and suggested that the provision of security services or heating/cleaning services, independent of the lease requirements, for specific charge would not be an activity of holding investments. As it was where services are provided under the lease then that may be deemed to be connected with and incidental to holding investments. [*IHTA 1984, s 105(3)*]. In a more recent case a woman owned a number of shares in a company which owned more than 100 different properties. Her executors claimed business property relief. HMRC rejected the claim on the basis that the shares were not 'relevant business property', because the company's business consisted mainly of 'making or holding investments', within *IHTA 1984, s 105(3)*. The executors appealed, contending that because the company carried out maintenance work on the properties, it should not be treated as falling within *s 105(3)*. The Special Commissioner rejected this contention and dismissed the executors' appeal, holding that 'the company's maintenance activity is not the separate provision of services; it is inherent in property ownership'. On the evidence, the company's business consisted 'mainly of holding investments'. See *Clark (executors of Clark deceased) v HMRC* [2005] STC SCD 823 Sp C 502. However, in a more recent case the activities of a money lender which encompassed lending to various family companies 'was in the business of making loans and not in the business of investing in loans . . . the loans were not investments for their own sake but the provision of a finance facility to the other companies'. Accordingly, the shares in the money lending company qualified for business property relief. *Phillips and Others (Phillips' Executors) v HMRC* [2006] STC SCD 639 Sp C 555.

In contrast, the decision of the Commissioners in *Stedman's Executors v CIR* [2002] STC SCD 358 Sp C 323 determined that, as '72% of the site fees goes in overheads (*sic*) . . . most of which relate to the provision of upkeep of the common parts', this was 'the provision of services and not the business of holding investments'. The Court of Appeal upheld this decision with Carnwath LJ stating that, on the evidence, the holding of property as an investment was only one component of the business, and did not prevent the company from qualifying for business property relief (*George & Loochin (Stedman's Executors) v CIR* CA [2003] EWCA Civ 1763; [2004] STC 147). As this was only the second time the Court of Appeal had considered BPR, the previous case being *Fetherstonaugh and others v CIR* [1984] STC 261, it is interesting to note Carnwath LJ's comment in conclusion:

> 'I find it difficult to see any reason why an active family business of this kind should be excluded from business property relief, merely because a necessary component of its profit making activity is the use of land.'

The decision in *HMRC v Personal Representatives of Pawson deceased* [2013] UKUT 50 (TCC) related to a seaside bungalow let on a weekly basis as holiday accommodation. It was a standard holiday let business, in that the property was fully furnished and equipped, and it was cleaned between lets and freshly laundered bedding provided on each occasion. The appeal was allowed by the First-tier Tax Tribunal on the basis that significant services were provided, such that 'an intelligent businessman would not regard the ownership of a holiday letting property as an investment and would regard it as involving far too active an operation for it to come under that heading'. That decision was reversed on appeal by HMRC. The Upper Tribunal stated that the First-tier Tribunal did not explain how an intelligent businessman could conclude that the services elements in the business outweighed the investments elements and the only conclusion reasonably open to the Tribunal on the facts was that the property was mainly held as an investment. *Personal Representatives of Pawson deceased v HMRC* [2013] UKUT 50 (TCC).

Further attempts have been made to secure business property relief for furnished holiday lets. In *Green v HMRC* [2015] UKFTT 236 (TC), the *Pawson* case was distinguished on the basis that the business comprised a number of let units so that the average annual income was far higher at £87,000 as opposed to around £6,100 in the *Pawson* case. Furthermore, if the properties had been let on assured shorthold tenancies, the income produced would be around £35,000, so that the additional £52,000 of annual income must be produced by the services provided. However, the Tribunal upheld HMRC's argument that the size of the business is irrelevant and the services did not produce the level of income suggested since the investment element in the business was predominant. Relief was therefore denied. In *Ross (Executors of the Estate of Marjorie) (Dec'd):* TC05959 [2017] UKFTT 507 (TC), there was an on-site handyman for eight let cottages, plus other staff and receptionist services. Guests had the option of taking some meals in a nearby hotel, or having bar meals delivered. The Tribunal held that the business was mainly one of letting land so that no relief was available. In *Executors of the late Sheriff G L Cox v HMRC* [2020] UKFTT 442 (TC), the letting of three holiday flats was held not to qualify for relief on the basis that the substantial work involved was the management of the flats as an investment.

A rare success was achieved in *G J Graham deceased v HMRC* [2018] UKFTT 306 (TC). Four flats were let by the deceased as self-catering holiday accommodation and in addition, two guest bedrooms within the house occupied by her were used occasionally for the provision of bed and breakfast accommodation. There was a sauna, barbecue area, games room and laundry plus a swimming pool and covered areas housed a golf buggy and bicycles which were made available to guests for payment. Inside the house was a separate guest lounge with a collection of books and open fire (in season). At the start of each visit, each flat was supplied with a range of goods and supplies. Running the business in season required in total about 200 hours work per week. The Tribunal concluded that this was an exceptional case and the business was not one which consisted wholly or mainly of holding investments. The services provided in the package more than balanced the mere provision of a place to stay. Accordingly, business property relief was allowed.

In *Trustees of David Zetland Settlement v HMRC* TC/2010/05387, trustees held a commercial building divided into small office units let to tenants for periods normally ranging between one and five years, although these terms were operated on a flexible basis so that they might be terminated earlier. The senior trustee had an office on site and was engaged for much of his time on the management of the premises. There was also a team of staff, including a receptionist, cleaner, handyman and porters, each employed by the trustees. On the premises were a café, operated with the support of the trustees, and other facilities such as bicycle park and meeting rooms available for hire on a daily or hourly basis. The trustees also carried out conversion work to suit the tenants and dilapidations work on termination of each tenancy, some of which produced profits for the trust. It was contended that the business was eligible for business property relief in view of the fact that the trustee and the staff were mostly engaged on providing their services to the tenants. The First-tier Tribunal held that the business in the round was one of holding an investment and was not eligible for business property relief. This decision was referred to in *Butler v HMRC* [2023] UKFTT 872 (TC) where a venue hired out for weddings was also held to be mainly an investment business not eligible for relief. A crucial point was that customers had to contract separately with third-party caterers so the principal activity of the wedding business was the provision of the premises.

In *Best (Exor of Buller deceased) v HMRC* [2014] UKFTT 77 (TC) a company held and managed a business centre comprising approximately 10% offices, and the balance being two thirds warehousing used by retailers or wholesalers and one third light industrial use. In total there were approximately 400 people in or around the Centre on a typical working day. The deceased spent considerable time each week at the Business Centre dealing with the everyday matters that might arise with occupiers. On his death the company employed a full-time replacement as a site administrator. Units were occupied under licence agreements not conferring exclusive possession of a unit. Twenty-four hour security was provided along with a receptionist, forklift driver, maintenance person, office facilities, meeting rooms, central telephone switchboard and various other business facilities. Nevertheless it was held that the investment activity of letting the units was the predominant activity and the company was therefore mainly an investment company. The claim to business property relief on the shares was therefore refused.

In *Vigne deceased (Personal Representatives of) v HMRC* [2017] UKFTT 632 (TC), a claim for business property relief was successful in relation to a livery business operated by the deceased on approximately 30 acres of land. The services provided included worming of the horses, provision of hay feed, removal of manure and daily check of the health of the horses. Some of the owners of the horses did not attend the premises regularly enough to ensure the proper care of the animal concerned and thus Mrs Vigne and her staff were on hand each day to ensure that an acceptable level of care was provided in the absence of the owner. The First-tier Tax Tribunal held that 'no properly informed observer could or would have said that the deceased was in the business of holding investments'.

Claims for relief for other livery businesses may currently be subjected to particular scrutiny by HMRC. These businesses range from those where full care and provision of the horses, as in the *Vigne* case above, is undertaken by the owner of the business to those where little more than stabling is provided with the owners of the horses being required to provide the care of them. The latter, commonly known as DIY liveries, will not benefit from business property relief since they are akin to a property rental business. The former should qualify for relief. Many liveries have elements of both types of business and these may experience reluctance by HMRC to allow relief.

In an appeal to the Special Commissioners' decision in 2008, a claim for BPR was made for land let under a conacre agreement. A widow (M) inherited 33 acres of farmland on the death of her husband. She did not farm the land herself, but let it to local farmers under an agreement of this type. She died in 1999. HMRC issued a notice of determination charging IHT on her estate. Her personal representatives appealed, contending that the farmland qualified for BPR. The Special Commissioner rejected this contention and dismissed the appeal, holding that although M was carrying on a business on the land, that business consisted mainly of making or holding investments, within *IHTA 1984, s 105(3)*, so that the land was not 'relevant business property'. The Commissioner observed that 'the activities of the business consisted of the making available of its major asset to other persons for payment without the separate provision of any substantial other goods or services'. *PN McCall & BJA Keenan (Personal Representatives of Mrs E McClean) v HMRC* [2008] STC (SCD) 752. Subsequently in *McCall (personal representatives of McClean, decd) v HMRC* [2009] STC 990, the decision was appealed and LJ Girvan in dismissing the appeal said 'The special commissioner was fully entitled to conclude that this was not to be viewed as a business of providing grass but rather a business of holding an investment.'

A different conclusion was reached in *Executors of Gill deceased v HMRC* [2019] UKFTT 650 (TC) where a full-time farmer managing land on a grazing agreement, including care for the animals owned by a third party, was held not to have a business of holding the land as an investment, such business property relief was due on the farm assets.

Holding of 'investments': cash reserves

Where relatively substantial amounts of surplus cash have been accumulated in a business, it must first be determined whether or not the business has become mainly one of holding investments, and if not whether all or part of the cash reserves are 'excepted assets'. In the Special Commissioner's decision in *Brown's Executors v CIR* [1996] STC SCD 277 Sp C 83 it was held that the sale of a night club, an asset of the proprietor's unquoted UK company Gaslight, resulting in capital being held on deposit interest account pending the further investment in a future premises was not a change in the nature of the business carried on by the company. HMRC had contended that at the time of the proprietor's death the company's business consisted wholly or mainly in the making and holding of investments and therefore excluded the shares from being qualifying business property. However, the Commissioner found in favour of the taxpayer because the proprietor intended to purchase suitable alternative premises and the deposit account holding the proceeds was of necessity short term to conclude a purchase. In the case of *Beckman v CIR* [2000] STC SCD 59 Sp C 226 monies in a business remaining a capital account on retirement of a partner was held on death to be 'simply those of a creditor of the business' and would therefore not qualify for BPR. The retention of large sums of money in the business after retirement should be avoided because there is no reason *per se* for such a retention which might be expected to be paid out.

Market maker

A '**market maker**' is a person who holds himself out at all normal times in compliance with the rules of either The Stock Exchange or, after 22 March 1992, traders on the London Financial Futures and Options Exchange (LIFFE) who are recognised by LIFFE (Administration and Management) as willing to buy and sell securities etc. With effect from 31 December 2012 the business of traders on any regulated market elsewhere in the EEA, which has been notified to the European Commission and who are recognised by that market, is also within the meaning of 'market maker'. [*IHTA 1984, s 105(4)(7); FA 1986, s 106; SI 1992/3181; SI 2012/2903*].

Relevant business property

[6.4] Business property qualifying for relief is in the following classes. See IHT 17, p 3.

(a) Unincorporated businesses

An unincorporated business is a property consisting of a qualifying business (see **6.3** above) or interest in such a business (e.g. sole trade, profession, share in partnership). [*IHTA 1984, s 105(1)(a)*]. The value of a business or of an interest in a business is the net value of the business or interest therein, i.e. the value of the assets used in the business including goodwill, less the business liabilities. A loan to a business in the ownership of a third party does not represent an interest in that business (*Beckman v CIR* [2000] STC SCD 59 Sp C 226 and see IHTM25152). In valuing an interest in a business, regard must only be had to assets and liabilities by reference to which the net value of the entire business would fall to be ascertained. Liabilities and outstanding rent due under a lease were held to be deductible from the value of the business in *Williams and Coleman (executors of D S Coleman deceased) v HMRC* [2018] UKFTT 0136 (TC).

In *Ninth Marquess of Hertford and others (Executors of eighth Marquess of Hertford deceased) v CIR*, [2005] STC SCD 177 Sp C 444 part of a historic house was open to the public, while part was used as a private residence and not open to the public. The freeholder died in 1997. HMRC issued a notice of determination charging IHT on 22% of the value of the house, on the basis that only 78% of the house was open to the public and thus only 78% of the house qualified for business property relief. The freeholder's executors appealed, contending that the house was a single asset and that the effect of *IHTA 1984, s 110(b)* was that the whole of the house qualified for business property relief even though 22% of the house was not open to the public. The Special Commissioner accepted this contention and allowed the appeal, observing that *s 110* made no provision for apportionment.

See also **30** NATIONAL HERITAGE. Also, HMRC state 'If the business owed any money to the deceased, often through a loan account, you must **not** add that value to the value of the capital and current accounts. A loan does not qualify for business relief.' [*IHTA 1984, s 110*]. See also *Hardcastle & Hardcastle (Vernede's Executors) v CIR*, [2000] STC SCD 532 Sp C 259 and *Mallender & Others (Drury-Lowe's Executors) v CIR*, Ch D [2001] STC 514 below.

In *Brander (Representative of the fourth Earl of Balfour) v HMRC* [2009] UKFTT 101 (TC) the appellant succeeded in integrating a property business within the overall estate and the whole qualified for BPR. The Scottish estate in question, Whittingehame, was owned by a trust founded by the first Earl. The Fourth Earl had the liferent (i.e. under Scottish trust law giving a right to the income of the estate and the power, within limits, to manage it). The estate was a typical one for Scotland, including farms (both managed by the estate and leased), woodland, shooting and 28 leased cottages. In late 2002 the Earl succeeded in having the trust wound up, the property becoming his absolutely. He then put it into a partnership that he managed jointly with his heir, his nephew. In June 2003 the Earl died. His executors claimed BPR on the Earl's share in the partnership, to reduce the taxable value of the Estate. HMRC sought to deny the relief but the Judgment stated 'Most estates of the type under discussion are heavily based on farming and to some extent on forestry and woodland management and related shooting interests. The letting side was ancillary to the farming, forestry, woodland and sporting activities. The farming activities, albeit they include agricultural tenancies, occupied by far the greater area of the estate' (see, for example, *Farmer (Farmer's Executors) v IRC* [1999] STC (SCD) 321).

The Nelson Dance case

In *Nelson Dance Family Settlement Trustees*, Ch D [2009] STC 802 Sp C 682, a farmer in 2002 transferred some farmland, which had development value, to the trustees of a family settlement. HMRC issued a ruling that 'none of the value transferred was attributable to the value of relevant business property'. The trustees appealed. The Special Commissioner allowed the appeal and held that:

> 'everything turns on the loss in value to the donor's estate, rather than what is given or how the loss to the estate arises, except where the identity of the recipient is crucial to a particular exemption.'

But that the business property relief was

> 'much more concerned with values than property. Although the attribution is to the net value of the business as a whole, this does not imply that the value transferred must relate to the whole business. Indeed the exclusion for value attributed to excepted assets in *s 112* shows that the value transferred may need to be attributed to the value of particular business assets (although that would equally be the case if the relief were restricted to transfers of the whole business). Presumably the attribution to the net value of the business is to put a ceiling on the relief to prevent a transferor giving away the total assets of the business, claiming business relief for them, while retaining the liabilities and paying them out of other assets (although that seems to be possible for agricultural relief as the relief is given in terms of attribution to the agricultural value of agricultural property).'

IHTA 1984, s 104 should be construed as meaning that 'all that is required is that the value transferred by the transfer of value is attributable to the net value of the business'. Accordingly, the transfer of the farmland qualified for 100% business property relief. HMRC's appeal was dismissed. *See* also **4.1** AGRICULTURAL PROPERTY and **55** TAX CASES.

Example 2

D and his wife W have owned and farmed 700 acres of land in Northern England since 1980 under a partnership agreement with the land being partnership property. This land is farmed for arable crops and there are a number of cottages let on assured shorthold tenancies together with a building let for commercial use by a local business. 100 acres of the land which includes the commercial letting and a let cottage and has development potential. D and W form a family trust for their children and the trustees become partners in the partnership. They then transfer the 100 acres to the trust. The agricultural value of this land is £10,000 per acre, the let buildings transferred with it have a value of £500,000 and the development potential is valued at £500,000.

		£
Valuations for IHT purposes		
100 acres at £10,000 per acre		1,000,000
Let buildings and development value		1,000,000
Total value of transfer into trust		2,000,000
The transfers subject to tax:		
(i) Agricultural value of land		
100 acres × £10,000	1,000,000	
Less agricultural property relief at 100%	(1,000,000)	—
(ii) Value of development potential and let buildings	1,000,000	
Deduct development potential and lettings attracting 100% BPR £1,000,000		
Chargeable at 20%		£Nil

Notes to the example

(A) In *Nelson Dance Family Settlement Trustees*, [2008] STC SCD 792 Sp C 682 the Special Commissioner found in favour of the taxpayer who had claimed 100% BPR in respect of the land transferred into the settlement. In examining *IHTA 1984, s 104(1)* the Special Commissioner stated that the assets comprised in the declarations of trust were attributable to the net value of the business as they were a component part of the assets used in the business contributing to the net value. Accordingly, the transfer of the farmland qualified for 100% business property relief.

(B) In the Court of Appeal, the Special Commissioner's decision was upheld and Sales J stated that 'the general principle governing the operation of the inheritance tax legislation is the loss to donor principle, which directs attention to changes in the value of the transferor's estate rather than in that of the transferee', and that 'any charge to tax does not turn upon what happens to property transferred when it is in the hands of the transferee'. *HMRC v Nelson Dance Family Settlement Trustees*, Ch D [2009] STC 802. The following example was given: 'Suppose that Mr dance had carried on his farming business in partnership with his wife on equal terms as to income and capital profits, and that all the land formed had been partnership property. Suppose that the partners had given away the land and cottages actually given in the instant case to the trustees. The interest in the business of Mr Dance and that Mrs Dance would have diminished in value as result of that disposition. Plainly, the value transferred by each of them would've been attributable to the value of his or her interest in the business'.

(C) Because the transfer to the trust is a chargeable transfer, all capital gains can be held over. No SDLT arises because the trustees are connected persons with D and W. In the event of the deaths of D and W, BPR on the gift to the trustees will not be withdrawn whilst the farming partnership continues between the trustees, D and W. It may be important to consider profit sharing after the gift to ensure that no reservation of benefit arises, although whilst the trade continues, BPR will ensure that no charge arises under this head, see **22.11**.

Settled property with interest in possession

In *Fetherstonaugh v CIR* CA, [1984] STC 261, it was decided that relief at what was then 50% in 1977 (now 100%) was available in relation to land of which a sole trader was life tenant and on which he had carried on a farming business prior to his death. HMRC's interpretation of this decision is that where there is a transfer of value of a life tenant's business or interest in a business (including assets of which he was life tenant which were used in that business) and 100% relief is available. Where, by contrast, the transfer of value is only of any land, building, machinery or plant, used wholly or mainly for the purposes of a business carried on by the life tenant and in which he has an interest in possession under a settlement, the relief is available only at 50% under '(d)(iii) Land, building, machinery or plant' below if the transfer takes place without the business itself being disposed of. Thus, relief under *IHTA 1984, s 105(3)(e)* applies only to lifetime transfers of such assets. Note that there is no limitation on the type of interest in possession relevant for these purposes, as there is no tie-in with the *FA 2006* changes to the treatment of interests in possession for IHT.

HMRC take the view that assets held on interest in possession trusts cannot have relief as partnership assets where they are used in a partnership business in which the life tenant is a partner because *IHTA 1984, s 49(1)* deems them to be in the beneficial ownership of the life tenant. They qualify for relief at 50% under *IHTA 1984, s 105(1)(d)*. See IHTM25154. It is uncertain whether 100% relief becomes available if the trustees also become partners in the business but since this does not impact on the deemed beneficial ownership by the life tenant, it would seem that this may not change the position for IHT.

Lloyd's Underwriters

In the case of **Lloyd's Underwriters** who converted to a NameCo, HMRC will by concession allow business property relief on the value of the underlying assets, subject to certain limitations, up to and including 31 December 2006. Previously, before Names converted to limited company status, it is understood that the CTO did restrict BPR treatment if assets so deposited were excessive compared with the underwriting undertaken. From 1 January 2007 regard must be had to the degree of likelihood that such assets that are put up as security will be drawn to meet the NameCo's losses. These may be met directly if they are third part Funds at Lloyd's (FAL) or indirectly if they are in the form of bank guarantee(s). The valuation of the assets needs to take into account the diminution in their value arising from the fact that the individual or his estate does not have unfettered use of the assets during the period the FAL requirements are in place or the guarantee(s) are available to be called upon. See Lloyd's Market Bulletin 86/411, 6 December 2003 and 31 May 2006. Also, the right to a share of the Lloyd's syndicate profit/loss is an asset/liability of the business and HMRC consider that the loss should be a liability incurred for the purpose of the business and is therefore taken into account for BPR purposes. In *Hardcastle v CIR* [2000] STC SCD 532 Sp C 259 this underwriting case concerned trading profits and losses. However, HMRC also claim that land (or the interest in the reversion) which is 'not used' in the underwriting business but supported a guarantee should be left out of account for BPR purposes. See *Hardcastle & Hardcastle (Vernede's Executors) v CIR* [2000] STC SCD 532 Sp C 259 and *CIR v Mallender and Others (Executors of Drury–Lowe deceased)*, Ch D [2001] STC 514. (See Lloyd's Market Bulletin, 8 May 2001). The business of corporate Lloyd's members may qualify for relief. The address of the CTO dealing with Lloyd's Underwriters' inheritance tax is Shares Valuation Division, Fitz Roy House, PO Box 46, Castle Meadow Road, Nottingham NG2 1BD. Tel 0115 974 2222, fax 0115 974 2197, DX 701203 Nottingham 4. See below for the position regarding settled property used in the business of a person with an interest in possession in that property.

(b) Partnership interests

The interest of a partner in the partnership business may qualify for business property relief if a qualifying business is carried on by the partnership (see **6.3**). The interest of the partner must be valued either by reference to the terms of the partnership agreement, if applicable, or if not by reference to the market value of the partner's interest in the partnership business at the relevant time. It will normally be necessary for the partnership accounts to be made up to the date concerned although HMRC may not require this if the normal accounting date is only a few weeks removed. See further **31** PARTNERSHIPS.

Land owned by a partner and used by the partnership for a qualifying business is eligible for 50% relief only whereas if the land is transferred into the partnership to become partnership property, 100% relief will be available. However, if all the value in an asset is declared to be held as partnership property but allocated to one partner alone, it is uncertain whether this is effective to allow 100% relief.

Business property relief is accepted as being available for partnership interests in the circumstances detailed in the table below:

	Event	IHT payable on	BPR available
1.	Partnership determines on death. Partnership assets realised and estate entitled to deceased's share of proceeds.	Value of partnership interest.	Yes
2.	Partnership continues with estate entitled to represent the deceased.	Value of partnership interest.	Yes

	Event	IHT payable on	BPR available
3.	Partnership continues with partnership share falling into the deceased's estate but with the option for other partners to acquire either on valuation or formula.	Value of partnership interest (valuation or formula).	Yes
4.	Partnership continues with the share of the deceased partner accruing to the surviving partners with the estate entitled to payment on valuation or formula.	Value of partnership interest (valuation or formula).	Yes
5.	A double option agreement is entered into under which the surviving partners have an option to buy and the PRs an option to sell, such options to be exercised within a stated period after the partner's death.	Value of partnership interest (valuation or formula).	Yes

Notes to the table

(A) Although the situation at 4 above has a similar effect to a buy and sell agreement, HMRC do not regard it as a binding contract for sale: see IHTM25292. Only the case where a deceased partner's interest passes to his or her executors, who are required to sell it to the continuing partners and they are required to buy it, falls to be regarded as a binding contract for sale.

(B) Concern has arisen in the past that the decision in *Spiro v Glencrown* [1991] 1 All ER 680 provided authority for an option to be a contract for sale (see items 3 and 5 in Table above) thereby resulting in no BPR being available. Early in 1996, the CTO confirmed that there had been no change in their opinion regarding SP 12/80 (see above) and that the case would not be cited as an authority for an option constituting a binding contract for sale. See also Key Points below.

Interests in Limited Liability Partnerships

HMRC's published view is that in the case of an LLP investing in unquoted shares in trading companies, it would be inappropriate to allow relief on the basis that the underlying assets constitute business property: the true position is that the nature of the business conducted by the LLP falls within *IHTA 1984, s 105(3)* (business wholly or mainly one of making or holding investments) so that relief is not available. See IHTM25094. HMRC's view has been further clarified in an ICAEW Technical release which confirms that an LLP cannot have the treatment as a holding company, for which special provision applies (*IHTA 1984, s 101(4)*), and so business property relief depends on whether or not the LLP itself carries on a qualifying business. If it does, then if any shares held are used in the business (rather than being held as investments), it is possible that the interest in the LLP may qualify for relief, provided that it does not fail the 'wholly or mainly' test of *s 105(3)*. The question of whether an asset is used in the business or held as an investment will be highly fact specific. For example, a professional farming partnership might be required to hold a minimum stake within a genetics company in order to get specific semen for their bovine herds, or in a crop company to get the best seed at the best price. If this stake is not held as an investment, but with the intention of ensuring that the trade continues and succeeds, then holding such a stake is unlikely to cause any restriction or removal of relief.

An LLP which only holds the shares in a company or in companies will have no relief, even if one of those companies is a trading company and the other companies hold the assets relevant to the trade (ICAEW Technical Release Tech 01/14 tax).

See further on this topic, an article by James Kessler QC and Oliver Marre in which they give their opinion that HMRC's analysis above is not correct and does not take into account the impact of the decision in the *Nelson Dance* case above. Relief is available to the members of the LLP on the basis that a transfer of an interest in the partnership is attributable to any relevant business property, that is any shares in unquoted trading companies, held by it. [*IHTA 1984, s 104(1)*]. (Taxation 20 March 2014, p 8).

Settled property used for partnership business

A deceased with a beneficial interest in possession of settled assets is treated as the beneficial owner of those assets for IHT purposes. They cannot therefore be contributed to a partnership as partnership assets and gain 100% relief under *IHTA 1984, s 105(1)(a)*. Instead, where they are used in a partnership in which the deceased was a partner, they can only obtain 50% business property relief under *s 105(1)(d)*.

(c) Shares and securities

From 6 April 1996, the relief for shares or securities of a company carrying on a qualifying business (see **6.3** above) is as follows:

(i) if they are quoted and (either with or without other such shares or securities owned by the transferor) gave the transferor *control* of the company immediately before the transfer, they qualify for 50% relief;
(ii) in the case of unquoted shares the relief is at 100%;
(iii) in the case of unquoted securities which (either by themselves or with other such securities or unquoted shares owned by the transferor) gave the transferor control of the company immediately before the transfer, relief is at 100%. [*IHTA 1984, s 105(1)(b)(bb)* and *(cc); F(No 2)A 1992, s 73, Sch 14 paras 2(1)–(3), 8; FA 1996, s 184(2), Sch 41 Pt VI*].

There is no business property relief for the amount due on a director's loan account with a trading company. The loan will therefore reduce the value of the company for the purposes of calculating the amount of business property relief, and the loan account will be an asset of the director's estate not benefiting from relief. A solution to this problem is to convert the loan account to redeemable preference shares which can qualify as unquoted shares eligible for relief. If this can be done by way of rights issue in respect of ordinary shares already held for two years, the preference shares may immediately, after issue, qualify for relief.

Where a control test applies, it is not necessary for either the transferor or the transferee to have control after the transfer. Loan stock not carrying rights which contribute to control will not qualify for relief (see IHTM25171). Note that, in relation to transfers of value made, and other events occurring before 6 April 1996, different rates of relief apply as in **6.16** below.

For the purposes of inheritance tax 'quoted' means listed on a recognised stock exchange and 'unquoted' means not so listed. The words 'recognised stock exchange' include those exchanges defined as such for the purposes of *ITA 2007, s 1005* previously *ICTA 1988, s 841* as amended by *Financial Services and Markets Act 2000, s 287*. See also *EU Directive 2001/34/EC* and www.gov.uk/guidance/recognised-stock-exchanges. In addition there are a number of other stock exchanges which have not yet have been designated by the Board for the purposes of *ITA 2007, s 1005* previously *ICTA 1988, s 841*. In practice, however, recognition for IHT purposes depends on whether the law of the country where it is situated recognises the exchange or market in question and whether it provides an adequate trading floor (this last requirement is now becoming obsolete). Both tiers of the NASDAQ stock market have recognised stock exchange status and securities traded thereon are quoted for IHT purposes but with effect from 28 November 2001 shares admitted to EU junior markets and to NASDAQ Europe are regarded as unquoted (see IHTM25192).

Holding companies

For the purposes of the relief a company and all its subsidiaries are members of a group [*IHTA 1984, s 111*] and 'holding company' and 'subsidiary' have the same meanings as in the *Companies Act 2006, s 1159, Sch 6*. [*IHTA 1984, ss 103(1)(2), 104*]. Under the *Companies Act 2006, s 1159(1)*, a company is a 'subsidiary' of another company, its 'holding company', if that other company:

(a) holds a majority of the voting rights in it; or
(b) is a member of it and has the right to appoint or remove a majority of its board of directors; or
(c) is a member of it and controls alone, pursuant to an agreement with other members, a majority of the voting rights in it,

or if it is a subsidiary of a company that is itself a subsidiary of that other company.

A holding company is not excluded from relief so long as its business consists wholly or mainly in holding one or more companies whose businesses themselves are within the relief. [*IHTA 1984, s 105(4)(b)*]. But the value of any subsidiary which does not carry on a qualifying business must be excluded, unless its business is wholly or mainly holding land or buildings occupied by other group members who are carrying on a business which qualifies for relief. [*IHTA 1984, s 111*].

Therefore shares in holding companies which own shares in trading subsidiaries benefit from the relief. However, there are categories of excepted assets that are left out of account when calculating whether there is an entitlement to business property relief and reference should be made to these circumstances below. [*IHTA 1984, s 112(2)*].

In published correspondence between HMRC and the Chartered Institute of Taxation dated 10 January 2011, HMRC confirmed that the following activities are indicative of the business of a holding company:

(a) holding the shares in subsidiaries;
(b) co-ordinating the activities of those subsidiaries by means of voting control and the ability to control subsidiary boards;

(c) provision of loan and other finance to those subsidiaries;
(d) providing strategic direction and oversight of the activities of subsidiaries and ensuring that they work together to achieve a common aim;
(e) monitoring the financial performance of subsidiaries; providing a 'treasury' function, and co-ordinating guarantees and cross-group collateral;
(f) providing a structure to allow ring-fencing of the activities of subsidiaries, nurturing new activities within them, and reorganising their businesses as they change and grow;
(g) managing relations with shareholders on behalf of all subsidiaries.

The correspondence states that: 'If these or similar activities predominate and the subsidiaries are non-investment companies, then business property relief would normally be available for the shares in the holding company. In this connection intra-group loans are regarded as non-investment where the funds are used by subsidiaries for their non-investment businesses and the amounts are reasonable in the context of the whole group.'

Definition — 'control'

'*Control*' is defined by *IHTA 1984, s 269* and means control of powers of voting on all questions affecting the company as a whole which if exercised would yield a majority of the votes capable of being exercised on them. See *Walding and Others (Executors of Walding, deceased) v CIR* [1996] STC 13 and 32.8 PAYMENT OF TAX. In determining whether the transferor has control, any shares or securities which are related property (see **53.21** VALUATION: RELATED PROPERTY) must be added. However in the *Walding* case shares in the name of the deceased's grandson, aged 4 years, were *not* to be excluded from the overall calculations of votes, notwithstanding the fact that due to his age he lacked capacity to exercise his voting rights. The Judge held that *s 269(1)* allowed relief where the deceased controlled the powers of voting on all matters affecting the entire company. In this connection, the capabilities of persons in whose name the shares were registered was not an issue. The relief was denied. See 55 TAX CASES. See also IHT 400 Notes and *Walker's Executors v CIR* [2001] STC SCD 86 Sp C 275 where the casting vote gave control and entitlement to BPR.

There is no relief if the company is being wound up or otherwise in the process of liquidation at the time of the transfer unless the business of the company is to continue after a reconstruction or amalgamation which is either the purpose of the winding up etc. or takes place not later than one year after the transfer [*IHTA 1984, s 105(5)*].

Example 3

A has owned, for many years, 60,000 shares in X Ltd, a trading company now listed on the Alternative Investment Market (AIM), whose issued share capital is 100,000 shares of £1 each. All shares carry full voting rights. A gifts to his son 20,000 shares in June 2013, a further 20,000 in June 2015 and the remaining 20,000 in June 2017. The son agrees to pay any IHT on all gifts. A dies in May 2020, at which time his son still owns the shares. Each gift qualifies for 100% business property relief. The same would apply if A had made a single gift of all his shares and that event the following further advantages could be obtained:

- the option to pay tax by instalments. [*IHTA 1984, ss 227(1)(b), 228(1)(a)*];

- the transfer of any buildings or plant and machinery where the transferor controlled the company immediately before the transfer would attract 100% relief under *IHTA 1984, ss 104(1)(a), 105(1)(b)*.

Example 4

A owns all the share capital of H Ltd, an unquoted company with no assets other than two wholly-owned subsidiary companies S Ltd and P Ltd. S Ltd is a trading company and P Ltd is a residential property investment company. The issued share capital of H Ltd is 100,000 ordinary shares of £1 each valued at £8 per share before any possible discounts. The value of the issued shares in S Ltd is £500,000 and the shares in P Ltd are worth £300,000.

A gave 10,000 shares in H Ltd to his son in August 2018. He had already made chargeable transfers using up his basic exemptions. His son agreed to pay any IHT. A dies in January 2020, at which time his son still owns the shares. Before any possible discounts, the IHT calculation is as below.

	£	£
Value of gift		80,000
Deduct business property relief 100% × £80,000	80,000	
Less $100\% \times 80{,}000 \times \dfrac{£300{,}000}{£800{,}000}$	30,000	
		50,000
PET becoming chargeable transfer on death		£30,000

Note to the example

It is possible to achieve relief for investment assets, for example, let properties or investment portfolios within trading groups, sometimes with remarkable results as illustrated by Example 6 below. To maximise relief, the main principle is that all subsidiary companies in the group should be either wholly or mainly non-investment in nature (ie., not within IHTA s105(3)) so that investment assets within them should be of lower value than the trade assets. The distinction between investment and trading does not apply to any minority holdings of shares, that is holdings in companies which are not sufficient to qualify as subsidiaries. Minority holdings should have a value below that of the subsidiary companies.

Example 5

Assume that in Example 4 the holding of shares in P Ltd was less than 50% and the holding is worth £600,000. P Ltd is now also wholly a trading company. On these facts, there may be no business property relief for the shares in H Ltd because it is not wholly or mainly the holding company of a subsidiary or subsidiaries which are non-investment companies. P Ltd is not a subsidiary and its value is greater than that of the trading subsidiary.

It may be arguable that the asset values of S Ltd and P ltd are not the only factors to be taken into account, for example, management time of directors should also be considered.

Example 6

Assume that in Example 5 H Ltd has another subsidiary R Ltd which is mainly a trading company worth £1m and this value includes non-trade investments of £400,000. The holding in P Ltd is worth £1.2m and the company is an investment company. The subsidiary S Ltd is trading and is worth £500,000 as before.

The shares in H Ltd should now qualify for business property relief in full because it is wholly or mainly the holding company of subsidiaries which are not carrying on businesses outside the scope of the relief. The holding in P Ltd does not restrict the relief because it is not a subsidiary and it is not an excepted asset if it is used for business purposes of H Ltd, as will usually be the case. Although the total investment assets of H Ltd are worth £1.6m compared to the trade assets of £1.1m, this is not relevant in establishing whether or not H Ltd qualifies for relief.

(d) Land, building, machinery or plant

Land, building, machinery or plant which, immediately before the transfer, was used wholly or mainly for the purposes of a qualifying business (see **6.3** above) carried on by:

(i) a company controlled by the transferor; or
(ii) a partnership of which he then was a partner; or
(iii) the transferor and was settled property in which he was then beneficially entitled to an interest in possession (but see below). [*IHTA 1984, s 105(1)(d)(e)*].

Any assets under this heading *owned by the transferor* and used wholly or mainly for the purposes of a business under (i) to (iii) above, qualify for relief only if that business, or the transferor's interest in it, or the shares or securities in the company are also relevant business property. For example, in cases where an asset is owned personally by a partner and used in his partnership (which would qualify for 50% BPR), the inheritance tax position would be improved if the asset brought into the partnership and held as a partnership asset where it will attract 100% BPR. [*IHTA 1984, s 105(6)*].

HMRC consider that (iii) above applies only to lifetime transfers as in the case of transfers on death 100% relief will normally apply to the whole of the business interest including the settled assets used by a life tenant in the business. If however the interest in possession arose after 21 March 2006 under a lifetime settlement, the reasoning for 100% relief would not seem to apply since the trust will be a relevant property trust, although HMRC manuals do not cover the point.

See below for binding contracts for sale. And see **6.7** (excepted assets) as regards the requirement that an asset provided for use by a company or partnership as in (i) and (ii) above must have been used by that entity for at least two years, or be a replacement for property previously so used, before relief is available.

Example 7

M has for many years owned a factory used in the business of Q Ltd, of which he has control. In September 2020, M gives the factory to his son S when its value is £700,000. He has made no previous chargeable transfer, but made a gift of £3,000 in 2009/10. M dies in October 2021, when the factory is being used for business purposes by the partnership of which S is a member. S agreed to pay any IHT on the gift.

	£
Value of gift	700,000
Deduct business property relief (50%)	350,000
	350,000
Deduct annual exemption (2020/21)	(3,000)
PET becoming chargeable transfer on death	£347,000
IHT payable at full rates* (death within 3 years)	£8,800

* 6 April 2021 nil rate band of £325,000 (table **37.1** 2011.A1)

Notes to the example

(A) If M wishes also to dispose of shares in Q Ltd by sale or gift after which he would no longer have control, he should give the factory to his son *before* disposing of the shares, otherwise business property relief would not be available on the gift of the factory.

(B) If the factory had been used by Q Ltd at the date of M's death, no business property relief would be available on the gift since the factory would not be relevant business property as regards S at the date of death. Reservation of benefit also needs to be considered.

HMRC clearances

[6.5] Non-statutory clearance applications will be accepted from business owners and their advisers where there is demonstrable material uncertainty about the IHT-BPR consequences of a transfer of value that follows a transaction affecting their business on areas of material uncertainty arising within four Finance Acts of the introduction of any new legislation. Alternatively, clearance applications will be accepted where legislation preceding the last four Finance Acts and there is material uncertainty around the tax outcome of a real issue of commercial significance to the business itself, determined by reference to the scale of the business and the impact of the issue upon it. For a clearance to be binding on HMRC the taxpayer must provide IHT-BPR Clearances Team, at the time the clearance is sought, with the full facts and context of the transaction, and set out the legislative uncertainty in question. If the taxpayer has applied for a non-statutory clearance, but has not received it by the time that an IHT account is due to be submitted, then the account must still be sent in before the time limit. If this occurs the taxpayer should complete the account according to their own view of the correct tax treatment of the particular transaction. The normal interest and penalty rules will apply if an account is incorrect, whether or not the transactions have been the subject of a clearance.

HMRC aim to provide clearances within 28 calendar days that will give certainty to business owners as to the IHT-BPR consequences of their transactions. HMRC consider the taxpayer is able to rely on any clearance, however for a clearance to be considered binding on HMRC, all the relevant facts should be set out and attention drawn to all the issues in the application. HMRC expect businesses to interpret this relatively broadly, for example, by providing information on related transactions where relevant. IHT does not arise as a consequence of the commercial transaction itself but of a later event if that event is a transfer of value. In these circumstances, HMRC's view of the application of inheritance tax law to the availability of business property relief for a business, an interest in a business, certain shares and securities or certain business assets applies to the facts and circumstances existing at the date of the commercial transaction. HMRC will not be bound by a clearance given if there is a change in circumstances between the date of the commercial transaction and a later transfer of value. A change of circumstances includes a change in the nature of the business or the structure of the business, a change in the nature of the interest held by the person to whom the application applies, or a change in the legislation relating to business property relief.

Example 8

Lin Wong holds all the shares in an unquoted trading company which trades oriental and Chinese rugs from Hong Kong. Rather than tie up money in working capital or premises, Lin Wong placed liquid funds on call at the bank amounting to £250,000 in comparison with a turnover of £600,000. The funds are earmarked for the purchase and import of granite Chinese garden statues and pagodas, a new business. At the time of the proposed purchase of the stock for the new enterprise business the Chinese currency increases in value relative to the pound sterling and the funds are kept on deposit and she switches her exploration of suppliers of granite statues and pagodas to Japan. Lin Wong, the proprietor wishes to pass on both businesses to her son and evidence is put forward that there had been consideration given to acquiring a new enterprise associated with imports from Japan some eight months ago. A question arises whether the £250,000 cash on deposit was required for the purposes of the business and is consequently relevant business property. In considering also *IHTA 1984, s 112(2)(b)*, i.e. whether the cash is a category of *excepted* assets that is left out of account when calculating whether there is an entitlement to business property relief, surplus cash, notwithstanding it is held by a limited company, is an excepted asset but those monies should be earmarked or used for 'some palpable business purpose'.

Lin Wong, with advice from her advisers, makes a non-statutory clearance application for 100% BPR in respect of the new business as well as the existing one, citing the Special Commissioner's case *Brown's Executors v CIR* [1996] STC SCD 277 Sp C 83 where it was held that the sale of a night club resulting in capital being held on deposit interest account pending the further investment in a future premises was not a change in the nature of the business carried on by the company. Also, distinguishing these circumstances from *Barclays Bank Trust Co Ltd v CIR* [1998] STC SCD 125 Sp C 158 where the Commissioner held that, for the purposes of *s 112*, 'required' did not include 'the possibility that the money might be required should an opportunity arise to make use of the money in two, three or seven years' time . . . The word "required" implies some imperative that the money will fall to be used upon a given project or for some palpable business purpose' and that indeed is the case with regard to the current application. See 55 TAX CASES.

Binding contracts for sale

[6.6] If at the time of the transfer a binding contract for sale has been entered into, the property will not qualify as relevant business property unless:

(i) it is a business or an interest in a business and the sale is to a company which is to carry on the business and is in consideration wholly or mainly for shares or securities in the company; or
(ii) it is shares or securities in a company and the sale is for the purpose of reconstruction or amalgamation. [*IHTA 1984, s 113*].

HMRC consider there is a binding contract for sale where partners or shareholder directors of companies enter into an agreement (known as a 'buy and sell' agreement) whereby, in the event of the death before retirement of one of them, the deceased's personal representatives are obliged to sell and the survivors are obliged to purchase the deceased's business interest or shares (IHTM25292). Funds for the purchase are frequently provided by means of life assurance policies. (HMRC Statement of Practice SP 12/80, 13 October 1980). In order to circumvent the 'buy and sell' agreements constituting binding contracts, the use of an option to purchase that does not constitute a binding contract for sale should be considered as an alternative to protect the BPR. See also the Table at **6.4**(B).

Excepted assets

[6.7] The value of any relevant business property which is attributable to 'excepted assets' does not qualify for relief.

Apart from business property relief qualifying under (c)(i) or (c)(ii) above only, '*excepted assets*' are those neither:

(i) used wholly or mainly for the purposes of the business concerned throughout the last two years before the transfer (or since acquisition if more recent); nor
(ii) required at the time of the transfer for the future use of the business.

[*IHTA 1984, s 112(2)(a), (b)*].

Where the business concerned is carried on by a group company, the use of an asset for the purposes of a business carried on by another company which at the time of use and immediately before the transfer was also a group member is treated as use for the purpose of the business concerned unless that other company's membership of the group is disregarded under *IHTA 1984, s 111*.

An asset is not relevant business property by virtue only of **6.4**(d)(i) or (d)(ii) above (use by controlled company or partnership) unless:

(A) it was used for the purpose of the business carried on by the company or partnership throughout the two years immediately preceding the transfer; or
(B) it replaced another asset so used and it and the other asset and any asset directly or indirectly replaced by that other asset were so used for periods comprising at least two years within the five years immediately before the transfer.

The qualifying period under (A) or (B) above is adjusted in the case of successive transfers (see **6.9** below) provided the asset (or it and the assets replaced by it) was or were so used throughout the period between the earlier and subsequent transfer (or throughout the part of that period during which it or they were owned by the transferor or his spouse or civil partner). [*IHTA 1984, s 112(3); FA 2005, s 103; The Tax and Civil Partnership Regulations 2005, SI 2005/3229, Reg 21*].

An asset which is wholly or mainly used for the business cannot be an excepted asset even though there may be substantial, albeit less than 50%, non-business use of it. But where a property is not used wholly or mainly for the business, although a part of it is so used exclusively, that part qualifies for relief [*IHTA 1984, s 112(4)*]. See IHTM25354:

> 'Land or building which is only partly used for the business must be separated into qualifying and non-qualifying parts for the purposes of relief. Qualifying parts would include a room or rooms in a doctor's house used as his waiting room and surgery, or the ground floor of a three-storey building used by its owner as a shop, provided they were exclusively used for business purposes.'

For the above purposes, an asset is deemed not to have been used wholly or mainly for the purposes of the business concerned at any time when it was wholly or mainly for the personal benefit of the transferor or a person connected with him. [*IHTA 1984, s 112(6)*]. See *Barclays Bank Trust Co Ltd v CIR* [1998] STC SCD 125 Sp C 158 where the deceased held half the shares in an unquoted trading company which traded in bathroom and kitchen fittings. It had substantial liquid funds on call at the bank amounting to £450,000 in comparison with a turnover of £600,000. The proprietor died and evidence was put forward that there had been consideration given to acquiring a new enterprise some eight months before her death. The target company was later liquidated with no further progress. Ultimately, seven years later the company spent £350,000 purchasing goods from China. The question arose whether all the cash on deposit at the time of death was required for the purposes of the business. The Special Commissioners held that the £300,000 was not required for the purpose of the business. This case is considered by HMRC to be authority for the proposition that in considering *IHTA 1984, s 112(2)(b)*, i.e. (ii) above, surplus cash is an excepted asset unless it is earmarked or used for 'some palpable business purpose'. However, it may be arguable that the bank account is one indivisible asset and either the whole of it is an excepted asset, or none of it (the apportionment rule applying only to land or buildings).

See also HMRC's published view that additional surplus cash held by a company as an additional reserve in a time of recession remains an excepted asset unless it is held for an identifiable future business purpose. (ICAEW Technical Release Tech 01/14 tax).

Where a company is entitled to BPR because it is mainly engaged in trading activities but is also involved in holding investments, it may be that there are no excepted assets. See SVM111220: 'If a company does carry on an investment business ancillary to its trading business, it cannot be said that the investments made have not been used for the purposes of the hybrid (mainly trading, partly investment) business. Thus those investments cannot be regarded as excepted assets'.

Minimum period of ownership

[6.8] The property described in **6.4** above will not qualify for relief unless:

(i) it was owned by the transferor for a minimum period of two years immediately preceding the transfer; or

(ii) it replaced other property which qualified (apart from the two-year period) immediately before the replacement and both properties together (or all properties if other qualifying property had been previously replaced directly or indirectly) were owned by the transferor for at least two years out of the five years immediately preceding the transfer. See also *AM Brander (Earl of Balfour's Personal Representative) v HMRC* [2010] UKUT 300 (TC), TC00069. [*IHTA 1984, ss 106, 107(1)*].

It should be noted that the period of ownership relates to the 'relevant business property' and not the particular assets used in the business concerned. Hence if a sole trader, who has owned the business for over two years, uses personal cash resources to buy new assets used in the trade, those assets immediately benefit from 100% business property relief. Similarly, it does not matter if the nature of the activity carried on has changed in the two-year period so long as a business of some kind has been carried on for that time (see IHTM25303).

A subscription for additional unquoted shares within **6.4**(c)(ii) above does not in itself qualify as replacement property but where such shares owned by the transferor immediately before the transfer would be identified with other shares previously owned by him for capital gains tax purposes under *TCGA 1992, ss 126–136* (reorganisations of share capital, conversions, amalgamations and reconstructions), the combined period of ownership may be taken for the purposes of (i) above or the additional requirement for substantial minority shareholdings below. [*IHTA 1984, s 107(4); FA 1996, s 184(3), Sch 41 Pt VI*]. A technical defect in the drafting of the Finance Bill clause meant that the replacement facility available to controlling shareholdings ((i) and (ii) above) would have been withdrawn. As this was not intended, amendments were made to allow both the existing replacement facilities for majority and minority holdings to be available to all unquoted holdings regardless of size. (See Inland Revenue Press Release 26 March 1996). [*IHTA 1984, s 107(4); FA 1996, s 184(3)*]. See also *Mrs MA Vinton & Mrs JJ Green (Mrs M Dugan-Chapman's Executors) v HMRC* [2008] STC SCD 592 Sp C 666; Ch D [2010] EWHC 904.

Example 9

From January 2014, A owns 85% of the share capital of Glum Ltd, i.e. 85,000 shares, an unquoted trading company valued at £150,000 until January 2018 when he exchanges his shares for AIM Happy Ltd shares. AIM Happy Ltd is an AIM-listed company. These replacement shares comprise one ordinary share in AIM Happy Ltd for each share in Glum Ltd. The AIM Happy Ltd shares are sold on the Stock Exchange when they become listed in December 2018. A holds the proceeds in cash and in July 2019 the whole of the cash is reinvested in buying further AIM-listed shares in Despondent Ltd, which is a trading company. The cash was held in a specific reinvestment account prior to the purchase of the Despondent Ltd shares. See *Barclays Bank Trust Co Ltd v CIR* [1998] STC SCD

125 Sp C 158 above. A dies in January 2020 when the shares are valued at £150,000 and his other worldly assets at £850,000. By the terms of his will he leaves the AIM shares to his son and also £325,000 to his son and the balance of assets to his widow.

Over the last five years (see (ii) above) A has owned unquoted shares, AIM listed shares, quoted shares, cash and then AIM-listed shares in that order. Working backwards, the shares currently held in Despondent Ltd have only been held for seven months and do not come within the two-year period of ownership within *s 106*. Prior to that, cash was held for six months and this is not relevant business property within *s 105* and neither were the quoted shares that were sold by A within the month of their becoming quoted. The original unquoted shares in Glum Ltd were transferred to AIM Happy Ltd shares and were both held for a total period of five years to qualify under (ii) above. However, when looking at the requirement in *IHTA 1984, s 107(1)(a)*

> '. . . it replaced other property and it, that other property and any property directly or indirectly replaced by that other property were owned by the transferor for periods which together comprised at least two years falling within the five years immediately preceding the transfer of value . . . '

the Glum Ltd shares do qualify for the two-year period within the last five years. Under *IHTA 1984, s 107(1)(b)* requires that 'any other property concerned . . would have been relevant business property in relation to the transfer' and in this respect the cash and quoted securities do not comply. As Glum Ltd shares were exchanged for AIM-listed shares but then for AIM Happy Ltd quoted shares, the eventual replacement property, i.e. the quoted shares, are not relevant business property.

Therefore, under this strict interpretation the inheritance by the son of the shares in the Despondent Ltd shares do not qualify under the two-year rule within the last five years under *s 107(1)*. Had A, on receiving notice of the quotation of the AIM-listed shares liquidated the investment prior to quotation on the stock exchange, and had not invested in cash subsequently, the criteria for *s 107(1)(b)* would have been met and BPR relief on the currently held AIM shares in Despondent Ltd would have attracted 100% BPR.

Notes to the example

(A) Where such shares owned by the transferor immediately before the transfer would be identified with other shares previously owned by him for capital gains tax purposes under *TCGA 1992, ss 126–136* (reorganisations of share capital, conversions, amalgamations and reconstructions), the combined period of ownership may be taken for the purposes of (i) and (ii) above.

(B) IHTM para 25303 notes that the nature of the business carried on by or on the *s 105(1)* business property need not be the same throughout the two-year period. But there must have been a business throughout that period e.g. if a company carried on a farming business until one year before a transfer and then changed its activity to providing recreational facilities for families, the shares in it would be relevant business property if the transferor had owned them for the two years before the transfer. For companies, if the company's business had changed from a non-qualifying business such as investment to a non-investment business within two years of the date of transfer, it is arguable that the two-year test applies only to the holding of the shares and not to the conduct of trading activities by the company.

(C) A could perhaps have considered reinvestment of the cash in, say, commercially managed woodlands, which attract both CGT exemption and qualify for 100% BPR. [*TCGA 1992, s 250(1)*]. Currently, small parcels of commercial woodlands can be bought and sold through specialist agents which qualify the purchaser for 100% BPR. In this way, A would have had relevant business property throughout the two-year qualification period and, in the unexpected case of his demise, the relief under *s 125* would have been available to his son as well as the 100% BPR.

Relief cannot be more than what it would have been had the replacement (or any one or more of the replacements) not taken place (i.e. increases in value by replacement are ignored). For this purpose, changes resulting from formation, alteration or dissolution of a partnership, or from the acquisition of a business by a company controlled by the former owner of a business, are disregarded. [*IHTA 1984, s 107(2)(3)*].

Example 10

In January 2018, A owns 85% of the share capital of Glum Ltd i.e. 85,000 shares, an unquoted company valued at £150,000. A transfers his business to Happy Ltd in exchange for shares. The replacement shares are comprised of one ordinary share in Happy and one share in its wholly-owned subsidiary company Sad Ltd for each share in Glum Ltd. Happy Ltd and Sad Ltd are trading companies. The issued share capital of Happy Ltd is 100,000 ordinary shares of £1 each valued at £1.50 per share. The value of the 100,000 issued shares in Sad Ltd is £30,000.

A gives half his new shares to his son in August 2018. He had already made chargeable transfers using up his basic exemptions. His son agreed to pay any IHT. A dies in January 2021, at which time his son still owns the shares.

	£	£
Value of gift to son		90,000
Deduct business property relief 100% × £90,000	90,000	
Less 100% × 90,000 × $\frac{£30,000}{£180,000}$	15,000	
		75,000
PET becoming chargeable transfer on death		£15,000

Note to the example

(A) The value of Happy Ltd shares at A's death will attract business property relief on their value but under *IHTA 1984, s 107(2)* the business property relief is not to exceed what it would have been had the replacement shares or any one or *more* of the replacements not taken place. Therefore on the death of A HMRC will require evidence of the prior value of Glum Ltd and a similar computation will apply in respect of the value of the shares not attracting BPR as shown in the example above. Under *IHTA 1984, s 109* operates to extend BPR where *s 106* would deny relief (i.e. minimum period of ownership not met), however, *s 109(3)* similarly operates so as not to increase the amount of BPR available.

Inherited property is treated as being owned from the date of death. If the spouse or civil partner inherits then ownership includes the period owned by the deceased spouse or civil partner. [*IHTA 1984, s 108; FA 2005, s 103; The Tax and Civil Partnership Regulations 2005, SI 2005/3229, Reg 19*].

Successive transfers

[6.9] Relief is given on relevant business property not owned for the minimum period under (i) or (ii) above by the transferor if:

(a) he or his spouse or civil partner acquired property (or part) by an earlier transfer on which business property relief was, or would have been, due; and
(b) that property, or any property directly or indirectly replacing it, would (apart from the two-year qualifying period) have been relevant business property in relation to the subsequent transfer; and
(c) either the earlier transfer or the subsequent transfer took place on death.

Relief cannot be more than what it would have been had the replacement (or any one or more of the replacements) not taken place (i.e. increases in value by replacement are ignored). For this purpose, changes resulting from formation, alteration or dissolution of a partnership, or from the acquisition of a business by a company controlled by the former owner of a business, are disregarded. [*IHTA 1984, s 109*].

Liabilities to acquire business property

[6.10] For transfers of value made or treated as made on or after 17 July 2013, it is no longer possible to reduce the value of an asset for IHT purposes by securing a loan on it where the loan is used to acquire or maintain (directly or indirectly) another asset which qualifies for certain IHT reliefs, including business property relief. Instead the loan will be primarily deductible from the asset qualifying for relief. These rules have equal effect for charges on settlements holding relevant property within *IHTA 1984, s 58*. But they apply only to the transferor of the IHT transfer of value, and so do not apply to a liability within an investment company taken on in order to use the loan proceeds to buy trading assets.

This rule applies to any liability incurred on or after 6 April 2013. In the case of any such liability incurred in respect of business property, the loan is to be primarily deducted from the value of that property before any applicable reliefs for such property are given. If the business property is gifted during lifetime the loan is to be deducted only from the value of that property if the lifetime gift is or becomes a chargeable transfer, so that the liability cannot also be deducted from the estate on death. But if the lifetime gift is a PET and the donor survives for seven years, retaining liability for the loan, it may then be deducted from the estate on death.

A loan is considered by HMRC to indirectly finance an asset where it is initially used to buy asset 1 which is later sold and the proceeds reinvested in asset 2. The loan then indirectly finances asset 2 (see HMRC IHT Manual para

IHTM28018). On this view it is not possible to circumvent the disallowance by first acquiring non-business property with a loan, subsequently selling that property and then acquiring agricultural property with the proceeds.

Where a liability is incurred partly for relievable property, as described above, and partly for other assets not qualifying for the reliefs, any part repayments of a liability are to be attributed first to the proportion of it incurred for the non-relievable property. For HMRC's view on apportionments of liabilities between relievable and non-relievable property, see IHT Manual para 28021. See also **53.19** for further analysis. [*IHTA 1984, ss 162A* and *162B*].

Further conditions for lifetime transfers

[6.11] Business property relief is available where any part of the value transferred by a POTENTIALLY EXEMPT TRANSFER (**35**) proves to be a chargeable transfer only if, in addition to the conditions in **6.3** to **6.8** above, the conditions listed below are also satisfied. Similarly, where a chargeable lifetime transfer, other than a potentially exempt transfer, made within seven years of the transferor's death is reduced under the business property relief provisions, the additional tax chargeable by reason of death must be calculated as if the relief had not been received unless the following conditions are satisfied. The impact on the cumulative total of the transferor is explained further below.

Subject to the provisions below for replacement property, the additional conditions are:

(a) that the original property was owned by the 'transferee' throughout the period beginning with the date of the chargeable transfer and ending with the transferor's death or, if earlier, the transferee's death; and

(b) in relation to a notional transfer of value made by the transferee immediately before the death in (a) above, the original property would, ignoring the minimum period of ownership requirement in *IHTA 1984, s 106* (see **6.8** above), be relevant business property unless, for transfers made, and other events occurring, after 16 March 1987, the original property consists of shares or securities:
    (i) which were 'quoted' at the time of the chargeable transfer; or
    (ii) fell within **6.16** below in relation to the transfer and were 'unquoted' throughout the period referred to in (a) above.

Thus for shares in an unquoted trading company, it does not matter if, after a lifetime gift of the shares, the company ceases to trade and becomes an investment company. On the death of the donor within seven years of the gift the only requirement to prevent clawback of relief on the gift is that the company continues to be unquoted (*IHTA 1984 s 113A(3)(a)*).

'*Transferee*' means the person whose property the original property became on that chargeable transfer or, where on the transfer the original property became or remained settled property in which no qualifying interest in possession subsists, the trustees of the settlement.

Example 11

X transfers his shares in Amalgam Ltd (a trading company listed on the Alternative Investment Market) to his son Y, being a 25% interest which he has held for ten years; he also transfers land and buildings used by his partnership to his other son Z on 16 June 2017. X has already used up his annual exemptions for the current year and the previous one. The shares are valued at £640,000 and the land and buildings at £676,000. In February 2019, Amalgam Ltd becomes quoted on the London Stock Exchange and Y's share value increases to £1 million.

Z sells the land and property to one of the partners in May 2019 and invests the whole proceeds in an unquoted company receiving shares to the value of £800,000. X dies on 6 June 2020.

Theoretical computations on death, assuming in the case of the shares in Amalgam Ltd that they had remained unquoted for IHT purposes.

	£	Gross	Tax
Value of shares given to Y	640,000		
Deduct BPR 100%	640,000	Nil	Nil
Partnership assets given to Z	676,000		
Deduct BPR 50%	338,000		
	338,000		
PET becoming chargeable transfer on death	£338,000	13,000	5,200

The tax payable on failed BPR and PETs that have become chargeable because of X's death within seven years:

Computation on death.

X's early death within three years of the gift of a non-controlling shareholding in Amalgam Ltd results in the loss of relief. Although Y did not own the shares for a minimum period of two years, i.e. June 2017 to February 2019 before they became quoted, this does not matter for the purposes of *IHTA 1984, s 113A*: see *subsection (3)(b)* of that section.

	£	£
Value of shares given to Y	640,000	
Deduct annual exemption	Nil	
		640,000
Value of property given to Z after BPR	338,000	
Deduct annual exemption	Nil	338,000
		978,000
Less nil rate band		(325,000)
		640,000 × 40% = £256,000

Apportionment of tax

Gift to Y

$$\frac{\pounds 640{,}000}{\pounds 978{,}000} \times \pounds 256{,}000 = \qquad \underline{\pounds 167{,}526}$$

Gift to Z

$$\frac{\pounds 338{,}000}{\pounds 978{,}000} \times \pounds 256{,}000 = \qquad \underline{\pounds 88{,}474}$$

Z has sold the business assets in the partnership and reinvested the proceeds in other relevant business property which attracts 100% BPR (i.e. unquoted shares) as opposed to 50% for the original assets (i.e. land and buildings) in the partnership. Z's replacement of the partnership assets with unquoted shares qualifies for replacement property relief: *IHTA 1984, s 113B*. However, Z's position is affected by Y's loss of 100% BPR in respect of the transfer of shares to Y by X.

Notes to the example

(A) In light of these circumstances Y and Z have tax liabilities on X's death that arise from a quotation on the London Stock Exchange of Amalgam Ltd shares.

(B) Z could have taken the view that his position was vulnerable to Y's decision to accept quoted shares (with no control) and X's death within seven years of the gifts. Insurance on a reducing basis could have been taken out by Z to protect his position and cover the liability of £83,274 (i.e. £88,474 – £5,200).

Where any shares owned by the transferee immediately before the death would either be identified with the original property under the provisions of *TCGA 1992, ss 126–136* (reorganisations of share capital, conversion of securities and company reconstructions and amalgamations) *or* were issued to him in consideration of the transfer of a business or an interest in a business consisting of the original property (or part), the shares are treated as if they were the original property (or part).

Where part only of the original property satisfies the conditions in (a) and (b) above, proportionate relief is given.

There is no mechanism to reduce the rate of relief, such as where unquoted shares were given but they become a quoted controlling holding before the death of the donor. The only requirement is that the shares remain relevant business property.

Impact on transferor's cumulative total. In the case of a potentially exempt transfer of business property which becomes a chargeable transfer on the death of the transferor within seven years, the cumulative total of the transferor will be revised if business property relief is subject to clawback on the death due to the operation of the rules set out above. Thus although the property may have qualified for full relief at the time of the gift, if the donee triggers the clawback provisions, the calculation of IHT on the donor's estate will be radically affected by the loss of all relief on the failed PET. The position is however different for a lifetime gift which was a chargeable transfer at the time it was made, for example a gift into a discretionary trust. In this case the additional tax chargeable on the gift by reason of the death is calculated without relief if a clawback of relief applies but there is no further provision by which the cumulative total of the transferor must be revised.

Example 12

Arthur gives AIM shares worth £325,000 which he has held for two years to his son, who immediately sells them to pay for a holiday home. Arthur dies within seven years of the gift. On Arthur's death, his nil rate band will be absorbed by the failed PET to his son in respect of which no BPR now applies.

George gives AIM shares worth £325,000 which he has held for two years to discretionary trustees for his son, who immediately sell them to pay for a holiday home for the son to use. George dies within seven years of the gift. On George's death, no tax is payable on the gift because it is within the nil band, and his estate also has a full nil band because George's cumulative total is not revised even though the chargeable transfer to the trustees no longer qualifies for 100% relief.

[*IHTA 1984, s 124A(1) and (2)*].

Replacement property

[6.12] Where the transferee has disposed of all or part of the original property before the death of the transferor and applied the whole of the consideration received in acquiring a replacement property within the 'allowed period' after the disposal of the original property or part (or has entered into a binding contract to acquire replacement property within that time), then, provided the disposal and acquisition are both made at arm's length or on terms such as might be expected to be included in such a transaction, the conditions in (a) and (b) above are taken as satisfied if:

(i) the replacement property is owned by the transferee immediately before the transferor's death (or immediately before the transferee's death if earlier); and
(ii) throughout the period beginning with the date of the chargeable transfer and ending with the death (disregarding any period between the disposal and acquisition) either the original property or the replacement property was owned by the transferee; and
(iii) in relation to a notional transfer of value made by the transferee immediately before the death, the replacement property would, ignoring the minimum period of ownership requirement, be relevant business property.

If the transferor dies before the transferee and all or part of the original property has been disposed of before the transferor's death (or is excluded by the provisions relating to binding contracts for sale under **6.4** above from being relevant business property in relation to the notional transfer under (iii) above) then if the replacement property is acquired (or a binding contract entered into) after the transferor's death but within the 'allowed period' after the disposal of the original property, or part, condition (i) above does not apply and any reference to a time immediately before the death is taken as a reference to the time when the replacement property is acquired.

Where any shares owned by the transferee immediately before the death would either be identified with the replacement property under the provisions of *TCGA 1992, ss 126–136* (above) *or* were issued to him in consideration of the transfer of a business or an interest in a business consisting of the original property (or part), the shares are treated as if they were the replacement property (or part).

Where a binding contract for the disposal of any property is entered into at any time before the disposal of the property, the disposal is regarded as taking place at that time.

'*Allowed period*' means the period of three years or such longer period as the Board may allow. In relation to transfers of value made, and other events occurring, before 30 November 1993, the legislation effectively provided for the allowed period to be twelve months. [*IHTA 1984, ss 113A, 113B; FA 1986, Sch 19 para 21; FA 1987, s 58(1)(2), Sch 8 para 8; F(No 2)A 1992, s 73, Sch 14 paras 3, 8; FA 1994, s 247(1)(3)*]. The three-year (or longer) allowed period will apply not only to transfers of value made after 29 November 1993 but also to charges or further charges to IHT arising on a death after that date in respect of a transfer of value made before 30 November 1993 (HMRC response in ICAEW Faculty of Taxation Memorandum TAX 9/94).

Where business property which is relevant business property is replaced shortly before the owner's death by agricultural property, the period of ownership of the original property will be relevant for applying the minimum ownership condition to the replacement agricultural property. If all the conditions for agricultural property relief (see 4 AGRICULTURAL PROPERTY) are satisfied relief will be available on the replacement agricultural property. (HMRC Tax Bulletin December 1994 p 183).

Transitional provisions

[6.13] The amendments made to *IHTA 1984* by *FA 1987, Sch 8* (broadly amendments to the status of Unlisted Securities Market shares and securities, business property, agricultural property and payments by instalments with effect in relation to transfers of value made, and other events occurring, after 16 March 1987) are disregarded in determining under (a) and (b) and (i)–(iii) above whether any property acquired by the transferee before 17 March 1987 would be relevant business property in relation to a notional transfer of value made after 16 March 1987. [*FA 1987, s 58(3)*]. In broad terms, this protects the position of shares and securities dealt in on the Unlisted Securities Market which were the subject of a transfer before 17 March 1987 in circumstances where the transferor died after 16 March 1987 and within seven years of the transfer.

Further provisions, which are to be read as one with the business property provisions of *IHTA 1984*, apply where by reason of a death occurring after 9 March 1992:

(1) a potentially exempt transfer made before 10 March 1992 proves to be a chargeable transfer, or

(2) additional tax falls to be calculated in respect of a chargeable transfer (other than a potentially exempt transfer) made before 10 March 1992 and within seven years of the death.

In these circumstances, then, for the purposes of the replacement property provisions of *IHTA 1984, ss 113A, 113B* above, it is to be assumed that the amendments made by *F(No 2)A 1992, Sch 14* (broadly amendments to business property relief (including the status of Unlisted Securities Market shares and securities and increased relief in certain cases), agricultural property relief, payment by instalments and gifts with reservation with effect in relation to transfers of value made, and other events occurring, after 9 March 1992) came into effect at the time the transfer was made, and, in a case within (2) above, that so much of the value transferred as would have been reduced in accordance with the business property relief provisions as amended by *F(No 2)A 1992, Sch 14* was so reduced. Where disregarding the amendments made by *F(No 2)A 1992, Sch 14*, any shares or securities transferred fell within *IHTA 1984, s 105(1)(b)* (see **6.4**(b) above) in relation to the transfer, those amendments are disregarded in determining whether (b) (i) and (ii) above apply to the shares or securities. [*F(No 2)A 1992, s 73, Sch 14 para 9*]. In broad terms, this protects the position of a transferee who receives Unlisted Securities Market shares and securities before 10 March 1992 out of a majority holding where the company acquires a recognised stock exchange listing, and the transferor dies, after 9 March 1992 and within seven years of the transfer.

In order to remove doubt that has arisen in the past a new *IHTA 1984, s 113A(7A)*, is inserted by *FA 1996, s 184(5)*, so that the availability of business relief is to be disregarded in determining whether a transfer falls within the rules in *s 113A*. The clawback rules will apply in respect of any potentially exempt or chargeable transfer to which *s 113A* applies and is effective after 27 November 1995. [*IHTA 1984, s 113A; FA 1986, Sch 19 para 21; FA 1996, s 184(5)*].

Business property — payment of tax by instalments

[6.14] Where IHT payable is attributable to the value of either:

(a) a business or interest in a business carried on for gain; or
(b) shares or securities in certain circumstances; or
(c) land of any description, wherever situated,

the person paying the tax may elect to pay it in ten equal yearly instalments if the transfer is made on death, *or* if it is one on which tax is charged on settled property under *IHTA 1984, Pt III* and the property concerned remains in the settlement, *or* if the tax is borne by the person benefiting from the transfer [*IHTA 1984, ss 227, 228*]. In this context, the nature of the business is not relevant as there is no requirement that it should be a trade. Hence, a business of property management or investment holding is eligible under (a) above. See **32.5** PAYMENT OF TAX for full details.

Interest on tax payable by instalments

[6.15] With certain exceptions, interest on tax payable by instalments which is attributable to any shares or securities, business or interest in a business runs from the date of each instalment [*IHTA 1984, s 234*]. See **32.9** PAYMENT OF TAX.

Historical rates and conditions

Conditions prior to 6 April 1996

[6.16] The percentage rates appropriate to the different classes of relevant property detailed in **6.4** above are as follows in relation to transfers of value made, and other events occurring, after 9 March 1992 and before 6 April 1996:

(a)	Unincorporated business (**6.4**(a) above)	100%
(b)	Shares or securities giving control of an 'unquoted' company (**6.4**(c)) above)	100%
(c)	Shares giving more than 25% voting control of an 'unquoted' company not within (b) above (see (i) below)	100%
(d)	Shares or securities giving control of a 'quoted' company (**6.4**(c) above)	50%
(e)	Shares in an 'unquoted' company not within (b) or (c) above (**6.4**(c)(ii))	50%
(f)	Land, buildings, machinery or plant in a partnership or in a controlled company or in a settlement (but see **6.4** and **6.4**(d) above)	50%

In relation to transfers of value made, and other events occurring, after 16 March 1987 and before 6 April 1996, minority holdings are classified as follows.

(i) Substantial minority holdings, i.e. holdings not falling within (b) above which (either with or without other such shares or securities owned by the transferor) gave the transferor control of over 25% of the powers of voting on all questions affecting the company as a whole and for this purpose there was included any shares or securities which were related property, see **53.21** VALUATION. Where shares or securities were comprised in a settlement, any voting powers which they can give to the trustees were deemed to be given to the individual (if any) beneficially entitled in possession to those shares or securities. Where there were shares or securities of any class with voting powers only on the winding up of the company and/or on any question primarily affecting that class, the reference above to 'all questions affecting the company as a whole' was to be read as referring to all such questions except those to which the powers of the particular class applied. [*IHTA 1984, s 105(1)(bb), (1A), (1B); FA 1987, s 58, Sch 8 para 5* as repealed by *FA 1996, Sch 41 Pt VI*].

(ii) Shares were excluded from the relief if they were insufficient by themselves, without other property, to satisfy the 25% test above immediately before the transfer *and* their value was reduced because of a qualifying sale within three years of death, see **53.22** VALUATION. [*IHTA 1984, s 105(2A); FA 1987, s 58, Sch 8 para 5* as repealed by *FA 1996, Sch 41 Pt VI*].

(iii) Other minority holdings not falling within **6.4**(b) or (i) above. [*IHTA 1984, s 105(c); FA 1987, s 58, Sch 8 para 5* as repealed by *FA 1996, Sch 41 Pt VI*].

In relation to transfers of value made, and other events occurring, after 9 March 1992 and before 31 March 1996, then, in relation to any shares or securities within **6.4**(b) above or shares within this paragraph, 'unquoted' meant not so quoted and for these purposes the Alternative Investment Market (AIM) was treated as unquoted. [*IHTA 1984, s 105(1ZA); F(No 2)A 1992, s 73, Sch 14 paras 2(4), 8* (see *HMRC Press Release, 20 February 1995*)]. This definition only applied for the purposes of defining relevant business property above and payment by instalments (see **32.5** PAYMENT OF TAX). Prior to 6 April 1996 shares or securities were excluded from relief if they were insufficient by themselves, without other property, to give control immediately before the transfer and their value is reduced because of a qualifying sale within three years of death, see **53.22** VALUATION. [*IHTA 1984, s 105(2); F(No 2)A 1992, s 73, Sch 14 paras 2(5), 8*]. (The shares by themselves may qualify for relief as minority holdings of '*unquoted*' shares.) From 6 April 1996 onwards quoted shareholdings and unquoted securities are only subject to the 'control' test and value reduction method. [*IHTA 1984, s 105(2); FA 1996, Sch 14 Pt VI*].

See **6.11** above for certain transitional reliefs where shares or securities have changed their status in relation to transfers of value made, and other events occurring after 9 March 1992 and before 6 April 1996.

Additional requirement for substantial minority shareholdings prior to 6 April 1996

To qualify for relief in relation to transfers of value made, and other events occurring, after 16 March 1987 and before 6 April 1996 as a substantial minority shareholding under **6.16** below, the 25% control test must have been satisfied throughout the two years immediately before the transfer or, where the rules relating to inherited property or successive transfers above apply and the transferor owned the shares for a period of less than two years immediately before the transfer, throughout that lesser period. [*IHTA 1984, s 109A; FA 1987, s 58, Sch 8 para 7* now repealed by *FA 1996, Sch 41 Pt VI*].

'Ownership' is not defined but would have its meaning in normal usage and includes both beneficial and legal ownership so that the two-year rule must be satisfied by the life tenant in a settlement and by the trustees in a discretionary trust (Official Report Standing Committee E, 24 June 1976 cols 1275/1276).

Conditions after 16 March 1987 and before 10 March 1992

In relation to transfers of value made, and other events occurring, **after 16 March 1987 and before 10 March 1992:**

(A)	Unincorporated business (**6.4**(a) above)	50%
(B)	Shares or securities giving control of a company (**6.4**(c) above)	50%
(C)	Shares giving more than 25% voting control of an 'unquoted' company not within (B) above	50%
(D)	Shares in an 'unquoted' company not within (B) or (C) above	30%

(E)	Land, buildings, machinery or plant in a partnership or in a controlled company or in a settlement (but see **6.4** and **6.4**(d) above)	30%

Meaning of 'quoted' and 'unquoted'

In relation to any shares or securities within the Table above '*quoted*' means quoted on a recognised stock exchange or dealt in on the Unlisted Securities Market and '*unquoted*' means neither so quoted nor so dealt in. [*IHTA 1984, s 272; FA 1987, s 58(2), 8 Sch 17*]. This definition applied for all IHT purposes, and *still* continues to do so, in relation to transfers of value made, and other events occurring, after 9 March 1992 for purposes *other* than defining relevant business property above and payment by instalments.

See **6.11** above for certain transitional reliefs where shares or securities have changed their status in relation to transfers of value made, and other events occurring after 16 March 1987 and before 10 March 1992.

Conditions before 17 March 1987

In relation to transfers of value made, and other events occurring, **before 17 March 1987**:

(1)	Unincorporated business (**6.4**(a) above)	50%
(2)	Shares or securities giving control of a company (**6.4**(c) above)	50%
(3)	Shares in a company not within (2) above and not 'quoted' on a recognised stock exchange (**6.4**(d) above)	30%
(4)	Land, buildings, machinery or plant in a partnership or in a controlled company or in a settlement (but see **6.4** and **6.4**(d) above)	30%

In relation to transfers of value made, and other events occurring, before 17 March 1987, the classification of minority holdings was simply to shares in a company which were not within the Table at (2) above and which were not quoted on a recognised stock exchange. Shares in companies dealt in on the Unlisted Securities Market were *not* treated as quoted securities for this purpose and qualified for relief under this category. (HMRC Statement of Practice SP 18/80, 23 December 1980).

'*Quoted*' and '*unquoted*' have the same meanings as in **6.4**(d) above subject to *FA 1996, Sch 38 para 2(1)(2)*. [*IHTA 1984, ss 104, 105; FA 1987, s 58, Sch 8 para 4; F(No 2)A 1992, s 73, Sch 14 paras 1, 2, 8*].

The increases in the relief from 30% to 50%, and from 50% to 100%, mentioned above will be interpreted as applying not only to transfers of value made after 9 March 1992 but also to charges or further charges to IHT arising on a death after that date in respect of a transfer of value made before 10 March 1992 (HMRC Press Release, 10 March 1992 and correspondence with the publisher).

Key points concerning business property

[6.17] Points to consider are as follows.

- There is often a risk of actively sheltering too many non-qualifying business assets within a qualifying business and the whole enterprise failing the BPR test because it becomes wholly or mainly an investment holding business. The facts of each individual case should be carefully considered, as should the relevant case law. However in *Brander (Representative of the fourth Earl of Balfour) v HMRC* [2009] UKFTT 101 (TC) the appellant succeeded in integrating a property business within the overall estate such that the whole qualified for BPR (see **6.4**(a) above).
- Normally where a director shareholder or a partner in a business enters into a 'buy and sell' agreement so that surviving directors and partners within the business have to buy the shares or partnership interest from the deceased's personal representatives then if this is a mutual *requirement* to sell the interest or shares or the surviving shareholders or partners are *obliged* to buy the shares or interest then this would constitute a 'binding contract for sale' and no BPR would be available. [*IHTA 1984, s 113*]. However, HMRC have stated that certain circumstances where there is an *option* then in their view it would not constitute a 'binding contract for sale'. *IHTA 1984, s 113* would not apply where:
  - (i) the deceased's interest passes to the surviving partners, who are required to pay the personal representatives a particular price; or
  - (ii) the deceased's interest falls into the estate, but with an option for the surviving partners to purchase it.

    Also, statement of practice SP12/80 states that an *option* for personal representatives to sell the deceased's interest to the survivors is not to constitute a binding contract for sale. BPR would in such circumstances be available providing the terms of the agreement stipulate a *requirement* i.e. a two-way option, to sell or buy is clearly evident. See IHTM25292 and SP12/80.
- In relation to shareholdings in unquoted trading companies, if further shares are acquired within the reorganisation of share capital provisions applicable for capital gains tax purposes (see *TCGA 1992, ss 126–136*), and the existing holding has been held for two years, then all of the shares qualify. In *Vinton v Fladgate Fielder (a firm)* Ch D [2010] EWHC 904, this condition was satisfied in relation to the 300,000 shares which a widow had acquired immediately before her death albeit not specifically under a rights issue because she acquired them in the right of her

ownership of a holding of 750,000 shares. However, the shares that the widow acquired on the renunciation by a fellow director and relative (Mrs Vinton) of her rights, and the shares which the widow acquired under the offer for subscription, were not acquired by her in the right of any existing holding of hers; they were acquired by her for reasons entirely unconnected with her existing holding. They were a new purchase of shares.

- The *Nelson Dance* case at **6.4** above permits relief to be given for assets used within a business which are the subject of a gift, i.e. it is not necessary for part of the business itself to be the subject of the gift.
- Nil rate band trusts are still used for some estates but they need careful handling where the estate includes business property (or agricultural property). A legacy of the largest sum which can be left in trust without incurring liability to IHT is a cash legacy and not a gift of business property, even if the executors should decide to appropriate business property to the trust in satisfaction of the sum due. The result is that, if the business property is not otherwise specifically bequeathed by the will, the business property relief must be apportioned over all the gifts by the will in accordance with the rules set out at **7.8**. This will reduce the sum due to the nil rate band trust and if some of the estate passes to the surviving spouse, some of the relief may be wasted against the spouse exemption. If it is wished to ensure that the business property goes into the nil rate band trust, the gift should be drafted in terms of 'all my property eligible for business property relief at 100 per cent and in addition the largest sum which may be bequeathed to my trustees without incurring liability to inheritance tax'.

7

Calculation of Tax

Cross-references. See 1 INTRODUCTION AND BASIC PRINCIPLES; 4 AGRICULTURAL PROPERTY; 6 BUSINESS PROPERTY; 21 EXEMPT TRANSFERS; 22 GIFTS WITH RESERVATION; 35 POTENTIALLY EXEMPT TRANSFERS; 36 QUICK SUCCESSION RELIEF; 37 RATES OF TAX; 48 TRANSFERS OF VALUE; 49 TRANSFERS ON DEATH; 50 TRANSFERS WITHIN SEVEN YEARS BEFORE DEATH; 54 WOODLANDS.

Simon's Taxes. See I3.256, I3.5, I4.1, I4.231–I4.243.

Other Sources. Tolley's Tax Computations; IHTM26000.

Introduction to the calculation of tax

[7.1] Inheritance tax is levied on the value transferred by a 9 CHARGEABLE TRANSFER at the rate or rates applicable at the time of the transfer. The transfer is treated as the highest part of the aggregate of the chargeable amount plus the values transferred by any previous chargeable transfers made by the transferor in the period of seven years ending with the date of transfer. [*IHTA 1984, ss 1, 7*].

Rates of tax

Only one table of rates is set out in the legislation and this is applicable to transfers on death. These are charged at a flat rate of 40% on the excess of the transfer over the available nil rate band or bands. Chargeable lifetime transfers are charged at one-half of the death rates (i.e. 20%). Transfers made within seven years of death are charged at the death rates but in the case of chargeable transfers made in that period and more than three years before death, the tax charge (note, *not* the value of the gift) is tapered. [*IHTA 1984, s 7*]. See **37** RATES OF TAX and **50** TRANSFERS WITHIN SEVEN YEARS OF DEATH. There is no subsequent credit or repayment for tax paid on a transfer *before* a reduction in the scale rates even if less tax would have been payable if the transfer had been made after the reduction in rates. In certain cases, where tax is chargeable by reference to an event before a reduction of tax by the substitution of new rate tables, *IHTA 1984, Sch 2* provides that the new rates are to be used. See **30.14** and **30.27** NATIONAL HERITAGE, **40.17** SETTLEMENTS: DISCRETIONARY TRUSTS AND OTHER TRUSTS OF RELEVANT PROPERTY, **50.1** TRANSFERS WITHIN SEVEN YEARS BEFORE DEATH and **54.5** WOODLANDS.

The value transferred is the loss in value to the transferor's estate, that is, the amount by which the value of the transferor's estate immediately after the disposition in question is less than it would be but for that disposition. [*IHTA 1984, s 3(1)*].

Chargeable transfer

A chargeable transfer is any transfer of value made by an individual, other than an EXEMPT TRANSFER (**21**). [*IHTA 1984, s 2(1)*]. Certain lifetime transfers are designated potentially exempt transfers. A potentially exempt transfer is a transfer of value made by an individual after 17 March 1986 which would otherwise be a chargeable transfer and which is either a gift to another individual or a trust for a disabled person, or prior to 22 March 2006 a gift into an accumulation and maintenance trust. From 22 March 2006 a gift into a bereaved minor's trust on termination of an immediate post-death interest is also potentially exempt. In relation to transfers of value made, and other events occurring, after 16 March 1987, certain gifts by individuals into and out of settlements with interests in possession are also included. See **35.1** POTENTIALLY EXEMPT TRANSFERS for full details. A potentially exempt transfer made seven years or more before the transferor's death is an exempt transfer and any other potentially exempt transfer is a chargeable transfer. A potentially exempt transfer is assumed to be an exempt transfer during the seven years following the transfer (or, if earlier, until immediately before the transferor's death). In the event of death within seven years of a lifetime gift, the nil rate band applying at the time of death, and not the time of the gift, is applicable. [*IHTA 1984, s 3A; IHTA 1864, Sch 2; FA 1986, Sch 19 para 1; F(No 2)A 1987, s 96*].

Transferor bearing tax

Where the transferor bears the tax on a lifetime transfer, the inheritance tax liability is taken into account in calculating the reduction in the value of his estate. [*IHTA 1984, ss 3(1), 162(3)*]. The 'net' transfer is grossed up at the appropriate rate(s) in order to arrive at the amount of the chargeable transfer. The chargeable transfer is always the gross, not the net, figure. See **37** RATES OF TAX for grossing-up tables. Where the transferee bears the tax on lifetime transfers, no grossing-up is required as the tax liability is not part of the reduction in value of the transferor's estate.

On death the tax is charged on the value of the deceased's estate immediately before his death and grossing-up is not required.

There are special rules for allocating the tax where the transfer is partly chargeable and partly exempt, see **7.6** below.

As the tax is charged on a cumulative basis, a careful record must be kept of all chargeable transfers made and the tax thereon.

Lifetime transfers — examples

[7.2]

(i) With transferor bearing the tax.

A transfers £69,000 to a discretionary trust on 1 May 2020, £265,000 on 31 December 2020 and a further £43,000 on 1 February 2021. He bears the tax and he has made no other chargeable transfers. His inheritance tax position is as follows.

	£	£
Gift on 1 May 2020		69,000
Deduct Annual exemption 2020/21	3,000	
Annual exemption 2019/20	3,000	6,000
		63,000
Covered by nil rate band of £325,000		
Gift on 31 December 2020		265,000
(*Note*. Annual exemption already used for 2020/21)		
Cumulative net transfers		£328,000
Tax thereon (see grossing-up table at **37.1** 2010.B2)		
0 – 325,000		
325,001 – 328,000 (£3,000 × 1/4)		750
Tax on gift		£750

Gift on 1 February 2021

	Gross	Tax	Net
Cumulative totals	328,750	750	328,000
Add Latest net transfer of £43,000	53,750	10,750*	43,000
	£382,500	£11,500	£371,000
*Tax on £371,000 per table **37.1** 2010.B2			
0 – 325,000			
325,001 – 371,000 (£46,000 × 1/4)		11,500	
		11,500	
Deduct Tax on previous transfers		750	
Tax on latest gift		£10,750	

(ii) With transferee bearing the tax on the latest gift.

If, in example (i) above, the trustees agree to pay the tax on the latest gift, the tax will be calculated on that transfer (without grossing-up) using the table at **37.1** 2010.B1 RATES OF TAX as follows.

	£
Previous chargeable transfers	328,750
Chargeable transfer on 1 February 2021	43,000
	£371,750
Tax on £43,000 is	
328,750 – 371,750 (£43,000 × 20%)	£8,600

(iii) For transfers under the CTT provisions and more than 7 years before lates transfer, see previous editions.

Transfers on death — example

[7.3]

A dies on 5 September 2020 leaving an estate valued at £338,000, of which he bequeaths £103,000 to his wife and the balance elsewhere. His lifetime chargeable transfers in the seven years before death totalled £97,265. Tax due from his estate (using the table at **37.1 2010.A1**) is as follows.

	£	£
Previous chargeable transfers		97,265
Value of estate at death	338,000	
Deduct exempt bequest to wife	103,000	
Chargeable residue		235,000
Total cumulative chargeable transfers		£332,265
Tax due from estate on £235,000		
97,265 – 325,000 (£227,735 at nil%)		
325,001 – 332,265 (£7,265 at 40%)		2,906

Potentially exempt transfers and cumulation with prior chargeable transfer

[7.4]

Jeremiah, who died on 1 December 2023, made the following lifetime gifts:

- £325,000 into a trust for his son Jeremy on 1 January 2010.
- £300,000 to his niece Jezebel on 31 December 2016.
- No tax was payable on the gift into trust because it was within the nil band.
- The gift to Jezebel was potentially exempt and becomes chargeable on Jeremiah's death because it was within seven years of his death. The gift in January 2010 must now be cumulated with it so that no nil band is available against this gift in December 2016. Tax is therefore payable in respect of it at the death rate of 40% of the amount due: £120,000.
- On Jeremiah's death, the gift into trust in January 2010 falls out of account because it was more than seven years prior to the death. But the gift to Jezebel uses £300,000 of the nil band so that only £25,000 is available against the estate on death.
- If Jeremiah had survived until 1 January 2024 and died on that day, no tax would have been payable on the lifetime gifts and the full nil band would have been available against the estate on death.

Potentially exempt transfers, change of rates and additional tax liability on death — example

[7.5]

A made the following lifetime transfers on which he paid any tax as appropriate.

January 1979	Gift to individual C	£50,000
December 1985	Gift to individual D	£65,000
May 1992	Gift to individual C	£96,000
November 1992	Gift to discretionary trustees	£117,000

He died in November 1994 leaving his estate valued at £320,000 to his sons C and D.

Tax payable following lifetime transfers

			£	£	
Gift to C in January 1979				50,000	
Deduct	Annual exemption	1978/79	2,000		
		1977/78	2,000		
	Small gifts exemption		100	4,100	
Cumulative net transfers				£45,900	
Tax thereon				£2,128	
Gross transfer				£48,028	
Gift to D in December 1985				65,000	
Deduct annual exemption 1985/86			3,000		
1984/85			3,000	6,000	
				£59,000	
Tax on latest gift of £59,000 (*Note.* There has been a change in tax rates)					
			Gross	Tax	Net
Gross transfers in previous ten years adjusted for change in rates applicable after 5 April 1985			48,028		48,028
Add latest net transfer of £59,000			66,824	7,824*	59,000
			£114,852	£7,824	£107,028
*Tax on £107,028 at grossing-up rates applicable after 5 April 1985					
0 – 85,700				3,300	
85,701 – 107,028 (£21,328 × 7/33)				4,524	
				7,824	
Deduct tax on transfers in previous ten years at rates applicable after 5 April 1985					
Tax on latest gift				£7,824	
Gift to C in May 1992					

The gift of £96,000 is a potentially exempt transfer to the extent it exceeds the available annual exemption (£3,000 for 1992/93 and £3,000 for 1991/92 brought forward), i.e. £90,000 (see **35.2** POTENTIALLY EXEMPT TRANSFERS), but incurs no immediate liability to tax.

Gift to discretionary trustees in November 1992

Tax on gift of £117,000

(*Note.* There has been a change in tax rates and the gift in January 1979 is more than seven years before the latest gift)

	Gross	Tax	Net
Gross transfers in previous seven years adjusted for change in rates applicable after 9 March 1992	66,824		66,824
Add latest net transfer of £117,000	125,456	8,456*	117,000
	£192,280	£8,456	£183,824

*Tax on £183,824 at grossing-up rates applicable after 9 March 1992 (see table at **37.1** 1992.B2 RATES OF TAX)

0 – 150,000	
150,000 – 183,824 (£33,824 × 1/4)	8,456
	8,456
Deduct tax on transfers in previous seven years at rates applicable after 9 March 1992	
Tax on latest gift	£8,456*

Tax payable following death in November 1994

Gift to C in January 1979

Gift to D in December 1985

These gifts are before 18 March 1986 and more than three years before death. No additional tax is payable (see **51.6** TRANSITIONAL PROVISIONS).

Gift to C in May 1992

The potentially exempt transfer of £90,000 (see above) becomes a chargeable transfer following A's death within seven years. Since it is made not more than three years before death, there is no reduction in tax rate (see **50.1** TRANSFERS WITHIN SEVEN YEARS BEFORE DEATH). The gift to D in December 1985 is within seven years of the gift and must be aggregated.

There has been a change in tax rates at death.

	Gross	Tax	Net
Gross transfers in previous seven years adjusted for the change in rates applicable after 5 April 1992	66,824		66,824
Add latest gross transfer	90,000	2,730*	87,270
	£156,824	£2,730	£154,094

*Tax on £156,824 at rates applicable on death after 9 March 1992

0 – 150,000	
150,001 – 156,824 (£6,824 × 40%)	2,730
Tax payable by C	£2,730

Gift to discretionary trustees in November 1992

Additional tax is due following A's death within seven years. However, the gift is made not more than three years before death, so there is no reduction in tax rate. The gifts in December 1985 and May 1992 are within seven years of the gift of £117,000 and must be aggregated.

	Gross	Tax	Net
Gross transfers in previous seven years	156,824	2,730	154,094
Add latest gross transfer of £125,456	125,456	50,182*	75,274
	£282,280	£52,912	£229,368

*Tax on £282,280 at rates applicable on death after 9 March 1992	
0 – 150,000	
150,001 – 282,280 (£132,280 × 40%)	52,912
	52,912
Deduct tax on transfers in previous seven years at rates applicable after 9 March 1992	2,730
	50,182
Deduct tax already paid	8,456
Additional tax payable by trustees	£41,726

Transfer on death in November 1994

The gift to D in December 1985 is made more than seven years before death. The gifts made in May 1992 and November 1992 must be aggregated with the death estate as they are both made within seven years of death. These gifts entail gross transfers of £90,000 and £125,456 respectively resulting in cumulative chargeable transfers of £215,456 immediately prior to death.

Cumulative chargeable transfers in previous seven years	215,456
Value of estate	320,000
Total cumulative chargeable transfers	£535,456
Tax due from estate of £320,000	
215,457 – 535,456 (£320,000 × 40%)	£128,000

Partly exempt transfers

[7.6] Where a transfer is partly exempt and partly chargeable, special provisions apply to allocate the tax chargeable and the benefit of the exemption. The circumstances will arise mainly with transfers on death but may also apply where, for example, property is distributed out of a 'relevant property' settlement (see 40 SETTLEMENTS: DISCRETIONARY TRUSTS AND OTHER TRUSTS OF RELEVANT PROPERTY) between exempt and non-exempt beneficiaries. On death, a common situation is where, after specific chargeable gifts, the residue of the estate is left to the widow or charity and is therefore exempt. The provisions are contained in *IHTA 1984, ss 36–42*. '*Specific gift*' means any gift other than a gift of residue or any share in residue, and therefore rather confusingly includes both specific legacies and general cash legacies. [*IHTA 1984, s 42(1)*]. In Scotland, legal rights claimed by a person entitled to claim such rights are treated as a specific gift which bears its own tax. In determining the value of such legal rights, any tax payable on the estate of the deceased is left out of account. [*IHTA 1984, s 42(4)*]. Any liability of the transferor which is not taken into account in arriving at the value of his estate (including liabilities non-deductible or abated under *FA 1986, s 103*, see **49.9** TRANSFERS ON DEATH) is treated as a specific gift. [*IHTA 1984, s 38(6); FA 1986, Sch 19 para 13*]. Any value transferred which is not a specific gift is made out of residue. [*IHTA 1984, s 39*].

Where there is a gift of an asset outside the UK, this is a specific gift which does not bear its own tax. Thus, in strictness, a will which disposes of UK and foreign property may be one in which part of the specific gifts are paid out of property bearing its own tax, and part out of assets which do not bear their own tax. In practice, HMRC will normally allow the gifts to be allocated to those assets not bearing their own tax.

Various problems of construction can arise with partly exempt estates. Some of these are highlighted by the cases of *Re Benham* and *Re Ratcliffe* discussed below. In *RSPCA v Sharpe* [2010] STC 975, where the charity was given the residue of an estate after legacies to family and friends, the alternative possibilities gave the charity either 38.88% of the estate with an IHT liability equal to 11.83% thereof, or 68.48% of the estate and a nil IHT liability. The issue, in this case, arose because one of the chargeable gifts was an amount equal to the maximum which could be given without IHT being due and the question was whether this gave the whole of the available nil band or the nil band after it was applied to first other chargeable gifts. It was held that on the proper interpretation of the will, the deceased intended the whole of the nil band to be applied to the gift of the maximum amount.

See below for the application of business and agricultural property reliefs.

Attribution of value to specific gifts

[7.7] If a specific gift is fully exempt (e.g. gift of specified property or a cash legacy to spouse) then that gift will not bear any tax. The legislation achieves this by stating that the value of that gift is to correspond to that same amount ('such part') of the total value transferred. By contrast an exempt residuary gift (e.g. gift of residue to spouse) may suffer the tax on a specific gift which does not bear its own tax (a tax-free gift). Where residue is part exempt and part chargeable (e.g. part to spouse and part to son), the exempt part is not to bear any tax attributable to the chargeable part. [*IHTA 1984, ss 38(1), 41*]. See *Re Benham's Will Trusts; Lockhart v Harker, Read and the National Lifeboat Institution* Ch D, [1995] STC 210 in which the testatrix listed A and B beneficiaries and those in List A were to receive 3.2 times as much as List B beneficiaries, 'in each case for their own absolute and beneficial use and disposal'. Each list included some charities. The Court's view of the testatrix's intention was that each beneficiary of the respective lists, whether charitable or not, should receive the same amount from the express terms of the will as the other beneficiaries within the same list. In view of this the beneficiaries who were not charities received grossed up shares so that they achieved equality after deduction of IHT with the charitable beneficiaries.

However, *Holmes v McMullen & Others Re Ratcliffe deceased* Ch D [1999] STC 262 in the Chancery Division did not follow *Benham*. Under the terms of the will, after payment of debts and funeral and testamentary expenses, the residue was to be distributed as to a one-half share to members of the deceased's family and to the other half share to certain charities. Blackburne J held that an equal division of disposable residue between relatives and charities meant that the IHT attributable to the relatives' shares had to be borne by those shares, since 'to subject the charities . . . share to any part of that burden was prohibited'.

HMRC appear to accept that the decision in *Re Ratcliffe* should normally be followed unless the will makes a clear statement that all shares of residue net of any IHT are to be of equal amount (see IHTM26172). The distinction between the two approaches is illustrated in the following Example.

Example

Assume that the residue in an estate of £200,000 is to be divided equally between a charity and the surviving son and the will is silent as to how the IHT should be dealt with. Assume for illustration purposes an estate rate is 40%.

The options:

- Divide the residue equally so that the charity gets £100,000 and the son gets £100,000 and he then bears the tax of £40,000 out of the share he receives. This is the Charity's beneficial option, applying *Re Ratcliffe* which is now generally preferred.

	£
Charity	100,000
Son	60,000
HMRC	40,000
Total	£200,000

- Under the *Re Benham*, calculation gross up the son's share so that the charity and the son end up with the same net amount after the son's share has suffered tax i.e. the £200,000 divided in the proportions 60:60:40 as follows:

	£
Charity	75,000
Son	75,000
HMRC	50,000
Total	£200,000

In the example, IHTA 1984, s 41(b) precludes calculating the tax on the £100,000 (son's share) and that tax of £40,000 then being deducted from the £200,000, leaving £160,000 divided equally between the charity and the son who each get £80,000. This would result in the exempt share of residue bearing tax attributable to the chargeable part of the estate which is prohibited by s 41(b). The second calculation which follows *Re Benham* results in higher IHT being payable. The son's share, grossed up at 40% is £125,000 so that the tax on it is £50,000. In other cases, the grossing up would be at whatever the estate rate is, for example with an estate rate of 15% the proportions are 15 tax, 85 non-exempt share and 85 exempt share, total for denominator 185.

Will drafting post-Benham

(1) As to one share absolutely for my wife (husband) [*or give name already defined as such*] if she(he) survives me for 28 days.

(2) As to another share (or as to the whole if the preceding gift fails) for all of my children as are alive at my death [and reach the age of 18] and if more than one in equal shares PROVIDED that if any child of mine [is already dead or] dies before me [or before reaching that age] but leaves a child or children alive at the death of the survivor of my child and me who reach the age of [*18*] or marry under that age then such equal shares so much of the Trust Fund as that child of mine would have taken on attaining a vested interest.

AND the shares given by (1) and (2) above shall be such shares as before [after] the deduction of any inheritance tax attributable to them respectively are of equal value [or are of equal values bearing to one another in the proportions (2:1) the larger share being given by (1)(2)].

Where two or more specific gifts are in excess of an exemption limit, relief for the exemption is given to gifts bearing their own tax before other gifts. Any excess relief is allocated to the other gifts in proportion to their values. [*IHTA 1984, s 38(2)*].

Where specific gifts which do not bear their own tax are the only chargeable part of a transfer the tax on them (found by grossing-up) is borne by the residuary estate. [*IHTA 1984, s 38(3)*].

Example 1

A dies in July 2010 leaving estate valued at £386,000. He leaves a tax-free legacy to his daughter of £331,000 and the residue to his widow. He has made no previous chargeable transfers.

	£
Tax-free legacy	331,000
Tax thereon (see table at 37.1 2010.A2) is (6,000 × 2/3)	4,000
Grossed-up legacy	£335,000
Value of estate	386,000
Deduct chargeable estate	335,000
Exempt residue to widow	£51,000

Where tax-free specific gifts are not the only chargeable gifts very complex rules must be followed. An assumed rate of tax must be calculated on a hypothetical chargeable estate for the purpose of allocating values to the chargeable and exempt parts of an estate. [*IHTA 1984, s 38(4)(5)*].

Example 2

A dies in July 2020 leaving an estate valued at £535,000. He leaves a tax-free legacy to his daughter of £341,000, a property worth £10,000 bearing its own tax to a nephew, and the residue of his estate equally between his widow and his son. He has made no previous chargeable transfers.

	£	£
Hypothetical chargeable estate:		
Tax-free specific gift to daughter		341,000
Tax thereon (as if legacy was the only chargeable gift – £16,000 × ²⁄₃)		10,666
Grossed-up specific gift to daughter		351,666
Specific gift bearing own tax to nephew		10,000
Total of specific gifts		361,666
Chargeable residue		
Gross estate	535,000	
Deduct total of specific gifts	361,666	
Residue	£173,334	
Half-share of residue to son		86,667
Hypothetical chargeable estate		£448,333
Calculation of assumed tax rate		
Tax on £448,333 would be (see table at **37.1** 2010.A1 RATES OF TAX)	£49,333	
Assumed rate is		

$$\frac{£49,333}{£448,333} \times 100 = 11.00365\%$$

Re-gross tax-free legacy to daughter using assumed rate

$$£341,000 \times \frac{100}{100 - 11.00365} = £383,162$$

Calculate chargeable estate and tax thereon		
Grossed-up value of tax-free legacy		383,162
Specific gift bearing own tax		10,000
Total of specific gifts		393,162
Chargeable residue:	535,000	
Deduct total of specific gifts	393,162	
Residue	£141,838	
Half-share of residue to son		70,919
Hypothetical chargeable estate		£464,081
Tax on chargeable estate of £464,081 (see table at **37.1** 2010.A1 RATES OF TAX) is		£55,632

$$\text{Estate rate is } \frac{55,632}{464,081} \times 100 = 11.98756\%$$

		£	£
Distribution of estate			
Specific gifts payable:	to daughter		341,000
	to nephew		10,000
			351,000
Tax on gift to daughter			
Gift grossed at assumed rate on £393,162 (see above)			
Tax thereon at estate rate of 11.98756%			47,131
Note. The nephew pays the tax on his gift of £10,000 at the estate rate of 11.98756% which is £1,198			
Total specific gifts plus tax			£398,131
Gross estate			535,000
Deduct total specific gifts plus tax			398,131
Residue			£136,869
Allocation of estate			
Widow (one half residue)			68,434
Son (one half residue)		68,435	
Tax on son's share at estate rate			
£68,435 at 11.98756%		8,203	
Payable to son			60,232
Legacies to daughter and nephew			351,000
Tax borne by residue (£47,131 + £8,203)			55,334
			£535,000

Application of business and agricultural property relief where transfers partly exempt

[7.8] With respect to transfers of value made after 17 March 1986, the rules for apportioning the value of an estate between specific gifts and residue (in order to determine the exempt and chargeable parts) are modified for transfers including property qualifying for business and agricultural property reliefs.

(a) Specific gifts of business or agricultural property are to be taken at their value as reduced by the business or agricultural property relief attributable to such property.

(b) Any other specific gifts not within (a) above are to be taken to be the fraction of their value given by the formula:

$$\frac{V-S}{E-P}$$

where:

V = Total value transferred (i.e. as reduced by business and agricultural property reliefs)
S = Specific gifts within (a) above as reduced by the attributable relief
E = Total value transferred *before* deduction of business and agricultural property reliefs
P = Specific gifts within (a) above *before* deduction of the attributable relief

For the purposes of the above provisions, the value of a specific gift of relevant business or agricultural property does not include the value of any other gift payable out of that property (e.g. a pecuniary legacy charged on the relevant property) and that other gift is not itself treated as a specific gift of relevant business or agricultural property.

IHTA 1984, ss 38 and *39* (see above) have effect subject to the above provisions. [*IHTA 1984, s 39A; FA 1986, s 105*].

Example 3

A dies in July 2010 leaving an estate valued at £405,000. The estate includes a sweet shop business valued at £30,000 (for which 100% business property relief is available) and a small tenanted farm valued at £10,000 (for which only 50% agricultural property relief is available as the tenancy commenced before 1 September 1995). He leaves a tax-free legacy to his daughter of £350,000, the tenanted farm bearing its own tax to his nephew and the residue of his estate equally between his widow and his son. He has made no previous chargeable transfers.

Application of business and agricultural property reliefs: Under (a) above, the value of the specific gift of the tenanted farm is taken as the value of it as reduced by the applicable agricultural property relief, i.e. £10,000 – £5,000 = £5,000.

Under (b) above

V = £405,000 – £30,000 – £5,000	=	£370,000
S = £10,000 – £5,000	=	£5,000
E	=	£405,000
P	=	£10,000

The value of the tax-free specific gift to the daughter is reduced to:

$$\frac{£370{,}000 - £5{,}000}{£405{,}000 - £10{,}000} \times £350{,}000 = £323{,}418$$

£26,582 (£350,000 – £323,418) of business property relief has therefore been allocated to the tax-free specific gift to the daughter, leaving £3,418 (£30,000 – £26,582) of business property relief to be allocated to residue.

	£	£
Hypothetical chargeable estate:		
Tax-free specific gift to daughter		323,413
Tax thereon (as if legacy was the only chargeable gift – £3,418 × 2/3)		2,279
Grossed-up specific gift to daughter		325,697
Specific gift bearing own tax to nephew		5,000
Total of specific gifts		330,697
Chargeable residue		
Gross estate	405,000	
Deduct total of agricultural and Business property reliefs	35,000	
Value transferred after reliefs	370,000	
Deduct total of specific gifts	330,697	
Residue	£39,303	
Half-share of residue to son		19,651
Hypothetical chargeable estate		£350,348

The calculation of the assumed tax rate, chargeable estate and tax thereon, distribution of the estate and allocation of the estate then proceed in the same manner (but with different amounts) as in *Example* 2 above. Agricultural and business property reliefs will be apportioned as above in the distribution of the estate.

Note to the example

Example 3 shows that business property relief will be apportioned to the exempt half-share of residue transferred to the widow and thereby effectively wasting some of the relief otherwise available. In this and similar situations, the wastage can be avoided by ensuring that all agricultural and business property are subject of specific gifts to non-exempt beneficiaries if part of the estate is destined to go to an exempt beneficiary such as the widow/widower or a charity, as it is understood that HMRC insist on the strict application of *IHTA 1984, s 39A*. Also see Example at **4.19** AGRICULTURAL PROPERTY.

Abatement

Abatement not attributable to tax

[7.9] Where a gift would be abated because of an insufficiency of assets under the normal rules for the administration of estates, the abated value will be taken for the purposes of inheritance tax. [*IHTA 1984, s 37(1)*].

Abatement for tax — specific gifts

[7.10] Where the grossed-up value attributable to specific gifts (see **7.6** above) exceeds the value transferred, they are treated as reduced to the extent necessary to reduce their value to that of the value transferred in the order in which, under the terms of the relevant disposition or any rule of law, the reduction would fall to be made on a distribution of assets. [*IHTA 1984, s 37(2)*].

Gifts made separately out of different funds

[7.11] Where there are gifts taking effect on a death both out of the deceased's own estate and out of a settled fund, the provisions in **7.6** and **7.9** above are applied separately to each fund. [*IHTA 1984, s 40*]. HMRC consider that the rate of tax to be used for grossing up should be found by looking at each fund separately and in isolation: see IHTM26211.

Example

A dies in June 2020 with a nil cumulative total. Of his free estate of £1,000,000, the sum of £330,000 free of tax is left to his son and the residue is left to his widow. A was the life tenant of a settlement the funds of which were worth £500,000 at the date of his death. His interest under the settlement passed to his grandchildren. The chargeable estate and tax thereon would be calculated as follows.

	£
Hypothetical chargeable estate	
Tax-free specific gift to son	330,000
Tax thereon (see table at **37.1** 2010.A2) is (£5,000 × $^2/_3$)	3,333
Grossed-up specific gift to son	333,333
Life interest in settlement bearing own tax and passing to grandchildren	500,000
Hypothetical chargeable estate	£833,333
Calculation of assumed tax rate	
Tax on £833,333 would be (see table at **37.1** 2010.A1)	£203,333
Assumed rate is	

$$\frac{203,333}{833,333} \times 100 = 24.39996\%$$

No further re-grossing is required and the assumed rate becomes the estate rate	
Distribution of estate	
Tax-free gift to son	333,333
Grossed-up gift to son is £333,333 and tax on this at the estate rate of 24.39996% is	81,333
Life interest bearing its own tax (so that trustees will be liable for tax on it at the estate rate, i.e. £122,000)	500,000
Widow's exempt residue	585,334
	£1,500,000

Tax chargeable in certain cases of future payments

[7.12] Special provisions apply where a disposition made for a consideration in money or money's worth is a transfer of value and any payments made or assets transferred *by the transferor* in pursuance of the disposition are made more than one year after the disposition i.e. the provisions apply where the transferor acquires property at an overvalue.

Tax is charged as if any payment made etc. was made in pursuance of a separate disposition made, without consideration, at that time and the amount of the payment etc. was the 'chargeable portion' of the full payment.

The '*chargeable portion*' of any payment etc. is such proportion of its value at that time as is found by multiplying it by the fraction

$$\frac{A}{B}$$

where

A = the value actually transferred by the disposition as a whole; and
B = the value, at the time of that disposition, of the aggregate of the payments etc. made or to be made by the transferor.

[*IHTA 1984, s 262*].

Example

M acquires property from P on 1 January 2020 which is worth £30,000 but for which he agrees to pay £20,000 immediately and two further instalments of £10,000 each on 1 January 2021 and 1 January 2022. The discounted value of the two future instalments on 1 January 2020 at, say, 10% interest, is £17,355 (£9,091 + £8,264).

The value transferred by the disposition as at 1 January 2020 is

	£
Immediate payment	20,000
Present value of future instalments	17,355
	37,355
Value of property received from P	30,000
Value transferred by disposition	£7,355

The chargeable portion of each of M's payments is

$$\frac{7{,}355}{37{,}355} = 19.69\%$$

i.e. the potentially exempt transfers are (ignoring annual exemptions)

On 1 January 2020 £20,000 × 19.69%	= 3,938
On 1 January 2021 £10,000 × 19.69%	= 1,969

	£
On 1 January 2022 £10,000 × 19.69%	= 1,969
	£7,876

Note to the example

If M dies whilst instalments are due, there is a liability in his estate for the outstanding amount. But the whole of this amount may not be deducted for IHT purposes, only the chargeable portion of them. It may also be appropriate to apply a discount for the liability not being due immediately. See IHTM28120.

Chargeable transfers affecting more than one property

[7.13] Where more than one property is comprised in a chargeable transfer, the tax which is attributable to each separate property is in the proportions which the separate values bear to the whole (subject to any provisions reducing the amount of tax attributable to the value of any particular property). [*IHTA 1984, s 265*].

More than one chargeable transfer on one day

[7.14] Where more than one lifetime chargeable transfer is made on the same day by the same person, the transfers are treated as made in the order which results in the lowest value chargeable and the rate of tax charged on each transfer is the effective rate (total tax divided by total transfers) which would apply if there has been one transfer of the total amount. The same rules regarding transfers on the same day apply to chargeable transfers from settlements without interests in possession if they are made out of property comprised in the same settlement. [*IHTA 1984, s 266*]. The previous CTO Advanced Instruction Manual stated that:

> 'It is important to bear in mind that a gift by cheque is not complete until the cheque itself is cashed . . . and thus where transfers are made by way of several cheques I*HTA 1984, s 266(1)/IHTA 1984, s 43(2)* will operate only if the cheques are **cleared** on the same day. The date on which the cheque is **drawn** is immaterial.'

See also *Curnock (Curnock's Personal Representative) v CIR* [2003] STC SCD 283 Sp C 365 where a cheque issued before the date but not cleared until after death still formed part of the deceased's estate on death. See **55** TAX CASES.

Transfers reported late

[7.15] Provisions are made to deal with the situation which arises where a transfer ('the earlier transfer') is not notified to the Board by an account or other information within the required period (see **2.15** ACCOUNTS AND RETURNS) and is not discovered until after the tax on a later transfer has been paid and accepted by the Board (or if no tax was payable, when the later transfer was notified in an account).

The provisions are as follows.

(a) Where the transfer which is reported late ('the earlier transfer') is made within the seven years preceding the later transfer, the tax payable on the earlier transfer is the amount which would have been payable on that transfer if it had been reported at the correct time (i.e. using the table of rates applicable at that time) plus the additional tax that would have been charged on the later transfer if the earlier transfer had been taken into account. Where a later transfer (A) is itself an earlier transfer in relation to a subsequent later transfer (B), the additional tax chargeable on (A) by virtue of its being an earlier transfer in relation to (B) is left out of account in the calculation required when (A) itself is a later transfer.

(b) Where two or more transfers in the seven-year period are reported late, the additional tax on a later transfer is apportioned between them on a pro rata basis; but if one of these unreported transfers is discovered after the liability on another has been settled, any further tax is payable on the latest transfer to be reported.

(c) Where the earlier transfer is made more than seven years before the later transfer, the tax payable on the earlier transfer is still the amount which would have been payable on that transfer if it had been reported at the correct time. The tax payable on the later transfer is not affected because of the seven-year cumulation rule.

(d) Where no account of a person's excepted estate is required by the Board, an account of that estate shall, be treated as having been delivered on the last day of the prescribed period in relation to that person. See **2.15** ACCOUNTS AND RETURNS.

[*IHTA 1984, s 264*].

Note. The legislation still refers to a ten-year period in (a) and (b) above but this should presumably be amended due to the reduction in the cumulation period from ten to seven years. The principle is, however, unaffected.

A transfer is discovered (i) if notified by an account etc. after the required period, on the date so notified or (ii) in any other case, on the date when the Board give notice of a determination (see **14.1** DETERMINATIONS AND APPEALS). [*IHTA 1984, s 264(9)*].

Interest on tax overdue will run from the due date of payment (see **32** PAYMENT OF TAX), but from that date to six months after the date of discovery the interest will be on the amount of tax which would have been payable if the transfer had been reported at the proper time. Thereafter, the interest will be on the actual tax payable. [*IHTA 1984, s 264(6)*].

Exemption limits

[7.16] If the earlier transfer would have been wholly or partly exempt because it was within the limits of an exemption and the later transfer actually received the benefit of the same exemption, the later transfer is not disturbed and the exemption which would have applied to the earlier transfer is reduced accordingly. [*IHTA 1984, s 264(7)*].

Settled property

[7.17] The provisions of *IHTA 1984, s 240(3)* apply to cases where any fraud, wilful default or neglect by the settlor of a **40** SETTLEMENTS: DISCRETIONARY TRUSTS AND OTHER TRUSTS OF RELEVANT PROPERTY comes to the knowledge of the Board. For the position regarding penalties in respect of return periods starting on or after 1 April 2009 where the return is due on or after 1 April 2010 see **32.20** PAYMENT OF TAX and **33.2** PENALTIES. In consequence, the provisions relating to transfers reported late do not apply to such settled property for IHT purposes.

8

Capital Gains Tax

Cross-reference. See **53.5** VALUATION for valuation at death for capital gains tax purposes.

Simon's Taxes. See **C3.501–C3.505, I3.611–I3.615, I5.1151.**

Other Sources. Tolley's Capital Gains Tax.

Introduction to capital gains tax

[8.1] A *lifetime* disposition may give rise to a chargeable gain subject to capital gains tax. There is no capital gains tax on property passing on death. For the purposes of inheritance tax no account is taken of any capital gains tax borne by the transferor in determining the reduction in value in his estate. *Section 5(4)* makes it clear that the value of a transferor's estate immediately after the transfer of value 'do not include his liability (if any) for any other tax or duty resulting from the transfer.' [*IHTA 1984, s 5(4)*].

Example 1

A makes a gift of land worth £100,000 to the trustees of a discretionary settlement in which he retains an interest. The gift incurs capital gains tax liability of £15,000. The transfer of value for inheritance tax purposes (subject to grossing-up for the IHT payable) is £100,000 (i.e. the same as if A had sold the land and given the £100,000 proceeds to the trustees). The capital gains tax liability is not relevant to the calculation of the chargeable transfer.

Relief for CGT against IHT

[8.2] Capital gains tax paid is taken into account for IHT purposes in the following circumstances.

(a) If the transferor fails to pay all or part of the capital gains tax within twelve months of the due date, an assessment may be made on the donee [*TCGA 1992, s 282 as amended by FA 2004, s 116*] and the amount of such tax borne by the donee is treated as reducing the value transferred. There is a similar effect when the transfer is from a settlement but this only applies if the capital gains tax is borne by a person who becomes absolutely entitled to the settled property concerned. [*IHTA 1984, s 165(1)(2)*].

> *Example 2*
>
> In the Example in 8.1 above, if A fails to pay the £15,000 capital gains tax and it is borne by the trustees, the value transferred by A is £85,000 for the purposes of inheritance tax.

(b) Where a person sells, or is treated as having sold, national heritage property on the breach or termination of an undertaking (see 30.10 NATIONAL HERITAGE) any capital gains tax payable is deductible in determining the value of the asset for IHT purposes. [*TCGA 1992, s 258(8)*].

(c) Where the transferee pays the CGT rather than the transferor then the CGT paid by the transferee may be deducted from the value transferred in determining the loss to the *transferor's* estate for IHT purposes. [*IHTA 1984, s 165(1)*].

If IHT becomes payable in circumstances [other than the above], there is no relief for any of the CGT payable on the transfers.

Relief for IHT against CGT

[8.3] Where capital gains tax on a disposal not at arm's length has been held over under *TCGA 1992, s 165* (relief for gifts etc. of business assets), or where *TCGA 1992, s 260* (relief for gifts on which inheritance tax is chargeable) applied, the transferee may deduct in the capital gains tax calculation on subsequent disposal the lesser of the IHT paid in respect of the gift and the amount of the chargeable gain on the disposal by the transferor. The relief applies even though the IHT liability was paid by the donor and not by the donee. A similar relief applies to hold over under the provisions of *FA 1980, s 79* as extended by *FA 1981, s 78* and *FA 1982, s 82* (general relief for gifts etc. before 14 March 1989). The IHT deductible may be that arising on a potentially exempt transfer within these CGT reliefs which becomes a chargeable transfer on the transferor's death within seven years and where the inheritance tax is re-determined in consequence of the transferor's death within seven years of the chargeable transfer or is otherwise varied, all necessary adjustments are to be made whether by assessment, discharge or repayment. [*TCGA 1992, ss 67(2)(3), 165(10)(11); FA 2004, s 116*].

The foregoing relief is subject to the anti-avoidance provisions regarding private residence relief which is subject to a hold-over election under *TCGA 1992, s 260*. [*TCGA 1992, s 260(7)(8); FA 2004, s 116, Schs 21, 22*].

For full details of capital gains tax, see Tolley's Capital Gains Tax.

Key points concerning capital gains tax

[8.4] Points to consider are as follows.

- Where there is a chargeable transfer of an asset into trust and an IHT liability arises on the disposal, the trustees may deduct the amount of the IHT payable in the calculation of the gain when they dispose of that asset, but not so as to create a loss. If the IHT was paid by the settlor/transferor, the trustees should request a note of the amount paid for future reference so that relief for the IHT can be claimed on a future disposal giving rise to CGT. It does not matter in this case whether or not a hold-over relief claim was actually made on the gift into trust. However, in the case of a disposal within *TCGA 1992, s 165*, it is important to make a hold-over claim in all cases because the allowance for any IHT paid is dependent on the hold-over claim having been made. If there is actually no gain to hold over, or in fact if a loss arises on the gift, a hold-over claim can still be made and then if IHT liability arises on the death of the transferor within seven years of the gift, credit for it can be claimed in the donee's CGT calculation. It is understood that if the donee makes a part disposal of the asset gifted, HMRC accept that all the IHT paid can be claimed as a deduction in the CGT calculation up to the amount of the gain arising. An apportionment of the IHT between the part sold and the part retained is not necessary.

- For shares in private investment companies, the capital gains tax liability on a gift can be reduced by making a gift of a minority interest in the company. Unlike the IHT rules, the value for capital gains tax purposes of the holding gifted takes no account of the size of the shareholding from which the gift is made. If the gift is to a relevant property trust for the benefit of children or grandchildren, the transferor could retain control as a trustee if need be and he would also be able to make payments of any IHT by ten yearly instalments for transfers of assets detailed at **32.6** and **32.7** PAYMENT OF TAX.

9

Chargeable Transfer

Simon's Taxes. See **I3.101–I3.113, I3.311, I3.312, I3.511, I3.521, I3.531, I4.101.**

Definition of chargeable transfer

[9.1] A chargeable transfer is any **48** TRANSFER OF VALUE made by an individual other than an exempt transfer (see **21** EXEMPT TRANSFERS). [*IHTA 1984, s 2(1)*]. *Note.* A transfer of value can be made by a person, thus including a company, but a chargeable transfer can be made only by an individual, although individual participators in a close company may be charged in respect of certain transfers made by the company (see **11** CLOSE COMPANIES). Inheritance tax is charged on the value transferred by a chargeable transfer. [*IHTA 1984, s 1*]. The exit charges arising on relevant property trusts (see **40** SETTLEMENTS – DISCRETIONARY TRUSTS AND OTHER TRUSTS OF RELEVANT PROPERTY) are also chargeable transfers although not charges under *IHTA 1984, s 79* in relation to conditionally exempt property.

Certain lifetime transfers are designated as potentially exempt transfers. A potentially exempt transfer is a transfer of value made by an individual after 17 March 1986 which would otherwise be a chargeable transfer and which is either a gift to another individual, a gift into a bereaved minor's trust on the coming to an end of an immediate post-death interest, or gift into a trust for a disabled person. In relation to transfers of value made, and other events occurring, after 16 March 1987, certain gifts by individuals into and out of settlements with interests in possession are also included. See **35** POTENTIALLY EXEMPT TRANSFERS for full details. A potentially exempt transfer made seven years or more before the transferor's death is an exempt transfer and any other potentially exempt transfer is a chargeable transfer. A potentially exempt transfer is assumed to be an exempt transfer during the seven years following the transfer (or, if earlier, until immediately before the transferor's death). [*IHTA 1984, s 3A; FA 1986, Sch 19 para 1; FA 2010, s 53(2)*].

The estate of a deceased person is treated as a transfer of value equal to the value of his estate made immediately before his death and is chargeable to inheritance tax. See 49 TRANSFERS ON DEATH for detailed provisions.

Seven-year cumulation period

[9.2] Chargeable transfers are cumulated over a seven-year period. After seven years transfers drop out of the cumulative total. The rate of tax on any chargeable transfer is determined from the tables at 37 RATES OF TAX by reference to the transferor's cumulative total of chargeable transfers within the previous seven years (including, where appropriate, potentially exempt transfers previously made becoming chargeable and chargeable transfers made before 18 March 1986 under the rules relating to CTT). [*IHTA 1984, s 7; FA 1986, Sch 19 para 2*].

Nil rate tax band

[9.3] The first £325,000 of chargeable transfers in the seven-year cumulation period are taxable at nil per cent for the period 6 April 2009 onwards. See 37 RATES OF TAX. The total of chargeable transfers is calculated after making any allowance for the annual exemptions. Where a potentially exempt transfer becomes a chargeable transfer on the death of the donor within seven years of the gift, it must be remembered that chargeable transfers within the seven years prior to the gift must be cumulated with it to establish the tax payable on the gift, charged at 40%. But if those prior chargeable transfers were made more than seven years before the death, they are then left out of account in calculating the lifetime cumulative total taken into account on the estate on death. See 7.5 CALCULATION OF TAX.

Time of gift

[9.4] As a basic rule, no chargeable transfer can take place until there has been a disposition resulting in a reduction in the estate of an individual.

Voidable transfers

[9.5] Where it can be shown that the whole or part of a chargeable transfer has been set aside by virtue of any enactment or rule of law as voidable or otherwise defeasible, a claim may be made for the transfer to be treated as void so that it never took place. The tax paid can then be reclaimed within a four-year time limit (with interest free of tax from the date of the claim). This provision covers matters such as transactions set under the *Insolvency Acts*, or the *Matrimonial Causes Act 1973*. The tax rate applied to later chargeable transfers must be recalculated. [*IHTA 1984, s 150*].

Repayment cases

[9.6] A similar claim may also be made for the repayment of inheritance tax in respect of any other chargeable transfer made before the claim that would not have been payable if the transfer that has been set aside had been void initially.

Again, the liability is extinguished if the tax has not been paid. In the case of an amount which is repayable on a claim under *IHTA 1984, s 150*, the repayment interest start date is the date on which the claim is made. A claim under this section must be made not more than four years after the claimant knew, or ought reasonably to have known, that the relevant transfer has been set aside. [*IHTA 1984, ss 150, 236(3); FA 1989, s 179(1); FA 2009, Sch 51 para 8, Sch 54 para 11*].

Pools syndicates and other similar arrangements

[9.7] There is no chargeable transfer where football winnings, National Lottery (now Lotto) etc., are shared among the members of the syndicate in accordance with the terms of an agreement drawn up before the win (HMRC Statement of Practice **E14**). The prior agreement can be verbal or written and it is recommended that a written record is made but it is not necessary to lodge this with HMRC. Providing an agreement is in existence any winnings by the syndicate leader which are passed on to the members of the syndicate are not chargeable to IHT.

However, in the event of a big win by a syndicate then HMRC may wish to see something similar to the following:

Agreement between the members of the [XYZ] Lottery* Syndicate

We, the parties hereunder, contributing [equal] amounts on a **weekly**/monthly/yearly* basis to the syndicate hereby confirm that the winnings from such game of chance will be distributed in **equal**/proportionate* shares to the stake contributed by each individual member as shown **below**/in the accompanying schedule*. Such stakes/contributions applied in the purchase of such tickets or the winnings arising therefrom and distributed by the appointed manager in accordance with the agreed shares shall not be a gift within *IHTA 1984, ss 2, 3A* but shall be treated as having no liability to inheritance tax in accordance with Inland Revenue Statement of Practice E14. The above shall apply to the members of this syndicate including the appointed manager being the first named member below.

Syndicate member.	Stake/contribution.	% share of prize	Date
1) X. Signed Mill Cottage, Netherington, Wilts SP4 8QS Address	£3 per **week**/month/year	33.3%	23 April 2010
2) Y *Etc.*	£3 per **week**/month/year	33.3%	26 April 2010

* deleted as appropriate.

10

Charities

Cross-references. See **21.2** and **21.4** EXEMPT TRANSFERS for gifts to charities

Simon's Taxes. See **I3.333, I4.215, I5.642, I5.643, I5.644.**

Other Sources. Tolley's Income Tax; Tolley's Capital Gains Tax; Foster's Inheritance Tax, Parts C3.33, D2.15; IHTM11101.

Introduction to charities

[10.1] Under *Recreational Charities Act 1958, s 1* amended by *Charities Act 2006, s 5*, the provision, in the interest of social welfare, of facilities for recreation or other leisure time occupation, is deemed to be charitable (subject to the principle that a trust or institution to be charitable must be for the public benefit). See in this connection *Guild v CIR* HL, [1992] STC 162, a CTT case where it was initially held in the SC that the phrase or for 'some similar purpose in connection with sport' in a bequest made to a sports centre might include non-charitable purposes and thus would not be 'for charitable purposes only' within *FA 1975, Sch 6 para 10* (now *IHTA 1984, s 23*). However, this was overturned in the HL, Lord Keith stating that, on a 'benignant construction', where the first part of the bequest (i.e. to the sports centre) was charitable, the phrase in the second part (i.e. 'or some similar purpose'), meaning the provision of facilities for the public at large, must also be charitable. For examples of purposes held to be charitable, see *Tolley's Income Tax*. See *Tolley's Capital Gains Tax* for tax relief for gifts of qualifying investments and interests in land to a charity by an individual. Also gifts to Community Amateur Sports Clubs are exempt for inheritance tax purposes as well as capital gains tax. [*ICTA 1988, s 587B inserted by FA 2002, s 43 and ICTA 1988, s 587C inserted by FA 2002, s 97; ITA 2007, ss 23, 24(1), 431(1), 445(1), Sch 1 paras 328, 536*].

Definitions

'*Charity*' means a body of persons or trust that is established for charitable purposes only meets the jurisdiction condition (i.e. EU, etc.), meets the registration condition (i.e. *Charities Act 1993, s 3*) and meets the management condition (i.e. its managers are fit and proper). [*Charities Act 2006, s 1; ICTA 1988, ss 505, 506(1); IHTA 1984, s 272 now repealed; ITTOIA 2005, s 878(1); FA 2006, ss 55, 56; ITA 2007, ss 519, 543(1); CTA 2009, s 1319; FA 2010, s 30, Sch 6*].

'*Charitable purposes*' comprise a purpose which is for the public benefit or falls within any of the following descriptions of purposes the prevention or relief of poverty, the advancement of education, the advancement of religion and a many other charitable purposes within *Charities Act 2006, s 2(2)*. A purpose falling within *s 2(2)* must be for the public benefit if it is to be a charitable purpose and in any reference to the public benefit is a reference to the public benefit as that term is understood for the purposes of the law relating to charities in England and Wales but it is not to be presumed that a purpose of a particular description is for the public benefit. The Charity Commission for England and Wales must issue guidance in pursuance of its public benefit objective within *Charities Act 2006, s 6*.

UK charity tax reliefs were extended, with effect from 6 April 2010, by *FA 2010, Sch 6* to certain organisations which are equivalent to charities and Community Amateur Sports Clubs in the EU and in the European Economic Area countries of Norway and Iceland. These charities had to be registered with any regulators in their home country which the law requires the organisation to register with, similar to the Charity Commission in England and Wales, and have managers that are fit and proper persons. This extension of charitable reliefs is withdrawn for transfers of value made on or after 1 April 2024. For an organisation which has not asserted its status as a charity, relief is withdrawn for transfers of value made on or after 15 March 2023. To have asserted its status as a charity, the organisation must have made a valid claim in reliance on its status as a charity, for example, a charitable tax repayment claim. [*F(No 2)A 2023, s 344*].

In *Routier and Venables (as executors of the late Beryl Coulter) v HMRC* [2016] EWCA Civ 938 the deceased was domiciled in Jersey but held assets of £1.8m in the UK. She left her estate to a Jersey charitable trust. It was accepted that the trusts qualified as charitable under English law but HMRC denied relief on the basis that the trust must be governed by the law of the United Kingdom and subject to the jurisdiction of the United Kingdom courts. The Court of Appeal upheld the decision of the High Court Chancery Division in favour of HMRC on this point. A further argument for the executors that the denial of relief was an unlawful restriction on the movement of capital under European law was left for a further hearing and subsequently the Supreme Court held that the EU rules on the free movement of capital apply, Jersey being a third country for the purpose of the transfer of capital from the UK. The refusal of the charity relief for IHT under *IHTA 1984, s 23* was an unlawful restriction on the freedom of movement. The relief was therefore to be allowed: [2019] UKSC 43.

Gifts

[10.2] Gifts to charities are generally exempt from inheritance tax including the gifts of qualifying investments introduced by the *Finance Act 2000* for capital gains tax purposes (see above). From 6 April 2012 where 10% or more of any component of an estate has been given to charity, a reduced rate of inheritance tax (36%) will apply to that component. There is no charge to tax when certain settled property becomes held for charitable purposes only without limit of time. See details at **21.2** and **21.4** EXEMPT TRANSFERS.

Example 1

Betty is very wealthy and wishes to benefit her village to a great extent and has discussions with the leader of the Parish Council and they agree the following:

- to provide £250,000 in a Trust Fund for the education and benefit of local children;
- to build a church annex for Sunday school worship costing £75,000;
- to provide £500,000 for a centre for the training and welfare of the community;
- a gift of £250 to every individual in the village.

In order to ensure that Betty falls within the requirements of *IHTA 1984, s 23* so that her gifts are for charitable purposes only she must not take any benefit. This is likely to be the case as even though she is resident in the village she will not be likely to benefit from the subject of her gifts e.g. the educational trust, Sunday school and the training/welfare centre. Whilst this is not a matter that is going to cause a problem for IHT purposes with regard to *s 23(4)* it might have done for income tax purposes under *FA 1990, s 25(2)*.

Note that in the case of the training/welfare charitable donation above it may be too widely drawn so as to preclude relief. A trust for the relief of unemployment is not charitable whereas the relief of poverty is charitable as is the furtherance of education. Again, care needs to be taken when setting up the necessary trust deed. However, with the introduction of gifts to Community Amateur Sports Clubs (CASCs) being exempt for inheritance tax purposes as well as capital gains tax she might consider this option as an answer to bullet point three above. CASCs must be open to the whole community and provide facilities for, and promote participation in, one or more eligible sports. These clubs must be registered with HMRC.

For guidance setting up a charity, see www.gov.uk/setting-up-charity/charitable-purposes.

Trusts

[10.3] Where a charity takes the usual form of a trust in which there is no interest in possession i.e. a discretionary trust, special rules apply. Where the trusts on which property is held require part of the income to be applied for charitable purposes, a corresponding part of the settled property is regarded as held for charitable purposes, for the purposes of the rules in *IHTA 1984, Part III, Ch III* relating to **40** SETTLEMENTS: DISCRETIONARY TRUSTS AND OTHER TRUSTS OF RELEVANT PROPERTY (other than the provisions of *ss 78, 79* relating to conditionally exempt occasions and exemption from ten-yearly charge for National Heritage property). [*IHTA 1984, s 84*]. Provided the property is held for charitable purposes only, whether for a limited time or otherwise, it is not 'relevant property' and there is no ten-year anniversary charge under *IHTA 1984, s 64* (see **40.3** and **40.6** SETTLEMENTS: DISCRETIONARY TRUSTS AND OTHER

TRUSTS OF RELEVANT PROPERTY). In addition, if the property becomes held for charitable purposes without any time limit, there is no charge to tax at other times (proportionate charge to tax) on distributions. See **10.4** below for property leaving temporary charitable trusts.

Case law — Deed of variation

In the case of *St Dunstan's v Major* [1997] STC (SCD) 212 Sp C 127 the gift to the Charity by way of Deed of Variation and the claiming of gift aid relief by the personal representative was precluded. But where a bequest is part of a will or the assets are left to someone to make the gift to the charity then the charity exemption is in point under *IHTA 1984, s 23* and where the beneficiary makes a subsequent transfer to the charity gift aid relief will also be available; the charity being able to claim the basic rate relief in respect of the gift aid and the higher rate relief being claimed by donor who has been a beneficiary under the will and benefited the charity. Alternatively, providing the above procedures are adhered to the opportunity to claim gift aid relief and exemption under *s 23* will be available.

In relation to deeds of variation in favour of a charity, it is a requirement that the charity has been notified of the gift to it under the deed.

Property leaving temporary charitable trusts

[10.4] Property which is held on charitable trusts only until the end of a specific period (whether defined by date or in some other way) is subject to a charge when either:

(a) it ceases to be held for charitable purposes otherwise than by being applied for charitable purposes (but see also **21.4** EXEMPT TRANSFERS for certain situations where there is no charge when property becomes that of a qualifying political party or a national body mentioned in *IHTA 1984, Sch 3* or, under certain conditions, a body not established or conducted for profit), or

(b) the trustees make a 'disposition' (otherwise than for charitable purposes) which reduces the value of the settled property. '*Disposition*' includes an omission to exercise a right, unless not deliberate, which is treated as made at the latest time that the right could be exercised. [*IHTA 1984, ss 70(1)(2)(10), 76*].

No charge arises

(i) if, under (b) above, the trustees do not intend to confer gratuitous benefit and either the transaction is at arm's length between persons not connected with each other (see **12** CONNECTED PERSONS) or is such as might be expected in such a transaction; or

(ii) if, under (b) above, the disposition is a grant of a tenancy of agricultural property in the UK, Channel Islands or Isle of Man, for use for agricultural purposes and made for full consideration in money or money's worth; or

(iii) on the payment of costs or expenses attributable to the property; or

(iv) where any payment is, or will be, income for income tax purposes of any person (or, in the case of a non-resident, would be if he were so resident); or

(v) in respect of a liability to make a payment under (iii) or (iv) above.

'*Payment*' includes a transfer of assets other than money.

[*IHTA 1984, ss 63, 70(3)(4)*].

Tax is charged on the amount by which the trust property is less immediately after the event giving rise to the charge than it would have been but for the event (i.e. the loss to the donor principle), grossed-up where the settlement pays the tax.

The rate at which tax is charged is the aggregate of the following percentages for each complete successive quarter in 'the relevant period'.

	Cumulative Total
0.25% for each of the first 40 quarters	10%
0.20% for each of the next 40 quarters	8%
0.15% for each of the next 40 quarters	6%
0.10% for each of the next 40 quarters	4%
0.05% for each of the next 40 quarters	2%
Maximum rate chargeable after 50 years	30%

The rate charged may be reduced if any of the property is, or was, **20** EXCLUDED PROPERTY, see **10.5** below.

Definitions

'*Relevant period*' is the period beginning with the day on which the property became (or last became) held on charitable trusts, or 13 March 1975 if later, and ending on the day before the chargeable event. Where property in respect of which tax is chargeable was relevant property (see **40.3** SETTLEMENTS: DISCRETIONARY TRUSTS AND OTHER TRUSTS OF RELEVANT PROPERTY) immediately before 10 December 1981 (e.g. in a discretionary trust) and became (or last became) comprised in a temporary charitable trust after 9 December 1981 and before 9 March 1982, the relevant period begins with the day on which the property became (or last became) relevant property before 10 December 1981 or 13 March 1975 if later. [*IHTA 1984, s 70(5)(6)(8)(9)*].

'*Quarter*' means a period of three months. [*IHTA 1984, s 63*].

See also **40.19** and **40.22** SETTLEMENTS: DISCRETIONARY TRUSTS AND OTHER TRUSTS OF RELEVANT PROPERTY which also apply to temporary charitable trusts.

Example 2

On 1 January 1972 A settled £100,000 on temporary charitable trusts. The income and capital were to be applied for charitable purposes only for a period of 25 years from the date of settlement, and thereafter could be applied for charitable purposes or to or for the settlor's grandchildren. On 1 January 2011 the trustees paid £50,000 to charity and the balance of the settlement, valued at £75,000, to the three grandchildren.

The relevant period is the period from settlement of the funds or, if later, 13 March 1975 to 1 January 2011, i.e. 143 complete quarters, and the amount on which tax is charged is £75,000 gross.

The rate of tax is:

	%
0.25% for 40 quarters	10.00
0.20% for 40 quarters	8.00
0.15% for 40 quarters	6.00
0.10% for 23 quarters	2.30
	26.30%

IHT payable is 26.30% × £75,000 = £19,725

Example 3

Assume the same facts as in the above Example 2 except that the trustees apply £75,000 net for the settlor's three grandchildren, and the balance to charity.

The rate of tax is, as before, 26.30%

IHT payable is $\frac{26.30}{100 - 26.30} \times £75{,}000 =$ £26,764

The gross payment to the beneficiaries is £75,000 + £26,764 = £101,764.

Excluded property

[10.5] Where the whole or part of the amount on which tax is charged as in 10.4 above is attributable to property which was 20 EXCLUDED PROPERTY at any time during the relevant period, then, in determining the rate at which tax is charged in respect of that amount or part, no quarter throughout which the property was excluded property is to be counted. [*IHTA 1984, s 70(7)*].

Key points concerning charities

[10.6] Points to consider are as follows.

- In some cases, it is possible to obtain both income tax and IHT relief and for the charity or collecting agency such as the Charities Aid Foundation to obtain increased funds. This situation arises when a testator makes a pecuniary legacy to a beneficiary and expresses in his or her will that he or she wishes the beneficiary to benefit a charity but this is a non-binding request. If the beneficiary, in turn, makes a gift to the charity within two years of the death, both IHT and income tax reliefs will be due. The IHT relief is by virtue of *IHTA 1984, s 143*. The beneficiary receives an extension in the basic rate band of tax and if a higher rate tax payer will receive tax relief on the amount over and above the basic rate band under gift aid relief. The charity reclaims the basic rate tax relief and benefits from the gift which was treated as donated net of basic rate. Where an interest in freehold land is transferred by a devisee to a charity and it is claimed that *IHTA 1984, s 143* applies, HMRC's instructions require this to be reviewed by their technical specialists (IHTM35173).
- The *Charities Act 2011, s 3* sets out the meaning of 'charitable purposes' and lists 13 categories. Care needs to be taken when drawing up a will that benefits a charity to ensure that the charity does in fact comply so that IHT relief is obtained. Some of the categories (i.e. d to l) are new and of uncertain scope.

11

Close Companies

Cross-references. See **4.14** AGRICULTURAL PROPERTY for agricultural companies; **6** BUSINESS PROPERTY; and **20.5** EXCLUDED PROPERTY for Government securities held by close companies.

Simon's Taxes. See **I6.1**.

Other Sources. Tolley's Corporation Tax 2023–24, Chapter 13; Foster, Part F1; IHTM14851.

Introduction to close companies

[11.1] A company can make a **48** TRANSFER OF VALUE as a *person* but only an individual can make a **9** CHARGEABLE TRANSFER. However, where a close company makes a transfer of value that value is apportioned among its participators and treated as if each had made a transfer of the apportioned part (except to the extent that the transfer is to that participator). [*IHTA 1984, s 94(1)*]. Also, where unquoted share or loan capital (or any rights attached thereto) is altered, the participators are treated as having made a disposition, see **11.8** below.

Definitions

'*Close company*' is as defined by *ICTA 1988, s 414* for the purposes of corporation tax with the addition that companies resident outside the UK are treated as close companies if they would otherwise be within the definition. Broadly, a company is close if it is under the control of five or fewer participators or participators who are directors. [*IHTA 1984, s 102(1)*].

'*Participator*' in a company (whether resident in the UK or not) is as defined by *ICTA 1988, s 417* for the purposes of corporation tax but with the exclusion of a person who is a participator by reason only of being a loan creditor. [*IHTA 1984, s 102(1)*]. The definition includes any person

(i) possessing, or entitled to acquire, share capital or voting rights; or
(ii) possessing, or entitled to acquire, a right to receive, or to participate in, distributions; or
(iii) entitled to ensure that present or future income or assets of the company will be applied; directly or indirectly, for his benefit.

See Tolley's Corporation Tax 2023–24 for full definitions of '*close company*' and '*participator*'.

Apportionment

[11.2] The value transferred (see **11.4** below) by the company is apportioned among the participators according to their respective 'rights and interests' in the company *immediately before the transfer* and any amount so apportioned to a close company is further apportioned among its participators, and so on.

Exceptions

[11.3] The following are not apportioned.

(a) Any value attributable to any payment or transfer of assets to any person who brings it into account for the purposes of his income tax or corporation tax computations (including UK company dividends and other distributions not chargeable to income tax or corporation tax under *ICTA 1988, s 208*).
(b) Any amount apportionable to an individual domiciled outside the UK which is attributable to any property outside the UK.

[*IHTA 1984, s 94(2)*].

Definitions

'*Rights and interests*' in a company include those in the assets of the company available for distribution among the participators in a winding-up or in any other circumstances. They do not include:

(i) preference shares (as defined by *ICTA 1988, s 210(4)*) where any transfer of value by the company or any other close company has only a small effect on their value compared with the effect on the value of other parts of the company's share capital; or
(ii) the rights and interests of 'minority participators' of a subsidiary company which disposes of an asset, as a transfer of value, to another 'group' company (within the terms of *TCGA 1992, ss 171(1), 171A(2)*) and that transfer has only a small effect on the value of the rights and interests of the minority participators compared with those of other participators.

A '*minority participator*' is a participator of the transferor company which is not, and is not a person connected with, a participator of the 'principal company' (before 14 March 1989, 'principal member') of the group or of any of the principal company's (before 14 March 1989, principal member's) participators.

'*Principal company*' and '*group*' are as defined in *TCGA 1992, s 170 as amended by FA 2000, Sch 29 para 14*. Before 14 March 1989, the '*principal member*' of a group is the member of which all the other members are '75% *subsidiaries*' (within *ICTA 1988, s 413(3)*).

[IHTA 1984, ss 96, 97, 102(2); FA 1989, s 138(6); FA 2000, Sch 29 para 14; FA 2001, s 106; FA 2002, s 42(3)].

Value transferred

[11.4] A transfer of value made by a close company is the amount by which the value of its assets immediately after a disposition is less than it would be but for the disposition, and this reduction (ignoring dispositions of **20** EXCLUDED PROPERTY) is the value transferred for apportionment among its participators. See **48** TRANSFER OF VALUE generally and **48.2** in particular for dispositions which are not transfers of value. The surrender by a close company of surplus advance corporation tax or losses within a group under *ICTA 1988, ss 240 (now repealed), 402* is not treated as a transfer of value. [*IHTA 1984, ss 3(1), 10, 94(3), 98(1)*]. A bonus issue of shares will not be a transfer of value nor will a genuine commercial transaction. In *Postlethwaite's Executors v HMRC* where a FURBS payment was not within *IHTA 1984, s 94* and that the payment was a disposition not intended to confer gratuitous benefit, within *IHTA 1984, s 10*. See **55** TAX CASES.

A dividend paid by a subsidiary to its parent is not a transfer of value nor is a transfer of assets between a wholly-owned subsidiary and its parent or between wholly-owned subsidiaries. (HMRC Statement of Practice E15).

Example 1

The ordinary shares of companies A and B are held as follows (in January 2021)

		A	B
Individuals	X	80%	
	Y	20%	
	Z		10%
Company A			90%

Company B is non-resident and Z is domiciled in the UK. Company A sells a property valued at £220,000 to a mutual friend of X and Y for £20,000. The following month, company B sells a foreign property worth £100,000 to X for £90,000.

Company A

	£
The transfer of value is £220,000 – £20,000	200,000
Apportioned to X 80% × £200,000	160,000
Y 20% × £200,000	40,000
	£200,000

Company B

The transfer of value of £10,000 is apportioned	
To X 80% × 90% × £10,000	7,200
Deduct increase in X's estate	10,000
	—

To Y 20% × 90% × £10,000	1,800
To Z 10% × £10,000 note (C)	1,000
	£2,800

Notes to the example

(A) If the sale by company A were to X (or Y), there would be no apportionment because the undervalue would be treated as a net distribution, thus attracting income tax.

(B) On the sale by company B, X would not be liable to income tax.

(C) If Z were not domiciled in the UK, his share of the transfer of value would not be apportioned to him. [*IHTA 1984, s 94(2)(b)*].

Charge on participators

[11.5] Where a close company makes a transfer of value which is apportioned among its participators as above, inheritance tax becomes chargeable as if each such participator who is an individual had made a transfer of value after deduction of tax (if any) equal to the amount apportioned to him, less the amount (if any) by which his estate is more than it would be but for the company's transfer. For this purpose his estate is treated as not including any rights or interests (see **11.2** above) in the company. [*IHTA 1984, s 94(1)*].

Example 2

Assume the values transferred by X, Y and Z above in **11.4** and that X and Y have each made previous chargeable transfers in excess of £325,000 since January 2014 and have used up their annual exemptions for 2019/20.

	X	Y	Z
Company A			
	£	£	£
Value transferred	160,000	40,000	
Annual exemptions 2020/21	(3,000)	(3,000)	
	157,000	37,000	
Tax (25% of net)	39,250	9,250	
Gross transfer	£196,250	£46,250	
IHT	£39,250	£9,250	
Company B			
Value transferred	7,200	1,800	1,000
Deduct increase in X's estate	(10,000)	—	—
		1,800	1,000
Deduct annual exemption		—	1,000
		1,800	—
Tax (25% of net)		450	
Gross transfer		£2,250	
IHT		£450	

Note to the example

(A) Although it is understood that HMRC would follow this method of calculation in the above example, there is an alternative view which follows the exact wording of *IHTA 1984, s 94(1)*. This view is that the grossing-up should take place before the increase in X's estate is deducted. In the above example, it makes no difference as the gross transfer would still be less than the increase in X's estate. But suppose that X held 90% of the ordinary shares in Company A. His value transferred would then be £8,100 (90% × 90% × £10,000) and this alternative method would proceed as follows.

	£
Value transferred	8,100
Tax (25% of net)	2,025
	10,125
Deduct increase in X's estate	(10,000)
	£125
IHT thereon at 20%	£25

Where a close company makes a transfer of value to another company and an individual is a participator in both companies, any amount apportioned to him of the transferor company's transfer may be reduced by his apportioned part of the increase, due to the transfer, in the estate of the transferee company. [*IHTA 1984, s 95*].

Trustees

[11.6] Where a person is a participator in his capacity as trustee of a settlement, any amount apportioned to him less the amount (if any) by which the value of the settled property is more than it would be apart from the company's transfer (leaving out of account the value of any rights or interests in the company) is treated as follows.

(a) If a qualifying interest in possession subsists in the settled property, a part of that interest corresponding to the amount apportioned (as reduced) is treated as having come to an end on the making of the transfer.

(b) If no qualifying interest in possession subsists in the settled property, the trustees are treated for the purposes of the rules relating to **40** SETTLEMENTS: DISCRETIONARY TRUSTS AND OTHER TRUSTS OF RELEVANT PROPERTY as having made, at the time of the transfer, a disposition as a result of which the value of the settled property is reduced by a corresponding amount.

[*IHTA 1984, s 99*].

Note. For transfers within (b) above the amount is grossed-up under *IHTA 1984, s 65(2)* (see **40.12** SETTLEMENTS: DISCRETIONARY TRUSTS AND OTHER TRUSTS OF RELEVANT PROPERTY) where the trustees pay the tax.

Where the amount apportioned to a person is not more than 5% of the value transferred, it is to be disregarded in determining the rate of tax on any later transfers made by him. [*IHTA 1984, s 94(4)*].

Exemptions

[11.7] A participator can set his annual exemption against any amount apportioned to him but not the exemptions for small gifts, normal expenditure gifts, or gifts in consideration of marriage because these do not apply to deemed transfers of value. The exemptions for gifts to charities and political parties and for national purposes or public benefit are available. [*IHTA 1984, ss 3(4), 19(5), 20(3), 21(5), 22(6), 94(5)*].

Alteration of share capital, etc.

[11.8] Where there is an alteration in the share or loan capital of a close company not consisting of quoted shares or securities (for transfers and other events occurring before 17 March 1987, shares or securities quoted on a recognised stock exchange) or in any rights attaching to its unquoted shares or debentures (for transfers and other events occurring before 17 March 1987, shares or debentures not quoted on a recognised stock exchange), the alteration is treated as having been made by a disposition by the participators whether or not it would otherwise fall to be so treated. Such a disposition is not a POTENTIALLY EXEMPT TRANSFER, and is therefore in all cases a chargeable transfer, subject to the application of any available exemptions. Alterations are not to be taken to have affected the value of the unquoted shares etc. immediately before the alteration. '*Alteration*' includes extinguishment. [*IHTA 1984, s 98; FA 1986, Sch 19 para 20; FA 1987, s 58, Sch 8 para 2*]. Any decrease in value arising from an alteration brought about by a death is to be disregarded in arriving at the value of the estate on death. [*IHTA 1984, s 171(2)*].

Example 3

In January 2021, the share capital of company H, an investment company, is owned by P and Q as follows:

P	600	
Q	400	
	1,000	ordinary £1 shares

The shares are valued at £10 per share for P's majority holding and £4 per share for Q's minority holding.

The company issues 2,000 shares at par to Q and the shares are then worth £3.50 per share for Q's majority holding and £1.50 per share for P's minority holding. P has previously made chargeable transfers in excess of £325,000 since January 2004 and has utilised any available annual exemptions.

The transfer of value for P is

	£
Value of holding previously	6,000
Value of holding now	900
Decrease in value	5,100
Tax (25% of net)	1,275
Gross transfer	£6,375
IHT thereon at 20%	£1,275

Notes to the example

(A) P's transfer of value is *not* a potentially exempt transfer. [*IHTA 1984, s 98(3)*].

(B) An alternative charge may arise under *IHTA 1984, s 3(3)* (omission to exercise a right) but the transfer would then be potentially exempt and only chargeable if P died within seven years.

For the above purposes, and in relation to transfers and other events after 16 March 1987, '*quoted*', in relation to any shares or securities, means quoted ('*listed*' from 1 April 1996) on a recognised stock exchange or dealt in on the Unlisted Securities Market, and '*unquoted*', in relation to any shares or securities, means neither so quoted nor so dealt in. [*IHTA 1984, s 272; FA 1987, s 58(2), Sch 8 para 17; FA 1996, Sch 38 para 2*]. In relation to transfers and other events after 9 March 1992, Unlisted Securities Market shares and securities are only treated as unquoted for the purposes of defining relevant business property (see **6.4** BUSINESS PROPERTY), loss on sale of unquoted shares (see **53.24** VALUATION), and payment of tax by instalments (see **32.5** PAYMENT OF TAX). For all IHT purposes, and in relation to transfers and other events before 17 March 1987, Unlisted Securities Market shares and securities were not regarded as quoted on a recognised stock exchange (Inland Revenue Statement of Practice SP 18/80, 23 December 1980).

It is understood (see Law Society's Gazette 11 September 1991) that HMRC treat deferred shares issued after 5 August 1991 which subsequently come to rank equally, or become merged with, another class of shares as an alteration of rights within *IHTA 1984, s 98(1)(b)* (alteration in rights attaching to unquoted shares or debentures, etc.). Previously such an issue 'could' (the original statement by the former Inland Revenue said 'would' but it is understood they accepted 'could' as appropriate) have been treated as within *IHTA 1984, s 98(1)(a)* (alteration in unquoted share or loan capital).

HMRC have refused to confirm that either a purchase, redemption or repayment of a company's own shares or the alteration to any Articles of Association to enable it to make such a purchase etc. will not give rise to a transfer of value under *IHTA 1984, s 94*. (CCAB Memorandum, 22 June 1982). See **45.10** SHARES AND SECURITIES.

Trustees

[11.9] Where a person is a participator in his capacity as trustee and the disposition would, if he were beneficially entitled to the settled property, be a transfer of value made by him, the following consequences arise.

(a) *If an individual is beneficially entitled to an interest in possession* (e.g. a life interest) in the whole or part of so much of the settled property as consists of unquoted shares or securities of the close company (before 17 March 1987 shares or securities of the close company not listed on a recognised stock exchange), part of the individual's interest (equal to the amount of the decrease in value of the shares etc. in which the interest subsists) is treated as coming to an end. The amount of the decrease in value is the decrease caused by the alteration and is not grossed-up. [*IHTA 1984, s 100; FA 1987, s 58, Sch 8 para 3*].

(b) *If no individual is beneficially entitled to an interest in possession* in the whole of so much of the settled property as consists of the unquoted shares etc. then a charge to tax automatically arises under *IHTA 1984, s 65(1)(b)* (see **40.12** SETTLEMENTS: DISCRETIONARY TRUSTS AND OTHER TRUSTS OF RELEVANT PROPERTY).

Liability for tax

[11.10] Liability for tax is treated as follows:

(a) **On a transfer of value by the company apportioned to participators** (see **11.2** above). The company is primarily liable for the tax chargeable on amounts apportioned but, if it is unpaid by the time it ought to have been paid (see **32** PAYMENT OF TAX), the persons to whom any amounts have been apportioned and any individuals benefiting from the transfer become liable subject to the following limitations.
   - (i) A person to whom not more than 5% of the value transferred is apportioned is not liable for any of the tax.
   - (ii) Each of the other persons to whom any part of that value has been apportioned is liable only for the corresponding proportion of the tax.
   - (iii) A person benefiting from the transfer by an increase in value of his estate is liable only to the extent of that increase. [*IHTA 1984 s 202*].

   Note. Whoever pays the tax, it is the participators (except those within (i) above) whose cumulative totals of transfers are increased. [*IHTA 1984, ss 3(4), 94(4)*].

   A taxation warranty may be in order where transfers in shares in a close company are involved. In spite of the heading to *IHTA 1984, s 94* which states 'charge on participators' *IHTA 1984, s 202(1)(a)* makes it clear that tax is payable by the company. However, if the tax remains unpaid it can be collected from the participators by reason of *IHTA 1984, s 202(1)(b)*. In order to counteract the possibility of such a charge the following warranty may be inserted:

Taxation Warranty

1. General

All returns computations and payments which should or should have been made by the Company for any fiscal purpose have been prepared on a proper basis and submitted within the prescribed time limits and are up to date and correct and none of them is now the subject or likely to be the subject of any dispute with HMRC and will not give rise to any disallowance . . .

8. Inheritance Tax

The Company has made no transfer of value within the IHTA 1984, sections 94 or 99 in respect of close companies and charges on participators respectively.

No person has the power under IHTA 1984, section 212 to raise any capital transfer tax or inheritance tax by the sale of or charge over any of the Company's assets.

There is no unsatisfied liability to capital transfer tax or inheritance tax attached to or attributable to the assets of the Company or the shares of the Company and neither the assets nor the shares are subject to HMRC/Capital Taxes charge as is mentioned in IHTA 1984, section 237.

Note: *Further conditions apply to the Taxation Warranty that are not relevant to this work.*

(b) **On an alteration of share capital or rights** (see **11.8** above). The participators who own the shares or debentures are liable for the tax on the disposition made by them. [*IHTA 1984, s 98(1)*].

Interest in UK residential property held by close company

[11.11] With effect from 6 April 2017, an interest in a close company, including a non-resident company which would be a close company if UK resident, is not to be treated as excluded property to the extent that the value of the interest is attributable to UK residential property. Any loan to such a company is treated as a participator interest in the company. For more detailed analysis, see **20.2** EXCLUDED PROPERTY. The examples below are reproduced from the Questions on *IHTA 1984, Sch A1* with HMRC comments published on 27 February 2020 jointly by the main professional bodies.

Example 4

Mr L, who is resident and domiciled in Malaysia, purchases a buy to let flat in Battersea for £1 million through a wholly-owned BVI company. The BVI company owns no other assets. He borrows £600,000 of the purchase price from his bank in Malaysia which he then lends to the company together with £400,000 from his own money. The bank loan is formally secured on a portfolio of investments belonging to Mr L and held by the Malaysian bank worth £1.8 million. On Mr L's death, the UK property is worth £1.5 million. Mr L's interests in the BVI company include the loans of £1 million and the equity in the company which is now worth £500,000. These interests will be subject to inheritance tax on his death (£1.5 million). This is comprised of his interest as a participator by reason of being a loan creditor, and the equity in the property. In addition, the loan from the bank is a relevant loan (see **20.2** EXCLUDED PROPERTY) as it is a loan to an individual which has been used to acquire an interest (in this case, the onward loan to the company) in a close company which in turn uses the money to acquire a UK residential property interest. Inheritance tax will therefore potentially also be payable on the value of the collateral up to the amount of the loan (£600,000). The total potential value subject to inheritance tax on Mr L's death is therefore £2.1 million (£1.5 million plus £600,000).

However, HMRC agree that, for the purposes of these charging provisions only, all the loan from the bank of £600,000 is wholly deductible from the collateral. Therefore the value chargeable to IHT is £1.5 million.

Example 5

The facts are the same as in Example 4 above except that the bank has made the loan direct to the BVI company (but still secured on Mr L's portfolio). The loan to the BVI company is not a relevant loan as it is not made to an individual, a partnership or the trustees of the settlement. Mr L's collateral is not therefore subject to inheritance tax on his death. In addition, the loan is deductible from the value of the property in calculating the value of Mr L's interest in the BVI company. The value of his interest in the BVI company is therefore £900,000 (£1.5 million minus £600,000). The total amount on which inheritance tax is payable on Mr L's death is £900,000.

Interest in possession owned by close company

[11.12] Where a close company is entitled to an interest in possession in settled property, the participators of that company are treated, for the purposes of inheritance tax (except for the provisions of *IHTA 1984, s 55* relating to the acquisition by a person of a reversionary interest expectant on an interest to which he is already entitled), as being entitled to that interest according to their respective rights and interests in the company. Where the company becomes entitled to the settled property or disposes of the interest, the conditions of *IHTA 1984, s 52(2)* and *s 53(2)* are regarded as satisfied (HMRC Statement of Practice E5).

If such participators include the trustees of a settlement and a person is beneficially entitled to an interest in possession in the whole or part of the settled property, that beneficiary is treated as entitled to the whole or a corresponding part of the interest to which the trustees would otherwise be treated as entitled. For consideration of this provision, see *Powell-Cotton v CIR* Ch D, [1992] STC 625 where an interest in possession for the life of P in part of settled property was held by a close company shares in which were gifted to a charity by P who held a life interest in the remaining part of the settled property. It was held that there had been a termination of P's interest (which he was deemed to hold by virtue of *IHTA 1984, s 101*). [*IHTA 1984, s 101 as amended by FA 2006, Sch 20 para 26*].

From 22 March 2006 where a close company is entitled to an interest in possession in settled property, that interest in possession will also include an immediate post-death interest (IPDI) or a transitional serial interest (TSI). Where there is a disposal of rights and interests in the close company to 'a later participator' then for these purposes the later participator will be entitled to that interest in possession according to their respective rights and interests in the company. See **39** SETTLEMENTS WITH INTERESTS IN POSSESSION for full details. [*IHTA 1984, s 101 as amended by FA 2006, Sch 20 para 26*].

Note: In cases where property is held on **39** SETTLEMENTS WITH INTEREST IN POSSESSION which are settled on or after 22 March 2006, not being an IPDI or a TSI, whereby the close company acquired the interest for full consideration in money or money's worth from an individual who was beneficially entitled to it then it is not relevant property for the purposes of *IHTA 1984, s 58(1C)*. [*FA 2006, Sch 20 para 19(3)*].

Employee benefit trusts (EBT)

Property held in TRUSTS FOR EMPLOYEES (**52**) is not relevant property including property held on SETTLEMENTS WITH INTERESTS IN POSSESSION (**39**) which is settled on or after 22 March 2006 which is not an IPDI, a TSI or a disabled person's interest.

The transfer of the shares into an EBT is an exempt transfer if the value transferred is attributable to shares or securities in the company provided:

- the beneficiaries of the trust include all or most of the person's employed by holding office with the company;
- within one year the trustees hold more than half of the ordinary shares of the company having majority voting powers (there being no provision or agreement affecting this without the trustees consent);
- the trust does not permit any of the settled property to be applied for the benefit of a participator in the company or a participator in another close company that has benefited the same trust or any person connected with the previously mentioned.

[*IHTA 1984, s 28*].

The settled property is held on trusts for the benefit of the persons employed in the company and spouses or civil partners or relatives of the employees using a settlement along these lines:

THIS SETTLEMENT is made the . . . . day of . . . . BETWEEN (1) [Settlor] of [address] ('the Settlor') and (2) [trustees] of [addresses] ('the Original Trustees')

WHEREAS

The Settlor wishes to make provision for the employees of [..........] and companies in the same group (if applicable) and has transferred into the names of the Original Trustees the investments specified in the first schedule ('the Investments') to be held by the Original Trustees and their successors as trustees for the time being of this settlement on and with and subject to the following trust powers and provisions

NOW THIS DEED WITNESSES as follows:

1. Definitions and interpretation

    1.1 In this settlement unless the context otherwise requires the following expressions shall have the following meanings

1.1.1 'the Trustees' means the Original Trustees . . . *continues*

1.1.2 'the Trust Fund' means the Investments . . . *continues*

1.1.3 'the Beneficiaries' means such of the following persons (not being an Excepted Person) as shall for the time being during such period of 80 years be in existence namely:

1.1.3.1 persons for the time being and from time to time employed by or holding office with a Group Company and any wife husband widow widower or child or other issue or dependant of any such employee or officer or of any deceased employee or officer

1.1.3.2 any person who at any time has been or shall have been employed by or has held or shall have held office with a Group Company and any wife husband widow widower or child or other issue or dependant of any such past employee or officer

and 'Beneficiary' means any one of the 'Beneficiaries

The Precedent continues

There are a number of important uses of an employee trust; the trust offers a non-quoted company the opportunity of creating a market for the sale and purchase of shares. These trusts can also be used to build up large shareholdings in sympathetic control so that the company will be protected against unwanted takeovers and outside interference. The employee trust will also build up good relations between staff and the employer. The trust provides for protection of workers and ex-workers in times of hardship or ill health. [*IHTA 1984, s 13*]. Sums paid to the employee benefit trust will also be deductible for corporation tax purposes when 'qualifying benefits' are provided from the scheme to employees i.e. a payment or transfer of cash or assets that attracts tax and NICs or on termination of an employee's termination of employment. [*CTA 2009, ss 1290–1296*]. Therefore special care should be taken in the wording of the deed so that the funds are 'for the sole purpose' or 'with the dominant intention of' their being potential emoluments. See *Dextra Accessories Ltd and Others v MacDonald* CA [2004] STC 339; HL [2005] UKHL 47 and *Sempra Metals Ltd v HMRC* CA [2008] STC SCD 1062. See also the disguised remuneration provisions of *FA 2011, Sch 2*.

In order to qualify for favoured treatment an employee trust must satisfy the conditions set out in *IHTA 1984, s 86* and the necessity that all or most of the employees must be within a class of potential beneficiaries (see above). If the trust falls outside *IHTA 1984, s 28* (or *ss 13, 86*) then contributions to the trust may be a transfer of value. If *IHTA 1984, s 86* does not apply then the trust will be subject to a ten-year anniversary charge and an exit charge when capital is distributed. An exit charge will in certain circumstances arise under *IHTA 1984, s 72*.

Sometimes the EBT does not hold more than 50% of the shares in the employing company and therefore the exemption will not apply. [*IHTA 1984, s 28(2)*]. However, there are a number of options in that within the year the trustees may be able to purchase the sufficient quantity of shares from a third party but whether the other party is going to agree to this is probably dependent on a number of factors.

Inheritance tax charges in relation to employee trusts

Revenue and Customs Brief 18/11 issued on 4 April 2011 confirmed views previously expressed by HMRC in its Brief 61/09 concerning inheritance tax charges in respect of employee benefit trusts. Where a close company makes a transfer of value (*IHTA 1984, s 3*) to an employee benefit trust an inheritance tax charge arises under *IHTA 1984, s 94* unless, broadly, the disposition:

- is not a transfer of value under *IHTA 1984, ss 10* (dispositions not intended to confer gratuitous benefit), *12* (dispositions allowable in computing profits for corporation tax) or *13* (dispositions by close companies for benefit of employees);
- is eligible for other relief.

Where there is a transfer of value it is apportioned between the individual participators according to their respective rights and interest in the company immediately before the contribution to the Employee benefit trust is made. There is an immediate charge of 20% on the value transferred (the contribution) in excess of the participator's unused nil rate band. The liability for the charge to inheritance tax that arises under *IHTA 1984, s 94* is the company's or, so far as the tax remains unpaid, the participator's (*IHTA 1984, s 202*).

In relation to the possible application of *IHTA 1984, s 10*, HMRC consider that it will not apply if there is the slightest possibility of gratuitous intent at the date the contribution is made. Furthermore, To meet the terms of *s 10* the transaction must either:

- have been made at arm's length between persons not connected with each other (as defined in *IHTA 1984, s 270*);
- was such as might be expected to be made in a transaction at arm's length between persons not connected with each other.

An employee benefit trust is a discretionary trust and to satisfy the conditions of *IHTA 1984, s 86* the trustees' discretion must remain unfettered. Given that the potential beneficiaries under an employee benefit trust normally include the participators themselves; the employees or former employees; and/or the wives, husbands, civil partners, widows, widowers, surviving civil partners and children and step-children under the age of 18 of such employees and former employees HMRC is of the view that it will normally be difficult to show that the conditions of *IHTA 1984, s 10* are met. See however the decision in *Postlethwaite's Executors v HMRC* [2007] STC (SCD) 83 in which, contrary to the foregoing view of HMRC, it was held that a transfer by a small company set up by an engineer to an employer financed retirement benefit scheme for his benefit was within *IHTA 1984, s 10* as dispositions not intended to confer gratuitous benefit.

In relation to the possible application of *IHTA 1984, s 12*, HMRC consider that relief under this section cannot be given provisionally while waiting to see whether the contribution will become allowable for corporation tax purposes; and is only available to the extent that a deduction is allowable to the company for the tax year in which the contribution is made.

In relation to the possible application of *IHTA 1984, s 13*, this exclusion does not apply where (amongst other things) the contributions by the Close Company are made to an employee benefit trust that does not satisfy *s 86*, and the participators in the company and any person connected with them are not excluded from benefit under the terms of the Employee Benefit Trust and so *s 13(2)* applies.

Relief from inheritance tax may, however, be available where the value transferred is attributable to relevant business property. The relevant requirements must however be satisfied, so that the business must not be an excluded one, for example a company the business of which consists wholly or mainly of making or holding investments and the value of the relevant business property transferred must not be attributable to any excepted assets.

Key points concerning close companies

[11.13] Points to consider are as follows.

- Close companies are not within the basic charge to IHT which covers a chargeable transfer made by an individual and the estate of any person on death. Neither of these is applicable to a company. However, close companies may still give rise to IHT liabilities in a variety of ways.
- A close company has an estate for IHT purposes. Under *IHTA 1984, s 5*, 'estate' is defined as the aggregate property to which a person is entitled and a company is a person for UK tax purposes. However, it is out of the scope of charge to IHT on its assets as noted above.
- A gift to a close company will be a chargeable transfer to the extent that it increases the value of the estates of other shareholders. The gift cannot be a potentially exempt transfer because it is not a gift to another individual and although it may have the effect of increasing the estate of another shareholder, it also increases the estate of the company, thereby precluding treatment as a PET – see *IHTA 1984, s 3A(2)(b)*. An incorporation of a company may be made by gift with CGT hold-over relief under *TCGA 1992, s 165* and the IHT consequences of an incorporation by this method should be reviewed.
- Where a close company enters into a transaction which reduces its 'estate', this may be apportioned among the participators, subject to the exception for amounts brought into account for other UK tax purposes and for dispositions without gratuitous intent. Grossing up applies to any apportioned amount. For a trading company,

business property relief may prevent any IHT liability where the conditions for the relief are satisfied. The apportioned amount cannot be a potentially exempt transfer but exemptions may apply, for example, spouse exemption, charitable gift exemption, or exemption for gifts for national purposes. The company is primarily liable for IHT on any apportioned amounts.

- Where there is any alteration to the share or loan capital of a close company, as for example where shares are issued to a new shareholder for less than market value, or where the rights shares or debentures in a close company are altered, the participators are treated as making a disposition which is in all cases a chargeable transfer and not a PET; *IHTA 1984, s 98*. In this case, the company has no liability for the tax due. Business property relief may be available in appropriate cases but it should be noted that if the participator dies within seven years of the chargeable disposition, the relief would appear to be subject to a clawback. This is because clawback is prevented only if 'the original property' continues to be owned by the transferee at the time of the death, the original property being the 'relevant business property' in relation to the chargeable transfer. The charge under *s 98* is, however, purely a deemed disposition by reference to the loss in value of the participator's interest in the company which does not seem to fall into the requirements for escaping clawback.

12

Connected Persons

Simon's Taxes. See **C2.110, I3.142.**

Other Sources. Foster, Parts C1.42 and F2; HMRC Customer Guide to Inheritance Tax; IHTM04442.

[*IHTA 1984, s 270; TCGA 1992, s 286; FA 2005, s 103; ITA 2007, ss 993, 994, Sch 1 para 411*].

Introduction to connected persons

[12.1] For many tax purposes, certain persons are treated as being so closely involved with each other that either they must be viewed as the same person or transactions between them must be treated differently from transactions 'at arm's length'. Any question of whether a person is connected with another is determined for the purposes of *IHTA 1984*, as it is for the purposes of capital gains tax, by *TCGA 1992, s 286 as amended by The Tax and Civil Partnership Regs 2005, SI 2005/3229, Reg 121* but with modification to the meaning of 'relative', 'settlement', 'settlor' and 'trustee'. [*ITA 2007, ss 993, 994*].

Relatives for the purposes of the IHT definition of connected persons include uncles, aunts, nephews and nieces, unlike the equivalent definition for capital gains tax purposes.

The meanings of 'settlement', 'settlor', and 'trustee' have the same meanings as in the IHT legislation, although in practical terms this meaning will normally coincide with that applicable for capital gains tax purposes.

Provisions in IHT legislation which refer to connected persons are as follows:

- *IHTA 1984, s 10(1)* dispositions between persons not connected with each other and on arm's length terms.
- *IHTA 1984, s 13(2)(c)* dispositions by close companies for the benefit of employees, and exclusion of persons connected with participators and certain others.
- *IHTA 1984, s 23(4)(a)* gifts to charities and requirement of connected persons not to have entitlement to occupy land donated.

- *IHTA 1984, s 52(3)* transactions between trustees and a person who is connected with a beneficiary having an interest in possession in settled property.
- *IHTA 1984, s 112(6)* business property relief and excepted asset, where land is used for personal benefit of connected person.
- *IHTA 1984, s 131(3)* depreciation relief for transfers within seven years of death and exclusion for sales to connected persons.
- *IHTA 1984, s 176(3)(c)* loss on sale relief for related property and exclusion of relief for sale to connected person.
- *IHTA 1984, Sch A1 para (2)(4)* close company holding UK residential property interest and inclusion of connected persons' interests for the purposes of ascertaining interests in the company.

Individuals

[12.2] An individual is connected with his spouse or civil partner, or with relatives (including their spouses) of his or of his spouse or civil partner. It appears that a widow or widower is no longer a spouse (*Vestey's Exors and Vestey v CIR* HL 1949, 31 TC 1). Spouses divorced by decree nisi remain connected persons until the decree is made absolute (*Aspden v Hildesley* Ch D 1981, 55 TC 609). See definition of relative in **12.6** below. [*ITA 2007, s 993(2)*].

Settlements

[12.3] A trustee of a settlement, in his capacity as such, is connected with:

(a) the settlor (see **12.6** below) if an individual; and
(b) any person connected with the settlor; and
(c) a body corporate connected with the settlement (see **12.6** below).

HMRC have confirmed (a) above applies as regards the time when a settlement is created and property first transferred to it. On the death of the settlor, neither (a) nor (b) apply (former Inland Revenue Tax Bulletin February 1993 p 56). [*ITA 2007, s 993(3)*].

Partner

[12.4] A partner is connected with any person with whom he is in partnership and with the spouse/civil partner or a relative of that person, except in relation to acquisitions and disposals of partnership assets pursuant to bona fide commercial arrangements. In the case of a civil partnership recognised under the *Civil Partnership Act 2004* from 5 December 2005 the individuals in such a union will be treated as 'connected persons' as they will be close relatives of each other.

Company

[12.5] A company is connected with another company if:

(a) the same person controls both, or
(b) one is controlled by a person [A] who has control of the other in conjunction with persons connected with him [A], or

(c) a person [A] controls one company and persons connected with him [A] control the other, or
(d) the same group of two or more persons control both, or
(e) a group of two or more persons has control of each company and the groups can be regarded as the same by treating one or more members of either group as replaced by a person with whom he is connected.

[*ITA 2007, s 993(5)*].

A company is connected with another person if that person (either alone or with persons connected with him) has control of it.

[*ITA 2007, s 993(6)*].

Control

[12.6] Persons acting together to secure or exercise control of a company are treated in relation to that company as connected with one another and with any person acting on the directions of any of them to secure or exercise such control. Control may be 'exercised' passively, see *Floor v Davis* HL 1979, 52 TC 609.

[*ITA 2007, s 993(7)*].

'*Relative*' means brother, sister, ancestor or lineal descendant, uncle, aunt, nephew and niece. In the circumstances regarding the taxation of 'pre-owned' assets within *FA 2004, s 84, Sch 15* 'relative' shall, as well as the definition of 'relative' in *ITA 2007, s 993(2), Sch 1 para 411* (formerly *ICTA 1988, s 839*), be extended to include uncle, aunt, nephew and niece. See **22.1** GIFTS WITH RESERVATION. [*ICTA 1988, s 839; TCGA 1992, s 286(8); IHTA 1984, s 270; FA 2004, Sch 15 para 2; The Tax and Civil Partnership Regs 2005, SI 2005/3229, Reg 121; ITA 2007, s 993(2), Sch 1 para 411*].

'*Company*' includes any body corporate or unincorporated association but does not include a partnership. [*TCGA 1992, s 288(1); ITA 2007, s 994(1)*].

'*Settlement*' and '*settlor*' are defined in *IHTA 1984, ss 43, 44* (see **38.1** SETTLEMENTS — GENERAL).

'*A body corporate connected with the settlement*' is a close company (or one which would be close if resident in the UK), the participators in which include the trustees of the settlement, or a company controlled by such a close company etc. 'Control' is as defined in *ITA 2007, s 995(1)–(3)* (formerly *ICTA 1988, s 840*), i.e. the power of a person by shareholding or voting power (whether directly or through another company), or under Articles of Association or other regulating documents, to secure that the company's affairs are conducted according to his wishes. See also *Walding and Others (Executors of Walding, deceased) v CIR* [1996] STC 13 and **6.4** BUSINESS PROPERTY; TAX CASES (55). [*ICTA 1988, s 682A(2)*].

Application

[12.7] Persons acting together to secure or exercise control of a company are treated in relation to that company as connected with one another and with any person acting on the directions of any of them to secure or exercise such control. Control may be 'exercised' passively, see *Floor v Davis* HL 1979, 52 TC 609.

Circumstances where the connected persons rules apply for IHT are relatively limited compared to the wider significance of the rules for capital gains tax purposes.

For the purposes of the exclusion for dispositions which are not intended to confer gratuitous benefit, it must be shown that the transaction concerned was at arm's length between persons not connected with each other, or such as might be expected between such persons. [*IHTA 1984, s 10*]. See **48.2**.

The relief for dispositions by close companies for the benefit of employees contains a condition that the trusts must not permit the settled property to be applied for the benefit of a person who is connected with a participator in the company, past or present [*IHTA 1984, s 13*]. A similar exclusion applies for the purposes of the relief for gifts by individuals on employee trusts. [*IHTA 1984, s 28*]. See **52.4** and **52.6**.

There is a charge where a transaction between trustees of an interest in possession settlement and a person who is, or is connected with, persons having certain interests under the settlement. [*IHTA 1984, s 52(3)*]. See **39.10**.

For the purposes of the excepted assets rules for business property relief, an asset is not to be treated as used wholly or mainly for the purposes of a business at any time when it was used wholly or mainly for the personal benefit of the transferor or of a person connected with him. [*IHTA 1984, s 112(6)*]. See **5.7**.

13

Deeds of Variation and Disclaimers

Cross-reference. See **49.15** TRANSFERS ON DEATH.

Simon's Taxes. See **I4.411–I4.423, I5.254.**

Other Sources. Foster, Part D4; HMRC IHT Newsletter, August 2002, April 2004, August 2004 and April 2006; HMRC Customer Guide to Inheritance Tax; IHTM35011.

Disclaimers and Variations

[13.1] A disposition by a deceased person (by will, on an intestacy or otherwise) may be disclaimed or varied after the death by 'an instrument in writing' by the person who benefits under the disposition. Quite commonly, the variation is made by deed in which it should be drafted by a solicitor or barrister but this is not necessary to satisfy the requirements of the relevant inheritance tax and capital gains tax provisions. HMRC will accept a variation made by letter signed by the beneficiary under the will so long as it satisfies all the conditions set out in HMRC's published checklist on Form IOV2, the principal conditions being that it is signed by all beneficiaries adversely affected and dated within two years of the death, contains any appropriate stamp duty exemption certificate in relation to shares and contains an election for either or both the IHT and CGT purposes. The deed is effectively a lifetime gift by the legatee but, if the following conditions are met, the disclaimer or variation is treated for inheritance tax purposes as if made by the deceased, and any disclaimed benefit is treated as if never conferred, nor is the disclaimer or variation treated as a transfer of value. [*IHTA 1984, ss 17(a), 142(1)*].

Example 1

A dies in December 2020 leaving his estate of £354,000 to his wife absolutely. His wife, having an index-linked widow's pension and other assets of her own, agreed with her sons, B and C, that they could benefit from the estate to the extent of the nil rate band in the sum of £325,000 in equal shares, i.e. £162,500 each. As this is a variation after 31 July 2002 a separate election/statement is not required and instead it is sufficient for the instrument itself to state that a variation is to have effect for inheritance tax purposes only where additional tax is due. A had made no chargeable transfers before his death.

	£
Exempt transfer to widow	29,000
Transfer to B	162,500
Transfer to C	162,500
	£325,000
IHT payable	Nil

Notes to the example

(A) If A's widow died five years later when her estate was valued at, say £354,000, IHT payable would be £11,600 (assuming the £325,000 nil rate band is in force). If no instrument including a variation had been made on A's death and his widow's estate was, as a result, £679,000 (i.e. £325,000 going to the sons now added to £354,000 in her estate in five years), the IHT payable on her death would have been £141,600. However the introduction of the transferability of the nil rate band now results in the personal representatives of the widow's estate being entitled to claim the late husband's nil rate band which would be up to £325,000 ensuring that the total estate of the widow is covered by the two nil rate bands. The instrument has in this case increased the IHT liability by £11,600 but has ensured that the sons received their £162,500 five years earlier than would have been the case if the widow had retained her late husband's property until her death. See Note (B) below. [*IHTA 1984, s 8A; FA 2006, s 155; FA 2008, s 10, Sch 4 para 2*].

(B) In a case as above where no instrument is effected A's estate would have been added to that of his wife and, say through judicious investment, had increased to £340,000 making a total estate on the wife's death of £694,000, then A's transferable nil rate band with that of his wife would have resulted in IHT of £17,600. The nil rate band utilised by effecting the variation in favour of the sons utilised the whole of the £325,000 at the date of A's death. If no variation had been made and the nil rate band was £325,000 at the date of death of the wife, then this is the potential claimable amount. [*IHTA 1984, s 8A(3); FA 2008, s 10, Sch 4 para 2*].

(C) It may be appropriate in a case where the widow or widower might remarry to use the nil rate band discretionary trust by the use of a deed of variation so that the assets subject to the deed are secured outside of the survivor's estate. In this case, both the sons benefit from the father's estate subject to their mother not having a depleted income.

Disclaimers

[13.2] A disclaimer of an interest in the estate of a deceased person must:

(a) be made in writing within two years of the death.

(b) not be made for any consideration in money or money's worth, except the making, in respect of another of the deceased's dispositions, of another disclaimer or variation which is treated as made by the deceased. See IHTM35100. Therefore costs in drawing up and effecting the disclaimer should not be met by the recipient out of non-estate assets.

[*IHTA 1984, s 142(1)(3)*].

A similar provision relating to a disclaimer of an interest in settled property is not subject to the two year time limit, even though the settlement may be created by will, however it remains the case for both this provision and for disclaimers of an interest in an estate that any disclaimer must be valid as a matter of general law. This requires that no benefit should have been taken from the interest.

[*IHTA 1984, s 93*].

THIS DEED OF DISCLAIMER is made by. . . . . of. . . . . ("Mr A")

WHEREAS

(A) [. . . . .] died on . . . . ("the Testator")

(B) The Testator left a will dated . . . . ("the Will")

By clause 3(1) of the Will the Testator left Mr A a pecuniary legacy of ten thousand pounds (£10,000) ("the Legacy")

Mr A. wishes to disclaim the Legacy

NOW THIS DEED WITNESSES as follows:

Mr A disclaims the Legacy

Mr A confirms that he has accepted or received no benefit from the Legacy

EXECUTED AS A DEED on . . . . 2010.

SIGNED as a deed and delivered	)
by [Mr A] in the presence	)
of:	)

Notes to the Precedent

(A) The deed should be unilateral. The personal representative should not be a party.

(B) There is no need (or reason) to recite details of the grant of probate if it has already been obtained, or to endorse a memorandum on the disclaimer subsequently if it has not.

(C) A minor cannot make a disclaimer without a court order. The disclaimer may also have adverse consequences such as grossing up in cases of a residuary estate being partially exempt or where BPR or APR is adversely affected.

(D) The precedent assumes that Mr A is not a residuary beneficiary, as the disclaimed legacy will fall into residue.

(E) No elections are required; *ss 62(6)* and *142(1)* have automatic effect.

Variations

[13.3] Variations are treated as follows:

(a) The variation must be made in writing, by any of the persons who benefit or would benefit from the dispositions, within two years of the death.

(b) For variations where the death of the deceased occurred on or after 6 April 2012, and where the variation is to any extent in favour of a charity or charitable trust, it is a requirement that the charity or charitable trustees must be notified of the existence of the variation.

(c) For instruments dated after 31 July 2002, it is not necessary for an election to be made and notified to HMRC. Instead, the instrument itself should contain a statement by the 'relevant persons' that they intend that the provisions of *IHTA 1984, s 142* shall apply to the variation. The relevant persons are those making the variation and, where it results in additional IHT being payable, the personal representatives. In *Vaughan-Jones v Vaughan Jones* [2015] EWHC 1086 this statement was erroneously omitted from a deed of variation and the Court ordered that the document be rectified by inserting the necessary words, although it declined to insert the similar wording in relation to capital gains tax. Where the variation results in additional tax being payable, any of the persons in (b)(i) or (ii) above shall, within six months after the day on which the instrument is made, deliver a copy of it to the Board of HM Revenue and Customs and notify them of the additional tax that is due. [*IHTA 1984, s 218A; FA 2002, s 120(2)*]. The penalty for not complying with *s 245A(1A)* is an amount not exceeding £100 and a further penalty of £60 for every day after the day on which the failure was declared by the court or Special Commissioners and up until the day before the day on which the requirements are complied with. In addition to the preceding penalty under *s 245A(1A)* a further penalty can arise where a disposition on death is varied by the beneficiaries and gives rise to an additional tax IHT liability. In these circumstances where there is a continuing failure to deliver an instrument varying a disposition and notification of additional tax payable within 18 months after the day on which the instrument is made, a penalty of up to £3,000 may be charged. No penalty arises under any of the above provisions where there is 'reasonable excuse' for the failure unless the failure is not remedied without unreasonable delay after the excuse has ceased. Also see **33.14 PENALTIES**. [*IHTA 1984, s 245A(1A)(1B)(5); FA 2002, s 120(3); FA 2004, s 295(3)*].

(d) The variation must not be made for any consideration in money or money's worth, except the making, in respect of another of the deceased's dispositions, of another variation or disclaimer which is treated as made by the deceased. See, however, IHTM35100 which states: 'The bar against consideration relates only to extraneous consideration and will not prevent a rearrangement of assets within the will'. In a recent case the residue of a will was left to the surviving spouse but subject to a substantial legacy to a son from a previous marriage. The stepson renounced his legacy. Had the renunciation been tax-effective, it would have increased the spouse-exempt portion of the estate, and reduced the overall IHT borne by the estate. The proceeds of the estate were paid to the widow in cash. Three days later she made a cash gift to her stepson of £1 million. HMRC reviewed documents and considered that the variation of the estate and the subsequent payment to the stepson were related. The widow and the stepson contended that the cash payment was made as a separate gift — to set him up in business. The Commissioners decided that the disclaimer was made for consideration, and therefore *IHTA 1984, s 142(1)* did not apply. See *Mrs M Lau (W Lau's executor) v HMRC* [2009] STC SCD 352 Sp C 740. See also Note (D) in Example in **4.19** AGRICULTURAL PROPERTY.

[*IHTA 1984, s 142(1)–(3) as amended by FA 2002, s 120(1)*].

General conditions

[13.4] HMRC have also specified the conditions which they consider must be satisfied before an instrument of variation can come within *IHTA 1984, s 142*. The instrument must clearly indicate the dispositions that are the subject of it, and vary their destinations as laid down in the will, or the law of intestacy, or otherwise. It is not necessary that the instrument should purport to vary the will or intestacy provisions themselves, nor does it have to operate by deleting clauses in the will and substituting new clauses: it is sufficient if the instrument identifies the disposition to be varied and varies its destination.

Under Scots law, there are certain circumstances in which a residuary legatee can make a partial disclaimer. Where this is possible, HMRC accept that *IHTA 1984, s 142* applies (see HMRC Statement of Practice E18). The same treatment may apply to partial disclaimers made under English law since they are thought to be valid where the part disclaimed is not onerous and either the legacy concerned is a pecuniary one or the will states expressly or by implication that partial disclaimers can be made (Tolley's Practical Tax 1994, pp 31 and 56).

Deed of Variation in intestacy

THIS DEED OF VARIATION dated . . . . 2022 . . . . is made between:

(1) 'the Administrators' . . . . [Names]. . . . . [Addresses] . . . .

(2) 'the Personal Representatives' [of, say, the widow/widower (*see note (A) below in* ***Notes to the Deed***)]

(3) 'the substituted Beneficiary' . . . . [Name]. . . . . [Address]. . . . .

WHEREAS

1.1 XY ('the Deceased') died intestate on . . . . [Date] . . . . and Letters of Administration of his estate were granted to the Administrators by the Principal . . . . [Name]. . . . . District Probate Registry on . . . . [Date]. . . . .

1.2 AB (the widow/widower of the deceased) was entitled to the whole of the deceased's estate.

1.3 AB died on . . . . (2021). . . . . and a grant of representation was made to the Personal Representatives by the Principal . . . . [Name]. . . . . District Probate Registry on . . . . [date].

(4) The Personal Representatives and the substituted Beneficiary:

2.1 agree that the provisions of the Schedule to this Deed shall be construed as if they constituted the deceased's will and his/her estate shall be administered accordingly;

2.2 direct the Administrators to distribute the estate of the deceased in accordance with the provisions of the Schedule.

(5) The parties elect for [section 142 of the Inheritance Tax Act 1984] and [section 62 of the Taxation of Chargeable Gains Act 1992] as amended by Finance Act 2002, section 120 and/or section 52 to apply to this deed.

(6) It is certified that this instrument falls within category M in the schedule to the Stamp Duty (Exempt Instruments) Regulations 1987.

SCHEDULE

Signed as a Deed by the Administrators in the presence of . . . . [Name] . . . .

. . . . [Address] . . . .

Signed as a Deed by the Personal Representatives in the presence of . . . . [Name] . . . .

. . . . [Address] . . . .

Signed as a Deed by the substituted Beneficiary in the presence of . . . . [Name] . . . .

. . . . [Address] . . . .

Notes to the Deed

(i) It will not necessarily be the case that the widow/widower will be entitled to the whole estate (see **49.23** TRANSFERS ON DEATH) and therefore references to widow/ widower of the deceased would be replaced by the 'original beneficiary' and the 'substituted beneficiary'.

(ii) A schedule to the deed is required to set out the operative provisions.

Where there is more than one variation in relation to the same will or intestacy, HMRC consider that an election validly made is irrevocable and that an instrument will not fall within *IHTA 1984, s 142* if it *further* redirects any item (or part of any item) that has already been redirected by an earlier instrument. (Law Society's Gazette 22 May 1985). This has been confirmed by the decision in the case of *Russell and Another v CIR* Ch D, [1988] STC 195. However, in *Lake v Lake and others* Ch D, [1989] STC 865 an originating summons was sought for rectification of an original deed of variation where HMRC had claimed that a later deed entered into was inoperative following *Russell* above. The order for rectification was granted as it was shown that the original deed did not carry out the intentions of the parties concerned. See also in this connection *Matthews v Martin and others* Ch D 1990, [1991] BTC 8048 where an order for rectification was granted as the original deed did not reflect the agreement reached between the parties because of errors in the preparation of the draft for execution. See also *Wills v Gibbs and Others* [2007] unreported but summarised at **55** TAX CASES.

HMRC have confirmed that they do not regard a deed as having been made for a consideration in money's worth where it is entered into solely to avoid or compromise a claim under the *Inheritance (Provision for Family and Dependants) Act 1975*. See also Note (D) in Example in **4.19** AGRICULTURAL PROPERTY.

HMRC have also made it clear that under *s 142(1)(a)* the words 'or otherwise' can apply to the automatic inheritance of a deceased owner's interest in jointly held assets by the surviving joint owner(s) (Inland Revenue Tax Bulletin, October 1995, p 254). It is not necessary for a variation in these circumstances to state that the joint tenancy is severed, although it may do so for the sake of clarity.

Example 2

A family home is owned by mother and son as beneficial joint tenants and, on the mother's death, her interest is passed by survivorship to the son who then becomes the sole owner of the property. The son could vary his inheritance of his mother's interest by redirecting it to his children and this would enable the half share of the property to skip one generation on transfer.

Where a variation to which the above provisions apply results in property being held in trust for a person for a period of not more than two years after the death, the disposition which takes place at the end of that period is treated as if it had taken place at the beginning of that period, but any distribution or application of property occurring in that period is unaffected (i.e. will be chargeable to inheritance tax under the provisions relating to settled property). In Scotland, property which is subject to a proper liferent is deemed to be held in trust for the liferenter. [*IHTA 1984, s 142(4)(7)*]. See also *Soutter's Executry v CIR* [2002] STC SCD 385 Sp C 325 where a woman (S) died in November 1999 and the value of her estate was less than the IHT threshold. She owned a house, in which she lived with a friend (G). Under her will, she gave G the right to live in the house, rent free. G died in November 2000. In an attempt to reduce the IHT due on G's death, S's executors and G's executors purported to execute a deed of variation of S's estate, under *IHTA 1984, s 142*, removing the provision whereby G could live in the house rent free. The former Inland Revenue issued a notice of determination that the purported deed of variation was ineffective because the deed of variation was not a disposition of property and had no effect. S's executors appealed. The Special Commissioner dismissed the appeal, observing that 'the executors of a liferentrix have nothing they can vary'. G's executors 'had neither right, title or interest to any liferent'. They 'could not have continued to receive the liferent so they had nothing to give up or vary. The liferent was not and could not be assigned to them . . . a purported assignation of an expired liferent has no reality'. Some commentators suggest that the view that there was nothing to vary is incorrect and there is conceptually no difference between the position where a beneficiary has spent a gift or sold a gifted asset before the execution of a variation, which would be allowed, and the case in point. See Taxation Magazine, 22 May 2003, p 197. See also HMRC IHT Newsletter, December 2001.

The above provisions regarding disclaimers and variations apply whether or not the administration of the estate is complete or the property concerned has been distributed in accordance with the original dispositions. They apply to 'property comprised in a person's estate' immediately before his death which term includes 20 EXCLUDED PROPERTY but not any settled property in which the deceased had only an interest in possession nor property to which he was treated as entitled under the provisions relating to 22 GIFTS WITH RESERVATION. [*IHTA 1984, s 142(5)(6); FA 1986, Sch 19 para 24*].

Example 3

Assume H dies in June 2017, leaving his entire estate of £300,000 to his wife W, whose estate is valued at £250,000. W marries J, a widower with no children, in December 2020. J dies in July 2022 leaving his estate of £325,000 to W. J had already made PETs in 2017 to relatives amounting to £175,000, apart from other gifts using annual exemptions. W then dies in May 2023 leaving her entire estate to her children. W's personal representatives are entitled to claim H's unused nil rate band of £325,000 and also the transferable nil rate band of J in an amount of £150,000. However, the personal representatives can only claim a maximum of £325,000 from either or both previous deceased spouses. Therefore it is more beneficial to claim the transferable nil rate band of H of £325,000 and effect a deed of variation benefiting the children within the two-year time limit in respect of £225,000 of J's assets otherwise bequeathed to his wife W on his death in July 2022. The variation must be made in writing, by any of the persons who benefit or would benefit from the dispositions, within two years of the death, i.e. by July 2024. The variation results in additional tax being payable, the personal representatives shall, within six months after the day on which the instrument is made, deliver a copy of it to the Board of HM Revenue and Customs and notify them of the additional tax that is due. [*IHTA 1984, s 8A(5)(6); FA 2008, s 10, Sch 4 para 2*]. Without the deed of variation the estate of W would have had an IHT liability of £90,000 (i.e. £250,000 + £300,000 (H's estate) + £325,000 (J's estate) = £875,000 − 650,000 × 40%) whereas if the variation was made in respect of J's assets the position would be as follows:

	£
W's estate	250,000
H's estate	300,000
From J's estate	100,000
Total	650,000
Less Nil rate bands	(650,000)
Chargeable	£Nil
IHT payable	Nil

	£
J's estate	325,000
PETs failed	175,000
Total	500,000
Less Nil rate band	(325,000)
Less spouse exemption (£325,000 – £225,000)	(100,000)
Chargeable	£75,000
IHT payable	£30,000

THIS DEED OF VARIATION is made. . . . . January 2024.

BETWEEN

1. "the Wife's Executors"	Namely. . . . . and . . . . both. . . . . solicitors of. . . . .
2. "the Husband's Executors"	Namely. . . . . and . . . . both. . . . . solicitors of. . . . .
3. "the Children"	Namely: (1). . . . . of . . . . (2). . . . . of . . . . (3). . . . . of . . . .

WHEREAS

(A) J ("the Husband") late of. . . . . died on. . . . .

(B) The Husband's Executors are the executors appointed under his will ("the Will") probate to which was granted by the Leeds District Probate Registry on. . . . .

(C) In his will the Husband left his entire estate to W ("the Wife")

(D) W late of. . . . . died on. . . . .

(E) The Wife's Executors are the executors appointed under her will dated . . . . and who will be applying for Probate a memorandum of which will be endorsed on this deed

(F) The Children are the residuary beneficiaries entitled between them to the entire estate of the Wife.

(G) The parties wish to vary the dispositions of the Husband's estate as follows

(H) Such variation will leave the estate of the Wife solvent and capable of answering all debts taxes liabilities and testamentary expenses

NOW THIS DEED WITNESSES

(1) The Will shall be deemed to read and always to have read as if in it the Husband had left (subject to tax) a pecuniary legacy of one hundred and fifty thousand pounds (£150,000) to each of the Children

(2) It is certified that this instrument falls within category L in the schedule to the Stamp Duty (Exempt Instruments) Regulations 1987.

(3) The parties elect for [section 142 of the Inheritance Tax Act 1984] and [section 62 of the Taxation of Chargeable Gains Act 1992] as amended by section 120 and/or section 52 of the Finance Act 2002 to apply to this deed.

EXECUTED AS A DEED on the day and year first above written

SIGNED etc.

Notes to the example

(A) The recital that the second estate will still be left solvent is considered advisable.

(B) Often, the executors of the estates of married persons will be identical. They should be listed as two separate parties. There is no difficulty in the executors being parties twice to the deed in distinct capacities (see *Rowley, Holmes & Co v Barber* [1977] 1 All ER 801). This could be the case here and as the children may be the executors even though they will have a liability in respect of the variation of J's estate, they will benefit from the fact that there is no IHT liability in respect of W's estate (which includes J's assets).

(C) From 1 December 2003, any deed of variation involving a land transaction falls within the Stamp Duty Land Tax regime and is exempt from charge [*FA 2003, s 125*]. An instrument of variation which alters the destination of stocks and shares or marketable securities may also be certified as exempt from stamp duty.

(D) Where it is not practicable for all the beneficiaries of W's estate whose entitlements in practical terms are being varied, to join in the deed, perhaps because they are numerous and geographically diverse, it ought to suffice for the executors in the second estate to get clear authorities from each beneficiary to enter into the deed and then simply to recite that they are duly authorised and directed by all of those relevantly entitled to benefit under the will to enter into the variation.

No specific provision has been included to deal with the income position.

(E) Income tax has not been addressed in this precedent.

(F) The question arises whether the variation may be ineffective with regard to J's assets within W's estate, but this will only be the case where, say, W was the life tenant in settled property under J's will and whilst she would be capable of disposing of her life interest during her lifetime that life interest is deemed incapable of being disposed of after her death. HMRC suggest that 'in the real world' the interest ceases to exist on death and therefore there is nothing to vary with regard to W's estate. Clearly, a variation in these circumstances on the terms of J's will becoming immediately known should have been made during W's lifetime. However, as this is not a case of settled property with a life interest being redirected then the problem does not arise. See also *Soutter's Executry v CIR* [2002] STC SCD 385 Sp C 325.

Case law

The case of *Marshall v Kerr* HL, [1994] STC 638 concerned the effects on what is now *TCGA 1992, s 87* (overseas resident trusts) on what is now *TCGA 1992, s 62(6)* (see Tolley's Capital Gains Tax 2010–11 under Death). Under this last provision, it is possible to vary or disclaim dispositions of the deceased so that, for capital gains tax purposes, a variation or disclaimer is ignored as a disposal and a variation is treated as made by the deceased and a disclaimed benefit is treated as never having been conferred. It was held that the person executing the variation was the settlor of the chose in action which comprised the property disposed of under the variation and there was nothing in the deeming provisions of *TCGA 1992, s 62(6)* which required any assumption to the contrary; see now the provisions of *TCGA 1992, s 68C*. The decision that the person making the variation was the settlor of the property varied is of no application to inheritance tax since the deeming provisions of *IHTA 1984, s 142* are by reference to 'this Act' (i.e. *IHTA 1984*) whereas the relevant deeming provisions of *TCGA 1992, s 62* are by reference to 'this section'. On this view, confirmed by the former Inland Revenue Tax Bulletin February 1995, p 195, a variation or disclaimer would therefore for all inheritance tax purposes be deemed to be made by the deceased (e.g. for deciding whether settled property is **20.2** EXCLUDED PROPERTY).

Under Scots law there are certain circumstances in which a residuary legatee can make a partial disclaimer. Where this is possible HMRC accept that *IHTA 1984, s 142* applies. The same treatment may apply to partial disclaimers made under English law since they are thought to be valid where the part disclaimed is not onerous and either the legacy concerned is a pecuniary one or the will states expressly or by implication that partial disclaimers can be made (Tolley's Practical Tax 1994, pp 31 and 56).

See **49.15** TRANSFERS ON DEATH for other alterations of dispositions on death which are not transfers of value. For waiver of loans to be effected by deed, see **19.1** ESTATE.

Planning

[13.5] Under *FA 2004, s 84, Sch 15 para 16* relating to 'Pre-owned assets' provides that under *IHTA 1984, s 17* where beneficiaries of a deceased's estate agree between themselves to vary the will or the intestacy provisions then any party to the variation is not to be taxed as a former owner by reason of having had an interest under the original will or intestacy provisions. There was some doubt expressed whether the wording of *FA 2004, s 84, Sch 15 para 16* protected a widow/widower from a charge where an interest in possession in a house is taken but subsequently that interest in possession is terminated and occupation still continues. HMRC have confirmed in an exchange of correspondence with the CIOT that such situations will be excluded from charge:

> . . . all instruments of variation to which section 142(1) IHTA 1984 applies will come within the protection afforded by paragraph 16 of Schedule 15.

IHT/CGT charge on share transfers

The situation may arise where one spouse/civil partner may transfer shares to another spouse/civil partner on a nil gain/nil loss basis and the transferee spouse/civil partner dies sometime later leaving those same shares to the surviving spouse/civil partner with the attaching increased probate value unencumbered by the burden of an historic acquisition price, saving a substantial CGT charge and enjoying the benefit of the inter-spousal/civil partnership transfer exemption under *IHTA 1984, s 18*. However, if the transferee spouse/civil partner dies within days/weeks of the gift and the shares pass back by survivorship to the original donor then for transfer purposes the date of acquisition is the date of death and the surviving spouse's/civil partner's acquisition falls within the 30 days matching period for share disposals. [*TCGA 1992, s 106A(5)*]. This may give rise to a substantial CGT liability in the donor spouse's disposal computation. See example below.

Example 4

Wife W acquired 1,000 shares in Dido Ltd in June 1987 for £90,000. W gives her husband H the holding of shares on 1 August 2020. H then dies on 30 August 2020 leaving his estate to W. The shares are valued at that time to be £342,000 and are left to his wife along with all his other assets. The inter spouse exemption rules out any IHT charge but under the matching CGT rules for shares, the disposal on 1 August must be matched with the acquisition at the date of death on 30 August thereby negating any probate value uplift. Had H died one day later the shares would have been uplifted from the original cost of £90,000 (indexation no longer applying) to £342,000 with the opportunity for W to sell at that uplifted base value with little or no CGT.

In order to rectify this problem a deed of variation might be entered into by the parties; the deed of variation alters the late spouse's (H) will to create an interest in possession trust for the surviving spouse (W) enabling the trustees to pay capital to the surviving spouse. The deed of variation must be made before the shares are sold and within two years of the date of death. The result is that, even if the shares have been transferred to the surviving spouse, they will be treated as being acquired by the trustees at the value on death of the transferee spouse (H). [*TCGA 1992, s 62(1)*]. Subsequently the trustees make a capital appointment of the transfer of the shares to the surviving spouse (W) who acquires the shares at market value at the date of appointment and will not have reacquired them within 30 days of having given them to the late spouse thereby avoiding the matching rules. If the value of the shares has increased in the period between the date of death and appointment this may be covered by the annual CGT exemption or unused personal losses or there may be a loss to carry forward arising out of the appointment from the trust depending on the rise or fall in the market for those shares.

Rearrangement in contradiction of Testator's wishes

The beneficiaries of a will may decide amongst themselves to rearrange the distribution of the estate to effect different inheritance tax consequences by the use of a deed of variation or a disclaimer or by application to the Court either under the *Inheritance (Provision for Family and Dependants) Act 1975* or if they are *sui juris* under the *Variation of Trusts Act 1958*. See also Note (A) in the Example below. In this latter case the Court's consent which is embodied in a Court Order must be made within two years. In the case of *Goulding and Another v James and Another* [1997] 2 All ER 239 the rearrangement of the beneficial interests to take advantage of tax planning schemes was successful despite the testatrix's previous intentions that the assets should devolve to the beneficiaries in another way. Such was the rearrangement that not only did it rearrange the division of the assets in contradiction of the testatrix's wishes but that there was also the subsidiary insertion of a tax planning scheme for the management of the funds. Note that in *Glowacki's Personal Representatives v HMRC* [2008] STC SCD 188 Sp C 631 the Commissioner held that *IHTA 1984, s 142* 'cannot operate to remove property from a person's estate so that it is no longer part of the estate subject to the deemed transfer of value on death under *s 4*. What *s 142* must vary is the destination of the estate on its deemed transfer under *s 4*'.

Legacy to charity

In a Special Commissioners case a deed of variation redirecting a legacy to a charity was claimed as a gift by the original beneficiary eligible for gift aid relief for income tax purposes because the *FA 1990, s 25(2)(a)(e)* provisions for relief were met—this was disputed by the Inspector of Taxes. Also the transfer of value arising from the deed of variation was exempt from inheritance tax to the extent that the value transferred was attributable to property which is given to charities. [*IHTA 1984, s 23(1)*]. In this particular case the legacy of £20,000 to the charity, who had renounced probate and the deceased's son had applied for a Grant of Letters of Administration, was payable out of the property bequeathed to the son, W. The terms of the will were that the residue was to be held in trust for the son, W. By effecting the deed of variation and reducing the inheritance tax by £8,000 (i.e. £20,000 @ 40%) the residue of the estate was £8,000 more than it would have been had the gift to the charity been made without taking advantage of *IHTA 1984, s 142*. As sole residuary beneficiary W ultimately benefited from the inheritance tax saving notwithstanding that the residue available to W had been reduced by £12,000. The charity's position remained unaffected in that it claimed repayment of tax from HMRC of £6,666.67 being the tax withheld at basic rate on the gift although the charity's appeal against the former Inland Revenue's assessment to recover this amount was dismissed. W therefore was by the timeous election under *s 142* able to redirect a legacy to the charity claiming gift aid relief for income tax purposes and relief for charitable donations under *IHTA 1984, s 23*. It is thought that if it can be arranged for the inheritance tax to accrue to a third party, or to be added to the gift to the charity, the scheme should succeed. See *St Dunstans v Major* [1997] STC SCD 212 Sp C 127 and **10.3** CHARITIES.

Breach of duty

On another matter, the fact that a solicitor failed to advise a testatrix of the possibility of executing a deed of arrangement under *s 142* and, on the testatrix's death, advising her residuary beneficiaries of the contents of the will in time for them to effect an election under that section; it was held by the court not to be a breach of duty in not advising the testatrix about the tax avoidance schemes of another estate and also the executor owed no duty to inform a legatee that there was a prospective legacy. Accordingly in this case there was no obligation on the executor to advise of the possibility of tax mitigation by way of *IHTA 1984, s 142*. However, a duty of care to an intended beneficiary is clear from Lord Nolan's dictum in *White v Jones* [1995] 1 All ER 691 and this might extend to advising a beneficiary of circumstances that might jeopardise a claim being submitted under *s 142* (see *Cancer Research Campaign v Ernest Brown & Co*, Ch D [1997] STC 1425).

Variations involving a life interest

In drawing up an Instrument of Variation, an interest in a will should be distinguished between an absolute one or a life interest only. In the case of an absolute interest passed on to the survivor who in turn dies, the property passed on subsists in the donee's estate and it is possible for those inheriting on the second death to redirect the estate of the first person to die provided the second death is within two years of the first death. Contrast this with the position where the survivor is given a life interest in property on the first death that interest expires on the death of the life tenant and there is no property capable of disposition. Therefore where there is a life tenancy comprising part of an estate and that person dies, then as the variation is made after the death of the life tenant, at that time there is no interest in existence and hence no opportunity to redirect. In such a case a variation to assign a life interest might be considered. See *Soutter's Executry v CIR* [2002] STC SCD 385 Sp C 325 above and example below.

Example 5

H dies on 31 August 2019 leaving an estate comprising farmland to his widow for life and thereafter to his two adult sons if they survive her, with substitution provisions in favour of grandchildren (those in existence being minors). The estate is non-chargeable because of the inter-spousal exemption but there is a potential problem that if the widow dies in excess of two years after the death of the husband, there can be no variation of the husband's estate even if that proves to be beneficial to gain the benefit of APR on the farmland. The widow can, however, vary her life interest in favour of her sons to ensure that they benefit from any available APR. The widow's personal representatives will in due course be able to claim some or the entire transferable nil rate band of H which is unutilised.

THIS DEED OF VARIATION is made. . . . . 2020.

BETWEEN

1.	"the Mother"	Namely. . . . . . . of. . . . .
2.	"the Sons"	Namely. . . . . of. . . . . .
		Namely. . . . . of. . . . . .
3.	"the Executors"	Namely:
		(1). . . . . of . . . .
		(2). . . . . of . . . .
		(3). . . . . of . . . .

WHEREAS

(A) . . . . of. . . . . ('the father') died on . . . . [2019]

(B) The Father's will dated . . . . ('the Will') appointed Executors to be executors and trustees of his estate.

(C) The Executors obtained probate of the Will from the [. . . . .] District Probate Registry on . . . . [2019]

(D) Under the Will the Mother is by Clause 3 entitled to the net income of the residuary estate for the remainder of her life ('her Life Interest')

(E) The property detailed in the schedule ('the Property') is comprised of the residuary estate of the Testator

(F) The Mother wishes to vary the dispositions of the Will as follows:

NOW THIS DEED WITNESSES

(1) The Will shall be deemed to read and always to have read (so far as on account of the contingent remainders such is possible) as if the Property has been left (subject to tax) to the sons as tenants in common in equal shares absolutely

(2) In furtherance of clause 1 the Mother assigns to the Sons her Life Interest to the extent of the Property (and no more) to hold the same unto themselves as tenants in common in equal shares absolutely

(3) The parties elect for [section 142 of the Inheritance Tax Act 1984] and [section 62 of the Taxation of Chargeable Gains Act 1992] as amended by Finance Act 2002, section 120 and/or section 52 to apply to this deed.

EXECUTED AS A DEED on the day and year first above written

the Schedule

. . . . and . . . . being

end of the Schedule

SIGNED etc.

Notes to the example

(A) A variation to give an immediate absolute entitlement to the land is not possible as the consents of the minors and unborns are unavailable. It should be remembered that where any potential beneficiaries are minors, or are otherwise *sui juris*, it will be necessary for any variation to be approved on their behalf by the courts. This could include unborn children if the wording of the will is wide-ranging. Even though HMRC will normally accept that a woman who is aged over 55 is past child-bearing age this is not necessarily true in practice. [*Variation of Trusts Act 1958; Trusts (Scotland) Act 1961*].

(B) Pending the mother's death title to the land would remain in the trustees unless some arrangement were reached between the trustees and the sons to transfer title on a protected basis.

14

Determinations and Appeals

Cross-reference. See 3 ADMINISTRATION AND COLLECTION.

Simon's Taxes. See A3.7, A5.3, A5.6, I11.301–I11.315, I11.373.

Other Sources. Foster, Part L3; IHTM37000.

Introduction to determinations and appeals

[14.1] Although IHT assessments are issued by HMRC, these are no more than calculations of the tax due and requests for payment. Appeals are not made against an assessment, but instead any points of disagreement are raised in correspondence in reply to the assessment received. The starting point with an appeal in relation to IHT liability will be the issue of a determination by HMRC. Once that has been issued, the taxpayer may enter an appeal against it and either request a review or notify the appeal to the Tax Tribunals. The tax in dispute will not be collected once the appeal to the Tribunal has been made and it is not necessary to make application for postponement of payment as is the case with other direct tax appeals. However, interest will be running and a deposit of tax may be made to stop the interest accruing thereafter. Appellants should expect the appeal process to be time consuming and arduous. There are long delays due to the volume of tax appeals and HMRC may adopt an adversarial stance from the outset, not just at the hearing itself which is obviously to be expected, but also in the preliminary steps of putting together document bundles and a statement of agreed facts.

Notice of determination

[14.2] Where it appears to the Board that a transfer of value has been made (or a claim received in respect of such a transfer), it may issue a notice in writing to any person who appears to be the transferor, the claimant or to be liable for any of the tax chargeable stating that they have determined the matters specified in the notice. The matters are all or any of:

(a) the date of the transfer;
(b) the value transferred and the value of any property to which the value transferred is wholly or partly attributable;
(c) the transferor;
(d) the tax chargeable and the persons who are liable to pay it;
(e) the amount of any payment made in excess of the tax for which a person is liable and the date from which, and the rate at which, tax or any repayment of tax overpaid carries interest; and
(f) any other matter that appears to the Board to be relevant.

This also applies to occasions on which tax is chargeable under the rules in *IHTA 1984, Pt III, Ch III* relating to 40 SETTLEMENTS: DISCRETIONARY TRUSTS AND OTHER TRUSTS OF RELEVANT PROPERTY, to events or occasions on which tax is chargeable under *IHTA 1984, s 32* or *s 32A* on conditionally exempt 30 NATIONAL HERITAGE property and to disposals of growing timber (see 54 WOODLANDS) left out of account on a previous death which gives rise to a charge under *IHTA 1984, s 126*.

The notice of determination will be based on any account or return which the Board are satisfied is correct or, otherwise, will be made according to the Board's best judgment. The notice must state the time and manner in which an appeal may be made. See *Two Settlors v CIR* [2004] STC SCD 45 Sp C 385; *Thomson (Thomson's Executor) v CIR* [2004] STC SCD 520 Sp C 429.

[*IHTA 1984, s 221(1)–(4)(6); FA 1985, Sch 26 para 5; The Transfer of Tribunal Functions and Revenue and Customs Appeals Order 2009, SI 2009/56, paras 120, 121*].

Conclusive nature of determination

[14.3] Subject to any variation agreed in writing or on appeal or later adjustments for underpaid or overpaid tax, a notice of determination is conclusive against the person on whom it is served. If it is served on the transferor and specifies the value of the transfer, or earlier transfers, it is also conclusive in respect of later transfers of value (whether or not made by the transferor) against any other person. [*IHTA 1984, s 221(5)*].

For all matters relating to the administration and collection of IHT, a notice of determination which can no longer be varied or quashed on appeal is sufficient evidence of the matters so determined. [*IHTA 1984, s 254(1)*].

Appeals against determinations

Review and Appeal to the Tax Tribunals

[14.4] An appeal may be made against a notice of determination within 30 days of its service, stating the grounds for it. See *Jacques v HMRC* [2006] STC SCD 40 Sp C 513 in which an appeal was struck out because the appellant refused to state the grounds on which it was made. The legislation provides for the appeal to be given to 'the Board' being the Commissioners of Inland Revenue, but in practical terms it will be sent to HMRC in reply to the correspondence giving the determination. Where an appeal is made, there is a statutory right given to the appellant to require HMRC to review 'the matter in question', being defined by as the matter to which an appeal relates. In practice, the notification requiring a review will usually be given by the agent acting for the appellant and that will be accepted by HMRC. If the appellant chooses to have a review, it is important not to put in an appeal to the Tax Tribunal at that stage because that prevents any review from going ahead [*IHTA 1984, s 223B*].

HMRC must then notify the appellant of their conclusions following the review within 45 days of the day on which notification is received by HMRC requiring the review, assuming that HMRC made the offer of a review (which will their normal procedure). Alternatively, the 45 days runs from the day on which HMRC gave their view of the matter. [*IHTA 1984, s 223E*].

Although the general experience is that any review upholds the view already given by HMRC, there is little to be lost by requiring it as there is always the chance that a different conclusion will be reached. After the review, if the appellant is not satisfied with the conclusion reached, the appeal may then be sent to the Tax Tribunal. The Notice of Appeal to the Tribunal, reproduced later in this chapter, is completed by the taxpayer and sent direct to the Tax Tribunals Service.

The First-tier Tax Tribunal will generally hear appeals (but see **14.5** and **14.6** below for exceptions) and their decision is final except on a point of law (but see *Edwards v Bairstow and Harrison* HL 1955, 36 TC 207 as a leading case on jurisdiction of court on questions of fact) and they may confirm, vary or quash the determination appealed against. [*IHTA 1984, ss 222(1)(2), 224(5); Transfer of Tribunal Functions and Revenue and Customs Appeals Order 2009, SI 2009/56, para 115*].

On an appeal before the Tribunal, they may allow the appellant to put forward any ground of appeal not specified in the notice of appeal and may take it into consideration if satisfied that the omission was not wilful or unreasonable. From 1 April 2009, if an appeal is notified to the Tribunal it must confirm the determination appealed against (or that determination as varied on a review under *s 223E*) unless the Tribunal is satisfied that it ought to be varied (or further varied) or quashed. [*IHTA 1984, s 224(4); Transfer of Tribunal Functions and Revenue and Customs Appeals Order 2009, SI 2009/56, para 118*]. See IHT 14, p 21.

Appeal direct to High Court

[14.5] An appeal may be made direct to the High Court (or Court of Session in Scotland and Court of Appeal in Northern Ireland) if the appellant and the Board agree. If the Board does not agree, the High Court may, on application by the appellant, give leave for appeal direct to that Court if it is satisfied the matters to be decided are likely to be substantially confined to questions of law. [*IHTA 1984, s 222(3)(5)*]. In these circumstances, the High Court has the same powers to confirm, vary or quash a determination of the Board as the Special Commissioners would have had if the appeal had gone first to them. (*Jon Ernst & Cie SA v CIR* Ch D 1979, [1979] STC 478).

In *Bennett v CIR* Ch D 1994, [1995] STC 54, it was stated that whilst a precondition of the grant of leave is that the appeal is substantially confined to questions of law there will be instances where the case's 'novelty or importance or otherwise' is such that it can and should proceed to the High Court in the interests of justice.

Appeal to Lands Tribunal [now part of the Upper Tribunal]

[14.6] From 1 June 2009, the Lands Tribunal has transferred to the Upper Tribunal, it is now the Lands Chamber of the Upper Tribunal. If and so far as the question in dispute on any appeal under this section which has been notified to the Upper Tribunal or the High Court is a question as to the value of land in the United Kingdom, the question shall be determined on a reference to the appropriate Lands Chamber. Appeal may be [notified] to the High Court, on an application made by the appellant, where the Board is satisfied that the matters to be decided on the appeal are likely to be substantially confined to questions of law and gives leave for that purpose. See *Prosser (personal representatives of Jempson deceased) v CIR* [2003] STC SCD 250 Sp C 362. Guidance on property valuations for IHT purposes may be obtained from the Royal Institution of Chartered Surveyors (RICS) in the form of their leaflet GN21. See also HMRC Tax Bulletin Issue 63 'Guidance on Property Valuations'. [*IHTA 1984, s 222(4)–(4B); FA 1993, s 200(1)(3); Transfer of Tribunal Functions and Revenue and Customs Appeals Order 2009, SI 2009/56, para 115; Transfer of Tribunal Functions (Lands Tribunal and Miscellaneous Amendment) Order 2009, SI 2009/1307, Sch 1 para 167*]. The Tribunal may be required to state a case for the Court of Appeal or the Court of Session in Scotland. [*Lands Tribunal Rules SI 1963/483*].

Late appeals

[14.7] A late appeal may be accepted by the Board. The Board must consent to the appeal if satisfied there was reasonable excuse for the delay and that the application was made thereafter without unreasonable delay. If HMRC do not agree to allow the late appeal, the taxpayer may refer the matter to the Tax Tribunal. [*IHTM 37101; IHTA 1984, s 223*].

'Leapfrog' procedures

[14.8] See **14.5** above for appeal direct to the High Court. It is also possible to bypass the Court of Appeal and to appeal direct from the High Court to the House of Lords in certain cases where the appeal concerns a point of law of general public importance. [*Administration of Justice Act 1969, Pt II*].

Tribunals

First-tier Tribunal

[14.9] The Tax Chamber of the Tribunals Service has its own judiciary, Rules of Procedure and a new location for processing direct tax appeals. It is independent of HMRC and appeals are sent direct to HM Courts and Tribunals Service, First-tier Tribunal (Tax Chamber), PO Box 16972, Birmingham, B16 6TZ and that office notifies HMRC of the appeal. A Notice of Appeal, reproduced in this chapter, form can be accessed on the website at https://appeal-tax-tribunal.service.gov.uk/appeal. An appeal may be withdrawn at any time before the hearing. There are a network of hearing centres across the country and the facility for additional hired venues. In cases of Complex hearings there will be limited locations for hearings.

There are four procedural tracks depending on the complexity of the appeal.

Upper Tribunal

The route of appeal from the First-tier will be to the Upper Tribunal, which is a superior court of record similar to the High Court. Appeal to the Upper Tribunal will be on a point of law only, and with permission of the First-tier or the Upper Tribunal. The exception to this will be those extremely rare cases which start in the Upper Tribunal, where onward appeals will be to the Court of Appeal or the Court of Sessions in Scotland.

Tribunal Procedure Committee (TPC)

The Tribunal Procedure Committee (TPC) have set out a number of rules that govern the operation of the Tribunal system as well as specific rules for the area of taxation. Invariably many appeals including most IHT appeals against HMRC decisions will be, in the first instance, to the First-tier Tribunal. The initial appeal against a decision by HMRC will have been to them within 30 days of their decision and then failed to agree or asked for a review (*The Tribunal Procedure (First-tier Tribunal)(Tax Chamber) Rules 2009, SI 2009/273, rules 25 and 26*). Where an appeal is being made against the decision by HMRC, it will be made in writing to the Tax Tribunal situated in Birmingham within 30 days of receiving the reviewing officer's decision letter. The Tax Tribunal will then manage the case by liaising with the parties to the dispute. Appeals should be notified to the Tribunal online at www.gov.uk/tax-tribunal/appeal-to-tribunal; by e-mail to taxappeals@justice.gov.ukor by post to the HM Courts and Tribunals Service, First-tier Tribunal (Tax Chamber), PO Box 16972, Birmingham B16 6TZ. A Notice of Appeal form (T240) can be downloaded from www.gov.uk/government/publications/notice-of-appeal-ask-a-tax-judge-to-examine-a-dispute-form-t240 or obtained from the Tribunals Service by phoning 0300 123 1024. [*IHTA 1984, s 223A–I; Transfer of Tribunal Functions and Revenue and Customs Appeals Order 2009, SI 2009/56, paras 116, 117*].

Categories of appeals

Once the appeal has been received by the Tax Tribunal it will be allocated to one of four case categories (*The Tribunal Procedure (First-tier Tribunal) (Tax Chamber) Rules 2009, SI 2009/273, rule 23*) i.e. default paper, basic, standard and complex. The category of default will be decided on written evidence submitted and HMRC's Statement of case and an oral hearing may be requested and any decision may be listed for hearing if the decision is not agreed. Detailed information on the default paper process is issued on form ARTG8370.

A basic appeal may be one which involves a penalty for an incorrect return. The taxpayer who appeals against the imposition of a penalty is not required to pay any penalty before a penalty appeal has been determined. The Tribunal may substitute its own decision for that of HMRC and if it does so, it may rely on the use of the special reduction for certain circumstances to which HMRC have recourse. If the Tribunal considers the decision by HMRC on the special reduction is flawed then the Tribunal may substitute its own decision. [*FA 2009, Sch 56 paras 13–15*]. See also **33.2** PENALTIES.

Hearings procedure

Information on the basic process is at ARTG8350 and subsequent paragraphs. Basic cases are listed for a relatively informal hearing within the broader Tribunals Service. The Tribunals Service will be able to arrange hearings in local hired venues, in the courts estate or arrange video conferencing on the basis of post code as given on the notice of appeal. The hearings will normally be listed for a morning (10.00am) or an afternoon session (2.00pm) in a Tribunals hearing centre, with other tax cases (Basic or default paper).

A standard appeal will cover most contentious appeal cases that do not come within the default and basic categories. It is likely that a majority of IHT appeals will come into this category. HMRC will provide a Statement of case within 60 days of being notified by the Tax Tribunal. At this stage, the parties then have 42 days to provide a list of papers which will be relied upon at the hearing. Decisions will normally be made in writing to the parties but may be made on the day of the hearing.

Complex cases usually involve lengthy and involved issues or large amounts of tax and are likely to be heard in the first instance by the Upper Tribunal. HMRC will provide a Statement of case within 60 days of being notified by the Tax Tribunal. At this stage, the parties then have 42 days to provide a list of papers which will be relied upon at the hearing (*The Tribunal Procedure (First-tier Tribunal) (Tax Chamber) Rules 2009, SI 2009/273, rules 25 and 27*). Decisions will normally be made in writing to the parties but may be made on the day of the hearing.

As regards costs, there will be no awards in the First-tier Tribunal except where either side has acted unreasonably or the case is a complex one. Costs can be awarded in complex cases though the appellant (not HMRC) can opt out of this before the hearing. In contrast, the Upper Tribunal will have a full costs regime. Hearings are normally held in public and only in rare cases will the Tribunal agree to a private hearing, these being where this is justified in the interests of public order, national security, or to protect confidentiality of sensitive information. The fact that the taxpayer is well-known will not be relevant to a request for a private hearing, nor to a request for an anonymised decision.

Point of law appeal

If HMRC, the appellant or another party to the proceedings think that the Tribunal's decision is wrong on a point of law, then an appeal may be made to the Upper Tribunal. At this stage, the tax in dispute must, if that is not already the case, be paid. If the appellant is successful, the amount will be repaid. A refusal of appeal by the First-tier Tribunal must be accompanied by an explanation why and an option to have the rejection reviewed by the Upper Tribunal. Costs may be awarded to the other party to the appeal where it was considered that one party had acted 'unreasonably' or the case was within the complex (*The Tribunal Procedure (First-tier Tribunal) (Tax Chamber) Rules 2009, SI 2009/273, rule 10*). A party may opt out of the costs within 28 days of the case being categorised (*The Tribunal Procedure (First-tier Tribunal) (Tax Chamber) Rules 2009, SI 2009/273, rule 10 para 1*). Therefore in most cases that are Default paper, Basic or Standard will have no costs rule attaching.

Judicial review

[14.10] A taxpayer who is dissatisfied with the exercise of administrative powers may in certain circumstances (e.g. where HMRC have exceeded or abused their powers or acted contrary to the rules of natural justice or where the Special Commissioners have acted unfairly or improperly) seek a remedy in one of the prerogative orders of mandamus, prohibition or certiorari. This is now done by way of application for judicial review under *Supreme Court Act 1981, s 31* and *Order 53* of the *Rules of the Supreme Court.*

There was held to have been no unfairness in two cases where the former Inland Revenue resiled from assurances given by its officers as to its course of action to be taken in regard to intended transactions put to it in 'advance clearance' form by the taxpayer where the latter, having received the assurances, subsequently entered into actual transactions similar to those envisaged in the request for clearance. In order to bind HMRC to any such assurances, it would seem necessary not only to make complete, clear, correct and unqualified representations of the circumstances in a written request and subsequently enter into actual transactions on all fours with those envisaged in the request but to ensure that request is sent to the appropriate HMRC officer or office (*R v CIR (ex p MFK Underwriting Agencies Ltd & Others)* QB 1989, 62 TC 607; *Matrix-Securities Ltd v CIR* HL, [1994] STC 272). See further Revenue Tax Bulletin August 1994, p 137.

The first step is to obtain leave to apply for judicial review from the High Court. Application for leave is made ex parte to a single judge who will usually determine the application without a hearing. The Court will not grant leave unless the applicant has a sufficient interest in the matter to which the application relates. See *CIR v National Federation of Self-employed and Small Businesses Ltd* HL 1981, 55 TC 133 for what is meant by 'sufficient interest' and for discussion of availability of judicial review generally.

Applications must be made within three months of the date when the grounds for application arose. The Court has discretion to extend this time limit where there is good reason, subject to conditions, but is generally very reluctant to do so. Grant of leave to apply for review does not amount to a ruling that application was made in good time (*R v Tavistock Commrs (ex p Worth)* QB 1985, 59 TC 116).

Parliamentary history of legislation

[14.11] Following the decision in *Pepper v Hart* HL, [1992] STC 898, the Courts are prepared to consider the parliamentary history of legislation, or the official report of debates in Hansard, where all of the following conditions are met.

(i) Legislation is ambiguous or obscure, or leads to an absurdity.

(ii) The material relied upon consists of one or more statements by a Minister or other promoter of the Bill together if necessary with such other parliamentary material as is necessary to understand such statements and their effect.

(iii) The statements relied upon are clear.

15

Diplomatic Immunity

Simon's Taxes. See I9.327.

Introduction to diplomatic immunity

[15.1] Diplomatic agents (i.e. heads of mission or members of diplomatic staff) of foreign states are exempt from all duties and tax except, *inter alia*, taxes on:

(a) private immovable property situated in the UK;
(b) capital taxes on investments made in commercial undertakings in the UK; and
(c) 'estate, succession or inheritance duties' on property in the UK except on movable property which is in the UK solely due to the presence of the deceased as a member of the mission or as a member of the family of a member of the mission. [*Diplomatic Privileges Act 1964, s 2*].

Head of mission

The head of a diplomatic mission will normally supply the Foreign and Commonwealth Office with a list of the staff of the mission etc. and, once such persons have been accepted as *persona grata*, exemption from liability will apply where appropriate. See The London Diplomatic List, December 2009. Any question which arises as to whether a person is entitled to privilege or immunity is to be settled conclusively by a certificate issued by or under the authority of the Secretary of State. [*DPA 1964, s 4; ITA 2007, s 841*]. See also IHTM11270.

Diplomatic family members

Relief is extended to members of the families of diplomatic agents (provided they are not UK nationals) and members of the administrative and technical staff of the mission, together with their families (provided they are not nationals or permanent residents in the UK).

OECD treaty models

In interpreting inheritance tax and estate treaties between the UK and any other country consideration should be given as to whether the treaty was based on the OECD 1966 Estate Tax Draft Model or the OECD 1982 Estate Tax Model.

This is because when interpreting certain terms in a treaty, either based on the 1966 Model or the 1982 Model, the 1982 version had a close relationship in application terms to the 1977 OECD Income Tax Model. Commentaries on the articles will vary significantly depending on the original model that was used. In the case of diplomatic and consular officials the 1982 Model refers to them in *Art 13*, whereas the 1966 Model refers to them in *Art 14*. *Article 13* of the 1982 Model convention provides that the convention does not affect the fiscal privileges of diplomatic agents or consular officials under the general rules of international law or under *special agreements*.

Consular officers, their families and staff

[15.2] Similar provisions apply as to diplomatic agents except that the *Consular Relations Act 1968, Arts 49, 51* expressly exclude from exemption 'duties on transfers' unless on movable property belonging to a deceased and in the UK solely because of his presence as a member of the consular post etc.

A *member of a consular post* means a consular officer, a consular employee or a member of the service staff. A *consular officer* means the person charged with the duty of acting as head of a consular post and any other person entrusted with the exercise of consular functions. A *consular employee* means any person employed in the administrative or technical service of a consular post; and a *member of the service staff* means any person employed in the domestic service of the consular post. [*CRA 1968, Sch 1 para 1*].

Officials of international organisations

Officials of international organisations including representatives, members of committees or missions etc. may be specified by Order in Council as exempt from certain taxes. [*International Organisations Act 1968; Arms Control and Disarmament (Privileges and Immunities) Act 1988, s 1(2)*]. The position of **officials etc. of the European Communities** is covered by the *Protocol on the Privileges and Immunities of the European Communities 1965*. [*European Communities Act 1972*].

16

Domicile

Cross-reference. See **18** DOUBLE TAXATION RELIEF.

Simon's Taxes. See **I9.201–I9.206.**

Other Sources. Tolley's Tax Planning; Foster, Part J2; HMRC publication HMRC6 and 17 April 2002 Treasury Budget Report; HMRC Customer Guide to Inheritance Tax; IHTM13000.

Introduction to domicile

[16.1] Chargeability to UK inheritance tax depends on where a person is domiciled or 'deemed' to be domiciled, this fundamental point having been brought forward from capital transfer tax and before that estate duty dating back to its introduction in 1894. In the majority of cases, it is quite clear where a person is domiciled but inevitably cases of dispute do arise and it can then require detailed research into the person's family history. In addition, where a person with a UK domicile of origin moves abroad, the question then arises as to whether or not he or she has replaced the UK domicile with a domicile of choice elsewhere. Forming conclusions in these cases can be exceedingly difficult and there is no mechanism for obtaining a ruling on the matter, nor agreeing the position with HMRC (see the decision in *Stuart Gulliver* [2017] UKFTT 222 (TC) where a previous agreement with HMRC on the taxpayer's domicile was held to be non-binding in relation to a subsequent tax enquiry). The announcement as part of the 2024 Budget that from April 2025 domicile would cease to be relevant for IHT purposes and instead liability would be based upon long-term residence for tax purposes should therefore be welcomed despite the anomalies which it can produce in certain cases. There appears to be political consensus for this major reform and it is therefore expected to be implemented notwithstanding any change of government. See **23** INHERITANCE TAX PLANNING for potential planning in 2024/25 ahead of the anticipated new regime.

Under the current regime, if a person is domiciled or deemed domiciled in the UK that person is liable to IHT on their worldwide assets wherever situated. Also, those individuals who are *not* domiciled in the UK are nonetheless liable to IHT on assets situated in the UK, or in relation to structures to hold UK residential property treated in the same manner as assets situated in the UK.

A person must be domiciled in a single legal jurisdiction, for example, either England, Scotland or Northern Ireland, or one of the states comprising the United States of America. There are a number of specific classes of UK domicile as follows:

(i) domicile of origin;
(ii) domicile of dependency;
(iii) domicile of choice; and
(iv) deemed domicile.

Every person receives at birth a *domicile of origin*. A legitimate child born in the lifetime of his or her father has the father's domicile at the time of their birth and that is determined by the father's permanent homeland; in other cases the domicile of origin is that of the mother at the time of the child's birth. A child may in certain circumstances take the domicile of the mother up until the age of sixteen. See **16.3** below. *Domicile of dependency* occurs where, say, a father (or mother in circumstances in **16.3** below) changes their domicile before the child has attained the age of sixteen and consequently the child's domicile changes with that of the father (or mother). *Domicile of choice* can arise where a person is sixteen or over and takes up residence in a new jurisdiction with the intention of fixing his sole or chief residence there permanently or indefinitely. Strong evidence is required for a change of a person's domicile of origin to that of choice and convincing steps must be taken to show a different country has become their homeland and all ties with the UK have been severed. See *Gaines Cooper v HMRC* [2008] STC 1665 and the Supreme Court refused Gaines Cooper's application for leave to appeal, so the CA decision is now final. Where a domicile of choice is abandoned, the domicile of origin automatically revives.

Up to 5 April 2017 *deemed domicile* applies for UK IHT purposes where a person has been resident in the UK for 17 out of the last 20 tax years but see **16.5** below for new rules to take effect from 6 April 2017 and for cases where a person has been UK domiciled within the preceding three *calendar* years. This latter case is likely to apply where a person has changed their UK domicile status to one of choice but will still be within the IHT net for that period. In future HMRC will consider opening an enquiry where domicile could be an issue, or making a determination of Inheritance Tax in such cases, only where there is a significant risk of loss of UK tax.

General case law

[16.2] A person may have only one place of domicile at any given time denoting the country or state considered his permanent home. He acquires a *domicile of origin* at birth (normally that of his father). It may be changed to a *domicile of choice*, but this must be proved by subsequent conduct. See *Re Clore (deceased) (No 2), Official Solicitor v Clore and Others* Ch D, [1984]

STC 609 for a case where English domicile of origin was retained as a result of failure to establish a settled intention to reside permanently in Monaco. Actual settlement abroad is necessary as well as intention; see *Plummer v CIR* Ch D, [1987] STC 698. If a domicile of choice is established but later abandoned (by actual action, not by intention or declaration only, see *Faye v CIR* Ch D 1961, 40 TC 103) reversion to domicile of origin is automatic as recently confirmed in *Barlow Clowes International Ltd (in liquidation) and Others v Henwood* [2008] EWCA Civ 577. A case of this was *Civil Engineer v CIR* [2002] STC (SCD) 72 where the abandonment of a Hong Kong domicile of choice, thereby reviving a UK domicile, resulted in a chargeable transfer in respect of the setting up of a discretionary trust in the interim that relied on the taxpayer's perception that he was non–UK domiciled. See also *Anderson (Anderson's Executor) v CIR* [1997] 1998 STC SCD 43 Sp C 147 in which a domicile of choice of England in place of Scotland (origin) suggested by HMRC failed due to the insufficient persuasive elements of the abandonment of Mr Anderson's roots in Scotland. See *Allen & Hateley (executors of Johnson) v HMRC* [2005] STC SCD 614 Sp C 481 where the Special Commissioners determined whether a person of UK origin had lost her domicile of choice in Spain by coming to reside in England in order to be cared for by a relative (domicile held not to have been lost). In *Gulliver v HMRC* [2017] UKFTT 222 (TC), it was held that a previous specific agreement by HMRC that the taxpayer had acquired a domicile of choice in Hong Kong did prevent HMRC from contending, in relation to a later tax year, that he had never acquired any such domicile of choice. In *Henkes v HMRC* [2020] UKFTT 00159 (TC), the taxpayer, who was 75, maintained that he had not settled permanently or indefinitely in the UK despite residing here for early 50 years and would leave the UK on retiring, although he had no plans to end work. It was held that he had acquired a UK domicile of choice.

Domicile is a concept of private international law and does not correspond with either residence or nationality. See *Earl of Iveagh v Revenue Commissioners* SC (RI), [1930] IR 431; *Fielden v CIR* Ch D 1965, 42 TC 501 and *CIR v Cohen* KB 1937, 21 TC 301. This last case shows how difficult it is to displace a *domicile of origin* by a *domicile of choice* but contrast *In re Lawton* Ch D 1958, 37 ATC 216. See also *In re Wallach* PDA 1949, 28 ATC 486, *Buswell v CIR* CA 1974, 49 TC 334, *Steiner v CIR* CA 1973, 49 TC 13, *CIR v Bullock* CA 1976, 51 TC 522 and *In re Furse decd., Furse v CIR* Ch D, [1980] STC 597; *A Beneficiary v CIR* [1999] STC SCD 134 Sp C 190; *Moore's Executors v CIR* [2002] Sp C 335.

Minors

[16.3] The domicile of a minor normally follows that of the person on whom he is legally dependent. Under *Domicile and Matrimonial Proceedings Act 1973, s 3* (which does not extend to Scotland), a person first becomes capable of having an independent domicile when he attains 16 or marries under that age. Under *s 4* thereof, where a child's father and mother are alive but living apart, his domicile is that of his mother if he has his home with her and has no home with his father. For Scotland, see *Family Law (Scotland) Act 2006, s 22* by which where the parents of a child are domiciled in the same country and the child has a home with a parent or a home with both of them, up to the age of 16 the child's domicile is the same as that of the parents. Otherwise the child is domiciled in the country with which he or she has the closest connection.

Married women

[16.4] Up to 31 December 1973, a woman automatically acquired the domicile of her husband on marriage. From 1 January 1974 onwards, the domicile of a married woman is to be ascertained 'by reference to the same factors as in the case of any other individual capable of having an independent domicile' except that a woman already married on that date will retain her husband's domicile until it is changed by acquisition or revival of another domicile. [*Domicile and Matrimonial Proceedings Act 1973, ss 1, 17(5)*]. A woman married before 1974 does not reacquire her domicile of origin and retains her husband's domicile unless she subsequently establishes her own domicile of choice. See *CIR v Duchess of Portland* Ch D 1981, 54 TC 648 and Form D31 of IHT 100. In the House of Lords decision involving a matrimonial case *Mark v Mark* HL, [2005] UKHL 42 it was decided that the legality of a wife's presence in the UK was irrelevant when considering her domicile of choice within *Domicile and Matrimonial Proceedings Act 1973, s 5(2)* and therefore it was held that it is possible for someone who is present in the UK illegally to have a domicile of choice in the UK.

Deemed domicile for IHT

[16.5] For the purposes of IHT only, an individual may be treated as domiciled in the UK at a time (the 'relevant time') when he is domiciled abroad under general law. From 6 April 2017, this applies where:

(a) he was domiciled (under general law) in the UK at any time during the three years immediately preceding the relevant time;
(b) he is a formerly domiciled resident (see below) for the tax year in which the relevant time falls; or
(c) he was resident (see below) in the UK in not less than 15 of the 20 tax years (i.e. years ending on 5 April) immediately preceding the relevant tax year and for at least one of the four tax years ending with the relevant year; or
(d) the terms of a double tax treaty do not operate to override this rule (see below under 'double tax agreements').

But (c) above does not apply if a person is not resident in the UK for the relevant tax year and has not been in any tax year beginning after 5 April 2017. This assists those who would become deemed domiciled in 2017/18 but left the UK before 6 April 2017.

A formerly domiciled resident is an individual who was born in the UK, whose domicile of origin is in the UK, who is UK resident for the tax year and was UK resident for at least one of the two preceding tax years. As a result, those who were born in the UK and have a UK domicile of origin but who have acquired a domicile of choice elsewhere will be treated as UK domiciled if they return to live in the UK for more than one tax year. The excluded property trust rules for IHT are also changed so that they do not apply during the period of time that such a person is UK resident. This will be the case even for trusts that are set up offshore while the individual was not domiciled or resident in the UK (and would therefore be excluded property for IHT purposes under the current rules).

For the years up to 2016/17, the deemed domicile rule at (c) above was that the individual was resident in the UK in not less than 17 of the 20 years of assessment ending with the year of assessment in which the relevant time fell. The above 15 out of 20 years test is different, therefore, in that it counts the years preceding the relevant tax year, and not up to and including it as before. Also, up to 5 April 2017, deemed domicile did not apply to a person who had not been UK domiciled at any time since 9 December 1974; this no longer applies after 5 April 2017. [*IHTA 1984, s 267(1)*].

In the circumstances regarding the taxation of 'pre-owned' assets within *FA 2004, s 84, Sch 15* 'domicile' for the purposes of the scope of the charge, includes deemed domicile within *IHTA 1984, s 267*, so that such treatment will include UK and, in some circumstances, overseas property. [*FA 2004, Sch 15 para 12*].

Exclusions

The above provisions do not apply:

(i) in determining whether exempt government securities which are in the beneficial ownership of a non-domiciled person (or are settled property to which such a person is entitled to a qualifying interest in possession) are excluded property, see **20.5** EXCLUDED PROPERTY;
(ii) in determining whether certain savings to which persons domiciled in the Channel Islands or Isle of Man are beneficially entitled are excluded property, see **20.8** EXCLUDED PROPERTY;
(iii) where the domicile of a person is determined under the terms of a double taxation agreement which related to estate duty (and CTT) and still applies for IHT purposes. The agreements concerned are currently those with France, Italy, India and Pakistan and in general the treaty override applies only in respect of the charge on death — see further **16.6** below;
(iv) in determining whether settled property which became comprised in a settlement before 10 December 1974 is excluded property, see **20.2** EXCLUDED PROPERTY; and
(v) in determining the settlor's domicile for the purposes of *IHTA 1984, s 65(8)* in relation to property which became comprised in the settlement before 10 December 1974, and whether for the purpose of that section, the conditions in *IHTA 1984, s 82(3)* are satisfied in relation to the settled property; see **40.13** SETTLEMENTS: DISCRETIONARY TRUSTS AND OTHER TRUSTS OF RELEVANT PROPERTY.

Election to be treated as UK domiciled for IHT

An individual who is not, or has not been, domiciled in the UK, but whose spouse or civil partner is so domiciled, may, from 6 April 2013, elect to be treated as UK domiciled for IHT purposes. The purpose of making such an election is to enable the full spouse exemption to apply to transfers of value from the domiciled to the non-domiciled party.

The election may be either a '*lifetime election*' or a '*death election*'. A lifetime election is one made by a non-domiciliary who at any time on or after 6 April 2013 and during the period of seven years ending with the date of the election had a spouse or civil partner who was UK domiciled. A 'death election' is one made within two years, or such longer time as HMRC may allow, of the death on or after 6 April 2013 of a person who at any time after that date and within the seven-year period ending with the death was UK domiciled but whose spouse or civil partner was not so domiciled. Both elections are irrevocable, although they cease to have effect if the person who made the election becomes non-UK resident for income tax purposes for four successive tax years after the time that the election was effective. A death election may be made by the personal representatives of a non-domiciled individual whose spouse or civil partner predeceased.

An election will not impact on the exemptions for Government securities and foreign currency bank accounts in relation to non-UK domiciled owners or trust beneficiaries (see **20.5** EXCLUDED PROPERTY), nor will it affect relief available under double tax treaties which were in force prior to 17 July 2013. An election is also ignored for the purposes of the deemed domicile provisions of *IHTA 1984, s 267* so as to prevent adverse interaction between the two sets of provisions.

There is no specified format for an election but HMRC require it to include the full name and address of the person making it, their date of birth, the date from which the election is to take effect and the full name and date of birth of the UK domiciled spouse or partner. Elections should be sent to Trusts and Estates Risk Team (Elections), Inheritance Tax, Ferrers House, Castle Meadow Road, Nottingham NG2 1BB.

Where an election has effect from a previous date, it may result in gifts made by that person since the effective date becoming chargeable transfers. In such cases the due dates for submitting an account of the transfer and for payment of tax are modified so that the date of the election is substituted for the date of the transfer.

[*IHTA 1984, ss 267ZA, 267ZB*].

UK residence before 1993/94

Residence in the UK for years of assessment before 1993/94 was determined as for income tax purposes, but without regard to any dwelling-house available in the UK for the person's use. After 1992/93, residence in the UK is determined simply as for income tax purposes, but in practice the position may be unchanged because of the amendments for 1993/94 and subsequent years made by *FA 1993, s 208(1)(4)* to *ICTA 1988, s 336* (now *ITA 2007, s 831*) for income tax purposes so as to provide that the residence status of temporary residents in the UK be decided without regard being had to the availability of the use of living accommodation in the UK. Registration and voting as an overseas elector are removed from determination of domicile for tax purposes under *IHTA 1984, s 267(1)(a)*. [*IHTA 1984, s 267; FA 1993, s 208(3)(5), Sch 23 Pt V; FA 1996, s 200; ITEPA 2003, s 722, Sch 6 paras 1, 48*].

IHT 100

An account on Form IHT 100 is required and also when there is a transferor who is non-UK domiciled and has transferred property that is not excluded property (i.e. asset held outside the UK) then supplementary form D31 should be completed as part of the IHT 100. This form asks for details of chargeable events if the transferor is domiciled in a foreign country or if the transferor is treated as domiciled in the UK. In addition, if the transferor was not ordinarily resident in the UK at the date of the chargeable event UK government securities that are authorised as being exempt from tax is also treated as excluded property for these purposes. Even though the Channel Islands and Isle of Man are treated as not being included in the UK, if a transferor was domiciled in one of those jurisdictions at the date of the chargeable event, War Savings Certificates, National Savings Certificates, Ulster Savings Certificates, Premium Bonds, Save As You Earn schemes and deposits with the National Savings & Investments (NS & I) are treated as excluded property.

Definition — United Kingdom

The United Kingdom comprises England, Scotland, Wales and Northern Ireland. The Channel Islands (Jersey, Guernsey, Herm, Brecqhou, Jethou, Lithou (which is not inhabited), Alderney and Sark) and the Isle of Man are not included. Great Britain comprises England, Scotland and Wales only.

Double tax agreements

[16.6] The concept of domicile when considered with other countries with which the UK has agreements (see **18.2** double taxation relief) can give rise to some disparate domicile treatment. Note, however, that from 6 April 2017, these treaties will not prevent the IHT charge on foreign assets deriving value from UK residential property if there is no tax payable in the overseas country concerned. However, this treaty override does not apply to individuals of foreign domicile who are deemed domiciled in the UK: see Key Points below.

(a) **Ireland** (1978/1107), the definition of domicile includes the deemed domicile rules of *IHTA 1984, s 267* but introduction of the Irish capital acquisitions tax (CAT) should be referred to in terms of residence superseding domicile. [*Irish Finance Act 2000*].
(b) **India** (1956/998), the UK deemed domicile rules of *IHTA 1984, s 267* cannot be applied to the worldwide assets of someone who dies with an Indian domicile under local law.
(c) **Pakistan** (1957/1522), the UK deemed domicile rules of *IHTA 1984, s 267* cannot be applied to the worldwide assets of someone who dies domiciled in Pakistan under local law. However, the foregoing does not apply to Bangladesh.
(d) **USA** (1979/1454), where an individual does not have a permanent home in the UK or USA he is deemed to be domiciled in the country in which he has his centre of vital interests rather than the country of habitual abode.
(e) **France** (1963/1319), under *Article V(2)* where the deceased was domiciled in Great Britain the French succession duty is not applied to property situated outside of France.

(f) **Italy** (1968/304), domicile is determined under the provisions of *Article II*.

Key points concerning domicile

[16.7] Points to consider are as follows.

- The location of assets is key after establishing non-UK domicile status. Only UK situated assets come within chargeability and overseas assets are excluded. Table of asset locations:

Asset	Location/situs
Land, buildings and leases including any share in land or a building.	Where the land is physically situated.
Registered shares and securities (but see Government stocks above).	Where the shares or securities are registered or traded.
An interest in an unincorporated business or an interest in a partnership.	Where the business is carried out.
Chattels and personal possessions.	Where the item is situated at the time of the transfer or at the date of death.
Debts owed to the deceased.	Where the debtor lives at the time of transfer or on death.
Bank accounts.	Where the bank or branch holding the account is situated.

- Pre-1975 agreements with France, Italy, India and Pakistan (see **18.2**) may preclude adverse treatment on death in respect of deemed domicile. There is treaty override in relation to residential property interests but this has limited effect. In Questions and HMRC answers published by the main professional bodies on 16 May 2019, it was agreed by HMRC that the double tax treaty override in *IHTA 1984, Sch A1 para 7* (residential property interests) applies only to the extent a person is liable to IHT by virtue of *para 1* or *para 5* of the *Sch A1*, and therefore as a person not UK domiciled for IHT purposes. In relation to a person who is deemed domiciled in the UK and whose interests in foreign companies are not excluded property irrespective of *Sch A1*, the treaty override at *para 7* therefore has no relevance. The excluded property rules are not disapplied by virtue of *para 1* or *5* but simply do not apply in the first place. The following example at para 29 of the published Questions and Answers was provided and agreed by HMRC: Two brothers Jeremy and John are both foreign domiciled. John is deemed domiciled for UK tax purposes. Both are domiciled in India under common law. Both hold UK residential properties through offshore companies. They are killed in an accident and their non-UK estates are dealt with under Indian Wills. In these circumstances on the death of John (who is deemed domiciled), treaty relief is available to exempt the company shares from IHT. This is because the treaty override in *para 7* is not effective for a deemed domiciliary as his interests in foreign companies are not excluded property so Sch A1 is not applicable. In the case of Jeremy (who is not deemed domiciled) nothing in the treaty prevents *Sch A1* from applying to his interests in the offshore companies since for IHT purposes the shares are otherwise excluded property.

- If a person intends to change their domicile of origin of the UK to that of a domicile of choice elsewhere there are a number of core rules regarding changes to their personal circumstances that must be adhered to as an absolute requirement. These include:
  - (i) cut all ties with the UK e.g. sell UK property, close bank accounts, cancel club subscriptions, liquidate or transfer investments out of UK jurisdiction, etc;
  - (ii) reinstate items at (i) above in new country;
  - (iii) ensure that all friends and relatives appreciate the new choice of domicile;
  - (iv) change passport to take up new citizenship in the country of choice;
  - (v) make sure that visits to the UK are limited or fleeting after giving up UK domicile;
  - (vi) ensure that everyday actions indicate a permanent attachment for the country of choice;
  - (vii) ensure that a foreign will is drawn up and burial/cremation wishes show an attachment to the country of choice; and
  - (viii) business interests in the UK are concluded.

The above matters will not be conclusive and each case will be treated on its own merits but the points above will assist in proving a domicile of choice. See also *Gaines-Cooper v HMRC* [2008] STC 1665 in which the taxpayer who had permanently settled in the Seychelles was held to not have lost his UK domicile due to the retention of a home in the UK despite a chain of eminent witnesses confirming that his permanent home was no longer in the UK and the taxpayer fiercely contesting the decision reached.

An area often overlooked is the treatment for IHT of gifts to a non-domiciled spouse or civil partner. Under *IHTA 1984, s 18(2)*, the spouse or civil partner gift exemption is restricted, following *FA 2013*, to the nil band amount of £325,000. Therefore, where a UK domiciled spouse transfers over £325,000 to their non-UK domiciled partner or spouse on death, all or part of their nil rate band of £325,000 will have to be utilised. Unfortunately, such gifts in lifetime up to the £325,000 limit do not come within the PETs regime under *IHTA 1984, s 3A* since they are fully exempt, not potentially exempt and once the £325,000 has been fully utilised, it is never again reinstated as it is a lifetime allowance. However, the PETs regime will apply to lifetime gifts in excess of £325,000 and if the UK domiciled spouse survives seven years following the gift to the spouse, then the gift will fall out of account within *IHTA 1984, s 3A*. Where spouses are UK domiciled and gifts are made between them and then one becomes non-UK domiciled, those previous gifts will be set against the £325,000 limit and any excess will be a PET but with the possibility that there may be a charge to IHT on death if seven years have not elapsed since the original transfer. This follows from *IHTA 1984, s 18(2)* 'shall not exceed the exemption limit at the time of the transfer *less any amount* previously taken into account for the purposes of the exemption conferred by this section'. Emphasis added.

17

Double Charges Reliefs

Simon's Taxes. See **I3.556, I3.557, I5.558, I3.559, I3.560, I4.163.**

Other Sources. HMRC Customer Guide to Inheritance Tax; Foster, Part C5.13.

Introduction to double charges reliefs

[17.1] Without specific relief, a double charge to IHT could arise in various circumstances, for example where a donor makes a gift to a donee who subsequently makes a gift back to the donor, and the donor dies within seven years of making the initial gift. Regulations made in 1987 (see *SI 1987/1130*) contain provisions to eliminate the potential double charge in the main circumstances which arise in practice. They work by a process of calculating the IHT chargeable on alternative bases, each one disregarding the other potentially chargeable amount, and then preserving the higher of the tax charges under the two calculations.

The circumstances covered by the Regulations

Relief from double charge is provided for in four specified cases.

(a) Where property given by a potentially exempt transfer is subsequently returned (otherwise than for full consideration) by the donee to the transferor and, as a result of the transferor's death, both that property and the potentially exempt transfer become chargeable to tax. See **17.2** below.

(b) Where property given by a transfer of value which is chargeable when made is returned (otherwise than for full consideration) by the donee to the transferor and that property is also chargeable as part of the transferor's estate on his death. See **17.3** below.

(c) Where a transfer of value is or subsequently becomes a chargeable transfer and, at the transferor's death, his estate owes to the transferee a debt which under the rules relating to such liabilities falls to be abated or disallowed in determining the value of the estate chargeable on the death. This relief is detailed at **49.11** TRANSFERS ON DEATH.

(d) Where there is a transfer by way of gift which is, or subsequently becomes, a chargeable transfer, but the gift is also caught by the reservation of benefit provisions on the death of the donor so that it is taxable twice, once as a chargeable transfer and secondly as part of the estate on death by reason of the reservation of benefit. This relief is detailed at **22.15** GIFTS WITH RESERVATION.

A fifth category of relief from double charges was introduced as part of the pre-owned assets provisions: see **17.4** below.

Potentially exempt transfers and death

[17.2] Relief from double charge to tax is given where, after 17 March 1986, an individual ('the deceased') makes a transfer of value to a person 'the transferee') which is a potentially exempt transfer that proves to be a chargeable transfer and where immediately before his death the deceased was beneficially entitled to property:

(a) which he acquired from the transferee otherwise than for full consideration in money or money's worth after making the potentially exempt transfer; *and*

(b) which was transferred to the transferee by the potentially exempt transfer or which is property directly or indirectly representing that property; *and*

(c) value attributable to which is a chargeable part of his estate on death.

Where the above conditions are fulfilled, there must be separately calculated the total tax chargeable as a consequence of the death of the deceased:

(i) disregarding so much of the value transferred by the potentially exempt transfer as is attributable to the value of property within (c) above which is included in the chargeable transfer on death; and

(ii) disregarding so much of the value of the property within (c) above which is included in the chargeable transfer on death as is attributable to property value of which is transferred by the potentially exempt transfer.

If charging the relevant property as part of the death estate under (i) above produces a higher amount of tax than would be payable if the charge on the potentially exempt transfer under (ii) was taken instead, the value transferred by the potentially exempt transfer is reduced by reference to the amount of the value of that property which is included in the chargeable transfer on death. Conversely, the potentially exempt transfer is charged if it produces the higher amount of tax with a corresponding reduction in the value of that property which is included in the chargeable estate on death. Where the amount calculated under (i) above is higher, to avoid the value of the same property entering twice into the tax calculations, this reduction applies for all IHT purposes.

Where the total tax chargeable under (i) and (ii) above is identical, calculation (i) is treated as producing a higher amount. [*FA 1986, s 104(1)(a); SI 1987/1130, Regs 4, 8*].

Example

A makes a potentially exempt transfer of £60,000 (annual exemptions having been used) to B in July 2004. In March 2006 A makes a gift of £281,000 (after annual exemptions of £3,000 × 2) into a discretionary trust and the trustees pay IHT of £1,200. He makes a further gift of £55,000 (before annual exemption for the year) to the same trust in August 2006, the trustees paying IHT of £10,400.

B dies in January 2007 and the 2004 potentially exempt transfer returns to A. A dies in May 2010. His death estate of £310,000 includes the 2004 potentially exempt transfer, returned to him in 2006, which at the time of A's death is worth £216,000. It is assumed for the purposes of this computation that tax rates and bands remain as those pertaining from 6 April 2010.

First calculation: charge the returned potentially exempt transfer in A's death estate and ignore the potentially exempt transfer made in 2004

	IHT payable
	£
July 2004	
Potentially exempt transfer £60,000 ignored	—
March 2006	
Gift £281,000	
Tax £NIL less £1,200 already paid (see note)	—
August 2006	
Gift £52,000 as top slice of £333,000	
Tax £NIL less £10,400 already paid	—
May 2010	
Death estate £310,000 as top slice of £643,000	127,200
Total tax due as a result of A's death	£127,200

Second calculation: charge the potentially exempt transfer made in 2004 and ignore the value of the returned potentially exempt transfer in A's death estate

	IHT payable
	£
July 2004	
Potentially exempt transfer £60,000	
Tax £NIL	—
March 2006	
Gift £281,000 as top slice of £341,000	
Tax £1,600 less £1,200 already paid	400
August 2006	

Gift £52,000 as top slice of £393,000	
Tax £20,800 less £10,400 already paid	10,400
May 2010	
Death estate £94,000 as top slice of £487,000	37,600
Total tax due as a result of A's death	£48,400

The first calculation gives the higher amount of tax. The potentially exempt transfer made in 2004 will be ignored, and tax on other transfers will be as in the first calculation.

Note

In the first calculation, the tax of £127,200 on death does not allow for any 36 QUICK SUCCESSION RELIEF that might be due by reference to any tax charged in connection with B's death. Such relief could reduce the tax given by the first calculation. Credit for the tax already paid on the March 2006 and August 2006 gifts is restricted to the lower of the tax already paid and the tax payable as a result of death i.e. Nil. There is no repayment of the excess.

Chargeable transfers and death

[17.3] Relief from double charge to tax is given where, after 17 March 1986 and within seven years before his death, an individual ('the deceased') makes a transfer of value to a person ('the transferee') which is a chargeable transfer and where immediately before his death the deceased was beneficially entitled to property:

(a) which he acquired from the transferee otherwise than for full consideration in money or money's worth after making the chargeable transfer; *and*
(b) which was transferred to the transferee by the chargeable transfer or which is property directly or indirectly representing that property; *and*
(c) value attributable to which is a chargeable part of his estate on death.

Where the above conditions are fulfilled, there must be separately calculated the total tax chargeable as a consequence of the death of the deceased

(i) disregarding so much of the value transferred by the lifetime chargeable transfer as is attributable to the value of property within (c) above which is included in the chargeable transfer on death; *and*
(ii) disregarding so much of the value of the property within (c) above which is included in the chargeable transfer on death as is attributable to property, value of which is transferred by the lifetime chargeable transfer.

If charging the relevant property as part of the death estate under (i) above produces a higher amount of tax than would be payable if the charge on the lifetime chargeable transfer under (ii) was taken instead, the value transferred by the lifetime chargeable transfer is reduced by reference to the amount of the value of that property which is included in the chargeable transfer on death. Conversely, the lifetime chargeable transfer is charged if it produces the higher amount of tax with a corresponding reduction in the value of that property which is included in the chargeable estate on death.

Where the higher amount is calculated under (i) above

(A) credit is available for tax already paid on the lifetime chargeable transfer which is attributable to the value disregarded under that calculation (but not exceeding the amount of tax due on death attributable to the value of the property in question); and
(B) to avoid the value of the same property entering twice into the tax calculations, the reduction applies for all IHT purposes other than a ten-year anniversary charge or a proportionate charge to tax on a discretionary settlement arising before the death of the deceased.

Where the total tax chargeable under (i) and (ii) above is identical, calculation (i) is treated as producing the higher amount. [*FA 1986, s 104(1)(d); SI 1987/1130, Regs 7, 8*].

Double charges following election into IHT under the pre-owned assets provisions

[17.4] The pre-owned assets regulations relating to income tax now include provisions to avoid a double charge to IHT where a chargeable person elects that the gift with reservation provisions apply to the relevant property. [*FA 1986, s 104(1); Charge to Income Tax by Reference to Enjoyment of Property Previously Owned Regulations 2005, SI 2005/724, Reg 6; Inheritance Tax (Double Charges Relief) Regulations 2005, SI 2005/3441, Reg 3*]. A double charge can arise where the chargeable person makes a gift of property or a debt that is a potentially exempt transfer for IHT purposes. If that same property is then liable to the income tax charge the person may decide to make an election on Form IHT500 that the property is subject to the IHT reservation of benefits rules. If that person then dies within seven years of the original gift a double charge to IHT may arise, firstly, by reason of the original transfer and secondly when the property is added back into the death estate for the purposes of the gift with reservation rules. The new provision avoids the double charge by opting for the IHT on transfer that produces the highest overall amount of IHT and thereby reduces the other transfer to nil.

Relief is given where a double charge to IHT arises in situations where arrangements are caught by the pre-owned assets income tax provisions in *FA 2004, Sch 15* which are subsequently dismantled by the individual but he/she dies within seven years. The conditions for double charge relief in these circumstances are as follows:

(a) the disposal condition or the contribution condition is met as respects the relevant property; and
(b) the deceased makes a transfer the result of which a third party becomes entitled to the benefit of a debt owed to the deceased; and
(c) before the deceased's death, any outstanding part of the debt is wholly written off, waived or released, and the write off, waiver or release is made otherwise than for full consideration in money or money's worth;

(d) further conditions apply so that:
  (i) the deceased dies on or after 6 April 2005; and
  (ii) on the deceased's death, the transfer of value treated as made immediately before the deceased's death included the relevant property, or any property representing that relevant property; and
  (iii) as a result of the deceased's death, the transfer of value referred to in (b) above has become a chargeable transfer.

See IHTM14701–14 for HMRC examples of how the double charge reliefs work in practice. [*Inheritance Tax (Double Charges Relief) Regulations 2005, SI 2005/3441*].

18

Double Taxation Relief

Cross-references. See **16** DOMICILE; **46.5** SITUS.

Simon's Taxes. See **I9.123, F4.1.**

Other Sources. Tolley's Tax Planning; Foster, Part J5; IR Leaflet IHT 18; HMRC Customer Guide to Inheritance Tax; IHTM27000.

Introduction to double taxation relief

[18.1] Where inheritance tax is chargeable in the UK, and tax of a similar character or which is chargeable on or by reference to death or gifts inter vivos is also charged by another country (an 'overseas territory') on the same property, relief may be available:

(a) under the specific terms of a double tax agreement between the UK and that other country, or
(b) under the unilateral double tax relief provisions contained in the UK legislation. [*IHTA 1984, ss 158(1), 159(1)*].

Double tax agreements

[18.2] An agreement with another country is made by Order in Council after a draft has been approved by resolution by the House of Commons and may give retrospective relief.

The Board is authorised to exchange with the other government any information required provided the Board or its authorised officer is satisfied as regards confidentiality. This authority has been further enhanced by changes in the *FA 2003* which relax the obligations of secrecy and insert changes to the wording governing the exchange of information by changing the wording *in IHTA 1984, ss 158(1A), 220A* from 'necessary for the carrying out of' to 'foreseeably relevant to the administration or enforcement of'. [*IHTA 1984, ss 158(1A), 220A inserted by FA 2000, s 147(1) and as amended by FA 2003, ss 197, 198*].

Domicile not affected by *IHTA 1984, s 267*

Any provisions relating to estate duty in an existing agreement are extended to capital transfer tax and inheritance tax payable on a death (but not on lifetime transfers). Provisions in such agreements relating to the determination of domicile are not affected by *IHTA 1984, s 267* which treats certain persons as domiciled in the UK when they are domiciled abroad under the general law, see **16.5** DOMICILE. [*IHTA 1984, s 158*].

The existing estate duty agreements which now apply to inheritance tax on death are (country and statutory instrument year and number).

France (1963/1319), **India** (1956/998), **Italy** (1968/304), **Pakistan** (1957/1522) and **Switzerland** (1957/426) (see also 1994/3214 below).

The existing capital transfer tax agreements which now apply to inheritance tax on chargeable lifetime transfers and death are (country and statutory instrument year and number).

Ireland (1978/1107), **South Africa** (1979/576), **Sweden** (1981/840 with amending protocol 1989/986) and **USA** (1979/1454).

Inheritance tax agreements entered into in respect of chargeable transfers on death are (country and statutory instrument year and number).

Switzerland (1994/3214), **Netherlands** (1980/706 with amending protocol 1996/730).

The specific provisions of the particular agreement concerned must be studied carefully. For instance, the agreement with France does not extend to Northern Ireland, the Pakistan convention remains in force despite the abolition of the death duties law in 1978 and the agreement with India remains in force despite the abolition of Indian estate duty law in 1985, see **16.6** DOMICILE. See HMRC Tax Bulletin, June 2001.

UK and Netherlands Protocol

See also UK and Netherlands Protocol which entered into force on 3 June 1996 amending the Convention signed in The Hague on 11 December 1979. (*Treaty Series No 73 (1996) Cmnd 3336*).

HMRC have stated:

> 'As both countries may have the right to tax the assets, these agreements usually have rules that say which country may tax the different assets. We will not give up our right to tax any assets until we have evidence from the foreign authority that the assets have been included for tax in the foreign country and tax has been paid. If you feel that certain assets should not be taxed in the UK because an agreement says so, you should let us have evidence that foreign tax has been paid on the assets as soon as you can'

Unilateral relief by UK

[18.3] Where relief is not available under a double tax agreement, relief may be obtained by means of a credit for the overseas tax against the UK inheritance tax. This unilateral relief is also applied if greater relief is obtained than under an agreement. The relief is as follows.

(a) Where the property is situated in the overseas territory and not in the UK, the credit is the whole amount of the overseas tax.

Example 1

Where property is situated in an overseas territory only

A, domiciled in the UK, owns a holiday home abroad valued at £396,000 which he gives to his son in July 2010. He is liable to local gifts tax of, say, £8,830. He has made no previous transfers and does not use the home again at any time before his death in February 2015. Assumes that nil rate band in force at that time is £325,000. See 37 RATES OF TAX.

Market value of holiday home		396,000
Annual exemption 2010/11	(3,000)	
Annual exemption 2009/10	(3,000)	
Chargeable transfer		£390,000

IHT payable at 60% of full rates by son (death between 4 and 5 years after gift) £65,000 × 40% × 60%	15,600
Unilateral relief for foreign tax	(8,830)
IHT borne	£6,770

Note to the example

(A) If the overseas tax suffered exceeded the UK liability before relief, there would be no IHT payable but the excess would not be repayable.

Example 2

Where property is situated in both the UK and an overseas territory

M, domiciled in the UK, owns company shares which are regarded as situated both in the UK and country X under the rules of the respective countries. On M's death in June 2010 the shares pass to M's son S. The UK IHT amounts to £5,000 before unilateral relief. The equivalent tax liability arising in country X amounts to £2,000.

Apply the formula

$$\frac{A}{A+B} \times C$$

shown below

The unilateral relief available is

$$\frac{5{,}000}{5{,}000+2{,}000} \times £2{,}000 = £1{,}429$$

IHT payable = £5,000 – £1,429 = £3,571

(b) Where the property is:

(i) situated neither in the UK nor the overseas territory; or

(ii) situated both in the UK and the overseas territory,

the credit is in accordance with the following formula.

$$\frac{A}{A+B} \times C$$

where:
A = the amount of inheritance tax;
B = the overseas tax; and
C = whichever of A or B is the smaller.

(c) Where tax is imposed in two or more overseas territories in respect of property which is:
 (i) situated neither in the UK nor in any of those territories; or
 (ii) is situated in the UK and in each of those territories,

the formula above applies but:
A = the amount of inheritance tax;
B = the aggregate of the overseas tax imposed in each of those territories; and
C = the aggregate of all, except the largest, of A and the overseas tax imposed in each of them.

Where credit is allowed under (a) above or under the terms of a double tax agreement in respect of overseas tax imposed in one overseas territory, any credit under (b) above in respect of overseas tax imposed in another is calculated as if the inheritance tax at A in the formula were reduced by that credit. Similarly, where in the case of an overseas territory within (b) or (c) above, credit is allowed against the overseas tax for tax charged in a territory in which the property is situated, the overseas tax at B in the formula is treated as reduced by the credit.

References to tax imposed in an overseas territory are references to tax chargeable under the laws of that territory and paid by the person liable to pay the tax. [*IHTA 1984, s 159*].

Example 3

Where tax is imposed in two or more overseas territories on property situated in the UK and each of those territories

Assume the facts in the example in 2 above except that a third country imposes a tax liability on the death as the shares are regarded as also situated in that country.

UK IHT before unilateral relief	£5,000
Tax in country X	£2,000
Tax in country Y	£400

Apply the formula

$$\frac{A}{A+B} \times C$$

shown above

The unilateral relief available is

$$\frac{5{,}000}{5{,}000 + 2{,}000 + 400} \times (2{,}000 + 400) = £1{,}622$$

IHT payable £5,000 – £1,622 = £3,378

19

Estate

Cross-references. See **26** LAND for estates of land; **38** SETTLEMENTS — GENERAL, **39** SETTLEMENTS WITH INTERESTS IN POSSESSION, **43** SETTLEMENTS: TRUSTS FOR BEREAVED MINORS and **53** VALUATION.

Simon's Taxes. See **I3.211, I3.212, I5.201, I5.214, I5.256, I5.726.**

Introduction to estate

[19.1] 'Estate' is one of the key concepts of IHT because of the loss to donor principle which underlies the tax. (See **1** INTRODUCTION AND BASIC PRINCIPLES for general exposition). During life, the value transferred by a transfer of value is the amount by which the transferor's estate is reduced by that transfer. On death, a person is treated as having made a transfer of value equal to the value of their estate immediately before their death. [*IHTA 1984, ss 3(1), 4(1)*].

Definition — person's estate

A person's estate, for IHT purposes, is the aggregate of all the 'property' to which the person is *beneficially entitled*, except that the estate of a person immediately before death does not include **20** EXCLUDED PROPERTY or property to which *IHTA 1984, ss 71A, 71D* (i.e. bereaved minor's trust and an 'aged 18–25 trust') apply. Also, a person's estate does not include, from 22 March 2006, certain interests in possession commencing on or after that date other than an immediate post-death interest (IPDI), a transitional serial interest (TSI), and a disabled person's interest under trust for their benefit within *IHTA 1984, s 89B*. See *Anand v IRC* [1997] STC (SCD) 58 Sp C 107 and *O'Neill v IRC* [1998] STC (SCD) 110 Sp C 154. '*Property*' includes rights and interests of any description but does not include a 'settlement power' being a power of appointment exercisable over settled property, nor does it include property to which a person is entitled as a corporation sole (e.g. as Archbishop of Canterbury). A person's liabilities, including the liability for IHT (but not any other tax or duty) on the value transferred, are taken into account in determining the value of an estate. However, a liability not incurred for a consideration in money or money's worth is left out of account unless it is a liability imposed by law. [*IHTA 1984, ss 5(1)(3)–(5), 47A, 271, 272; FA 2006, Sch 20 para 10, 28*].

Although excluded property forms part of the estate during lifetime, no account is to be taken of any loss to the estate by virtue of a lifetime disposition of such property [*IHTA 1984, s 3(2)*].

Where a dormant asset has been transferred to an authorised reclaim fund the right of recovery which a claimant may have against the fund is to have the same treatment for IHT purposes as the original asset transferred to the fund. This is effective from 6 June 2022. [*IHTA 1984, s 159A*].

Joint bank accounts

There are no specific provisions in the IHT legislation dealing with joint bank accounts. HMRC's practice is to treat the funds in such an account as belonging to the joint owners in the proportions representing their own contributions to the account less withdrawals made from the contributions. Thus, where all the funds are provided by one of the joint owners, that person's share in the account will normally be regarded as the whole of the account, notwithstanding the fact that the other joint owner has the ability to draw on the funds at any time (see notes on form IHT404 and IHTM15042). If the other joint owner does make withdrawals, HMRC regard these as lifetime gifts by the account holder who provided the funds. A different approach might apply if there is evidence of an intention to make a gift of the funds when the joint account was set up or if both joint account holders have to sign or participate electronically in relation to withdrawals (IHTM15043).

This treatment has some support from the decisions in *O'Neill v IRC* [1998] STC (SCD) 110 Sp C 154 and *Sillars v IRC* [2004] STC (SCD) 180 Sp C 401, although in both these cases, the other joint owners did not know of the existence of the accounts. See also *Ms S Taylor (Executrix for Mrs K Boland) v HMRC* [2008] STC (SCD) 1159 Sp C 704 and *Matthews v HMRC* [2012] UKFTT 658.

For joint accounts where all joint owners make frequent contributions and withdrawals, it is thought that they may be regarded as having equal ownership of the funds, unless the facts indicate otherwise.

Joint interests in property

Except in the case of joint tenancies (where all entitlements are by definition equal), the interests of joint owners of freehold or leasehold property will normally be set out in a Declaration of Trust. Where the interests cannot be identified in this way, it is necessary to ascertain the intentions of the parties by conducting research into any relevant documents or correspondence.

Loans as part of estate

Where a loan is made between individuals, HMRC will not accept that the loan has been waived and the estate of the lender reduced unless the waiver was effected by deed (Law Society's Gazette, 18 December 1991). See also *Moggs (Moggs' Executor) v CIR* [2005] STC (SCD) 394 Sp C 464. A suitable precedent is set out below.

THIS DEED is made by:

(1) "Father" namely [ ] of [ ]
In favour of
(2) "Son" namely [ ] of [ ]

RECITALS

(A) Son is indebted to Father for the loan brief details of which are set out in the schedule below ("the Loan")
(B) By this waiver Father intends to utilise the annual exemption available to him under section 19 of the Inheritance Tax Act 1984

WAIVER

(1) Father waives and releases in favour of Son Three Thousand pounds (£3,000.00) of the Loan
(2) The continuing balance of the indebtedness due under the Loan following t waiver is set out in part 2 of the schedule

The Schedule

Part 1 – [details of "the Loan"]

Part 2 – balance now [ ]

EXECUTED AS A DEED	)
and DELIVERED on	)
2010	)
FATHER in the presence of	)

Note to the waiver

It is important that waivers of loan are made by Deed. Estoppels apart (which should not be relied on), waivers underhand, by letter etc. are simply ineffective due to a lack of consideration.

Estate on death

[19.2] There are additional rules for the valuation of a person's estate immediately before their death. See 49.2 TRANSFERS ON DEATH.

General powers

[19.3] A person who has a 'general power' (or would have if he were *sui juris*) to dispose of, or to charge money on, any property other than settled property is treated as beneficially entitled to the money or property. '*General power*' means a power or authority enabling a person by whom it is exercisable to appoint or dispose of property as he thinks fit. [*IHTA 1984, s 5(2)*]. See *Kempe and Roberts (personal representatives of Lyon, deceased) v CIR* [2004] STC (SCD) 467 Sp C 424. In the case of a Power of Attorney [now Lasting Power of Attorney] care should be exercised as applying *dicta* of Russell J in *Re Reckitt*, CA [1928] 2 KB 244, 'the primary object of a power of attorney is to enable the attorney to act in the management of his principal's affairs. An attorney cannot, in the absence of a clear power to do so, make presents to himself or to others of his principal's property.' See *McDowall & Others (McDowall's Executors) v CIR* [2004] STC (SCD) 22 Sp C 382. As settled property is specifically excluded, the existence of a general power of appointment in a trust deed does not result in the settled property being deemed to be included in the estate of the trustee. It has been held that a right reserved by the settlor to require his trustees to revest in him settled property was property forming part of his estate immediately after the settlement. This could have resulted in 'double counting' because the person entitled to an interest in possession in the settled property would have been treated as beneficially entitled and the general power of appointment would be property of the appointor's estate. *Melville v CIR*, [2000] STC 628; CA [2001] STC 1271. In this case, the position has now been rectified by legislation in *FA 2002, s 119(4)*. The section reverses the effects of the *Melville* case from 17 April 2002 by providing expressly that powers over trusts are not to be treated as property; that is, they do not form an asset capable of being part of a person's estate. Powers which have been acquired for money or money's worth will not be disregarded for IHT purposes by reason of *FA 2002, s 119(3)* inserting new *IHTA 1984, s 55A*.

In *Sillars v IRC* [2004] STC (SCD) 180 Sp C 401, the deceased transferred her building society account into the names of herself and her two daughters. In putting the account into their joint names, the deceased had intended to make an immediate gift. The daughters did regard a one-third share of the balance in the account as being theirs. Withdrawals from the account were made either to or for the benefit of the mother until her death. On the mother's death the whole of the account formed part of her estate. Although the deceased's power over the account was not a *general power* in the ordinary sense, it did fit the definition. The deceased was able to dispose of the balance as she thought fit and there was no accounting to see whether more than one-third was being extracted from the account. The daughters did not therefore have a general power over the account 'enabling the person by whom it is exercisable to dispose of or appoint property as he thinks fit'. See also **5.1** ANTI-AVOIDANCE.

Settled property

[19.4] A person who is beneficially entitled to an interest in possession in settled property, which interest commenced before 22 March 2006, is treated as beneficially entitled to the property in which the interest subsists, i.e the person's estate for IHT purposes includes the value of any settled property in which there is such an interest (and not the actuarial value of the interest itself). [*IHTA 1984, s 49(1)*].

Example 1

X, a widower, who has a life interest in a settlement since 1995, dies in June 2020 with his nil rate band of £325,000 available but having used the available annual exemptions. On his death, X has a free estate of £302,000. The value of his trust fund is £263,000, making a total value of £565,000. X has a power of appointment over the trust fund, and by the terms of his will, he appoints the fund to his nephew and leaves the personal estate of £302,000 to his daughter.

Although the nil rate band available of £325,000 would have meant that his daughter received the whole of the personal estate of X free of IHT, the trust fund has to be taken into account. The result is that the nil rate band must be apportioned between the personal estate and the trust fund so that both the trustees of the settlement and the executors will have a liability for IHT as follows:

Calculation on death of X

Value of X's estate at June 2020 *IHTA 1984, s 49(1)(1A)* (see above).	£
Value net free estate	302,000
Add Trust fund	263,000
	£565,000

IHT on chargeable gift of £565,000 is charged in the nil rate band up to £325,000.

	£
£0–325,000 at Nil%	Nil
Estate chargeable @ 40%	240,000
Tax due on death of X	£96,000
Calculate estate rate: £96,000/565,000 × 100 = 16.99115	
Executors' portion £302,000 × 16.99115% =	£51,313
Trustees' portion £263,000 × 16.99115% =	£44,687
IHT payable	£96,000

Notes to the example

(A) Under *IHTA 1984, s 49A* the niece has an IPDI which arises under the will of X and she is treated as beneficially entitled to an interest in possession in settled property in which the interest subsists. See **39** SETTLEMENTS WITH INTERESTS IN POSSESSION.

(B) Testators may wish the benefit of the whole of the available nil bands to be allocated to the free estate in priority to the settled property. Unfortunately, this is prevented by *IHTA 1984, s 265* which requires the tax to be apportioned according to the respective values of the free estate and the aggregated trust fund.

See **49.2** TRANSFERS ON DEATH for exceptions to the above where settled property reverts to the settlor, or in certain circumstances to the settlor's spouse, on the death of a person entitled to an interest in possession in that property. For the position from 22 March 2006 see **38** SETTLEMENTS — GENERAL and **39** SETTLEMENTS WITH INTERESTS IN POSSESSION.

A reversionary interest

A reversionary interest in settled property is generally **20 EXCLUDED PROPERTY**, i.e. it forms part of the estate of the person entitled to the reversionary interest, except immediately before the person's death (see **19.1** above, so it is not liable to tax as part of the estate on death). For lifetime transfers, the interest is not taken into account in determining the value transferred by any transfer of value. The exceptions to this rule are (i) where the reversionary interest has been retained by a settlor, spouse or civil partner; (ii) where it has been acquired for consideration in money or money's worth; and (iii) where certain anti-avoidance provisions apply (*IHTA 1984, s 74A*). Where a person entitled to an interest (whether in possession or not) in any settled property acquires a reversionary interest expectant (whether immediately or not) on that interest, the reversionary interest is not part of the person's estate. See also **5 ANTI-AVOIDANCE**. [*IHTA 1984, ss 3(1)(2), 5(1), 48, 55(1); FA 2006, Sch 20 para 10*].

Trustees of settled property

A trustee of settled property is the legal, not the beneficial, owner of the property so the property does not form part of the estate. See **19.3** above for the position where a trustee has general powers of appointment etc. Where a trustee is remunerated for his services by an interest in possession in settlement property (e.g. an annuity) the interest is not part of his estate except to the extent that it represents more than reasonable remuneration. [*IHTA 1984, s 90*].

HMRC normally expect to deal with the reversionary interest but the DV may be asked by HMRC whether or not consideration paid by the lessee represented the full consideration for the grant of the lease for life. It is only these cases that the DV will be involved in the use of Life Tables in order to arrive at the required value. HMRC will inform the DV of the age and sex of the person by reference to whose death the lease will determine. (VOA IHT manual, section 8, para 8.22).

Key points concerning estate

[19.5] Points to consider are as follows.

- Powers of appointment are usually either a special power or a general power. In addition, there is also recourse to hybrid powers which may be categorised as coming within a general power or special power. Under the new *Perpetuities and Accumulations Act 2009, s 11* a 'general power' and 'special power' are defined as follows:
  (i) a *general power* of appointment is one which is exercisable by one person alone, and under which that person could exercise the power to appoint the entire trust to themselves, without the consent of anyone else or compliance with any other condition; and

(ii) a *special power* is any power of appointment which is not a general power of appointment (i.e. it entitles the holder to appoint the trust to whomever they like).

The new *Perpetuities and Accumulations Act 2009, s 11* extends the perpetuity period for trusts created after 5 April 2010 to 125 years and means it is no longer necessary to have a life in being as the basis of the perpetuity period and consequently drafting a Royal life clause is not relevant.

- An immediate post-death interest in possession of settled property (see **39.2**) has the result that the settled property in which the interest subsists forms part of the beneficiary's estate. If, therefore, both the trust and the beneficiary with the interest in possession in it hold ordinary shares in an unquoted company, the shares in the trust and the personal holding of the same shares must be combined for the purposes of valuing the total of the two holdings for IHT.
- It should be remembered that a general power under which the donee has a power to appoint over settled property is not beneficially entitled to that property for IHT purposes. This results from *IHTA 1984, s 5(2)* which applies to powers to dispose of property 'other than settled property'.

20

Excluded Property

Cross-references. See **46** SITUS; **48** TRANSFER OF VALUE.

Simon's Taxes. See **I5.702, I5.724, I5.725, I5.728, I9.3.**

Other Sources. Foster, Parts C2.17, C4.43, D1.21, E7.02, J3; HMRC Customer Guide to Inheritance Tax; IHTM04251.

Introduction to excluded property

[20.1] Excluded property is outside the scope of charge to inheritance tax. The value transferred by a transfer of value does not take account of the value of any excluded property ceasing to form part of a person's estate as a result of a disposition [*IHTA 1984, s 3(1)(2)*] and a person's estate immediately before his death (on which inheritance tax is payable) does not include excluded property. [*IHTA 1984, s 5(1)*]. Similarly, if the excluded property is settled property, the termination of an interest in possession in it is not taxable (see **39** SETTLEMENTS WITH INTERESTS IN POSSESSION) and nor is it relevant property for the purposes of the rules for **40** SETTLEMENTS: DISCRETIONARY TRUSTS AND OTHER TRUSTS OF RELEVANT PROPERTY. [*IHTA 1984, ss 53(1), 58(1)*]. The types of excluded property are described below.

Property abroad

Foreign assets of non-domiciliaries

[20.2] Property which is not comprised in a settlement (but including a reversionary interest in settled property, see **20.4** below) and which is situated outside the UK is excluded property if the person beneficially entitled to it is an individual domiciled outside the UK and not deemed domiciled in the UK (see **16.5**). [*IHTA 1984, ss 6(1)(1A), 48(3), (3A)* as inserted by *FA 2003, s 186(2)(3)*]. A double tax treaty may specify where property is situated. [*IHTA 1984, s 158(1)*]. See **16.5** DOMICILE for special provisions and **46** SITUS for situation of property generally.

UK residential property interests

With effect from 6 April 2017, offshore structures which hold interests in UK residential property will not qualify as excluded property up to the value of the residence concerned. An interest in a partnership (including Limited Liability Partnerships and entities similar to partnerships) or a close company (including a non-resident company which would be a close company if UK resident) is not to be excluded property to the extent that the value of the interest is directly or indirectly attributable to a UK residential property interest. There is a disregard of interests in both partnerships and companies where the value of the interest is less than 5% of the total value of all the interests in the partnership or company. HMRC guidance indicates that normal valuation rules and discounts apply for the purposes of such valuations and the comparison is not with value of a 100% interest in the company but with the aggregate value of all other interests. In the case of a company, 'interests' includes those in the assets available for distribution on winding up or otherwise and HMRC consider that a loan to a close company is therefore an interest in it for these purposes. The values of any interests of connected persons (see **12** CONNECTED PERSONS) must be taken into account. In determining the value of rights or interests in a company, liabilities of the company are to be apportioned rateably over all its assets, even if secured on the UK residence.

An interest is indirectly attributable to a UK residential property interest if it is held via an underlying company or partnership, as for example where a partnership holds shares in a non-resident company which holds a UK residence or has made a 'relevant loan' to another (see below). For further examples in relation to close company interests, see **11** CLOSE COMPANIES.

A UK residential property interest means an interest in UK land where the land consists of a dwelling. If the land includes other premises, such as a shop with a flat above, the provisions will apply only to the extent that the land includes a dwelling. Interests under a contract for an off-plan purchase are residential property interests. For contracts generally, prior to completion, the value is subject to a deduction for the consideration due on completion. The extent to which land includes the dwelling is to be determined on a just and reasonable basis. Dwelling has the meaning given by *TCGA 1992, Sch B1, para 4* and therefore means any building which is suitable for use as a dwelling or which is in the process of being constructed or adapted for such use. Land which is occupied or enjoyed with a dwelling as its garden or grounds is taken to be part of the dwelling. *Schedule B1, para 4* contains a number of exclusions, such as residential accommodation or school pupils or armed forces or children etc.

Example

Robin and Pauline are non-UK domiciled and own all the shares in a BVI company, each having 50 shares. They are not married but have lived together for many years. The company holds the following assets:

- UK residence worth £1,000,000, purchased with bank loan secured on it of £500,000;
- UK commercial property worth £1,200,000.

Up to 5 April 2017, the shares were excluded property. From 6 April 2017, the shares will not be excluded property to extent that the value of them is attributable to the UK residence.

Assuming the value of each 50% shareholding is to be based on asset value, less a discount of 20% for lack of control, each shareholding is valued at:

£1,700,000 × 50% × 80% = £680,000.

That percentage of the bank loan to be attributed to the UK residence is as follows:

$$\frac{£1,000,000}{£2,200,000} = 45.45\%$$

Thus 45.45% of the loan of £500,000 is deductible from the value of the residence, which is £227,250. The value of each shareholding which is not excluded property is therefore:

Value of residential interest: £1,000,000 – £227,250 = £772,750.

Value of shares not qualifying as excluded property: £772,750 × 50%, less 20% discount = **£309,100.**

Note to the example

If Robin and Pauline were married, the 20% valuation discount would not apply as each holding of shares would be related property (see **53.21**) and the calculation would be £772,750 × 50% = **£386,375.**

The rights of a creditor under a loan arrangement will not be excluded property if it is a 'relevant loan', defined as a loan if and to the extent that the money made available under the loan is used by an individual, a partnership or settlement trustees to finance directly or indirectly:

(a) the acquisition of a UK residential property interest; or
(b) the acquisition of a partnership interest or close company interest as referred to above, including making a relevant loan to such entities; or
(c) the maintenance of, or enhancement of the value of, a UK residential property interest.

Loans to close companies are not therefore relevant loans and fall to be treated as a participator interest in the company; by this means the loan will not be excluded property to the extent that it is attributable to a UK residential property interest. However, loans to partnerships are relevant loans, and therefore not excluded property, if used to finance the purchase of a UK residential property interest. Funds borrowed to service interest on a relevant loan are also treated as relevant loans.

From 6 April 2017, assets given as collateral, security or guarantee for a relevant loan are also not excluded property up to amount of the relevant loan. Interests in partnerships and closely held companies will also not be excluded property to the extent that they derive their value from a loan to acquire direct or indirect interests in UK residential property. Hence, where a non-domiciled individual has a portfolio of non-UK investments, and borrows on the security of the portfolio to buy a UK residence, the value of the residence less the loan is part of the individual's estate for IHT purposes as well as the value of the portfolio as collateral but capped to the value of the outstanding borrowing against it.

If a loan is initially made to finance the acquisition of an asset which is not within these provisions, but subsequently the proceeds of sale of that asset are then used directly or indirectly to finance the purchase of a UK residential property interest, the loan then becomes a 'relevant loan' and thereafter falls within these provisions. At such time as the residential property interest is disposed of, wholly or partly, the loan ceases to be a relevant loan either wholly, or to the extent of the partial disposal of the property.

Where an interest in a closely held company or partnership within these provisions is disposed of for money or monies worth, or a relevant loan is repaid or disposed of for money or monies worth, the proceeds will not count as excluded property for a period of two years beginning with the date of disposal. This applies notwithstanding the fact that the funds will be placed on a qualifying foreign currency bank account (see **20.13**). Any asset which directly or indirectly represents such proceeds of sale, or the repayment of the loan, is also caught by the two-year rule up to the value of the sale proceeds or the amount paid in respect of the loan. No similar two-year period applies in relation to the release of collateral, security or guarantee assets, or to the disposal proceeds of a UK residence within a close company or partnership.

A general anti-avoidance provision is to apply so that any arrangements which have a purpose or a main purpose of securing a tax advantage by avoiding or minimising the effect of these provisions is to be disregarded.

There is also a treaty override provision. Nothing in any double tax relief arrangements is to be read as preventing a person from being liable for inheritance tax under this legislation. See, however, **16.7** (Key points concerning domicile, second item) for the limitations of this in the case of treaties which override the UK deemed domicile provisions.

A transitional provision allows trustees' returns affected by liability under this legislation to be made at the later of the normal due date for the return and 31 December 2017. Interest on chargeable transfers similarly affected also runs from the end of 31 December 2017, if that is later than the normal date. [*IHTA 1984, Sch A1*].

Settlements made by non-domiciliaries

Subject to the provisions referred to below concerning formerly domiciled residents and the provisions referred to above in relation to UK residential property interests, settled property situated outside the UK was, prior to FA 2020, excluded property if the settlor was domiciled outside the UK and not deemed domiciled when the settlement was made. If the settlor added funds to the trust at a time when he was UK domiciled, or had become deemed domiciled, the added funds were not considered by HMRC to be excluded property although there were arguments against this view. This point was referred to by the Court of Appeal in *Barclays Wealth Trustees (Jersey) Ltd and*

Dreelan v HMRC [2017] STC 2465 but left open for a decision in a case specifically on the point. Since the position was unclear, it has been dealt with by an amendment to *IHTA 1984, s 48(3)(a)* for charges on settled property arising on or after 22 July 2020. Settled property situated outside the UK is now excluded property if the settlor was not UK domiciled and not deemed domiciled in the UK at the time the property became comprised in the settlement. This test has full retrospective effect so that it must be applied to additions to the settlement made in all past years. There are no tracing provisions set out in the legislation and trustees will therefore need to make the best analysis they can of transactions within the trust where there have been past additions made when the settlor was UK domiciled. Accumulations of income are treated as becoming comprised in the settlement at the time when the property from which they arise became comprised in the settlement.

It remains the case that the domicile status of beneficiaries of the trust, or the residence of the trustees, is irrelevant in determining whether any of the settled property is excluded property.

Where settled property is transferred to another relevant property settlement and it had excluded property status before the transfer, it will continue to be excluded property after the transfer only if the settlor of the original settlement continues to be non-UK domiciled at the time of the transfer. See **40.23** for more detailed analysis.

Authorised unit trusts and shares in open-ended investment companies are also excluded property in trusts created by a foreign domiciled settlor. See *A Beneficiary v CIR* [1999] STC SCD 134 SpC 190. For property in a settlement before 10 December 1974, the special provisions relating to domicile in *IHTA 1984, s 267* (see **16.5** DOMICILE) do not apply. The status of excluded property is determined immediately before vesting (*Von Ernst and Cie SA v CIR* IRC [1980] 1 All ER 677, CA 1979, [1980] STC 111, CA).

A reversionary interest in a trust of assets qualifying as excluded property is also excluded property if the individual entitled to it is domiciled outside the UK.

Where UK assets in a settlement made by a non-domiciled settlor are sold and the proceeds reinvested in overseas assets, no IHT exit charge arises (see *IHTA 1984, s 65(7)*). Defective drafting of *s 65(7)* did not originally prevent an exit charge where funds not qualifying as excluded property were reinvested in authorised unit trusts or shares in open-ended investment companies, but this defect was corrected with full retrospective effect to 15 October 2002 by *FA 2013, s 175*.

Where the settlor or settlor's spouse has an initial interest in possession in a settlement created after 26 March 1974, such that the life interest causes the settled property to be in the estate of the life tenant for IHT purposes, two conditions must be satisfied if any of the trust assets are to continue to be excluded property in any relevant property trust after the life interest ends. The first condition ('condition A') is that the settlor must be non-domiciled and not deemed domiciled when the property concerned became comprised in the settlement and also that the settlor's spouse must be non-domiciled and not deemed domiciled when the life interest terminates. The second condition ('condition B') is neither of them must be *formerly domiciled residents* for the tax year in which the relevant time falls. [*IHTA 1984, s 81B*]. The condition in relation to formerly domiciled residents has effect from 6 April 2017 [*IHTA 1984, s 48(3E)*]. The conditions in relation to the person who originally created the settlement do not apply to authorised unit trusts in a settlement created before 22 July 2020.

[*IHTA 1984, s 81B(7)*].

A *formerly domiciled* resident is an individual who was born in the UK, whose domicile of origin is in the UK, who is UK resident for the tax year and was UK resident for at least one of the two preceding tax years.

Provisions to block avoidance schemes

Because the domicile status of trust beneficiaries is irrelevant for the purposes of determining whether trust assets are excluded property, it was possible to avoid IHT liability by purchasing an interest in an excluded property trust. To prevent such schemes, an initial draft of anti-avoidance measures were introduced with effect from 5 December 2005 to prevent UK domiciled individuals who become entitled to interests in pre-existing foreign trusts originally settled by non-UK domiciliaries which are treated as excluded property within *IHTA 1984, s 48(3)* from being treated as excluded property if it is acquired for money or money's worth. It is immaterial whether the consideration is given by the person acquiring the interest in possession in the settlement or someone else or whether the entitlement arises by way of will or intestacy. Any IHT arising as a result of this avoidance provision applying from 5 December 2005 to the day before enactment of the *FA 2006* on 19 July 2006 will be due 14 days after enactment. If the acquired interest is subsequently resettled by someone who is domiciled outside the UK relief may still be available under *IHTA 1984, s 48(3)* in respect of the new settlement.

In summary therefore *FA 2006* anti-avoidance has provided that property is not excluded property if:

(a) an individual is, or has been, beneficially entitled to an interest in possession in the property at any time;
(b) the individual is, or was, domiciled in the UK at the time; and
(c) their entitlement arose directly or *indirectly* as a result of a disposition for consideration in money or money's worth made on or after 5 December 2005. It does not matter whether the consideration was given by the individual with the interest in possession or by someone else (this also includes cases in which an entitlement arose indirectly including entitlements arising under a will or the law relating to intestacy).

[*IHTA 1984, s 48(3B)(3C)*].

See *Salinger and Kirby v HMRC* ([2016] UKFTT 677 (TC)) in which interests in an Isle of Man trust settled by a company domiciled outside the UK were purchased in 2009 by a UK domiciled beneficiary who died thereafter in 2011. The main trust interest purchased was as the sole income and capital beneficiary for the trust period of 150 years, but subject to a trustee's power to accumulate, hence the provisions above did not apply. The First-tier Tax Tribunal accepted that the acquisition of this interest was a commercial bargain and so did not give rise to a chargeable transfer.

To deal with the loophole exposed by the case of *Salinger and Kirby*, this anti-avoidance legislation was extended by *FA 2012, s 208*, with effect from 20 June 2012 for arrangements entered into on or after that date, to cover cases where a UK domiciled individual, or a close company in relation to which the individual is a participator, acquires an interest in excluded property (or property which was foreign situs property at any time during the arrangements), other than an interest in possession which forms part of the individual's estate. For this purpose there is an interest in settled property if the property, or any derived property, is, will or may become payable to, or applicable for the benefit of, the individual or the individual's spouse or civil partner in any circumstances, or if the individual or the individual's spouse or civil partner enjoys a benefit deriving (directly or indirectly) from the property or any derived property. There must also be a 'relevant reduction' in the individual's estate, broadly a reduction in value by virtue of entering into the arrangements to acquire the interest. Where *s 208* applies to arrangements, not only is the excluded property status of foreign trust assets withdrawn, but in addition the individual purchasing the trust interest makes a chargeable transfer equal to the amount by which the scheme reduces his estate for IHT purposes. If the scheme relates to the individual's interest in possession in settled property within *IHTA 1984, s 49(1)*, and it reduces the value of the settled property, a corresponding chargeable transfer is treated as made by the beneficiary and he is liable for any tax due as a result together with the trustees.

[*IHTA 1984, ss 48(3D–F), 74A–C*].

Liabilities to finance excluded property

For transfers of value made or treated as made on or after 17 July 2013, it is no longer possible to reduce the value of an asset for IHT purposes by securing a loan on it where the loan is used to acquire or maintain (directly or indirectly) excluded property. Instead the loan is not to be taken into account for IHT purposes. This rule has equal effect for charges on settlements holding relevant property within *IHTA 1984, s 58*.

The rule applies to liabilities whenever incurred. If the excluded property is subsequently disposed of for full consideration, the liability may then be deductible for IHT purposes to the extent that the proceeds of the disposal are not used to acquire or maintain other excluded property, or to pay off another loan which cannot be taken into account by virtue of this provision. A liability may be taken into account to the extent that it exceeds the value of any of the excluded property not disposed of, but not where this excess is attributable to arrangements to secure a tax advantage, an increase in the amount of the liability, or a disposal of any of the excluded property. For example, if a loan is taken out to buy shares in a foreign incorporated company, and arrangements are then made for tax reasons to reduce the value of those shares, the loan will remain non-deductible.

A loan is considered by HMRC to indirectly finance an asset where it is initially used to buy asset 1 which is later sold and the proceeds reinvested in asset 2. The loan then indirectly finances asset 2 (see HMRC IHT Manual para IHTM 28018). On this view it is not possible to circumvent the disallowance by first acquiring UK property with a loan, subsequently selling that property and then acquiring excluded property with the proceeds. Equally where a loan is taken out to buy a UK asset, say a painting, and that asset becomes excluded property, for example by being removed from the UK, the loan is deductible only to the extent that it exceeds the value of that asset and subject also to there being no arrangements to secure a tax advantage.

See further commentary at 53.19.

Situs

[20.3] See 46 SITUS for the rules determining where property is situated.

Table of asset locations:

Asset	Location/situs
Land, buildings and leases including any share in land or a building.	Where the land is physically situated.
Registered shares and securities (but see Government stocks above).	Where the register is kept on which the shares or securities are registered.
An interest in an unincorporated business or an interest in a partnership.	Where the business is carried out.
Chattels and personal possessions.	Where the item is situated at the time of the transfer or at the date of death.
Debts owed to the deceased (other than specialty debts).	Where the debtor lives at the time of transfer or on death.
Bank accounts.	Where the bank or branch holding the account is situated.

Reversionary interest

[20.4] A reversionary interest is excluded property unless:

(a) it has at any time been acquired (whether by the person entitled to it or by a person previously entitled) for a consideration in money or money's worth; or

(b) it is the interest expectant on the determination of a lease which is treated as a settlement because the lease is for life or lives, or for a period ascertainable only by reference to death, or which is terminable on, or at a date ascertainable only by reference to, a death, and was not granted for full consideration in money or money's worth. Where a lease, not granted at a rack rent, is at any time to become a lease at an increased rent, it shall be treated as terminable at that time; or

(c) for a settlement made after 15 April 1976, it is one to which either the settlor or his spouse or civil partner is (or, for a reversionary interest acquired after 9 March 1981, has been) beneficially entitled.

(d) where the anti-avoidance provisions of *IHTA 1984, s 74A(1)* apply (that is, in relation to avoidance schemes involving the purchase of an interest in an excluded property trust), the interest acquired is a reversionary interest in the trust concerned but another interest in that trust is or can be acquired.

If a reversionary interest falls into one of the exceptions in (a)–(c) it may still be excluded property in certain circumstances if it is situated outside the UK. See **20.2** above. Additionally, a reversionary interest is to be treated as excluded property where the reversioner to that property is non-UK domiciled. This assists non-UK domiciled individuals who have a reversionary interest but die before that interest falls in and will no longer have the threat of an IHT charge in those particular circumstances for instance. [*IHTA 1984, s 48(3A)(b)* as inserted by *FA 2003, s 186(3)*].

Where more than one person is the settlor in relation to a settlement and the circumstances so require, the above provisions apply as if the settled property were comprised in separate settlements. HMRC normally apply this general rule, that is the circumstances are normally regarded as requiring it.

[*IHTA 1984, ss 43(3), 44(2), 48(1)(2)(3A)(b); FA 2003, s 186(3)*].

Government securities

[20.5] The inheritance tax exemption for Government securities is summarised as follows by HMRC at IHTM27241:

- FOTRA securities (that is, those free of tax to persons resident abroad) issued before 29 April 1996 and acquired before 6 April 2013 will be exempt provided the beneficial owner is both domiciled and ordinarily resident outside the UK.
- 3½% War Loan 1952 or after acquired before 6 April 2013 will only be exempt if the beneficial owner is both domiciled and ordinarily resident outside the UK, even if the chargeable event is after 6 April 1998.
- All other government securities issued before 6 April 1998 without FOTRA conditions will be exempt from that date if acquired before 6 April 2013 provided the beneficial owner is ordinarily resident outside the UK. Domicile is no longer relevant.
- All other government securities issued after 29 April 1996 and acquired before 6 April 2013 will be exempt provided the beneficial owner is ordinarily resident outside the UK. Domicile is no longer relevant.
- In relation to all categories listed above, for securities acquired after 6 April 2013 the requirement as to ordinary residence is removed and replaced with a condition that the beneficial owner is resident outside the United Kingdom.

Thus in the circumstances set out above the securities are excluded property if:

(a) they are beneficially owned by such a person and are not settled property; or

(b) they are settled property and such a person is entitled to a qualifying interest in possession in them. If a close company is the person entitled, the participators in the company are treated as being entitled to the interest according to their respective rights and interests in the company; or

(c) they are settled property in which there is no qualifying interest in possession (see **40.1** SETTLEMENTS: DISCRETIONARY TRUSTS AND OTHER TRUSTS OF RELEVANT PROPERTY) and all known persons for whose benefit the settled property or income from it has been or might be applied or who are or might become beneficially entitled to an interest in possession in it are of a description specified in the condition in question. See *Montague Trust Co (Jersey) Ltd and Others v CIR* Ch D [1989] STC 477.

Where:

(i) after 19 April 1978 and before 10 December 1981 property ceased to be comprised in one settlement and, by the same disposition, became comprised in another settlement; or

(ii) after 9 December 1981 property ceased to be comprised in one settlement and became comprised in another without any person in the meantime having become entitled to the property (and not merely to an interest in possession in it),

the property in the second settlement will only be excluded property if these requirements are satisfied by both settlements. However, this does not apply where a reversionary interest in the property expectant on the termination of a qualifying interest in possession subsisting under the first settlement was settled on the trusts of the second settlement before 10 December 1981.

A charity cannot be a 'known person for whose benefit the settled property . . . might be applied' (*Von Ernst & Cie SA and Others v CIR* CA 1979, [1980] STC 111).

Note that in the few cases where domicile remains relevant for the purposes of this exemption (FOTRA securities issued before 29 April 1996), the deemed domicile provisions of *IHTA 1984, s 267* are disapplied [*IHTA 1984, s 267(2)*].

[*IHTA 1984, ss 6(2), 48(4)–(7), 101(1), 267(2); FA 1996, s 154, Sch 28 paras 7, 8*].

Overseas pensions

Transfers on death only

[20.6] Any pension receivable from a fund set up under the *Government of India Act 1935, s 273* (or a corresponding fund under *Overseas Pensions Act 1973, s 2*) is to be left out of account in determining the value of a person's estate immediately before his death.

Transfers generally

[20.7] Any pension, gratuity, sum payable on or in respect of death or a return of contributions (including interest thereon) paid from certain pension funds relating to service in overseas territories is to be treated as paid by the government of the territory concerned. It will thus constitute property situated outside the UK (see **46** SITUS) and will be excluded property if the pensioner is domiciled overseas (see **20.2** above). The pensions are those:

(a) paid out of any fund established in the UK by the government of any country which at the time the fund was established was, or formed part of, a colony, protectorate, protected state or 'UK trust territory' for the sole purpose of paying pensions etc. in respect of service under that government e.g. DFID Overseas Pensions Department;

(b) paid out of the Central African Pension Fund established by *Federation of Rhodesia and Nyasaland (Dissolution) Order in Council 1963, s 24*;
(c) paid under a scheme made under *Overseas Pensions Act 1973, s 2* which is constituted by the *Pensions (India, Pakistan and Burma) Act 1955* (or similar);
(d) paid under the scheme constituted under *Overseas Pensions Act 1973, s 2* by *Overseas Service Act 1958, ss 2, 4(2)* (or similar); and
(e) for which the UK has assumed responsibility within the meaning of *Overseas Pensions Act 1973, s 1* exclusive of any increase in the pension under *Pensions (Increase) Act 1971* or any enactment repealed by that Act.

'*UK trust territory*' means a territory administered by the UK government under the trusteeship system of the United Nations.

[*IHTA 1984, s 153*].

Persons domiciled in Channel Islands or Isle of Man

Savings

[20.8] The following savings to which persons domiciled in the above Islands are beneficially entitled are excluded property.

(a) War savings certificates.
(b) NS&I National savings certificates (including Ulster savings certificates).
(c) NS&I Premium bonds.
(d) NS&I Deposits with the National Savings Bank or with a trustee savings bank.
(e) Any certified contractual savings scheme (e.g. SAYE schemes with qualification in the prospectus) within the meaning of *ICTA 1988, s 326(2)(6)* and *ITEPA 2003, Sch 3 para 48(1)* as replaced by *ITTOIA 2005, ss 702(1), 703(2)(3), 704(2), 705(1), 707(1)*.

For the above purposes, the special provisions relating to domicile in *IHTA 1984, s 267* (see **16.5** DOMICILE) does not apply.

[*IHTA 1984, ss 6(3), 267(2)*].

Visiting forces

[20.9] Emoluments paid by the Government of a country designated by Order in Council to a member of a visiting force of that country (including the member of a civilian component) are excluded property provided that member is not a British citizen, a British Dependent Territories citizen or a British Overseas citizen. Any tangible movable property in the UK solely because of the presence of that member is also excluded. [*Visiting Forces (Inheritance Tax) (Designation) Order 1998, Art 1; ITA 2007, s 833*].

A period during which any such member is in the UK by reason solely of his being such a member is not treated for inheritance tax purposes as a period of residence in the UK or as creating a change of residence or domicile. [*IHTA 1984, ss 6(4), 155*].

The *Visiting Forces (Inheritance Tax) (Designation) Order 1998, SI 1998/1516* comes into effect in respect of the following countries on the later of the date the country becomes party to the agreement or the day after the date on which the Order was made (i.e. 25 June 1998).

Designated countries:

- Armenia
- Austria
- Azerbaijan
- Belarus
- Finland
- Georgia
- Kazakhstan
- Kyrgyzstan
- The Former Yugoslav Republic of Macedonia
- Moldova
- Russia
- Switzerland
- Turkmenistan
- Ukraine
- Uzbekistan

Special discretionary trusts

[20.10] Where tax is charged when property leaves certain trusts, no account is taken of any quarter throughout which the property was excluded property when determining the appropriate rate of tax. [*IHTA 1984, ss 70(7), 71(5), 72(5), 73(3), 74(3)*]. See **10.5** CHARITIES; **42.5** SETTLEMENTS: INTERESTS HELD ON PROTECTIVE TRUSTS; **44.5** SETTLEMENTS: TRUSTS FOR DISABLED PERSONS; and **52.9** TRUSTS FOR EMPLOYEES.

Chevening Estate and Apsley House

[20.11] Inheritance tax does not apply to property held on trusts under the *Schedule* to the *Chevening Estate Act 1959* or rights conferred by the *Wellington Museum Act 1947*. [*IHTA 1984, s 156*].

Non-UK domiciles (AUT and OEIC investments)

[20.12] Investments in authorised unit trusts (AUTs) or open-ended investment companies (OEICs) are excluded property whilst held by non-domiciled and non-deemed domiciled individuals. Similarly, such investments held by trusts of which the settlor was non-UK domiciled at the time the settlement was made are excluded property, save that this ceases to apply for any tax year in which the settlor is a formerly domiciled resident for that year (**20.2** SETTLEMENTS MADE BY NON-DOMICILIARIES). These provisions were introduced to boost the competitiveness of UK-authorised funds in the international market place. The treatment of such investments as excluded property applies to IHT occasions of charge on or after 16 October 2002.

The IHT anti-avoidance measures mentioned in **20.2** above apply from 5 December 2005 to prevent UK domiciled individuals who purchase interests in pre-existing foreign trusts originally settled by non-UK domiciliaries which benefit from the exemption attaching to such property or under *IHTA 1984, s 48(3A)* relating to holdings in AUTs and OEICs from obtaining the benefit of excluded property. It is immaterial whether the consideration is given by the person with the interest in possession in the settlement or someone else arising by way of will or intestacy. Any IHT arising as a result of this avoidance provision applying from 5 December 2005 to the day before enactment of the *FA 2006* on 19 July 2006 will be due 14 days of enactment. If the acquired interest is subsequently resettled by someone who is domiciled outside the UK relief may still be available under *IHTA 1984, s 48(3A)* in respect of the new settlement. See **20.2** above. [*IHTA 1984, ss 6(1A), 48(3A)(a)* as inserted by *FA 2003, s 186(3)* and amended by *FA 2006, s 157(3)–(6)*].

Non-residents' bank accounts

[20.13] On the death prior to 6 April 2013 of a person not domiciled, resident or ordinarily resident in the UK immediately before his death, the balance on any 'qualifying foreign currency account' is not included in the value of his estate immediately before his death. This also applies to such an account held by trustees of settled property in which the deceased held a beneficial interest in possession unless either (a) the settlor was domiciled in the UK at the time the settled property became comprised in the settlement, or (b) the trustees are either domiciled or resident in the UK at the time of the beneficiary's death.

With effect for deaths on or after 6 April 2013, this exemption continues to apply but is modified to delete the requirements relating to ordinary residence outside the UK. The conditions for exemption of a foreign currency bank account held by a person at the time of death are therefore that he is not domiciled and not resident in the UK immediately before his death.

For transfers of value on or after 17 July 2014, a liability which is attributable to financing an account within this exclusion from IHT is not deductible from the value of the account holder's estate on death. If the liability exceeds the balance on the account, the excess is deductible so long as it does not arise from arrangements made either to secure a tax advantage or to increase the liability for example by rolling up interest on the loan. [*FA 2014, Sch 25 para 3*].

See **53.20** for further details.

Awards for gallantry

[20.14] A decoration or other award is excluded property if it was awarded for valour or gallant conduct and no interest in it has ever changed hands for money or money's worth. This was previously the subject of HMRC Extra-statutory Concession F19, which was enacted with effect from 6 April 2009. With effect from 3 December 2014 the exclusion was extended to include a decoration or other similar award:

(a) that is designed to be worn to denote membership of (i) an Order that is, or has been, specified in the Order of Wear published in the London Gazette, or (ii) an Order of a country or territory outside the United Kingdom;

(b) that is, or has been, specified in the Order of Wear;

(c) that was awarded for, or in connection with, a person being, or having been, a member of, or employed or engaged in connection with the armed forces of any country or territory;

(d) that was awarded for, or in connection with, a person being, or having been, an emergency responder within the meaning of *IHTA 1984, s 153A* (death of emergency service personnel, see **21.20**); or

(e) that was awarded by the Crown or a country or territory outside the United Kingdom for, or in connection with, public service or achievement in public life.

[*IHTA, s 6(1B), (1C); FA 2015, s 74*].

21

Exempt Transfers and Other Reliefs

Cross-references. See 4 AGRICULTURAL PROPERTY; 6 BUSINESS PROPERTY; 10 CHARITIES; 13 DEEDS VARYING DISPOSITIONS ON DEATH; 15 DIPLOMATIC IMMUNITY; 30 NATIONAL HERITAGE; 35 POTENTIALLY EXEMPT TRANSFERS; 52 TRUSTS FOR EMPLOYEES.

Simon's Taxes. See I3.154, I3.155, I3.3, I4.2, I4.445, I4.446, I5.336.

Other Sources. Form P11(Notes); Foster, Parts C and D; IHT 110; IHT 400 Notes; IHTM11000; HMRC Customer Guide to Inheritance Tax; IHTM43001–IHTM43035.

General exemptions

Nil rate tax band

[21.1] Currently, the first £325,000 of chargeable transfers in any seven-year period are taxable at nil%. However, this is not to be regarded as an exemption, it is an amount chargeable but at nil rate. See **9.3** CHARGEABLE TRANSFER and **37** RATES OF TAX.

Gifts to charities

[21.2] Gifts to charities are exempt from inheritance tax. [*IHTA 1984, s 23(1)*]. [**Case Study 9**]. See also **21.4** below for transfer of property from certain trusts to charities. See IHTM11101.

Property is given to a charity if it becomes the property of the charity or is held on trust for charitable purposes only. [*IHTA 1984, s 23(6)*]. Where the value transferred (i.e. the loss to the transferor's estate as a result of the disposition) exceeds the value of the gift in the hands of the charity (or political party), the exemption extends to the whole value transferred. (See HMRC Statement of Practice E13.)

'*Charity*' has the meaning given by *ITA 2007, ss 519, 543(1)* for income tax purposes, i.e. 'any body of persons or trust established for charitable purposes only' and was considered by HMRC to exclude all foreign charities. For transfers of value from 6 April 2010 up to 31 March 2024, charity tax reliefs were extended by FA 2010, Sch 6 to certain organisations which are equivalent to charities and Community Amateur Sports Clubs in the EU and in the European Economic Area countries of Norway and Iceland. However, this is withdrawn for transfers of value made on or after 1 April 2024 and, in relation to transfers of value made on or after 15 March 2023, for gifts to charities which have not by that date asserted their status as a charity by making a valid claim for a charitable tax relief to HMRC. A community amateur sports club if it is a registered club, will be treated as a charity for inheritance tax purposes. Following *Finance Act 2002* the '*charity*' exemption is also extended to include a club that is registered as a community amateur sports club, and is required by its constitution to be, and is a club that (a) is open to the whole community; (b) is organised on an amateur basis; and (c) has as its main purpose the provision of facilities for, and the promotion of participation in, one or more eligible sports. [*FA 2002, Sch 18 paras 1–3, 9(2); ITA 2007, s 430(1)(d)*]. See *Dreyfus (Camille & Henry) Foundation Inc v CIR* HL 1955, 36 TC 126. [*IHTA 1984, s 272; F(No 2)A 2023, s 344*]. See also **10** CHARITIES.

Reduced rate for certain estates with 10% gifts to charities

For deaths on or after 6 April 2012 inheritance tax is charged on the net chargeable value of an estate at a rate of 36% where 10% or more of that estate has been left to charity.

Where the estate comprises only the deceased's 'free estate', the value of the estate on which the 10% threshold is based, (the 'baseline') is the value of the net estate charged to IHT after deducting all available reliefs, exemptions and available nil rate band, but excluding the charitable legacy itself. The total amount of charitable legacies is compared with the baseline amount to see if the estate qualifies for the reduced IHT rate (the '10%').

In cases in which the estate for IHT purposes includes assets additional to those in the 'free estate', the 10% test is applied to each category of assets, described as a 'component', that makes up the aggregate estate. The components are:

(a) the 'general component' being the free estate passing under the terms of the will. This excludes other components listed below and also gifts with reservation of benefit chargeable on the death;
(b) the 'survivorship component' being jointly owned assets passing by survivorship (in England, Wales and Northern Ireland), or under a special destination in Scotland, or under corresponding provisions of any applicable foreign law;
(c) the 'settled property component', being settled property comprised in the estate by virtue of an interest in possession to which the deceased was beneficially entitled.

If the assets passing to charity from one component exceed 10% of the baseline, other components may be merged with it to give an aggregate baseline. This merging of components requires an election to be made by all those who are 'appropriate persons' for each of the components involved; the appropriate persons are the personal representatives in relation to the general component, the settlement trustees in relation to the settled component and the surviving joint owner or owners in relation to the survivorship component.

The value of the assets passing to charity from a particular component are compared to the baseline amount for that component. The baseline amount is calculated after deducting from that component all available reliefs, exemptions and the appropriate proportion of the available nil rate band, as increased by the transfer of nil rate band provisions. If the 10% test for a component is passed, IHT is charged on that particular component at 36%.

The reduced rate of IHT will apply automatically if the estate or component passes the 10% test. If it does not, IHT is charged at the full rate. However, personal representatives and other relevant persons may elect for the reduced rate not to apply if, for example, the benefit obtained from applying the reduced rate is likely to be minimal and they do not wish to incur additional costs of valuing items left to charity.

These provisions apply equally to charitable legacies made by will or by an Instrument of Variation. The conditions for an Instrument of Variation to be taken into account for IHT purposes are amended so that the reduced rate applies only if it is shown that the charity has been notified that the devolution of the estate has been varied in its favour. [*FA 2012, s 209; IHTA 1984, Sch 1A*].

Example 1

The estate of Percival who dies after 6 April 2012 is valued at £425,000, comprising quoted investments and cash. He leaves a legacy of £10,000 to the National Trust and the residue of £415,000 less IHT passes to his children. The IHT payable will be £90,000 at 36% – £32,400 because 10% of the estate after deduction of the nil-band is left to charity. So the gift to the charity reduces the residue by only £2,400 (£10,000 gift less IHT reduction £40,000 – £32,400). If Percival died on 5 April 2012 the IHT payable would be £36,000.

Exceptions

[21.3] The exemption above does not apply under any of the following circumstances.

(a) If the testamentary or other disposition giving the property:
  - (i) takes effect on the termination of any interest or period after the transfer is made (e.g. a gift to a person for life and then to the charity); or
  - (ii) depends on a condition which is not satisfied within twelve months after the transfer; or
  - (iii) is defeasible. (For this purpose, any disposition which has not been defeated within twelve months of the transfer and is not defeasible after that time is treated as not being defeasible (whether or not it was capable of being defeated before that time).)

(b) If the property is:
  - (i) an interest in other property and that interest is less than the donor's; or
  - (ii) an interest in other property and that property is given for a limited period; or
  - (iii) an interest in possession in settled property and the settlement does not come to an end in relation to that settled property on the making of the transfer (unless the transfer is a disposition whereby the use of money or other property is allowed by one person to another) (see *Powell-Cotton v CIR* Ch D, [1992] STC 625); or
  - (iv) land or a building given subject to an interest reserved or created by the donor entitling him, his spouse or civil partner or a person connected with him to possess or occupy the whole or part of the property rent-free or at a rent less than obtainable in an arm's length transaction between unconnected persons; or
  - (v) not land or a building and is given subject to an interest reserved or created by the donor other than an interest created by him for full consideration in money or money's worth or an interest which does not substantially affect the enjoyment of the property by the person or body to whom it is given; or
  - (vi) property of which any part may become applicable for purposes other than charitable purposes or those of a body within **21.5** to **21.8** below; or
  - (vii) given in consideration of the transfer of a reversionary interest which under *IHTA 1984, s 55(1)* (see **19.4** ESTATE) does not form part of the estate of the person acquiring that interest.

(c) If immediately before the time when it becomes the property of the charity, the property is comprised in a settlement and, at or before that time but after 11 April 1978, an interest under the settlement is or has been acquired for a consideration in money or money's worth by that or another charity or body within **21.5** to **21.8** below (otherwise than *from* another charity or body within **21.5** to **21.7** below). For these purposes, a person is treated as acquiring an interest for a consideration in money or money's worth if he becomes entitled to it as a result of transactions which include a disposition for such consideration (whether to him or another) of that interest or other property. The exception does not apply if the transfer is a disposition whereby the use of money or other property is allowed by one person to another.

In (b)(i) above any question whether any interest is less than the donor's and in (b)(iv) and (v) above whether property is given subject to an interest, is decided at a time twelve months after the transfer.

See **48.3** TRANSFER OF VALUE for modification of the above where the transfer of value is an uncommercial loan. See also **21.24** below.

[*IHTA 1984, ss 23(2)–(5), 56(1)(3)–(6)(8); F(No 2)A 1987, Sch 7 para 2; FA 1998, s 143(2)(a); FA 2002, Sch 18 para 9(2)*]. See *Bailhache Labesse Trustees Ltd & Others v HMRC* [2008] STC (SCD) 869.

Settled property becoming held for charitable purposes

[21.4] No charge to tax arises when property ceases to be relevant property in a **40** SETTLEMENTS: DISCRETIONARY TRUSTS AND OTHER TRUSTS OF RELEVANT PROPERTY or ceases to be comprised in a temporary charitable trust (see **10.4** CHARITIES), a maintenance fund for historic buildings (see **30.23** NATIONAL HERITAGE, **41** SETTLEMENTS: ACCUMULATION AND MAINTENANCE TRUST, **42** SETTLEMENTS: INTERESTS HELD ON PROTECTIVE TRUST, **44** SETTLEMENTS: TRUST FOR DISABLED PERSONS, or **52** TRUST FOR EMPLOYEES) and becomes property held for charitable purposes only without limit of time (defined by date or otherwise). Also exempt is the settlement on discretionary trusts by a person's will of property which then becomes held, within two years of death, for charitable purposes only without limit of time. See **49.15** TRANSFERS ON DEATH. See also Tolley's Income Tax for information on gifts to charity from certain settlements. [*FA 2000, s 44*].

The exemption does not apply under the following circumstances.

(a) The disposition is defeasible. (For this purpose any disposition which has not been defeated within twelve months of the transfer and is not defeasible after that time is treated as not being defeasible (whether or not it was capable of being defeated before that time).)
(b) The property or any part of it can be applied otherwise than for charitable purposes or the purposes of a body within **21.6** to **21.8** below (but see *FA 1998, s 143(4)*).
(c) At or before the time of the disposition, an interest in the settlement is, or has been, acquired for a consideration in money or money's worth (or as a result of transactions which include a disposition for such consideration, whether to that body or another person, of that interest or other property) by a charity or body within **21.6** to **21.8** below otherwise than *from* a charity or body within **21.6** or **21.7** below.

If the amount on which tax would otherwise be charged (before grossing-up if applicable and before **6** BUSINESS PROPERTY relief or **4** AGRICULTURAL PROPERTY relief) exceeds the value of the property immediately after it becomes the property of the recipient body (less any consideration for the transfer received by the trustees), the amount on which tax is charged is restricted to the excess. [*IHTA 1984, ss 76(1)(3)–(8), 144; FA 1998, s 143*].

These provisions also apply where the settled property mentioned above becomes that of the bodies within **21.6** to **21.8** below. See also **40.22** SETTLEMENTS: DISCRETIONARY TRUSTS AND OTHER TRUSTS OF RELEVANT PROPERTY.

Gifts to housing associations

[21.5] Transfers of value after 13 March 1989 to registered social landlords (within the meaning of *Housing Associations Act 1985* or *Housing (Northern Ireland) Order 1981, Part VII (SI 1981/156)* and *Housing Act 1996, Part I*) are exempt to the extent that the value transferred is attributable to land in the United Kingdom. [*IHTA 1984, s 24A(1)(2); FA 1989, s 171*]. See IHTM11211.

Exceptions are the same as those applying to gifts to charities, see **21.2** above [*IHTA 1984, ss 23(2)–(5), 24(3), 56(1)(3)–(6)(8); FA 1998, s 143(3)*].

Gifts for national purposes

[21.6] Gifts to certain national bodies (see list under **30.29** NATIONAL HERITAGE) are exempt from inheritance tax. [*IHTA 1984, s 25(1), Sch 3*]. See IHTM11221.

Exceptions are the same as those applying to gifts to charities, see **21.2** above, but **21.3**(b)(i) and (ii) do not prevent the exemption from applying in relation to property consisting of the benefit of an agreement restricting the use of land. [*IHTA 1984, ss 23(2)–(5), 25(2), 56(1)(3)–(6)(8)*].

See also **21.4** above which applies equally to settled property becoming the property of a national body under *IHTA 1984, s 25(1)*. [*IHTA 1984, ss 76(1)(3)–(8), 144; FA 1998, s 143(4)*].

Gifts to political parties

[21.7] All gifts made to qualifying political parties after 14 March 1988 are exempt from inheritance tax. For gifts made before 15 March 1988 exemption was limited to £100,000 if made on or within one year of death. Certain uncommercial loans which were transfers of value were not subject to the £100,000 limit. See **48.3** TRANSFER OF VALUE. A political party qualifies for exemption if, at the last general election (i.e. by-elections are ignored) preceding the transfer of value:

(a) two members of that party were elected to the House of Commons, or
(b) one member of that party was elected to the House of Commons and not less than 150,000 votes were given to candidates who were members of that party.

[*IHTA 1984, s 24(1)(2); FA 1988, s 137*].

Qualifying parties are listed in HMRC's Inheritance Tax Manual at para 11197. It should be noted that if a gift is made to a party not qualifying for exemption of any sort it will be a chargeable transfer, not a potentially exempt transfer as it does not increase the estate of another individual. Exceptions are the same as those applying to gifts to charities, see **21.2** above. [*IHTA 1984, ss 23(2)–(5), 24(3), 56(1)(3)–(6)(8)*].

In *Banks v HMRC* [2018] UKFTT 0617 (TC), concerning substantial donations to the UK Independence Party, the restrictions on this relief were challenged on the grounds that they were in breach of the European Convention of Human Rights, amounting to discrimination by reference to political views, and also they were in breach of the UK's obligations under the Treaty on European Union. It was held that the lack of exemption for gifts to UKIP could not be objectively justified, but the appeal failed because the Tribunal could not rewrite the statutory provision and was not able to make a declaration of incompatibility with the Human Rights legislation.

See also **21.4** above which applies equally to settled property becoming the property of a qualifying political party. [*IHTA 1984, ss 76(1)(3)–(8), 144; FA 1998, s 143(4)*].

Gifts for public benefit

[21.8] Up to 16 March 1998, gifts of eligible property to bodies not established or conducted for profit were, if the Board so directed (whether before or after the transfer), exempt from inheritance tax. [*IHTA 1984, s 26(1); FA 1985, s 95*]. Exceptions were the same as those applying to gifts to charities, see **21.2** above. [*IHTA 1984, ss 23(2)–(5), 26(7), 56(1)(3)–(6)(8)*]. These provisions were repealed with effect from 17 March 1998, due in the main to the unrestricted exemption on transfers to charitable bodies existing elsewhere in the legislation. [*FA 1998, s 143(4)*].

Transfers between spouses or civil partners

[21.9] Transfers of value between spouses or civil partners are exempt from inheritance tax:

(a) where property becomes comprised in the transferee's estate, by the amount by which the transferor's estate is diminished; or
(b) in any other case (e.g. payment by the transferor of his spouse's or civil partner's debt), by the amount by which the transferee's estate is increased.

For these purposes, property is given to a person if it becomes his property or is held in trust for him. For the purposes of the exemption, HMRC consider the following to be spouses:

(a) those legally married to each other, including same sex couples;
(b) those legally registered as same sex couples;
(c) those legally married but separated at death;
(d) those within a valid polygamous marriage.

[*IHTA 1984, s 18(1)(4); The Tax and Civil Partnership Regulations 2005, SI 2005/3229, Reg 7*].

£325,000 domiciliary gift limit

If, immediately before the transfer, the transferor, but not the transferor's spouse or civil partner, is domiciled in the UK the spouse exemption is subject to an upper limit. [*IHTA 1984, s 18(2)*]. This is a lifetime limit and once fully absorbed by lifetime gifts it cannot thereafter be restored. Any such lifetime gift, if not within some other exemption, will be primarily allocated to the limited exempt amount and only when that limit is exceeded will the gift be a potentially exempt transfer. Equally, gifts in excess of the exemption have no protection from the IHT reservation of benefit rules (see 22 GIFTS WITH RESERVATION). On the death of a UK domiciled spouse or civil partner, exemption for assets passing to a non-UK domiciled surviving spouse or civil partner will therefore be subject to the applicable limit, less the amount of lifetime gifts which have already been allocated to this exempt amount. Note that it is not only gifts which the deceased made in lifetime to his or her surviving spouse which must be included in the reckoning but also gifts made by the deceased to any spouse during previous marriages, whether the spouse concerned was UK domiciled or not (IHTM 11033). This means that personal representatives will need to try and identify the totality of lifetime gifts by the deceased to any spouse, an undertaking which may be impossible to carry out with any certainty. From 1982 to 5 April 2013 the limit was £55,000, and with effect for deaths and transfers on or after 6 April 2013, the limit is equal to the IHT nil band and is therefore £325,000. Therefore if there were lifetime gifts before 5 April 2013 which absorbed the £55,000 allowance, on death of the transferor after that date the balance of the higher allowance from that date will be available, currently £270,000. If the entire estate who dies after 5 April 2013 passes to the surviving spouse or civil partner and there have been no lifetime gifts, anything in excess of £325,000 is a chargeable legacy. In such cases where the net estate is above the nil rate band plus £325,000 there will be no nil rate band to transfer. Where the net estate is less than the nil rate band plus £325,000, there will still be an amount of nil rate band available to transfer. See also IHTM11011, IHTM11033. [*FA 2013, s 178*].

From 6 April 2013 an individual who is not domiciled in the UK (disregarding the IHT deemed domicile provisions of *IHTA 1984, s 267*, but whose spouse or civil partner is so domiciled, may elect to be treated as UK domiciled. The election may be either:

(a) a 'lifetime election' made at any time when the person making the election is non-UK domiciled but the person's spouse or civil partner is UK domiciled, or

(b) a 'death election' made within two years of the death on or after 6 April 2013 of the person's UK domiciled spouse or civil partner. This election may be made by the personal representatives of the non-UK domiciled spouse, in the event of that person's death.

Both elections are irrevocable, and apply only for IHT purposes so that they will have no application to the remittance basis rules for other tax purposes. An election has effect on the date specified in it, which must be on or after 6 April 2013. Subject to this, a lifetime election may specify a date which is within the period of seven years ending with the date on which it is made, and a death election may specify a date which is within seven years of the death of the UK domiciled spouse. In both cases the parties must have been married or civil partners throughout the period covered by the election.

The effect, on the death of a domiciled spouse leaving his or her estate to a surviving non-domiciled spouse, will be to allow full spouse exemption on that death, but on the death of the surviving spouse foreign assets of that spouse will not be excluded property for IHT purposes. However an election will cease to have effect if the person who made it becomes non-UK resident for income tax purposes for four successive tax years after the time that the election was effective. It will also not have any effect on the excluded property status of assets transferred into trust by the non-domiciled spouse before an election takes effect, nor on excluded property within *IHTA 1984, ss 6(3)* or *48(4)* (FOTRA gilts) and s *6(3)* (certain National Savings products). HMRC state that elections will need to be made in writing to them but there will be no prescribed form.

Example 2

George is UK domiciled and owns a house in the UK worth £3 million. His wife Monique is not domiciled in the UK for inheritance tax purposes and has only foreign assets worth £2 million. George dies on 1 August 2013 leaving his estate to Monique.

The IHT on the death of George is:

£3,000,000 less the spouse exemption £325,000 less the nil band £325,000, chargeable amount therefore £2,350,000. IHT liability is £940,000.

On death of Monique on 1 September 2018 when her domicile status for IHT remains unchanged, IHT will once again be due on the UK house. Assuming that its value has not changed, and that the IHT on George's death was paid from her overseas assets, the IHT on Monique's estate will be £3 million less £325,000, chargeable amount £2,675,000. IHT liability on that amount is £1,070,000, giving total liability on both deaths of £2,010,000.

If Monique had elected within two years of the death of George to be treated as domiciled in the UK with effect from 1 August 2013, no IHT would be payable on George's death. On Monique's death, IHT would then be due on both her UK and foreign assets. If they remain unchanged from George's death and having the same values, the IHT liability would be on £5,000,000 less her nil band and less George's nil band transferred to her estate, chargeable amount £4,350,000. The IHT liability on her estate would then be £1,740,000.

An election has no impact on the relief available under double tax treaties were in force prior to the introduction of this new provision.

Where an election has effect from an earlier date, it may cause dispositions already made by that person to become chargeable transfers. In that event the time limit for delivery of an account to HMRC for those chargeable transfers is extended to twelve months from the end of the month in which the election is made.

Exceptions

[21.10] Unless the transfer of value is a loan of money or property (see 48.3 TRANSFER OF VALUE) the spouse above exemption does not apply:

(i) if the testamentary or other disposition giving the property takes effect on the termination of any interest (e.g. a life interest in settled property) or period after the transfer is made, but this does not exclude a gift which is dependent on the spouse/civil partner surviving the donor spouse/civil partner by a specified period; or

(ii) if it depends on a condition which is not satisfied within twelve months after the transfer is made; or

(iii) if property is given in consideration of the transfer of a reversionary interest which under *IHTA 1984, s 55(1)* (see **19.4** ESTATE) does not form part of the estate of the person acquiring that interest. [*IHTA 1984, ss 18(3), 56(1)*].

Where a spouse purchased a reversionary interest in settled property after 15 April 1976 for a consideration in money or money's worth, the exemption does not apply on the falling in of the reversion by the termination of the interest on which the reversionary interest is expectant unless a loan of money or property is involved, see **48.3** TRANSFER OF VALUE. For these purposes, a person is treated as acquiring an interest for a consideration in money or money's worth if he becomes entitled to it as a result of transactions which include a disposition for such consideration (whether to him or another) of that interest or other property. [*IHTA 1984, s 56(2)(5)–(7); F(No 2)A 1987, Sch 7 para 2*].

See also **21.24** below.

Gifts on trusts for employees

Subject to detailed conditions, a gift of shares or securities into trust for employees is an exempt transfer. With effect from 6 April 2014, the exemption extends to certain gifts into an employee ownership trust. See **52** TRUSTS FOR EMPLOYEES.

Sums paid under the Equitable Life (Payments) Act 2010

[21.11] The value of any right to a payment under the *Equitable Life (Payments) Act 2010* is to be left out of account in determining (a) the value of a person's estate on death, and (b) the value of relevant property on a ten-year anniversary, in each case where the payment is made after the date of the chargeable event.

Lifetime transfers only

Annual gifts

[21.12] Annual gifts are treated as follows:

(a) **Annual exemption.** Transfers of value during the lifetime of a person up to a total of £3,000 per fiscal year are exempt from inheritance tax; this amount has remained unchanged since 1981. See IHTM14141, IHT110 and 210. [*IHTA 1984, s 19(1)(4)*].
Where the gifts (if any) fall short of the above limit, the shortfall is carried forward to the next following year and added to the allowance *for that year only*.

Where the gifts exceed the limit, the excess must:

(i) if the gifts were made on different days, be attributed, so far as possible, to a later rather than an earlier transfer; and

(ii) if the gifts were made on the same day, be attributed to them in proportion to the values transferred by them.

[*IHTA 1984, s 19(2)(3)*].

(b) Where a transfer of value is a **35** POTENTIALLY EXEMPT TRANSFER, in the first instance it is left out of account for the above purposes. However, if it proves to be a chargeable transfer, it is taken to have been made in the year in which it was made later than any transfer of value which is not a potentially exempt transfer. [*IHTA 1984, s 19(3A); FA 1986, Sch 19 para 5*]. The relevance of this provision is discussed at **35.2** POTENTIALLY EXEMPT TRANSFERS. See also **19.1** ESTATE for loan waiver using annual exemption.

For the purposes of the pre-owned assets anti-avoidance legislation within *FA 2004, Sch 15*, the disposal of any property which is an outright gift to an individual and is for the purposes of *IHTA 1984* a transfer of value that is *wholly* exempt by reason of *s 19* will be an excluded transaction. [*FA 2004, Sch 15 para 10(1)(e), (2)(e)*].

Example 3

S, who has made no other transfers of value, made gifts to his sister of £5,000 on 1 June 2018 and £4,000 on 1 May 2019. S dies on 1 September 2020 with an estate valued at £325,000. See **37** RATES OF TAX.

Annual exemptions are available as follows

2018/19	£	£
1 June 2018 Gift		5,000
Deduct 2018/19 annual exemption	3,000	
2017/18 annual exemption (part)	2,000	
		5,000
		Nil

2019/20	£
1 May 2019 Gift	4,000
Deduct 2019/20 annual exemption	3,000
PET becoming chargeable on death	£1,000

The PET, having become a chargeable transfer as a result of death within seven years, is covered by the nil rate band but is aggregated with the death estate in computing the IHT payable on death and therefore £1,000 is chargeable at 40%.

(c) **Small gifts to same person.** Transfers of value during the lifetime of a person up to a total of £250 per fiscal year *to any one person* are exempt from inheritance tax; this amount has remained unchanged since 1980. The gifts must be outright (i.e. not settled) but include free use of property (see **48.3** TRANSFER OF VALUE). This exemption is in addition to the annual exemption under (a) above and applies to any number of gifts up to £250 to separate persons but it cannot be used to cover part of a larger gift, i.e. the exemption will only apply where the value of all gifts in a year *to any individual* does not exceed £250. Form P11(Notes) states that 'This exemption covers gifts at birthdays and Christmas' but is not actually solely restricted to such gifts. [*IHTA 1984, s 20*]. See IHTM14180.

Notes to (a) and (b) above.

(i) The exemptions apply separately to husband, wife or civil partner.

(ii) The value of gifts is calculated without tax (i.e. they are not grossed up). [*IHTA 1984, ss 19(1), 20(1)*]. The exemptions apply only to transfers actually made (i.e. during lifetime) and not where deemed to have been made (such as on death or on a transfer by a settlement), but (a) does apply to transfers of value by a close company which are apportioned among its participators (see **11.5** CLOSE COMPANIES) and to the value chargeable on the termination of an interest in possession in settled property (see **39.9** SETTLEMENTS WITH INTERESTS IN POSSESSION). [*IHTA 1984, ss 3(4), 19(5), 20(3), 57, 94(5)*].

(iii) For the purposes of the pre-owned assets anti-avoidance legislation within *FA 2004, Sch 15,* the disposal of any property which is an outright gift to an individual and is for the purposes of *IHTA 1984* a transfer of value that is *wholly* exempt by reason of *s 20* will be an excluded transaction. [*FA 2004, Sch 15 para 10(1)(e), (2)(e)*].

Gifts in consideration of marriage or civil partnership

[21.13] Gifts in consideration of any one marriage or civil partnership by any one transferor (e.g. husband and wife are treated separately) are exempt from inheritance tax on the value transferred without tax (i.e. there is no grossing-up) up to the following limits, which have remained unchanged since 1975:

(a) £5,000 by a parent of either party to the marriage or civil partnership.

(b) £2,500 by one party to the marriage or civil partnership to the other or by a grandparent or remoter ancestor.

(c) £1,000 in any other case.

Any excess of gifts over the above limits is attributed in proportion to the values transferred. Form P11(Notes) prior to the civil partnership legislation being introduced stated that the gift should be made 'on or shortly before the marriage' and 'to be fully effective on the marriage taking place'. The common usage form of '...on the occasion of the marriage . . . ' is also acceptable. See IHTM14201 where HMRC state:

> 'Gifts or settlements made **after** marriage or civil partnership do not qualify for the exemption unless made in the fulfilment of a binding promise **before** marriage or civil partnership. You may assume that there is a binding promise for this purpose whenever the transferor has definitely told the donee that they were going to make the gift if the marriage or civil partnership takes place'.

Gifts must be outright to a party to the marriage or civil partnership, or settled gifts exclusively for the following persons who are or may become entitled to any benefit under the settlement (using Form 222).

(i) The parties to the marriage or civil partnership, issue of the marriage or civil partnership, or a wife or husband or civil partner of any such issue.
(ii) A subsequent spouse or civil partner of a party to the marriage or civil partnership, or any child of the family, or the spouse or civil partner of any such child, of a subsequent marriage or civil partnership of either party.
(iii) As respects a reasonable amount of remuneration, the trustees of the settlement.

'*Child of the family*' above includes in relation to parties to a marriage or civil partnership, a child of one or both of them. [*The Tax and Civil Partnership Regulations 2005, SI 2005/3229, Reg 8(6)*].

'*Issue*' includes any person legitimated by a marriage, or adopted by husband and wife jointly. [*IHTA 1984, s 22(1)–(5)*].

The exemptions apply only to actual lifetime gifts, not to transfers deemed to have been made (but include a loan of money or property, see **48.3** TRANSFER OF VALUE) and to the value chargeable on the termination of an interest in possession in settled property (see **39.9** SETTLEMENTS WITH INTERESTS IN POSSESSION). [*IHTA 1984, ss 3(4), 22(6), 57*]. See IHTM14201 for examples of non-qualification vis:

> 'Where before the marriage or civil partnership the donor has taken steps towards making the gift, for example, by instructing their solicitors or brokers, but the gift is not completed until after the marriage or civil partnership, it does not qualify.'

Note

The exemption will not be lost:

(A) if some other person can benefit from the settlement only in the event of any child to the marriage or civil partnership dying without attaining a specified age; or
(B) on the operation of a protective trust to which a person within (i) or (ii) above is the principal beneficiary.

Dispositions for maintenance of family

[21.14] A disposition is not a transfer of value if it is made during lifetime:

(a) by one party to a marriage or civil partnership for the maintenance of the other party; or
(b) by one party to a marriage or civil partnership for the maintenance, education or training of a child of either party for a period up to 5 April after attaining the age of eighteen or, if later, after ceasing full-time education or training. '*Child*' includes step-child and adopted child; or
(c) by any person for the maintenance, education or training of a child not in the care of a parent of his for a period up to 5 April after attaining the age of eighteen or, if the child has been in the care of the disponer for substantial periods before that age, after ceasing full-time education or training; or

(d) in favour of an illegitimate child of the person making the disposition and is for the maintenance, education or training of the child for a period up to 5 April after attaining the age of eighteen or, if later, after ceasing full-time education or training; or

(e) as a reasonable provision for the care or maintenance of a dependent relative (i.e. a relative of self, spouse or civil partner who is incapacitated by old age or infirmity from maintaining himself or his mother or father or his spouse's or civil partner's mother or father). By concession, such a disposition is also exempt if made by a child in favour of his unmarried mother if she (although not so incapacitated) is genuinely financially dependent on that child. See *R McKelvey (personal representative of D V McKelvey) v HMRC* [2008] STC SCD 944 Sp C 694. (See Extra-statutory Concession F12.)

'*Marriage*' or '*civil partnership*' includes a former marriage or civil partnership where a disposition has been made on its dissolution or varied later.

'*Step-child*' in relation to a civil partner is the meaning given within *Civil Partnership Act 2004, s 246.*

For the purposes of the pre-owned assets anti-avoidance legislation within *FA 2004, Sch 15,* the disposal of any property which is a disposition falling within the requirements of this paragraph will be an excluded transaction. [*FA 2004, Sch 15 para 10(1)(d), (2)(d)*].

If a disposition as above only partially satisfies the conditions, it will be separated into exempt and non-exempt parts. An exempt disposition which is a disposal of an interest in possession in settled property is not treated as terminating that interest so as to make it chargeable to tax under *IHTA 1984, s 51(1)* (see **39.9** SETTLEMENTS WITH INTERESTS IN POSSESSION). [*IHTA 1984, ss 11, 51(2); The Tax and Civil Partnership Regulations 2005, SI 2005/3229, Reg 4*] The non-exempt part may qualify as a **35** POTENTIALLY EXEMPT TRANSFERS.

Normal expenditure out of income

[21.15] A transfer of value during lifetime is exempt if, or to the extent that, it is shown:

(a) that it was made as part of the normal (i.e. typical or habitual) expenditure of the transferor; and
(b) that (taking one year with another) it was made out of his income; and
(c) that, after allowing for all transfers of value forming part of his normal expenditure, the transferor was left with sufficient income to maintain his usual standard of living.

[*IHTA 1984, s 21(1)*].

To qualify as having been made out of income, the gift cannot be a gift of an asset unless it was acquired out of income for the purpose of making the gift. Details of income and expenditure should be provided on form IHT403 to support any claim under *IHTA 1984, s 21.*

The exemption applies only to transfers actually made and not where deemed to have been made. [*IHTA 1984, ss 3(4), 21(5)*]. The first gift in a series can qualify as 'normal' provided there is clear evidence that further gifts are intended.

'Income' for the purposes of exemption, means net income after income tax and is determined in accordance with normal accountancy rules rather than income tax rules (IHTM14250 and see also Key Points at **21.25**). Funds received from a lifetime care plan taken to finance care costs in ill health or old age are regarded by HMRC as capital repayments rather than income. The same applies to withdrawals for single premium bonds and funds from a discounted gift trust (IHTM14250).

Gifts should be comparable in amount but small differences will be accepted. Premiums paid on a life policy taken out for the benefit of a family member may be regarded as normal expenditure except where the policy was taken out when the payer's life expectancy was short.

Where a lifetime care plan has been purchased with a lump sum to provide for future care home fees, HMRC do not regard any subsequent monthly payments out of the scheme as income and the care fees payable remain part of the normal expenditure of person in care.

In *Bennett v CIR* Ch D 1994, [1995] STC 54, Lightman J stated that a pattern of gifts is intended to remain in place for more than a nominal period and for a sufficient period (barring unforeseen circumstances). Also, the amount of the expenditure need not be fixed nor the individual recipient be the same but a pattern established by proof of the existence of a prior commitment or resolution or by reference only to a sequence of events. In this particular case the deceased had adopted a pattern of expenditure in respect of the surplus income which was part of her normal expenditure despite her death just over one year after executing a form of authority to distribute her surplus income.

In *McDowall (executors of McDowall, deceased) v IRC* [2004] STC (SCD) 22, SpecComm, the deceased had granted power of attorney to his wife which on her death passed to his son. The son used the power to make a number of gifts from the deceased's bank accounts including five payments of £12,000 to the children of the deceased. The evidence was that the attorney intended to make similar gifts to the children in future years. On this basis, the Special Commissioners held that the five payments were potentially within the exemption for normal expenditure out of income, but on the facts the attorney had acted outside the scope of the power and so they were not validly made. See also *Nadin v CIR* [1997] STC SCD 107 Sp C 112 at **55** TAX CASES.

A premium on a life insurance policy

[21.16] **A premium on a life insurance policy** on his own life paid directly or indirectly by the transferor is not part of his normal expenditure if at any time an annuity was purchased on his life, unless it is shown that the purchase of the annuity and the making or varying of the insurance (or any prior insurance for which the first-mentioned insurance was directly or indirectly substituted) were not associated operations (see **5.5** ANTI-AVOIDANCE) (i.e. were not 'back to back'). [*IHTA 1984, s 21(2)*]. The practice 'is to regard policies and annuities as not being affected by the associated operations rule if, first, the policy was issued on full medical evidence of the assured's health, and, secondly, it would have been issued on the same terms if the annuity had not been bought'. (Official Report, Standing Committee A, 5 February 1975 Col 872). See also **28.9** LIFE ASSURANCE POLICIES.

Income does not include the capital element of a life annuity purchased after 12 November 1974. [*IHTA 1984, s 21(3)(4)*].

Loans of property etc.

[21.17] Loans of money or other property etc. are exempt from inheritance tax if the transfer was a normal one on the part of the transferor and they were left with sufficient income to maintain their usual standard of living. What constitutes normal for this purpose is not defined but that HMRC interpret it as meaning typical or usual. Notwithstanding this exemption, it remains arguable that an interest-free loan of money has no gift element because uninvested money produces no return. See **48.3** TRANSFER OF VALUE. [*IHTA 1984, s 29(1)(4)*].

Transfers allowable for income tax or conferring retirement benefits

[21.18] A disposition is not a transfer of value if:

(a) it is allowable in computing profits or gains for income tax or corporation tax; or

(b) it is a contribution to an approved retirement benefit scheme (occupational pension scheme); or

(c) it is to provide:
  - (i) benefits on or after retirement for a person not connected with the transferor who is or has been in his employ; or
  - (ii) benefits on or after the death of such a person for his widow or dependants or surviving civil partner; or

(d) it is a contribution after 22 July 1987 under approved personal pension arrangements entered into by an employee of the person making the disposition.

Where benefits under (c) are greater than could be provided under (b), the excess is a transfer of value. Dispositions under more than one of the kinds described in (b), (c) and (d) in respect of service by the same person, are exempt only to the extent that the benefits do not exceed what could be provided by a disposition of the kind described in any one of those subparagraphs. For the purposes of (c) above, the right to occupy a dwelling at a rent less than would be expected in a transaction at arm's length between persons not connected with each other is regarded as equivalent to a pension equal to the additional rent that might be so expected.

If a disposition as above only partially satisfies the conditions, it will be separated into exempt and non-exempt parts. From 6 April 2006 a person's contributions to an employees' registered pension scheme or scheme within *ICTA 1988, s 615(3)* will also not be a transfer of value as above. Contributions by an employer to a registered pension scheme or *ICTA 1988, s 615* scheme in respect of an employee are not treated as transfers of value. Also, contributions to a qualifying non-UK pension scheme by an employer for an employee will not be chargeable to IHT. [*IHTA 1984, s 12; F(No 2)A 1987, s 98(2)(3); FA 2004, s 203(2); The Tax and Civil Partnership Regulations 2005, SI 2005/3229, Reg 5; FA 2006, Sch 22 para 2; FA 2008, Sch 29 para 18*].

The above exemptions apply to lifetime dispositions only. (Official Report Standing Committee E, 29 June 1976 Col 1435).

Transfers on death only

Death on active service, etc.

[21.19] No inheritance tax is payable on the death of a person from wound, accident or disease contracted whilst on active service against an enemy (or on service of a similar nature) during that time or from aggravation during that time of a previously contracted disease. See IHTM11281. For deaths on or after 19 March 2014, the relief is extended to provide exemption from charge on the death for lifetime potentially exempt transfers and chargeable transfers. This exemption only applies when HMRC receive a valid certificate issued by the Ministry of Defence. These types of certificate are detailed at IHTM11301 and IHTM11302 and may be obtained from:

Defence Business Services
Joint Casualty and Compassionate Centre (Attn SO3 Deceased Estates)
Imjin Barracks
Innsworth
Gloucester
GL3 1HW
(Tel 01452 712 612 Extension 5680/8174)

The following information should be provided:

- the deceased's service number;
- a copy of the death certificate;
- any relevant supporting medical evidence such as a post-mortem report.

Exemption applies to a person certified by the Defence Council or the Secretary of State as dying from the above causes inflicted or incurred whilst in the armed forces, or if not a member of those forces, whilst subject to the law governing any of those forces by reason of association with or accompanying them. [*Armed Forces Act 1981; IHTA 1984, s 154*]. The wound does not have to be the only or direct cause of death, provided it is a cause (*Executors of 4th Duke of Westminster (otherwise Barty-King) v Ministry of Defence* QB 1978, [1978] STC 218). The exemption applies to the estates of those killed on active service in the Falklands conflict (HMRC Press Release 23 June 1982) and, with effect for deaths on or after 19 March 2014, to those responding to emergency circumstances in the course of the person's duties as a member of the armed forces or as a civilian subject to service discipline. Where a common seaman, marine or soldier died before 12 March 1952 in the service of the Crown and his estate was wholly exempt from estate duty and under his will he left a limited life interest, no inheritance tax is charged on such exempted property which passes under the terms of the will on the termination of the limited interest. (HMRC Extra-statutory Concession F13.)

Transferable nil rate band

Since the introduction of the transferable nil rate band (TNRB) the opportunity to claim the relief on the second death has required a clarification of the above rules. For deaths before 12 March 1952, two separate schemes of relief from

Estate Duty for those killed or missing in action were in force. One was a *complete exemption* relief and the another *conditional remission*. The service rank of the person killed or missing determined which scheme applied. Complete exemption applied to all ranks up to and including Corporal (Army and Royal Air Force: a Lance Sergeant was treated as a corporal), Chief Petty Officer (Royal Navy) and Sergeant in the Royal Marines, as well as Fleet Air Arm ratings. The conditional remission applied to all service ranks not eligible for complete exemption. Remission also applied on the death of any person who was drowned or killed, within a period of twelve months, by reason of injuries received as a result of operations of war in the period from 3 September 1939 to 31 March 1948. The aim of the extension was to provide relief to the estates of civilians killed in the blitz, or drowned following the torpedoing of a ship. Where complete exemption applies, the whole of the nil rate band is transferred for use on the death of the surviving spouse. In these cases, the application for TNRB need contain only the killed or missing person's rank and proof that he or she died in service. The remission was limited to the first £5,000 of property comprised in the estate for Estate Duty purposes. Where the value of the property passing to specified relatives and/or property passing to other people exceeded £5,000, Estate Duty was charged on the balance at a reduced rate. For estates in England or Wales, the Grant will show the amount of any Estate Duty paid when the Grant was taken out. If any duty was paid, no TNRB will be available. See also April 2009 HMRC Inheritance Tax and Trusts Newsletter at http://www.hmrc.gov.uk/cto/newsletter.htm.

Death of emergency service, police or armed forces personnel

[21.20] Certain exemptions are provided for deaths on or after 19 March 2014 of emergency personnel and those in the police or armed forces where, in broad terms, the death arose by virtue of their status as such persons.

The reliefs are:

(a) that no potentially exempt transfer made by the person becomes a chargeable transfer because of the death;
(b) that the estate on death is not chargeable to IHT; and
(c) that no additional IHT becomes due because of a chargeable transfer made by the person within seven years of the death, although tax already paid is not refundable.

The reliefs for *emergency personnel* apply where he or she:

(a) dies from an injury sustained, accident occurring or disease contracted at a time when that person was responding to emergency circumstances; or
(b) dies from a disease contracted at some previous time, the death being due to, or hastened by, the aggravation of the disease during a period when that person was responding to emergency circumstances.

'*Emergency circumstances*' means circumstances which are present or imminent and are causing or likely to cause (a) the death of a person or animal, (b) serious injury to, or the serious illness of, a person or animal, (c) serious harm to the environment or to any property, or (d) a worsening of any such injury, illness or harm.

A person is 'responding to emergency circumstances' if the person (a) is going anywhere for the purpose of dealing with emergency circumstances occurring there, or (b) is dealing with emergency circumstances, preparing to do so imminently or dealing with the immediate aftermath of emergency circumstances.

Emergency personnel within the reliefs are:

(a) those in the fire services or fire and rescue services;
(b) those in search services or rescue services (or both);
(c) those providing medical, ambulance or paramedic services;
(d) those in police service;
(e) those providing services for the transportation of organs, blood, medical equipment or medical personnel; or
(f) a person engaged by the government of a state or territory, an international organisation or a charity in connection with the provision of humanitarian assistance.

The reliefs for *constables, former constables and those in the armed forces* apply where he or she:

(a) dies from an injury sustained or disease contracted in circumstances where the person was deliberately targeted by reason of his or her status as a constable or armed service person, or former constable or armed service person; or
(b) dies from a disease contracted at some previous time, the death being due to, or hastened by, the aggravation of the disease by an injury sustained or disease contracted in circumstances mentioned above.

The relief for armed service personnel requires a certificate by the Defence Council or the Secretary of State.

[*IHTA 1984, ss 153A, 155A; FA 2015, s 75*].

Compensation for victims of World War II persecution

[21.21] Extra-statutory concession F20, which was introduced in 2001 to provide an exemption from IHT for ex gratia payments to those held as prisoners of war in World War II, is replaced by a statutory provision of broadly similar scope and with effect from 1 January 2015. The exemption applies on the death of the person to whom compensation was due, and is structured as a credit against the IHT due on the death, the credit being IHT at death rates on the sum received, or the amount of IHT due on the chargeable transfer on death, whichever is the lower. Payments eligible for this relief are those made to the deceased before death or to his or her estate, or to his or her spouse, and which fall within the categories below:

(a) the German foundation known as 'Remembrance, Responsibility and Future' in respect of a person who was a slave or forced labourer;
(b) the Swiss Bank Settlement (Holocaust Victim Assets; Litigation) in respect of the slave or forced labourers;
(c) the Austrian Victims of National-Socialism Fund and the Austrian Reconciliation Fund;

(d) the Swiss Refugee Programme under the Swiss Bank Settlement (Holocaust Victim Assets Litigation;
(e) the Dutch Maror Fund;
(f) the French Orphan Scheme;
(g) the German Child Survivor Fund and Hardship Fund;
(h) the UK Far Eastern Prisoners of War Ex Gratia Scheme.
(i) For deaths occurring on or after 1 January 2019, a one-off payment of a fixed amount from the Kindertransport Fund established by the Government of the Federal Republic of Germany.

[*IHTA 1984, s 153ZA, Sch 5A; FA 2020, s 74*].

Other compensation

[21.22] Compensation fund payments arising out of the 11 September 2001 terrorist attacks that comprise part of the UK victims' estates are not subject to IHT. The Victim's Compensation Fund of 2001 was established by the US government as an alternative to any legal proceedings that the victims' estates could take under the law as it stood on 11 September. The legislation was actually passed after 11 September 2001 but claims under the compensation fund have no value at that date for IHT purposes. Payments made after that date are not chargeable to IHT in any case so that part of a victim's estate comprising of the compensation fund payment is not subject to IHT.

Relief from IHT is available for payments made under (1) the Windrush Compensation Scheme or (2) the Troubles Permanent Disablement Payment Scheme, except where made after the death of the person concerned and to someone other than the person's personal representatives. [*FA 2020, Sch 15, para 5*]. There are different effective dates for these two reliefs: the relief under (1) is for deaths on or after 3 April 2019, and the relief under (2) is for deaths on or after 29 May 2020.

Relief from IHT is available for compensation paid to those wrongly convicted of fraud following the introduction of the Post Office Horizon accounting system. This is effective for payments made on or after 22 July 2021. The effective date for similar payments under a Group Litigation Order is 1 August 2022. [*SI 2023/184*].

Relief from IHT is available for compensation paid under the Infected Blood Interim Compensation Scheme. This is effective for payments made on or after 28 October 2022. [*SI 2023/184*].

Non-residents' bank accounts

[21.23] See **49.6** TRANSFERS ON DEATH for the exemption of certain foreign currency bank or Post Office accounts held by persons not domiciled, resident or ordinarily resident in the UK at death. For deaths on or after 6 April 2013 the requirement as to ordinary residence was removed by *FA 2013, Sch 46 para 118*.

'Bank' for this purpose takes the same meaning as *ITA 2007, s 991* (formerly *ICTA 1988, s 840A*) and includes the Bank of England and any institution authorised by the *Financial Services and Markets Act 2000, Part 4*.

Abatement of exemptions

[21.24] Where a transfer on a death after 26 July 1989 is wholly or partly exempt under any of **21.2** or **21.5–21.9** above or under **30.23**, **30.24** NATIONAL HERITAGE or **52** TRUSTS FOR EMPLOYEES, and the recipient of the property (the trustees where applicable) disposes of property not derived from the transfer on death in settlement of all or part of a claim against the deceased's estate, the exemption for the transfer on death is abated. The (otherwise exempt) gift on death is treated instead as a chargeable specific gift not bearing its own tax, up to the lower of:

(i) the value of the property transferred in that gift;
(ii) the amount by which the estate of the recipient of the property immediately after the disposition settling the claim is less than it would be but for the disposition.

In determining the value of the recipient's estate for the purposes of (ii), no deduction is made for the claim, no account is taken of any liability of the recipient for any tax on the disposition, and the provisions giving relief for AGRICULTURAL PROPERTY (**4.1**) and BUSINESS PROPERTY (**6.1**) are disregarded.

The abatement does not apply to the extent that the claim against the deceased's estate is in respect of a liability to be taken into account in determining the value of that estate for inheritance tax purposes. See **49.9** TRANSFERS ON DEATH for liabilities to be taken into account.

[*IHTA 1984, s 29A; FA 1989, s 172*].

Key points concerning exempt transfers

[21.25] Points to consider are as follows.

- Where on a death normal expenditure out of income under *IHTA 1984, s 21* is claimed, the personal representatives will normally be asked to provide full details on form IHT403 detailing all income and outgoings for each of the years in which the gifts were made. Income details may in most cases be obtained from previously submitted tax returns but non-taxable income such as ISAs should also be taken into account. Where income is taxable, the net of tax figure is the appropriate for the calculations. Surplus income may be carried forward from one year to the next, but not for more than two years when it is considered by HMRC to become capital. Since the exemption requires a pattern of giving, either established or envisaged but not fulfilled due to untimely death, advisors should consider issuing IHT403 to any client to complete during lifetime when the exemption is to be claimed for certain gifts the client is making.
- Exemption under *IHTA 1984, s 154(1)(b)* (Death on active service) should be considered as in **21.19** above. In this connection, a person may die many years after the conflict in which they

sustained their injuries but if a link exists then it may well be worth making a claim. HMRC manual states 'the exemption applies only if the Defence Council or the Secretary of State certifies that the deceased was within one of the exempted categories of service when he or she received the injury, contracted the disease or suffered the aggravation of the disease which caused the death'. At first sight, there may appear only a tenuous link between the death and the original injury but for instance, the case of mustard gas attacks on the trenches in the first world war led to deaths from respiratory diseases. Recent wars have a high incidence of post-war traumatic stress syndrome and similar to the *Executors of 4th Duke of Westminster (otherwise Barty-King) v Ministry of Defence* QB 1978, [1978] STC 218, it may be possible to show a link as was the case in Westminster when the Duke died of cancer in 1967 after sustaining a wound whilst on active service in 1944.

- Where one spouse is UK domiciled and the other is not, and the UK domiciled spouse is the first to die, a decision must be taken about whether the survivor should elect to be treated as UK domiciled for IHT purposes, thereby allowing the full spouse exemption to apply at that time. In principle, if the main asset in their estates is a UK home and that is likely to remain the case, then the election will normally be worthwhile. If, however, this is not the case, it is unlikely that the election will be beneficial unless either the non-domiciled spouse expects to become deemed domiciled in due course or else the two have failed to take any advice about potential inheritance tax liabilities. If the survivor is expected to become deemed domiciled, then all that person's worldwide assets can equally be expected to be liable to IHT on death, including those inherited from the deceased spouse (subject to the availability of quick succession relief); in such circumstances the spouse exemption on the first death is likely to be an important relief. If, however, the survivor can preserve non-domiciled status for IHT purposes, and tax advice is taken in good time, it may not be worth making the election and thereby forgoing all the potential advantages for IHT purposes through holding excluded property, even if it means that liability to IHT arises on the death of the domiciled spouse leaving all assets to the survivor.

22

Gifts with Reservation

Cross-references. See **2.9** ACCOUNTS AND RETURNS; **5.5** ANTI-AVOIDANCE for associated operations; **27.5** LIABILITY FOR TAX; **34.2** PENSION SCHEMES.

Simon's Taxes. See I3.4, I7.170, I7.382.

Other Sources. Form P11(Notes); IHT 110; Foster, Parts C4 and C5; HMRC Customer Guide to Inheritance Tax; IHTM14301.

Introduction to gifts with reservation

[22.1] Before 17 March 1986 it was possible to make a gift of an asset with the IHT position in relation to the gift being unaffected by any continuing benefits to the donor from the gift. A typical example was a gift into a discretionary trust where the settlor was one of the potential beneficiaries. To prevent the effectiveness of such arrangements for IHT purposes, legislation was introduced to ensure that the gifted assets remain within the donor's estate on death if the reservation of benefit continues up to that time. If it ceases before then, a potentially exempt transfer is treated as occurring. Pre-17 March 1986 arrangements continue to be outside the reservation of benefit provisions, but, subject to exclusions, the legislation applies to all gifts after that date.

Any potential reservation of benefit should be considered with all lifetime gifts, particularly because the gift remains effective for all other tax purposes (capital gains tax, for example) whereas it will be counted back into the estate on death if there is a continuing benefit to the donor at that time. The result is a full inheritance tax charge on the death but without the tax-free uplift for capital gains tax purposes.

The rule is that, subject to the exceptions in **22.2** below, where, after 17 March 1986, an individual disposes of any property (by way of gift or otherwise) and either:

(a) possession and enjoyment of the property is not *bona fide* assumed by the donee at or before the beginning of the 'relevant period'; or

(b) *at any time* in the relevant period the property is not enjoyed to the entire exclusion, or 'virtually' to the entire exclusion, of the donor; or

(c) *at any time* in the relevant period the property is not enjoyed to the entire exclusion, or virtually to the entire exclusion, of any benefit to the donor by contract or otherwise (and for this purpose a benefit which the donor obtained by virtue of any associated operations (see **5.5** ANTI-AVOIDANCE), of which the gift is one, is treated as a benefit to him by contract or otherwise);

then, if and so long as any of the conditions in (a) to (c) above apply, the property is referred to (in relation to the gift and the donor) as '*property subject to a reservation*'. See *HD Lyon's Personal Representatives v HMRC; Trustees of the Alloro Trust v HMRC* [2007] Sp C 616 where the manner in which a trust, set up by the settlor, had been operated meant that the 'possession and enjoyment of the property' within (a) above had not been 'bona fide assumed by the donee at the beginning of the relevant period', within *s 102(1)(a)*.

Any question where property falls within (b) or (c) above is, so far as that question depends on the identity of the property, determined by reference to the property which is at that time treated as comprised in the gift. See **22.3** to **22.7** below for special rules where the property changes after the gift or the donee predeceases the donor.

The effect of the above is that:

(i) if, immediately before the donor's death, there is any property which, in relation to him, is property subject to a reservation then, to the extent that the property would not otherwise form part of his estate immediately before death, it is treated as property to which he was beneficially entitled at that time; and

(ii) if at any time before the end of the relevant period, any property ceases to be property subject to a reservation, the donor is treated as having at that time made a disposition of the property by a disposition which is a POTENTIALLY EXEMPT TRANSFERS (**35**).

The benefit must be referable to the gift. Thus, where an individual owns shares in a company which he gives away, and the company owns a property in which he lives and continues to do so after the gift, there is no reservation of benefit. The occupation of the property is not referable to the gift (IHTM14334).

Definitions

'*Relevant period*' is the period ending on the date of the donor's death and beginning seven years before that date or, if later, on the date of the gift.

'*Virtually*' is not defined but it is intended to prevent the rules applying where the benefit enjoyed by the donor is small. HMRC have published the following examples of situations which they consider a benefit to the donor may be disregarded:

(a) a house which becomes the donee's residence but where the donor subsequently stays, in the absence of the donee, for not more than 2 weeks each year, or stays with the donee for less than one month each year;
(b) social visits, excluding overnight stays made by a donor as a guest of the donee, to a house which they had given away, such visits being no more than would have taken place without the gift;
(c) a temporary stay for some short term purpose in a house the donor had previously given away, such as while the donor convalesces after medical treatment; while the donor looks after a donee convalescing after medical treatment; while the donor's own home is being redecorated;
(d) a house together with a library of books which the donor visits less than five times in any year to consult or borrow a book, but not where the books are used regularly, for example in connection with work.
(e) visits to a house for domestic reasons, for example baby-sitting by the donor for the donee's children;
(f) a motor car which the donee uses to give occasional (less than three times a month) lifts to the donor;
(g) land which the donor uses to walk their dogs or for horse riding provided this does not restrict the donee's use of the land.

Life policies. Any property comprised in a gift made after 17 March 1986 falls within the reservation of benefit provisions if the gift consists of or includes, or is made in connection with, a policy of insurance on the life of the donor or his spouse/civil partner or their joint lives *and* the benefits which will or may accrue to the donee as a result of the gift vary by reference to benefits accruing to the donor or his spouse/civil partner (or both) under that or another policy. Policies on joint lives include those on joint lives and the life of the survivor. Benefits accruing to the donor or his spouse/civil partner (or both of them) include benefits accruing by virtue of the exercise of rights conferred on either or both of them. For HMRC's understanding of when an insurance is made, see **29.2** TIME OF DISPOSITION.

Gift of unquoted shares or a business interest. HMRC guidance states that:

> The continuation of existing reasonable commercial arrangements in the form of remuneration and other benefits for the donor's services in a business entered into before the gift does not amount to a reservation provided the benefits are in no way linked to, or affected by, the gift.
>
> What is "reasonable" will depend on all the facts but, broadly, you should test this by reference to what might reasonably be expected under arm's length arrangements between unconnected parties.
>
> If, however, as part of the overall transaction, including the gift, new remunerative arrangements are made you will need to examine all the facts to determine whether the new package amounts to a reservation 'by contract or otherwise'.

(IHTM14337).

Exceptions to the GWR rule

[22.2] The above provisions do not apply in the following circumstances.

(a) To the extent that the disposal by way of gift is an exempt transfer by virtue of:

(i) *IHTA 1984, s 18 as amended by FA 2003, s 185(2)* (transfers between spouses/civil partners except where provided by *FA 1986, s 102(5A)(5B)*, see **21.9** EXEMPT TRANSFERS);

(ii) *IHTA 1984, s 20* (small gifts, see point (b) at **21.12** EXEMPT TRANSFERS);

(iii) *IHTA 1984, s 22* (gifts in consideration of marriage, see **21.13** EXEMPT TRANSFERS);

(iv) *IHTA 1984, s 23* (gifts to charities, see **21.2** EXEMPT TRANSFERS);

(v) *IHTA 1984, s 24* (gifts to political parties, see **21.7** EXEMPT TRANSFERS);

(vi) *IHTA 1984, s 24A* (gifts to housing associations, see **21.5** EXEMPT TRANSFERS);

(vii) *IHTA 1984, s 25* (gifts for national purposes, see **21.6** EXEMPT TRANSFERS);

(viii) *IHTA 1984, s 27 as amended by FA 1998, s 144* (maintenance funds for historic buildings, see **30.23** NATIONAL HERITAGE); or

(ix) *IHTA 1984, ss 28 and 28A* (employee trusts, see **52** TRUSTS FOR EMPLOYEES).

[*FA 1986, s 102(5); The Tax and Civil Partnership Regulations 2005, SI 2005/3229, Reg 44*]. *Note.* The annual exemption (see further **35.2** POTENTIALLY EXEMPT TRANSFERS) and the normal expenditure out of income exemption are not included.

(b) If the disposal by way of gift is made under the terms of a policy issued in respect of an insurance made before 18 March 1986 *unless* the policy is varied on or after that date so as to increase the benefits secured or extend the term of the insurance. Any change in the terms of the policy made in pursuance of an option or other power conferred by the policy is deemed to be a variation of the policy except for the exercise of an indexation option with respect to benefits or premiums before 1 August 1986 if the option or power could only be exercised before that date. [*FA 1986, s 102(6)(7)*].

(c) In the case of property which is an interest in land, any occupation by the donor of the whole or any part of the land is disregarded for the purposes of **22.1**(b) and (c) above if:

(i) it results from a change in circumstances of the donor since the time of the gift, being a change which was unforeseen at that time and was not brought about by the donor to receive the benefit of this provision;

(ii) it occurs at a time when the donor has become unable to maintain himself through old age, infirmity or otherwise;

(iii) it represents a reasonable provision by the donee for the care and maintenance of the donor; *and*

(iv) the donee is a relative of the donor or his spouse/civil partner. [*FA 1986, Sch 20 para 6(1)(b); The Tax and Civil Partnership Regulations 2005, SI 2005/3229, Reg 46*].

(d) the gift of an undivided share in land (being land held under a tenancy in common, not a joint tenancy) on or after 9 March 1999 will not be treated as a gift with reservation where either:
- the donor does not occupy the property, for example where it is let;
- the donor occupies the land to the exclusion of the donee for full consideration in money or money's worth; or
- the donor and donee occupy the land and the donor receives no material benefit, other than a negligible one, by or at the donee's expense in connection with the gift. [*FA 1986, s 102B(4)*]. For further analysis, see Key points at the end of this chapter.

(e) In the case of property which is an interest in land or a chattel (corporeal movable in Scotland), retention or assumption by the donor of actual occupation of, or actual enjoyment of an incorporeal right over, the land or actual possession of the chattel (corporeal movable in Scotland) is disregarded for the purposes of **22.1**(b) and (c) above if it is for full consideration in money or money's worth. [*FA 1986, Sch 20 para 6(1)(a),(3)*]. In the case of a partnership, where one partner transfers land occupied rent free by the partnership to another partner, HMRC accept that there is no reservation of benefit if the transferee's profit-sharing ratio is suitably increased in connection with the gift (IHTM14341). For Chattels, see lease precedent set out below. HMRC consider that for this exception to apply, full consideration should be provided throughout the relevant period (see **22.1** above), so that any rent passing should be reviewed at appropriate intervals to reflect market changes (IHTM 14335). According to HMRC Bulletin, November 1993, p 98, any consideration passing will be treated as full if it lies within a range of values reflecting normal valuation tolerances although the IHT manual does not contain confirmation of this. Note that the full consideration exception to the reservation of benefit provisions is not considered by HMRC to apply to any other types of asset and is confined to interests in land or a chattel. See further analysis under Key points at the end of this chapter.

CHATTEL LEASE

PARTIES:

1. 'The Parents' namely, ...
2. 'The Children' namely . . . .

BACKGROUND

A. The Children are the beneficial owners of the chattels set out in the Schedule below ('the Chattels')

B. The Children wish to allow the Parents the use and enjoyment of the Chattels on the basis of full consideration payable by the Parents

AGREEMENT

1. Bailment

The Children grant a lease of the Chattels to the Parents for the following term and generally on the terms and conditions following:

2. The Term

The term of the lease shall be equal to the joint lives and life of the survivor of the Parents, terminable earlier:

2.1 Upon six months written notice given by either party

2.2 Immediately upon default of any obligations contained in clause 9

2.3 Immediately upon both the Parents or the survivor of them becoming mentally incapable within the meaning of section 94 (2) of the Mental Health Act 1983.

3. Ownership

3.1 The Children retain the ownership of the Chattels

3.2 The Children reserve the right to fix any plating or other means of identification to the Chattels or any of them

3.3 The Parents covenant not (nor take steps) to sell, deal, charge or part with the Chattels in any other way contrary to the ownership of the Children

3.4 The Parents will immediately pay any sum required to remove any lien which may arise over the Chattels.

4. Enjoyment and Housing

4.1 The Children covenant with the Parents (provided the Parents pay the rent and perform the Parents' covenants) that the parents shall peaceably hold and enjoy the Chattels during the term without any interruption by the Children or any person rightfully claiming under or in trust for any of them

4.2 The Chattels shall be housed at . . . . [Name of property] . . . . or at other locations from time to time agreed between the Parents and the Children

5. Rental

5.1 The initial annual rental for the Chattels shall be £. . . . . . . per annum (which is agreed by the Children and the Parents to reflect . . . . . . % of the current open market value of the Chattels)

5.2 The rental shall be paid annually; the first year's rental is due on the signing of this agreement (and the Children acknowledge receipt of it); further annual rental payments shall be due on the anniversaries of this agreement. Such adjustment as is necessary on the termination of the agreement by the death of the survivor of the Parents shall be made as is required; otherwise there shall be no adjustment

5.3 The rental shall be reviewable by agreement at three yearly intervals (*see note (A)*) from the date of this agreement to ensure that the Parents give full consideration for the use and enjoyment of the Chattels. In default of agreement, the reviewed rent shall be determined by a valuer appointed by the President for the time being of the Incorporated Society of Valuers and

Auctioneers acting as expert and not an arbitrator; either party shall be at liberty to request the President to make such an appointment.

6. Insurance

 6.1 The Parents will insure the Chattels for their full replacement cost comprehensively against all risk with the interest of the Children noted on the Policy and will duly and punctually pay all premiums and on request will promptly produce the insurance policy and proof of payment of premiums to the Children. All claims under such insurance policy will be dealt with in accordance with the written direction of the Children. All claims and moneys received by the Parents under such insurance policy shall be held by the parents in trust for the Children

7. Preservation and Repair

 7.1 The Parents undertake to preserve the Chattels

 7.2 The Parents undertake to keep the Chattels clean and in good and substantial repair and will bear the cost of any repairs not covered by insurance

 7.3 The Parents will permit the Children and any person authorised by them at any reasonable hour to view or survey the state and condition of the Chattels

 7.4 The Parents will forthwith after being required to do so by the Children make good any want of repair in the Chattels

PROVIDED that nothing in this clause shall require the Parents to maintain the Chattels in anything other than their current condition or require the Parents to improve or put the Chattels into first rate condition

8. Security

 8.1 The Parents undertake to put in place, maintain and bear the cost of such security arrangements as are from time to time agreed between the Parents and Children or as are reasonably stipulated by the Children to reflect the requirements of any relevant insurance company, advice from the Police or advice otherwise specifically received from a specialist security company engaged for the purpose

9. Default

If the Parents default in the punctual payment of any of the instalments of rent provided for, or default in the payment of the insurance premiums as provided for, or default in the performance of any of the terms and conditions of this agreement, the Children may immediately retake possession of the Chattels, without notice to the Parents, with or without legal process, and the parents by this agreement authorise and empower the Children to enter the premises or other places where the Chattels may be found and to take and carry away the Chattels. All moneys due under this agreement shall become immediately due and payable plus all reasonable costs of repossession

EXECUTED on 2010

Signed by . . . .

Note to the Precedent

(A) The initial rent should be arrived at preferably by written negotiation between two competent valuers aware of the terms of the lease, the value and condition of the chattels, cost of insurance and security, etc. The draft agreement provides for rent reviews every three years but advice should be taken as to whether or not this is the appropriate period of time for the reviews.

(B) The agreement is said to be a chattel lease as that is the common understanding. Strictly it is a bailment agreement though nothing turns on that.

Case law — *Ingram* Schemes

In the case of *Ingram v IRC*, [2000] 1 AC 293, [1999] STC 37, HL; the case revolved around the transfer of property on 29 March 1987 by Lady Ingram to her Solicitor who then, as nominee, granted Lady Ingram 20-year leasehold interests and then transferred the land subject to the leases to Trustees to hold on trust for specified beneficiaries. The widow continued to live at the property until her death in 1989. HMRC treated the transfer as a gift with reservation and issued a notice of determination accordingly. The House of Lords allowed the executors' appeal. Lord Hoffmann held that:

> 'although (*s 102*) does not allow a donor to have his cake and eat it, there is nothing to stop him from carefully dividing up the cake, eating part and having the rest. If the benefits which the donor continues to enjoy are by virtue of property which was never comprised in the gift, he has not reserved any benefit out of the property of which he disposed.'

For these purposes, 'property' was 'not something which has physical existence like a house but a specific interest in that property, a legal construct, which can co-exist with other interests in the same physical object. *Section 102* does not therefore prevent people from deriving benefit from the object in which they have given away an interest. It applies only when they derive the benefit from that interest'. The policy of *s 102* was to require people to 'define precisely the interests which they are giving away and the interests, if any, which they are retaining'. The interest, which the widow retained, was 'a proprietary interest, defined with the necessary precision'. The gift was 'a gift of the capital value in the land after deduction of her leasehold interest in the same way as a gift of the capital value of the fund after deduction of an annuity'.

The *Ingram* case therefore laid down an important principle for the purposes of the legislation, commonly described as the 'carve out principle'. If an interest in asset to be given away is carved out and retained by the donor, with there being no benefit retained in the remaining interest in that asset, the reservation of benefit provisions do not apply to the interest given away.

Buzzoni and Others v IRC [2013] EWCA Civ 1684, involved a leasehold property rather than a freehold. An individual held a lease for 100 years less one day in respect of a residential property and on 21 November 1997 she granted an underlease commencing on future date to a nominee company. The underlease was then transferred to a trust for her sons. The superior landlord consented to the grant of the underlease on condition that the underlease contained the usual covenants on the part of the underlessee. The covenants which were contained in the underlease mirrored many of those contained in the headlease, e.g. payment of the service charges and an undertaking to keep the property in good repair, these all taking effect on the date when the underlease fell into possession. Both the First Tier Tax Tribunal and the Upper Tribunal held that the covenants were a clear benefit reserved to the headlessee out of the gift of the underlease and so there was a reservation of benefit. However, the Court of Appeal reversed those decisions. The central point is whether or not the donee's enjoyment of the property gifted is to the exclusion of any benefit to the donor. The focus is not primarily on the question whether the donor has obtained a benefit from the gifted property but whether the donee's enjoyment of that property remains exclusive. In this case any benefit to the donor did not have any impact on the donee's enjoyment of the property and therefore the reservation of benefit rules were not in point.

An arrangement similar to that in *Buzzoni v IRC* was the subject of an appeal in *Viscount Hood v CIR* [2016] UKFTT 059 (TC) but with one crucial difference. The deceased, Lady Hood, gave a reversionary sub-lease of a property to her sons and they in turn gave covenants to her which were identical to those which were in favour of the freeholder and contained in the head lease, retained by Lady Hood until her death. Because the covenants by the sons were given in favour of Lady Hood rather than directly to the freeholder, it was held that the sons, as donees, had given a benefit to the deceased as donor and therefore the arrangements were caught as a gift with reservation.

See **5.4** for HMRC's views on reversionary lease schemes under the general anti-avoidance rule enacted in *Finance Act 2013*.

Post-8 March 1999 anti-avoidance

From 9 March 1999 the scheme in the *Ingram* case, as described above was blocked by new counter avoidance measures. These apply where there is a disposal of land by way of gift on or after that date and the donor or his spouse/civil partner enjoys a significant right or interest, or is a party to a significant arrangement, in relation to the land. A right, interest or arrangement in relation to the land is significant only if it entitles the donor to occupy all or part of the land, or enjoy a right in relation to it, otherwise than for full consideration in money or money's worth. However an interest retained is not significant, and thus these anti-avoidance provisions do not apply, if:

- it does not and cannot prevent the enjoyment of the land to the entire exclusion (or virtually the entire exclusion) of the donor;
- it does not entitle the donor to occupy all or part of the land immediately after the gift, but would do so were it not for the interest gifted; or
- it was granted or acquired more than seven years before date of the gift.

The first of these exclusions appears to deal with retained interests which are de minimis. The second of the above deals with the case where a person gives another an immediate lease over land by way of gift; this is not an arrangement to which the legislation was intended to apply and hence the second exclusion takes it out of the scope of the provisions. The third exclusion is considered to permit most deferred lease schemes to escape the reservation of benefit provisions. For example a deferred lease of a property, commonly for 999 years, to commence in say 20 years' time should be outside the scope of the 1999 legislation if the donor's retained freehold interest was acquired more than seven years prior to the gift. Reversionary lease schemes are accepted by HMRC as being outside the 1999 legislation where the donor's freehold interest was acquired more than seven years previously and the lease contains no beneficial covenants, but as a result they fall within the pre-owned assets charge (see ?.6) (IHTM14360).

It is considered that the provisions of *FA 1986, s 102A* focus on rights in relation to the use and enjoyment of the land itself and not rights in relation to any income from the letting of the land. Enjoyment of income from the land, for example where it is in a settlement where the settlor is a beneficiary, must be considered under *FA 1986, s 102* and that is subject to the principle of carve out highlighted in the *Ingram* case. See IHTM14360.

Post-19 June 2003 anti-avoidance: Eversden schemes

In *CIR v Eversden and another (executors of Greenstock deceased)* [2003] STC 822 the Court of Appeal held that the reservation of benefit provisions did not apply where there was a gift on (pre-22 March 2006) interest in possession trusts for the spouse which later terminated in favour of discretionary trusts from which the settlor could benefit. This was because the reservation of benefit provisions contain a complete exclusion from their scope for gifts by which the estate of the spouse is increased. See TAX CASES (55).

Accordingly a targeted anti-avoidance now applies to bring such 'Eversden trusts' within the scope of the reservation of benefit provisions. From20 June 2003 this anti-avoidance provision ensures that the reservation of benefit provisions will apply where a gift is made on or after that date and:

(a) the property becomes settled property by virtue of the gift; and
(b) the trusts of the settlement give an interest in possession to the donor's spouse/civil partner, so that the gift is exempt from IHT because the exemption for transfers between spouses/civil partners and the rule that treats an interest in possession as equivalent to outright ownership; and
(c) between the date of the gift and the donor's death the interest in possession comes to an end; and
(d) when that interest in possession comes to an end, the beneficiary does not become beneficially entitled either to the settled property, or another interest in possession in it.

The anti-avoidance provisions also apply to ensure that *FA 1986, s 102(5B)* is to apply as if the gift had been made immediately after the relevant beneficiary's interest in possession has ended so that it is only the circumstances after that date which determine whether the property is subject to reservation even in the case where the donor dies within seven years. In addition, *FA 1986, s 102(5C)* duplicates the rule in *FA 1986, s 51(b)* which treats an interest in possession as coming to an end when it is disposed of and reinforces the fact that a reference to property or an interest in property includes part of any property or interest. [*FA 1986, s 102(5)(A), (B), (C); FA 2003, s 185(3); The Tax and Civil Partnership Regulations 2005, SI 2005/3229, Reg 44*].

The above provisions do not make the gift of land a gift with reservation where:

- the gift was itself an exempt transfer covered by the main exemptions from inheritance tax in *FA 1986, s 102(5)* (including transfers between spouses) until 19 June 2003. See *Essex and another (executors of Somerset deceased) v CIR* [2002] STC (SCD) 39 and *Eversden*; or

- due to unforeseen circumstances, the donor occupies the land because he/she becomes unable to maintain himself/herself through old age, infirmity or otherwise, and, the interest in land represents reasonable care and maintenance provided by the donee, who is a relative.

Example 1

Alistair, aged 79 years, owns a property that is valued at £640,000. He gives the property to his daughter on 31 March 2017 at the time he enters a nursing home as an infirm resident. However, on 31 June 2020, the nursing home closes due to the financial impact of the COVID-19 pandemic. In view of the fact that there is a shortage of nursing home beds available in the vicinity, Alistair returns to the former family home to live with his daughter who gives up her job to care for him full time. Under *FA 1986, Sch 20 para 6(1)(b)* Alistair's occupation of the property, now owned by his daughter, will not be treated as a gift with reservation because:

(a) the change resulting in the reoccupation of the property arose out of 'unforeseen' circumstances which were not brought about by the donor; and

(b) it occurs at a time when the donor is unable to maintain himself because of old age, infirmity or otherwise; and

(c) the gift represents reasonable care and maintenance provided by the donee which in this case can be equated with the loss of earnings by the daughter; and

(d) the daughter is a relative.

Alistair dies on 16 June 2013. Providing that within (c) above it can be determined that the care and maintenance was 'reasonable' and the other factors within (a), (b) and (d) are in point, the donor's occupation and enjoyment of the gifted land will be disregarded concerning the provisions on gifts with reservation. HMRC do not state what 'reasonable' equates to but states in a letter dated 19 February 1987 'What is *reasonable* will of course depend on the facts of the case'. However, in Tax Bulletin, Issue 9 November 1993 within *FA 1986, Sch 20 para 6(1)(b)* a definition is made by comparison with the shorter Oxford English Dictionary and the corollary of this when defining 'reasonable' would be that the care and maintenance is 'as much as is appropriate or fair; moderate'. In these circumstances the care and maintenance which is full time might be argued to be appropriate and fair for an infirm person commensurate with nursing home standards.

[*FA 1986, ss 102(1)–(5)(5A)–(5C), 102A–B, Sch 20 para 6(1)(c)(2), 7; FA 1999, s 104; FA 2003, s 185(2)(3); The Tax and Civil Partnership Regulations 2005, SI 2005/3229, Regs 44, 45*].

Notes

(1) The disposition by which the property becomes subject to a reservation may itself be a chargeable transfer (e.g. a gift to a discretionary trust with the settlor among the class of beneficiaries). Provided certain conditions are met, regulations provide for the avoidance of a double charge to tax in these circumstances. See **22.15** below.

(2) The amount of the benefit or enjoyment retained by the donor is not important. If a gift falls within the provisions the value of all the property subject to the reservation is taken into account.
(3) Any property which the donor's spouse/civil partner enjoys or benefits from does not automatically fall within the above provisions.
(4) See 35.2 POTENTIALLY EXEMPT TRANSFERS for HMRC treatment of the annual exemption in relation to the potentially exempt transfer deemed to be made as in (ii) above.

Example 2

On 19 June 2002, D gave his house and contents to his grandson G, but continued to live in it alone paying no rent. The agreement between D and G read as follows:

> I give to . . . . [Grandson G]. . . . . my house known as . . . . [Postal address]. . . . . that constitutes my principal private residence but subject to his bearing any inheritance tax attributable to its value. I also give to . . . . [Grandson G]. . . . . those of my personal chattels, specified in the schedule annexed hereto, in my house known as . . . . [Postal address] . . . . which constitute furniture or articles of household use or ornament; jewellery or articles of personal use or adornment; books photographs and articles relating to any sport hobby or other pastime also subject to his bearing any inheritance tax attributable to their value.

The house and contents were valued at £230,000. On 5 May 2015, D remarried, and went to live with his new wife F in a property owned by her. G immediately moved into the house he had been given, which was then valued at £633,000.

On 3 January 2020 D died, leaving his estate of £400,000 equally to his granddaughter H and his wife F.

Gift 19 June 2002

As the gift was made more than seven years before death, it is a PET which has become exempt.

5 May 2015 release of reservation

The release of D's reservation is a PET which becomes chargeable by reason of D's death between 4 and 5 years later. IHT is charged, at 60% of full rates on the basis of the Table of rates in force at the time of death, on the value of the house at the date of release of reservation.

		£	£
Gift			633,000
Deduct annual exemptions	2014/15*	Nil	
	2015/16*	Nil	
* see note (C) below			
			Nil
Chargeable transfer			£633,000
Tax thereon (assuming no change in rates)			
0–325,000 at nil%		—	
325,001–333,000 at 40%		123,200	
		£123,200	
IHT payable at 60% of full rates, 60% × £123,200 =			£73,920

Death of D on 3 January 2020

IHT is charged at full rates on the chargeable estate of £200,000 (£200,000 passing to the wife is exempt) with the nil band having been used by the deemed PET above. But downsizing relief of £175,000 is available in respect of the lifetime gift.

Tax thereon	
£25,000 at 40%	£10,000

Notes to the example

(A) The agreement between the D and his grandson G above is not ideal as there are likely to be a number of factors that might be open to dispute, particularly the schedule if it does not have, say, an insurance valuation and photographs attaching.

(B) The deemed PET on cessation of reservation of benefit is not reduced by any available annual exemptions. See IHTM14343. This is due to *IHTA 1984, s 19(5)* which effectively prevents the annual exemption being given in respect of deemed transfers of value.

(C) Downsizing relief is available as *IHTA 1984, s 8H(4D)* treats the cessation of reservation of benefit as a lifetime gift to the grandson by D. The relief is not given against the deemed lifetime gift but is given to the extent that the estate on death is closely inherited (*IHTA 1984, s 8FB*). In this case, that condition is satisfied because of the gift of half the residue to the granddaughter.

Post-5 April 2005 anti-avoidance

Further anti-avoidance measures apply from 6 April 2005 have been introduced following a short consultation period on the consultation document 'The Tax Treatment of Pre-Owned Assets' to counteract the free continuing use of assets that have been ostensibly gifted. Subsequently, a Technical Guidance note was issued on 17 March 2005. Further Technical Guidance Notes were subsequently issued, the latest being on 2 November 2007 at www.hmrc.gov.uk/poa/poa_news.htm. See also **5.6** ANTI-AVOIDANCE. HMRC's consultative document concentrated mainly on a charge to income tax, under *Sch D Case VI* [now see *ITTOIA 2005*], on former owners of assets on the benefit of using the asset(s) unless the asset has been sold to an unconnected party at arm's length. [*FA 2004, Sch 15 paras 4, 7, 9; Charge to Income Tax by Reference to Enjoyment of Property Previously Owned Regulations 2005, SI 2005/724, Regs 2–4*]. Taxpayers who have existing schemes that come within the charge may, by the relevant filing date i.e. 31 January in the year of assessment immediately following the initial year or such later date as HMRC may allow, elect for special transitional relief that allows them to avoid the charge to income tax by dismantling the original gift scheme. [*FA 2004, Sch 15 para 23(3)* as amended by *FA 2007, s 66*]. For IHT 500 election form see below. This will then ensure that the asset is treated as part of the individual's taxable estate for IHT purposes in accordance with the gifts with reservation rules while the individual continues to enjoy the property. Under those rules the property would be potentially eligible for IHT reliefs and exemptions (e.g. APR and BPR) providing the necessary requirements for those reliefs and exemptions were met. However, it may still in certain circumstances be appropriate to suffer the income tax charge under existing schemes and avoid the IHT charge. In addition, the charging provisions do not apply to property within an 'exemption from charge' or to the extent that it comes within an 'excluded transaction' category.

Substitutions and accretions of unsettled property

[22.3] Special rules are required to cover cases where the property changes hands after the gift or the donee predeceases the donor.

Basic rule

Where the donor makes a gift, other than a sum of money in sterling or any other currency then if at any time before the 'material date' the donee ceased to have the possession and enjoyment of any of the gifted property, the property, if any, received by him in substitution for that property is treated as if it had been comprised in the original gift instead of the property of which the donee ceased to have possession and enjoyment. This includes, in particular:

(a) in relation to any property disposed of by the donee, any benefit received by him by way of consideration for the sale, exchange or other disposition; and
(b) in relation to a debt or security, any benefit received by the donee in or towards the satisfaction or redemption thereof; and
(c) in relation to any right to acquire property, any property acquired in pursuance of that right. Any consideration given by the donee, in money or money's worth, is allowed as a deduction in valuing the original gift at any time after the consideration is given. This does not apply to any part (not being a sum of money) of that consideration which is property comprised in the same or another gift from the donor and is treated either as forming part of his estate immediately before death or as being attributable to the value transferred by a potentially exempt transfer made by him.

The '*material date*' is the date of the donor's death, or, if earlier the date on which the property ceases to be property subject to a reservation.

Spouse exemption

[22.4] Where an asset is gifted in a lifetime to, say, a child of the donor and is subject to reservation of benefit to the donor, the fact that the donor's estate on death is wholly within the spouse exemption does not eliminate a charge to IHT under the reservation of benefit provisions. This is because the lifetime gift is not property given to the spouse and does not become part of the spouse's estate on death.

Although a gift within the spouse exemption cannot be within the reservation of benefit provisions, this will not apply where the spouse is non-UK domiciled and the gift exceeds £325,000 in value. Such gifts are outside the scope of the spouse exemption and could therefore easily become subject to the reservation of benefit charge, given that assets held by each of them will often be used for the benefit of both. A gift of cash will not normally be subject to reservation of benefit since the tracing rules do not apply to cash sums, but the cash itself could be subject to reservation of benefit if it is retained as cash and not applied to purchase another asset.

Gift by donee

Where, before the material date, the donee makes a gift of the property comprised in the gift to him or otherwise voluntarily divests himself of it (except under compulsory purchase) for less than the value of the property at that time, then, unless he does so in favour of the donor, he is treated as continuing to have possession and enjoyment of that property. For these purposes, the donee is treated as divesting himself, voluntarily and without consideration, of any interest in property which merges or is extinguished in another interest held or acquired by him in the same property. [*FA 1986, Sch 20 paras 1, 2(1)–(5), 3(1)*].

The effect of the above is as follows:

(i) If the original gift subject to a reservation is of money in sterling or other currency it appears that the reservation ceases when the money is spent on acquiring any property.

(ii) If the disposal by the donee is for full consideration, the property received in substitution is treated as the original gift. As drafted, one interpretation is that this provision only applies to the first substitution and that on a second substitution (e.g. the application of the proceeds of sale of the original property for full consideration) the reservation ceases. It is understood that HMRC do not agree with this interpretation, and their view is that the property received on second and subsequent substitutions is also treated as the original gift. This point is unlikely to be resolved until the matter is tested in the courts.

(iii) If the disposal by the donee is for less than full consideration, the donee is treated as continuing to have possession and enjoyment of the original property.

Shares and debentures

[22.5] Where any shares in or debentures of a body corporate are comprised in the original gift and the donee is issued with, or granted rights to acquire, further shares or debentures (in the same or any other body corporate) otherwise than by way of exchange, the further issue or rights granted are treated as having been comprised in the gift in addition to the original property. (Where the shares etc. are issued by way of exchange, the *basic rule* above applies.)

This applies where the issue or grant of rights is:

(a) made to the donee as holder or as having been the holder; or

(b) made to him in pursuance of an offer or invitation made to him as being or having been the holder; or

(c) an offer or invitation in connection with which any preference is given to him as being or having been the holder. [*FA 1986, Sch 20 para 2(6)(7)*].

Consideration by donee

Any consideration given by the donee, in money or money's worth, for the issue or grant of rights to acquire shares in a company is allowed as a deduction in valuing the original gift at any time after the consideration is given. This does not apply to any part of that consideration:

(i) which, not being a sum of money, is property comprised in the same or another gift from the donor and is treated either as forming part of his estate immediately before death or as being attributable to the value transferred by a potentially exempt transfer made by him; or
(ii) as consists in the capitalisation of reserves or in the retention of any property distributable by the body corporate; or
(iii) is otherwise provided (directly or indirectly) out of the assets or at the expense of the body corporate or any associated body corporate. For this purpose, two bodies are deemed to be associated if one has control of the other or if another person has control of both. [*FA 1986, Sch 20 para 5*].

Early death of donee

[22.6] Where there is a gift and the donee dies before the material date (see 22.3 above) the provisions of 22.3 and 22.5 above apply to any property comprised in the gift as if:

(a) the donee had not died and the acts of his personal representative were his acts; and
(b) property taken by any person under his testamentary dispositions or his intestacy (or partial intestacy) were taken under a gift made by him at the time of his death. [*FA 1986, Sch 20 para 4*].

Application to settlements

Settlement by donor

[22.7] Where there is a disposal by way of gift and the property becomes settled property by virtue of the gift, the provisions relating to gifts with reservation apply as if the property comprised in the gift consisted of the property in the settlement on the 'material date' except insofar as that property neither is, nor represents, nor is derived from, property in the original gift. In practical effect this means that there is automatic tracing of reservation of benefit through all the changes which may later take place in the underlying assets in the trust. For these purposes:

(a) any property comprised in the settlement on the material date which is derived, directly or indirectly, from a loan made by the donor to the trustees is treated as derived from property originally comprised in the gift; and
(b) where, under any trust or power relating to settled property, income arising from that property after the material date is accumulated, the accumulations are not treated as derived from the property.

The '*material date*' is the date of the donor's death or, if earlier, the date at which the property ceased to be property subject to a reservation.

If the settlement comes to an end before the material date as respects all or any part of the property which, if the donor had died immediately before that time, would be treated as comprised in the gift, then

(i) the property in question (other than property to which the donor then becomes absolutely and beneficially entitled in possession); and
(ii) any consideration (not consisting of rights under the settlement) given by the donor for any of the property to which he so becomes entitled,

is treated as comprised in the original gift in addition to any other property so comprised. [*FA 1986, Sch 20 para 5(1)(2)(4)(5)*].

Where a gift is made into trust, the retention by the settlor of a reversionary interest under the trust is not considered to constitute a reserved benefit, whether the retained interest arises under the terms of the trust, or by operation of law, such as a resulting trust where the trust deed fails to declare the ultimate beneficiary of the funds (IHTM14392).

HMRC accept that the interaction of *FA 1986, s 102(3)* in **22.1**(i) above and *IHTA 1984, s 48(3) as amended by FA 2006, s 157* (see **20.2** EXCLUDED PROPERTY) is such that if a non-UK domiciled settlor creates a discretionary settlement of assets situated outside the UK and is included as a possible beneficiary, the gifts with reservation rules do not apply because the excluded property provisions are paramount. The fact that the settlor becomes domiciled in the UK after creating the settlement would also not give rise to the operation of *FA 1986, s 102(3)* should he die while so domiciled. Should the settlor become so domiciled and then cease to be a beneficiary, there is deemed to be a potentially exempt transfer of the settled assets but if they are excluded property this will prevent any liability arising on death within seven years (IHTM14396).

Spouse exemption

[22.8] HMRC have confirmed that spousal exemption applies to settled property subject to a reservation of benefit if, on the death of the settlor, the settlor's spouse becomes beneficially entitled to the property in the settlement either under the terms of the settlement itself or under a subsequent deed of appointment made prior to the death of the settlor. The same would apply if the spouse's entitlement on the death of the settlor were to a qualifying interest in possession. However, spousal relief cannot apply if the reservation ceases during the lifetime of the settlor (*STEP Briefing Note dated 24 February 2021*).

Settlement by donee

[22.9] Where the donor's gift is not settled property but the property is settled by the donee before the material date, the above provisions for settlements by the donor apply as if the settlement had been made by the original gift. For this purpose, property which becomes settled property under any testamentary disposition of the donee or his intestacy (or partial intestacy) is treated as settled by him. [*FA 1986, Sch 20 para 5(3)*].

Continuing benefit after termination of life interest

[22.10] Up to 21 March 2006 there was no reservation of benefit where a life interest was terminated and following that termination discretionary trusts followed under which the former life tenant could benefit. This was because the termination was not treated as a gift by the life tenant.

Accordingly new provisions were introduced to bring such arrangements within the scope of the reservation of benefit provisions. From 22 March 2006, where an interest in possession is in one of the categories which result in the life tenant being treated as beneficially entitled to settled property for IHT purposes (for example, a life interest which commenced before that date) and that interest comes to an end during that person's lifetime then the termination is to be treated as if it was a gift for the purposes of the gifts with reservation rules. Therefore where the interest in the property has terminated and the individual with the former interest in possession either receives or may receive benefits thereafter from the assets concerned then the gifts with reservation rules may apply in the same way as if the life tenant had made a gift of those assets personally. This is subject to the application of the exclusions from charge noted above. [*FA 1986, s 102ZA*].

Agricultural property and business property

[22.11] Where there is a gift of an asset which at the time of gift qualifies for agricultural property relief or business property relief, and the gift is caught by the reservation of benefit provisions, a special rule applies to determine whether either of those reliefs may apply to any potentially exempt transfer treated as taking place when the reservation ceases, or alternatively to the charge in respect of those assets on the death of the donor. In very broad terms either of these reliefs will only apply at the later time if the asset concerned continues to be within the relief in the hands of the donee. Thus relief will be available for a business asset if it continues to be used for a qualifying business by the donee, but if it is used by him for non-business purposes, any reservation of benefit charge on the donor will not be reduced by business property relief. The donor's and the donee's periods of ownership are aggregated for the purposes of establishing whether the applicable period of ownership test is satisfied.

In more detail, where there is a disposal by way of gift which, in relation to the donor, is at that time:

(a) relevant business property (see **6.4** BUSINESS PROPERTY); or
(b) agricultural property to which *IHTA 1984, s 116* applies (see **4.4** AGRICULTURAL PROPERTY); or
(c) shares or securities in agricultural companies to which *IHTA 1984, s 122(1)* applies (see **4.13** AGRICULTURAL PROPERTY),

and that property is subject to a reservation, then, subject to the exception below, any question as to the availability and appropriate percentage of agricultural or business property relief on the 'material transfer of value' is determined as if, so far as it is attributable to the gifted property, the transfer was made by the donee. For these purposes only, in determining whether the requirements as to minimum period of ownership and/or occupation are fulfilled (see **4.3** AGRICULTURAL PROPERTY and **6.8** BUSINESS PROPERTY) the donor's ownership prior to the gift is treated as the donee's and any occupation by the donor (before or after the gift) is treated as occupation by the donee.

The exception is that any question as to whether, on the material transfer of value, any shares or securities qualify for business property relief where control or 25% voting control is an issue is determined as if the shares or securities were owned by the donor and had been owned by him since the gift.

Where the gift falls within (c) above, agricultural property relief is not available (for transfers and other events occurring before 17 March 1987 the above provisions did not apply) unless *IHTA 1984, s 116* (see **4.4** AGRICULTURAL PROPERTY) applied in relation to the value transferred by the disposal *and* throughout the period from the gift to the 'material date' the shares and securities are owned by the donee. For this purpose only, in determining whether the requirements of **4.13**(c) AGRICULTURAL PROPERTY are fulfilled the requirements as to the ownership of the shares or securities there mentioned are assumed to be fulfilled.

The '*material transfer of value*' is, as the case requires, the transfer of value on the donor's death or on the property concerned ceasing to be subject to a reservation and '*material date*' is construed accordingly.

Early death of donee

[22.12] If the donee dies before the material transfer of value, then, as respects any time after his death, references to the donee include references to his personal representatives or, if appropriate, the person by whom the property or shares etc. concerned were taken under a testamentary disposition made by the donee or under his intestacy (or partial intestacy). [*FA 1986, Sch 20 para 8; FA 1987, s 58, Sch 8 para 18; F(No 2)A 1992, s 73, Sch 14 para 7*].

Estate duty cases

[22.13] The estate duty legislation contained similar, but not identical, provisions relating to gifts with reservation. It appears to be accepted that the estate duty cases are relevant for IHT purposes, particularly in relation reservation of benefit. In *Pearson v CIR* HL, [1980] STC 318, it was held that the meaning of 'interest in possession' for estate duty purposes was not necessarily the same for CTT purposes. But in more recent cases, such as *Ingram v IRC*, [2000] 1 AC 293, [1999] STC 37, HL and *Viscount Hood v CIR* [2016] UKFTT 059 (TC), the estate duty authorities were extensively reviewed and no suggestion was made that they did not apply to the current reservation of benefit provisions. The following decisions in estate duty cases must, therefore, be considered subject to this background.

(a) *Exclusion of the donor from enjoyment under* **22.1**(b) *above.* This condition is not fulfilled if at some later date after the gift the property or income therefrom is voluntarily applied by the donee to the donor, even if the latter is under an obligation to repay sums used by him (*New South Wales Commissioners of Stamp Duties v Permanent Trustee Co. of New*

South Wales Ltd PC, [1956] AC 512). The deceased may remain as a guest in a house he has given without tax being attracted provided that there was no agreement to this effect and it was a *bona fide* gift (*A-G v Seccombe* KB, [1911] 2 KB 688—contrast *Revenue Commissioners v O'Donohoe* SC (RI), [1936] IR 342) but this proposition is open to question following *Chick v New South Wales Commissioners of Stamp Duties* PC, [1958] AC 435 in which held that: 'Where the question is whether the donor has been entirely excluded from the subject matter of the gift that is the single fact to be determined. If he has not been so excluded, the eye need look no further to see whether his non-exclusion has been advantageous or otherwise to the donee'.

(b) *Exclusion of the donor from any benefit under* **22.1**(c) *above*. Arrangements between the donee and a third party to give the donor benefit is within this provision, but retention of rights under a contract made prior to the gift and quite separate from it, is not. The gift of land already subject to a lease to the donor is not a gift with reservation as the lease is not part of the gift (*Munro v New South Wales Commissioners of Stamp Duties* PC 1933, [1934] AC 61). But compare *Nicholas v CIR* CA, [1975] STC 278 where the donor's lease was acquired at the same time as the gift. (*Note*. The question of whether the owner of property (in particular, land) can grant a lease to himself or a nominee for himself may need to be answered by reference to the legal jurisdiction concerned. In the Scottish stamp duty case of *Kildrummy (Jersey) Ltd v CIR* CS, [1990] STC 657 the grant of a lease of land by the owners of the freehold interest to a nominee for themselves prior to the transfer of the freehold reversion to a third party was declared a nullity on the ground that a person cannot contract with himself. In the English law of property case of *Rye v Rye* HL 1961, [1962] AC 496 it was held that *Law of Property Act 1925, s 72(3)* does not enable a person or persons who are the freeholders of land to grant a lease to himself or themselves but, although not at issue, the judgment of Radcliffe LJ suggests the use of a nominee in such circumstances would be valid. These cases may be pertinent when considering the *Munro* decision in the context of IHT and gifts with reservation.)

Examples of 'benefit' include a covenant by the donee to pay the donor's debts and funeral expenses (*Grey (Earl) v A-G* HL, [1900] AC 124); a power reserved to the donor to charge a capital sum on the subject matter of the gift (*Re Clark*, (1906) 40 ILT 117); a collateral annuity to the donor secured by personal covenant (*A-G v Worrall* QB 1894, [1891–94] All ER 861); remuneration paid to the settlor as trustee, but *not* money spent on maintenance and education of the donor's children (*Oakes v New South Wales Commissioners of Stamp Duties* PC 1953, [1954] AC 57).

(c) *Settlements*. A reservation of benefit arises where a settlor is included as a potential beneficiary under a discretionary trust (see *A-G v Heywood* QB, [1887] 19 QBD 326; *A-G v Farrell* CA, [1931] 1 KB 81; and *Gartside v CIR* HL, [1968] AC 553; *HD Lyon's Personal Representatives v HMRC; Trustees of the Alloro Trust v HMRC* [2007] Sp C 616) but not necessarily where a spouse is included. The inclusion of the spouse may have income tax disadvantages (unless the trust contains non-income producing assets) but the inclusion of a widow or widower will not do so (*Lord Vestey's Executors and Vestey v CIR* HL 1949, 31 TC 1). Trustees are treated as having possession on behalf of the beneficiaries (*Oakes v New South Wales Commissioners of Stamp Duties* PC 1953, [1954] AC 57). A settlement of shares in favour of an infant child with absolute gift provided he reached the age of 21 but with a resulting trust to the donor if the child failed to reach that age is not a gift with reservation as the property comprised in the gift is the equitable interest which the donor had created in the shares (*New South Wales Commissioners of Stamp Duties v Perpetual Trustee Co. Ltd* PC, [1943] AC 425).

Variations and disclaimers

[22.14] The provisions relating to variations and disclaimers in *IHTA 1984, s 142* (see **13.1** DEEDS OF VARIATION AND DISCLAIMERS) do not apply to property to which the deceased was treated as entitled under the gifts with reservation rules. [*IHTA 1984, s 142(5); FA 1986, Sch 19 para 24*].

Double charges — gifts with reservation and death

[22.15] Without specific relief, a double charge to tax could arise where there is a transfer by way of gift of property which is or subsequently becomes a chargeable transfer and the property is, by virtue of the rules relating to gifts with reservation, subject to a further transfer which is chargeable as a result of the transferor's death. The pre-owned assets regulations relating to income tax now include provisions to avoid a double charge to IHT where a chargeable person elects that the gift with reservation provisions apply to the relevant property. [*FA 1986, s 104(1); Charge to Income Tax by Reference to Enjoyment of Property Previously Owned Regulations 2005, SI 2005/724, Reg 6; Inheritance Tax (Double Charges Relief) Regulations 2005, SI 2005/3441, Reg 3*]. A double charge can arise where the chargeable person makes a gift of property or a debt that is a potentially exempt transfer for IHT purposes. If that same property is then liable to the income tax charge the person may decide to make an election on form IHT500 under *FA 2004, Sch 15 para 21* that the property is subject to the IHT reservation of benefits rules. If that person then dies within seven years of the original gift a double charge to IHT may arise, firstly, by reason of the original transfer and secondly when the property is added back into the death estate for the purposes of the gift with reservation rules. The new provision avoids the double charge by opting for the IHT on transfer that produces the highest overall amount of IHT and thereby reduces the other transfer to nil. See Example 3 below.

Relief from double charge to tax is given where the following conditions are fulfilled.

(a) An individual ('the deceased') makes a transfer of value by way of gift of property after 17 March 1986 which transfer is or proves to be a chargeable transfer.
(b) The property in relation to the gift and the deceased is property subject to a reservation.

(c) *Either*:
   (i) the property is treated as property to which the deceased was beneficially entitled immediately before his death (as the property is then subject to a reservation); *or*
   (ii) the property ceases to be property subject to a reservation and is the subject of a potentially exempt transfer at that time.

(d) *Either*:
   (i) the property is comprised in the estate of the deceased immediately before his death and value attributable to it is a chargeable part of this estate on death; *or*
   (ii) the property is property transferred by the potentially exempt transfer in (c)(ii) above, value attributable to which is transferred by a chargeable transfer.

Where the above conditions are fulfilled, there must be separately calculated the total tax chargeable as a consequence of the death of the deceased:

(A) disregarding so much of the value transferred by the transfer of value under (a) above as is attributable to property to which (d) above refers; and

(B) disregarding so much of the value of property to which (d) above refers as is attributable to property to which (a) above refers.

Whichever of the two calculations produces the higher amount of IHT as a result of the death remains chargeable and the value of the other transfer is reduced by reference to the value of the transfer which produced that amount.

Where the higher amount is calculated under (A) above:

(I) credit is available for tax already paid on the lifetime chargeable transfer which is attributable to the value disregarded under that calculation (but not exceeding the amount of tax due on death attributable to the value of the property in question); and

(II) to avoid the value of the same property entering twice into the tax calculations, the reduction in value applies to all IHT purposes except a ten-year anniversary charge or proportionate charge to tax on a discretionary trust arising before the transferor's death if the transfer by way of gift was chargeable to tax when made.

Where the total tax chargeable under (A) and (B) above is identical, calculation (A) is treated as producing the higher amount. [*FA 1986, s 104(1)(c); SI 1987/1130, Regs 5, 8*].

Relief is given where a double charge to IHT arises in situations where arrangements are caught by the pre-owned assets income tax provisions in *FA 2004, Sch 15* which are subsequently dismantled by the individual but he/she dies within seven years. The conditions for double charge relief in these circumstances are as follows:

(a) the disposal condition or the contribution condition is met as respects the relevant property; and

(b) the deceased makes a transfer the result of which a third party becomes entitled to the benefit of a debt owed to the deceased; and

(c) before the deceased's death, any outstanding part of the debt is wholly written off, waived or released, and the write off, waiver or release is made otherwise than for full consideration in money or money's worth, and

(d) the following conditions must be fulfilled:
   (i) the deceased dies on or after 6 April 2005; and
   (ii) on the deceased's death, the transfer of value treated as made immediately before the deceased's death included the relevant property, or any property representing that relevant property; and
   (iii) as a result of the deceased's death, the transfer of value referred to in (b) above has become a chargeable transfer.

See HMRC's IHT Manual at IHTM14711–14 for HMRC examples of how the double charge relief works in practice. [*Inheritance Tax (Double Charges Relief) Regulations 2005, SI 2005/3441*].

Example 3

A entered into a lifetime loan scheme, commonly known as a 'double trust' scheme, in June 2006. He then sold his house to a trust fund for £500,000 and he is a life tenant of that trust fund. The trustees do not pay the purchase price but give A an IOU instead. A then gifts the IOU to a second trust for the benefit of his children B and C. A remains in occupation of the property but the outstanding debt will reduce A's estate on death under *IHTA 1984, s 162* by the amount of the loan. Under *FA 2004, Sch 15* A makes an election under *ibid* paragraph 21 so that the value of the house becomes subject to the gifts with reservation rules. A dies in July 2010 and the house at that date is valued at £750,000 and A's estate is worth £500,000. See 50 TRANSFERS WITHIN SEVEN YEARS OF DEATH. However, the house is also chargeable within the estate because it constitutes a gift with reservation following the election under *FA 2004, Sch 15, para 21*.

As a double charge would now arise each calculation should be considered in isolation.

First calculation: charge to tax using the original gift in the death estate.

Transfer in June 2006	£	£
Taxable gift	500,000	
Less Nil rate band using the table at 37.1 2010.A1	(325,000)	
Taxable balance	175,000	
Tax payable @ 40%	70,000	
Less Taper relief @ 40% (i.e. between 4 and 5 years)	(28,000)	42,000
Taxable estate	500,000	
Tax payable @ 40%	200,000	200,000
Total IHT payable		242,000

Second calculation: charge to tax using the gifts with reservation rules in the death estate (ignoring PET in June 2006).

	£	£
Estate	500,000	
Add Gift with reservation	750,000	
Taxable balance	1,250,000	
Less Nil rate band using the table at 37.1 2010.A1	(325,000)	
	925,000	
Tax payable @ 40%	370,000	
Total IHT payable		370,000

Notes to the example

(A) The charge to tax using the gift with reservation will be used by HMRC and the charge using the original gift will be reduced to nil by using the double charge relief. [*Inheritance Tax (Double Charges Relief) Regulations 2005, SI 2005/3441, Reg 4(4)*].

(B) It should be noted that the double charge relief provisions will not always apply when a perceived double charge arises. This will happen where an election is made in respect of the property subject to an '*Eversden*' type scheme (see **5.2** ANTI-AVOIDANCE) with the result that one spouse/civil partner has made a potentially exempt transfer and the other spouse's/civil partner's estate includes property subject to a reservation so that both charges are unaffected by the double charge relief provisions. The provisions only apply where there is a double charge in respect of one individual.

Example 4

A made a potentially exempt transfer of £150,000 to B in January 1998. In March 2005, A made a gift of land worth £336,000 into a discretionary trust of which he is a potential beneficiary. The gift was a gift with reservation but also a chargeable lifetime transfer on which IHT of £14,600 would have been paid at rates current at the time assuming there were no other previous transfers; the trustees paid the tax; no annual exemptions were available.

A dies in February 2010 without having released his interest in the trust. His estate is valued at £440,000 including the land in the discretionary trust currently worth £360,000.

First calculation: charge the land subject to the gift with reservation in A's death estate and ignore the gift with reservation.

	IHT payable £
January 1998	
Potentially exempt transfer (now exempt)	—
March 2005	
Gift with reservation (ignored)	—
February 2010	
Death estate £440,000	
Tax £46,000 less £14,600 already paid on the gift with reservation*	31,400

	IHT payable £
Total tax due as result of A's death	£31,400

* Credit for the tax already paid cannot exceed the amount of the death tax attributable to the value of the gift with reservation property i.e.

$$\frac{360,000}{440,000} \times £31,400 = £25,691.$$

Credit is therefore given for the full amount of tax paid £14,600.

Second calculation — charge the gift with reservation and ignore the land in the death estate

	IHT payable £
January 1998	
Potentially exempt transfer (now exempt)	—
March 2005	
Gift with reservation £336,000	
Tax £2,640 less £14,600 already paid (see note (A))	Nil
February 2010	
Death estate £80,000 (ignoring gift with reservation land) as top slice of £416,000	32,000
Total tax due as result of A's death	£32,000

Notes to the example

(A) 60% of the full rate for the date of death for a transfer more than 4 years but not more than 5 years before death i.e. 60% × 40% × (£336,000 – £325,000).

(B) The second calculation gives the higher amount of tax. In the first calculation the value of the gift with reservation transfer is reduced to nil and tax on death is charged with credit for the tax already paid. However, the credit provisions do *not* affect the choice of calculation, even if they operate to turn what was the higher amount of tax into the lower amount. See IHTM14571.

Key points concerning gifts with reservation

[22.16] Points to consider are as follows.

- Gifts to family members are often not formalised by deed of gift and this may cause the gift to fail if possession does not immediately pass to the donee. For instance, there may be informal arrangements whereby family members take possession of certain chattels of the deceased on the basis of a prior understanding that ownership had already been passed to the beneficiaries before the death. Whilst verbal agreements are commonplace, the gift of a chattel should be by deed or delivery. Therefore in the absence of both the gift cannot be perfected because there is no deed and the chattel still remains in possession of the donor and lacks delivery. Even if there were a gift, it would be one with reservation of benefit under *FA 1986, s 102(1)*. For a documented gift, see the Chattels Lease precedent at **22.2**.

- It is a common fallacy that any reservation of benefit can be dealt with by the donor giving full consideration in respect of it to the donee. The provision for any benefit to be disregarded where full consideration is given for it applies only to gifts of an interest in land or a chattel. Gifts of other types of assets, such as shares in a family company, are outside the statutory provision and therefore in the view of HMRC, it is not possible to make good a benefit from the shares or the company by giving full consideration. This view derives from the decision of the Privy Council on similar legislation in *Chick v Commissioner of Stamp Duties of New South Wales* [1958] AC 435 (see **22.13**). This gives the harsh result that once there is some enjoyment by the donor of the asset given, a benefit has arisen and nothing can be done to correct it.
- Consider the following example. John and Julia live together but are not married. John owns the house they occupy. John decides to give the house to Julia whilst continuing to live there. John has thereby made a gift with reservation and so the house remains in his estate for IHT purposes. This does not mean, however, that the house cannot also be in Julia's estate as there is no rule to state that if an asset is caught by the reservation of benefit provisions, it is prevented being part of the donee's estate. For this same reason, a gift with reservation to discretionary trust does not prevent IHT ten-year and exit charges arising on the trust.

After taking advice, Julia decides to give the property back to John. This reverses John's gift with reservation as the property is now back in his estate. But instead Julia now makes a gift reservation so the position is not improved at all. On further advice, they get married to benefit from the spouse exemption. However, the marriage does not have any impact on the IHT position of gifts made prior to it. So the position is still not improved and only caused arguments about the advice. If they both then die in the same car accident, up to 80% IHT could be payable on the value of the property if John is younger than Julia (see **49.14**). It is hard to see a sensible solution to this matter which theoretically could blight their tax position for ever after. HMRC state that although the property does not pass on death under the will or intestacy, exemptions that are available on death such as spouse exemption and charity exemption will be applicable to the transfer deemed to be made on death if, on death, the property passes to an exempt beneficiary (IHTM14303). One can hope that on Julia's death HMRC regard the property as passing to John although in fact it is already in his estate.

If John had given only a half share to Julia so that they own it as joint tenants, he might have hoped that the sharing exemption in *FA 1986, s 102B* would prevent any reservation of benefit. However, the sharing exemption applies to gifts as tenants in common in undivided shares. Changing the ownership to tenants in common after the gift does help because *FA 1986, s 102B* requires the original gift to be as tenants in common. John has therefore made a gift with reservation of a half share and if Julia gives it back to John she makes a gift with reservation. Julia could, however, avoid her reservation of benefit by severing the joint tenancy first, so that her gift back then falls within *FA 1986, s 102B*. They could now start again with John making a gift as tenants in common. This is all well and good for a main residence but CGT will arise for other properties. There can be SDLT as well if the property is mortgaged. At one time, it was thought that HMRC applied *FA 1986, s 102B* to all types of co-ownership, however, it is uncertain whether this is still the case as there has been a report that the *FA 1986, s 102B* exclusion was denied in a joint property case.

23

Inheritance Tax Planning

Introduction to inheritance tax planning

[23.1] This chapter contains a summary of the more common arrangements currently used in estate planning. It should be borne in mind that the arrangements are described in outline only, focusing primarily on inheritance tax issues, although other relevant tax consequences are mentioned where appropriate. However, all estate planning requires professional advice specific for the client and there may be other tax issues not mentioned here which will be relevant in the particular case concerned. This chapter is therefore intended as an initial guide only so that possible planning techniques appropriate to the client may be investigated further. In general, arrangements relevant to clients not domiciled in the UK are not included as this is a more complex area and significant changes to the relevant IHT provisions are expected in 2025.

The requirements for disclosure of tax avoidance schemes (see 5.7) should be considered in relation to all IHT planning which involves contrived or abnormal steps, a test which is completely subjective and incapable of definition. Disclosure can be required for established planning techniques which HMRC are clearly already aware of, if there is any modification of the steps involved. The disclosure requirement does not mean that the arrangements may not work; only that HMRC require notification about it.

Transition to residence basis of taxation

[23.2] A technical note issued by HM Treasury on 23 April 2024 set out proposals for liability to inheritance to be based on a residence test in place of the current application to those domiciled or deemed domiciled in the UK, with extension to assets with UK situs. The note summarises the proposals, to be effective from 6 April 2025, as follows:

> 'It is envisaged that the new rules will involve charging IHT on worldwide assets owned outright when a person has been resident in the UK for 10 years (the "residence criteria"), with a provision to keep a person in scope for 10 years after leaving the UK (the "tail" provision). The design of the system (including consideration of further criteria such as other connecting factors) will be subject to consultation. UK situs assets will remain in charge on the same basis as at present, regardless of residence.
>
> For trusts, it is envisaged that the new rules for chargeability of assets comprised in a settlement will depend upon whether a settlor meets the residence criteria or is within the tail provision at the time the assets are settled and/or when charges such as 10-year anniversary charges or exit charge arises.'

There is broad political agreement to this change although the IHT treatment of existing trusts made by non-domiciliaries remains a contentious matter and a more harsh regime is expected under a new government. UK domiciliaries who have been resident abroad for whatever reason will be able to escape liability to inheritance tax by ensuring that they remain outside the UK for the ten-year period. If, however, they become UK residents again before achieving ten years of non-residence, this significant opportunity will be lost and it appears that it will take another ten years of non-residence before it is restored.

Those domiciled outside the UK will become fully liable to inheritance tax five years before the current time, which is after 15 years of UK residence (deemed domicile), and their position is considerably worsened on leaving the UK. Currently, an individual who is deemed domiciled in the UK escapes liability to IHT after three complete tax years of residence outside the UK assuming he or she remains non-resident for the fourth year outside the UK. Under the forthcoming regime, the proposal is that liability to inheritance tax will continue for ten years after leaving the UK. That requires them to keep records of lifetime gifts, notify HMRC of funds put into foreign trusts and comply with the complexity of the IHT rules for the ten-year 'tail'.

Planning for the forthcoming regime is clearly difficult in the absence of more information and detail about it, but close attention to how the ten-year rule may affect any particular individual may be the best that can be done for 2024/25.

The main residence and other property interests

[23.3] Reversionary lease arrangements may, in appropriate circumstances, be outside the scope of the legislation introduced in the wake of the House of Lords decision in favour of the taxpayer in *Ingram v CIR* [2000] 1 AC 293, [1999] STC 37, HL, and appearing at *FA 1986, s 102A*. As an example, the arrangement works by parents granting a lease of the home to their children to come into effect on the expiry of 21 years at the latest, or on the death of the surviving parent whichever is the earlier. The lease will commonly be for at least 99 years, and may be for a longer period. So long as the parents originally purchased a freehold interest in the property more than seven years prior to the grant of the reversionary lease, *FA 1986, s 102A* will not apply provided that the lease contains no covenants of benefit to the freeholders. Hence there is no gift with reservation of benefit. See however *Viscount Hood v CIR* [2017] UKUT 0276 (TCC) for a case involving a leasehold property, rather than a freehold, and as a result it was caught as a reservation of benefit owing to the covenants to the head leaseholder contained in the sublease. A similar arrangement did however succeed in *Buzzoni (executor of the estate of Mrs Lia Kambi, deceased) v CIR* [2011] UKFTTT 267(TC), [2011] SFTD 771, [2011] SWTI 1946 where the sublessee's covenants were given direct to the freeholder.

Where the arrangements involve the freehold of a property occupied by those granting the lease, there will be a liability under the pre-owned asset legislation at *FA 2004, Sch 15*. However the value of the reversionary lease will initially be very low and should be within the de minimis exception for at least the first five years. If the property is not occupied by the freeholder, for example a commercial property, there will be no liability under *FA 2004, Sch 15*.

The main downside is that the capital gains tax base cost of the reversionary lease will be very low so that as the years pass and the reversionary lease acquires value, thereby depressing the value of the freehold interest, the reduction in inheritance tax is counter-balanced by a capital gains tax liability on the holders of the reversionary lease should they ever dispose of the property. Unless they are living at the property (in which event an alternative scheme may be better) the gain in their hands cannot be within the main residence exemption. Because of this, the scheme is best suited for a property which it is intended will remain in the ownership of the family indefinitely.

More sophisticated versions of the arrangement use a trust to hold part of the freehold interest of the home, with the reversionary lease being granted to a separate fund within the trust. This provides full capital gains tax exemption for the reversionary lease. However such arrangements require very careful drafting of the documentation.

It should be noted that HMRC's DOTAS guidance issued on 29 March 2018 suggests that these arrangements are notifiable under DOTAS with effect from 1 April 2018. It is unclear why HMRC require to be notified of schemes which they are already very familiar with.

Equity release

[23.4] An alternative arrangement in relation to the family home would be to take out a commercially available equity release arrangement and to make a gift of the cash to the next generation as a lifetime potentially exempt transfer. A commercial equity release which involves a sale is an excluded transaction for the purposes of the pre-owned assets legislation, and there are no capital gains tax issues with this arrangement. Nevertheless if the equity release is by way of loan, it must be acknowledged that people who have spent their lifetimes paying off a mortgage on their own home will not readily relish taking out a new mortgage in their later years for inheritance tax planning purposes. But if there is a wealthy family member, it may be that the loan could be arranged with that person, so long as the borrower has not previously made substantial gifts to him or her (in which case *FA 1986, s 103* would apply).

A borrowing on the home need not necessarily be given away to achieve IHT savings. The sum obtained could be transferred to a qualifying non-UK pension scheme for the benefit of the home-owners. Funds in such a pension scheme are left out of account in valuing a person's estate on death (*IHTA 1984, s 151*) and this applies with immediate effect from the time of funding the scheme.

Joint ownership

[23.5] Where children continue to be resident with their parents and this is likely to remain the case, the parents could put the property into the joint ownership of themselves and the children resident with them. Although there is a gift involved with this arrangement and therefore a potentially exempt transfer, it would be outside the reservation of benefit provisions so long as the conditions in *FA 1986, s 102B(4)* are satisfied, these being that the donors do not receive any benefit, other than a negligible one, which is provided by or at the expense of the donees for some reason connected with the gift. In practical terms, this means that the donees must not bear more than a fair proportion of the running expenses of the home. Ideally, this issue can be avoided entirely if the parents continue to pay all outgoings.

It should be noted that the legislation does not deal with the question of what fractional shares in the property may be held in order to be within the exclusion from reservation of benefit. Equal ownership by all parties is undoubtedly acceptable, but one can expect a challenge from HMRC if children are given substantially greater shares in the property than the parents retain. Such a challenge can only be on the basis that there is an implied condition in the legislation and that seems to be rather a weak proposition.

The family debt scheme

[23.6] If the home is owned by, say, the husband, he could sell it to his wife for full market value with the proceeds remaining outstanding as a debt. He then gives away the debt to his children as a lifetime gift. This arrangement is simply a variation on the widely marketed home loan arrangements which ultimately culminated in the introduction of the pre-owned assets legislation. However, that legislation contains an exemption for situations where the property concerned is transferred to the spouse and hence this arrangement does not give rise to an annual income tax charge.

There is however no exemption from the stamp duty land tax provisions for a sale between married persons and so there can be liability to that tax.

The arrangement can be adapted for other properties in the ownership of one of the spouses because there can be no capital gains tax payable where the disposal is to the spouse.

The erstwhile home loan schemes, sometimes known as double trust schemes, are no longer considered by HMRC to be effective for IHT purposes. The reasons given are (1) the debt is not deductible because it is created by a disposition made by the taxpayer and is caught by *FA 1986, s 103*; (2) the failure of the donee trustees to call in the loan, or the tacit understanding with them not to do so, amounts to a reserved benefit in the trust; and (3) the *Ramsay* approach applies. Clients need to be warned that any arrangements of this type will face strong opposition from HMRC and in *Pride v HMRC* [2023] UKFTT 316 (TC), the argument that *s 103* applies was upheld.

The terms of the debt need careful consideration as if it is payable on demand, but the children to whom it is given agree not to call for payment of it during the lifetimes of their parents, it would seem easier to allege that a benefit has been reserved out of the gift by associated operations. As an alternative the loan could have a fixed repayment date, or in some cases it may be structured as a relevant discounted security.

With effect from 1 April 2018, this type of arrangement should be notified under the DOTAS provisions.

Let properties

[23.7] A share in a let property may be given away to a settlor interested trust with the result that the share in the trust is outside the settlor's estate for inheritance tax purposes by virtue of *FA 1986, s 102B(3)*. As the trust is settlor-interested, capital gains tax holdover relief will not be applicable and accordingly, the capital gains tax position on the transfer into the trust will require review. Also the income will be treated as that of the settlor for income tax purposes, and it may therefore be sensible to give the settlor an entitlement to income. It follows that, if the entire title to a let property is shared between two such trusts, there will be no reservation of benefit whereas if only one trust holds all the title, the reservation of benefit provisions can apply. If the property is jointly owned by husband and wife, a settlement made by them, to which the property is transferred, will be treated as two settlements for IHT each containing the share transferred to it by its settlor. All the title to the property will therefore come within *FA 1986, s 102B(3)*.

Although the gift into the trust is not within the reservation of benefit rules, it is nevertheless a chargeable transfer for inheritance tax purposes, and should therefore be confined to the settlor's available nil rate band if an initial inheritance tax liability is to be avoided. Ten-year charges on the settlement will apply in the normal way.

Other lifetime trusts

[23.8] It may be appropriate to use up the available inheritance tax nil rate band by making a gift into a trust that is not settlor-interested. The advantage of this is that it enables assets which have accrued but unrealised capital gains to be held over into the trust, and equally on distribution out of the trust at some later time hold over can once again apply.

Assets which do not currently have any capital gain but which are expected to appreciate in value in the future may be sold to a family trust with the proceeds left outstanding as a debt due to the vendor. There will be no significant inheritance tax transfer of value with this arrangement, but there will be a disposal for capital gains tax purposes, and equally a sale for the purposes of stamp duty land tax if the asset is a property interest. Assuming that the debt is not given away, this arrangement amounts to an estate freezing operation so that only the growth in value is outside the vendor's estate, and for that reason he or she must not be a beneficiary of the trust.

Even so, if the loan is interest-free, there are various cases, such as *Jenkins v IRC* 26 TC 265, which indicate that the settlement will be settlor-interested for income tax purposes whilst the debt remains outstanding. For IHT purposes, HMRC's view is that an interest-free loan has an element of gift but is not in itself a gift with reservation. However, *FA 1986, Sch 20, para 5* treats any property derived from a loan to the trust as also derived from any gift to the trustees made by that same individual. It would therefore be appropriate to ring fence repayment of the debt away from any income or income accumulations in the trust and to have the initial gift into the trust made by some other party, for example, the husband or wife of the person who makes the loan. Alternatively, to sidestep these issues, the debt can be given away as a potentially exempt transfer.

Chattels and works of art

[23.9] These may be given away to the next generation with custody of the items retained by the donor on payment of a commercial 'rent' to the donees. The capital gains tax position on the gift will need to be reviewed. The main advantage of these arrangements is that the payments due to the donees may be quite low owing to the onerous obligations on the person retaining the use of the chattels in relation to safe keeping and insurance. At one time it was thought that HMRC would accept approximately 1% of the value of the items per annum as being full consideration, although more recently there have been reports that HMRC no longer accept that payments at this level are sufficient. It has always been advised that level of rent should be determined by donor and donees appointing valuers to negotiate the amount payable on behalf of their clients. If full consideration is given on an annual basis, there will be no reservation of benefit issues for inheritance tax purposes, although of course the initial gift will be a transfer of value. Also, full consideration takes the arrangement out of the charge to pre-owned assets tax.

A key point is ensuring that ownership of the chattels passes to the donees, and this normally requires a declaration of gift together with delivery of the items to them. If they remain in the possession of the donor, there will be no delivery and no effective gift. This issue may be dealt with either by following the formalities under the *Bills of Sale Act 1878*, which are fairly convoluted and many will find them off-putting. An alternative is for there to be a sale under the *Sale of Goods Act 1979*, with payment of nominal consideration to the vendor.

For non-domiciliaries holding valuable art or other moveable property in the UK, they could consider holding the items in a foreign partnership. The asset in the estate of the non-domiciliary is then the interest in the foreign partnership, and not the art or moveable property in the UK. So long as each partner remains non-domiciled and not deemed domiciled in any part of the UK, the partnership interests will be excluded property.

Exempt assets

[23.10] Investment of cash funds in assets qualifying for 100% relief such as agricultural property or shares in unquoted trading companies may be considered. These are not exempt and so form part of the gross estate on death, with consequent impact on the residence nil rate band (see **49.16**) but for most practical purposes, the 100% relief has the same effect as an exemption. There are commercially available schemes by which cash funds are invested in a managed portfolio of shares listed on the Alternative Investment Market. These will benefit from inheritance tax business property relief after two years of ownership, whereas investment in agricultural property requires seven years of ownership if the land is let under a farm business tenancy, the two-year test for agricultural land applying only if it is farmed by the owner. It must be remembered that if business assets or let agricultural land are given away in lifetime, the donee must retain the gifted property, or suitable replacement property, for seven years or until the death of the donee, whichever is the shorter period. This is to ensure that the relief given on the gift remains available in relation to a failed PET on the death of the donor. A further point to bear in mind is that the relief for let agricultural land may not survive the change of government as it has been suggested that it is an unwarranted relief for investors.

Another commercially marketed arrangement designed to secure business property relief within two years works by setting up a wholly-owned company which enters into property development partnerships with other investors. The developments are managed so as to minimise risks, whilst providing an income return which can be drawn out of the company by way of dividend.

It should be noted that following the new rules on deductibility of debts in *FA 2013*, any borrowings taken out after 5 April 2013 to finance the acquisition of agricultural or business property are to be deducted primarily from the value of that property for IHT purposes, notwithstanding the fact that they may be secured on other assets.

Exempt gilts

[23.11] All UK Government securities issued after 29 April 1996 and acquired after 6 April 2013 are exempt from inheritance tax as excluded property if the beneficial owner is resident outside the United Kingdom: see **20.5**. There is no two-year ownership test for the securities. Accordingly, if surplus cash is invested in such securities by an individual who is not ordinarily resident in the UK, they may then be given to a family trust from which the settlor should be excluded, or given directly to the next generation. This will not involve any transfer of value for inheritance tax purposes.

Divorce settlements

[23.12] So long as a settlement agreed between parties on divorce is within the exemption in *IHTA 1984, s 10* (dispositions not intended to confer gratuitous benefit), the funds concerned may be transferred directly into a trust for the recipient, rather than being paid to that person outright. The transfer into trust will not be a chargeable transfer nor will the funds within the trust be within the estate of any person for inheritance tax purposes. The reservation of benefit provisions will not apply because neither of the parties has made any gift. A Court Order may therefore require a home to be transferred from one party into a number of trusts for the other for life and then the children of the marriage so as to keep the property out of the spouse's estate and to keep the value in each trust below the nil rate band.

Share freezing arrangements

[23.13] If the business of a family company does not qualify for inheritance tax business property relief (for example if it is a property investment company) it is possible to freeze the value of the existing ordinary share capital by issuing a new class of shares which takes the rights to (a) all annual profits above a stated level, being approximately the current level of profit, and (b) all growth in assets values above the current asset value of the company. This requires extensive rewriting of the Articles of Association of the company and it must also be borne in mind that the alteration in the share or loan capital of a close company can result in a chargeable transfer being made by the existing shareholders by virtue of *IHTA 1984, s 98*. The relevant thresholds for the share freezing operation therefore need to be carefully set. The new class of shares is likely to have a nil base cost for capital gains tax purposes.

Freezing other assets with an option

The grant of an option to buy an asset likely to appreciate in value, such as a property, is a means of freezing the value for IHT purposes. This arrangement is discussed by HMRC in the inheritance tax manual at IHTM09772–09777 where it is confirmed that so long as full consideration is paid for the option, it will be taken into in valuing the property on the next time of charge to IHT where this is within the duration of the option granted. Whether or not the option is exercised is not relevant to the valuation. The option price will initially be chargeable to CGT as a disposal of an asset, namely the option itself (and not a part disposal of the underlying asset), but this is subject to treatment as part of the acquisition price of the asset concerned if the option is exercised. On exercise of an option over UK land, stamp duty land tax may be chargeable depending on the exercise price. If the option is never exercised, the grantee will make a transfer of value for IHT purposes and it will be necessary to review whether or not it falls to be treated as a PET, which it will not be if the omission enlarges the estate of the grantor whilst it is in administration. It will be appreciated that freezing an asset in this way simply swaps an IHT charge for a CGT charge on eventual disposal of the asset concerned, subject to any available reliefs at the time of disposal.

Insurance-based schemes

[23.14] The main insurance-based estate planning schemes fall into two categories, these being gift and loan trusts and discounted gift schemes.

Under a gift and loan trust, a discretionary trust is created with a nominal sum and the client then makes a loan to the trustees with the funds being invested in a single premium life insurance bond. The trustees take the 5% annual withdrawals which are available from the bond and use this to repay the loan owing to the client over the next 20-year period. The remaining funds within the bond grow free of inheritance tax outside the estate of the client.

It will normally be preferable for the client not to be the person who forms the discretionary trust with the nominal sum. This is to prevent the arrangement involving any gift by the client with the loan repayments being a benefit reserved out of it.

Discounted gift schemes involve the contribution of a lump sum payment to a trust set up for the benefit of the next generation and under the terms of the trust the settlor retains an entitlement to a predetermined level of cash withdrawals during his or her lifetime. Because the settlor has carved out a fixed entitlement and given away the balance of the funds to the other beneficiaries the scheme is outside the inheritance tax gift with reservation of benefit provisions. The settlor's entitlement to the payments for the rest of his life discounts the value of the gift to the next generation for inheritance tax purposes. The other beneficiaries may have absolute entitlements, in which case the gift to them counts as a potentially exempt transfer, or alternatively they may take their benefits under a discretionary trust, in which case the value of the gift into the trust will be a chargeable transfer and should be structured so as to fall within the available nil rate band. These schemes are very popular because they effectively enable a gift of capital to be made with retained rights to income but outside the reservation of benefit regime. HMRC accept the validity of the arrangements, although they have challenged the discount figure in relation to the value of the potentially exempt transfer in some cases at the tax Tribunals. Revenue and Customs Brief 22/13 and the HMRC Trusts and Estates Newsletter December 2013 contain further guidance on HMRC's views. As a general rule, the scheme is most suitable for retired persons in their 70s. It should be borne in mind that it is inflexible and may be difficult to unwind if the settlor should later wish to do so.

Short term trust for surviving spouse

[23.15] One of the complications of estate planning is often the capital gains tax liability which arises on gifts of assets during lifetime to the next generation. This problem can be quite acute under the current capital gains tax regime where the rate of tax on a gain on a residential property such as a holiday home is likely to be 24%, with the possibility of a higher rate being introduced under the new Government, so that substantial 'dry' tax liability can arise on a gift of an asset with a low base cost. If one spouse is in poor health whereas the other remains in good health, or alternatively where one spouse is considerably older than the other, it may be appropriate for the spouse with the shorter life expectancy to leave assets on trust for the surviving spouse for a short period of time, say one year. This secures the spouse exemption on the death and also a tax-free uplift in base costs for capital gains tax purposes. On termination of the trust for the spouse, so long as the assets pass absolutely to other beneficiaries, there will be a potentially exempt transfer by the surviving spouse. As to the length of time which should be set for the spousal interest, IHTM11023 states that a gift by will to the spouse should be accepted without investigation if it takes effect immediately in possession on the death and is not subject to any conditions; on this basis, any such interest in possession, however short, is sufficient to qualify as an exempt gift.

It is preferable for this arrangement to be set up by Will rather than by deed of variation since for the latter, the trust for the surviving spouse must remain in place for more than two years because of the provisions of *IHTA 1984, s 142(4)*. It is worth noting that HMRC's GAAR guidance Part D contains an example of assets in the name of one spouse being transferred to the other shortly prior to the death of the donee spouse, so that they may be received back under the will with the capital gain eliminated. The arrangement is outside the scope of the general anti-avoidance rule although the published guidance contains the proviso that this is 'so long as Mrs Jones was in full capacity at the time of the gift'. Presumably where the donee is not in full capacity, the objection is that the donor will inevitably receive back what was given and the avoidance is circular in nature.

Double dip

[23.16] Assets qualifying for 100% relief may be left by will to a family discretionary trust, with other investment assets passing to the surviving spouse. After the death, the surviving spouse may then sell investment assets to the trustees having a value equal to that of the assets in the discretionary trust. The sale proceeds will be satisfied by the transfer of the trust assets to the spouse. See Example at **4.19**. This transaction will be a disposal of both types of asset for both capital gains tax and stamp duty land tax, or stamp duty, purposes. However, all assets from the estate will have a probate value base cost and so no gain may arise. After a further period of time, two years in the case of business assets, the assets acquired from the trust will once again qualify for relief in the estate of the surviving spouse. A variation of this arrangement involves leaving all assets on discretionary trusts, with those not qualifying for 100% relief being appointed on IPDI trusts for the spouse within two years of the death. If the IPDI trusts are formulated as a sub-fund of the discretionary trusts, the trustees may then exchange assets by way of sale between the two funds with no capital gains tax or stamp duty land tax issues arising due to the treatment of both funds as one settlement for the purposes of those taxes.

Death bed planning for business owners

[23.17] The test for business property relief works in a different way to that for agricultural property relief. The requirement for business relief is that the business concerned, or the shares concerned, must have been held for a two-year qualifying period. There is no requirement that the assets used in the business must have been held for the same two-year period. Accordingly, if surplus available funds are invested in a business by the owner of it, or by a partner in it, shortly prior to his or her death, those funds will immediately become eligible for business property relief. The funds must be used to acquire assets used in the business or alternatively, it must be demonstrated that they are required for future use in the business. This strategy cannot be used for an asset used by a partnership unless it is purchased with capital put into the partnership; this is because *IHTA 1984, s 112(3)* treats an asset as an excepted asset if it has been provided for use by a partnership for less than two years, and it does not replace an asset previously so used.

For family companies, the funds must be used to subscribe further shares by way of rights issue on shares already held for a two-year period: see *Vinton and Green v HMRC* [2008] STC SCD 592.

For agricultural property relief, there is a requirement that the land concerned has been held for a two-year period if farmed in hand. However, it may be that business property relief can be claimed for such acquisitions during that two-year period.

Ten inappropriate or ineffective IHT planning ideas

[23.18] To conclude this review of IHT planning, set out below are ten inappropriate or ineffective IHT planning steps which are most commonly promoted by those not fully conversant with the complexities of IHT. Some may appear to be very obvious but lack of understanding of the IHT rules results in more people falling into these traps than ought to be the case.

Transferring the home into the joint names with children

Unless the children are living with the parents and continue to do so, this will be a gift with a reservation and so ineffective to save IHT on death. The reservation of benefit can be dealt with by the payment of full market rent for the share given away, but if any such rent is found to be below market level by HMRC, it will achieve nothing. Any degree of reservation of benefit collapses the whole gift for IHT purposes.

Putting the home into a trust to save care fees

People may be advised to transfer their home into a trust for themselves and their children in the hope that it will then not count as an asset of their estates and also so that they will be able to claim assistance with care fees in old age.

Whether or not it works for that purpose may be debatable, but unless the home is within available nil rate bands, there will be a chargeable transfer into the trust notwithstanding the fact that it is a gift with reservation of benefit. Also, ten-yearly charges will apply. It is a common misconception that where a gift is caught by the reservation of benefit rules, there can be no chargeable transfer at the time it was made, nor ten-year charges.

Gift with reservation of shares

HMRC allow the continuation of normal commercial remuneration from a company after shares in it have been given away, for example to children. In that case, there is no reservation of benefit. However, if they do not accept that the remuneration is within such limits, there will be a reservation of benefit. It might be thought that some sort of payment could be made to the children to remove the reservation of benefit, but such payments apply only to use of properties and chattels. They will have no effect where the gift was shares. A possible argument is that the benefits received are not referable to the gift.

Gifts by the elderly within the nil band

A gift within the band simply reduces or eliminates the nil rate band available on death. Accordingly, no IHT at all is saved if the donor dies within seven years of the gift. Tapering does not apply because tapering relates to tax payable on death and if there is no tax on the gift, there is no tapering.

Wasting business property relief

If an estate is partly exempt, for example where a share in residue is left to the widow and other shares go to chargeable beneficiaries or a nil rate band will trust, any business property relief on assets in the residuary estate will be apportioned between the exempt and chargeable portions. Some of it will therefore go to waste. It does not matter that the business property may in fact be appropriated to the chargeable beneficiaries by the executors. Therefore, the better strategy would be to ensure that there is a specific gift of the business property to the chargeable beneficiaries.

Losing the benefit of the residence nil rate band

If an estate includes the residence of the deceased, any hope of claiming the residence nil right band will be lost if children or other descendants receive cash legacies and the residue goes to other beneficiaries or perhaps to a family trust. In order for the residence nil rate band to be available, the property or a share in it must be left to the descendants. It will make no difference if the executors appropriate the property to the descendants in settlement of the legacies.

The position is different under downsizing relief. In this case, the relief can apply to cash legacies to descendants.

Deed of variation to recycle assets

A beneficiary of an estate may attempt to gain a benefit by entering into a deed of variation by which his or her legacy is redirected to the surviving spouse, who agrees to pass the funds on in due course. This arrangement will not be acceptable to HMRC. The same can apply where a deed of variation leaves funds in trust for the spouse on interest in possession trusts lasting for at least two years from the date of death, and where there is an intention to end the trusts thereafter and release the funds back to the original legatee.

Gift to a company partly owned by the donor

It might be thought that a gift of assets to a company which is not wholly owned will count as a potentially exempt transfer to the extent that the value increases the interests of the other shareholders. Unfortunately, this is not the case because the requirement for a potential exempt transfer is that no other person's estate is increased by the transfer. With a gift to the company, the company's estate is increased and so the transfer cannot be potentially exempt. It is therefore chargeable.

Trust capital distributions within the IHT nil band

Capital distributions transferred within the previous ten years are taken into account in the IHT calculation on the ten-year anniversary date and so if they are within the IHT nil band, they produce no saving in IHT. This applies to all such transfers in the entire ten-year period running up to the anniversary date which may seem unfair given that normal IHT rules only count gifts in a prior seven-year period.

In fact, such capital distributions can lead to an increase in IHT chargeable overall if they were subject to an IHT exit charge when they were made, as might be the case between ten-year anniversaries. There is the exit charge to be paid, which is not deductible in any way from the subsequent ten-year charge, and the distributions also reduce the nil band available on that anniversary. Thankfully, the unfairness of this is mitigated by the fact that IHT rates on relevant property are tolerably low.

Distribution of estate assets which have lost value

The IHT provisions allow for loss in value relief to be claimed as a deduction for IHT purposes where shares, land or property are sold by the 'appropriate person'. The sale must be within one year of the death for quoted investments and three years for land or a property (with an extension in certain cases to four years). If such assets are distributed out of the estate before sale, this relief is lost as the beneficiary will not be the 'appropriate person', even if that same person is the executor.

24

Interest in Possession

Cross-references. See **38** SETTLEMENTS — GENERAL; **39** SETTLEMENTS WITH INTERESTS IN POSSESSION; **40** SETTLEMENTS: DISCRETIONARY TRUSTS AND OTHER TRUSTS OF RELEVANT PROPERTY.

Simon's Taxes. See **I5.141–I5.148, I5.201**.

Other Sources. Foster, Part E2; HMRC Customer Guide to Inheritance Tax; IHTM16000.

Introduction to interest in possession

[24.1] Up to 21 March 2006, a person with an interest in possession in all or part of settled property was treated as beneficially entitled to the property or part in which his interest subsisted. Alternatively, if there was no interest in possession the special charging rules relating to settlements of 'relevant property' apply (see **40.1** SETTLEMENTS: DISCRETIONARY TRUSTS AND OTHER TRUSTS OF RELEVANT PROPERTY). [*IHTA 1984, ss 49, 50, 58, 59*]. For IHT purposes it was therefore important to establish into which category a settlement fell.

From 22 March 2006 an interest in possession to which a person becomes beneficially entitled on or after that date will result in that person being treated as beneficially entitled to the property concerned only if it is either (i) an immediate post death interest (see **39.2** SETTLEMENTS WITH INTERESTS IN POSSESSION), (ii) a disabled person's interest (see **44** SETTLEMENTS: TRUSTS FOR DISABLED PERSONS), or (iii) a transitional serial interest (see **39.2**). [*IHTA 1984, s 49 as amended by FA 2006, Sch 20 para 4*]. These are described as qualifying interests in possession [*IHTA 1984, s 59*]. From 9 December 2009, this treatment was also extended to trust interests in possession for which full consideration was paid by the beneficiary to the settlor, this being intended to block an avoidance scheme [*IHTA 1984, s 5(1B)*].

Interests in possession which arose before 22 March 2006 and which continued thereafter were unaffected by the above changes introduced in *FA 2006* and therefore the beneficiary continues to be treated as beneficially entitled to the settled property in which the interest subsists for so long as that same interest endures.

The IHT treatment of settlements with interests in possession is detailed further at **39** SETTLEMENTS WITH INTERESTS IN POSSESSION.

Meaning of 'interest in possession'

[24.2] There is no statutory definition of 'interest in possession' in the IHT legislation (except see **24.3** below for Scotland). The explanation of the expression 'qualifying interest in possession' (see **40.1** SETTLEMENTS: DISCRETIONARY TRUSTS AND OTHER TRUSTS OF RELEVANT PROPERTY) merely clarifies what is meant by 'qualifying'. What is meant by an interest in possession is therefore a matter of general law as interpreted by the courts in the light of the specific IHT legislation.

The authoritative statement on the meaning of the term for CTT (and therefore IHT) purposes is to be found in the majority opinions in the House of Lords in *Pearson and Others v CIR* HL, [1980] STC 318. The salient facts to be derived from this case are as follows.

(a) There must be a **present right to the present enjoyment** of certain settled property for there to be an interest in possession in that property. So a person with an interest in possession must have an immediate right to trust income as it arises. It should be noted that it is of no consequence that no income actually arises so it is not necessary to ensure that a life tenant actually receives income in order to establish the interest in possession. See *Oakley & Hutson (Jossaume's Personal Representatives) v CIR* [2005] STC SCD 343 Sp C 460 at **55** TAX CASES.

(b) If the trustees have **any power to withhold income** as it arises there is no interest in possession. There is a distinction between a power to terminate a present right to present enjoyment and a power which prevents a present right of present enjoyment arising. It follows that:
   - (i) *a power to accumulate income* is sufficient to prevent a beneficiary from having an interest in possession. (*Note.* per Inland Revenue Press Release 12 February 1976, if any accumulations must be held solely for the person having the interest or his personal representatives, this does not amount to a power to withhold income.) The position is the same if there is a trust to accumulate. Whether or not income is in fact accumulated is irrelevant.
   - (ii) *an overriding power of appointment* which could be used to defeat the interest of a beneficiary does not prevent that interest from being in possession if it does not affect the right of the beneficiary to the income which has already arisen.
   - (iii) *the possibility of future defeasance* of an interest does not prevent it from being in possession until the occurrence of the relevant event.

(iv) *a power of revocation* does not prevent an interest from being in possession until it is exercised.

(c) There is a distinction between trustees' **administrative powers**, such as those to pay duties, taxes etc. and their **dispositive powers** to dispose of the net income of the trust. The existence of the former does not prevent an interest from being in possession. Any interest in possession will be in the net income of the trust after deduction of administrative expenses.

HMRC's view was previously expressed in their Press Release of 12 February 1976 which they regard as not inconsistent with the majority HL opinions in *Pearson*.

Scotland

[24.3] **In Scotland**, any reference to an interest in possession in settled property is a reference to an interest of any kind under a settlement by virtue of which the person in right of that interest is entitled to the enjoyment of that property, or would be so entitled if the property were capable of enjoyment, (including an interest of an assignee under an assignation of an interest of any kind in property subject to a proper life rent, other than a reversionary interest) and that person is deemed to be entitled to a corresponding interest in the whole or any part of the property comprised in the settlement. [*IHTA 1984, s 46*]. For further background on Scottish Trusts see HMRC Trust Manual at www.gov.uk/hmrc-internal-manuals/trusts-settlements-and-estates-manual/tsem6520.

In a Scottish case, an individual (D) transferred certain securities and investments to trustees in 1962. The income arising from the trust was treated for tax purposes as income of the settlor under *FA 1958, s 22* (now *ITTOIA 2005, ss 624–628*). D died in 1981 and then his wife died in 2002. HMRC issued a notice of determination on the basis that she had enjoyed an interest in possession in the settled property. The trustees appealed. The Special Commissioner dismissed the appeal, finding that D's widow had effectively enjoyed 'a power of veto: the whole of the free annual income of the trust fund had to be paid or applied to her or for her benefit from year to year unless or until she should concur with a consideration by the trustees that it was proper and expedient for a lesser amount to be so paid or applied'. Accordingly the trust deed had conferred an interest in possession. See *Trustees of the Douglas Trust (for Mrs I Fairbairn) v HMRC* [2007] STC SCD 338 Sp C 593.

Trustee Act 1925

[24.4] *Trustee Act 1925, s 31* provides for the accumulation of income during the infancy of a beneficiary who has an interest in trust property, and upon attaining the age of 18, the income is then to be paid to the beneficiary if he or she does not at that time otherwise become entitled to it. The operation of *s 31* can therefore give rise to an interest in possession when the beneficiary attains the age of 18.

Sole object of discretionary trust

[24.5] The fact that income from trust funds is to be held upon 'protective trusts' to be paid to or applied for a class of beneficiaries at the trustees' absolute discretion has been held not to give the sole existing beneficiary a protected life interest. Nor does that beneficiary have an interest in possession by virtue of being the sole current existing object of a discretionary trust if the trusts are for a class of beneficiaries which has not closed and there is a reasonable possibility of other members of the class coming into existence. The possibility, however remote, that another discretionary object could come into existence is sufficient to prevent him from having the necessary immediate entitlement to trust income as it arises. (*Moore and Osborne v CIR* Ch D, [1984] STC 236.)

Occupation of dwelling-house by beneficiary

[24.6] Trustees under a will or settlement may have power to allow a beneficiary to occupy a dwelling-house comprised in the trust on such terms as they think fit. Where there is no interest in possession in the dwelling house HMRC do not regard the exercise of the power as creating one if the effect is merely to allow non-exclusive occupation, or to create a contractual tenancy for full consideration. The creation of a lease for a term or a periodic tenancy for less than full consideration does not create an interest in possession, though it may give rise to a charge under *IHTA 1984, s 65*. (See **40.12** SETTLEMENTS: DISCRETIONARY TRUSTS AND OTHER TRUSTS OF RELEVANT PROPERTY.) On the other hand, if the power is drawn in terms wide enough to cover the creation of an exclusive or joint right of residence, albeit revocable, for a definite or indefinite period, and is exercised with the intention of providing a particular beneficiary with a permanent home, HMRC will normally regard the exercise of the power as creating an interest in possession; see HMRC Statement of Practice SP10/79. A lease for life for less than full consideration will also be regarded as an interest in possession. (In another context see *Harrison and Another v Gibson and Others* Ch D [2005] TLR 24 January 2006 where the testator's intentions as to occupancy of his bungalow 'in trust to my wife' did not give an absolute interest to his wife under *Administration of Justice Act 1982, s 22*.) A similar view will be taken where the power is exercised over property in which another beneficiary had an interest in possession up to the time of the exercise.

As noted at **24.1**, since 22 March 2006, the creation of an interest in possession in settled property on or after that date has no consequence for IHT purposes as regards lifetime settlements. However, in the case of trusts as arising under a will, allowing a beneficiary to occupy a property as his or her home may create an immediate post-death interest – see case law below. This will have further implications if the beneficiary ceases to occupy the property in due course; a termination of the interest in possession will then arise, which will be either a potentially exempt transfer or a chargeable transfer depending on the nature of the continuing trusts for the property.

Case law

In the case of *Judge and another (personal representatives of Walden deceased) v HMRC* [2005] STC SCD 863 Sp C 506 a deceased husband's will gave his house to trustees, with a declaration that they should allow his widow (W) to occupy the house 'for such period or periods as they shall in their absolute discretion think fit'. W previously had no interest in the property and continued to occupy the house until her death in 2003. HMRC issued a notice of determination on the basis that her husband's will had given her an interest in possession in the house (see also Inland Revenue Statement of Practice SP 10/79, 15 August 1979). Her personal representatives appealed. The Special Commissioner allowed their appeal, holding that the effect of W's husband's will was that she 'had no right to occupy the property but the trustees were given a discretion (but not a duty) to allow her to occupy'.

Accordingly, the widow did not have an interest in possession in the property. Despite the case being found in favour of the taxpayer and the husband's will being held to create discretionary trusts with no tax being payable by the estate, it has not dealt with all uncertainties in this area, partly because it is a decision of the Special Commissioner which is not a binding precedent, and partly because all similar cases will depend on the particular wording of the trusts concerned. Further issues will arise where the trust relates to a share in the property where the surviving spouse holds the remaining interest. In order to reduce any inference that an interest, trustees should perhaps regularly reconsider their discretionary powers documenting such deliberations in writing for record. Another possibility is to grant the surviving spouse a shorthold lease for minimal rent, which SP10/79 acknowledges prevents an interest in possession from applying; alternatively, consider creating a formal licence to occupy. (Inland Revenue Statement of Practice SP 10/79.) See also Taxation Magazine, 20 May 2004, p 183.

See also *CIR v Lloyds Private Banking Ltd* [1998] STC 559 in which a will included a clause stating that 'while my Husband ... remains alive and desires to reside in the [matrimonial home] and keeps the same in good repair and insured comprehensively to its full value with Insurers approved by my Trustee and pays and indemnifies my Trustee against all rates taxes and other outgoings in respect of the property my Trustee shall not make any objection to such residence and shall not disturb or restrict it in any way'. This was held to create an interest in possession in the property.

In *Vincent v HMRC* [2019] UKFTT 657 (TC), a property was jointly owned by a married couple with another family member, Mr Thom, who had a five-eighths share. After the deaths of both of the married couple in 2001, their three-eighths share in the property was to be held 'upon trust to permit Mr Thom to reside therein for so long as he shall desire free from rent but he being responsible for general rates, water rates, insurance and maintenance repairs of an income nature'. It was held that this gave Mr Thom an interest in possession in that share so that the whole of the property formed part of his estate on his death. He had a right to reside at the property by virtue of being a co-owner and the provision allowing rent-free occupation was designed to give him additional protection, amounting to an interest in possession.

In *Hall (as trustees of the Carolina Raboni estate) v HMRC* [2023] UKFTT 32 (TC), a friend of the deceased had been granted a right of occupation of the deceased's home by her will. However, as the property was the only asset in the estate, apart from minimal other funds, the IHT liability of over £15,000 could not be paid without either a sale of the property, or raising funds some other way. A sale of the property would have resulted in the right of occupation falling away as there was no provision for the purchase of an alternative property. The solution agreed between the executors and the residuary beneficiaries was that they would personally provide the funds to pay the IHT. Nevertheless, in these circumstances, it was held that there was no interest in possession in the property because the occupation rights under the will were unenforceable.

Precedent for occupation of trust property

Where two or more beneficiaries have interests in possession in a property held in trust and it is agreed that one shall have exclusive occupation of it, making a compensatory payment to the other beneficiary or beneficiaries, the agreement set out below may be adapted to suit the case.

Agreement between the Trustees and Beneficiary for the occupation of trust property [pursuant to ***Trusts of Land and Appointment of Trustees Act 1996, section 13*****]**

THIS AGREEMENT is made the . . . . . . day of . . . . . . 2010. . . . . . between

. . . . [Trustee]. . . . . of . . . . [Address] . . . . and . . . . [Trustee]. . . . . of . . . . [Address]. . . . . hereinafter known as 'the Trustees' and . . . . [Beneficiary]. . . . . of . . . . [Address]. . . . . hereinafter known as 'the Beneficiary'.

WHEREAS

(1) The Trustees are the present Trustees of:

(a) a conveyance ('the Conveyance') dated . . . . [date] . . . . . . and made between the parties and

(b) a settlement ('the Settlement') of even date with and made between the same parties in the same order as the Conveyance.

(2) The freehold property (the 'Property') described in the schedule is vested in the Trustees and is held on trusts under which the Beneficiary is entitled to an interest in possession.

(3) The Trustees have determined in accordance with the provisions of the Trusts of Land and Appointment of Trustees Act 1996, section 13 that the Beneficiary may occupy the Property on the following terms and conditions including the payment by the Beneficiary to . . . . [Name of second Beneficiary] . . . . of . . . . [Address]. . . . . hereinafter known as . . . . [Name]. . . . . (who is also entitled to an interest in possession under the trusts affecting the Property) of such annual sums as are stated in this agreement.

NOW IT IS AGREED as follows:

1 *Licence*

The Trustees permit the Beneficiary to reside in and occupy the Property until the agreement is determined in accordance with the provisions below.

2 *Tenant not to assign*

This licence is personal to the Beneficiary and he/she shall not assign it or allow any other person or persons to occupy the whole or any other part of the property.

3 *Payment*

The Beneficiary undertakes to pay to . . . . [Name] . . . . the annual sum of £. . . . . by equal half yearly instalments payable in arrears throughout the currency of this licence so long as . . . . [Name]. . . . . is entitled to an interest in possession under the Trusts affecting the property, the first such instalment to be paid on . . . . [Date]. . . . . and the subsequent instalments to be paid on . . . . [Date]. . . . . and . . . . [Date]. . . . . in each year and the last payment to be made on the termination of the licence or on such earlier date as . . . . [Name]. . . . . ceases to be entitled to an interest in possession under the trusts affecting the property (whether due to the death of . . . . [Name]. . . . . or for any other reason) and to be a proportionate payment.

Notes to the Agreement

(A) Further provisions on powers, proper law, etc. and full administrative provisions are required to effect this agreement.

(B) Note that in the above agreement the second Beneficiary is excluded from occupying land under the *Trusts of Land and Appointment of Trustees Act 1996, s 13(1)* but he/she still retains an interest in possession in that land. On the death of the occupying Beneficiary and upon the second Beneficiary becoming sole life tenant of the trust fund he/she can no longer be excluded from occupation under *s 13(1)* nor will he/she be required to pay compensation (see point 3 'Payment' in Agreement above) under *s 13(6)*.

(C) The payment of compensation does not affect the capital gains tax main residence exemption for the property.

Power to augment income out of capital

[24.7] Where a trustee exercises a power to augment the income of a beneficiary out of capital, this will have no immediate IHT effect if the beneficiary is a life tenant who has an interest in possession, as by virtue of *IHTA 1984, s 49(1)* he is already treated as beneficially entitled to the property. In other circumstances, the exercise of the power is likely to give rise to a tax charge under *IHTA 1984, s 52(1)* or a charge under *IHTA 1984, s 65(1)(a)*. If the life tenant is the surviving spouse of a testator who died before 13 November 1974, exemption might be available as set out at **51.2** TRANSITIONAL PROVISIONS. (See HMRC Statement of Practice E6.)

Time of creation of interest in possession

Age of majority

[24.8] Under *Family Law Reform Act 1969, s 1*, the age of majority is reduced from 21 to 18 although for settlements created before 1 January 1970, the relevant age of majority remains 21. Where an interest is created by a special power of appointment made after 31 December 1969 under a settlement made before 1 January 1970, HMRC regard the beneficiary's interest in possession as arising at 18.

Administration period

[24.9] Where a person would have been entitled to any interest in possession in the whole or part of the residue of the estate of a deceased person had the administration of the estate been completed, he is regarded for inheritance tax purposes as becoming entitled to an interest in possession in the unadministered estate and in the property representing ascertained residue, or a corresponding part of it, on the date as from which the whole or part of the income of the residue would have been attributable to his interest had the residue been ascertained immediately after the date of death. In practical terms, this means that where a person would have had an immediate post-death interest (a life interest) in another estate, but he or she dies before the administration of the other estate is completed, for IHT purposes, the estate of the deceased life tenant should include the assets in the unadministered estate valued on the date of the life tenant's death less the outstanding debts and liabilities of that estate on that date. If the interest was in part of the other estate only, then that fraction of the assets and liabilities in it should be included. The appropriate supplementary schedule is IHT415 [*IHTA 1984, s 91*].

Survivorship clauses

[24.10] Where under the terms of a will or otherwise property is held for any person on condition that he survives another for a specified period not exceeding six months, the disposition taking effect at the end of the period (or on death if the person does not survive until then) is treated as having had effect from the beginning of the period. This has no effect on distributions etc. occurring before the disposition. [*IHTA 1984, s 92*].

Usufructs

[24.11] Usufructs are a type of property ownership found in overseas civil law jurisdictions. They give the right of enjoyment of a property which is in another person's ownership. HMRC's published view is that a usufruct is to be treated as a settlement for IHT purposes and the interest of the person having the right to enjoyment of the property for life is an interest in possession. This means that where such a property interest is acquired or set up after 21 March 2006, the property becomes subject to a relevant property settlement for IHT and a chargeable transfer arises, unless it is excluded property: see 40 SETTLEMENTS – DISCRETIONARY TRUSTS AND OTHER TRUSTS OF RELEVANT PROPERTY. HMRC's view is controversial and not generally accepted because 'there is no settlement into trust or state of affairs equivalent to a trust in relation to the property concerned' (Peter Harris, barrister), although James Kessler QC regards it as 'a toss of a coin matter'. HMRC note that 'it is possible that the value for tax that emerges from applying HMRC's approach may not be (so) very different from the value offered by the taxpayer, particularly where there are encumbrances against the property; but each case will need to be considered on its own merits'. [IHTM27054]. This seems to suggest that a negotiated settlement of the tax position is normally achieved.

25

Interest on Tax

Cross-references. See **7.15** CALCULATION OF TAX for transfers reported late and **32** PAYMENT OF TAX.

Simon's Taxes. See **I11.405, I11.411, I11.430.**

Other Sources. Foster, Part L5.31–2; IHTM36000.

Interest on tax overdue

[25.1] Interest is chargeable on unpaid inheritance tax from the due date (see **32.1** PAYMENT OF TAX) to the date of payment at the rates available online at: www.gov.uk/government/publications/rates-and-allowances-hmrc-interest-rates-for-late-and-early-payments/rates-and-allowances-hmrc-interest-rates.

Where inheritance tax or additional inheritance tax arises virtue of the changes to deemed domicile made by *F(No 2)A 2017, s 30*, or the changes to the IHT treatment of UK residential property interests made by *F(No 2)A 2017, Sch 10*, interest runs from the normal due date or 1 January 2018, whichever is the later. [*F(No 2)A 2017, s 30(14) and (16)*].

Interest is payable gross and it is not deductible in computing income, profits or losses for tax purposes. It is refundable to the extent that the tax concerned is subsequently cancelled.

For the above purposes, where:

(a) additional tax becomes chargeable as a result of the transferor's death within seven years of a chargeable transfer (including tax payable under the provisions relating to **40** SETTLEMENTS: DISCRETIONARY TRUSTS AND OTHER TRUSTS OF RELEVANT PROPERTY because of the settlor's death within that period), and
(b) a political party is liable for tax on the death of the transferor within one year after a gift in excess of £100,000 made before 15 March 1988,

the chargeable transfer is deemed to have been made on death.

Acceptance of property in satisfaction of tax

Where after 16 March 1987, the Board agree to accept property (acceptance by the AIL Panel of Resource) in satisfaction of any IHT, CTT or estate duty (see **32.10** PAYMENT OF TAX) on terms that the value to be attributed to the property for the purposes of the acceptance is determined at a date earlier than that on which the property is actually accepted, the terms of the agreement may provide that the amount of tax which is satisfied by the acceptance of the property does not carry interest from that earlier date. [*IHTA 1984, ss 233, 236(1)(1A); FA 1986, Sch 19 paras 32, 33; FA 1987, s 60; F(No 2)A 1987, s 97; FA 1988, Sch 14; FA 1989, ss 178, 179; SI 1985/560; SI 1986/1944; SI 1987/887; SI 1988/1230; SI 1988/1623; SI 1989/1002; SI 1989/1297; SI 1989/1298*].

Example 1

B died on 10 February 2020. The executors made a payment on account of IHT of £70,000 on 30 June 2020 on delivery of the account. The final notice of determination was raised by HMRC on 19 June 2021 in the sum of £102,500. The rate of interest for these purposes is assumed to be 5% for the purpose of this example.

Date of chargeable event (death) — 10 February 2020
Date on which interest starts to accrue — 1 September 2020

	£
IHT payable	102,500
Payment made on account 30 June 2020	70,000
Balance due	£32,500
Assessment raised by HMRC 19 June 2021	
Interest payable (1.9.2020 to 19.6.2021)	
£32,500 at 5% for 292 days	£1,300

Example 2

F gave his holiday home in Cornwall to his granddaughter G on 7 August 2016. On 23 May 2020 F died. He had made no use of the property at any time after 7 August 2016. G made a payment of £15,000, on account of the IHT due, on 1 January 2021. The liability was agreed at £27,000, and the balance paid, on 17 February 2021. The rate of interest for these purposes is assumed to be 5%.

Date of PET — 7 August 2016
Date on which PET becomes chargeable — 23 May 2020
Date on which IHT is due — 1 December 2020

	£
IHT payable	27,000
Payment made on account 1 January 2021	15,000
Balance due	£12,000
Interest payable	
On £27,000 from 1.12.2020 to 1.1.2021	
£27,000 at 5% for 31 days	115
On £12,000 from 1.1.2021 to 17.2.2021	
£12,000 at 5% for 47 days	77
Total interest payable	£192

Where HMRC delay their reply to a letter or other enquiry for no good reason, and the delay in total exceeds by more than six months its 28-day target for replies, then no interest will be charged on tax that was unpaid during the period of the delay, and any reasonable costs incurred directly because of the delay will be reimbursed (HMRC Code of Practice 1).

Interest on tax repaid

[25.2] From 22 August 2023, the interest repayable in respect of IHT overpaid is 4.25%. Any repayment of tax or interest paid will carry interest from the date of payment until the order for repayment is issued at the above rates and such interest will be tax-free. [*IHTA 1984, s 235*]. Where inheritance tax is repaid as a result of an order that is made under the *Inheritance (Provision for Family and Dependants) Act 1975, ss 2, 19* as amended by the *Family Law Act 1996, s 66* special treatment applies, see **25.4** below.

Where there has been unreasonable delay on the part of HMRC, and the delay has caused a liability for interest on tax to build up, HMRC may waive payment of the interest charge (DMBM 404020). Unfortunately, the current extensive delays at HMCTS Probate in dealing with applications for Grant of Probate, frequently leading to delays in realising estate assets to pay IHT, are not recognised by HMRC as a reason to waive interest for any period since there is no provision for a reasonable excuse defence in relation to interest on late-paid tax.

Interest on payment by instalments

[25.3] See **32.9** PAYMENT OF TAX.

Special cases concerning interest on tax

[25.4] Tax overpaid or underpaid in consequence of the *Inheritance (Provisions for Family and Dependants) Act 1975* (or NI equivalent) (see **49.19** TRANSFERS ON DEATH) does not carry interest before the date of the order. [*IHTA 1984, ss 146(1), 236(2)*].

Interest will normally become payable on the unpaid inheritance tax six months after the end of the month in which the chargeable event occurred (see **32.1** PAYMENT OF TAX), but special provisions are sometimes made, as was the case in 2001 with the outbreak of foot and mouth disease which affected farming businesses. It is now provided that where there is a disaster or emergency, interest on unpaid tax may be deferred where the Commissioners agree such a case warrants it. [*FA 2008, s 135*].

26

Land

Cross-reference. See **14.5** DETERMINATION AND APPEALS re land valuation.

Simon's Taxes. See **I4.312, I7.302, I7.401, I8.342.**

Introduction to land

[26.1] Land includes (unless the contrary intention appears) buildings and other structures, land covered with water, and any estate, interest, easement, servitude or right in or over land, but does not include any estate, interest or right by way of mortgage or other security. In *Chelsea Yacht and Boat Co Ltd v Pope*, CA [2001] 2 All ER 409 where a houseboat moored to a pontoon and embankment wall by ropes constituted a chattel and not part of the land which consequently would affect the option to pay by instalments. In contrast in *Cinderella Rockerfellas Ltd v Rudd* [2003] All ER 219 a floating nightclub permanently attached to the land by ropes and chains would constitute part of the land which consequently would affect the option to pay by instalments. See **32.5** PAYMENT OF TAX. In any Act passed before 1 January 1979, 'land' includes messuages, tenements and hereditaments, houses and buildings of any tenure. [*Interpretation Act 1978, s 5, Sch 1, Sch 2 para 5(b); IHTA 1984, s 272*]. See also IHTM23001. The Land Registry Office is the preferred source of information for HMRC. See www.landregistry.gov.uk.

Chargeable transfers of land

[26.2] Inheritance tax applies to chargeable transfers of land situated in the UK and to land situated abroad but in which an interest is held by a person domiciled or deemed domiciled in the UK. Certain special provisions apply as below.

Agricultural land and business land

[26.3] Until the amending legislation in *FA 2009*, agricultural relief applied only to land in the UK, the Channel Islands or the Isle of Man. Relief was then extended with effect from 22 April 2009 to land in a European Economic Area State and the legislation included a provision for retrospective relief where tax was due or was paid on or after 23 April 2003. There was a similar extension of deferral relief under *IHTA 1984, s 125* to woodlands in an EEA state. Where claims for repayment resulted in a refund of tax, interest would be added. Claims had to be made within the four-year time limit in *IHTA 1984, s 241* or 21 April 2010, whichever was the later. [*FA 2009, s 121*]. This extension of relief for agricultural property is now withdrawn in relation to chargeable events arising on or after 6 April 2024 and furthermore, land in the Channel Islands or the Isle of Man no longer qualifies, so from 6 April 2024, the relief applies only to land in the UK. [*F(No 2)A 2024, s 11*].

There is no similar restriction for land used for the purposes of a business and this therefore qualifies for business property relief wherever it is situated, subject to satisfaction of the normal rules for the relief: see **6** BUSINESS PROPERTY. Accordingly, although agricultural relief or woodlands deferral relief may no longer be claimed for land outside the UK, if such land is used for the purposes of a business, it may qualify for BPR.

In the case of agricultural or business property that may qualify for 100% relief, HMRC state that the open market value should still be used. Personal representatives may consider using their own estimate of the value of the property in the expectation that the business will, in any case, be covered by the 100% relief. A reason for using a nominal value may be the cost of a professional valuer's fees to the estate. However, nominal or ill-considered values should be avoided because if relief is not due for some reason and there is an uplift in the nominal value put on the business by the personal representatives, then the consequent uplift to the correct value may incur a penalty. Also, for the purposes of *TCGA 1992, s 274*, the value for CGT purposes should be 'ascertained' and not a nominal estimated value. See example in **6.3** BUSINESS PROPERTY.

Case law

In *Tapp v HMRC* [2008] EW Lands TMA/284/2008 a Lands Tribunal case shows the necessity of documentation, including photographs, regarding the state of repair of property at the time of death but a subsequent visit by the District Valuer at a later date may indicate a higher value which was not reflected at the time of death. See IHTM23203. This may also apply to land which, say, adjoins a potential gravel extraction site which is subject of planning consent at the time of the death valuation. At the time of the District Valuer's visit a public enquiry has recommended to the Secretary of State that the appeal by the gravel extraction company should be dismissed hence resulting in a higher market valuation at the time of the inspection visit. For special valuation matters concerning minerals see IHTM23197.

The *conacre* (derivation from 'corn acre') system is unique to Ireland and around a third of all farmland in Northern Ireland is let informally to farmers in this way, often from 20 to 30-acre farms now too small to be commercially viable. APR of 100% applies to the ordinary value of farmland however, where farmland has development potential but is still farmed by letting in conacre, it attracted a second relief – business property relief – also at 100% on that additional development value. Following the Northern Ireland Court of Appeal hearing in *McCall (Personal Representatives of Mrs E McClean (deceased)) v HMRC*, CA (NI) [2008] STC 990 Sp C 678 that business may now consist mainly of making or holding investments, within *IHTA 1984, s 105(3)*, so that the land is not 'relevant business property'. *See* **4.1** AGRICULTURAL PROPERTY and 55 TAX CASES.

Free use of land

[26.4] A transfer of value may arise where an owner allows the use of land to another person for a fixed or minimum period for inadequate consideration. See 48.3 TRANSFER OF VALUE for details.

Housing associations

[26.5] Gifts of land in the UK to registered housing associations after 13 March 1989 are exempt. See 21.5 EXEMPT TRANSFERS.

National heritage land

[26.6] Land and buildings which are of outstanding historic or other interest may be exempt from inheritance tax under certain conditions, see 30 NATIONAL HERITAGE.

Payment of tax by instalments

[26.7] Under certain conditions, where a liability to inheritance tax arises on the transfer of land and buildings of any description, wherever situated, an election to pay the tax by ten annual instalments may be made. See 32.5 PAYMENTS OF TAX for details and HMRC Customer Guide to Inheritance Tax.

Sales within three (or four) years after death

[26.8] Special provisions apply to allow a relief for loss on sale, see 53.9 VALUATION.

See 50 TRANSFERS WITHIN SEVEN YEARS BEFORE DEATH for special provisions.

UK residential property interests

[26.9] With effect from 6 April 2017, the value of an interest in a closely held company or a partnership is not to be excluded property to the extent the interest concerned derives its value from UK residential property. These provisions also apply to loans to acquire such property interests and collateral for such loans, but not to interests in commercial property. For further details, see 20.2.

Woodlands

[26.10] See 54 WOODLANDS for special provisions.

Key points concerning land

[26.11] Points to consider are as follows.

- The open market value of agricultural property may exceed its agricultural value where the land has planning permission or there is development or amenity value, or mineral value (such as gravel or sand extraction potential). The difference between the open market value and the agricultural value often occurs on farms where there are ranges of traditional buildings suitable for conversion into residential or commercial use. Agricultural relief will not be available in respect of the excess value but business relief may be available for it. Care should be taken to confirm that the parts of the farm with excess value for non-agricultural use are actually used as an asset of a qualifying business if business relief is to be claimed. Problems frequently arise with traditional buildings suitable for development that are obsolete for modern farming methods and have not been used for the business for some considerable time and do not qualify for 100% BPR or APR.
- Where land is situated in the United Kingdom, HMRC rely on professional advice from the Valuation Office Agency (VOA), or the Valuation and Lands Agency (VLA) in Northern Ireland, in arriving at a valuation unless specifically stated otherwise. Although most land in the UK which is chargeable to tax on the death is referred to the VOA, there are some exceptions such as land subject to a binding contract for sale at the date of death. The role of the District Valuer (DV) is to agree the agricultural value and in cases where, the property has value for development or value for other non-agricultural uses or there is an imposing farmhouse in a location that would appeal to non-farming purchasers e.g. 'lifestyle farmers', the DV will also agree an open market value for the property. The DV bases his valuation at inspection on local knowledge, or on the basis of information provided by the parties and the inspection itself.
- It would be advantageous to receive the development land at a high value for CGT purposes for any future disposal but this is only of benefit where the land is covered by the APR or BPR 100% exemptions. Where hope value arises out of development potential or change of use then such excess value will not attract agricultural relief. As the excess value may attract business relief but a claim for business relief on the value of agricultural property on the excess over its agricultural value — e.g. farmland with planning permission, development value or mineral value (such as gravel and sand)

is dependent on it being 'relevant business property'.

27

Liability for Tax

Cross-references. See **11.10** CLOSE COMPANIES for liability of participators; **30.10** NATIONAL HERITAGE for persons liable on a chargeable event; **32** PAYMENT OF TAX; **34.2** PENSION SCHEMES; **49.21** TRANSFERS ON DEATH for liability where legitim is claimed in Scotland; **54.4** WOODLANDS for person liable on a disposal.

Simon's Taxes. See **Part I10, I11.211**.

Other Sources. Foster, Part K; HMRC Customer Guide to Inheritance Tax; IHTM28000.

More than one person liable

[27.1] According to the nature of a chargeable transfer, more than one person may be liable for the tax and if any one does not discharge the liability, then other persons may be liable up to certain limits and with a right of recovery. Except as provided otherwise, where two or more persons are liable for the same tax, each of them is liable for the whole of it. [*IHTA 1984, s 205*].

Lifetime transfers

[27.2] Subject to the rules in **27.7** below for lifetime transfers within seven years of death, the primary person liable is the transferor. If the tax remains unpaid after it ought to have been paid, the following persons are also liable.

(a) Any person the value of whose estate is increased by the transfer.
(b) Any 'person in whom the property is vested' (whether beneficially or otherwise) or who is beneficially entitled to an interest in possession in it at any time after the transfer (e.g. a nominee, trustee, life tenant, but see **27.10** below) to the extent that the tax is attributable to the value of that property. See **27.5** below for the extension of the meaning of 'person in whom property is vested' which also applies to lifetime transfers.

(c) Where by the chargeable transfer any property becomes comprised in a settlement, any person for whose benefit any of the property or income from it is applied.

References to property include any property directly or indirectly representing it.

Limitation of liability

[27.3] The liability of persons within (a) to (c) above is limited to the tax which would be payable on the value transferred as reduced by the tax remaining unpaid (i.e. the liability cannot be for a greater amount than tax on the property transferred without grossing-up). Liability is further limited as follows.

(i) In the case of a trustee, it is limited to the value of the property he has received, disposed of or has become liable to account for to the beneficiaries and any other property as is for the time being available in his hands for the payment of tax (or might have been so available but for his own neglect or default).
Note. For income tax purposes, the income of a settlement is treated as that of the settlor where he might benefit directly or indirectly from the settlement. HMRC do not take the view that, solely because the trustees have power to pay, or do in fact pay, inheritance tax due on assets which the settlor puts into the settlement, the settlor has an interest in the income or property of the trust and any income should be treated as the settlor's. (Former Inland Revenue Statement of Practice SP 1/82 6 April 1982.)

(ii) A person within (b) above, other than a trustee, is only liable to the extent of the property concerned.

(iii) A person within (c) above is liable only to the extent of the property or income (as reduced by income tax borne by him in respect of that income) applied for his benefit by the trustees. [*IHTA 1984 ss 199(1)(4)–(5), 204(2)(3)(5)(6)*].

Example 1

A settled £78,000 on discretionary trusts in December 2010, having previously made chargeable transfers on 31 March 2010 totalling £325,000.

A's liability is as follows	£
Gift	78,000
Deduct 2010/11 annual exemption	3,000
	£75,000
Grossed at 20%	£93,750
IHT thereon at 20%	£18,750

Example 2

Transferee

In the example above A pays only £10,000 of IHT and defaults on the balance of £8,750, so that the trustees become liable as transferee.

The trustees' liability is not, however, £8,750 but is as follows

	£
Original gross	93,750
Deduct IHT unpaid	8,750
Revised gross	£85,000
IHT thereon at 20%	17,000
Deduct IHT paid by A	10,000
Now due from trustees	£7,000

Example 3

Person in whom property is vested

In January 2011 C transferred to trustees of a discretionary trust shares in an unquoted property company worth, as a minority holding, £50,000. However, the transfer deprives C of control of the company with the result that the value of his estate is reduced by £210,000. He has already used his nil rate band and annual exemptions.

C's liability is as follows	£
Net loss to him	210,000
Grossed at 20%	262,500
IHT thereon at 20%	52,500

C fails to pay so that the trustees become liable, as follows

	£
Original gross	262,500
Deduct unpaid IHT	52,500
	£210,000
IHT thereon at 20%	£42,000

Notes to the example

(A) The trustees' liability cannot exceed the value of the assets which they hold, namely the proceeds of sale of the shares, less any CGT and costs incurred since acquisition, plus any undistributed income in their hands.

(B) Prior to 2004/05 when there was a differential between the marginal income tax rate (40%) and the rate applicable to trusts (34%) a further liability on the beneficiary could arise. If the trustees had already distributed net income of £2,000 to beneficiary D who is liable to pay additional higher rate income tax of £182 thereon (i.e. £3,030 × 6%), D could have been made to pay IHT of £1,818, being the net benefit received by him. From 6 April 2004 this will not arise as the rate applicable to trusts was increased to 40%. From April 2010 the rate applicable to trusts increased to 50% and the dividend rate is now 42.5%. [*ICTA 1988, s 686(1A)* as amended by *FA 2004, s 29(2)* and *ITA 2007, s 9(1)(2)*; *FA 2009, s 6*].

Transferor's spouse or civil partner

[27.4] Where a transferor is liable for tax on a chargeable transfer and has made another, separate transfer to his spouse or civil partner and both transfers took place while they were married to each other, the spouse or civil partner is also liable for the tax on the chargeable transfer. The liability of the spouse or civil partner is limited to the market value of the gift to the spouse or civil partner at the time of the spouse/civil partner transfer. In addition, where the transfer to the spouse or civil partner is *before* the chargeable transfer and the property transferred to the spouse or civil partner is not tangible movable property, the liability of the spouse or civil partner is limited to the market value of the gift received *at the time of the chargeable transfer* (or if the gift has been sold, its market value at the time of the sale) if this is lower than the market value at the time of the spouse/civil partner transfer. [*IHTA 1984, s 203; The Tax and Civil Partnership Regulations 2005, SI 2005/3229, Reg 36*]. This is an anti-avoidance provision to enable tax to be recovered from the spouse or civil partner where it cannot be recovered from the transferor or other person as above.

Transfers on death

[27.5] The persons liable are as follows.

(a) *The deceased's 'personal representatives'* in respect of property not comprised in a settlement immediately before death and settled land in the UK which devolves upon or vests in them. The liability is a personal rather than a representative liability of the personal representatives (see also Personal Contact manual, para 3.19 issue 12/94), and their non-UK residence does not prevent either liability or the UK courts' jurisdiction to deal with IHT claims (*CIR v Stype Investments (Jersey) Ltd*; *Re Clore (deceased)* CA, [1982] STC 625 and *CIR v Stannard* Ch D, [1984] STC 245). However, the liability is limited to the unsettled assets received and the UK land settled immediately before the death and available at any time in their hands for the payment of tax (or such assets and land which might have been available but for their own neglect or default). In Scotland, an executor is not liable under this provision for tax on any heritable property vested in him under *Succession (Scotland) Act 1964, s 18*. The European Convention on Human Rights and *Human Rights Act 1998* which came into effect on 2 October 2000 has now confirmed that HMRC cannot seek penalties from the personal representatives of a deceased person who was liable for a penalty. In addition any such penalties already collected must now be repaid and these repayments should include repayment interest at the rate applicable under *IHTA 1984, s 233*. Such interest would run from the date the penalties are paid to the date of repayment by HMRC.
The liability of the personal representatives extends to joint property passing by survivorship. There is concurrent liability by the surviving joint tenant as a person in whom the property vests upon the death. The liability is not a testamentary expense (see *IHTA 1984, s 211(1)*) and so under *IHTA 1984, s 211(3)*, it is recoverable from the surviving joint tenant if not paid by that person direct to HMRC.

Under certain wills, the deceased may not have given any indication of how the burden of inheritance tax is to be allocated among the items of property in the estate. Where personal representatives are liable for tax on chargeable transfers on death, then, subject to any contrary intention in the will, any tax payable on the value of unsettled UK property which vests in them is to be treated as part of the general testamentary and administration expenses of the estate. Where any tax paid by the personal representatives does not fall to be treated in this way, the tax must, where necessary, be repaid to them by the person in whom the property is vested. References to tax include interest on tax.

(b) *The trustees of a settlement* which immediately before death comprised property passing on the death. The liability is limited to the value of the property the trustees have received, disposed of or have become liable to account for to the beneficiaries and any other property for the time being as is in their hands for the payment of tax (or might have been so available but for their own neglect or default).

(c) *Any person in whom property is vested* (whether beneficially or otherwise) *or who is beneficially entitled to an interest in possession in it* at any time after the death (but see **27.10** below) to the extent that tax is attributable to the value of the property. The liability is limited to the extent of the property.

(d) *Any person for whose benefit any of the property or income comprised in a settlement immediately before death was applied after death*. The liability is limited to the property or income (as reduced by income tax borne by him on that income) applied for his benefit by the trustees.

(e) *The administrator of any registered pension scheme in respect of funds which are chargeable under IHTA 1984, ss 151A, 151C or 151D*. The liability is intended to apply in the case where individuals use alternatively secured pension (ASP) to pass on tax-privileged retirement savings to their dependants rather than to provide a pension in retirement. See **34.2** PENSION SCHEMES.

References to property include any property directly or indirectly representing it. See also *MB Smith v HMRC (and related appeals)* [2009] STC SCD 132 Sp C 742.

For the above purposes, entitlement to part only of the income of any property is deemed to be entitlement to an interest in the whole property. The whole tax attributable to the property can therefore be recovered from any beneficiary. [*IHTA 1984, s 200(3)*].

Personal representatives cannot distribute the estate, leaving HMRC to recover the inheritance tax due from the beneficiaries under (d) above. See *Harris as personal representative of H N McDonald deceased* [2018] UKFTT 0204 (TC) in which the personal representative was held to be liable for the IHT on an estate despite distributing the funds to a beneficiary who had said he would pay the tax due.

[*IHTA 1984, ss 200(1), 204(1)–(3)(5), 209(1), 210, 211; FA 2006, s 160, Sch 22 para 5; FA 2008, Sch 28 para 11*].

Example 4

Personal representatives of E, who died on 30 September 2010, received the following assets.

	£
Free personal property	155,26
Land bequeathed to F (which, under the terms of the will, bears its own IHT)	29,73
Private residence, bequeathed to spouse/civil partner	51,00

A trust in which E had a life interest was valued at £154,000. Under the will of E, legacies of £15,000, each free of IHT, were given to F and G and the residue was left to H. E had made no chargeable transfers during his lifetime.

	Persons liable	£	IHT £
IHT is borne as to			
Chargeable transfer			
Free personal property	PRs	155,265	2,565
Land bequeathed to F	F	29,735	491
Private residence to spouse/civil partner	—	Exempt	Nil
Trust fund	Trustees	154,000	2,544
		£339,000	£5,600

The residue left to H is as follows	£	£
Free personal property		155,265
Deduct IHT	2,565	
Legacies to F and G	30,000	32,565
		£122,700

Note to the example

(A) If the will had not directed that the IHT on the land bequeathed to F be borne by F, the IHT would be payable out of residue. [*IHTA 1984, s 211*].

Definitions

'*Personal representative*' includes any person by whom or on whose behalf an application for a grant of administration or for the resealing of a grant made outside the UK is made; and also includes persons within (i) below. [*IHTA 1984, s 272*].

'*Persons in whom the property is vested*' includes (i) any person who becomes liable as executor or trustee by taking possession of or intermeddling with property (or in Scotland, intromits with property or has become liable as a vitious intromitter) and (ii) any person to whom the management of property is entrusted on behalf of a person not of full legal capacity. [*IHTA 1984, ss 199(4), 200(4)*].

A person who transfers the sale proceeds of English property belonging to the estate of a deceased person out of English jurisdiction has been held to have intermeddled with the estate and to be liable for IHT as *executor de son tort* (*CIR v Stype Investments (Jersey) Ltd Re Clore (deceased)* CA, [1982] STC 625).

Gifts with reservation

[27.6] Where property is treated as forming part of a deceased person's estate under the rules relating to **22** GIFTS WITH RESERVATION, a personal representative is only liable for the tax on that property if it remains unpaid for twelve months after the end of the month in which death occurs and, subject to that, only to the extent mentioned in (a) above. [*IHTA 1984, s 204(9); FA 1986, Sch 19 para 28*].

Lifetime transfers with additional liability arising through death

[27.7] For transfers of value before 15 March 1988, if death occurred within one year of a gift to a political party (see **21.7** EXEMPT TRANSFERS) in excess of £100,000, the tax due on death was the liability of the political party only. [*IHTA 1984, s 206; FA 1988, Sch 14*].

Death within seven years

[27.8] Where a transferor dies within seven years of making a **35** POTENTIALLY EXEMPT TRANSFERS or a chargeable lifetime transfer, the persons liable for the tax on the value transferred by the potentially exempt transfer or the additional tax on the chargeable transfer are as follows.

(a) The personal representatives but only to the extent that
   - (i) no other person within (b) below is liable for the tax because of their limitation of liability as detailed below; or
   - (ii) tax remains unpaid twelve months after the end of the month in which death occurs.

   Subject to the above, the personal representatives are liable only to the extent of the unsettled assets received and the UK land settled immediately before death and available at any time in their hands for the payment of tax (or such assets and land which might have been available but for their own neglect or default).

   Without prejudice to the application of *IHTA 1984, s 199(2)*, HMRC will not usually pursue personal representatives who, having obtained a certificate of discharge (see **32.15** PAYMENT OF TAX) and distributed the estate before a chargeable lifetime transfer comes to light, have made the fullest enquiries that are reasonably practicable in the circumstances to discover lifetime transfers and done all in their power to make a full disclosure of them to HMRC (letter from Capital and Valuation Division reproduced at [1991] STI 238).

(b) Any person within 27.2(a) to (c) above subject to the limitation of liability as in 27.3(i) to (iii) above (but *not* the preambles thereto). In broad terms this means that the recipient of the lifetime potentially exempt transfer has primary liability for the IHT payable in respect of it, but limited to the value of the gift.
HMRC's Inheritance Tax Manual at IHTM10211 states:

> 'The transferee is accountable (*IHTA 1984, s 216 (1)(bb)*). This is because the person who receives the gift is liable for any tax on a PET that proves to be a chargeable transfer. In strictness, the transferee is required to specify all appropriate property received and the value of that property. The account to be used is the IHT 100. The time limit for delivering the account is 12 months from the end of the month in which the transferor's death occurred.'

In practice, if the donee does not pay the tax due within 12 months of the death, HMRC will not take any action to recover the amount from that person but instead will then look to the personal representatives for payment because they have secondary liability as noted above.

[*IHTA 1984, ss 199(1)(2)(5), 204(1)–(3)(5)(7)(8); FA 1986, Sch 19 paras 26, 28*].

Where additional tax is due on the death, a fall in value relief may be claimed if the asset gifted has depreciated in value between the gift and the date of death. See Example 6 and more detailed analysis at **50.2** TRANSFERS WITHIN SEVEN YEAR BEFORE DEATH.

Example 5

On 31 December 2018, H, who had made no earlier chargeable transfers other than to utilise his annual exemptions for 2018/19 and earlier years, transferred £368,000 into a discretionary trust and, a month later, settled an asset worth £20,000 into the same trust. H paid the appropriate IHT. On 30 June 2021, H died.

The trustees become liable to further IHT as follows

	£	£
Original net gift	£368,000	£20,000
Grossed-up at half of full rates	£378,750	£25,000
IHT (paid by H). See **37.1** rates 2010.B2	£10,750	£5,000
IHT at 80% of death rates applicable in June 2021 on original gross (death between 3 and 4 years after gifts)	17,400	8,000
Deduct IHT paid originally by H	10,750	5,000
Now due from trustees	6,650	£3,000

Note to the example

(A) The additional IHT on death is calculated using the rates in force at the date of death which in this case are the same as at the time of the gift. See **37.1** rates 2010.A1. If the IHT at the new death rates, as tapered, was less than the IHT paid on the original chargeable transfer, there would be no repayment as in this case.

Example 6

The second gift in the example above had fallen in value to £18,000 by the time of H's death.

The trustees may claim to reduce the IHT payable as follows

	£
Original gross gift	25,000
Deduct drop in value (£20,000 – £18,000)	2,000
Revised gross	£23,000
IHT thereon at 80% of death rate applicable in June 2021	7,360
Deduct IHT paid by H	5,000
	£2,360

Settled property

[27.9] Where a chargeable transfer is made, or is deemed to be made, out of settled property, the persons liable for the tax are:

(a) the trustees of the settlement (to the extent shown in **27.5**(b) above), or, if they do not pay;

(b) any person entitled (whether beneficially or not) to an interest in possession in the settled property (but liability of a person entitled to a beneficial interest is limited to the extent of the property); and

(c) any person for whose benefit any of the settled property or income from it is applied at or after the time of transfer (but liability is limited to the extent of the property or income (as reduced by income tax borne by him in respect of that income) applied for his benefit by the trustees); and

(d) the settlor, where the chargeable transfer is made during his lifetime and the trustees are not for the time being resident in the UK except that:

  (i) where the chargeable transfer is made within seven years of the death of the transferor but, after 16 March 1987, is not a potentially exempt transfer, the settlor is not liable for the extra tax due because of the death within seven years; and

  (ii) there is no liability where the settlement was made before 11 December 1974 if the trustees were resident in the UK when the settlement was made but have not been resident in the UK at any time between that date and the time of the transfer; and

  (iii) after 16 March 1987, there is no liability if a potentially exempt transfer proves to be a chargeable transfer where the settlement was made before 17 March 1987 if the trustees were resident in the UK when the settlement was made but have not been resident in the UK at any time between 16 March 1987 and the death of the transferor.

For these purposes, the trustees of a settlement are regarded as not resident in the UK unless the general administration of the settlement is ordinarily carried on in the UK and the trustees or a majority of them (including a majority of each class where there is more than one class of trustees) are for the time being resident in the UK. Where more than one person is a settlor in relation to a settlement, for these purposes the property is treated as comprised in separate settlements.

References to property include any property directly or indirectly representing it. [*IHTA 1984, ss 201, 204(2)(3)(5)(6); FA 1986, Sch 19 para 27; F(No 2)A 1987, Sch 7 para 3*].

Where a person having an interest in possession in settled property is made liable for the tax due under (b) above, that person is entitled to a charge over the settled property in the same way as if the tax had been raised by means of a mortgage to him. [*IHTA 1984, s 212(3)*].

A purchaser of property

[27.10] A 'purchaser' of 'property' and a person deriving title from or under such a purchaser, is not liable for any tax attributable to the property unless the property is subject to an HMRC charge (see **32.12** PAYMENT OF TAX). [*IHTA 1984, ss 199(3), 200(2)*].

'*Purchaser*' means a purchaser in good faith for consideration in money or money's worth other than a nominal consideration and includes a lessee, mortgagee or other person who for such a consideration acquires an interest in the property in question.

'*Property*' includes rights and interests of any description. [*IHTA 1984, s 272*].

Deed of inheritance tax indemnity

[27.11] PARTIES

1. "Father" namely
2. "Son" namely

RECITAL

Immediately after the execution of this deed Father intends to give Son a cheque for £ as a gift subject to inheritance tax ("the Gift")

IHT INDEMNITY

1. The Liability

   "The Liability" means any [additional] liability to inheritance tax probably chargeable in respect of the Gift arising or crystallising on or by reason of the death of Father

2. Incidence

   Son acknowledges that the burden of inheritance tax (if any) on the Gift shall be borne by Son

3. Covenant and Indemnity

   Son covenants with Father and his personal representatives to pay the Liability (whether by direct discharge to HMRC or by reimbursement to Father's estate or otherwise) immediately upon demand following an assessment on Father's estate and generally to keep Father and his personal representatives indemnified against the liability

4. Effluxion

The indemnity given by this deed shall lapse and be extinguished on the seventh anniversary of the date of the Gift if Father is still then living

5. Limitation

The indemnity given by this deed shall be limited to £ . . . .

EXECUTED as a deed on 2010

SIGNED AS A DEED AND)
DELIVERED by
FATHER in the presence of:—)

Witness' signature

Address

Occupation

SIGNED AS A DEED AND)
DELIVERED by
SON in the presence of:—)

Witness' signature

Address

Occupation

Note to the deed

An indemnity of this nature will be sufficient to ensure there is no grossing up and to mark for family purposes who carries the burden in the event of premature death. If there is any serious prospect of it having to be relied on through enforcement then further provisions may be needed e.g. dealing with interest after the due date, reporting, costs, etc.

28

Life Assurance Policies and Annuities

Cross-references. See **41.4** SETTLEMENTS: ACCUMULATION AND MAINTENANCE TRUSTS; **31.1** PARTNERSHIPS for partnership assurance policies.

Life assurance policies and annuities — application

[28.1] Where a life assurance policy matures on the death of the person who took out the policy and remained the beneficial owner, the policy monies are included in his estate for the purposes of inheritance tax. [*IHTA 1984, s 171(1)*]. See IHTM20000 at www.gov.uk/hmrc-internal-manuals/inheritance-tax-manual/ihtm02000.

Where the policy is expressed to be for the benefit of the spouse, civil partner or children under the *Married Women's Property Act 1882*, a trust is created in their favour so that the person whose life is assured never has an interest in the policy and the proceeds will not be included in his estate on his death. [*Married Women's Property Act 1882, s 11 as amended by Civil Partnership Act 2004, s 70*].

To [ ] Life Assurance Company

MWPA TRUST

This request is an integral part of the attached application and I declare that such application is made by me as settlor ("the Settlor") and request that the policy(ies) issued pursuant thereto shall be issued under the provisions of [Married Women's Property Act 1882] or [Married Women's Policies of Assurance (Scotland) Act 1880] or [Law Reform (Husband and Wife) Act (Northern Ireland) 1964] and subject to the powers and provisions in the Schedule below upon trust and for the benefit of:

I wish to appoint as trustees additional to myself the following persons whose concurrence is evidenced by execution hereto (and "the Trustees" shall be a reference to the trustees for the time being) of these trusts.

The receipt of the Trustees shall be a complete discharge to [. . .] for moneys payable under the policy.

Schedule of Further Trust Provisions

1. The Trustees shall have power to invest any moneys in their hands in or upon any investment of any nature and wherever situated and whether income producing or not and whether an investment strictly so called (including the effecting of policies of life assurance or annuities for the life of any beneficiary or other person and further including the purchase of freehold or leasehold land as an investment or the residence of a beneficiary) free from all duties of diversification as if the Trustees were the absolute beneficial owners

2. The Trustees shall have full power to surrender/convert/sell/auction or otherwise deal with any policy subject to these trusts notwithstanding that the sum assured may be increased or decreased

3. Section 31 of the Trustee Act 1925 shall apply as if:

   3.1 the words "may in all the circumstances be reasonable" had been omitted from paragraph (i) of subsection (1) and in substitution there had been inserted the words "the Trustees may in their absolute discretion think fit" and as if the proviso at the end of subsection (1) had been omitted

   3.2 in subsection (2) the words "as follows:—" and the paragraphs (i) and (ii) thereof had been omitted and replaced by "upon trust for that person absolutely"

4. Section 32 of the Trustee Act 1925 shall apply as if the words "one half" were omitted from proviso (a) to subsection (1)

5. The Trustees shall have power as they in their absolute discretion think fit to pay or apply any moneys for the time being subject to the trusts hereof (or borrowed hereunder) in or towards the discharge of any Inheritance Tax or other fiscal imposition the liability for which would otherwise fall either directly or indirectly on any beneficiary whether or not the interest or such beneficiary under the trusts hereof is absolute or contingent or vested in possession or in remainder or reversion PROVIDED that no such payment shall exceed the value of such beneficiary's interest at the time of such payment

6. The power of appointing new or additional trustees shall be exercisable by the Settlor during his lifetime

7. The receipt of a parent or guardian in respect of any benefit payable or transferable to a minor beneficiary shall be a sufficient discharge to the Trustees who shall be under no obligation to see to its application

8. Neither the Settlor nor the Trustees shall be under any obligation whatsoever to keep up any policy subject to these trusts or to reinstate the same if it becomes void and the Settlor shall have no right by way of lien or otherwise to reimbursement of any premiums paid or subsequently paid in respect of any policy subject to these trusts

9. These trusts shall be governed by and construed in accordance with the Law of England

Dated _______________ 2010 _______________

(The Settlor) Signed

(The further Trustees) Signed

Dated ______________ 2010 ______________

Where an annuity under an approved trust scheme or contract or, after 22 July 1987, under approved personal pension arrangements or, from 6 April 2006, a registered pension scheme (or *ICTA 1988, s 615(3)* scheme) is payable on a person's death to the widow, widower, surviving civil partner or dependant and the terms of the scheme etc. gave the deceased the option to have a sum of money i.e. cash payable to his personal representatives, he is not treated as having been beneficially entitled to that sum which is therefore not included in his estate. [*IHTA 1984, s 152; F(No 2)A 1987, s 98(5); FA 2004, s 203(5); The Tax and Civil Partnership Regulations 2005, SI 2005/3229, Reg 33*]. For the valuation of an annuity which is an interest in possession (IIP) chargeable on property, see **39.5** SETTLEMENTS WITH INTERESTS IN POSSESSION.

Compensation fund payments arising out the 11 September 2001 terrorist attacks that comprise part of the UK victims' estates are not subject to IHT. The Victim's Compensation Fund of 2001 was established by the US government as an alternative to any legal proceedings that the victims' estates could take under the law as it stood on 11 September. The legislation was actually passed after 11 September 2001 but claims under the compensation fund have no value at that date for IHT purposes. Payments made after that date are not chargeable to IHT in any case so that part of a victim's estate comprising of the compensation fund payment is not subject to IHT.

Transitional serial interest (TSI)

[28.2] Where a person (stipulated as being 'C' in the legislation) is beneficially entitled to a present interest in settled property in relation to a life insurance policy entered into before 22 March 2006, those rights under the contract or in property in the settlement directly or indirectly representing rights under the contract are, for the purposes of *IHTA 1984, Pt III, Ch III,* a transitional serial interest only if a number of conditions are satisfied:

- The first condition is that the settlement must have commenced before 22 March 2006 and the property comprised in the settlement was property which consisted of or included rights under the insurance contract to which 'C', or some other person, was beneficially entitled an interest in possession which for these purposes is designated 'the earlier interest';
- The second condition is either:
  that 'the earlier interest' in the insurance contract came to an end on or after 6 October 2008 on the death of the person beneficially entitled to it and 'C' became beneficially entitled to the present interest at one of the following times:
  (i) at the time of the ending of the earlier interest; or
  (ii) on the death of the person beneficially entitled to an interest in possession at the time of the ending of the earlier interest (i.e. (i) above); or

(iii) on the ending of a second or last in a series of unbroken consecutive sequences of interests in possession to the first where a person becomes beneficially entitled at the time of the ending of the earlier interest (i.e. (i) above) each of which has ended on the death of the person with beneficial entitlement;

or that 'C' became beneficially entitled to the present interest:

(i) on the coming to an end of an interest in possession that is a TSI under *s 49C* on the death of the person who is beneficially entitled to it. See **39.1** SETTLEMENTS WITH INTERESTS IN POSSESSION; or

(ii) on the ending of a second or last in a series of unbroken consecutive sequences of interest in possession the first of which is a TSI under *s 49C* each of which has ended on the death of the person with beneficial entitlement.

- The third condition is that rights under the contract of insurance were comprised in the settlement from 22 March 2006 to the date when 'C' became beneficially entitled;
- The fourth condition is that neither *IHTA 1984, s 71A* (bereaved minor's trust) applies to the property in which the interest subsists nor is the interest a disabled person's interest.

This TSI category relating to life assurance policies is more limited than the other two categories at **39.1** SETTLEMENTS WITH INTERESTS IN POSSESSION in that it does not apply to any property settled before 22 March 2006, but only to property settled which comprises rights under a contract of life insurance entered into before 22 March 2006. The benefit of this TSI category is that it can apply to more than one of a chain of successive interests in possession, provided each one qualifies as a TSI. Similarly to the category 2 spouse/civil partner TSI at **39.1** SETTLEMENTS WITH INTERESTS IN POSSESSION it only applies to TSIs falling into possession on the death of a person previously entitled to an interest in possession.

The legislation in *IHTA 1984, s 49E* above provides for TSI treatment to apply to contracts of insurance after 5 October 2008 for contracts set up before 22 March 2006 and pre-22 March 2006 settlements. The main purpose of this is to allow TSI treatment on premiums that continue to be paid after 22 March 2006 on a policy settled on IIP or accumulation and maintenance trusts before that date. However, if after 5 October 2008 a power of appointment is exercised to appoint any new beneficiary who is not absolutely entitled, this will result in the trust coming within the new regime. See Example 1 below.

[*IHTA 1984, s 49E; FA 2006, Sch 20 para 5; FA 2008, s 141*].

Pre-22 March 2006 life insurance within an IIP trust

[28.3] Where a life policy has been settled on an interest in possession (IIP) trust before 22 March 2006 but that premiums continue to be paid on that policy the whole of the value of the policy itself still qualifies for transitional protection as an asset of a trust in existence before 22 March 2006. This transitional treatment will continue to apply as long as the original terms of the policy continue. Also, where someone succeeds to the policy on the death of the policy holder then transitional protection will continue. [*IHTA 1984, s 46A; FA 2006, Sch 20 para 11*]. See Fosters Inheritance Tax, para E1.56.

PET treatment of premiums paid

[28.4] Care needs to be taken regarding the payment of further premiums as detailed in IHTM20331:

> 'If a transferor puts a policy into an accumulation and maintenance trust or a disabled trust and then pays the renewal premiums direct to the insurance company, PET treatment will therefore not be available. This is because the premiums as such do not become settled property. However, if the transferor makes payments to the trustees and they use those payments to pay the renewal premiums PET treatment is available – even if payment by the transferor is by a cheque which the trustees endorse in favour of the insurance company. The associated operations provisions should be invoked to deny PET treatment in these cases.'

Example 1

A is to pay premiums of £4,000 p.a. on a policy on his own life (policy 1) which commenced on 1 January 2006. He assigns the policy into trust in favour of a number of potential beneficiaries, including his wife, but A is excluded from all possible benefits. The market value of the policy at the date of gift is £3,000. A also pays annual premiums of £2,000 on a policy (policy 2) on his life which commenced on 2 January 2006 written in favour of his son S. The original policy terms permit a variation of beneficiaries and the policy is assigned on discretionary trust in favour of his grandson GS on 6 October 2008. The cumulative premiums paid to that date are £6,000 and the value of the policy is £4,000. In July 2014 A becomes gravely ill and the value of the policy at 2 January 2016 is £155,000. A has utilised his £275,000 of his nil rate band in the previous seven years to 2 January 2016. The nil rate band at that stage is assumed to be £350,000. See 37 RATES OF TAX.

Assignment of policy (policy 1)

The gift is valued either at

(i) market value (£3,000), or

(ii) the accumulated gross premiums paid (£4,000) if greater i.e. £4,000.

Continued premiums paid into a policy effected in trust before the Budget (22 March 2006) will not cause the policy to be subject to the new IHT trust provisions that apply to post-21 March 2006 trusts. Provided that the original policy terms permit, the terms of a policy can be varied post-21 March 2006 without causing the policy to be subject to the new IHT provisions. This means that the benefits can be increased or the term of the policy extended without changing the inheritance tax treatment of the policy. If one of the policy named (see extract above) becomes entitled to an interest in possession via an appointment to him before 6 October 2008 (a TSI), this will not cause the policy to be subject to the new IHT rules. If one of the named in A to F in the policy document becomes entitled to an interest in possession following the death of the previous holder of the interest in possession, this will not cause the policy to be subject to the new IHT rules provided the previous holder of the interest:

- held that interest on Budget day (22 March 2006); or
- held that interest as a TSI (so that it had been made via an appointment to him before 6 October 2008).

Annual premiums (policy 2)

The payment of an annual premium is regarded as an annual gift, the amount of the transfer being the net premium after deduction of any tax relief at source or the gross premium where paid without deduction. In this case no tax relief is due so £2,000 is the figure that is taken for these purposes. Continuing payment of premiums paid into a policy effected in trust before the Budget (22 March 2006) will not result in the policy becoming subject to the new IHT trust provisions that apply to post-21 March 2006 trusts. Premiums paid after Budget day to these trusts will continue to be treated as PETs and will not be chargeable lifetime transfers. Also, providing the original policy terms permit, the terms of a policy can be varied post-21 March 2006 without resulting in the policy becoming subject to the new IHT provisions. The result is that, in those circumstances, the benefits can be increased or the term of the policy extended without changing the inheritance tax treatment of the policy. Whilst the gifts of the premiums after 21 March 2006 where there has been a subsequent appointment of a new beneficiary will no longer be treated as PETs within *s 46A(4)* transfers should still be exempt under the annual exemption or gifts out of normal expenditure. See **21** EXEMPT TRANSFERS.

Re-assignment of policy (policy 2)

Where there is the possibility of a change in the named/default beneficiaries after 5 October 2008 it should be avoided unless the appointment is absolute. In this particular case the power to appoint a new beneficiary within the terms of the policy has been exercised in favour of GS after 5 October 2008 but on discretionary trusts and therefore brings the policy into the new regime of charge (see below) and triggers a chargeable lifetime transfer by the son S. Providing S's transfer was less than £10,000 per annum or £40,000 cumulative over the past ten years prior to 6 April 2007 it would not need to have been reported on Forms IHT100 and IHT100a but now see **2.5** ACCOUNTS AND RETURNS. This will depend on previous cumulative total of gifts to date and adding the accumulated premiums or the market value of the policy at that point.

Ten-yearly charge

Initial ten-yearly charge for period 6 October 2008 to 2 January 2016	£
Value of relevant property on 2.1.2016	155,000
Value of property in related settlements	—
	155,000
Assumed cumulative total	275,000
	£430,000
IHT at lifetime rates after assumed nil rate band of £350,000	£16,000
Effective rate $\frac{16,000}{430,000} = 3.72093\%$	
Rate of ten-year anniversary charge:	
3/10 × 3.72093% = 1.116279%	
Ten-year anniversary charge: 28*/40 × 1.116279% × £155,000	£1,211

* i.e. 28 complete quarters from 6 October 2008 to first ten-year anniversary.

Notes to the example

(A) Pre-22 March 2006 life policy trusts will not be subject to the new IHT taxing rules provided the original terms of the policy continue and where someone succeeds to the policy on the death of the policy holder then transitional protection will continue. The payment of ongoing premiums for life policies owned by trusts will not constitute additions to the trust thereby bringing them into the new IHT charging provisions. On the premature death of the wife prior to A the life policy trust above would still qualify as subsequent beneficiaries would be entitled and therefore the terms of the trust would not have altered since it was set up pre-22 March 2006 within the stipulations of *IHTA 1984, s 46A inserted by FA 2006, Sch 20 para 11.*

(B) In the case of the life policy trust assigned for the benefit of the grandson GS after 5 October 2008 as this is not an absolute appointment then the new taxing regime within *IHTA 1984, s 43(2)* will apply with the prospect of 20% life time charge (where gifts to the trust exceed the nil rate band) ten yearly charge on the value of the trust fund on the tenth anniversary of the policy and potential exit charge when the policy proceeds are paid out to the beneficiary. In this case the ill health of A prior to the first ten-yearly charge has resulted in a substantial revaluation of the policy.

(C) Existing accumulation and maintenance settlements that hold life policies needed to be reviewed before 6 April 2008.

Assignment of policy

[28.5] Where the benefits of a life policy (or contract for an annuity payable on a person's death) are assigned as a gift or for less than full value, there is a transfer of value and inheritance tax is chargeable (unless any reliefs may be claimed, see **21** EXEMPT TRANSFERS).

The value of a life policy or contract *transferred before death* is to be taken as not less than:

(a) the total premiums or other consideration paid at any time (under the policy or contract or any policy or contract for which it was substituted) before the transfer of value; *less*

(b) any sum received, at any time before the transfer of value, for a surrender of any right conferred by the policy or contract (or a policy or contract for which it was substituted).

This provision does not apply unless the policy or contract ceases to be part of the transferor's estate as the result of the transfer of value. [*IHTA 1984, s 167(1)(2); FA 1986, Sch 23 Pt X*].

The special rules for valuing a policy above do not apply where the policy is one under which the sum assured becomes payable only if the person whose life is insured dies (i) before the expiry of a specified term, or (ii) both before the expiry of a specified term and during the life of a specified person. Where under the policy the term ends, or can be extended to end, more than three years after the making of the insurance, if neither the person whose life is insured nor the specified person dies before the expiry of the specified term, the rules do not apply if the policy satisfies the conditions that the premiums are payable during at least two-thirds of that term and at yearly or shorter intervals, *and* the premiums payable in any one period of twelve months are not more than twice the premiums payable in any other twelve months. [*IHTA 1984, s 167(3)*].

Unit linked policies

[28.6] Where the benefit secured under a policy is expressed in units the value of which is published and subject to fluctuation and the payment of each premium secures the allocation to the policy of a specified number of such units, then the value to be taken as above will take into account any investment loss on those units. This is done by deducting from the total premiums etc. paid, the difference between the value of the units when they were first allocated and their value at the time of the transfer of value. [*IHTA 1984, s 167(4)*].

Settlements

[28.7] References above to a transfer of value include an event on which there is a charge to tax under the provisions relating to **40** SETTLEMENTS: DISCRETIONARY TRUSTS AND OTHER TRUSTS OF RELEVANT PROPERTY in *IHTA 1984, Pt III, Ch III* (except *s 79*, see **30.22** NATIONAL HERITAGE), other than an event on which tax is chargeable in respect of the policy or contract by reason only that its value is reduced otherwise than by these provisions. [*IHTA 1984, s 167(5)*].

Premiums continued by donor

[28.8] Where a policy is transferred and the donor continues to pay the premiums, or provides the money for this purpose, then a transfer of value occurs on each occasion, based on the decrease in value of the donor's estate (i.e. the special rules above for valuing the policy on its assignment do not apply to later payments of premiums). These payments may be exempt, see **21** EXEMPT TRANSFERS. HMRC take the view that where the payment of a premium on a life assurance policy is a transfer of value, the amount of the transfer is the net amount of the premium after deduction under *ICTA 1988, s 266(5)* (tax relief at source) or the gross premium where paid without deduction. (HMRC Press Release 17 January 1979.)

Example 2

A has paid premiums of £2,000 p.a. for six years on a policy on his own life. He gives the policy to his son B. The market value of the policy at the date of gift is £11,000 but due to a demutualisation policy enhancement is uplifted to £12,500 (see HMRC Tax Bulletin, April 1998, p 520). A also pays annual premiums of £2,000 on a policy on his life written in favour of his son.

Assignment of policy

The gift is valued either at:

(i) market value (£12,500); or

(ii) the accumulated gross premiums paid (£12,000) if greater (but they are not).

Annual premiums

The payment of an annual premium is regarded as an annual gift, the amount of the transfer being the net premium after deduction of any tax relief at source or the gross premium where paid without deduction.

Notes to the example

(A) The gifts are PETs. The assignment of the policy will only become chargeable if A dies within seven years, and only the annual premiums paid within seven years of A's death will be chargeable.

(B) Exemptions available for reduction of the chargeable transfer on assignment include the annual exemption and the marriage exemption.

(C) The normal expenditure exemption may be available to A for premiums paid and the annual exemption may also be claimed to exempt the gift in whole or in part.

(D) Normal expenditure relief is not available when a policy and annuity have been effected on a back-to-back basis (with certain exceptions).

Annuity purchased in conjunction with life policy

[28.9] The use of annuities in conjunction with life policies is known as 'back to back' arrangements.

Example 3

The purchase of an immediate annuity for a lump sum would reduce the purchaser's estate and provide him with an income for life. If he arranged an insurance on his own life but for the benefit of another person whom he wished to benefit at his death, the proceeds would be free of tax because they are not part of his estate. There would be further advantages if he paid the premiums on the policy and could obtain exemption from inheritance tax on them, e.g. as normal expenditure out of income (see **21.15** EXEMPT TRANSFERS).

The following provisions reduce the effectiveness of 'back to back' arrangements.

Where a life insurance is made, varied or substituted and an annuity on the life of the insured is purchased at any time before or after that date and the benefit of the insurance policy is vested in a person other than the purchaser of the annuity, the purchaser of the annuity is treated as making a transfer of value at the time the benefit of the policy became vested in the other person. The value transferred is the lesser of:

(a) the aggregate of (i) the value of the consideration given for the annuity and (ii) any premium paid or other consideration given under the policy on or before the transfer; and

(b) the value of the greatest benefit capable of being conferred at any time by the policy, calculated as if that time were the date of the transfer.

The above provisions also apply where an annuity payable on a person's death is substituted for 'life insurance policy'.

The above provisions do *not* apply if it can be shown that the purchaser of the annuity and the making, variation or substitution of the insurance were not associated operations (see **5.5** ANTI-AVOIDANCE). [*IHTA 1984, s 263*].

In practice, such policies and annuities are not regarded as being affected by the associated operations rule if the policy was issued on full medical evidence of the insured's health and it would have been issued on the same terms if the annuity had not been bought. (HMRC Statement of Practice E4.) See also *AC Smith v HMRC (and related appeals)* Ch D [2007] EWHC 2304, Sp C 605 at 55 TAX CASES.

If the transferor pays, either directly or indirectly, a premium on a life insurance on his life and an annuity on his life is purchased at any time, the premium will not be treated as part of his normal expenditure out of income unless it can be shown that the associated operations rule (see above) does not apply. [*IHTA 1984, s 21(2)*].

See **21.15** EXEMPT TRANSFERS for normal expenditure out of income and that chapter generally for exemptions which might be applied to the transfers of value mentioned above.

Key points concerning life assurance policies and annuities

[28.10] Points to consider are as follows.

- Schedule IHT410 of IHT400 requests details of life assurance policies the deceased was paying regular instalments on or lump sum payments whether on the life of the deceased or another life. If the policy was in connection with mortgage protection the details should be included on IHT410 but if it is a joint mortgage protection policy the details are to be included on form IHT404 *Jointly owned assets*.
- Life assurance policies are commonly written in trust for the benefit or potential benefit of other family members. This is important to ensure that the policy does not form part of the policyholder's estate.
- In certain circumstances Trustees may wish to protect the trust from a charge to IHT on the premature death of the policyholder. In such cases, level term assurance for seven years would be appropriate with the maturity value decreasing as the tapering provisions apply after the first three years reducing to zero after the expiry of the seventh year with a consequent diminishing of premiums.
- Where property in an estate is the right to claim a lump sum and an annuity and such a right is not assignable it will nonetheless still be valued on an assumption that it could be sold on the open market. On that basis a policy has a value appropriate to what it could be sold for on the open market with a discount so for instance in *DM Fryer & Others (Personal Representatives of Ms P Arnold) v HMRC* (see 55 TAX CASES) the Commissioner upheld HMRC's contention that 'the concept of a 'disposition' was widened by *s 3(3)* to

include passive dispositions, meaning omissions which resulted in the enhancement of another person's estate or of settled property in which no interest in possession subsisted'. The Commissioner held that the disposition should be treated as having taken place on the date of her death. The omission to exercise the right to take annuity benefits from the age of 50 (now this would be 55) had increased the value of the settled property, and the evidence showed that this had been intentional and *s 3(3)* applied.

29

Lifetime Transfers

Cross-references. See **1** INTRODUCTION AND BASIC PRINCIPLES; **2.5** ACCOUNTS AND RETURNS and **7** CALCULATION OF TAX.

Simon's Taxes. See **Part I3**.

Other Sources. HMRC Customer Guide to Inheritance Tax.

Introduction

[29.1] An individual is subject to inheritance tax on every **9** CHARGEABLE TRANSFER made by him after 17 March 1986. Chargeable transfers are any transfers of value made by an individual other than **21** EXEMPT TRANSFERS. For inheritance tax purposes, certain lifetime transfers are designated **35** POTENTIALLY EXEMPT TRANSFERS. Such a transfer made seven years or more before the death of the transferor is an exempt transfer and any other such transfer is a chargeable transfer.

For details of taper relief in relation to lifetime gifts made within seven years before death, and depreciation relief where the market value of a lifetime gift of an asset has reduced after the gift, see **50.2** TRANSFERS WITHIN SEVEN YEARS BEFORE DEATH.

The nil rate band is allocated to the earliest chargeable gift first and thereafter in chronological order. As to liability for any inheritance tax due on the gift, the donor can specify who should bear the liability. For example, on a gift into a lifetime trust, the settlor may accept liability for the tax, with consequent grossing up (see **7.1** CALCULATION OF TAX), or the settlor may make the gift on terms that the trustees shall discharge any tax due. With lifetime gifts which are potentially exempt when made but become chargeable on the death of the donor, the legislation sets out detailed rules as to who may be made liable to pay the tax due (see **27** LIABILITY FOR TAX), although in strictness, these rules concern the rights of collection of tax given to HMRC and not the question of who should ultimately bear the liability. Testators can include a provision in a will for any tax on lifetime transfers to borne by the estate and there is no grossing of the chargeable amount of the gift in such circumstances, although it may be that the IHT is itself a tax-free gift from the estate which requires grossing up where the estate is partly exempt: see **7.6**. In the absence of any provision concerning payment of the tax, it is generally thought that the tax should be borne by the donee although this can give rise to significant difficulties given that the donee may not have funds still available to pay the amount due.

The tax is normally levied on the value of the reduction in the transferor's **19** ESTATE caused by the chargeable transfer which includes the inheritance tax on the value of the gift where the transferor pays that tax (i.e. the value of the gift, after taking account of any exempt transfers, is grossed-up). If the transferee bears the tax, the transferor's estate is reduced only by the value of the gift itself (after exemptions). Dispositions not intended to confer gratuitous benefit are not transfers of value. See point (a) at **48.2** TRANSFER OF VALUE. For definition of estate, see **19** ESTATE. The chargeable transfers are aggregated during a seven-year period to arrive at the scale rate of tax applicable (see **7** CALCULATION OF TAX). [*IHTA 1984, ss 2(1)(2), 3, 3A, 7, 10; FA 1986, Sch 19 para 1; F(No 2)A 1987, s 96; FA 2006, Sch 20 para 9*].

See also IHTM14000 at www.gov.uk/hmrc-internal-manuals/inheritance-tax-manual/ihtm04000.

Time of disposition

[29.2] As a basic rule no **9** CHARGEABLE TRANSFER can take place until there has been a disposition resulting in a shift of value from one estate to another. The legal requirements that must be fulfilled to ensure such a shift vary depending on the subject matter of the gift. Usually all the requirements relating to the species of gift must be satisfied by the donor before the gift becomes effective. One common exception is where the donor has done all in his power to transfer the property e.g. signed a stock transfer form and delivered the scrip.

A gift of moveable property must have words of gift and a delivery of the subject matter of that gift to be effective. See Key Points at gifts with reservation (**22** GIFTS WITH RESERVATION) for an example where a words of the gift were conclusive but the actual delivery was not completed satisfactorily and therefore the GWR rules applied. See also *Irons v Smallpiece* [1819] 2 B & Ald 551.

Freehold or leasehold land

Freehold or leasehold land is gifted on the conveyance or assignment under seal or declaration of trust evidenced in writing.

Choses in possession

Choses in possession (e.g. motor cars, furniture) are gifted when the appropriate formalities are completed. This could be the execution of a deed, declaration of trust or actual or constructive delivery. In the case of chattels that are capable of being physically handed over by a donor then constructive delivery may be the preferred option in a formal presentation in, say, domestic surroundings. Where an item is large and not portable then it may still be the subject of a constructive delivery if the donor expresses to the donee that he is making the gift of the item to the donee and places his hands on the item in question (see *Rawlinson v Mort* (1905) 21 TLR 774). Alternatively, the donor may hand over the physical means of making the item the ownership of the donee by surrendering the keys to, say, a locked bureau (see *Dublin City Distillery Limited v Doherty* [1914] AC 823, 843). In the case of leases relating to chattels the anti-avoidance provisions introduced by *FA 1999, s 104* only apply to land and not chattels. Therefore leases of chattels are possible but the law of bailment should be taken into account as there is a suggestion that this counters such a lease arrangement. See also **22.1** GIFTS WITH RESERVATION for a standard Memorandum of Gift. See also *Torts (Interference with Goods) Act 1977, s 10(1)* and *Law of Property Act 1925, s 188.*

In cases where delivery of the chattels to the donee is not to take place, for example where the donee wishes to retain possession of them paying a market rent for the enjoyment of them, there should be either: (a) a document of transfer under Bills of *Sale Act 1878, s 4*, for which detailed conditions and formalities under that Act apply, as well as a requirement to register it at the Central Office of the Royal Courts of Justice, or (b) a sale under the *Sale of Goods Acts* for which documentation is not required for an effective transfer of title although payment of the purchase price is required, even though in the present case the transaction may be at substantial undervalue.

Choses in action

Choses in action (e.g. shares, insurance policies) are normally gifted on the completion of the appropriate transfer or assignment although negotiable instruments are transferable by delivery. A transfer of shares is not complete until all the requirements of the company's articles have been complied with or the individual has complied with them to the best of his powers (*Re Rose, Rose and Others v CIR* CA, [1952] 1 All ER 1217). See also *Companies Act 2006, s 544.*

Short form memorandum evidencing a gift of chattel(s)

[29.3] The gift of a chattel(s) during lifetime should normally be evidenced so that when the gift is called into question there is proof on both sides, the donor and the donee, that such a gift was effected at the time stated. The chattels may be in co-ownership either as joint tenants or as tenants in common and therefore it is important to attach a Schedule (see below) detailing the chattels and their ownership division. This may be useful not only for the purposes of determining future IHT liabilities but also in connection with bankruptcy, winding-up and divorce, for example. It is important that there is no reservation of benefit in the gift once it has been disposed for IHT purposes and a short form memorandum is detailed below:

MEMORANDUM OF GIFT OF CHATTEL(S)

THIS MEMORANDUM records that on the . . . . day of . . . . 2010 the undersigned [*Donor*] of [*Address*] ('the Donor') gave and by word of mouth expressed himself/herself to give to the undersigned [*Donee*] of [*Address*] ('the Donee') [all the furniture effects and moveable property] which [are] specified in the Schedule attached hereto ('the Chattel(s)') for the absolute sole use of the and benefit of the Donee and at the same time the Donor delivered the Chattel(s) to the Donee and placed the Donee in possession and unrestricted control of the Chattel(s) and at the same time the Donee accepted the gift.

Dated:

SCHEDULE

[Identification is made here of all chattels which have been given by the Donor]

Signed by [*Donor*]:

Signed by [*Donee*]:

Interests under trusts

[29.4] Interests under trusts are gifted when the necessary formalities have been completed. A disposition of an equitable interest must be in writing (*Grey and Another v CIR* [1960] AC 1, [1959] 3 All ER 603, HL and *Oughtred v CIR* HL, [1960] AC 206, [1959] 3 All ER 623, HL). See *Stenhouse's Trustees v Lord Advocate* CS 1983, [1984] STC 195, 1984 SC 12, Ct of Sess for position when trustees make an appointment which is in part in breach of trust until a later date.

Cheques

Cheques are gifted on payment (not when the cheque is received) i.e. the gift remains incomplete until the cheque is cleared by the paying bank (*Owen, Re, Owen v CIR* Ch D, [1949] 1 All ER 901, [1949] TR 189). See *Curnock (Personal Representative of Curnock, dec'd) v CIR* [2003] STC 283, SCD where monies represented by a cheque issued before the date but not cleared until after death still formed part of the deceased's estate on death. See TAX CASES (55).

Insurance policies

Insurance policies (e.g. where written to benefit a person other than the person insured or paying the premiums) are treated by HMRC as made when one party has unconditionally accepted an offer (or counter-offer) from the other party and has notified the other party accordingly (see Inland Revenue Press Release 18 March 1986).

Omission to exercise a right

[29.5] The omission to exercise a right (unless not deliberate) is treated as a disposition if it decreases the value of one person's estate and increases the estate of another person or the value of a settlement without an interest in possession. The disposition is treated as made at the time, or latest time, the right could have been exercised. [*IHTA 1984, s 3(3)*]. See *Macauley & Another v Premium Life Assurance Co Ltd*, Ch D 29 April 1999 unreported where a scheme failed to take account of *s 3(3)* so that the whole of the free estate became liable to IHT on death. A claim that the six-year time limit laid down by the *Limitation Act 1980* precluded liability was rejected by the court.

Voidable transfers

[29.6] Where it can be shown that the whole or part of a chargeable transfer has been set aside by virtue of any enactment or rule of law as voidable or otherwise defeasible, a claim may be made for the transfer to be treated as void initially and for any tax paid to be repaid: see 9 CHARGEABLE TRANSFER.

Lifetime transfers and IHT100

[29.7] An account on Form IHT 100 is required when there is a chargeable event described below.

- Lifetime transfers made by an individual that are chargeable to inheritance tax at the time they are made (supplementary event form IHT 100a).
- A potentially exempt transfer where the transferor has died within seven years bearing in mind that there is no requirement to tell HMRC regarding the transfer while the transferor is still alive.
- A termination of an interest in possession in settled property (supplementary event form IHT 100b) e.g. the ending of a life interest, which occurs during the life of the life tenant and is chargeable to inheritance tax at the time of the event. If the interest in possession is not chargeable at the time it is made then there is no requirement to advise HMRC unless the life tenant dies within seven years of the event.
- A termination of an interest in possession in settled property within seven years of the death of the life tenant.
- A termination of an interest in possession in settled property *arising* as a result of the life tenant's death.
- Property is given subject to a reservation where the reservation is retained until the death of the transferor.
- Property ceases to be held on discretionary trusts and there is a proportionate charge or exit charge (supplementary event form IHT 100c).
- A ten-year anniversary charge on a discretionary trust (supplementary event form IHT 100d).
- Assets are no longer held on special trusts (supplementary event form IHT 100e) e.g. the flat rate charge.
- Recapture charges are exigible e.g. the ceasing of an entitlement to conditional exemption (supplementary event form IHT 100f).
- Assets ceasing to benefit from conditional exemption and being subject to a recapture charge (supplementary event form IHT 100f) e.g. sale of trees, timber or underwood.

Initially IHT 100 is completed together with supplementary Forms D31 to D40 which provide for information on the assets where required. In addition, there is the Form IHT 100WS which can be used to calculate the tax that will be due regarding the chargeable event.

30

National Heritage

Cross-references. See **2.15** ACCOUNTS AND RETURNS for rendering an account on ending of conditional exemption; **21.6** EXEMPT TRANSFERS for gifts for national purposes; **21.8** EXEMPT TRANSFERS for gifts for public benefit.

Simon's Taxes. See **A4.620, I7.501–I7.508, I4.161A, I4.218, I5.337, I7.5, I11.430.**

Other Sources. VOA IHT manual, section 1, www.hmrc.gov.uk/heritage/.

Introduction to national heritage

[30.1] On certain conditions, transfers of national heritage property can be exempted from inheritance tax. In March 2005, following the Goodison Report, the Museum, Libraries and Archive's Acceptance in Lieu Panel which advises on items that are acceptable in lieu of tax was given more power under the Contracting Out (Functions in Relation to Cultural Objects) Order 2005 to act on behalf of the Secretary of State of the Department for Culture, Media and Sport (or the appropriate Minister outside England) to approve offers under *IHTA 1984, s 230* and allocation under the *National Heritage Act 1980, s 9.*

National heritage property may also be given or sold by private treaty without tax liability to specified national bodies or may be transferred to individuals or settlements with conditional exemption. The detailed provisions are stated below.

National heritage property

[30.2] The following types of property are within the term 'national heritage property' provided they are so designated by the Board.

(a) Any:
   (i) picture, print, book, manuscript, work of art or scientific object, or any other thing not yielding income, which appears to the Board to be pre-eminent for its national, scientific, historic or artistic interest (introduced by *FA 1965*);
   (ii) any collections or groups of objects within (i) above which, taken as a whole, appears to the Board to be so pre-eminent (introduced by *FA 1973, s 46*); and
   (iii) any objects where they are associated with a particular building and where the Secretary of State believes it is desirable for that object to remain associated with a particular building or where objects have a significant association with a particular place

(b) Land which, in the opinion of the Board, is of outstanding scenic or historic or scientific interest.

(c) A building for the preservation of which special steps should, in the opinion of the Board, be taken by reason of its outstanding historic or architectural interest.

(d) Land which, in the opinion of the Board, is essential for the protection of the character and amenities of such a building as is mentioned in (c) above.

(e) An object which, in the opinion of the Board, is historically associated with such a building mentioned in (c) above.

Definitions

'National interest' includes interest within any part of the UK.

'Pre-eminence'-in determining whether an object or collection is pre-eminent, any significant association with a particular place is to be taken into account ie the 'Waverley criteria'. The object or collection should be

central, rather than of merely marginal significance, in the context of display in a public collection or important historic building and should satisfy one or more of the following tests which follow those laid down by the AIL Panel:

- Does the object have an especially close association with our history and national life? This category includes foreign as well as British works, e.g. gifts from foreign sovereigns or governments and objects that have been acquired abroad in circumstances associated with our history. It also includes objects closely associated with some part of the United Kingdom, or with the development of its institutions and industries. Some objects that fall under this category will be of such national importance that they deserve to enter a national museum or gallery. Others may well be of a lesser degree of national importance although they will be significant in a local context. This category will also include works which derive their significance from a local connection and which may therefore qualify as 'pre-eminent' to a local authority or independent museum or gallery.
- Is the object of especial artistic or art-historical interest? This category includes objects deserving of entering a national museum or gallery as well as other objects that may not be pre-eminent in a national museum or gallery but will be pre-eminent in local authority, university or independent museums or galleries which do not already possess items of a similar genre or quality. For example, outstanding items of decorative or applied art would come within this category for consideration.
- Is the object of especial importance for the study of some particular form of art, learning or history? This category includes a wide variety of objects, not restricted to works of art such as engineering plans or models, which are of especial importance for the study of, say, a particular scientific development. The category also includes objects forming part of an historical unity series or collection either in one place or in the country as a whole. Without a particular object or group of objects, both a unity and a series may be impaired.
- Does the object have an especially close association with a particular historic setting? This category will include primary works of art, manuscripts, furniture or other items that have an especially close association with an important historic building. The category may include paintings, furniture especially commissioned for a particular house or a group of paintings having an association with a particular location including those being returned to their original setting.

(See also Inland Revenue Press Release 17/99, 11 February 1999.)

Pre-eminent and associated objects

Now HMRC refer offers of 'pre-eminent' or 'associated' objects (see (a)(iii) above) to the Acceptance in Lieu (AIL) panel, which is comprised of 18 people, a list of which can be found in the Cultural Gifts Scheme and Acceptance in Lieu Reports available on the website for the

Arts Council of England. The panel takes into account the views of independent experts and advises the Secretary of State whether the property offered is suitable for acceptance in lieu by the Commissioners of HMRC in terms of the objects' pre-eminence. The Arts Council has published a leaflet entitled 'Acceptance in Lieu' which summarises the workings of the scheme and the benefits of it.

For claims made before 31 July 1998, objects or collections within (i) and (ii) above could be designated if they appeared to the Board to be of national, scientific, historic or artistic interest. There was no requirement to satisfy the standard of 'pre-eminence' but only a lower standard of 'museum quality'.

[*IHTA 1984, s 31(1)(5); FA 1985, Sch 26 para 2(2); FA 1998, Sch 25 para 4*].

The introduction of the pre-eminence test under (a) above may have the effect, in certain circumstances, of rendering previously exempted objects chargeable to a latent estate duty previously deferred but now exigible. Also, in the Finance Bill Committee Stage Debates the Financial Secretary's answer to questions on the definition of 'pre-eminent' exacted the following reply:

> 'An object must be pre-eminent or associated with a historical building; it does not have to be both. If the collection is pre-eminent in its own right, it should qualify. If it is not, its connection with a building may allow it to qualify as pre-eminent.'

(Hansard, 16 June 1998, Col 896).

Conditionally exempt transfers

[30.3] The Board may, on a claim (see below), designate property as eligible under **30.2** above and a transfer of such property is exempt from inheritance tax if certain conditions are met and undertakings given. Such a transfer is called a 'conditionally exempt transfer'. The failure to observe an undertaking is a 'chargeable event' and tax will become chargeable (see **30.10** and **30.14** below). It is understood that HMRC review all conditionally exempt transfers of land under **30.2**(b) at five-yearly intervals to ensure that undertakings are observed (HC Written answer, Hansard 18 June 1992, Vol 209, Cols 629, 630). A gift cannot be conditionally exempt if it is entirely exempt as a gift to a spouse/civil partner or to a charity. See **21.2** and **21.9** EXEMPT TRANSFERS. [*IHTA 1984, ss 30(1)(2)(4), 31, 32(1)(2); FA 1985, s 95, Sch 26 para 1; FA 1998, Sch 25 para 7*].

Conditions

[30.4] Exemptions may be given for transfers on death and lifetime gifts but the latter are eligible only if:

(a) the transferor or his spouse or civil partner has been beneficially entitled to the property throughout the six years ending with the transfer; or
(b) the transferor acquired the property on a death and the acquisition was itself a conditionally exempt transfer.

[*IHTA 1984, s 30(3); The Tax and Civil Partnership Regulations 2005, SI 2005/3229, Reg 11*].

Interaction with potentially exempt transfers

[30.5] The above provisions are disregarded in determining whether a transfer is a POTENTIALLY EXEMPT TRANSFER (35). Where the transfer in question is a potentially exempt transfer, no claim under the above provisions can be made until the transferor has died. [*IHTA 1984, s 30(3A)(3B); FA 1986, Sch 19 para 7*]. If the transferor survives for seven years after the transfer, the potentially exempt transfer becomes an exempt transfer and there is no need to make a claim for conditional exemption. If the transferor dies within the seven-year period, a claim for conditional exemption may be made and the question whether any property is appropriate for designation is determined by reference to circumstances existing after the transferor's death. [*IHTA 1984, s 31(1A); FA 1986, Sch 19 para 8*]. There is no conditional exemption if the property has been disposed of by sale before the transferor's death [*IHTA 1984, s 30(3C); FA 1986, Sch 19 para 7*] but a potentially exempt transfer which would have proved to be a chargeable transfer is an exempt transfer to the extent that the property has or could be designated under **30.2** above and, after the transfer in question and before the transferor's death, has been disposed of by way of sale by private treaty or otherwise to one of the bodies listed in **30.29** below or has been accepted by the Board in satisfaction of tax (see **32.10** PAYMENT OF TAX). [*IHTA 1984, s 26A; FA 1986, Sch 19 para 6*].

Where only part of a property is granted conditional exemption it is the actual transfer of value which is exempted rather than the property itself. Accordingly, the District Valuer should value the entire property and then apportion this figure on a just and reasonable approach between the value attributable to the heritage property and that attributable to the taxable non-heritage property. (VOA IHT manual, section 20, para 20.13).

Undertakings

[30.6] An undertaking must be given, by such a person as the Board think appropriate in the circumstances of the case, that, until the person beneficially entitled to the property dies or the property is disposed of:

(i) in the case of property under **30.2**(a) above, the property will be kept permanently in the UK and will not leave it temporarily except for a purpose and a period approved by the Board; and such steps as are agreed with the Board will be taken for the preservation of the property and for securing reasonable access to the public (but confidential documents may be excluded altogether or to a limited extent from the public access requirement), and

(ii) in the case of land under **30.2**(b), such steps as are agreed with the Board will be taken for its maintenance and the preservation of its character, and for securing reasonable access to the public, and

(iii) in the case of buildings, amenity land or objects within **30.2**(c)–(e), such steps as are agreed with the Board will be taken for its maintenance, repair and preservation and for securing reasonable access to the public and, if it is an object within **30.2**(e) above, for keeping it associated with the building concerned.

[*IHTA 1984, ss 30(1), 31(2)–(4); FA 1985, s 95, Sch 26 paras 1, 2(3)*].

Where the transfer in question is a POTENTIALLY EXEMPT TRANSFER (35) which has proved to be a chargeable lifetime transfer and at the time of the transferor's death an undertaking has been given by the appropriate person under *IHTA 1984, Sch 4 para 3(3)* (maintenance funds for historic buildings, see **30.23** below) or *TCGA 1992, s 258* with respect to any of the property to which the value transferred by the transfer is attributable, that undertaking is treated as having been given under the above provisions. [*IHTA 1984, s 31(4G); FA 1986, Sch 19 para 8*].

Public access

Reasonable access to the public. For undertakings given on or after 31 July 1998, public access cannot be confined to access by prior appointment only. [*IHTA 1984, s 31(4FA); FA 1998, Sch 25 para 5*]. As a result, in the case of objects within **30.2**(a) above, the 'V & A list' procedure described below ceases to apply. Where an undertaking whether original or a replacement undertaking is given on or after 31 July 1998 then:

- public access to the tax-exempt assets cannot be restricted to 'appointment' access through the owner or his/her agent (see former Inland Revenue letter sent to owners of conditionally exempt chattels on 31 March 1999 below);
- the owner may be required to publicise the terms of the undertaking and any other information relating to exempt assets which will otherwise be considered confidential.

[*FA 1998, Sch 25 paras 5, 6*].

'*Public access*', above, means that all owners of exempt assets will have to provide a measure of 'open' access to those assets, but this will only be in accordance with the terms agreed with HMRC set out in the undertaking. The law requires 'public access' to be reasonable and this will depend upon the nature and type of the asset as well as the preservation and maintenance needs of that asset. See *Re Applications to Vary the Undertakings of 'A' and 'B'* [2005] STC SCD 103 Sp C 439 below. For example, the measure of access for a large building may not be reasonable in the case of a smaller building or, say, a delicate object. In this latter case, it may be appropriate to mix 'open' access with 'appointment' access if the preservation of the object requires it. In certain circumstances, it may be appropriate to suspend or exclude public access.

HMRC announced that closure of a property due to the COVID-19 pandemic was not considered to be a breach of undertakings given. When government advice changes, property owners should make up for lost days if possible.

Chattels exemption

For chattels exempt in their own right 'open' access may be provided by displaying the objects at:

- the residence of the individual or at the place the object(s) is kept (restricted to the area in which the object is displayed, unless the building itself is tax exempt in which case this facility will not apply);
- a museum or gallery to which the public have access (see Revised DCMS model loan agreement for AIL in-situ offer revised at 30 December 2002);

- any other building open to the public, e.g. a local Record office;
- the appropriate European Heritage Open Days event free of charge (i.e. Heritage Open Days (England), Doors Open Days (Scotland), London Open House, European Open Days in Wales and Northern Ireland); and
- local, regional or touring exhibitions.

Objects may be loaned for display in the public collection of a national institution, local authority, university or independent museum and this period will count as 'open'. Historically associated objects will normally be displayed in the building concerned.

HMRC have announced that if a conditionally exempted object is on loan to a venue which has to close due to the COVID-19 pandemic, this will not be considered to be a breach of undertakings given. This will apply even if it means that the item is not on show at all in 2020. Similarly, if access by appointment is withdrawn, this will not be a breach of undertaking until Government advice on the matter changes.

Public access should be for a suitable period and time each year, without the need for a prior appointment. This annual period should not normally be less than a month or so. Access should normally be supplemented with:

(a) access with a prior appointment at other times;
(b) willingness to make loans to public collections for special exhibitions;
(c) willingness to provide curators with images to help them in mounting exhibitions.

This supplementary access would not normally be necessary where the work of art was kept in a house owned by, for example, the National Trust or in a privately owned house that opened during most of the year. Neither would it be necessary where the work of art was on continuous long-term loan to a public collection.

Access disclosure

Publicising access and undertakings is a requirement of conditional exemption for heritage assets. HMRC will expect the individual to make such an undertaking available to any member of the public who asks to view it. The undertaking in relation to the building or exempt chattel may be displayed at the premises and HMRC may also enter the details on their internet website.

The information required for the website will be a description of each object, full address of the building and opening times, and name, address and telephone number of the contact person (i.e. owner, agent, etc.). In the case of land HMRC may also require a copy of the undertaking together with any related management plan to be given free of charge to any local authority in which the land is situated. The authority and HMRC's advisers (e.g. Countryside Commission) will be free to make this information available to members of the public. The owner of amenity land must show the location of the land including the National Grid references for all points of entry onto that land. HMRC also require the name, address and telephone number of the person who can give further details of the amenity land on request. In the case of scenic land the owner may be required to advertise the details in the local tourist office and/or town hall, display map boards at each point of entry to the land and waymark the permitted paths, bridleways, etc.

HMRC accept that no obligation exists for owners to make proposals regarding the variation of existing undertakings. It is dependent on HMRC to review existing undertakings and then make proposals for variations as well as leaving some existing arrangements in place under the old 'V & A List Arrangements'. See below. In addition, the personal circumstances of those dictated by existing undertakings are relevant in deciding whether it is 'just and reasonable' in all the circumstances' for the terms of the current undertakings to be altered. [*IHTA 1984, s 35A(2)(c) as inserted by FA 1998, Sch 25 para 10(1)*].

Owners of buildings open to the public may be required to publicise the public access arrangements by:

(1) advertising details in the local paper, tourist office and/or town hall;
(2) advertising details in one of the annual national guides to historic houses, i.e. *Hudson's Historic Houses and Gardens* and *Johansens Historic Houses Castles & Gardens*;
(3) placing a sign at the main entrance of the property with details of opening times; or
(4) informing appropriate local council and education authorities.

For undertakings given before 31 July 1998, HMRC issued guidelines on what was considered to be reasonable public access as regards works of art etc. within **30.2**(a) above. One option for securing access is for the owner to allow viewing by appointment and, subject to conditions, to lend it for special exhibitions on request to directors or curators of public collections for up to six months in any two-year period. A register ('the V & A list') of objects granted conditional exemption, computerised with database search, is available for public consultation at the Victoria and Albert Museum (London), National Library of Scotland (Edinburgh), National Museum of Wales (Cardiff) and Ulster Museum (Belfast). Access may be obtained through the internet on www.hmrc.gov.uk/gds/heritage/lbsearch.htm.

HMRC accepted that during the COVID-19 pandemic, it may not have been possible to produce publicity or promotional material, and this will not be regarded as a breach of undertakings given.

Additional undertaking for amenity land

[30.7] An *additional* undertaking is required for amenity land within **30.2**(d) above, called the '*relevant land*', which is over and above the requirement for an undertaking at (iii) above. The person seeking conditional exemption for the relevant land must provide (or secure, if necessary, from another person) undertaking(s) that until the death of the person beneficially entitled to the building for which the relevant land is an amenity or any other amenity land of that building which is either between it and the relevant land or physically closely connected with one of them, or until that property is disposed of, such steps as are agreed with the Board will be taken for the maintenance, repair, preservation and securing of reasonable public access to the building or other amenity land. Where different persons are entitled (either beneficially or otherwise) to the building and the other amenity land, separate undertakings are required in respect of each by whomever the Board think appropriate. These undertakings are required notwithstanding the fact that another undertaking is already effective for that building or other amenity land. Such undertakings will have been given with respect to the building etc., whereas the additional undertaking, although relating to the maintenance etc. of the building etc., is given with respect to the relevant amenity land. [*IHTA 1984, s 31(4A)–(4F); FA 1985, ss 94, 95, Sch 26 para 2(4)*].

Variations of undertakings

[30.8] Undertakings may be varied by agreement between the Board and the person bound by the undertaking. Failing such agreement, a Commissioner may approve a proposed variation by the Board:

- for any undertaking given on or after 31 July 1998; or
- for any undertaking given before 31 July 1998 (unless there has been a chargeable event after the giving of the undertaking and before that date) but only so as to impose wider requirements for:
  - (i) public access where existing undertakings are confined to access by prior appointment only; and/or
  - (ii) publication of details of the exemption.

For replacement undertakings sought on or after 31 July 1998 to preserve an existing exemption (IHT or CTT) the person will need to comply with the rules on undertakings in force on the date the undertaking is given. [*FA 1998, Sch 25 para 7*]. This does not affect any replacement undertakings given under the rules relating to estate duty. If the conditionally exempt item is sold there will normally be a charge to tax but a replacement undertaking may be given for another item. However, the Heritage Section of HMRC should be advised promptly of the change in such circumstances or they will be in breach of the undertaking. Form IHT100 (event form IHT 100f) should be completed where there is an ending of a conditional exemption and this should be delivered within six months from the end of month in which the event giving rise to the tax charge occurs. Form Cap100 is appropriate for the ending of a CTT conditional exemption. There is no prescribed form of account for the ending of an Estate Duty conditional exemption. In order to avoid interest and penalties an early submission of Form IHT 100 is recommended.

In *Re Applications to Vary the Undertakings of 'A' and 'B'* [2005] STC SCD 103 Sp C 439 HMRC had agreed that the owners of certain valuable works of art should have the benefit of 'conditional exemption' from IHT. Subsequently, HMRC made applications, under *IHTA 1984, s 35A*, to vary the undertakings so as to give wider publicity to the existence of the items, and wider access to them. The Special Commissioner dismissed HMRC's applications, holding that 'the accumulated burdens placed on the particular owner' would 'so outweigh the benefit to the public as to make it neither just nor reasonable for me to direct that the proposals take effect'. There would be 'a serious intrusion into the family lives of the owners', and 'the increased risks of theft and damage to the owners' possessions' would go 'beyond what Parliament had in mind when empowering the inclusion of extended access requirements and publication requirements'. [*IHTA 1984, s 35A (2)(c)*]. This has now been acknowledged by HMRC in their letter to owners and advisers and it is thought that HMRC will now make their requests for greater access less burdensome following the above case.

HMRC will consider changes to their proposals by the person bound but the law:

- requires the undertaking to be appropriate to the asset concerned, so when they consider the changes they have regard to any change in the personal circumstances of the person bound; and
- does not provide for any appeal if the proposals put forward cannot be accepted.

[*IHTA 1984, s 35A; FA 1998, Sch 25 para 8*].

Claims

[30.9] A claim should be made on Form IHT 420. Copies are available from HMRC, Nottingham at the address shown in **2.21** ACCOUNTS AND RETURNS. In relation to transfers of property after 16 March 1998, the claim must be made no more than two years after the transfer of value or, in the case of potentially exempt transfers, the date of death. In either case the Board may allow a longer period. [*IHTA 1984, s 30(3BA); FA 1998, Sch 25 para 2*]. The Board will consider each application to extend the two-year period on its own merits but have stated that any oversight or mistake on the applicant's part or their adviser's, or the making of a post-death variation, will not normally by itself be an acceptable reason to allow a late claim. A primary claim for agricultural or business property relief may delay matters beyond the two-year claim period in which case a protective claim may be advisable. Normally a claim may not be made in advance except in the cases of:

- any claim for exemption from the IHT ten-yearly charge on discretionary trusts, as such claims must be made, and assets designated, before the date of the charge, but note that this rule will cease to apply with effect from Royal Assent to the *Finance (No 2) Act 2015* following which a claim will be admissible within two years after the date of charge or such longer time as HMRC may allow; and
- approval of a proposed heritage maintenance fund.

[*IHTA 1984, s 79(3), Sch 4 para 1(2)*].

HMRC expect applicants to make their claims without undue delay.

Chargeable event

[30.10] Where there has been a conditionally exempt transfer of any property, tax is charged on the first occurrence after the transfer (or, if the transfer was a POTENTIALLY EXEMPT TRANSFER (35) after the transferor's death) of a chargeable event. Where properties are '*associated properties*' (i.e. a building within 30.2(c) above and any amenity land or objects within 30.2(d) or (e) related to that building), tax is chargeable on the first event after a conditionally exempt transfer (or, if the transfer was a potentially exempt transfer, after the transferor's death) of *any* of the associated properties (or part) on the *whole* of each of the associated properties (or part) for which the event is a chargeable event. Subject to exceptions below, there is a '*chargeable event*' on a material failure to observe an undertaking within **30.3** above, on the death of any person beneficially entitled to any property and on any disposal of any property. [*IHTA 1984, ss 32(1)–(3), 32A(1)–(4); FA 1985, Sch 26 para 4; FA 1986, Sch 19 paras 9, 10; FA 1998, Sch 25 para 7*].

Where a chargeable event arises in respect of heritage property which was allowed conditional exemption on the death of the owner, the lower 36% rate of IHT cannot be claimed on that event even if the remaining estate had satisfied the conditions for that rate (see **49.13**).

Exceptions

[30.11] There is no chargeable event in the following situations.

(a) If a failure to observe an undertaking or a disposal relates to one only of the associated properties or part of it, and the associated properties as a whole have not been materially affected, the Board may, if so satisfied, direct that the chargeable event be limited to the property or part actually affected by the failure of undertaking, etc. [*IHTA 1984, s 32A(10); FA 1985, s 95, Sch 25 para 4*].

(b) There is no chargeable event on death if within three years the personal representatives (or trustees or person next entitled if settled property, see **30.18** *et seq.* below) make a disposal of property by way of sale by private treaty or gift to one of the national bodies listed in *IHTA 1984, Sch 3*, or where the property is accepted in lieu of tax. A disposal is likewise not a chargeable event where it is one of this nature. Where there is then a subsequent death or disposal there is no chargeable event with respect to the property (or part) concerned unless there has been another, intervening, conditionally exempt transfer. The disposal of one or part of a group of 'associated properties' to a national body or in lieu of tax does not mean that the remaining associated properties are not chargeable. Conditional exemption only continues for the property retained if the necessary undertaking is given by such person or persons as the Board thinks appropriate. [*IHTA 1984, ss 32(4), 32A(5)–(7); FA 1985, Sch 26 para 4; FA 1998, Sch 25 para 7*].

(c) Death, or disposal otherwise than by sale, is not a chargeable event if the transfer of value thereby made is itself a conditionally exempt transfer or if the necessary undertaking is given by such person or persons as the Board think appropriate. [*IHTA 1984, ss 32(5)(5AA), 32A(8)(8A); FA 1985, Sch 26 para 4; FA 1998, Sch 25 para 7*].

(d) A disposal by sale of one or part of a group of associated properties gives rise to a chargeable event limited to that part of the associated properties actually disposed of (if it is not otherwise exempt) if the necessary undertaking is given by such person or persons as the Board think appropriate. [*IHTA 1984, s 32A(9); FA 1985, Sch 26 para 4; FA 1998, Sch 25 para 7*].

The person liable

The person liable to pay the tax chargeable is

(i) in the case of breach of undertaking or death, the person who, if the property were sold at that time, would be entitled to receive (whether for his benefit or not) the proceeds of sale or any income arising from them; or

(ii) in the case of disposal, the person by whom or for whose benefit the property is disposed of.

[*IHTA 1984, s 207(1)–(2B); FA 1985, Sch 26 para 10*].

Transferability of nil rate bands and the deferred charge, etc.

[30.12] From 9 October 2007, on the death of the survivor of a married couple or a civil partnership, a claim may be made to transfer any amount of the nil rate band which was not used in the estate of the one who predeceased (see **49.15** TRANSFERS ON DEATH). In cases where there has been a deferred charge on, say, heritage property such as in *IHTA 1984, ss 32(1)–(3), 32A(1)–(4)* and there is subsequently unused nil rate band available to the surviving spouse or civil partner, then that charge is taken into account before calculating the unused nil rate band of the surviving spouse or civil partner. See Example 1 below. If there is more than one deferred charge before the transfer of the nil rate band to the spouse or civil partner these deferred charges similarly reduce the nil rate band that may be claimed. See Example 2. Further, if there is a deferred charge after the nil rate band of the deceased has been claimed by the surviving spouse's personal representatives then any available nil rate band to be claimed against the deferred charge will be reduced by the amount claimed by the survivor's personal representatives. See Example 3 below. See also similar provisions described at **49.16** in relation to the interaction between the forthcoming main residence nil rate amount and conditional exemption charges. [*IHTA 1984, ss 8A, 8C as inserted by FA 2008, Sch 4 para 2*].

Example 1

Chargeable event during lifetime of surviving spouse or civil partner

C died in August 2002 having made chargeable transfers of £125,000 and previously, a conditionally exempt gift of heritage property to his brother, B. C had left the balance of his estate to his wife, D. In October 2008, the heritage property conditional exemption is breached when it is valued at £104,000. D dies in February 2010.

The claim for the unused nil rate band by D's personal representatives must be calculated after taking into account the proportion of C's nil rate band used to cover previous chargeable transfers and the heritage property conditional exemption breach. C had used ½ of his nil rate band on his death (i.e. (£250,000 – £125,000) ÷ £250,000 × 100%) so at the time of the chargeable event in October 2008 the current nil rate band is £312,000. As the amount on which tax is chargeable is £104,000 (see below) this is the amount referred to as TA below and the nil rate band at the date of breach is NRBME below. This is calculated to be one-third (i.e. £104,000 ÷ £312,000) and this is deducted from the amount of the available nil rate band on C's death i.e. $^1/_2 - ^1/_3$ = 16.667%. At the time of D's death when the nil rate band has increased to £325,000 the remaining portion of C's nil rate band available to D's personal representatives at that time is £54,168 (i.e. £325,000 × 16.667%). [*IHTA 1984, s 8C* as inserted by *FA 2008, Sch 4 para 2*].

Notes to the example

(A) The transferable amount of the unused nil rate band of the predeceased C to D in this example is calculated by applying the unused nil rate band under *IHTA 1984, s 8A(2)(4)* as follows:

$$\text{Percentage} = \left(\frac{E}{NRBMD} - \frac{TA}{NRBME}\right) \times 100$$

where:

M = maximum amount that could be transferred on the predeceased person's death where it is chargeable at the nil rate band at that time, i.e. £250,000;

VT = value actually transferred by the chargeable transfer or nil if applicable, i.e. £125,000;

E = the amount by which M above is greater than VT above, i.e. £125,000 (£250,000 – £125,000);

NRBMD = the nil rate band maximum applying at the time of the deceased spouse's or civil partner's death, i.e. £250,000;

TA = the amount on which tax is charged i.e £104,000;

NRBME = the nil rate band maximum at the time of the event giving rise to the deferred charge, i.e. £312,000.

(B) C's estate at death will be increased to take account of the chargeable event to determine the rates applicable to any later chargeable event as in Example 2 below. [*IHTA 1984, s 34(1)(2); FA 1985, Sch 26 para 5*].

	£
Cumulative total of previous chargeable transfers of relevant person C	125,000
Valuation of conditionally exempt property	104,000
Revised cumulative total for relevant person C	£229,000

Example 2

Two or more chargeable events during lifetime of surviving spouse or civil partner

C died in August 2002 having made chargeable transfers of £125,000 and previously, a conditionally exempt gift of heritage property to his brother, B. C had left the balance of his estate to his wife, D. In October 2008 and December 2008, the two items of conditionally exempt property are sold by B for £63,415 each and capital gains tax of £11,415 is payable. D dies in February 2011.

The claim for the unused nil rate band by D's personal representatives must be calculated after taking into account the proportion of C's nil rate band used to cover previous chargeable transfers and the heritage property conditional exemption breach. C had used ½ of his nil rate band on his death (i.e. (£250,000 – £125,000) ÷ £250,000 × 100%). At the time of the chargeable events in October and December 2008 the nil rate band is £312,000. As the amounts on which tax is chargeable after CGT is £52,000 on each chargeable event these amounts are referred to as TA below and the nil rate band at the date of sale is NRBME below. These amounts are each calculated to be one-sixth (i.e. £52,000 ÷ £312,000) and are deducted from the amount of the available nil rate band on C's death (i.e. ½ – ($^1/_6$ + $^1/_6$) = 16.667%). At the time of D's death, when the nil rate band has increased to £325,000, the portion of C's nil rate band still available to the personal representatives at that time is therefore £54,168 (i.e. £325,000 × 16.667%). [*IHTA 1984, s 8C(2)(3)* as inserted by *FA 2008, Sch 4 para 2*].

Notes to the example

(A) The transferable amount of the unused nil rate band of the predeceased C to D in this example is calculated by applying the unused nil rate band under *IHTA 1984, s 8A(2)(4)* as follows:

$$\text{Percentage} = \frac{E}{NRBMD} - \left(\frac{TA}{NRBME} + \frac{TA}{NRBME}\right) \times 100$$

where:

M = maximum amount that could be transferred on the predeceased person's death where it is chargeable at the nil rate band at that time, i.e. £250,000;
VT = value actually transferred by the chargeable transfer or nil if applicable, i.e. £125,000;
E = the amount by which M above is greater than VT above, i.e. £125,000 (£250,000 – £125,000);
NRBMD = the nil rate band maximum applying at the time of the deceased spouse's or civil partner's death, i.e. £250,000;
TA = the amount on which tax is charged, i.e. £52,000;
NRBME = the nil rate band maximum at the time of the event giving rise to the deferred charge, i.e. £312,000 but if the second sale had been in December 2009 this figure would have been £325,000 not £312,000.

		£
Cumulative total of previous chargeable transfers of relevant person C		125,000
Net sale proceeds of conditionally exempt property October 2008	63,415	
Deduct capital gains tax payable	(11,415)	52,000
Net sale proceeds of conditionally exempt property December 2008	63,415	
Deduct capital gains tax payable	(11,415)	
Chargeable transfer		52,000
Revised cumulative total for relevant person C		£229,000

Example 3

Chargeable event after the death of the surviving spouse or civil partner

C died in August 2002 having made chargeable transfers of £125,000 and previously, a conditionally exempt gift of heritage property to his brother, B. C had left the balance of his estate to his wife, D. D dies in February 2011 with an estate valued at £350,000. In October 2011, the conditionally exempt property is sold for £300,000 and capital gains tax of £54,000 is payable.

The claim for the unused nil rate band by D's personal representatives on form IHT402 (previously IHT216) has already been made by the time the conditionally exempt property is sold and becomes chargeable. C had used half of his nil rate band on his death (i.e. (£250,000 – £125,000) ÷ £250,000 × 100%) so D's personal representatives are entitled to claim ½ × £325,000. D's nil rate band of £325,000 added to the predeceased C's available nil rate band of £162,500 (i.e. (£250,000 – £125,000) ÷ £250,000 = ½ × £325,000) makes a total of £487,500. Of this amount, £350,000 is used to cover the estate of D of which £25,000 is part of C's original nil rate band. In October 2011, the property is sold by the brother B for £300,000 and capital gains tax of £52,000 is payable, making net proceeds of £248,000. Therefore, the unused proportion of C's nil rate band of £200,000 (i.e. (£125,000 + £25,000) – £350,000) is available to set against the net sale proceeds of the conditionally exempt property as below. [*IHTA 1984, s 8C(4)(5)* as inserted by *FA 2008, Sch 4 para* 2].

Notes to the example

(A) In a case of breach of undertaking or death the person who is liable to pay the tax is the person who, if the property were sold at that time, would be entitled to receive (whether for his benefit or not) the proceeds of sale or any income arising from them, i.e. B. The tax is due six months after the end of the month in which the disposal took place. [*IHTA 1984, s 226(4)*].

(B) If the relevant person is dead, the rate of tax will be the rate applicable to the property if it were added to the value of C's estate on death and formed the highest part of that value.

		£
Cumulative total of previous chargeable transfers of relevant person C		125,000
Value of property at date of sale in October 2011	300,000	
Deduct capital gains tax	(52,000)	
Chargeable transfer		248,000
Revised cumulative total for relevant person C		£373,000
Inheritance tax payable after deducting the available nil rate band (by reference to death rates in February 2010), i.e. £350,000 – £150,000 (£125,000 + £25,000) = £200,000 – £248,000 £48,000 at 40% = £19,200 payable by B		

Conditional exemption on death before 7 April 1976

[30.13] Similar rules apply in respect of conditional exemption granted under previous legislation on deaths before 7 April 1976. [*FA 1975, ss 32, 34(3)–(6); IHTA 1984, ss 35(2), 207(4)(5), Sch 5 paras 1, 3(1)–(4), Sch 6 para 4(2); FA 1985, Sch 26 paras 7, 13; FA 1986, Sch 19 para 12*].

Charge to tax

[30.14] Different provisions apply according to the date of the conditionally exempt transfer or occasion (see **30.18** below) on which the chargeable event arises. In each case the tax is due six months after the end of the month in which the chargeable event occurs. [*IHTA 1984, s 226(4); FA 1985, Sch 26 para 11*]. See **30.10** above for person liable to pay the tax.

A conditionally exempt transfer can arise during lifetime or on death. The tax on a subsequent chargeable event is on the value of the property at the time of the event (i.e. there is no 'grossing-up') and where the event is a disposal on a sale not intended to confer any gratuitous benefit on any person and at arm's length between unconnected persons (or on similar terms), the value is equal to the sale proceeds (with proportionate reduction where the conditional exemption applied only to part of the property) [*IHTA 1984, s 33(1)(a)(3)(4)*] less any capital gains tax chargeable. [*TCGA 1992, s 258(8)*].

The rate at which tax on a subsequent chargeable event is charged is determined by reference to the relevant person. [*IHTA 1984, s 33(1)(b)*].

Relevant person

The 'relevant person' is:

(i) if there has been only one conditionally exempt transfer or one conditionally exempt occasion (see **30.18** below) before the event, the person who made that transfer or the person who is the settlor in relation to the settlement in respect of which the occasion occurred;

(ii) if there have been two or more such transfers or occasions, and the last was before, or only one of them was within, the period of thirty years ending with the event, the person who made the last transfer or the person who is the settlor in relation to the settlement in respect of which the last occasion occurred;

(iii) if there have been two or more such transfers or occasions within that period, whichever person or settlor the Board may select. [*IHTA 1984, ss 33(5), 78(3)*].

The rate of tax will be, subject to the exceptions below,

(a) if the relevant person is alive, the rate applicable to the property if it were added to the cumulative total of his chargeable transfers at the date of the chargeable event and tax calculated using rates applicable to lifetime transfer. The amount is only notionally added for this purpose and does not affect the rate of tax on later transfers made by the relevant person unless he is also the person who made the last conditionally exempt transfer (see **30.16** below). The rates are not affected by the death of the relevant person after the chargeable event. [*IHTA 1984, ss 33(1)(b)(i)(2A), 34(1); FA 1986, Sch 19 para 11*].

(b) if the relevant person is dead, the rate applicable to the property if it were added to the value of his estate on death and formed the highest part of that value. If the relevant person made the conditionally exempt transfer on death (but the property was not treated as forming part of his estate under the rules relating to GIFTS WITH RESERVATION (**22**)) the death rates are used. In any other case, tax is calculated using the rates applicable to lifetime transfers. If the relevant person is the settlor and the settlement was created on his death, the death rates are used, if not tax is calculated using the rates applicable to lifetime transfers. If the chargeable event occurs after tax is reduced by the substitution of a new table of rates, the new rates are used. Where the relevant person died before 18 March 1986, nevertheless, the amount of tax payable is calculated as if the amendments to *IHTA 1984, s 7* in *FA 1986, 19 Sch 2* (rates of tax for transfers within seven years of death and tapering relief) had applied at the time of death. [*IHTA 1984, ss 9, 33(1)(b)(ii)(2), 78(4), Sch 2 para 5; FA 1985, Sch 26 para 5; FA 1986, Sch 19 paras 11, 19, 41*].

Exceptions

If the relevant person is determined as in (i) to (iii) above by reference to a conditionally exempt occasion (see **30.18** below)

(A) the rates under (a) and (b) above will be reduced to **30%** of the full charge if the occasion occurred before the first ten-year anniversary (see **40.6** SETTLEMENTS: DISCRETIONARY TRUSTS AND OTHER TRUSTS OF RELEVANT PROPERTY) to fall after the property became comprised in the settlement concerned and **60%** of the full charge if the event occurred after the first and before the second ten-year anniversary.

(B) the rate under (b) above is, where the relevant person died before 13 March 1975, and subject to (A) above, the rate applicable to the property as if the relevant person died when the chargeable event occurred and the chargeable amount were added to, and formed the highest part of, the value on which estate duty was chargeable when he in fact died. [*IHTA 1984, s 78(4)(5)*].

Conditionally exempt transfers or occasions in (i) to (iii) above do not include those made before any previous chargeable event on the same property or before any event mentioned in **30.10**(b) above. [*IHTA 1984, s 33(6); FA 1985, Sch 26 para 6*].

Tax credit

[30.15] Subject to below, where there is a chargeable transfer after a conditionally exempt transfer of the same property (wholly or in part), any tax charged is allowed as a credit:

(a) if the chargeable transfer is also a chargeable event (see **30.10** above), against the tax chargeable on that chargeable event;

(b) if the chargeable transfer is not also a chargeable event, against the tax chargeable on the next chargeable event on the property.

Where after a conditionally exempt transfer of any property there is a potentially exempt transfer of all or part of that property, and *either* the potentially exempt transfer is a chargeable event with respect to the property *or* after the potentially exempt transfer but before the transferor's death a chargeable event occurs with respect to the property, the tax charged under the above provisions on the chargeable event is allowed as a credit against any tax which may become chargeable by reason of the potentially exempt transfer proving to be a chargeable transfer. No relief is due under (a) or (b) above. [*IHTA 1984, s 33(7)(8); FA 1986, Sch 19 para 11*].

Example 4

Chargeable event during lifetime of relevant person

C, who has made previous chargeable transfers during August 2003 of £230,000, makes a conditionally exempt gift of property in February 2004. In October 2010, the property is sold for £500,000 and capital gains tax of £90,000 is payable.

		£
Cumulative total of previous chargeable transfers of relevant person		230,000
Net sale proceeds of conditionally exempt property	500,000	
Deduct capital gains tax payable	(90,000)	
Chargeable transfer		410,000
Revised cumulative total for relevant person		£640,000

Inheritance tax payable (by reference to lifetime rates in October 2010)
£315,000 at 20% = £63,000

Example 5

Chargeable event after relevant person is dead

D died in April 1995 leaving a taxable estate of £325,000 together with conditionally exempt property valued at £600,000 at the breach in October 2010.

	£
Value of relevant person's estate at death	350,000
Value of conditionally exempt property at date of breach	600,000
	£950,000

Inheritance tax payable (by reference to full rates applicable in October 2010)
£600,000 at 40% = £240,000

Example 6

Property inherited in 1984 from A's estate by B, who gave the necessary undertakings so that the property is conditionally exempt, is given in December 2009 by B to C. C agrees to pay any inheritance tax arising from the transfer but does not wish to give the necessary undertakings, so a chargeable event arises. B dies in March 2011.

	£
A's estate at date of death in 1984	180,000
B's cumulative chargeable transfers at date of chargeable event in December 2009 (all in 2009/10)	86,000
Value of property at date of chargeable event	266,000

Inheritance tax on chargeable event (subject to tax credit)

	£
Value of A's estate at date of death	180,000
Value of property at date of chargeable event	266,000
	£446,000

Inheritance tax payable
£121,000 (£446,000 – 325,000) at 40% = £48,400

Inheritance tax on B's gift

Cumulative total of previous transfers		86,000
Value of property gifted	266,000	
Deduct annual exemption 2010/11	3,000	263,000
		£349,000
Inheritance tax arising on gift of £263,000		£9,600
Tax credit		
IHT on B's gift		9,600
IHT on chargeable event	48,400	
Deduct tax credit	(9,600)	
		38,800
Total inheritance tax borne		£48,400

Effect of chargeable event on subsequent transfers

[30.16] The person who made the last conditionally exempt transfer before the chargeable event (not necessarily the relevant person) will have his cumulative total of chargeable transfers increased by the amount of the property on which tax is paid on the chargeable event and, consequently, the rate of tax applicable to all his subsequent chargeable transfers is increased. Where that person is dead, but he is the relevant person in relation to a later chargeable event, the value of his estate at death will be increased by the amount on which tax is paid on the first chargeable event to determine the rates applicable to the later chargeable event. [*IHTA 1984, s 34(1)(2); FA 1985, Sch 26 para 5*].

Settlor

[30.17] If the 'relevant person' is not the person who made the last conditionally exempt transfer of the property and at the time of the chargeable event, or at any time within the preceding five years, the property is or has been comprised in a settlement made within 30 years before that event and a person who is a settlor of that settlement has made a conditionally exempt transfer of the property within those 30 years (excluding any made before any previous chargeable event on the same property or before any event mentioned in **30.10**(b) above), then the amount of the property chargeable at the time of the chargeable event is added to the cumulative total of the settlor (and not to that of the person who made the last conditionally exempt transfer). [*IHTA 1984, s 34(3)(4); FA 1985, Sch 26 para 6*].

Where the last conditionally exempt transaction before a chargeable event was a conditionally exempt occasion (see **30.18** below) as opposed to a conditionally exempt transfer, the above does not apply. [*IHTA 1984, s 78(6)*].

Example 7

Multiple conditionally exempt transfers

D died in December 1983 leaving a conditionally exempt property to his son E. D's taxable estate at death was £230,000. In 1992 E gave the property to his daughter F. F gave the necessary undertakings so this transfer was also conditionally exempt. In December 2010 F sold the property for its market value of £500,000 and paid capital gains tax of £80,000. During 1992 E had made chargeable transfers of £20,000 and he has made no other transfers.

	£	£
Value of relevant person's estate at death		230,000
Net sale proceeds of conditionally exempt property	500,000	
Deduct capital gains tax	80,000	
Chargeable transfer		420,000
		£650,000
Inheritance tax payable by F		
£325,000 at 40% =		£130,000
Previous cumulative total of E		20,000
Add chargeable transfer		420,000
E's revised cumulative total		£440,000

Notes to the example

(A) There have been two conditionally exempt transfers within the period of 30 years ending with the chargeable event in December 2010. HMRC may select either D or E as the 'relevant person' for the purpose of calculating the tax due. The IHT liability will be higher if D is selected. [*IHTA 1984 ss 33(5), 78(3)*].

(B) As F receives the proceeds of sale, she is the person liable to pay the IHT [*IHTA 1984, s 207(1)*].

(C) Although the IHT is calculated by reference to D's cumulative total, it is E whose cumulative total is adjusted as he made the last conditionally exempt transfer of the property. [*IHTA 1984, s 34(1)*].

(D) As the chargeable event occurs after a reduction in the rates of tax, the new rates are used to calculate the tax payable. [*IHTA 1984, Sch 2 para 5*].

Settlements

Conditionally exempt occasions

[30.18] A national heritage property (see **30.2** above) comprised in a settlement without interests in possession (**40** SETTLEMENTS: DISCRETIONARY TRUSTS AND OTHER TRUSTS OF RELEVANT PROPERTY) may be transferred with exemption from inheritance tax provided:

(a) the property has been comprised in the settlement throughout the six years ending with the transfer, and

(b) on a claim being made, the property is designated by the Board as being within **30.2** above, and

(c) the requisite undertaking (or undertakings) in **30.3** above are given by such person as the Board thinks appropriate.

Any event, other than a transfer, which would otherwise give rise to a charge under the provisions relating to SETTLEMENTS WITHOUT INTERESTS IN POSSESSION **41**, is also exempt if the above conditions are satisfied. An exempt transfer or event as above, is a '*conditionally exempt occasion*'. [*IHTA 1984, s 78(1)(2); FA 1985, s 95, Sch 26 para 8*].

In relation to transfers of property or other events occurring after 16 March 1998, the claim under (b) above must be made no more than two years after the date of the transfer or other event in question, although the Board may allow a longer period. [*IHTA 1984, s 78(1A); FA 1998, Sch 25 para 3*].

Chargeable events

[30.19] Chargeable events giving rise to a tax liability are as in **30.10** above with appropriate modification so that references to a conditionally exempt transfer include references to a conditionally exempt occasion; references to a disposal otherwise than by sale include references to any occasion on which tax is chargeable under the provisions relating to settlements without qualifying interests in possession (other than the ten-year anniversary charge for which see **30.22** below); and references to an undertaking in **30.3** above include the undertaking in **30.18** above. [*IHTA 1984, s 78(3); FA 1985, Sch 26 para 8*].

Example 8

A, who is still alive, settled property and investments on discretionary trusts in September 1988, conditional exemption being granted in respect of designated property. In April 2002, the designated property was appointed absolutely to beneficiary C who gave the necessary undertakings for exemption to continue. However, in February 2011, C sold the property for £135,000 net of costs, suffering a capital gains tax liability of £20,000. At the time of C's sale, A had cumulative chargeable transfers of £40,000.

			£
Cumulative total of previous chargeable transfers of relevant person			40,000
Net sale proceeds of conditionally exempt property			115,000
			£155,000
Inheritance tax payable by C			
£110,000	At Nil	—	
£5,000	At 20%	1,000	
£115,000		£1,000	£1,000

Notes to the example

(a) A is the relevant person in relation to the chargeable event as he is the person to effect the only conditionally exempt transfer *and* the person who is settlor in relation to the settlement in respect of which the only conditionally exempt occasion arose. [*IHTA 1984, ss 33(5), 78(3)*].

(b) HMRC have discretion to select either the conditionally exempt transfer (by A to the trustees) in 1988 or the conditionally exempt occasion (from the trustees to C) in 2002 as the 'last transaction' for the purposes of determining who is the relevant person. A is the relevant person regardless of which is selected but HMRC are more likely to choose the earlier transfer as this will result in a greater amount of tax being collected. [*IHTA 1984, ss 33(5), 78(3)(4)*].

(c) The chargeable amount of £115,000 does not increase either A's cumulative total or that of the trustees for the purpose of calculating the IHT liability on any subsequent transfers. As the last conditionally exempt transaction before the chargeable event was a conditionally exempt occasion rather than a conditionally exempt transfer, the provisions of *IHTA 1984, s 34* (which allow for an increase in the cumulative total) do not apply. [*IHTA 1984, s 78(6)*].

Charge to tax

[30.20] The tax on a chargeable event is on the value of the property at the time of the event (i.e. there is no grossing-up) and where the event is a disposal on a sale not intended to confer any gratuitous benefit on any person and at arm's length between unconnected persons (or on similar terms), the value is equal to the sale proceeds (with proportionate reduction where the conditional exemption applied only to part of the property) [*IHTA 1984, ss 33(1)(a)(3)(4), 78(3)*] less any capital gains tax chargeable. [*TCGA 1992, s 258(8)*].

The rate of tax will be as in **30.14** above.

Where a chargeable event arises in respect of settled property which was allowed conditional exemption on an earlier death, the lower 36% rate of IHT cannot be claimed on that event even if the remaining estate had satisfied the conditions for that rate: see **49.13** TRANSFER ON DEATH. Tax is due six months after the end of the month in which the chargeable event occurs. [*IHTA 1984, s 226(4); FA 1985, Sch 26 para 11*].

Tax credit

[30.21] The same credit applies as in **30.14** above with the substitution of 'conditionally exempt occasion' for 'conditionally exempt transfer'.

Exemption from the ten-year anniversary charge

[30.22] Where, on or before the occasion on which property became comprised in the settlement, there has been:

(a) a conditionally exempt transfer of the property, or
(b) a disposal to which *TCGA 1992, s 258(4)* applies (capital gains tax relief for works of art etc.)

there is no liability to the ten-year anniversary charge (see **40.6** SETTLEMENTS: DISCRETIONARY TRUSTS AND OTHER TRUSTS OF RELEVANT PROPERTY) on any such anniversary that falls before such a time as where (a) applies a chargeable event occurs, or where (b) applies, property is treated as sold under *TCGA 1992, s 258(5)*.

Where (a) or (b) above do not apply but the Board have, on a claim, designated under **30.2** above relevant settled property (see **40.3** SETTLEMENTS: DISCRETIONARY TRUSTS AND OTHER TRUSTS OF RELEVANT PROPERTY) and the requisite undertaking or undertakings have been given, the ten-year charge will not apply but a charge will arise on the first occurrence of any event that would be a chargeable event under **30.10** above. Thereafter charges to tax under *IHTA 1984, s 64* will apply. No charge will arise, however, if after the property becomes settled property and before the occurrence of a chargeable event, there has been a conditionally exempt occasion (see **30.18** above) in respect of the property.

Tax is charged on the value of the property at the time of the event. The rate at which tax is charged is the aggregate of the following percentages for each complete successive quarter in 'the relevant period'.

	Cumulative Total
0.25% for each of the first 40 quarters	10%
0.20% for each of the next 40 quarters	8%
0.15% for each of the next 40 quarters	6%
0.10% for each of the next 40 quarters	4%
0.05% for each of the next 40 quarters	2%
Maximum rate chargeable after 50 years	30%

'*Relevant period*' is the period beginning with the latest of

(i) the day on which the settlement commenced; and
(ii) the date of the last ten-year anniversary of the settlement to fall before the day on which the property became comprised in the settlement; and
(iii) 13 March 1975

and ending with the day before the event giving rise to the charge.

'*Quarter*' means a period of three months.

Where National Heritage property became comprised in the settlement in the previous ten years and exemption from the ten-year anniversary charge on qualifying property has been obtained as above, the value of the consideration given for that property is nevertheless taken into account when calculating the rate at which tax is charged on the other (non-national heritage) property in the settlement. The amount is included under *IHTA 1984, s 66(5)(b)* as a previous chargeable transfer by the notional transferor (see **40.8** and **40.10** SETTLEMENTS: DISCRETIONARY TRUSTS AND OTHER TRUSTS OF RELEVANT PROPERTY).

[*IHTA 1984, ss 61(1), 63, 79(1)–(9); FA 1985, s 95, Sch 26 para 9*].

An account must be delivered within six months from the end of the month in which the chargeable event occurs and any tax payable is due at the expiration of that period. Interest on overdue tax runs from the due date (see **25** INTEREST ON TAX). [*IHTA 1984, ss 216(7), 226(4), 233(1)(c); FA 1985, Sch 26 para 11; FA 1989, s 179(1)*].

The persons liable for the tax are the trustees of the settlement and any person for whose benefit any of the property or income from it is applied at or after the time of the event occasioning the charge. [*IHTA 1984, s 207(3)*].

Example 9

Trustees own National Heritage property for which the necessary undertakings have been given and the property has been designated by the Treasury. The property was settled in July 1974 and is the sole asset of the trust. No appointments or advances of capital have been made. On 30 October 2010, there is a breach of the undertakings. At this date the property is valued at £150,000.

Ten-year anniversary charge

There is no liability in 1984, 1994 or 2004.

Breach in October 2010

Value of property at time of event	£150,000

The relevant period is the period from the date of settlement or, if later, 13 March 1975 to 29 October 2010, i.e. 142 complete quarters.

The rate of tax is

	%
0.25% for 40 quarters	10.00
0.20% for 40 quarters	8.00
0.15% for 40 quarters	6.00
0.10% for 22 quarters	2.20
	26.20%
IHT payable is 26.20% × £150,000 =	£39,300

Maintenance funds for historic buildings

[30.23] The capital transfer tax provisions detailing the conditions to be met to exempt transfers into maintenance funds for historic buildings were introduced, with effect from 2 May 1976, by *FA 1976, s 84* and amended in 1980 and 1981. These provisions were replaced in 1982 by legislation subsequently consolidated as *IHTA 1984, ss 27, 57(5), Sch 4 paras 1–7* in relation to events after 8 March 1982 although much of the previous legislation was reproduced. Previously existing exempt funds are treated as approved under the revised provisions relating to CTT and the provisions relating to IHT, and designations, undertakings and acceptances are likewise treated as having been made under *CTTA 1984, Sch 4 para 3(3)* or *IHTA 1984, Sch 4 para 3(3)*. [*IHTA 1984, Sch 4 paras 1(3), 3(5)*].

Provided the necessary conditions are met, there is no charge to inheritance tax either when the property is settled (but see **21.24** EXEMPT TRANSFERS for abatement of this exemption) or applied for approved purposes.

Qualifying conditions

[30.24] A transfer of value is an exempt transfer to the extent that the value transferred by it is attributable to property which by virtue of a transfer becomes, or immediately after the transfer remains, comprised in a settlement and in respect of which a Board direction has effect at or after the time of the transfer. The Board may give a direction in respect of property proposed to be comprised in the settlement. [*IHTA 1984, ss 27(1), 57(5), Sch 4 para 1(2)*]. Exemption will not apply to a transfer which falls within certain situations in *IHTA 1984, ss 23, 56*. See **21.2**(a), (b)(i)(ii)(iii)(vii) and point (c) at **21.2** EXEMPT TRANSFERS. [*IHTA 1984, ss 27(2), 56(1)(3)(4)*].

The Board *must* so direct (on a claim being made, see below) if they are satisfied:

(a) that its property during the six years from the date on which it became comprised in the settlement can only be applied:
  (i) for the maintenance, repair or preservation of, or making provision for public access to, property which is for the time being qualifying property as defined in **30.2**(b) above in relation to which the requisite undertaking has been given under **30.3** above and no tax has become chargeable since the last undertaking given, or for defraying the expenses of the trustees or for reasonable improvement of property so held; or
  (ii) as respects income not so applied or accumulated, for the benefit of a body mentioned in **30.29** below or a charity which exists wholly or mainly for maintaining, repairing or preserving for the public benefit, buildings of historic or architectural interest, land of scenic, historic or scientific interest or objects of national, scientific, historic or artistic interest; and

(b) that any property ceasing at any time in that period (or before the death of the settlor if earlier) to be comprised in the settlement can only devolve on a body or charity as mentioned in (ii) above; and

(c) that income arising from property in the settlement can at any time after the end of that period only be applied as mentioned in (i) and (ii) above; and

(d) that the property is of a character and amount appropriate for the purposes of the settlement.

The provisions as to variations of undertakings in **30.3** above also apply to undertakings under (a)(i) above. [*IHTA 1984, Sch 4 para (3A); FA 1998, Sch 25 para 8*].

Meaning of 'repair'

In (a)(i) above structural 'repair' to the heritage property will normally qualify but alterations will not unless they are 'necessary to preserve the existing property' such as a new roof but not the conversion of a new wing of a house. Running repairs and maintenance costs will normally qualify e.g. preservation of stonework and fabric, internal redecorations and general maintenance. Heating costs will qualify where they are necessary either to maintain or preserve the building or its qualifying contents or as a consequence of public access. Where land is concerned, clearance, provision of fences and firebreaks, upkeep of ditches and fences and provision of sluices are allowable. In the gardens, seeds, plants, materials, implements, greenhouse heating costs and gardeners' wages are allowed. (VOA IHT manual, section 20, para 20.24).

Claims, etc.

FA 1998, s 144 introduces *IHTA 1984, s 27(1A)* which imposes the need to make a claim no more than two years after the date of the transfer or such longer period as the Board may allow for transfers of value made on or after 17 March 1998. The requirement of *IHTA 1984, s 27(1A)* does not apply where property enters a maintenance fund from an interest in possession trust already in existence following the death of a person entitled to that interest — see **30.26** below.

Where the transfer into the maintenance fund was an exempt transfer made by a person entitled to a beneficial interest in possession in the property (the 'beneficiary') or the transfer fell within **30.26** below, for directions given after 16 March 1987 for the reference to the settlor in (b) above there is substituted a reference to either the settlor or the beneficiary.

If a trust has been, or is to be, set up for the maintenance etc. of a property within **30.2**(b)–(e) above but the property has not been subject to a conditionally exempt transfer, the Board can, on a claim, designate the property and accept the necessary undertakings and it will then be treated as qualifying property.

[*IHTA 1984, Sch 4 para 1(1), 2(1)(a), 3; FA 1985, s 95, Sch 26 para 12; FA 1987, s 59, Sch 9 paras 2, 5*].

Where property is transferred from one settlement to another and a tax charge is excluded under *IHTA 1984, Sch 4 para 9* (see **30.27**(iii) below) or would have been excluded but for *IHTA 1984, Sch 4 para 9(4)* (see **30.27**(iii)(b) below) then (a) and (b) above do not apply and (c) applies with the omission of 'at any time after the end of that period'. The full restrictions do, however, continue to apply until the qualifying conditions have been satisfied for a period of six years from the date on which the property became comprised in the earlier maintenance settlement. [*IHTA 1984, Sch 4 para 4*].

Where more than one person is the settlor in relation to a settlement and the circumstances so require *IHTA 1984, Sch 4 paras 1–7* apply as if the settled property was comprised in separate settlements. [*IHTA 1984, s 44(2)*].

The Board may, by notice in writing, withdraw the direction from a specified date if the facts cease to warrant its continuance. [*IHTA 1984, Sch 4 para 5; FA 1985, s 95*].

The trustees must:

(i) be approved by the Board;
(ii) include either a trust corporation (i.e. a person so constituted for the purposes of the *Law of Property Act 1925* or the *Administration of Estates (Northern Ireland) Order 1979, Article 9*), or a solicitor, or a member of an incorporated society of accountants or a member of such other professional body as the Board allow; and

(iii) at the time the direction is given, be resident in the UK. For this purpose, trustees are regarded as resident in the UK if the general administration is ordinarily carried on there and the trustees or a majority of them (including a majority of each class where there is more than one class of trustees) are resident there. Where a trust corporation is a trustee, residence is determined as for corporation tax.

The trustees must furnish the Board with such accounts and other information as it reasonably requires. The trusts on which the property is held are enforceable at the suit of the Board which has the rights and powers of a beneficiary regarding the appointment, removal and retirement of trustees.

[*IHTA 1984, Sch 4 paras 2(1)(b)(2)(3), 6, 7; FA 1985, s 95*].

Transfers from discretionary settlements etc

[30.25] A charge to tax under *IHTA 1984, s 65* does not arise where property comprised in a settlement without interests in possession (**40** SETTLEMENTS: DISCRETIONARY TRUSTS AND OTHER TRUSTS OF RELEVANT PROPERTY) (the original settlement) ceases to be relevant property and either:

(a) becomes comprised in a settlement in respect of which a direction under **30.24** above then has effect (the maintenance fund), or
(b) is transferred to an individual who in turn makes an exempt transfer to such a fund within the permitted period and the value of the exempt transfer is attributable to that property. The '*permitted period*' is 30 days from the date the property ceases to be relevant property or two years if that occasion was on the death of any person.

The exemption will not apply if:

(i) the amount on which tax would otherwise be charged (before grossing-up if applicable and before BUSINESS PROPERTY (**6**) relief or AGRICULTURAL PROPERTY (**4**) relief) exceeds the value of the property immediately after it becomes, in (a) above, property in respect of which the direction has effect or, in (b) above, comprised in the maintenance settlement (less any consideration received by the original trustees under (a) or the individual under (b)). In these cases, the amount on which tax is charged is restricted to the excess without grossing-up and ignoring business property relief and agricultural property relief, or
(ii) the trustees of the maintenance fund under (a) above acquired an interest under the original settlement, at or before the time when the property in question is transferred, for a consideration in money or money's worth or as a result of transactions which include a disposition for such consideration (whether to them or another) of that interest or of other property, or
(iii) the individual under (b) above has acquired the property for a consideration in money or money's worth or as the result of transactions which include a disposition for such consideration (whether to him or another) of that or other property.

[*IHTA 1984, Sch 4 paras 16–18*].

See also the provisions of **40.19** and **40.22** SETTLEMENTS: DISCRETIONARY TRUSTS AND OTHER TRUSTS OF RELEVANT PROPERTY which also apply to property settled or appointed on maintenance funds.

Transfers from interest in possession settlements following the death of the beneficiary

[30.26] Where a person dies after 16 March 1987 but before 22 March 2006 and immediately before his death he was entitled to an interest in possession in settled property, then, subject to the exceptions below, if, within two years after his death, the property becomes held on qualifying trusts within **30.24** above (whether in the same or a different settlement) the disposition is treated as having been made by the deceased. Accordingly, no disposition or other event occurring after his death and before the property becomes subject to those trusts is, so far as it relates to the property, a transfer of value or an occasion for a charge to tax.

Where a person dies on or after 22 March 2006 and immediately before his death he was entitled to an interest in possession in settled property, then, subject to the exceptions below, if, within two years after his death, the property becomes held on qualifying trusts within **30.24** above (whether in the same or a different settlement) the disposition is treated as having been made by the deceased but only if the interest in the settlement was:

(1) an immediate post-death interest (see SETTLEMENTS WITH INTERESTS IN POSSESSION (**39**)),
(2) a disabled person's interest (see SETTLEMENTS: TRUSTS FOR DISABLED PERSONS (**44**)), or
(3) a transitional serial interest or falls within *s 5(1B)* (see below and SETTLEMENTS WITH INTERESTS IN POSSESSION (**39**)).

Where the property becomes held on the qualifying trusts as a result of court proceedings (and could only have done so) the two year period is extended to three years. An amendment to *IHTA 1984, s 57A(1A)* was made by *FA 2010, s 53(5)* which allows relief for property passing into a maintenance fund to apply in relation to settled property but this is subject to the new *IHTA 1984, s 5(1B)* interest. This new *s 5(1B)* interest is an anti-avoidance section applying to exclude relief so that the pre-22 March 2006 rules (see (1)–(3) above) applying to settled property in which there is an interest in possession applies to settled property subject to an interest in possession to which a person domiciled in the UK became beneficially entitled on or after 9 December 2009 by virtue of a disposal falling within *IHTA 1984, s 10* (not conferring gratuitous intent) are disapplied. *Finance Act 2010* changes contain no exclusion of the periodic and exit charges on relevant property from applying to settled property subject to a *s 5(1B)* interest in possession and therefore IHT charges under the relevant property rules will be imposed in addition to any IHT charges arising as a result of this section. See ANTI-AVOIDANCE (**5**).

The provisions do not apply if:

(a) the disposition by which the property becomes held on qualifying trusts depends on a condition or is defeasible;

(b) the property which becomes held on those trusts is itself an interest in settled property;
(c) the trustees who hold the property on those trusts have, for a consideration in money or money's worth, acquired an interest under a settlement in which the property was comprised immediately before the death of the beneficiary or at any time thereafter; or
(d) the property which became held on those trusts does so for a consideration in money or money's worth, or is acquired by the trustees for such a consideration, or has at any time since the death of the beneficiary been acquired by any other person for such consideration.

If the value of the property when it becomes held on the qualifying trusts is lower than that part of the value transferred on the death which is attributable to the property, the provisions apply to the property only to the extent of the lower value.

For the purposes of (c) and (d) above a person is treated as acquiring property for a consideration in money or money's worth if he becomes entitled to it as a result of transactions which include a disposition for such consideration (whether to him or another) of that or other property. [*IHTA 1984, s 57A; FA 1987, s 59, Sch 9 paras 1, 4; FA 2006, Sch 20 para 17; FA 2010, s 53*].

Property leaving a maintenance fund

[30.27] A charge to tax arises on property in an approved maintenance fund:

(a) which is applied otherwise than for the purposes in **30.24**(a)(i) or (ii); or
(b) which devolves otherwise than on a body or charity as mentioned under **30.24**(a)(ii); or
(c) which devolves on a qualifying body or charity under **30.24**(a)(ii) above but, at or before the time of devolution, an interest under the settlement in which the property was comprised immediately before the devolution is or has been acquired for a consideration in money or money's worth (or as the result of transactions which include a disposition for such consideration, whether to that body, etc. or to another person) by that or another such body, etc. For this purpose, any acquisition from another such body, etc. is disregarded; or
(d) where, if (a) or (b) above do not apply, the trustees make a disposition which reduces the value of the settled property. '*Disposition*' includes an omission to exercise a right, unless not deliberate, which is treated as made at the latest time the right could be exercised.

[*IHTA 1984, Sch 4 para 8(1)–(3)(5)(6)*].

No charge arises under the following circumstances

(i) If, under (d) above, the trustees do not intend to confer a gratuitous benefit and either the transaction is at arm's length between persons not connected with each other (see **12** CONNECTED PERSONS) or is such as might be expected in such a transaction.
(ii) If, under (d) above, the disposition is a grant of tenancy of agricultural property in the UK, Channel Islands or Isle of Man, for use for agricultural purposes made for full consideration in money or money's worth.

(iii) If the property becomes comprised in another approved maintenance fund as a result of an exempt transfer under **30.24** above within the permitted period i.e. 30 days from the date on which tax would otherwise be chargeable *or* two years if that occasion was the death of the settlor. Where the transfer into the maintenance fund was an exempt transfer made by a person entitled to a beneficial interest in possession in the property (the 'beneficiary') or the transfer fell within **30.26** above, for occasions of charge or potential charge after 16 March 1987 for the reference to the death of the settlor there is substituted a reference to either the death of the settlor or the beneficiary.

This exemption is not available.

(a) if the person making the exempt transfer acquired the property for money or money's worth or as a result of transactions which include a disposition for such consideration (whether to him or another) of that or other property, or

(b) if the amount on which tax would otherwise be charged (before grossing-up, if applicable, and before BUSINESS PROPERTY (6) relief or AGRICULTURAL PROPERTY (4) relief) exceeds the value of the property immediately after it becomes comprised in the settlement (less any consideration for the transfer received by the person who makes the transfer). The amount on which tax is charged is, however, limited to the excess, without grossing-up or taking into account business property relief or agricultural property relief.

(iv) If the settlor or his spouse or civil partner become beneficially entitled to the property, or, if the settlor has died in the preceding two years, the settlor's widow or widower or surviving civil partner become beneficially entitled to it. This exemption is not available:

(a) if, at or before the time when the settlor, etc. becomes beneficially entitled to the property, he acquires or has acquired an interest under the approved maintenance fund for a consideration in money or money's worth or as the result of transactions which include a disposition for such consideration (whether to him or another) of that or of other property, or

(b) if the amount on which tax would otherwise be charged (before grossing-up, if applicable, and before BUSINESS PROPERTY (6) relief or AGRICULTURAL PROPERTY (4) relief) exceeds the value of the property immediately after it becomes the property of the settlor etc. (less any consideration for its transfer received by the trustees). The amount on which tax is charged is, however limited to the excess, without grossing-up or taking into account business property relief or agricultural property relief, or

(c) if the property was relevant property before it became, or last became held in the approved maintenance fund and, by virtue of **30.25**(a) or (b) above, no proportionate charge to tax arose (or no such charge would have arisen apart from **30.25**(i)) on its ceasing to be relevant property. See **40.3** and **40.12** SETTLEMENTS: DISCRETIONARY TRUSTS AND OTHER TRUSTS OF RELEVANT PROPERTY for '*relevant property*' and '*proportionate charge to tax*' respectively, or

(d) if, before the property last became comprised in an approved maintenance fund (the second fund) it was comprised in another such fund (the first fund) and it ceased to be comprised in the first fund and last became comprised in the second fund in circumstances such that by virtue of (iii) above no charge to tax arose (or no charge would have arisen but for (iii)(b) above), or

(e) unless the person who becomes beneficially entitled to the property is domiciled in the UK at the time when he becomes so entitled.

Where the transfer into the maintenance fund was an exempt transfer made by a person entitled to a beneficial interest in possession in the property (the 'beneficiary') or the transfer fell within **30.26** above, for occasions of charge or potential charge after 16 March 1987 the above provisions do not apply if the beneficiary had died at or before the time when the property became property subject to the charge to tax. Otherwise, the above provisions apply with the substitution of 'beneficiary' for 'settlor' wherever occurring. Where, however, the property becomes property to which the beneficiary's spouse, civil partner, widow or widower or surviving civil partner is beneficially entitled, the charge to tax is only avoided where the spouse etc. would have become beneficially entitled to the property on the termination of the interest in possession (but see **30.26** above) if the property had not then become held on maintenance trusts.

(v) Where the property becomes held for charitable purposes only without limit of time or the property of a political party qualifying for exemption under *IHTA 1984, s 24*, a national body mentioned in *IHTA 1984, Sch 3*, or, under certain conditions, a body not established or conducted for profit (see **21.4, 21.6–21.8** EXEMPT TRANSFERS).

[*IHTA 1984, s 76, Sch 4 paras 8(3), 9, 10, 15A; FA 1987, s 59, Sch 9 paras 3, 6; The Tax and Civil Partnership Regulations 2005, SI 2005/3229, Reg 39*].

Loss to the donor principle

Tax is charged on the amount by which the trust property is less immediately after the event giving rise to the charge than it would have been but for the event (i.e. the loss to the donor principle), grossed-up where the settlement pays the tax. [*IHTA 1984, Sch 4 para 8(3)*].

Note that for the purposes of the capital gains tax counter avoidance legislation within *FA 2004, s 117, Sch 22* where trustees acquire property with the benefit of *TCGA 1992, s 260* holdover relief and are denied the relief on disposal of the property, if it is property within the meaning of *IHTA 1984 Sch 4* the main residence relief is preserved on a subsequent disposal by them. [*TCGA 1992, s 226B as inserted by FA 2004, Sch 22 para 6*]. See Note C to the Precedent in **30.24** above.

Rates of tax

[30.28] The rate at which tax is charged depends upon whether or not the chargeable property has previously been relevant property comprised in a settlement without interests in possession (**40** SETTLEMENTS: DISCRETIONARY TRUSTS AND OTHER TRUSTS OF RELEVANT PROPERTY).

(A) Where the property chargeable was relevant property before it became (or last became) held in the approved maintenance fund and, by virtue of **30.25**(a) or (b) above, no proportionate charge to tax arose (or no such charge would have arisen apart from **30.25**(i)) on its ceasing to be relevant property, the rate at which tax is charged is the aggregate of the following percentages for each complete successive quarter in 'the relevant period'

	Cumulative Total
0.25% for each of the first 40 quarters	10%
0.20% for each of the next 40 quarters	8%
0.15% for each of the next 40 quarters	6%
0.10% for each of the next 40 quarters	4%
0.05% for each of the next 40 quarters	2%
Maximum rate chargeable after 50 years	30%

'*Relevant period*' is the period *beginning* with the latest of the date of the last ten-year anniversary of the settlement in which the property was comprised before it ceased (or last ceased) to be relevant property *or* the day on which the property became (or last became) relevant property before it ceased (or last ceased) to be such property *or* 13 March 1975 and *ending* on the day before the chargeable event. Where property in respect of which tax is chargeable has at any time ceased to be and again become property in an approved maintenance fund such that by virtue of (iii) above no charge to tax arose (or no charge would have arisen but for (iii)(b) above) it is treated for these purposes as having been the property of an approved maintenance fund throughout the permitted period in (iii) above.

'*Quarter*' means a period of three months.

[*IHTA 1984, Sch 4 paras 8(4), 11*].

(B) In all other cases, the rate at which tax is charged is the higher of:

(1) the aggregate of the percentages for each successive quarter in the relevant period as in the table in (A) above (but see below for the meaning of relevant period in this context), and

(2) if the settlor is alive, the effective rate applicable to the property if it were added to the cumulative total of his chargeable transfers at the date of the chargeable event and tax calculated using the rates applicable to lifetime transfers. The rate or rates determined in respect of any occasion are not affected by the death of the settlor after that occasion, and

(3) if the settlor has died since 12 March 1975, the effective rate applicable to the property if it were added to the value of his estate on death and formed the highest part of that value. If the settlement was made on death, the death rates are used, if not, the rates applicable to lifetime transfers are used, and

(4) if the settlor died before 13 March 1975, the effective rate that would be applicable to the property if the settlor dies when the chargeable event occurred and the chargeable amount were added to and formed the highest part of the value on which estate duty was chargeable when in fact he died. If the settlement was made on death, the death rates are used, if not, the rates applicable to lifetime transfers are used.

Where the transfer into the maintenance fund was an exempt transfer made by a person entitled to a beneficial interest in possession in the property (the 'beneficiary') or the transfer fell within **30.26** above, for occasions of charge or potential charge after 16 March 1987 for the reference in (1) to (4) above to the settlor there are substituted references to the beneficiary. Under (3) and (4) if the beneficiary had died at or before the time when the property became property subject to the charge, the death rates are used, if not the rates applicable to lifetime transfers are used.

Where (4) above applies or where under (3) above the settlor died before 18 March 1986, nevertheless, the amount of tax payable is calculated as if the amendments to *IHTA 1984, s 7* in *FA 1986, Sch 19 para 2* (rates of tax for transfers within seven years of death and tapering relief) had applied at the time of death.

'*Relevant period*' under (1) above means the period beginning with the day on which the chargeable property became (or *first* became) comprised in an approved maintenance fund and ending with the day before the event giving rise to the charge. For this purpose, any occasion on which the property became comprised in an approved maintenance fund and which occurred before an occasion of charge to tax under (a) to (d) above (other than the event currently giving rise to the charge or an occasion which would not be an occasion of charge but for (iii)(b) above) is disregarded.

'*Effective rate*' in (2) to (4) is the rate found by expressing the tax chargeable as a percentage of the amount on which it is charged.

For the purposes of (2) to (4) above, where tax is chargeable on property which has previously been comprised in another settlement and ceased to be comprised in that first settlement in circumstances such that, by virtue of (iii) above no charge to tax arose (or no charge would have arisen but for (iii)(b) above), '*settlor*' is construed as a reference to the person who was settlor of the first settlement, or, if the Board so determine, the current settlement. Where property has previously been comprised in more than one settlement and ceased to be comprised in each of them and became comprised in another or the current settlement in similar circumstances, '*settlor*' is construed as a reference to the person who was settlor of the first of the previous settlements, or, if the Board so determine, any other of the previous settlements or the current settlement. Similarly, for occasions of charge after 16 March 1987 where the transfer into the maintenance fund was an exempt transfer made by a person entitled to a beneficial interest in possession in the property (the 'beneficiary') or the transfer fell within **30.26** above, '*beneficiary*' may be, if the Board so determine, construed as a reference to the person who was settlor of the current settlement or, where the property has previously been comprised in more than one settlement, any of the previous settlements or the current settlement.

Where, in the period of seven years preceding the current charge, there has been a previous charge where the tax was calculated at the rate under (2) to (4) above and the person who is the settlor for the purposes of the current charge was the settlor for the purposes of the previous charge, the amount on which tax was charged on the previous charge (or if there have been more than one, the aggregate of the amounts on which tax was charged on each) is taken for the purposes of calculating the rate of the current charge:

(i) under (2) above, to be the value transferred by a chargeable transfer made by the settlor immediately before the occasion of the current charge; and

(ii) under (3) or (4) above, to increase the value there mentioned by an amount equal to the amount or aggregate on which tax was previously charged.

This applies whether or not the settlements are the same and, if the settlor is dead, whether or not he has died since the other charge. Where the transfer into the maintenance fund was an exempt transfer made by a person entitled to a beneficial interest in possession in the property (the 'beneficiary') or the transfer fell within **30.26** above, for occasions of charge or potential charge after 16 March 1987 for the references to the settlor there are substituted references to the beneficiary.

[*IHTA 1984, Sch 4 paras 12–14, 15A; FA 1986, Sch 19 paras 38, 42; FA 1987, s 59, Sch 9 paras 3, 6*].

In (3) and (4) above, where tax is reduced by the substitution of a new Table of rates between the date of death and the chargeable event, the new rates are used. [*IHTA 1984, Sch 2 para 6*].

Property in pre-*FA 1982* maintenance funds which are treated as approved under the current provisions by *IHTA 1984, Sch 4 para 1(3)* (see **30.23** above) is for the purposes of calculation of the rates of charge treated as having become property in an approved maintenance fund at the time of the original transfer of value. [*IHTA 1984, Sch 4 para 15*].

Example 10

On 1 January 1989 P settled £500,000 in an approved maintenance fund for his historic mansion during the lives of himself and his wife, W. P died in February 1994, his taxable estate and lifetime transfers chargeable on death amounting to £175,000. On 1 January 2010, the date of death of W, the fund, which has been depleted by extensive repairs to the mansion, is valued at £300,000. £80,000 is transferred to the National Trust, which also accepts the gift of the mansion, and the balance is paid to P's grandson G.

No IHT is payable on the £80,000 paid to the National Trust, but the balance passing to G is liable to IHT at the higher of a tapered scale rate (the 'first rate') and an effective rate calculated by reference to P's estate (the 'second rate'). [*IHTA 1984, Sch 4 paras 12–14*].

First rate

The property was comprised in the maintenance fund for 20 years, i.e. 80 quarters.

The scale rate is

	%
0.25% for each of the first 40 quarters	10.0
0.20% for each of the next 40 quarters	8.0
0.15% for each of the next 4 quarters	0.6
	18.6%

Second rate

The effective rate is calculated, using half Table rates applying on 1 January 2010 (taken as those rates applying on 6 April 2009), as if the chargeable amount transferred (£220,000) had been added to the value transferred by P on his death (£175,000) and had formed the highest part of the total. Half Table rates at **37.1 2009.A1** RATES OF TAX are used because the fund was set up in P's lifetime.

		£
£137,000	at nil	—
£83,000	at 20%	16,600
£220,000		£16,600

The effective rate is

$$\frac{16,600}{220,000} \times 100\% = \quad 7.55\%$$

IHT payable is £220,000 at 18.6% =

Gifts, etc. to national bodies

[30.29] Gifts to the following bodies (i.e. *Schedule 3* bodies) whether or not national heritage property are exempt from inheritance tax. For exceptions, see 21 EXEMPT TRANSFERS.

- The National Gallery.
- The British Museum.
- The National Museums of Scotland.
- The National Museum of Wales.
- The Ulster Museum.
- Any other similar national institution which exists wholly or mainly for the purpose of preserving for the public benefit a collection of scientific, historic or artistic interest and which is approved for this purpose by the Treasury. For a list of approved institutions, see IHTM11224.

- Any museum or art gallery in the UK which exists wholly or mainly for that purpose and is maintained by a local authority or university in the UK.
- Any library the main function of which is to serve the needs of teaching and research at a university in the UK.
- The Historic Buildings and Monuments Commission for England.
- The National Trust for Places of Historic Interest or Natural Beauty.
- The National Trust for Scotland for Places of Historic Interest or Natural Beauty.
- The National Art Collections Fund.
- The National Endowment for Science, Technology and the Arts.
- The Trustees of the National Heritage Memorial Fund.
- The Friends of the National Libraries.
- Nature Conservancy Council for England.
- The Historic Churches Preservation Trust.
- Nature Conservancy Council for Scotland.
- Countryside Council for Wales.
- Any local authority within *ITA 2007, s 838*.
- Any Government department (including the National Debt Commissioners).
- Any university or university college in the UK.
- A health service body within *CTA 2010, s 986*.

Since the 1984 Act similar national institutions are, with Treasury approval or the Board of HMRC, also included in the list of bodies within *IHTA 1984, Sch 3*.

[*National Heritage Act 1980; IHTA 1984, s 25(1), Sch 3; FA 1985, s 95; National Heritage (Scotland) Act 1985, Sch 2 para 4; National Health Service and Community Care Act 1990, s 61(5); Environmental Protection Act 1990, Sch 6 para 25; National Heritage (Scotland) Act 1991, Sch 2 para 9*].

See also **21.4** EXEMPT TRANSFERS which equally applies to settled property becoming the property of bodies listed above. [*IHTA 1984, s 76*].

Sales by private treaty to national bodies

[30.30] To encourage *sales* to approved bodies as above, the conditional exemption from IHT will not be lost on such a transaction (but see **30.10**(b) above for exception where there are associated properties). [*IHTA 1984, ss 32(4), 32A(5); FA 1985, Sch 26 para 4*]. Even if the work of art has not been formally exempted from IHT, a sale of this character by concession will not normally attract CGT. The price paid by the museum etc. in a private treaty sale is based on an agreed valuation of the picture or object in the open market or at auction. The amount the buyer offers to pay takes into account the tax exemption and divides the benefit of the exemption between both parties. The government has advised museums etc. that, in general, the seller should receive 25% (10% in the case of real property) of the benefit of tax exemption, subject to negotiations above or below this figure where flexibility is appropriate. It has been suggested that this amount of 25% should be increased to 50% by Resource's *Acceptance in Lieu: A Review* in January 2001, para 3.21. The final sum received will therefore be more than the net sum on an open market sale (i.e. gross value less tax) because the seller shares in the amount of tax saved. The addition is sometimes known as 'the douceur' (see also HMRC Capital Gains Tax Manual, para 73370) and the arrangement is an administrative not a statutory one.

A claim for exemption from inheritance tax on the transfer of a heritage object, whether in life or on death, is normally made on or shortly after the transfer. Where an estate includes an object in respect of which a claim might be made, and the executors or administrators wish to sell the object by private treaty while the estate is in the course of administration and before a claim has been made, nothing in the legislation prevents designation of the object as exempt before or on such sale. The price is a matter for free negotiation between the parties but there is no capital gains tax exemption where no undertaking has been given regarding maintenance, preservation and access unless allowed concessionally. (Hansard Vol 9 No 153 Col 697, Written Answer for 31 July 1981).

No CGT is charged if property is accepted in lieu of IHT although it is usually necessary for HMRC to calculate a notional charge in arriving at the approximate tax credit. (See also VOA IHT manual, section 20, para 20.60).

Acceptance in satisfaction of tax

[30.31] If IHT has to be paid on any assets, it may be possible to offer a work of art, chattel, etc. in satisfaction of the liability. This is known as acceptance in lieu and the work of art accepted is exempt from IHT, whether or not it has been formally exempted. If the Secretary of State agrees with advice received from the Acceptance in Lieu panel, then a particular item(s) may be accepted in lieu of tax. Each Secretary of State (England, Wales, Scotland and Northern Ireland) will be ultimately responsible for the decision. The standard of objects which can be so accepted is very much higher than that applicable for conditional exemption. They have to satisfy a test of 'pre-eminence' either in the context of a national, local authority, or university collection, or through association with a particular building. A further administration requirement has been introduced to ensure that due diligence procedure with respect to the provenance and title to the chattel offered in lieu of tax. This is a result of the claims for restitution of chattels by descendants of Holocaust victims.

The benefit of the tax exemption is taken into account by adding 25% (the douceur) of the value of that exemption to the estimated value of the object after payment of notional tax. The amount thus calculated is offset against the tax liability of the estate on other property.

Example 11

Trustees of deceased Lord Charles offer to the AIL Panel a chattel estimated to be worth £1 million at auction and seven acres of land with an arboretum designed by Capability Brown valued at £500,000. The IHT liability at 40% would be £400,000 on the chattel and £200,000 on the land. The douceur in the case of the chattel is 25% of the IHT due and in the case of the land is 10%. Therefore, the amount accepted in lieu of tax with douceur in these two circumstances would be as follows:

Chattel (auction value)	£1,000,000
Less: IHT @ 40%	£(400,000)
	£600,000
Add: Douceur at 25% × £400,000	£100,000
Sub-total	£700,000
Land (Valuation by the RICS)	£500,000
Less: IHT @ 40%	£(200,000)
	£300,000
Add: Douceur at 10% × £200,000	£20,000
	£320,000
Total acceptance in lieu (AIL) for chattel and land	**£1,020,000**

Persons wishing to offer a work of art in lieu of tax should send details to Wealthy and Mid-sized Business Compliance HMRC, SO842, Heritage Team (Ferrers House), Central Mail Unit, Newcastle NE98 1ZZ. See also **32.10** PAYMENT OF TAX.

When HMRC receive an offer in lieu of tax it normally seeks the following details relating to the taxable occasion for which the offer in lieu of tax relates.

(1) A full description of the items being offered, giving, where appropriate, the artist, the medium (oil on canvas, watercolour, porcelain, bronze, etc.) and dimensions. Any exhibition history, literature and provenance should also be supplied. For archival offers, a full calendar, if available, should be supplied. Where a calendar is not on hand, a detailed description should be provided with the number of pieces in each section of the archive.

(2) Three good quality photographs, preferably in colour, of each item being offered and condition report. This is not required for archival offers.

(3) The valuation at which each item is being offered and a justification of the value by reference to previous sales of that artist or the sale of similar works. Unless HMRC have agreed to the alternative, the valuation should be that for the date the offer is made to them.

(4) Information on where the item can be inspected and contact details; and where the item was located when the tax liability in respect of it arose.

(5) Evidence of ownership and details of ownership between 1933 and 1945.

(6) A statement explaining why the items are being proposed as pre-eminent or, where appropriate, the association with an historic property.

(7) A statement of any allocation wishes or conditions that are part of the offer.

(8) A note of whether the item has been given exemption from tax or duty in the past.

Estate duty

[30.32] On the occurrence of a chargeable event, estate duty may still be payable on heritage objects granted conditional exemption under the estate duty provisions. Where the object was conditionally exempt on an inter vivos gift the 'taper' relief of *FA 1960, s 64* is only given for clawback assessments made before 3 May 1984. (HMRC Press Release 3 May 1984). See also **51** TRANSITIONAL PROVISIONS.

Key points concerning national heritage

[30.33] Points to consider are as follows.

- *Enactment of Extra Statutory Concessions Order 2009, SI 2009/730* has been given statutory effect in *TCGA 1992, s 258(2)* to provide that private treaty sales to *IHTA 1984, Sch 3* bodies of pre-eminent works of art or heritage property of companies or other bodies are not subject to CGT or CT charge from 6 April 2009. The 'douceur' (see above at **30.30**) is also now available to companies and other bodies whose chargeable gains are assessed to corporation tax.
- Single items or collections can form the subject of an acceptance in lieu claim. The usual standard items might include pictures, archives, sculptures as well as scientific and historical items. However, modes of transport such as boats, classic cars, planes, etc. can be offered as well as others.

31

Partnerships

Cross-references. See **4** AGRICULTURAL PROPERTY and **6** BUSINESS PROPERTY for relief applicable to disposal of partnership assets; **12** CONNECTED PERSONS; **32.5** PAYMENT OF TAX for payment by instalments.

Simon's Taxes. See **I6.2.**

Other Sources. VOA IHT manual, sections 7, 19; Foster, Part F2.

Introduction to partnerships

[31.1] A partnership is the relationship which subsists between persons carrying on a business in common with a view of profit. [*Partnership Act 1890, s 1*]. It is a question of fact whether a particular person is truly a party to such a relationship or is merely a senior employee who is being held out as a partner. The usual tests must, therefore, be applied in order to establish the correct relationship. The absence of a formal partnership agreement under *Partnership Act 1890* is not definitive of the existence or non-existence of a partnership. See *Burrell* [1997] STC 1413. An English partnership is not a legal entity in the same way as a company, but a *collection of separate individuals*. This being so, the provisions of inheritance tax apply to each partner as an individual and to his interest in the firm's assets. (See also VOA IHT manual, section 19, para 19.8.)

IHT400 Schedule IHT413 should be completed in respect of any partnership interest and where there are separate partnership interests or assets in partnerships, then a separate IHT413 must be completed.

'Buy and sell' agreements

[31.2] See **6.4** BUSINESS PROPERTY for the effect of a partnership 'buy and sell' agreement on the availability of business property relief on the transfer of a partner's interest in the partnership.

Goodwill

[31.3] Where goodwill is ignored for incoming and outgoing partners then *IHTA 1984, s 10* would probably apply so that there is no transfer of value. It would also apply where consideration passes which is equal to the market value or the value which would pass between persons at arm's length. See also *A-G v Boden and Another* KB 1911, [1912] 1 KB 539; *A-G v Ralli* 1936, 15 ATC 523 and *Re White (deceased) White v Minnis and Another*, Ch D [1999] 2 All ER 663.

Value of partnership interest

[31.4] Under UK law a partnership, other than a Limited Liability Partnership, is not a legal entity such that it cannot hold property. Even so, the asset held in a partner's estate is the person's rights under the partnership agreement. For IHT purposes, the valuation of any such interest should be by reference to the value of the appropriate share of each asset in the partnership, less liabilities. The partnership agreement will identify the shares of each partner in the assets held on behalf of the partnership. In general, reliefs applicable to each asset will apply. In particular for a partnership which carries on a business eligible for business property relief, relief will equally apply to the partner's interest in the business to the extent that the value of the interest is attributable to business property (*IHTA 1984, s 104*). HMRC do not allow any deduction for potential costs of sale. But see below as regards the application of business property relief to limited liability partnerships holding interests in unquoted trading companies.

In the case of partnership property the starting point is the valuation of the whole, but it is recognised that because of the fragmented ownership, a purchaser would expect to pay a lower price than if the whole of the property had been available as a single entity. Note the discount should not exceed 10%. (VOA IHT manual, section 19, para 19.8 but also see **53.6** VALUATION.)

Partnership assurance policies

Partnership assurance policies taken out before 15 September 1976 (and not varied since that date) on normal business terms on trusts under English law or Scots law provided the policy does not directly or indirectly involve a partnership itself as a separate persona) will not be regarded as settlements for inheritance tax purposes if the premiums paid fall within *IHTA 1984, s 10* (see above). The exercise of a power of appointment under a 'discretionary' trust policy would not be regarded as a variation. (HMRC Extra-Statutory Concession F10.)

Scottish partnerships

Scottish partnerships are legal entities, so that provisions relating to individuals might not strictly apply, but in practice it is thought that the provisions would be applied as for the rest of the UK.

Foreign partnerships

The situs of a partnership controlled and managed abroad is outside the UK and accordingly the interest in it of a partner not domiciled and not deemed domiciled in the UK is excluded property for IHT purposes. This remains so even though some assets of the partnership may be in the UK, for example, a commercial property or moveable assets of any kind. However, with effect from 6 April 2017, an interest in a partnership which holds UK residential property will not qualify as excluded property to the extent that the value of the partnership interest is attributable to such property: see further details at **20.2** EXCLUDED PROPERTY. There is no provision which treats a partnership as transparent for IHT purposes and thus the existence of other types of UK assets within the partnership does not affect the excluded property status of the partnership interest for non-domiciliaries.

Limited Liability Partnership (LLP)

Limited Liability Partnership (LLP) members are treated as if they are partners in a partnership. This ensures that inheritance tax will be charged in respect of members' interests in a LLP as it relates to partners' interests in a partnership and that business property relief will be available on the same basis.

As regards family limited partnerships, these are used to hold family wealth as an alternative to a trust, thereby avoiding the IHT charges which arise under the relevant property regime. To the extent that a partner contributes assets in which other partners have an interest under the partnership deed, a potentially exempt transfer arises.

Property to which a limited liability partnership is entitled, or which it occupies or uses, shall be treated as property to which its members are entitled, or which they occupy or use, as partners and therefore comprises part of their chargeable estate for IHT purposes. Any trade or business carried by an LLP is treated as carried on in partnership by the members. The incorporation, change in membership or dissolution of an LLP is treated in the same way as if it were a partnership and any transfer of value by or to an LLP is treated as made by or to its members. [*IHTA 1984, s 267A*].

Notwithstanding this treatment under *s 267A*, an LLP does not have general treatment as a transparent entity for inheritance tax purposes, and thus the interests of the partners on death or lifetime transfer are in the partnership itself and not in the underlying assets. Accordingly, HMRC consider that if the main business of a LLP is to hold shares in unquoted trading companies, the partners' interests are not in those companies but in the partnership itself whose business is 'wholly or mainly holding investments' and therefore not eligible for business property relief (ICAEW Technical Release Tech 01/14 tax). This view is disputed by leading tax counsel; the partners' interests are attributable to the value of relevant business property, that is, the shares in unquoted trading companies [*IHTA 1984, s 104*]and so should qualify for relief (see article by James Kessler QC and Oliver Marre, Taxation, 20 March 2014, p 80).

Under the terms of ICAEW Technical Release Tech 01/14 tax, HMRC allow full business property relief if the main business of the LLP is to conduct a trade and shares in companies are held as part of the business operations. If they are not so held, HMRC will consider whether they fall to be treated as excepted assets within *IHTA 1984 s 112*.

Although property to which an LLP is entitled, or which it occupies or uses, is treated for inheritance tax purposes as property to which its members are entitled this provision has the crucial qualification that this is 'as partners'

(*IHTA 1984, s 267A*), so that the partners cannot claim personal entitlement to the underlying assets. Transfers of value are similarly treated made by the individual members and not by the LLP itself. [*LLPA 2000, s 11*].

Civil partnerships

[31.5] Under the *Civil Partnership Act 2004* (CPA 2004), same sex couples may have their relationship legally recognised following a registration process which will then entitle them to acquire legal rights similar to heterosexual married couples. There are certain restrictions and the individuals who must be of the same sex must be unmarried and not party to another civil partnership whilst also not being related to each other. [*CPA 2004, s 3, Sch 1*]. Once they have their registration certificate they will be treated similarly to married couples with regard to both legal and taxation matters including IHT. [*FA 2005, s 103; The Tax and Civil Partnership Regulations 2005, SI 2005/3229*].

In *Burden & Burden v United Kingdom* [2006] ECHR Case 13378/05, [2007] STC 252, two elderly sisters lived together in a jointly-owned house on land which they had inherited from their parents. They lodged a complaint with the ECHR, contending that the provisions of *IHTA 1984, s 18* (as amended by the *Tax and Civil Partnership Regulations 2005*) were a breach of *Article 14* of the *European Convention on Human Rights*, because when one of them died, the survivor would be required to pay IHT on her sister's share of their home, whereas no IHT would have been charged if they had lived together as a registered lesbian civil partnership. The ECHR rejected their application.

A civil partner can make application under *Inheritance (Provision for Family and Dependants) Act 1975* for reasonable financial provision. [*CPA 2004, Sch 4 paras 15–27*]. For tax purposes, civil partners will be treated the same way as married couples and tax charges and anti-avoidance rules apply in equal measures. For IHT purposes, transfers between the two of them will be exempt from tax during lifetime and on death.

Key points concerning partnerships

[31.6] Points to consider are as follows.

- Whilst agricultural property relief was originally restricted to agricultural land in the UK, and will once again be so restricted from 6 April 2024, business property relief has never been subject to that geographical restriction. Therefore partnership interests held abroad will qualify for 100% BPR where the qualification requirements are met.
- Although the change to the excluded property provisions in relation to UK residential property interests were part of wider changes, including the non-resident capital gains tax provisions, when those CGT provisions were extended in 2019 to cover all UK property interests, the excluded property provisions were not similarly extended. Hence, an interest in a non-resident partnership which holds commercial property in the UK (but no residential property) continues to be excluded property for an individual partner who is not domiciled or deemed domiciled in the UK.
- An individual partner's share in a partnership (subject to meeting the necessary requirements) will obtain 100% BPR on the death of that partner, whereas an individual partner's property that is used by the partnership attracts BPR at only 50%. HMRC may accept that where property is shown on the balance sheet of partnership accounts, it is partnership property and forms an asset of the business within 100% relief. The better approach to put the position beyond doubt is for there to be a deed of trust by those holding the legal title by which it is declared that the property is held on trust for the partnership. There will be no CGT consequences provided that there is no change in beneficial ownership through the partnership but the SDLT position is complicated by the fact that partnership shares are determined solely by reference to income profit sharing, and not capital sharing ratios and there can also be subsequent SDLT charges on withdrawal of capital within three years of transfer of land to a partnership and on transfer of partnership interests.

32

Payment of Tax

Cross-references. See 3 ADMINISTRATION AND COLLECTION; 25 INTEREST ON TAX; 27 LIABILITY FOR TAX.

Simon's Taxes. See I11.4, I11.5, I11.6.

Other Sources. Foster, Part K; IHTM30000.

Due date of tax

Lifetime transfers

[32.1] Subject to the exceptions listed below, inheritance tax is due six months after the end of the month in which the chargeable transfer is made unless made after 5 April and before 1 October in any year when tax is due on 30 April in the following year.

Exceptions

Tax chargeable on the ending of conditional exemption for works of art, historic buildings etc. on woodlands and on maintenance funds for historic buildings is always payable six months after the end of the month in which the chargeable event occurs. With effect for charges arising on or after 6 April 2014 under *IHTA 1984, Part 3, Chapter 3* (relevant property trusts etc.), the same due date for payment applies. [*IHTA 1984, s 226 (3C)* inserted by *FA 2014, Sch 25, para 5(2)*].

It should be noted that tax will often become payable before accounts (see 2 ACCOUNTS AND RETURNS) are due to be rendered.

Transfers on death

[32.2] Inheritance tax is due six months after the end of the month in which death occurs but personal representatives must pay the tax for which they are liable *on delivery of their account* (even if before the due date) and may also at the same time pay any other tax on the death at the request of the persons liable. The *FA 2007* changes make provision for situations where there is a left-over pension pot at the death of an ASP scheme member who was over the age of 75 on death and was traced after their death by the scheme administrator. In such cases the left-over ASP funds are brought within the charge to IHT by *IHTA 1984, s 151A(6)* but the scheme administrator has six months from the end of the month in which they discovered the scheme member's death to pay any IHT due. [*IHTA 1984, s 226(4)* inserted by *FA 2007, Sch 19 para 25*].

Lifetime transfers with additional liability on death

[32.3] Where tax or additional tax is due at death because:

(a) a 35 POTENTIALLY EXEMPT TRANSFER proves to be a chargeable transfer; or
(b) the transferor dies within seven years of making a chargeable lifetime transfer; or
(c) the settlor dies within seven years of the transfer and a further liability arises under the rules relating to 40 SETTLEMENTS: DISCRETIONARY TRUSTS AND OTHER TRUSTS OF RELEVANT PROPERTY,

the additional tax is due six months after the end of the month in which death occurs.

[*IHTA 1984, s 226(1)–(4); FA 1986, Sch 19 para 30; FA 1988, Sch 14*].

Without prejudice to the recovery of the remainder of any tax due, the Board may, in the first instance, accept or demand payment by reference to the value stated in an account delivered to them. [*IHTA 1984, s 226(5)*].

Banking details for payment of tax

[32.4] At one time, there were separate arrangements in England and Wales, Scotland and Northern Ireland for payment of IHT, but all payments should now be made as detailed below.

For online or telephone banking, and transfers by CHAPS or Bacs: sort code 08 32 10, account number 12001136, account name HMRC inheritance tax.

For payments at a bank or building society, sort code 25 61 21, account number 63495590. From an overseas bank account, the details required are: IBAN GB66BARC20114763495590, BIC BARCGB22, account name HMRC inheritance tax.

HMRC's banking address is:
Barclays Bank PLC
1 Churchill Place
London
United Kingdom
E14 5HP

Where personal representatives apply personally for a grant of representation (see **2.21** ACCOUNTS AND RETURNS for addresses) they will be told how much tax should be paid before the grant can be obtained and the address at which the tax should be paid.

Personal representatives can draw on funds held in the deceased's bank building society account, or NS&I account solely for the purpose of paying inheritance tax prior to the grant. In this connection, Form IHT 423 should be completed.

It is also possible to surrender holdings of Government stocks in payment of IHT. This facility is run by Computershare Investor Services, contact details by email: gilts@computershare.co.uk; phone 0370 703 0143; address:

British Government Stocks (Gilts)
Computershare Investor Services plc
The Pavilions
Bristol
BS99 6ZW

It is also possible to surrender heritage property in satisfaction of an inheritance tax liability (see further details at **32.10** below and **30.31** NATIONAL HERITAGE). It is essential to obtain an HMRC Inheritance Tax reference number before making any payment otherwise the payment will be held in a suspense account and considerable delay will result. Applications for a reference number can be online or by post with Form IHT 422.

Payment by instalments

[32.5] An election in writing to the Board may be made to pay the tax due by ten equal yearly instalments in respect of property listed below. The first instalment is payable on the due date on which the whole tax would otherwise be due if it were not payable by instalments, see **32.1** above. Where the transfer is on death, the first instalment is due six months after the end of the month in which death occurs even if the personal representatives must otherwise pay tax before that date.

The tax outstanding (with interest to the time of payment, see **32.9** below) may be paid at any time. If the whole or any part of the property concerned is sold or ceases to be comprised in a settlement, then the related tax still outstanding (with accrued interest) becomes payable forthwith unless (i) the sale precedes the date that the first instalment is due in which case the tax does not become due until that date; or (ii) the sale is by the transferee following a **35** POTENTIALLY EXEMPT TRANSFER and the transferee dies before the transferor. For these purposes, the sale of an interest in a business is treated as a sale of part of the business and payment of a sum in satisfaction of the whole or part of an interest in a business otherwise than on sale is treated as a sale of the interest or part at the time of payment. Where there is a delay between the dates of contract and completion, the sale for the purposes of *IHTA 1984, s 227(4)* is deemed to take place at the completion date (Tolley's Practical Tax 1991 p 200). *Note.* Where *IHTA 1984, s 107* (see **6.8** BUSINESS PROPERTY) allows for the extension of business relief to property which replaces relevant business property in a situation where a business is acquired by a company controlled by the former owner of the business, the right to pay by instalments is in practice not lost because of the 'sale' of the business to the company (Tolley's Practical Tax 1989 p 191).

Transfers on death

[32.6] The eligible property is:

(a) land and buildings of any description, wherever situated;

(b) listed or unquoted shares or securities which gave control of the company (see **32.8** below) to the deceased;

(c) unquoted shares or securities (in relation to transfers made, and other events occurring, before 17 March 1987, shares or securities not listed on a recognised stock exchange) not within (b) above:
   - (i) which attract (together with tax on any other transfer under (a) to (e) on which the same person is liable) not less than 20% of the tax liable by that person in the same capacity; or
   - (ii) if the Board are satisfied that the tax attributable to the shares or securities cannot be paid in one sum without undue hardship;

(d) unquoted shares (not securities) (in relation to transfers made, and other events occurring, before 17 March 1987, shares not quoted on a recognised stock exchange) not within (b) with a value exceeding £20,000 where either:
   - (i) their nominal value is not less than 10% of the total nominal value of all the shares of the company at the time of death; or

- (ii) they are ordinary shares (see **32.8** below) with nominal value not less than 10% of all ordinary shares of the company at the time of the death;

(e) the net value of a business (see **32.8** below) or an interest in a business carried on for gain, including a profession or vocation.

Lifetime transfers

[32.7] The right to elect to pay tax on lifetime transfers by instalments in respect of the property listed below is restricted to cases:

(i) where the tax is borne by the person benefiting from the transfer (understood to be taken by HMRC to mean the transferee) (but see (F) below); or

(ii) where the transfer is made under the settled property provisions in *IHTA 1984, Pt III* in respect of settled property which remains in the settlement.

In relation to transfers of value made, and other events occurring, after 16 March 1987, tax cannot be payable by instalments where a **35** POTENTIALLY EXEMPT TRANSFER proves to be a chargeable transfer or additional tax becomes payable due to the death of the transferor within seven years of the transfer unless *either* the property was owned by the 'transferee' throughout the period from the date of the transfer to the transferor's death (or, if earlier, his own death) *or*, for the purposes of determining the tax (or additional tax) due, the value of the property is reduced by agricultural or business property relief by virtue of the replacement property provisions. See **4.10** AGRICULTURAL PROPERTY and **6.11** BUSINESS PROPERTY. If the property consists of unquoted shares or securities, there is an additional condition that the shares or securities remained unquoted throughout the period from the date of the transfer to the transferor's death (or, if earlier, the transferee's death).

'*Transferee*' means the person whose property the qualifying property became on the transfer or, where on the transfer the property became comprised in a settlement in which no qualifying interest in possession subsists, the trustees of the settlement.

The eligible property is:

(A) land and buildings of any description, wherever situated;

(B) listed or unquoted shares or securities which gave control (see **32.8** below) of the company to the transferor or to the trustees of the settlement;

(C) unquoted shares or securities (before 17 March 1987 and after 9 March 1992, shares or securities not listed on a recognised stock exchange) not within (B) where the Board are satisfied (on the assumption that the shares etc. are retained by the person liable to pay the tax) that the tax attributable to the shares or securities cannot be paid in one sum without undue hardship;

(D) unquoted shares etc. — as for transfers on death under (d) above;

(E) the net value of a business (see **32.8** below) or an interest in a business carried on for gain, including a profession or vocation;

(F) trees or underwood left out of account on death (see 54 WOODLANDS) and later disposed of in a lifetime transfer. In this case the right to pay by instalments is available to both the transferor and transferee and does not cease if the timber is later sold.

[*IHTA 1984, ss 227–229; FA 1986, Sch 19 para 31; FA 1987, s 58, Sch 8 paras 15–17; F(No 2)A 1992, s 73, Sch 14 paras 5, 6, 8; FA 1996, Sch 38 para 5; FA 2009, Sch 53 para 7(2)*].

Example 1

F died on 17 December 2020, leaving a free estate of £395,000, including £75,000 (after business property relief at 50%) in respect of plant and machinery used in a partnership but not held as partnership property. An election is made to pay inheritance tax on the plant and machinery by 10 equal yearly instalments.

Inheritance tax on free estate			£
On first	£325,000		Nil
On next	£70,000	at 40%	28,000
	£395,000		£28,000

IHT applicable to business property

$$\frac{75,000}{395,000} \times £28,000 \qquad £5,316$$

1st instalment due 1.7.2021	£531
2nd instalment due 1.7.2022 and annually thereafter until 1.7.2030	£531

And so on

Example 2

On 1 December 2020, G gave his land used in a partnership of which G was a partner to his son S who agreed to pay any IHT on the transfer. The land was valued at £600,000. G had made prior chargeable transfers of £140,000 and had already used his 2019/20 and 2020/21 annual exemptions. G died on 31 December 2024 when the land continued to be eligible for business relief for S.

S elected to pay the IHT by ten yearly instalments and paid the first on 1 August 2025, and the second on 1 September 2026. On 1 December 2026, he sold the land and paid the balance of the IHT outstanding on 1 February 2027. It is assumed that the rate of interest on unpaid inheritance tax for this purpose is 3% p.a. throughout.

Inheritance tax on gift

	£
Value of land	600,000
Deduct business property relief at 50%	300,000
PET becoming chargeable on death	£300,000
IHT payable in the band £140,001–£440,000	

	£	
£140,001–325,000	Nil	
£325,001–440,000 at 40%	46,000	
	£46,000	
Total IHT payable at 60% of full rates (death between 4 and 5 years after gift)		£27,600
1st instalment due 1.7.2025	2,760	
Interest at 3% from 1.7.2025 to 1.8.2025		
$^{31}/_{366}$ × £2,760 × 3%	7	
		2,767
2nd instalment due 1.7.2026	2,760	
Interest at 3% from 1.7.2026 to 1.9.2026		
$^{62}/_{366}$ × £2,760 × 3%	14	
		2,774
Balance due on sale on 1.12.2026	22,080	
Interest at 3% from 1.12.2026 to 1.2.2027		
$^{62}/_{366}$ × £22,080 × 3%	112	
		22,192
Total IHT and interest		£27,733

Note to the example

(A) Interest on unpaid tax after 5 April 1998 is calculated using 366 days as the denominator rather than 365 days. See **25.1** INTEREST ON TAX.

Definitions

[32.8] Definitions relating to **32.5** above are as follows.

'*Control of company*' by a person is when he can exercise control of a majority of votes on all questions affecting the company as a whole, and for this purpose there will be included any shares or securities which are related property (see **53.21** VALUATION) and where shares or securities are comprised in a settlement, any voting powers which they give to the trustees of the settlement are deemed to be given to the individual beneficially entitled in possession to those shares or securities (or to the trustees if there is no such individual). See *Walker's Executors v CIR* [2001] STC (SCD) 86 Sp C 275. Where there are shares or securities of any class with voting powers only on the winding-up of the company and/or on any question primarily affecting that class, then the reference above to 'all questions affecting the company as a whole' are to be read as referring to all such questions except those to which the powers of the particular class apply. In the case of *Walding and Others (Executors of Walding deceased) v IRC* [1996] STC 13 where the point at issue was whether the deceased had 'the control of powers of voting on all questions affecting the company as a whole'. [*IHTA 1984, s 269(1)*]. The deceased's holding of 45 shares out of 100 gave control, in the view of the Executors, because 24 shares held by a four year old grandson of the deceased could not realistically be exercised in the voting rights of the company due to the minor's mental or physical incapacity. The judge held that *s 269(1)* allowed relief where the deceased controlled the powers of voting on all matters affecting the company. However, even though the grandson was too young to exercise his voting rights, *s 269(1)* required his company at the date of death. The court dismissed the Executors' appeal and no BPR relief was due; *IHTA 1984, s 269(1)* deals with the ambit of the powers of voting, no the capabilities of the shareholders in whose names the shares were registered. [*IHTA 1984, s 269; ITA 2007, s 995*].

'*Ordinary shares*' are shares which carry either (i) a right to dividends not restricted to dividends at a fixed rate or (ii) a right to conversion into shares carrying such a right as in (i). [*IHTA 1984, s 228(4); ITA 2007, s 989*].

In relation to transfers of value made, and other events occurring, after 9 March 1992, then, in relation to any shares or securities, '*quoted*' means quoted on a recognised stock exchange, and '*unquoted*' means not so quoted. [*IHTA 1984, ss 227(1AA), 228(5); F(No 2)A 1992, s 73, Sch 14 paras 5, 6, 8*]. This definition applies additionally for defining relevant business property (see **6.4** BUSINESS PROPERTY) but otherwise, for transfers of value made, and other events occurring, after 9 March 1992 does not apply generally for IHT purposes. In relation to transfers of value made, and other events occurring, after 16 March 1987 but before 10 March 1992, '*quoted*', in relation to any shares or securities, means quoted on a recognised stock exchange or dealt in on the Unlisted Securities Market, and '*unquoted*', in relation to any shares or securities, means neither so quoted nor so dealt in. [*IHTA 1984, s 272; FA 1987, s 58(2), Sch 8 para 17*]. This applied for all IHT purposes and *still*, in relation to transfers of value made, and other events occurring, after 9 March 1992, does so for purposes other than defining relevant business property and the above provisions. It should also be noted that as from 1 April 1996 the word '*quoted*' on a recognised stock exchange is substituted by the word '*listed*'. [*FA 1996, Sch 38 paras 2, 5*]. In relation to transfers of value made, and other events occurring, before 17 March 1987, shares and securities in companies dealt in on the Unlisted Securities Market were not treated as quoted on a recognised stock exchange for all IHT purposes (Inland Revenue Statement of Practice SP 18/80, 23 December 1980). See IR Press Release, 25 April 2001 for the proposed revised listing arrangements and its effect on the term 'recognised stock exchange'. The Alternative Investment Market (AIM) opened for business on 19 June 1995 with transitional arrangements until 29 September 1995 (see also IRPR 20 February 1995). This market replaced the USM which was wound up at the end of 1996.

Whilst *FA 2007* inserted new definitions of 'recognised stock exchange' for the purposes of income tax and capital gains tax, the change did not include inheritance tax. HMRC have in the past confirmed that AIM shares and the erstwhile PLUS quoted market were to be unlisted for the purposes of, for example, CGT taper relief (as they were not included on the UK official list, required by new *ITA 2007, s 1005(3)*). However, the new definition for IHT will not in itself mean that the treatment of such shares will change for IHT purposes as they continue to be treated as unquoted. IHTM 25192 confirms this in relation to AIM shares. [*ITA 2007, s 1005; FA 2007, s 109, Sch 26*].

'*Net value of a business*' is the value of the assets used in the business (including goodwill) reduced by the total amount of any liabilities incurred for the purposes of the business; and in ascertaining the net value of an interest in a business, (e.g. a partnership share), regard is to be had only to those assets and liabilities which would have been used in calculating the net value of the entire business. [*IHTA 1984, s 227(7)*].

Interest

[32.9] Interest on the unpaid portion of tax payable by instalments is added to each instalment where applicable and paid accordingly. Interest on the amount outstanding runs from the due date of the first instalment except where interest relief applies, for which see further below. See **25.1** INTEREST ON TAX above for rates of interest. [*IHTA 1984, ss 227(2), 233, 234(1); FA 1989, s 179(1); FA 2009, Sch 53 para 7(3)*].

Where interest relief applies, interest is charged on each instalment from its due date. Therefore if each instalment is paid on its due date, no interest will be payable. The cases where interest relief applies are:

(i) land or buildings where it forms part of a business under **32.6**(e) or **32.7**(E) above or is agricultural property reduced by **4** AGRICULTURAL PROPERTY relief;

(ii) any shares and securities under **32.6**(b)(c) and (d) and **32.7**(B)(C) and (D) except where the business of the company consists wholly or mainly of dealing in securities, stock or shares, land or buildings or making or holding investments, save that interest relief is available if the business of the company:
   - (a) is wholly that of a 'market maker' (before the stock exchange reform, a jobber) or that of a discount house and, in either case, is carried on in the UK; or
   - (b) is that of a holding company of one or more companies whose business is not wholly or mainly dealing in securities, stock or shares, land or buildings or making or holding investments;
   - (c) includes the holding of agricultural property qualifying for relief as such (**4** AGRICULTURAL PROPERTY), in which case interest relief is available for tax attributable to the agricultural value;

(iii) any business interests not qualifying for 100% business property relief; this can include property businesses or any other type of business so long as it is carried on for gain; and

(iv) woodlands to which deferral relief applies (see **54.1**) where tax subsequently arises due to a chargeable transfer of the woodlands.

Where inheritance tax or additional inheritance tax arises virtue of the changes to deemed domicile made by *F(No 2)A 2017, s 30*, or the changes to the IHT treatment of UK residential property interests made by *F(No 2)A 2017, Sch 10*, interest runs from the normal due date or 1 January 2018, whichever is the later. This applies equally to instalments of tax. [*IHTA 1984, ss 229 and 234; F(No 2)A 2017, s 30(15)*].

Acceptance of property in satisfaction of tax

[32.10] The Board may, if they think fit and the Ministers agree, on application of any person liable to pay tax, accept property within the following categories in whole or part payment of tax and interest (see VOA IHT manual, section 20, para 20.31 and also HMRC Statement of Practice 6/87).

(a) Land. In practice only land with a particular amenity value will normally be accepted. Agricultural land as such will not normally be accepted unless it is associated with an historic building. Buildings will normally only be accepted if they are of architectural or historic interest and can be put to amenity use such as display as part of the national heritage.

(b) Any objects which are or have been kept in any building (i) accepted in satisfaction of IHT, CTT or estate duty or (ii) belonging to the Crown or Duchies of Lancaster or Cornwall or (iii) belonging to, or used for the purposes of, a government department or (iv) protected under the *Ancient Monuments and Archaeological Areas Act 1979* or the *Historic Monuments Act (Northern Ireland) 1971* or (v) belonging to certain museums and other bodies specified in *IHTA 1984, Sch 3* (see list under 30.29 NATIONAL HERITAGE). It must appear desirable to 'the Ministers' for the objects to remain associated with the building.

(c) Any picture, print, book, manuscript, work of art, scientific object or other thing which the Ministers are satisfied is pre-eminent for its national, scientific, historic or artistic interest. This includes a collection or group of such objects. (The test of 'pre-eminence' is 'would the object be a pre-eminent addition to a public collection, whether national, local authority or university?'. The object must be something which stands out for its particular qualities and will attract special attention when displayed, and is not merely a normal addition to a public collection.) However, see Taxation, 10 November 1994, p 123 regarding restrictions on the acceptance of assets of national importance in lieu of tax where those assets are exempt for other reasons e.g. BPR.

[*National Heritage Act 1980, ss 12, 13; IHTA 1984, s 230*].

HMRC and DCMS requirements

If a claim is made under *IHTA 1984, s 230* for acceptance in lieu of tax but the offeror has already paid the IHT, HMRC will not accept a subsequent offer to transfer assets in lieu, except in the circumstances set out below:

- where all the tax has been paid in advance in order to obtain the grant or confirmation, provided that at or around the time of payment HMRC are notified of the possibility that an offer in lieu of the tax will be made; or
- where HMRC are holding money on account of a liability to pay interest and tax where the money is held to the taxpayer's order but remains unpaid.

Where HMRC agree under *IHTA 1984, s 230* to accept property in satisfaction of the amount, and under those terms the valuation of the property is determined at an earlier date then the amount of tax which is satisfied by the acceptance of the property does not carry late payment interest after that date. [*National Heritage Act 1980, ss 12, 13; IHTA 1984, s 230; FA 2009, Sch 53 para 14*].

The Department for Culture, Media and Sport has drawn up a model *in situ* loan agreement for use when drawing up a loan agreement covering Chattel(s) accepted in whole or part satisfaction of capital taxes and any other liabilities under the provisions of *IHTA 1984, s 230* but which are to be displayed to the public *in situ* at the Borrower's premises.

The special price at which the item is accepted is calculated from the value of the item on the date the property is offered unless the person liable for the tax which is to be satisfied by an acceptance in lieu notifies HMRC that he wishes them to adopt the value of the property on the date of acceptance. See Inland Revenue Statement of Practice SP 6/87, April 1987. Where the 'offer date' arrangements are chosen, interest on the tax satisfied by the item ceases to accrue on that date, see **25.1** INTEREST ON TAX.

A person having power to sell property in order to raise money for payment of tax may agree with the Board for the property to be accepted under the above conditions and such agreement shall be treated as a sale made under the said power. [*IHTA 1984, ss 231, 233(1A); FA 1987, s 60; F(No 2)A 1987, s 97*]. In order to facilitate the above, the *Exchequer Audit Department Act 1866, s 10* will be required to contain information about property accepted in lieu of tax on or after 1 April 1998. [*FA 1998, s 145*]. The appointed day for the purposes of this section is 4 November 1998. [*Finance Act 1998, s 145, (Appointed Day) Order 1998, SI 1998/2703*].

'*The Ministers*' means the Secretary of State and the Lord President of the Council. [*National Heritage Act 1980, s 12(1); IHTA 1984, s 230(5); SI 1986/600*].

For further details in relation to acceptance of property in satisfaction of tax, see **30.31** NATIONAL HERITAGE, the Valuation Office IHT Manual Appendix 29 and HMRC Statement of Practice 6/87.

Certificates of tax deposit

[32.11] Certificates of tax deposit Series 7, which enabled money to be set aside for payment of future tax liability, may still be used in payment of inheritance tax. Interest accrues on these certificates from the date of purchase until the date on which the tax in respect of which they are surrendered falls due. After a six-year period from the date of purchase, certificates cease to be eligible for further interest. Certificates ceased to be available for purchase from 23 November 2017 as the scheme is now closed for new purchases, but existing certificates will continue to be honoured until 23 November 2023.

HMRC charge

[32.12] Where any tax or interest is unpaid, an HMRC charge is imposed for that amount on:

(a) any property to which the tax is attributable by its transfer;
(b) any property comprised in a settlement where the chargeable transfer arises on property becoming comprised in the settlement or is made under *IHTA 1984, Pt III* in respect of settled property; and
(c) any property relating to heritage assets charged under the existing provisions of *IHTA 1984, ss 32, 32A, 79, Sch 4 para 8* or *Sch 5 para 1* or *3*. Where the event giving rise to the charge is a disposal to a purchaser of the property or object in question, no charge may be imposed on that property or object or any property for the time being representing it.

The charge may be imposed on any property directly or indirectly representing the above.

[*IHTA 1984, s 237(1)(2)(3B)(3C); FA 1999, s 107*].

HMRC charge not applying

No charge may be imposed on:

(i) personal or movable property in the UK (excluding leaseholds in relation to deaths after 8 March 1999) treated as transferred on the death of the beneficial owner (other than settled property in which the deceased was beneficially entitled to an interest in possession) and which vests in his personal representatives;
(ii) heritable property situated in Scotland (but where this is disposed of, any property representing it is subject to the charge).

[*IHTA 1984, s 237(3)(4); Trusts of Land and Appointment of Trustees Act 1996, Sch 14; FA 1999, s 107*].

Priority of charge

[32.13] An HMRC charge on any property is effective after any incumbrance thereon which is allowable as a deduction in valuing that property for the purposes of IHT e.g. a mortgage. [*IHTA 1984, s 237(5)*].

Validity of charge on disposition

[32.14] A disposition of property subject to an HMRC charge takes effect subject to that charge. However, property disposed of to a purchaser will not be subject to any HMRC charge if at the 'time of disposition'

(A) in the case of land in England and Wales, the charge was not registered as a land charge or, in the case of registered land, was not protected by notice on the register; or
(B) in the case of land in Northern Ireland the title to which is registered under the *Land Registration Act (Northern Ireland) 1970*, the charge was not entered as a burden on the appropriate register maintained under that *Act* or was not protected by a caution or inhibition or, in the case of other land in NI, the purchaser of the property had no notice of the facts giving rise to the charge; or
(C) in the case of personal property situated in the UK other than in (A) and (B) above, and of any property situated outside the UK, the purchaser had no notice of the facts giving rise to the charge; or

(D) in the case of any property, a certificate of discharge (now 'closure letter', see **32.15** below) had been given by the Board and the purchaser had no notice of any fact invalidating the certificate.

In the above circumstances, the charge ceases to apply to the property but then applies to the property representing it. (Note that the above does not apply to a donee who would receive property subject to any charge whether or not it was registered or he had notice of it.) [*IHTA 1984, ss 237(6), 238(1)*].

'*Time of disposition*' means (i) in relation to registered land, the time of registration of the disposition; and (ii) in relation to other property, the time of completion. [*IHTA 1984, s 238(3)*].

Where a **35** POTENTIALLY EXEMPT TRANSFERS proves to be a chargeable transfer, property concerned which has been disposed of to a purchaser before the transferor's death is not subject to an HMRC charge but property concerned which has been otherwise disposed of before the death and property which at the death represents any property disposed of to a purchaser is subject to the charge. [*IHTA 1984, s 237(3A); FA 1986, Sch 19 para 34*].

Where property is disposed of to a purchaser subject to an HMRC charge, such charge ceases to apply after six years from the later of the date on which the tax became due and the date on which a full and proper account of the property was first delivered to the Board in connection with the chargeable transfer concerned. [*IHTA 1984, s 238(2)*].

A closure letter (previously a certificate of discharge, see **32.15** below) cancels any HMRC charge applying to the property specified. [*IHTA 1984, s 239(3)*]. Applications for the cancellation of an HMRC charge entered on property under the *Land Registration Acts 1925–1971* should be made on Form Cap 37. See **2.9** ACCOUNTS AND RETURNS for automatic discharge of 'excepted estates' and **2.12** for 'excepted terminations' of settled property.

Clearance letters and certificates

[32.15] On application by the person liable for tax on the transfer of specified property, the Board may give a certificate to confirm that all IHT attributable to it has been, or will be, paid. Application is made on Form IHT30. For assets which were transferred on death or where the transferor has died, the person liable for the tax may require a certificate to be issued where HMRC are satisfied that the tax has been or will be paid, or that none is payable. A full account must have been delivered in all cases. An application with respect to the tax which is or may become chargeable by a **35** POTENTIALLY EXEMPT TRANSFERS may not be made earlier than two years after the transferor's death (except as allowed by the Board at any earlier time after death). Such a certificate will discharge the property from HMRC charge (see **32.12** above) on its acquisition by a purchaser. HMRC will however normally decline to give a certificate during the transferor's lifetime in respect of a chargeable lifetime transfer because further tax may be due in the event of the subsequent death of the transferor. [*IHTA 1984, s 239(1)(2)(2A)(3)(5); FA 1986, Sch 19 para 35*].

Application for clearance should not be made until the applicants are reasonably certain that all aspects of the estate have been settled. This means that executors should have checked with the trustees that the value of all settled property has been notified and agreed with HMRC. Trustees should have made similar enquiries of executors before lodging their application.

It is usual now for HMRC to issue a letter of clearance without specific request for it, before closing their file on a particular case. These letters are known as non-statutory assurances and have the same effect as a formal clearance certificate (IHTM40001). The letter will be unsigned but contains a reference code which is used to establish that the letter is genuine.

Effect of fraud or failure to disclose material facts etc

[32.16] The above certificates are invalid in a case of fraud or failure to disclose material facts and do not affect any further tax on further property afterwards shown to be included in a deceased's estate immediately before his death or arising from an alteration of dispositions under a deed of family arrangement or similar document. They are valid in favour of a purchaser of property who had no notice of any invalidation. [*IHTA 1984, s 239(4)*] A closure letter will also be invalid where a claim under *IHTA 1984, s 8A(3)* has been overstated.

For HMRC's practice regarding the liability of personal representatives previously issued with a closure letter who discover a further chargeable lifetime transfer, see 27.7 LIABILITY FOR TAX.

Excepted estates

[32.17] Subject to the same rules regarding fraud etc. (see above), where an estate is an excepted estate (see 2.9 ACCOUNTS AND RETURNS), if the Board do not issue a notice calling for an account, the personal representatives will automatically be discharged from any further claim for tax or charge on property at the end of the prescribed period. In these cases, there is no need to apply for a closure letter. If the Board issue a notice calling for details of the estate, automatic discharge does not apply and the normal course must be followed. [*SI 2002/1733*; Inland Revenue Press Release 2 July 1987].

Excepted terminations

[32.18] Where the termination of an interest in possession is an 'excepted termination' (see 2.12 ACCOUNTS AND RETURNS), unless within the period of six months from the termination the Board issue a notice requiring an account, the trustees will be discharged from any claim for tax on the value of that property. This provision does not discharge any person in a case of fraud or failure to disclose material facts. [*SI 1981/1440; SI 2002/1731*].

Recovery of tax

[32.19] No legal proceedings to recover tax or interest can be taken by the Board unless the amount has been agreed in writing or specified in an undisputed notice of determination (see 14 DETERMINATIONS AND APPEALS). Tax and interest may, without prejudice to any other remedy, be sued for and recovered in a Scottish sheriff court if the amount sought does not exceed the sum for the time being specified in the *Sheriff Courts (Scotland) Act 1971, s 35(1)(a)*.

Where proceedings to recover tax or interest are taken in a county court or sheriff court, the court may be addressed by any authorised officer of the Board, and a certificate by an officer of the Board that the tax or interest is due or that, to the best of his knowledge and belief, it is unpaid is sufficient evidence of that fact in any proceedings for its recovery.

If an appeal to the Tax Tribunal, or direct to the High Court, is pending, only agreed undisputed tax is recoverable. Where an appeal is taken a stage further, the disputed tax is payable (and adjusted after that appeal has been determined). [*IHTA 1984, ss 242–244, 254(2); FA 1993, s 200(2)(3)*].

Adjustment of tax

Underpayments

[32.20] Where too little tax has been paid, the deficiency is payable with interest whether or not the original payment was stated in a notice of determination; but where the payment was made and accepted in full satisfaction of tax in accordance with an account duly delivered to the Board no proceedings for any additional tax may be brought after six years from the later of:

(a) the date on which the payment (or last instalment) was made and accepted; and
(b) the date on which the tax (or last instalment) became due.

At the end of that period any liability for additional tax and any HMRC charge for that tax is extinguished. See also **32.15** above.

If there is fraud, wilful default or neglect by a person liable for tax, the six years begin when the Board first has knowledge of these circumstances. For periods starting on or after 1 April 2009 where the return is due on or after 1 April 2010 the six-year period is reduced to four years. In certain cases the six-year time limit remains in place in a case where there is a loss of tax brought about by 'careless' action by a person liable for the tax (or a person acting on behalf of such a person). Proceedings in such a case of 'careless' action may be brought at any time not more than six years after the later of the date on which the payment of tax was made (and accepted by HMRC) or the date tax was due and this includes payments made by the instalment option. Further, in a case involving a loss of tax brought about by 'deliberate' action by a person liable for the tax (or a person acting on behalf of such a person) may be brought at any time not more than 20 years after the later of those dates. [*Finance Act 2008, Schedule 40 (Appointed Day, Transitional Provisions and Consequential Amendments) Order 2009, SI 2009/571*].

This also applies to fraud by the settlor of a settlement in the case of tax chargeable under the rules relating to **40** SETTLEMENTS: DISCRETIONARY TRUSTS AND OTHER TRUSTS OF RELEVANT PROPERTY. In the case of a settlement the new provisions above apply to a person liable for the tax and are to be treated as including references to a person who is the settlor in relation to the settlement. [*IHTA 1984, s 240; FA 2009, Sch 51 paras 11, 12*].

Where the fraud etc. is by a settlor, HMRC have confirmed that they would not seek to recover the full amount of the additional tax due from the trustees of the settlement personally where the trustees had acted in good faith and had insufficient trust funds left with which to pay the tax. (Law Society's Gazette 12 December 1984).

HMRC's Concession A19 (Arrears of tax arising through official error) is unavailable where an inheritance tax liability is in point. The concession applies only to income tax, capital gains tax and class 4 National Insurance Contributions.

Overpayments

[32.21] Where an overpayment of tax or interest is proved to the satisfaction of the Board, repayment will be made provided the claim is made within four years from the payment (or last payment). Where the return was due before 1 April 2010, a six-year time limit applied. [*IHTA 1984, s 241; FA 2009, Sch 51 para 13* and see HMRC Statement of Practice SP 6/95].

If too much tax was paid because of a mistake by HMRC or any other government department, repayment can be claimed outside the statutory time limit (see HMRC Extra-statutory Concession B41). Due to the European Convention on Human Rights and *Human Rights Act 1998* which came into effect on 2 October 2000, HMRC cannot seek penalties from the personal representatives of a deceased person who was liable for a penalty. In addition, any such penalties already collected must now be repaid and these repayments should include repayment interest at the rate applicable under *IHTA 1984, s 233*. Such interest would run from the date the penalties are paid to the date of repayment by HMRC (IHTM36166).

For Scotland only, the time limits above do not apply to adjustments of tax arising due to a person claiming or renouncing his right to legitim. See **49.21** TRANSFERS ON DEATH. [*IHTA 1984, s 147(8)(9)*].

Payment by court

[32.22] Where IHT is attributable to any property in the possession or control of a court pending proceedings for its administration, the court must provide any unpaid tax, or interest, out of such property. [*IHTA 1984, s 232*].

Payment on previous view of law

[32.23] Any payment made and accepted in satisfaction of any liability for tax and on a view of the law then generally adopted, will only be disturbed on the same view of the law, notwithstanding that it appears from a subsequent legal decision or otherwise that the view was or may have been wrong. [*IHTA 1984, s 255*].

Foreign assets

Payment out of foreign assets

[32.24] Where, because of restrictions imposed by the foreign government, executors cannot immediately transfer to this country sufficient of the deceased's foreign assets for payment of the inheritance tax liability attributable to them, they are given the option of deferring payment until the transfer can be effected. If the amount in sterling that the executors finally succeed in bringing to this country is less than this tax, the balance is waived. (HMRC Extra-statutory Concession F6).

Foreign-owned works of art

[32.25] Where a work of art normally kept overseas becomes liable to inheritance tax on the owner's death solely because it is physically situated in the UK at the relevant date, the liability will be waived if the work was brought into the UK solely for public exhibition, cleaning or restoration. Despite the flexibility of concession F7 it is perhaps wise to ensure that HMRC is approached in these circumstances to ensure that no IHT liability will be attached if the foreign domiciliary dies with an artwork in the United Kingdom and a chargeable event arises. If the work of art is held by a discretionary trust (or is otherwise comprised in settled property in which there is no interest in possession) the charge to tax under *IHTA 1984, s 64* (ten-year anniversary charge) will similarly be waived.

Powers to raise tax etc.

[32.26] Any transferee or devisee who is liable to tax (including interest) on the value of any property may raise the money by sale or mortgage of, or a terminable charge on, that property whether or not the property is vested in him. A person with limited interest in the property who pays the tax is entitled to a similar charge on the property as if raised by a mortgage to him. [*IHTA 1984, s 212*].

Refund by instalments

[32.27] Where a person has paid tax which is or might at his option have been payable by instalments and he is entitled to recover part or the whole of it from another person, that other person (unless otherwise agreed between them) is entitled to refund the tax by the same instalments (and with the same interest thereon) as might have been paid to the Board. [*IHTA 1984, s 213*].

Certificates of tax paid

[32.28] A person who has paid tax not ultimately due from him may apply to the Board for a certificate specifying the tax paid and the debts and incumbrances allowed in valuing the property and any certificate is conclusive evidence of payment as between the payer and the person by whom the tax specified falls to be borne. [*IHTA 1984, s 214*].

33

Penalties

Simon's Taxes. See **I11.7.**

Other Sources. Foster, Part L7; Adjudicator's Leaflet AO 1; IHTM36000.

Introduction — IHT penalties

[33.1] A uniform penalty regime to apply across all taxes administered by HMRC is in the process of being introduced. Penalties will fall under three main headings:

(1) failure to deliver an account;
(2) inaccuracies in returns delivered;
(3) late payment of IHT due.

Other penalties apply to those who give false information to another person for the purposes of an account to be delivered by that person and failure to notify HMRC of an under-assessment issued by it. There is in addition a penalty for failure to make a return under *IHTA 1984, s 218* (formation of non-resident trusts).

The uniform penalty regime is to be brought into effect by Statutory Instruments. At present only the penalties for inaccuracies in returns, giving of false information and failure to notify under-assessments have been brought into effect; see *Finance Act 2008, Sch 40 (Appointed Day, Transitional Provisions and Consequential Amendments) Order 2009, SI 2009/571*. The existing IHT penalty regime in *IHTA 1984, Pt VIII* continues to apply to other compliance failures, until such time as the remaining aspects of the uniform penalty regime are brought into effect for IHT.

This chapter details the penalty regime as currently in force. The final part at Chapter 33 summarises aspects of the uniform penalty regime which have yet to be brought into effect.

Errors in accounts — the post-31 March 2009 penalty regime

[33.2] Where documents are to be filed with HMRC for inheritance tax purposes the penalty regime under *FA 2007, Sch 24* applies with effect for documents where the liability to pay IHT arises on or after 1 April 2010, or in the case of documents produced under the excepted estates regulations (see 2.11 ACCOUNTS AND RETURNS) where the death is on or after 1 April 2009. These penalties apply to errors in documents or information supplied for the purposes of an IHT return and where the error is either careless or deliberate. The previous IHT penalty regime will apply to events occurring before those dates. [*IHTA 1984, s 247(1), (2); FA 2007, s 97, Sch 249; FA 2008, Sch 40 para 21(c); FA 2009, s 106, Sch 55; Finance Act 2008, Sch 40 (Appointed Day, Transitional Provisions and Consequential Amendments) Order 2009, SI 2009/571*].

Definitions — Reasonable care, careless, deliberate and concealed

An inaccuracy is 'careless' if it is due to a failure to take reasonable care. References to negligence in the preparation of accounts only apply prior to the introduction of the uniform penalty regime. The reasonable care will be satisfied where personal representatives have followed HMRC written guidance, made suitable enquiries of asset holders, ensured valuations followed correct instructions and generally sought advice where necessary and cleared up inconsistencies in information received. HMRC consider the personal representatives should obtain at least one professional valuation of assets such as properties although there is no requirement to do so if the value can be clearly established by some other method. Where an agent is appointed by the personal representatives to do the work then on receiving the completed IHT400 or IHT205/207/C5 forms from the agent the personal representatives should check the forms to ensure that all relevant material details required have been included. Where IHT is payable other than in connection with a death by, say, a transferor or trustee then similarly they should ensure that all relevant material details required have been included even where completed. For instance, where an agent has been appointed to complete the necessary documentation this fact will not excuse the personal representatives, transferor or trustees from their responsibility to ensure that the documents supplied to HMRC are accurate and could result in a charge of carelessness and attract the appropriate penalty charge as shown in the table below.

If an inaccurate return is now submitted to HMRC then the inaccuracy may be reviewed to determine whether it can be categorised as *careless, deliberate but not concealed* or *deliberate and concealed*. HMRC consider reasonable care has been taken where accurate records have been kept to ensure returns are correct, checking what the correct position is when it is unclear and then advising HMRC promptly of any error. In defining 'reasonable care' HMRC state that 'it is simply a question of examining what the person did or failed to do and asking whether a prudent and reasonable person would have done that or failed to do that in those circumstances'. However, there will be different interpretations in certain unique circumstances and it will be a case which is in dispute that proceeds to the tribunals and courts. See *Cairns (personal representatives of Webb deceased) v R & C Commissioners* [2009] STI 1801 TC00008 where a summons alleging fraud and negligence was dismissed because *'Something more than the bare words of the relevant statute were required to ensure that fair notice was given'*. Also, the inaccuracy penalty percentage will depend on whether the nature of the disclosure was prompted or unprompted and the penalty adjudged depending on that circumstance. [See *FA 2007, Sch 24 para 3(1)(a)*]. See also Taxation Magazine 19 February 2009, page 172.

Level of penalty

As stated above, in considering the penalty position with regard to *careless*, *deliberate* or *deliberate and concealed*, HMRC will consider whether the disclosure of an inaccuracy was *prompted* or *unprompted*. In the table below, 'unprompted disclosure' means that the person has no reason to believe that HMRC have discovered or are about to discover the failure to pay the required contributions. 'Prompted disclosure' is likely to apply in all other cases. Where the person has made a prompted disclosure in a 'careless' case, this attracts a maximum 30% penalty of potential lost revenue but this may be reduced as in the table where the person liable then assists in determining the quantity of unpaid IHT and allowing HMRC access to records to check the amount unpaid tax that has been quantified. There are examples of how the reduction for disclosure will be calculated in the Compliance Handbook at CH82440 onwards.

Finance Act 2015, Sch 20 introduced amendments to the level of penalties and these apply to documents given to HMRC in relation to transfers of value made on or after 1 April 2016. The amendments restrict the table below to inaccuracies relating to 'domestic matters'. Where the inaccuracy relates to an 'offshore transfer' or an 'offshore matter', higher penalties apply, depending on the overseas territory concerned. 'Offshore matters' relate to assets situated in a territory outside the UK for inheritance tax purposes immediately after the relevant chargeable transfer. 'Offshore transfers' are those where the chargeable disposition involves a transfer of assets and after it is made, but before the filing date for the IHT return, the assets or part of them are transferred outside the UK with deliberate intent.

Four categories of overseas territories are stated in the legislation. The categories are designed to take account of the degree to which information exchange takes place with the territory concerned. The normal level of penalty, i.e. ranging from 30% to 100%, applies for a category 0 territory, which is for those adopting automatic exchange of information with the UK. The higher levels of penalty will be 37.5% for category 1 territories, 87.5% for category 2 territories and 125% for category 3 territories, reduced by up to one-half for prompted disclosure, and minimums for unprompted disclosures of 0% 25% and 40% respectively.

There are provisions for reduction of penalties because of special circumstances, suspension of penalties where this will help to avoid further penalties for careless inaccuracies, and a right of appeal to the Tribunal. However the power to mitigate under *TMA, s 102* is disapplied. [*FA 2008, Sch 40 (Appointed Day, Transitional Provisions and Consequential Amendments) Order 2009, SI 2009/571; TMA, s 103ZA*].

Since the only possibility for reducing a penalty for careless error to nil is where unprompted disclosure is made to HMRC, it follows that all such errors should be notified to HMRC as soon as they come to light. To reduce the need to make separate disclosure each time an amendment to an IHT account becomes necessary HMRC have stated that 'in future there will be no need to notify HMRC every time there's an amendment to the initial calculation. Provided the changes do not:

- total, individually or collectively, more than £50,000;
- comprise items of land/realty or unquoted shares;
- comprise loss on sale of land or shares claims;
- relate to a case that is subject to a compliance check,

they should be notified 18 months from the date of death or at the point the estate is finalised, whichever is earlier.

HMRC guidance states that 'penalties are not charged for inaccuracies on returns where a taxpayer has taken reasonable care to get it right. If an inaccuracy was due to reasonable care not being taken, we will not charge a penalty provided:

- you give us full details about the inaccuracy and why it happened by the dates specified above; and
- you had no reason to think we were about to discover the inaccuracy.

Penalties may be charged if applicable if the notification is incomplete or the original inaccuracy was deliberate or deliberate and concealed.'

[HMRC Trusts and Estates Newsletter April 2012].

Factor	Disclosure	Minimum Penalty	Maximum Penalty
Careless	Unprompted	0%	30%
Careless	Prompted	15%	30%
Deliberate, not concealed	Unprompted	20%	70%
Deliberate, not concealed	Prompted	35%	70%
Deliberate & Concealed	Unprompted	30%	100%
Deliberate & Concealed	Prompted	50%	100%

Errors related to avoidance arrangements

In establishing the level of penalty due, a presumption of carelessness applies to IHT returns and other accounts which under-declare liability by reason of tax avoidance arrangements. Note however that avoidance is very widely defined to include any arrangements having a main purpose of reducing the liability or increasing a relief so contrary to the normal meaning of avoidance it can include any conceivable steps to mitigate liability, however basic. There is an exclusion for arrangements which accord with established practice which HMRC accepted at the time the arrangements were entered into. Arrangements within DOTAS as considerably widened with effect from 1 April 2018 (see **5.10**), and arrangements counteracted under an anti-avoidance rule are always to be taken to be tax avoidance arrangements.

The foregoing applies to returns and other accounts given to HMRC on or after 16 November 2017 and which relate to a period for which IHT is charged that begins on or after 6 April 2017 and ends on or after 16 November 2017.

The presumption of carelessness does not apply to deliberate inaccuracies, nor does it apply if HMRC, or the Tribunal on appeal, is satisfied that reasonable care was taken. However the reasonable care defence is not available for 'disqualified advice', defined as advice given by an interested person (being, broadly, a person involved in setting up the avoidance arrangements); or advice given to a person as a result of arrangements between an interested person and the person giving the advice; or advice given by a person without appropriate expertise; or advice which took no account of the client's circumstances; or advice given to a third party. Disqualified advice given by a person who facilitated the avoidance arrangements may be taken into account if the adviser had appropriate expertise and took account of the client's circumstances, provided always that the arrangements fail only because an anti-avoidance rule (other than the GAAR) applies. However for this let-out to apply the arrangements must not be within DOTAS, which may assist for planning before 1 April 2018 but from that date most IHT planning is within DOTAS unless it has no contrived or abnormal steps (both terms are undefined).

These provisions are applied to the personal representatives of a deceased person in the same way that they apply to the deceased.

The foregoing applies to returns and other accounts given to HMRC on or after 16 November 2017 and which relate to a period for which IHT is charged that begins on or after 6 April 2017 and ends on or after 16 November 2017.

[*F(No 2)A 2017, s 64*].

Other penalties for errors

A penalty of 100% of potential lost revenue applies where a person deliberately supplies false information to, or deliberately withholds information from, another person for the purposes of an IHT account to be submitted by that other person. The penalty may be reduced to 30% for unprompted disclosure, and 50% for prompted disclosure. See *T C Hutchings v HMRC* [2015] UKFTT 9 (TC), TC04221in which a 50% penalty, amounting to £87,533, was upheld where the son of the deceased had received a substantial gift of cash offshore a few months before the death but failed to mention it to the executors in response to their enquiries about lifetime gifts. [*FA 2007, Sch 24 para 1A*].

A penalty of 30% of potential lost revenue applies where a person fails to take reasonable steps to notify HMRC of an under-assessment, or determination showing too little tax, issued by HMRC. HMRC must consider whether the person knew, or should have known, about the under-assessment. The penalty may reduced to 15% for prompted disclosure. [*FA 2007, Sch 24 para 2*].

The wide-ranging powers given to HMRC to give notice in writing requiring a person to provide information or to produce documents apply to inheritance tax from 1 April 2009. These can give rise to a tax-related penalty after fixed penalties have been issued but the failure by the taxpayer continues. This tax-related penalty can be a very substantial sum in the context of inheritance tax; see *HMRC v Tager* [2015] UKUT 0040 (TCC) in which a tax-related penalty of £1,171,020 was imposed by the Tribunal for failure to deal with HMRC enquiries in relation to a death in March 2005, with return submitted late in January 2009, and information notices issued in September 2011 not attended to. The penalty was subsequently reduced to £200,000 by the Court of Appeal.

Penalties for enablers of defeated tax avoidance were introduced by *F(No 2)A 2017, s 65*, designed to apply to the minority who devised aggressive avoidance schemes. The penalty is broadly equal to the fees charged.

Failure to make a return penalty

[33.3] Where a person liable to deliver an account fails to do so within the prescribed period he is liable to a penalty of £100. If no proceedings for declaration of the failure are commenced within six months of the date by which the account should have been delivered, and the accountable person has not delivered the account by the end of that six-month period, there is a further liability to a penalty of £100. These penalties are restricted, in total, to the amount of the taxpayer's IHT liability. There is a further penalty not exceeding £60 for every day after the day on which the failure has been declared by a court or the Tax Tribunal and before the day on which the account is delivered. This latter liability is avoided if the account is delivered before proceedings in which the failure could be declared are commenced. In addition to the foregoing penalties, if the failure to deliver an account continues after one year from the latest date by which it should have been delivered, and there would have been liability to tax shown in the account, a penalty not exceeding £3000 may be imposed. HMRC's standard calculation of penalties payable for late submission of accounts is set out at IHTM 36023.

Where a person has a reasonable excuse for the failure, he is not liable to a penalty unless he fails to remedy it without unreasonable delay after the excuse has ceased [*IHTA 1984, s 245*].

From 6 April 2016, penalties under this heading in relation to offshore matters and offshore transfers are brought within the scope of the scheme already existing for income tax and capital gains tax under *FA 2009, Sch 55*. This will introduce higher penalties for such cases at the same levels as described above for errors in returns.

[*FA 2015, Sch 20; Finance Act 2015, Schedule 20 (Appointed Days) Order 2016, SI 2016/456*]

Penalties for offshore matters

Offshore tax non-compliance

[33.4] Severe penalties may be incurred by any person who, at 5 April 2017, had any compliance failure, whether due to simple misunderstanding or for more serious reasons, or any outstanding undeclared liability to IHT, where:

(a) it involves an offshore matter, being assets situated or held in a territory outside the UK immediately after an occasion by reason of which IHT is payable, or activities carried on wholly or mainly in such a territory, or anything having effect as if it were such assets or activities;
(b) on 17 November 2017, the liability could lawfully have been assessed by HMRC (see time limits at **3.7**) and on the assumption that it has not been corrected by that date;
(c) there is further failure to correct the non-compliance by 30 September 2018, whether by making the necessary return, communicating the liability to an officer of HMRC in the course of an enquiry, or using any other agreed method.

The penalty is 200% of the potential lost revenue (as defined), which may be reduced for disclosure, but not below 100%. The penalty does not arise where there is a reasonable excuse for the failure but the provisions relating to reasonable excuse are set out in some detail, largely designed to encourage independent review of offshore structures before 30 September 2018. Relying on 'disqualified advice' will not be reasonable excuse. Such advice includes advice was given by a person without appropriate expertise, or advice which failed to take account of all the taxpayer's individual circumstances so far as relevant, or which was given to someone other than the taxpayer. Where offshore avoidance arrangements are concerned, advice is disqualified if it was given by an interested party (however eminent), being in broad terms a person who was involved in setting up the offshore structure. Avoidance arrangements are defined to mean anything which reduces tax liability, but not those which accord with established practice or in relation to which HMRC had indicated acceptance of them when they were set up.

It will be appreciated that with an inheritance tax liability of 40% and a minimum penalty of 100%, plus interest on the tax, these provisions could result in complete confiscation of the funds concerned. They are therefore of great importance where, for example, there is doubt concerning the domicile status of the settlor when a settlement was made (with consequent relevance as to whether funds involved are excluded property), or where there are other grey areas concerning the IHT treatment of assets held overseas. The reasonable excuse exclusions are probably directed at offshore employee benefit trusts but are not limited in any way. [*F(No 2)A 2017, Sch 18*].

Penalty for offshore asset moves

[33.5] With effect from 27 March 2015, a penalty applies where assets are moved on or after that date from a 'specified territory' to a 'non-specified territory' and the main, or one of the main purposes, of the movement is to prevent the discovery of a loss of revenue by HMRC. It is intended that territories will be 'specified' by Statutory Instrument once they have committed to exchanging information under the new Common Reporting Standard. There must be an 'original penalty' for a deliberate failure to correct an inaccuracy or make a return, followed by an offshore asset move to prevent or delay discovery by HMRC of the loss of tax. The 'original penalty' may be one arising under the provisions detailed above for offshore tax non-compliance.

Where an asset move has been made (see below), an additional penalty may be imposed where a person has been liable for an earlier penalty for a deliberate failure to make a return or for deliberate error in documents submitted. The additional penalty is 50% of the earlier penalty.

The asset moves giving rise to the additional penalty can be of various types: firstly, where the taxpayer remains beneficial owner of the asset even though the asset has moved from a specified territory to a non-specified territory; secondly, where the person holding the asset made a corresponding change of residence; and thirdly, where there has been a change in ownership arrangements of the asset. In applying the tests, any second or later asset purchased with all or part of the proceeds of sale of the original asset will be regarded as the original asset.

There is a right of appeal to the Tax Tribunals against the penalty. Also in two situations a person will not be liable to the additional penalty, these being where:

- the tax unpaid as a result of a deliberate error in a document giving rise to the original penalty has been assessed or determined before 27 March 2015; and
- the tax unpaid as a result of a failure to make a return giving rise to the original penalty has been assessed or determined before 27 March 2015 and the failure relating to it has been remedied by that date.

The reason for the introduction of this additional penalty is that as more overseas territories enter into agreements to provide greater automatic exchange of information with the UK under the new Common Reporting Standard, with first information exchanges to be made in 2017, HMRC consider that there is a risk that money and investments will be moved from those territories to others that have not entered into such agreements in order to continue to hide past failures to pay tax lawfully payable. [*FA 2015, Sch 21*].

[*FA 2015, s 121, Sch 21*].

Asset-based penalty for offshore inaccuracies

[33.6] Where the potential lost revenue for a deliberate compliance failure in relation to an offshore matter or offshore transfer exceeds £25,000, an asset-based penalty may be incurred. The penalty is the lower of 10% of the asset value or the offshore potential lost revenue multiplied by 10. For the purposes of inheritance tax, the asset concerned is the property disposed of giving rise to a transfer of value for IHT and as a result of which a standard offshore penalty has been charged (see *FA 2007, Sch 24* and *FA 2008, Sch 41*), or a penalty under the provisions detailed above for offshore tax non-compliance. [*FA 2016, Sch 22*].

Penalty assessment procedure

[33.7] Penalty assessment procedure — where a penalty has been assessed as payable, notified to the taxpayer as well as the period for which the penalty is assessed then the penalty must be paid within 30 days of the date on which the notice of penalty is issued. The procedure in these circumstances is the same as for existing assessments to tax. Supplementary assessments may be issued where an earlier penalty assessment was underestimated. The assessment must be made on or before the later of two stipulated dates: the first date is the last day of the period of two years beginning with the date in column 4 of the table at *FA 2009, Sch 56 para 1(4)* i.e. the last date on which payment may be made without incurring a penalty. See also **32.1** PAYMENT OF TAX. The second date is the last date of the period of twelve months beginning with the end of the appeal period of the assessment of tax to which the penalty applies, or if there is no assessment made the date on which the amount of tax is ascertained. A right of appeal is open to the taxpayer. See **14.1** DETERMINATIONS AND APPEALS.

Example

X dies on 26 November 2009 and the personal representatives (PRs) to the estate made the necessary return on Form IHT400 and paid the tax due within the six month period. Prior to his death X had been contacted by HMRC regarding omissions from his tax returns in connection with an offshore account (IHT421 Probate summary). X had ignored the enquiry letter and subsequent reminders prior to his death. The personal representatives have now received notification of the enquiry and after making investigations they produce a letter from an offshore account that although the address is the same as the deceased the name on the account is different to that of the deceased. Enquiries of the agent acting for the deceased unearth the fact that X sent the letter to him and asked what he should do. The agent stated that in his view the wrong address had been entered incorrectly by the offshore bank and unless X knew any differently the bank should be notified that they had sent the letter to the wrong address. X died before the agent could receive a reply from him as to the action he had taken.

Further enquiries and full documentation provided to HMRC by the PRs and agent regarding the deceased reveal that X was also known by an alternate name and the alias was included in the will when it was drawn up but was overlooked when the death certificate was drawn up and when the oath was sworn. The letter from the offshore bank states that the capital in the account amounts to £120,000. The outstanding IHT due on this is charged at 40% on the whole sum as the nil rate bands have been utilised and no exemptions exist in respect of the offshore account.

HMRC, apart from the ongoing income tax obligations, review the penalty situation

	£
The PRs have made a *prompted disclosure* of a *careless* inaccuracy.	
The Potential Lost Revenue (PLR) is £48,000*.	48,000
The percentage for the quality of the disclosure has been calculated as 60%. See Note C below.	
The maximum penalty is 30% and the minimum penalty is 15%. So the maximum disclosure reduction is 30% – 15% = 15%	
The actual reduction percentage for disclosure is 15% × 60% = 9%	
Penalty percentage to be charged is 30% – 9% = 21%	
The penalty to be charged is £48,000 × 21% =	10,080
Total IHT and penalty due	58,080
*IHT (PLR) on an omitted estate of £120,000 = £48,000	

Note to the example

(A) HMRC indicate in example 4 at CH82422 what a prompted disclosure is considered to be: 'During an enquiry into an inheritance tax account, we referred the value of the deceased's house to the Valuation Office Agency and tell the personal representatives that we have done so. The personal representatives subsequently correct the value upwards saying that they sold the property for the higher value shortly before submitting the account. This is a prompted disclosure.'

(B) The disclosure reduction is obtained by assessing the quality of each of the three elements of the disclosure i.e. timing, nature and extent of the disclosure. In this case HMRC have concluded that there was no initial disclosure so no discount applies but there was full assistance by the PRs (and agent) uncovering why the document was inaccurate and why HMRC were not told about the under-assessment with a positive approach to explaining the omission (30% discount). Finally, the extent of the disclosure was full and unreserved by the PRs (30% discount). See also CH82440, CH82450 and CH82460.

Summary of penalties under IHTA 1984

[33.8] Failure to deliver an IHT account under *IHTA 1984, s 216* or a corrective supplementary account under *IHTA 1984, s 217*. See **2.5** to **2.16** ACCOUNTS AND RETURNS.

A penalty of £100 applies unless the tax payable is less than £100 or there is a reasonable excuse (see below). A further penalty of £100 is due where proceedings in which the failure could be declared are not commenced within the period of six months from the date that the account was due to be delivered and where the account has not been delivered at the end of that six-month period. The total of these penalties cannot exceed the amount of tax payable.

A daily penalty of up to £60 applies from the date the failure is declared by a court or the Tribunal (now see **14.1** DETERMINATIONS AND APPEALS) until the account is delivered.

[*IHTA 1984, s 245*].

Failure to make a return under *IHTA 1984, s 218* (non-resident trustees) and failure to comply with a notice under *IHTA 1984, s 219 as amended by FA 2000, s 147(2)* (power to require information). See **2.18** and **2.19** ACCOUNTS AND RETURNS.

Penalty up to £300 applies plus a daily penalty of up to £60 from the date the failure is declared by a court or the Tax Tribunal until the return is made. [*IHTA 1984, s 245A*].

Failure to comply with a notice under *IHTA 1984, s 219A* (power to call for documents, etc.). See **2.19** ACCOUNTS AND RETURNS.

Penalty up to £50 applies plus daily penalty of up to £30 from the date the failure is declared by a court or the Tribunal until the notice is complied with.

Continued failure to deliver an IHT account under *IHTA 1984, s 216(6), (7)*. See **2.15** ACCOUNTS AND RETURNS.

A penalty charge of up to £3,000 applies if the failure to deliver an account continues after the anniversary of the filing dates within *IHTA 1984, s 216(6), (7)* unless there is a reasonable excuse for the late delivery.

Failure to comply with requirements of *IHTA 1984, s 218(A)*. See **13.3** DEEDS VARYING DISPOSITIONS ON DEATH.

A penalty can arise where a disposition on death is varied by the beneficiaries and gives rise to an additional tax liability. In these circumstances where there is a failure to deliver instrument varying a disposition and notification of additional tax payable within eighteen months. [*IHTA 1984, s 245A(1B)*].

No penalty arises where there is 'reasonable excuse' for the failure unless the person fails to make the return or comply with the requirements of *IHTA 1984, s 218A* without unreasonable delay after the excuse has ceased. [*IHTA 1984, ss 245(7) and 245A(5)*]. See also IHTM36023.

Definition — reasonable excuse

No penalty arises under the IHT penalty regime (but not the uniform penalty regime under *FA 2007, Sch 24*) where there is *reasonable excuse* for the failure unless the failure is not remedied without unreasonable delay after the excuse has ceased. But see *F(No 2)A 2017, s 64* for situations where there is no reasonable excuse as regards tax avoidance arrangements; see **33.2** above.

Note that unlike penalties under *s 245(2)(a),(3)*, penalties of up to £3,000 under *s 245(4A)* are not capped by the amount of tax on the account.

[*IHTA 1984, ss 245, 245A as amended by FA 1999, s 108; FA 2004, s 295(2), (3) and (5)–(8) and Transfer of Tribunal Functions and Revenue and Customs Appeals Order 2009, SI 2009/56, paras 120, 121*].

Fraudulent or negligent supply of information

[33.9] Fraudulent or negligent supply of information or documents to the Board. From 1 April 2009, penalties for inaccuracies in returns, information, documents, statements or declarations made to HMRC which result in the loss of tax or an over-repayment of tax are dealt with under the provisions of *FA 2007, Sch 24*. These provisions apply across all taxes and the penalties are tax-geared.

There is also a penalty payable by any person not liable for tax where that person fraudulently or negligently provides any incorrect information or document to HMRC. The penalty is a maximum of £3,000. [*IHTA 1984, s 247(3)*].

Discovery

[33.10] Errors discovered of a material respect in any information or document supplied by a person without fraud or negligence shall be treated as negligence under **33.9** parts (a)(ii) or (b)(ii) above unless remedied without unreasonable delay. 'Unreasonable delay' is not a fixed defined period but within HMRC's Compliance Handbook in relation to direct tax matters it refers to more than 30 days from the date of issue of the assessment. See CH81090. If any other person notices an error in a return etc. not submitted by him whereby tax for which that other person is liable has been or might be underpaid, he must inform the Board without unreasonable delay, otherwise he will be subject to the penalty for negligence under **33.9**(b)(ii) above. [*IHTA 1984, s 248*].

Procedure

[33.11] Penalty proceedings are by the Board (in Scotland, by the Board or the Lord Advocate) and may be commenced before the Special Commissioners [now Upper Tribunal] or in the High Court (or the Court of Session as the Court of Exchequer in Scotland) as civil proceedings by the Crown. An appeal may be lodged by either party against decisions by the Special Commissioners (see **33.2** above and **14.1** DETERMINATIONS AND APPEALS) on a question of law and by the defendant (or, in Scotland, the defender) against the amount of penalty awarded which may be confirmed, reduced or increased by the Court. Any penalty awarded by the Special Commissioners [now Upper Tribunal] is recoverable by the Board as a debt due to the Crown. [*IHTA 1984, ss 249, 252; Transfer of Tribunal Functions and Revenue and Customs Appeals Order 2009, SI 2009/56, para 122*]. *Summary penalties* may be awarded by the Special Commissioners in respect of **33.8** and **33.9** above with appeal available to the High Court (or Court of Session in Scotland). [*IHTA 1984, s 251; SI 1994/1813, Sch 1 para 22*]. The Board may mitigate penalties before or after judgment. [*IHTA 1984, s 253*].

Time limits

[33.12] No proceedings for penalties may be brought more than three years after notification by the Board of the tax properly payable in respect of the chargeable transfer concerned. The European Convention on Human Rights and *Human Rights Act 1998* which came into effect on 2 October 2000 has now confirmed that HMRC cannot seek penalties from the personal representatives of a deceased person who was liable for a penalty. In addition any such penalties already collected must now be repaid and these repayments should include repayment interest at the rate applicable under *IHTA 1984, s 233*. Such interest would run from the date the penalties are paid to the date of repayment by HMRC. [*IHTA 1984, s 250*].

False statements

[33.13] 'False statements to prejudice of Crown and public revenue' are indictable as a criminal offence (*R v Hudson* CCA 1956, 36 TC 561). In the case of *R v Fogon* [2003] STC 461 a question arose as to whether the appellant fell within *Criminal Justice Act 1988, s 71(4)* 'a person benefits from an offence' or *s 71(5)* 'a person derives a pecuniary advantage'. The Judge held that the prosecution's approach was correct and that the case was covered by *s 71(4)* as:

> 'He diverted the money to a concealed account for his own purposes and failed to declare it to the Inland Revenue.'

Therefore it was concluded that 'money transferred to the account [Company] was property obtained in connection with the commission of the offence' and came within *s 71(4)*.

Mitigation

[33.14] The *Finance Act 2007, Sch 24* introduced a new framework of penalty impositions from 1 April 2008 relating to direct tax matters including 'careless', 'deliberate' and 'concealed' actions which result in loss of tax; however, inheritance tax was initially excluded and had its own framework for penalty sanctions but now see above for the position from 1 April 2009 where documents (IHT400 or IHT205/207/C5) containing inaccuracies are to be filed with HMRC from 1 April 2010. [*IHTA 1984, s 253*].

In relation to the IHT penalty regime HMRC will normally exercise their statutory power under *IHTA 1984, s 253* to charge a lower penalty in a negotiated settlement. Starting with the maximum figure of penalty HMRC will reduce it depending on how much is disclosed to them, how co-operative the parties are and how grave the offence. The rule of thumb that HMRC use in their negotiations will be as follows:

Disclosure — a reduction in the penalty of up to 20% (or even up to 30% with full and voluntary disclosure). However, if there is denial that anything is wrong until the last possible moment then there will be little or no reduction. Full and voluntary disclosure without prompting from HMRC will attract the maximum reduction or thereabouts. HMRC indicated that in between these two extremes a wide variety of circumstances are possible and consideration will be given to the amount of information given, how soon it was given and how that information contributed to the settling of the enquiries by HMRC.

Co-operation — a reduction in the penalty of up to 40%. If information is supplied to HMRC promptly after discovery and questions are answered honestly and accurately then the maximum reduction will apply. In addition, the maximum reduction is dependent on the relevant facts being supplied and the tax, once it is calculated, being paid promptly. Delays, untrue or evasive answers, or nothing was done until HMRC took formal action will not attract a reduction at all.

Gravity — a reduction of 40%. HMRC take into account the reasons for failing to deliver an account and the amount of money involved. The less serious the matter the bigger the reduction in the penalty.

Penalties yet to be brought into effect

[33.15] Failure to make return penalties under *FA 2009, Sch 55* have yet to be brought into force for IHT by Statutory Instrument. It is understood that HMRC are continuing to work on the introduction of these penalties in conjunction with counsel. When brought into force, the uniform penalty applying across virtually all taxes administered by HMRC will apply to IHT. In summary, these provide that where a penalty has been assessed as payable, and failure continues after the end of the period of three months beginning with the penalty date a penalty of £10 for each day is charged whilst the failure continues during the period of 90 days beginning with the date specified in the notice of penalty given by HMRC. [*FA 2009, Sch 55 paras 2, 3 and 4*]. If the failure to pay the penalty continues after the end of the period of six months beginning with the penalty date, then a further loading penalty of 5% of any liability to tax which would have been shown in the return in question or £300 whichever is the greater. [*FA 2009, Sch 55 para 5*]. Where the failure to pay the penalty continues after the end of the period of 12 months beginning with the penalty date, then there is a further loading penalty. However, the penalty will depend on whether the original inaccuracy was deliberate but not concealed or deliberate and concealed. In the case of the former, the further loading penalty is 70% of any liability to tax which would have been shown in the return in question or £300 whichever is the greater. In the case of the latter, the further loading penalty is 100% of any liability to tax which would have been shown in the return in question or £300 whichever is the greater. In all other cases, there is a further loading penalty of 5% of any liability to tax which would have been shown in the return in question or £300 whichever is the greater.

[*FA 2009, Sch 55 para 6*].

Late payment of tax penalty

A new penalty regime is to be introduced for the late payment of inheritance tax. The regime was set up by *FA 2009, Sch 56* to apply across virtually all taxes administered by HMRC but has yet to be brought into force for IHT by Statutory Instrument. A right of appeal will be included and if it is determined that a reasonable excuse applies for the failure then the penalty may be discharged or mitigated. Also, if the taxpayer enters into a payment agreement with HMRC to pay the inheritance tax then any late payment penalty will be removed if the taxpayer meets the terms of the agreement. See also **32.1** PAYMENT OF TAX.

Under the forthcoming regime, a taxpayer will be liable to pay a penalty of 5% of the unpaid tax. If the amount of this tax remains unpaid after the end of 5 months beginning with penalty date then the taxpayer is liable to a penalty of 5% of that amount. Further, if any amount of that tax is still unpaid after the end of the period of 11 months beginning with the penalty date a further 5% penalty is payable. [*FA 2009, Sch 56 para 3*]. In certain cases where there are penalty provisions HMRC may stay the penalty or agree a compromise but this will not apply where the taxpayer is unable to pay the penalty or there is a potential loss of revenue which is balanced by a potential overpayment by another taxpayer. [*FA 2009, Sch 56 para 9*].

In a case where a taxpayer is subject to a tax charge makes a request of HMRC to defer the payment before the penalty date and HMRC agree to defer that charge before (or after) the date then the taxpayer is not liable to the penalty at that time. If the taxpayer breaks the agreement then the penalty will be due by reference to the date of issue of the original notice. Such an agreement between the taxpayer and HMRC is broken if the tax is not paid by the end of the deferral period or there is non-compliance by the taxpayer of a condition of the agreement. [*FA 2009, Sch 56 para 10*].

Key points concerning penalties

[33.16] Points to consider are as follows.

- The introduction of the uniform tax penalty regime in 2008 can give rise to very substantial penalties in the context of inheritance tax and any suggestion that the Tribunals would mitigate them to any great extent, given that inheritance tax liabilities are commonly significant amounts as compared to other taxes, is a serious misapprehension. The case of *Tager v HMRC* (see **33.2** 'Other penalties for errors') demonstrates that the Tax Tribunal will see nothing wrong with imposing a 100% penalty for failure to respond adequately to a notice to supply information where the tax liability is over £1,000,000 and the failure to supply information and make returns has persisted for some years, although the appellant in that case was fortunate enough to get the penalty substantially reduced on further appeal.
- We have yet to see the penalties for late payment of tax brought into effect for inheritance tax purposes, but no doubt the time is coming when that will take place. HMRC say that they are currently working on the practical issues involved. When these are brought into effect, the old regime under which interest only is charged will be replaced and the standard late payment of tax penalties applicable to self-assessment will apply to inheritance tax. Practitioners dealing with inheritance tax returns will need to take the utmost care in order to avoid such penalties being claimed from them personally by their clients.

34

Pension Schemes

Cross-references. See **20.6** EXCLUDED PROPERTY for overseas pensions; **21.18** EXEMPT TRANSFERS for dispositions conferring retirement benefits; **28** LIFE ASSURANCE POLICIES AND ANNUITIES.

Simon's Taxes. See **I4.125**, **I5.633–I5.635**.

Other Sources. Foster, Parts C1.55, D1.25, E6.36–37, K1.25.

Introduction to pension schemes

[34.1] Property held as part of a superannuation scheme or fund (including retirement annuity contracts) approved by HMRC for income tax purposes or, after 22 July 1987, held under approved personal pension arrangements and, from 6 April 2006, registered pension schemes (or *ICTA 1988, s 615(3)* schemes) or a qualifying non-UK pension scheme is not subject to inheritance tax under the provisions relating to settlements without interests in possession (**40** SETTLEMENTS: DISCRETIONARY TRUSTS AND OTHER TRUSTS OF RELEVANT PROPERTY). This remains the case where the funds remain in the pension scheme after the death of the scheme member.

However, if the funds are paid across to a pension bypass trust, usually formed by the pension scheme member for the purpose of protecting the fund against excessive withdrawals by the person entitled to the benefits after his or her death, such a trust will be a relevant property trust, liable to IHT charges in the normal way. Note also that the provisions relating to property moving between settlements will apply in such cases (*IHTA 1984, s 81*) so that the trust is treated as commencing when the member joined the original pension scheme, with consequent impact on the timing of ten yearly charges and other related IHT charges. If the funds are derived from different pension schemes, they will remain comprised in different settlements for IHT purposes and more than one nil rate band may be available.

Transitional relief is available for funds which are not in a registered pension scheme but to which exemption under *IHTA 1984, s 151* applied before 6 April 2006. If no contributions are made after that date, the exemption continues to apply and the funds will continue to be outside the relevant property provisions (see **40**). If contributions are made after that date only, a proportion of the funds will be exempt as above, as regards which a formula is used to calculate the 'protected proportion'. [*FA 2004, Sch 36, paras 56–58*].

The majority of approved pension schemes are outside the estate of the member of the scheme so that no liability to IHT arises on the member's death but this is not the case if the trustees of the scheme have no discretion over payment of benefits on the death.

Contributions

A contribution to a pension scheme is not a transfer of value for IHT purposes if it is allowable in computing profits or gains for the purposes of income tax or corporation tax. HMRC's view is that this applies to contributions by employers for their employees but not those made by the self-employed for whom contributions are given relief by reference to relevant earnings, and are not a deduction in calculating the amount of them for tax purposes. In most cases however, a transfer to a pension scheme is made without gratuitous intent, because the scheme member contributes in order to make provision for his or her retirement. It is not therefore a transfer of value by virtue of *IHTA 1984, s 10*. In exceptional circumstances, there may be gratuitous intent, for example where contributions are made at a time when the taxpayer is in poor health with a view to increasing the pension benefits available to children after decease. HMRC practice is to review contributions made within the two years prior to a death if they are substantial and not part of a regular pattern. These may be regarded as a transfer of value for IHT purposes if the purpose was to reduce the estate liable to IHT. See HMRC Inheritance Tax manual, para IHTM 17043.

Pension schemes — application

[34.2] Where a person is entitled to an interest in or under a scheme etc. which ends on his death, the interest will not be included in his estate if it:

(a) is, or is a right to, a pension or annuity, and
(b) is not an interest resulting from the application of any benefit provided under the fund or scheme otherwise than by way of a pension or annuity.

Other rights (e.g. a right to repayment of contributions or to a lump sum on death before retirement age) are chargeable to IHT. If the deceased's estate is entitled to other post-death payments as of right, for example, annuity payments which continue for a period of time after the death, their value as at the death is taxable as part of the estate on death.

A person entitled to a pension or annuity satisfying the conditions of (a) and (b) above is not treated as being beneficially entitled to the property in which the interest subsists. The fund is not, therefore, liable to IHT on his death. In the case of Guaranteed Annuities if the deceased was receiving payments under an annuity and died before the end of the annuity period, the right to receive the remainder of the payments is an asset of the estate and the value should be included on Form IHT 406 at page 1. See below. HMRC have prepared an annuity calculator on their website which calculates the open market value of remaining period.

Where a person has a general power to dispose of their benefits as they think fit, they are treated as beneficially entitled to the interest: see *IHTA 1984, s 151(4)* which modifies the provision relating to general powers of appointment *(s 5(2))* so that it will apply in the case of pension funds. In practical terms, this means that if the scheme member is able to make a binding nomination of the funds remaining on their death, those funds will be subject to IHT as part of the member's estate. If, however, a benefit passes only at the discretion of the trustees of the scheme and is not a legally enforceable claim by the personal representatives, there is no liability to inheritance tax. See *Kempe and Roberts (personal representatives of Lyon, deceased) v CIR* [2004] STC SCD 467 Sp C 424.

HMRC's Statement of Practice 10/86 confirmed that, in a UK registered scheme where the death benefit is held on discretionary trusts under the scheme rules, this will not be a gift with reservation where:

1. the deceased; or
2. the deceased's estate; or
3. the deceased's personal representatives,

   are potential beneficiaries. This practice continues in force but it should be noted that it does not apply to an unregistered pension scheme such as an EFRB.

Some older pension plans were not set up under trust, for example, retirement annuity policies under *Taxes Act 1970, s 226*. In such cases, death benefits may be payable to the estate of the plan holder and therefore be liable to IHT as part of the estate. To prevent this, the death benefit could be assigned into a discretionary trust. Where there is a tax liability, it is due from the pensioner or his personal representatives but not from the trustees of the scheme etc.

[*IHTA 1984, s 151*].

Cash options

[34.3] When a person dies and his widow or other dependant becomes entitled to an annuity under the terms of a superannuation scheme or fund (including annuity contracts) or, after 22 July 1987, the terms of approved personal pension arrangements or, after 5 April 2006, registered pension schemes (or *ICTA 1988, s 615(3)* schemes), or a qualifying non-UK pension scheme, the fact that the deceased could have chosen instead that a cash sum be paid to his personal representatives is not to be regarded as giving him the type of 'general power' within *IHTA 1984, s 5(2)* (see **19.3** ESTATE) which would result in that sum being included in his estate on death. [*IHTA 1984, s 152; F(No 2)A 1987, s 98(5); FA 2004, s 203(5); FA 2008, Sch 29, para 18*].

Benefits under pension schemes from 6 April 2011

[34.4] *FA 2011, Sch 16* removed the requirement to buy an annuity by the age of 75 and the alternatively secured pension rules were repealed, both with effect from 6 April 2011. Individuals are able to leave their pension funds invested after their retirement age and commence drawdown at any later time of their choosing.

From April 2015, there are, in principle, no restrictions on the amount of funds which can be taken after retirement. An income tax charge applies on funds withdrawn subject to a tax-free allowance equal to 25% of the fund, or 25% of the lump sum allowance if lower. This allowance is fixed at £268,275 from 6 April 2024. Death benefits from the funds held for those who die before age 75 and which are designated to drawdown within two years of the death remain tax-free. A lump sum and death benefit allowance of £1,073,100 applies from 6 April 2024 such that if death occurs before the age of 75, a lump sum taken from the fund is tax free up to this amount, but after deducting any tax-free lump sum taken in lifetime. Amounts taken in excess of the allowance are taxed at the beneficiary's marginal rate of income tax. Following the death of the scheme member who has attained the age of 75, nominated beneficiaries can alternatively take either a lump sum or periodic benefits from the pension scheme and these will be taxed at their marginal rate of income tax. Pension funds which fall under these flexible provisions can be nominated to a beneficiary post-death, and the use of previous pension bypass trusts is no longer necessary, although these should still be considered in certain circumstances such as where the fund is to be used to provide an income for a surviving spouse and after their death, to provide funds for children of a previous marriage.

Because of these changes with effect from 6 April 2011, inheritance tax ceased to apply to drawdown pension funds remaining under a registered pension scheme, including when the individual dies after reaching the age of 75. Also with effect from 6 April 2011, inheritance tax charges under *IHTA 1984, s 3(3)* (omission to exercise rights) that could otherwise apply to registered pension schemes and qualifying non-UK resident pension (QNUP) schemes where the scheme member omits to take their retirement entitlements (e.g. a failure to buy an annuity) were removed. Strictly this exemption did not apply where the rights had been exercised and the pension was in drawdown, but this drafting error is now corrected with retrospective effect by insertion of *IHTA 1984, s 12A*. Thus *IHTA 1984, s 12 (2A)–(2E)* and *ss 151A, 151B, 151BA, 151C, 151D, 151E* are all repealed with effect from 6 April 2011. These changes will also apply to superannuation funds that are occupational pension schemes by virtue of *TA 1988, s 615(3)*. [*IHTA 1984, ss 12(2ZA), 12A, 151*].

Funds in a registered pension scheme applied to pay lump sum payments are taken to be held for the purposes of the scheme until payment is made so that no IHT charge arises on payment. Funds in *ICTA 1988, s 615(3)* schemes and qualifying non-UK pension schemes will not attract charges under the relevant property regime if they are paid within the stipulated time frame of two years by the pension scheme trustees or persons having control of the scheme. The time allowed for the payment of lump sum by the scheme will run from the date on which the pension scheme is notified of the scheme member's death or, if earlier, when the scheme trustees or persons having control of the scheme could reasonably have been aware of that member's death. [*IHTA 1984, s 58(2A)*].

Pension transfers

[34.5] Those with pension benefits in defined benefit or final salary pension schemes may choose to transfer the cash equivalent transfer value (CETV) to a SIPP, albeit generally with a requirement to obtain specialist advice first.

HMRC consider that the transfer is a lifetime transfer by the scheme member but this has no IHT implications if the member is in good health at the time of transfer. If, however, the scheme member has health issues at that time, there may be donative intent if the transfer is designed to enhance the death benefits available to family members on death and a transfer of value arises under. In practice, this is not applied to transfers made more than two years prior to death, but IHT 409 must be completed where there is a transfer within that two-year period. If, after the transfer, the scheme member vests all the benefits in the transferee scheme, there will be no transfer of value because there can be no intention to enhance death benefits. In other cases of ill-health where a transfer is made within two years of death, it may be argued that there is no transfer of value because *IHTA 1984, s 10* applies (dispositions made without gratuitous intent, see **1.4**).

The argument that *s 10* applies was rejected by the Court of Appeal in *Revenue and Customs Comrs v Parry (as personal representatives of Staveley, decd)* [2017] UKUT 4 (TCC), [2017] STC 574, but ultimately upheld on the facts by the Supreme Court ([2020] UKSC 35) which noted that, notwithstanding the pension transfer, the funds in the policy would have gone to the same beneficiaries by one route or another. The facts were that the deceased was diagnosed with terminal cancer early in 2006. Subsequent to that, she transferred the funds in a *s 32* pension plan into a personal pension plan, the terms of which would allow the entire fund to be paid to her estate or to other beneficiaries. She was keen to ensure that her ex-husband could not benefit from the fund. She took no benefits from the policy prior to her death in December 2006 and nominated her two sons as the beneficiaries to receive the death benefits from the fund although strictly any payments remained payable at the discretion of the pension trustees.

HMRC considered that the transfer of funds from the *s 32* policy was a disposition within *IHTA 1984, s 3(1)* for IHT purposes but the executors argued that it was exempt as being made without gratuitous intent – the purpose was to ensure the fund could not benefit the ex-husband. The Supreme Court upheld the argument of the executors on this point. It is open to question whether the same decision would have been reached if the deceased had taken the decision not to draw benefits at the same time as, or after, the pension transfer.

HMRC also considered that the failure to take pension benefits was an omission to exercise a right within *IHTA 1984, s 3(3)* which caused an increase in the sons' estates. The Upper Tribunal rejected this argument because it could not be said that the sons' estates were necessarily increased; the pension trustees might have exercised their discretion to pay the funds to other potential beneficiaries. However, this decision was reversed by the Court of Appeal on the basis that the pension trustees would follow the express wishes of the deceased and provide the benefits to the sons. Their estates would, therefore, be increased as a result. The Supreme Court agreed on this point. This part of the decision is of limited application following the introduction of *IHTA 1984, s 12A* in 2016 which provides that *IHTA 1984, s 3(3)* no longer applies to the failure to take benefits from drawdown funds, but note that *s 12A* does not apply to EFRBs.

HMRC consider that where *s 10* does not apply, the transfer of value may be calculated as the value of the CETV less the value of the rights retained by the scheme member. Those retained rights are the tax-free pension cash lump sum available from the transferor scheme plus the value of the remaining funds net of the tax which would be payable if all drawn out. See further *Taxation* 4 January 2018, pp 12–15 and 8 October 2020, pp 12–16.

Case law applying up to 5 April 2011

[34.6] In *DM Fryer & Others (Personal Representatives of Ms P Arnold) v HMRC* [2010] UKFTT 87 (TC), TC00398, a woman was born in 1942 and in 1995 she set up a discretionary trust. Later that year, she took out a pension plan. It was agreed that if she died before taking her retirement benefits, then the value of those benefits would pass to her discretionary trust. In 2002, shortly before her 60th birthday, she was diagnosed as suffering with terminal cancer. She died in 2003 without having taken the available benefits. HMRC issued a determination charging IHT on the basis that, by failing to take her retirement benefits when she reached the age of 60 in 2002, she had made a disposition of value for the purposes of *IHTA 1984, s 3(3)*. Her personal representatives appealed, contending firstly that she should not be treated as having made any such disposition, and alternatively that if she had made such a disposition, it was not 'intended to confer a gratuitous benefit', so that *IHTA 1984, s 10(3)* applied. The First-tier Tribunal rejected these contentions and dismissed the appeal in principle, subject to a reduction in HMRC's valuation of the disposition. Clark J upheld HMRC's contention that 'the concept of a "disposition" was widened by *s 3(3)* to include passive dispositions, meaning omissions which resulted in the enhancement of another person's estate or of settled property in which no interest in possession subsisted'. He rejected HMRC's contention that the deemed disposition should be treated as having taken place on her 60th birthday (which was her normal retirement date under her pension policy), holding that the disposition should be treated as having taken place on the date of her death. Her omission to exercise her rights had increased the value of the settled property, and the evidence showed that this had been intentional. Accordingly, *IHTA 1984, s 10* did not apply. With regard to the appropriate valuation, Clark J reviewed the evidence in detail and found that the total benefits amounted to £119,800. He directed that this should be discounted by 25%, resulting in a chargeable consideration of £89,950.

Key points concerning pension schemes

[34.7] Points to consider are as follows.

- The *Finance Act 2011* transformed the tax treatment of registered pension schemes and the *Finance Act 2015* has now introduced total flexibility. Hence funds in a SIPP are, for many pensioners, no longer locked in the scheme and inaccessible (apart from the longstanding 25% lump sum withdrawal facility). Furthermore the fund remaining on the death of the pensioner, the whole of his or her pension fund can be used to provide a pension income to dependants. As an alternative the trustees of the pension scheme may pay the fund as a lump sum to beneficiaries and, assuming that they are payable at the discretion of the pension trustees, the taxation of these lump sum payments is:

(a) if the taxpayer dies before the age of 75 and before drawing benefits, the pension fund can be paid to beneficiaries as a lump sum free of tax up to the available lump sum and death benefit allowance. If designated to drawdown within two years of the death income withdrawals are tax-free;

(b) if the taxpayer dies after the age of 75 but before drawing benefits, the pension fund can be paid as a lump sum to beneficiaries subject to tax at their marginal rates, or to a trust with a tax charge of 45%, or may be used to provide income benefits taxed at marginal rates.

This makes private pension funds much more attractive in overall financial planning. For higher rate taxpayers the effective cost of providing a pension fund of £1,000 is now either £600, or £550 for those on the highest tax rate, subject of course to the limits on contributions. The fund can provide an income in retirement by means of indefinite drawdown plus lump sum and other benefits to heirs on death. £600 invested outside a pension scheme and left to the next generation might incur 40% inheritance tax on death, leaving only £360 available after tax. Lifetime inheritance tax planning and use of exemptions can of course have impact on this analysis, but the new pensions regime is certainly offers more encouragement to pension savings than previously. In simple terms, it may be better to use private savings to finance living expenses and to preserve the funds in a SIPP as far as possible as an IHT-free fund available for beneficiaries on death.

Qualifying non-resident pension schemes also have their attractions since they have equal IHT exemption on death of the pensioner, but without any tax charge applying, and they are free of the investment restrictions which apply to SIPPS. On the other hand, there are of course no tax reliefs for contributions. These schemes are available to both UK residents and non-residents and although in theory there is no limit on the amount which can be contributed, it is necessary to operate the QNUP as a pension scheme and not a family trust. Hence, the amount contributed should be suitable in terms of what it will provide as a pension income for the contributor. It is also essential that sums are not contributed by an employer, as in that event, other anti-avoidance legislation applies. There are no particular reliefs from capital gains tax and income tax anti-avoidance rules.

- It should not be overlooked that a pension transfer within two years of death can give rise to a charge to IHT on death and HMRC are unlikely to accept that the exception for dispositions without gratuitous intent applies. A deduction for the value of the retained rights under the scheme will however considerably reduce the amount of the chargeable transfer.

- Following the case of *Revenue and Customs Comrs v Parry (as personal representatives of Staveley)*, those with pension funds should take professional advice before making any transfer from one registered pension scheme to another, particularly if they are in poor health. An IHT liability can arise by virtue of the transfer if it cannot be shown to be made without any gratuitous intent. It might be supposed that pension funds are always now outside the scope of IHT but the *Parry* case shows that this is not necessarily correct.

35

Potentially Exempt Transfers

Cross-references. See **2.5** and **2.12** ACCOUNTS AND RETURNS; **4.10** AGRICULTURAL PROPERTY; **6.11** BUSINESS PROPERTY; **7** CALCULATION OF TAX; **25.1** INTEREST ON TAX; **27.7** LIABILITY FOR TAX; **30.3** NATIONAL HERITAGE; **32.1** PAYMENT OF TAX for due date of payment; **32.5** for payment by instalments; **32.12** for HMRC charges; **32.15** for certificates of discharge; **48.5** TRANSFER OF VALUE for the repayment of certain debts during lifetime being treated as potentially exempt transfers.

Simon's Taxes. See I3.311–I3.319, I3.322.

Other Sources. Foster, Parts C3, C4 and C5.

Introduction to potentially exempt transfers

[35.1] Except as provided to the contrary under 35.4 below, a potentially exempt transfer is a transfer of value made by an individual after 18 March 1986 which would otherwise be a chargeable transfer and which falls into one of the following categories.

(a) A gift to another individual of property which:
   - (i) becomes comprised in his estate; or
   - (ii) if not falling within (i) above, increases the value of his estate provided that it does not also become comprised in the estate of another person. The proviso is important: for example, a gift of an asset to a company may increase the value of another shareholder's estate, but this will not be a potentially exempt transfer because the gifted asset becomes comprised in the estate of the company. Note also that if the diminution in the transferor's estate is greater than the increase in the other individual's estate, the excess is a chargeable transfer.

   Included however is a gift made before 22 March 2006 by an individual into a settlement or which increases the value of settled property, and, in either case, another individual has a beneficial interest in possession in that settlement.

(b) A gift into an accumulation and maintenance trust before 22 March 2006 which gift, by virtue of the transfer, becomes *property* to which *IHTA 1984, s 71* applies, see **41.4** SETTLEMENTS: ACCUMULATION AND MAINTENANCE TRUSTS.

(c) A gift to a disabled trust which gift, by virtue of the transfer, becomes *property* to which *IHTA 1984, s 89* applies, see **44.1** SETTLEMENTS: TRUSTS FOR THE DISABLED.

(d) The disposal or termination by an individual of his beneficial interest in possession in settled property by gift before 22 March 2006 on which event:
   (i) another individual becomes beneficially entitled to the property in which the interest subsisted or an interest in possession in that property; or
   (ii) that property is settled on accumulation and maintenance trusts or trusts for the disabled; or
   (iii) the value of another individual's estate is increased.

(e) The disposal or termination by an individual of his beneficial interest in possession in settled property by gift on or after 22 March 2006 on which event another individual becomes beneficially entitled to the property in which the interest subsisted (but not to an interest in possession in that property). Note that any continuing powers of appointment exercisable by the trustees may prevent the individual from becoming immediately entitled to the settled property so that a chargeable transfer into a relevant property trust then arises.

(f) A gift into a trust for a bereaved minor (see **43.1**) on or after 22 March 2006 on the ending during the lifetime of the beneficiary of an immediate post-death interest (IPDI). The bereaved minor's trust must be a continuation of the trusts of the same settlement as that in which IPDI subsisted and IPDI must terminate during the life of the life tenant. [*IHTA 1984, s 3A(3B) inserted by FA 2006, Sch 20 para 9(5)*].

In addition to the above, a PET is deemed to arise where (i) a gift with reservation was made more than seven years before an individual's death and the reservation of benefit ceased within that seven-year period (see **43.1**) and (ii) there is a debt repayment and the debt was not deductible from the lender's estate by virtue of *FA 1986, s 103* (see **49.11**).

Proviso re 'identifiable property'

For the purposes of (b) and (c) above some identifiable property must become subject to the trusts, otherwise the gift remains a chargeable transfer. For example, the payment by the settlor of an insurance premium on a policy written for the beneficiaries of an accumulation and maintenance trust would be a chargeable transfer. If, however, the settlor provides the trust with the funds from which to pay the premiums, the gift would be a potentially exempt transfer. For the purposes of (d), however, there are certain transitional rules that ensure that new interests in possession which are created out existing ones before 6 October 2008 ('transitional serial interests') still will qualify as PETs. See **39** SETTLEMENTS WITH INTERESTS IN POSSESSION.

Summary of transfers qualifying as PETs

In summary therefore a PET will, from 22 March 2006, comprise lifetime gifts and transfers as follows:

- transfers by individuals to other individuals;
- transfers by individuals to certain trusts for the disabled (see **44** SETTLEMENTS: TRUSTS FOR DISABLED PERSONS);
- transfers on or after 22 March 2006 by an individual to a bereaved minor's trust on the coming to an end of an immediate post-death interest (see **43** SETTLEMENTS: TRUSTS FOR BEREAVED MINORS);
- transfers by an individual into an interest in possession trust in which, for transfers on or after 22 March 2006, the beneficiary has a disabled person's interest (see **44.1** SETTLEMENTS: TRUSTS FOR DISABLED PERSONS); and
- entitlements on the termination or disposal of an individual's beneficial interest in possession in settled property where one or more individuals then become absolutely unconditionally entitled to the funds.

With regard to the last point above, an anti-avoidance provision applies to an interest in possession to which a person domiciled in the UK became beneficially entitled on or after 9 December 2009 by virtue of a disposition falling within *IHTA 1984, s 10* (dispositions without gratuitous intent). This counteracts an avoidance scheme whereby an interest in possession in settled property was purchased for full value but then fell out of the purchaser's estate without any IHT charge due to the 2006 changes to the IHT treatment of trusts. Under the amendments made, the purchased interest in possession forms part of the purchaser's estate, but on termination, a chargeable transfer arises without the possibility of a potentially exempt transfer.

[*IHTA 1984, ss 3A(1)–(3)(6)(6A)(7), 3B, 5(1B); FA 1986, Sch 19 para 1; F(No 2)A 1987, s 96(1)–(3); FA 2006, Sch 20 para 9, Sch 26 Pt 6; FA 2010, s 53(2)(3)*].

Consequences of treatment as potentially exempt transfer

[35.2] A potentially exempt transfer made seven years or more before the death of the transferor is an exempt transfer and any other potentially exempt transfer is a chargeable transfer. [*IHTA 1984, s 3A(4); FA 1986, Sch 19 para 1*]. A potentially exempt transfer is assumed to be an exempt transfer during the seven years following the transfer or, if earlier, until immediately before the transferor's death. [*IHTA 1984, s 3(A)(5); FA 1986, Sch 19 para 1*].

As potentially exempt transfers are assumed to be exempt at the time of the transfer, no IHT is payable at that time. If the transferor makes a subsequent chargeable lifetime transfer (e.g. a gift to a discretionary trust) the earlier potentially exempt transfer does not enter into the transferor's cumulative total at that time. Where, however, the transferor dies within seven years of the potentially exempt transfer, it becomes a chargeable transfer at the actual date of the gift. Tax is calculated at the full death rates applying at the time of death, subject to taper relief, but there is no grossing up, even if the tax is payable out of the deceased's estate: see **50.1** TRANSFERS WITHIN SEVEN YEARS BEFORE DEATH. Tax on subsequent chargeable lifetime transfers may, therefore, not only need to be revised under the rules for TRANSFERS WITHIN SEVEN YEARS BEFORE DEATH (57) but will also be affected by the revision of the transferor's cumulative total.

Example 1

X makes a potentially exempt transfer to Y of £338,000 on 1 January 2004 and then on 1 August 2009 makes a chargeable transfer of £150,000 into the Z discretionary trust. X dies on 31 December 2010 with an estate valued at £500,000.

On the initial gift of the £338,000 to Y this will be a PET and no charge arises and no cumulation either. The subsequent gift to Z Trust is chargeable but at the time of the gift the nil rate band is greater than reduction in his estate by virtue of the gift. However, with the death of X the PET now becomes chargeable because the gift was within seven years of X's death and this will be a charge to tax at death rates after the reallocation of the nil rate band to the gift. This has a knock-on effect in that the chargeable gift into the Trust which was made later and was not subject to tax because of the nil rate band now becomes chargeable to inheritance tax at death rates.

		£		
Y's liability becomes:		338,000		
	Less 2003/04, 2002/03	6,000		
		332,000		
	Less nil rate band	325,000		
		£7,000	@ 40% =	£2,800
	Less taper relief (80% for surviving six years)			2,240
	Tax payable by Y			£560
Z Trust liability becomes:		150,000		
	Less 2009/10, 2008/09	6,000		
		144,000	@ 40% =	£57,600
X's death estate liability becomes:		£500,000	@ 40% =	£200,000

As the gift into the Trust was within three years of the death there is no taper relief. The liability arising on the gift to Y is primarily payable by Y but the personal representatives of X deceased have secondary liability if Y fails to pay the tax within 12 months after the end of the month in which X dies: see **27.8**. The example assumes that the tax on the gift to the Z trustees will be paid out of the settlement funds; if it were paid from the estate of X deceased grossing up would apply (IHTM 14541).

Where a potentially exempt transfer becomes chargeable on the death of the donor within seven years of the date on which it was made, it will be necessary to calculate the tax due by cumulating chargeable transfers made within the seven years previous to it. Some such earlier transfers may be outside the seven-year period up to the date of death. See Example 2.

Example 2

James made as gift into a discretionary trust on 1 January 2008 of £280,000. This was within the nil band £300,000 at the time and so no IHT was due.

On 1 May 2014, James gave £200,000 to his son Robert to assist him with the purchase of a house. This was a potentially exempt transfer when it was made.

James also uses his annual IHT exemption each year with other gifts.

On 1 February 2021, James dies leaving an estate of £300,000 to his other children. He has no transferable nil rate band which can be claimed, nor any entitlement to the residence nil rate band.

On the death of James within seven years of the gift to Robert, that gift becomes a chargeable transfer. It is within the nil band on death of £325,000 but the prior gift into trust must be cumulated for the purpose of working out the tax on the gift. This means that the cumulative value of the gift to Robert is now £480,000 so that the tax on the gift is the excess of that amount over the nil band at the time of death (£325,000). The chargeable amount is therefore £155,000. Tax thereon on 40% is £62,000 but taper relief reduces this by 80% to give an amount payable of £12,400.

In the estate of James, the gift into trust in 2008 falls out of cumulation. The lifetime cumulative total in the estate is therefore £200,000 being the gift to Robert. The estate therefore has a nil band of £125,000 notwithstanding the full nil band having been applied against the lifetime gifts.

Treatment of annual exemption in relation to a potentially exempt transfer

[35.3] Where a transfer of value is a potentially exempt transfer, in the first instance it is left out of account for the purposes of allocating the £3,000 annual exemption. However, if the transfer subsequently proves to be a chargeable transfer, it is taken to have been made in the tax year in which it was actually made but later than any transfer of value in the same year which is not a potentially exempt transfer (*IHTA 1984, s 19(3A)*). This provision appears to conflict with *IHTA 1984, s 3A(1)(b)* which states that a transfer of value may qualify as a PET only if it would otherwise be chargeable, and it would not be otherwise chargeable to the extent of any available annual exemption. HMRC practice is to disregard *IHTA 1984, s 19(3A)* in applying the annual exemption so that the exemption will be applied in strict order to all gifts in the same year, whether potentially exempt or immediately chargeable (IHTM 14143). This means that when considering the order of dispositions where there are annual exemptions available then a small benefit can be obtained by making any chargeable transfer first. See Key Points below.

HMRC's view is that where a potentially exempt transfer is treated as made under *FA 1986, s 102(4)* as a result of a reservation of benefit ceasing to exist in the donor's lifetime (see **22.1**), no deduction of annual exemption can be made if the potentially exempt transfer proves to be a chargeable transfer (IHTM 14141).

Exceptions

[35.4] The following transfers are not to be regarded as potentially exempt transfers.

(a) A transfer to the extent to which it would in any case be an EXEMPT TRANSFER (**21**). [*IHTA 1984, ss 2, 3A(1)(b); FA 1986, Sch 19 para 1; FA 2006, Sch 20 para 9*].

(b) A transfer on which tax is in any circumstances to be charged *as if* a transfer of value has been made other than, after 16 March 1987, a transfer made under *IHTA 1984, s 52* (charge on the termination of an interest in possession). [*IHTA 1984, s 3A(6); FA 1986, Sch 19 para 1; F(No 2)A 1987, s 96(1)(2)*]. This excludes from treatment as a potentially exempt transfer the charge on:
   (i) participators where a close company makes a transfer of value, see **11.1** CLOSE COMPANIES; and
   (ii) the termination of an interest in possession in settled property before 17 March 1987, see **39.9** SETTLEMENTS WITH INTERESTS IN POSSESSION.

(c) A disposition treated as having been made by the participators of a close company where there is an alteration in the share or loan capital of a close company not consisting of quoted shares or securities (in relation to transfers of value made, and other events occurring, before 17 March 1987, shares or securities quoted on a recognised stock exchange) or in any rights attaching to its unquoted shares or debentures (in relation to transfers of value made, and other events occurring, before 17 March 1987, shares or debentures not quoted on a recognised stock exchange). [*IHTA 1984, s 98(3); FA 1986, Sch 19 para 20; FA 1987, s 58, Sch 8 para 2*]. See **11.8** CLOSE COMPANIES.

(d) If made after 1 July 1986, the first transfer of value including woodlands on which estate duty was deferred on a death before 13 March 1975. [*FA 1986, Sch 19 para 46*]. Although this provision denies treatment as a potentially exempt transfer to all property comprised in a single transfer of value any part of which, however small, is woodlands subject to a deferred estate duty charge, by concession after 4 December 1990 it will be restricted in its scope to that part of a transfer of value which is attributable to such woodlands).

Key points concerning potentially exempt transfers

[35.5] Points to consider are as follows.

- When advising on gifts in a particular year where there will be PETs and chargeable transfers, the order in which they are made is important for two reasons. The first is that the annual exemption will be applied to them in the strict order in which they are made. So if a PET is made and subsequently a chargeable transfer is made (for example, a gift into trust), the annual exemption will be applied to the PET, whether or not it subsequently proves to be made within seven years of the death of the donor. If it turns out that the PET is made more than seven years before the donor's death, the annual exemption will be wasted against the PET which is not chargeable anyway. The second reason is that if a PET becomes a chargeable transfer by virtue of the death of the donor within seven years from the date on which it was made, the PET will be applied against any available nil rate band, thereby increasing the tax payable on subsequent chargeable transfers. Worse still the rate of tax payable on relevant property trusts made after the PET will change because the settlor's cumulative total at the time the trust was made is taken into account in calculating ten-year anniversary charges and exit charges on the trust.

- In the case above where a gift is made of a chattel, some form of documented transfer is essential if the item is not taken into the possession of the donee. Hence, either a deed of gift or a memorandum of gift with witness being present *at the time of the gift* will be required. Reservation of benefit issues will also need to be dealt with (see **22.2**):

THIS MEMORANDUM records that on the . . . . day of . . . . 2010 the undersigned [*Transferor*] of [*Address*] ('the Transferor') gave and by word of mouth expressed himself/herself to give to the undersigned [*Transferee*]of [*Address*] ('the Transferee) [all the furniture effects and moveable property] which [are] specified in the Schedule attached hereto ('the Chattel(s)) for the absolute sole use of the/and benefit of the Transferee and at the same time the Transferor delivered the Chattel(s) to the Transferee and placed the Transferee in possession and unrestricted control of the Chattel(s) and at the same time the Transferee accepted the gift.

Dated:

SCHEDULE

[*Identification is made here of all chattels which have been given by the Transferor*]

Signed by [*Transferor*]: ....

Signed by [*Transferee*]: ....

STATUTORY DECLARATION

I/We [..........](Declarant). . . . . of [..........]. . . . . do solemnly and sincerely DECLARE as follows;

1. I am [a Solicitor of the Supreme Court]/[over the age of 18 years] and competent to make this declaration.

2. On the . . . . day of . . . . 2010 at .... in the morning/afternoon I was present at . . . . [..........] . . . . where:

   (i) I saw [..........]. . . . . standing in the [hall of ....] and adjacent to a George III mahogany Serpentine sideboard on which he placed his hand at the same time [..........*(i.e. Transferor)*] . . . . stated to [..........*(i.e. Transferee)*] . . . . "I give you this George III Mahogany sideboard and you may remove it to your home in London". Immediately thereafter I saw [..........*(i.e. Transferor)*]. . . . . lock the sideboard by its key and hand the key to [..........*(i.e. Transferee)*] . . . . who then took it from him.

SECOND SCHEDULE.

Declaration of gifted items continues . . .

AND I make this solemn declaration conscientiously believing the same to be true and by virtue of the *Statutory Declarations Act 1835*

DECLARED at . . . .

this . . . . day of . . . .

(signature of declarant) ....

2010. . . . . .

Before me

(signature of person before whom declaration is made)

[A solicitor or A Commissioner for Oaths or as appropriate].

FIRST SCHEDULE

SECOND SCHEDULE

36

Quick Succession Relief

Cross-reference. See also **49** TRANSFERS ON DEATH.

Simon's Taxes. See **I4.165, I5.283**.

Other Sources. HMRC Customer Guide to Inheritance Tax; Foster, Part D1.65, D1.65, E2.83; IHTM22000.

Application

[36.1] Where there is a later transfer of any property within five years of an earlier transfer ('the first transfer') which increased the transferor's estate and the later transfer:

(a) arises on death; or
(b) is of settled property and (i) the transferor was entitled to an interest in possession in the property, (ii) the first transfer was of the same property, and (iii) the first transfer either was or included the making of the settlement or was made after the making of the settlement,

the tax payable on the later transfer is reduced by:

$$\text{Percentage} \times \frac{(G - T)}{G} \times T$$

where:

G = gross (chargeable first transfer);

T = tax on first transfer.

The percentages are as follows:

Period between transfers	*Percentage*
One year or less	100%
More than 1 year but not more than 2 years	80%
More than 2 years but not more than 3 years	60%
More than 3 years but not more than 4 years	40%
More than 4 years but not more than 5 years	20%

Where in relation to the first transfer there is more than one later transfer, if full relief cannot be given because the tax charge on the earliest of them is insufficient, credit may be given on later transfers in chronological order until credits representing the whole of (G – T) × T/G have been given. Credit of (for example) £1,200 on a later transfer after 2½ years represents £1,200/60% = £2,000, and the maximum relief on any later transfer would be limited to the appropriate percentage (60%, 40% or 20%) of ((G – T) × T/G – £2,000).

In calculating whether or to what extent the first transfer increased the value of the transferor's estate (i.e. (G – T)/G), any excluded property consisting of a reversionary interest to which he became entitled either on the occasion of, or before, that transfer is left out of account. [*IHTA 1984, s 141*].

Where the earlier occasion was a lifetime transfer and the transferee dies before the transferor, relief may still be available even though it cannot be determined whether any tax is in fact payable on the potentially exempt transfer (or further tax in respect of a lifetime transfer chargeable when made) until seven years have elapsed from the date of the gift or the transferor dies before the expiry of that period. Provided the transferee dies within five years of the gift, quick succession relief will be given in the transferee's estate in the normal way once the amount of the tax on the gift is quantified.

Where the later transfer qualifies to any extent for the lower 36% rate of IHT (see **49.13**: estates where 10% or more of any component is given to charity) any quick succession relief given to the estate as a whole must be divided between the relevant components by reference to the tax that is payable by each component, and not the capital value of those components. [*IHTA 1984, s 141A*].

Example

On 1 January 2011 A died with a net estate valued at £400,000. In December 2006 he had received a gift from B of £20,000. B died in November 2008 and A paid the IHT (amounting to £8,000) due as a result of B's potentially exempt transfer becoming chargeable within the three years before the death.

A was also entitled to an interest in possession in the whole of his father's estate. His father had died in February 2007 with a net estate of £306,000 on which the IHT paid was £2,400. On A's death, the property passed to A's sister and was valued at £145,000. A had made no previous transfers and left his estate to his brother.

	£
Free estate	400,000
Settled property	145,000
Taxable estate	£545,000
IHT on an estate of £545,000 = £88,000	

Quick succession relief

The gift from B was made more than four but not more than five years before A's death so quick succession relief at 20% is available.

QSR =	$20\% \times £8{,}000 \times \dfrac{12{,}000}{20{,}000}$	£960

Interest in possession in father's will trust	£
Net estate before tax	306,000
Tax	2,400
Net estate after tax	£303,600

A's death was more than two but not more than three years after his father's so relief is given at 60%.

QSR =	$60\% \times £2{,}400 \times \dfrac{303{,}600}{306{,}000}$	£1,428

Tax payable on death of A		£	£
IHT on an estate of £545,000			88,000
Deduct QSR			
On gift from B		960	
On father's estate		1,428	
			2,388
IHT payable			£85,612
On free estate	$\dfrac{400{,}000}{545{,}000} \times £85{,}612$		£62,834
On settled property	$\dfrac{145{,}000}{545{,}000} \times £85{,}612$		£22,778

Note to the example

(A) The relief is given only by reference to the tax charged on the part of the value received by the donee. Therefore, the tax paid must be apportioned by applying the fraction 'net transfer received divided by gross transfer made'.

Key points concerning quick succession relief

[36.2] Points to consider are as follows.

- If there are two successive charges on the settled property within a period of five years the tax payable on the second charge is reduced, and the reduction is a percentage of the tax payable on the earlier transfer. The second settled property charge must arise on the termination of an interest in possession, and the first such charge must have increased the estate of the life tenant who was the holder of that interest and be determined by reference to the same settled property. This latter condition means in effect that, where the life tenant's interest arose on or after 22 March 2006, it must be an IPDI, a disabled person's interest or a TSI and as a result increased the beneficiary's estate for IHT purposes.
- Form IHT415 should be used to claim quick succession relief if the administration of the earlier estate has not been completed and the deceased had not received their share of that estate before they died. If the deceased had already received their gift and relief is being deducted then you must enter:
- the IHT reference of the first person to die;
- their full name, and
- their date of death,

  in the Additional Information boxes on pages 15 and 16 of Form IHT400.
- Under *IHTA 1984, s 159* unilateral credit for overseas tax can be allowed not only on death but also in respect of lifetime dispositions where some type of gift tax is charged in that foreign country. The basic conditions to be satisfied in connection with a lifetime or death transfer are that both UK IHT and overseas tax must be chargeable by reference to the same event and attributable to the value of the same property, and that the foreign tax is similar in character to IHT. See **18** DOUBLE TAXATION RELIEF. Where QSR is allowed, the amount of IHT attributed to the property is the net amount after allowing the relief. Some countries such as Australia, Canada and New Zealand do not have estate taxes and the USA has federal and state estate taxes so examination of the prior gift and estate duty tax attaching to it is required.

37

Rates of Tax

Rates	37.1

Cross-references. See 7 CALCULATION OF TAX and 50 TRANSFERS WITHIN SEVEN YEARS BEFORE DEATH.

Simon's Taxes. See I3.5, I4.1.

Rates

[37.1] *Inheritance tax is levied on the value transferred by a* CHARGEABLE TRANSFER (9) at the rate or rates applicable to the highest part of the aggregate of that value and the values transferred by any chargeable transfers made by the transferor in the period of seven years ending with the date of the transfer. [*IHTA 1984, ss 1, 7(1)*].

Only one table of rates is enacted which is applicable to transfers on death. Chargeable lifetime transfers are charged at one half of those death rates throughout the range of rate bands. Transfers made within seven years of death are charged at the death rates but in the case of chargeable transfers made in that period but more than three years before death (including potentially exempt transfers which become chargeable transfers), the tax charged is tapered, see **50.1** TRANSFERS WITHIN SEVEN YEARS BEFORE DEATH. [*IHTA 1984, s 7(2)–(4), Sch 1; FA 1986, Sch 19 paras 2, 36*].

The rate of tax on death has been 40% throughout with effect from 15 March 1988 and a 20% rate applies for chargeable lifetime transfers. Before 15 March 1988, a scale of rates applied up to a top rate of 60%.

Tables are set out below to show the grossing-up calculations applicable from 5 April 2009. For a table of nil rate bands, see **49.15** TRANSFERS ON DEATH.

Indexation of rate bands

The rate bands are subject to a provision for annual indexation annually unless Parliament determines otherwise. Parliament has determined otherwise for more years than it has allowed the indexation to operate, so the provision has little practical significance. The way it operates is by reference to the Retail Prices Index as published by the Office of National Statistics for September as compared to that for the previous September. If there is an increase in the index, then from the following 6 April, the lower and upper limits of the rate bands in the tables applying in the previous year are increased by the same percentage as the percentage increase in the index. [*Transfer of Functions (Registration and Statistics) Order 1996, SI 1996/273*]. The figures are rounded up, if necessary, to the nearest £1,000. The Treasury specifies the new rate bands by statutory instrument before the start of the tax year in question. There is no provision for a reduction in the bands on a fall in the index. For years before 1994/95 the calculation was made by reference to the change in the Index during the year to the previous December. The indexing provisions are not applied for 1987/88, 1988/89, 1992/93, 1993/94, 1994/95, 1996/97 and 2002/03 but were relevant for 1995/96, 1997/98, 1998/99, 1999/2000, 2000/01, 2001/02, 2003/04, 2004/05 and 2005/06. The rate of the nil rate band for 2009/10 onwards has been fixed up to and including 2027/28, by which time the nil rate band will have remained unchanged for 19 years. [*IHTA 1984, s 8; FA 1986, Sch 19 para 3; FA 2010, s 8; FA 2014, Sch 21 para 2*].

Transferable nil rate band

Although only one table of rates is enacted, a table for chargeable lifetime transfers is also given below. Grossing-up tables are included to simplify calculations which involve net transfers. From 9 October 2007 married couples and those in civil partnerships may transfer any unused nil rate band on their death to the surviving spouse or civil partner. This may have been during the period when Capital Transfer Tax operated. See further details at **49.15**. [*IHTA 1984, ss 8A, 8C; FA 2008, Sch 4, paras 10, 11*].

TRANSFERS ON DEATH AFTER 5 APRIL 2009

2010.A1 Tax on transfers

	Gross taxable transfers £	Gross cumulative totals £	Rate
First	325,000	0–325,000	Nil
Above	325,000		40% for each £ over 325,000

2010.A2 Grossing-up of specific transfers on death which do not bear their own tax

	Net transfers £	Tax payable thereon £
0–	325,000	Nil
Above	325,000	Nil + 2/3 (66.666%) for each £ over 325,000

CHARGEABLE LIFETIME TRANSFERS AFTER 5 APRIL 2009

2010.B1 Tax on gross transfers

	Gross taxable transfers £	Gross cumulative totals £	Rate
First	325,000	0–325,000	Nil
			20% for each £ over 325,000
Above	325,000		

2010.B2 Grossing-up of net lifetime transfers

	Net transfers	Tax payable thereon
	£	£
0–	325,000	Nil
Above	325,000	Nil + 1/4 (25%) for each £ over 325,000

38

Settlements — General

Cross-references. See also **24** INTEREST IN POSSESSION; **39** SETTLEMENTS WITH INTERESTS IN POSSESSION; **40** SETTLEMENTS WITHOUT INTERESTS IN POSSESSION.

Simon's Taxes. See **Part I5**.

Other Sources. Foster, Parts E and M8; HMRC Customer Guide to Inheritance Tax; IHTM16000.

Introduction to settlements in general

[38.1] Although inheritance tax primarily applies to transfers of value by individuals, it is extended to occasions on which tax is chargeable on relevant property settlements. [*IHTA 1984, s 2(3)*].

Under the legislation, settlements are divided into two main categories.

- Settlements with qualifying interests in possession. In this case, the settled property is treated as being beneficially owned by the beneficiary with the interest in possession.
- Settlements without qualifying interests in possession. Subject to various exceptions, these are described as settlements of relevant property.

The charging provisions for the two types of settlement are completely different and are detailed at **39** SETTLEMENTS WITH INTERESTS IN POSSESSION; **40** SETTLEMENTS WITHOUT INTERESTS IN POSSESSION. See **24** INTEREST IN POSSESSION for meaning of '*interest in possession*'. A '*qualifying*' interest in possession is an interest in possession to which an individual (or a company in the business of acquiring such interests on commercial terms) is beneficially entitled. From 22 March 2006 a '*qualifying*' interest in possession will also include an immediate post-death interest (IPDI), a disabled person's interest, a transitional serial interest (TSI) or an interest in possession to which a company is beneficially entitled. [*IHTA 1984, s 59 as amended by FA 2006, Sch 20 para 20*].

'Settlement' means any disposition or dispositions of property, whether effected by instrument, by parol (i.e. verbal or oral) or by operation of law, or partly in one way and partly in another whereby the property is for the time being:

(a) held in trust for persons in succession or for any person subject to a contingency; or
(b) held by trustees on trust to accumulate the whole or any part of any income of the property or with power to make payments out of that income at the discretion of the trustees or some other person, with or without power to accumulate surplus income; or
(c) charged or burdened (otherwise than for full consideration in money or money's worth paid for his own use or benefit to the person making the disposition), with the payment of any annuity or other periodical payment payable for a life or any other limited or terminable period. [*IHTA 1984, s 43(1), (2)*].

In *Nader v HMRC* [2018] UKFTT 294 (TC), the First-tier Tribunal expressed the view that the definitions of 'settlement' and 'settlor' in *IHTA 1984, ss 43* and *44* do not require an 'element of bounty'.

'Settlor' includes any person by whom the settlement was made directly or indirectly and any person who has provided funds directly or indirectly for the purpose of or in connection with the settlement or has made with any other person a reciprocal arrangement for that other person to make the settlement. Where more than one person is a settlor in relation to a settlement, and the circumstances so require, the settled property is treated as if comprised in separate settlements for the purposes of the provisions relating to inheritance tax on settled property other than *IHTA 1984, s 48(4)–(6)* (exempt gilts, see **20.5** EXCLUDED PROPERTY). [*IHTA 1984, s 44*].

The words 'for the purpose or in connection with' contained in *IHTA 1984 s 44* imply that there must at least be a conscious association of the provider of funds with the settlement in question. It is insufficient that the settled funds should historically have been derived from the provider of them. If it were otherwise, anyone who gave funds unconditionally to another person which that other person later settled would fall to be treated as the settlor or as a settlor of the funds (*Countess Fitzwilliam v CIR (and related appeals) HL* [1993] STC 502).

A bare trust is not regarded as a settlement for IHT purposes. If *Trustee Act 1925, s 31* applies in relation to the income during the minority of a beneficiary, HMRC accept that this does not cause the trust to be a settlement for IHT purposes as one in which the income falls to be accumulated (IHTM16068).

Tax on settlements with interests in possession

[38.2] The normal charging provisions for transfers of value apply with some modification to any settlement with interest in possession which commenced prior to 22 March 2006 on the basis that the settled property is treated as beneficially owned by the beneficiary entitled to the interest in possession. On the termination or disposal of that interest tax is charged as if he had made a transfer of value of the property in which his interest subsisted. For interests created on or after 22 March 2006, this treatment applies only in the case of

(i) an immediate post-death interest;
(ii) a disabled person's interest; or

(iii) a transitional serial interest.

It follows that any post-22 March 2006 interest in possession not within any of those three categories will fall within the relevant property regime – see **40** SETTLEMENTS WITHOUT INTEREST IN POSSESSION, and as a result any change in entitlements to income will have no consequences for IHT. From 22 March 2006 a person beneficially entitled to an interest in possession in settled property which is terminated is charged to tax as if he had made a transfer of value of the property in which his interest subsisted only if his interest first arose prior to that date, or is an IPDI or a TSI. See **35.1** POTENTIALLY EXEMPT TRANSFERS. See **39** SETTLEMENTS WITH INTERESTS IN POSSESSION for full details regarding IPDIs and TSIs. [*IHTA 1984, ss 49, 49A–49D, 51, 51A, 52; FA 2006, Sch 20 paras 11–13*].

Tax on settlements without interests in possession

[38.3] There are separate charging regimes for settlements without interests in possession. The majority of such settlements will be discretionary trusts for which the charging provisions are detailed at **40** SETTLEMENTS WITHOUT INTERESTS IN POSSESSION.

For other types of settlements, see **10** CHARITIES; **30** NATIONAL HERITAGE; **34** PENSION SCHEMES; **41** SETTLEMENTS: ACCUMULATION AND MAINTENANCE TRUSTS; **42** SETTLEMENTS: INTERESTS HELD IN PROTECTIVE TRUSTS; **43** SETTLEMENTS: TRUSTS FOR BEREAVED MINORS; **44** SETTLEMENTS: TRUSTS FOR DISABLED PERSONS; **52** TRUSTS FOR EMPLOYEES.

Property entering settlement

[38.4] A settlement commences for IHT purposes when property first becomes comprised in it. For a case where a transfer into trust was made in the belief that no IHT would arise, but this proved to be incorrect and a substantial liability was due, see *Merwe v Goldman and HMRC* [2016] EWHC 790; the court set aside the transfer into trust on grounds of mistake.

A transfer made by an individual after 17 March 1986 and before 22 March 2006 was a potentially exempt transfer (PET) to the extent that it constituted a gift into an accumulation and maintenance trust or a trust for the disabled. In relation to transfers of value made, and other events occurring, after 16 March 1987 and before 6 October 2008, certain gifts by individuals into settlements with interests in possession are also included. In this latter case certain transitional rules apply to ensure that new interests in possession which are created out of existing ones before 6 October 2008 ('transitional serial interests') still will qualify as PETs. See **35.1** POTENTIALLY EXEMPT TRANSFERS for full details. Such transfers made seven years or more before the transferor's death are exempt transfers. Any other potentially exempt transfer is a chargeable transfer. [*IHTA 1984, ss 49, 49C–49E as amended by FA 2008, s 141*; *IHTA 1989, s 48A*.] See **39** SETTLEMENTS WITH INTERESTS IN POSSESSION; **40.22** SETTLEMENTS: DISCRETIONARY TRUSTS AND OTHER TRUSTS OF RELEVANT PROPERTY for property moving between such settlements.

Settlements not liable to IHT

[38.5] Broadly, settled property situated outside the UK is not liable to IHT if the settlor did not have a UK DOMICILE (**16**) or deemed UK domicile at the time when the property concerned first became comprised in it.

From 5 December 2005, anti-avoidance measures apply to prevent UK domiciled individuals who become entitled directly or indirectly to interests in pre-existing foreign trusts which were originally settled by non-UK domiciliaries and would be treated as excluded property within *IHTA 1984, s 48(3)* from benefiting from such treatment if that interest is acquired for money or money's worth. This also applies to the excluded property provisions regarding such property under *IHTA 1984, s 48(3A)* relating to holdings in AUTs and OEICs, [*IHTA 1984, s 48(3), (3A), (3B), (3C); FA 2006, s 157*]. See **20** EXCLUDED PROPERTY, **46** SITUS and former IR Tax Bulletin, February 1997, pp 398 and 399.

Multiple settlements and associated operations

[38.6] A settlor is free to choose whether to create one settlement or whether to create a number of settlements to which funds are transferred and if the latter, they cannot be treated as one settlement by associated operations.

See *Rysaffe Trustee Co (CI) Ltd v CIR* [2003] STC 536 where a settlor had executed five settlements within a period of 35 days, and transferred shares of equal value to each settlement. HMRC had issued a notice of determination that the five holdings should be treated as a single settlement for the purposes of the charge to tax under *IHTA 1984, s 64*. The company which acted as the trustee of the settlements appealed. The Ch D allowed the appeal, holding that there were five separate settlements for the purposes of *s 64*. Park J held that 'it is up to the settlor who places property in trust to determine whether he wishes to create one trust or several trusts, or for that matter merely to add more property to a settlement which had already been created in the past'. Each settlement was created by a 'disposition' within *IHTA 1984, s 43*. The 'associated operations' provisions of *IHTA 1984, s 268* did not apply, since their 'practical operation' was 'comparatively limited'. *IHTA 1984, s 268* was 'not an operative provision which of itself imposes inheritance tax liabilities. It is a definition of an expression (associated operations) which is used elsewhere. The definition only comes into effect in so far as the expression "associated operations" is used elsewhere, and then only if the expression in another provision is relevant to the way in which that other provision applies to the facts of the particular case'. This decision was upheld by the Court of Appeal and is now accepted by HMRC.

Other types of settlement

[38.7] The following are also treated as settlements.

(a) *A foreign settlement*. Any disposition which would fall within **38.1**(a) to (c) above if it were regulated by the law of any part of the UK, or if under foreign law the administration of the property is governed by provisions equivalent in effect. [*IHTA 1984, s 43(2)*]. See also **20.2** EXCLUDED PROPERTY.

(b) A lease of property for life or lives, or for a period ascertainable only by reference to a death, or which is terminable on, or at a date ascertainable only by reference to, a death, *unless* the lease was granted for full consideration in money or money's worth.
For this purpose a lease not granted at a rack rent which is at any time to become a lease at an increased rent is to be treated as terminable at that time.
In Northern Ireland, this does not apply to a lease in perpetuity within the meaning of the *Renewable Leasehold Conversion Act 1849, s 1* or a lease to which *s 37* of that Act applies. [*IHTA 1984, s 43(3)(5)*].

(c) *In Scotland*, (i) an entail; (ii) any deed by virtue of which an annuity is charged on, or on rents of, any property (the property being treated as the property comprised in the settlement); and (iii) any 'deed' creating or reserving a proper liferent of any property whether inheritable or movable (the property from time to time subject to the proper liferent being treated as the property comprised in the settlement). '*Deed*' includes any disposition, arrangement, contract, resolution, instrument or writing. [*IHTA 1984, s 43(4)*].

(d) *In Northern Ireland*, references to property held in trust for persons include references to property standing limited to persons. [*IHTA 1984, s 43(5)*].

(e) *Usufruct*: in the April 2013 HMRC *Trusts & Estates Newsletter*, it was stated that HMRC have always been of the view that a usufruct will 'more than likely fall to be treated as a settlement for IHT purposes, although HMRC recognise that the arrangements differ between jurisdictions and the circumstances of each need to be considered'. This means that, for a usufruct created on or after 22 March 2006, the property concerned may be considered to be held in a relevant property settlement, with consequent entry charge on creation and subsequent ten-yearly charges arising. Comments on the *Trusts Discussion Forum* concerning this statement have indicated that it is considered to be open to challenge.

Key points concerning settlements

[38.8] Points to consider are as follows.

- As the trust income tax rate is the highest marginal rate (45%) in a relevant property trust it may be advantageous to make a revocable appointment of an interest in possession in favour of a beneficiary who has a lower marginal rate than that of the trust. This has no effect on the treatment of the trust for IHT purposes.
- The date when a settlement is made is when property first becomes comprised in it under *IHTA 1984, s 48A*. This date of commencement is particularly important under the relevant property regime as this determines the when the ten-year periodic charge is applied. Property becomes comprised in a settlement when it is actually transferred to the trustees or held by nominees/trustees for them. The commencement of various settlements can be summarised as follows:

(i) the settlement of the *initial capital* notwithstanding later larger additions of capital sets the commencement date so if the settlement is within the relevant property regime the periodic ten-year anniversary charge will be by reference to the date the initial capital was introduced to the settlement;

(ii) a settlement created by will commences at the date of death under *IHTA 1984, s 83* but if a small pilot trust was set up before death and the will merely adds capital to that trust then the original pilot trust set up date will apply.

(iii) where a settlement is created by deed of variation within *IHTA 1984, s 142*, the date of commencement will be the date of death and not the date of the variation which may be up to two years later. However, for income tax the date will not necessarily be the same as IHT i.e. date of death, because income will have already been paid out for that interim period. Any CGT election may be made independently under *TCGA 1992, s 62*.

(iv) an interest in possession settlement arising before 22 March 2006, or an IPDI or disabled person's interest arising after 21 March 2006 commences on the date the settlor's or their spouse's/civil partner's beneficial interest in possession comes to an end. See **39** SETTLEMENTS WITH INTERESTS IN POSSESSION and *IHTA 1984, s 80*. However, the date of the ten-yearly anniversary charge is not affected as this is related to the original settlement commencement date under *IHTA 1984, s 61(2)*. See **40** SETTLEMENTS: DISCRETIONARY TRUSTS AND OTHER TRUSTS OF RELEVANT PROPERTY.

39

Settlements with Interests in Possession

Cross-references. See also **24** INTEREST IN POSSESSION; **28** LIFE ASSURANCE POLICIES AND ANNUITIES; **38** SETTLEMENTS — GENERAL; **40** SETTLEMENTS: DISCRETIONARY TRUSTS AND OTHER TRUSTS OF RELEVANT PROPERTY.

Simon's Taxes. See I3.524–I3.527, I5.201–I5.241, I5.2.

Other Sources. Foster, Parts E1–4; HMRC Customer Guide to Inheritance Tax; IHTM16000.

Introduction — Interest in possession (IIP)

[39.1] A person beneficially entitled to an interest in possession in settled property which commenced prior to 22 March 2006 is treated as beneficially entitled to the property in which the interest subsists, i.e. it is treated as part of his or her own estate. There is an IHT charge based on the value of the settled property in which his or her interest subsists when a beneficiary disposes of his or her interest or it otherwise comes to an end, i.e. either as a transfer on death or as a PET where the termination of the interest occurs during the lifetime of the tenant, for example, where there is an exercise of a power of appointment. [*IHTA 1984, ss 49(1), 51(1), 52(1); FA 2006, Sch 20 paras 11–13*]. See **35.1** POTENTIALLY EXEMPT TRANSFERS. See **24** INTEREST IN POSSESSION for meaning of 'interest in possession'. *Note* that the actual actuarial value of the interest is irrelevant except in the limited cases where an interest is acquired for money or money's worth. See **39.10** below.

Post-21 March 2006 interest in possession

From 22 March 2006 newly created IIP settlements will be treated under the relevant property taxing regime unless the interest is an immediate post-death interest (IPDI) or a transitional serial interest (TSI) or a disabled person's interest. See below and 28 LIFE ASSURANCE POLICIES AND ANNUITIES; 40 SETTLEMENTS: DISCRETIONARY TRUSTS AND OTHER TRUSTS OF RELEVANT PROPERTY. [*IHTA 1984, ss 49(1A), 51(1A); FA 2006, Sch 20 paras 4, 11; FA 2010, s 53(4)*]. Any new trusts created from 22 March 2006 which are not IPDI or TSI trusts will be subject to certain requirements before they qualify for exclusion from the relevant property regime. See SETTLEMENTS WITHOUT INTEREST IN POSSESSION (40) and SETTLEMENTS: DISCRETIONARY TRUSTS AND OTHER TRUSTS OF RELEVANT PROPERTY (44).

Immediate post-death interest (IPDI)

[39.2] An IPDI arises for IHT purposes where a person (stipulated as being 'L' in the legislation) is beneficially entitled on or after 22 March 2006 to an interest in possession in settled property and a number of conditions are satisfied. For such trusts set up by will or intestacy the following conditions must apply:

- the first condition is the requirement that the interest in settled property arises *immediately* on the death of the settlor by reason of will or intestacy;
- the second condition is that 'L' becomes beneficially entitled to an interest in possession on the death of the testator or intestate;
- the third condition is that rules regarding bereaved minor's trusts under *IHTA 1984, s 71A* do not apply in these circumstances to property in which the interest subsists and the interest is not a disabled person's interest-see SETTLEMENTS: TRUSTS FOR BEREAVED MINORS (43);
- the fourth condition is that at all times since 'L' became beneficially entitled to the interest in possession that neither *IHTA 1984, s 71A* (bereaved minor's trust) applies to the property in which the interest subsists nor is the interest a disabled person's interest.

[*IHTA 1984, ss 49(1), 49A, 51(1A), 52(2A), 53(2A); FA 2006, Sch 20 paras 5, 11–13; FA 2010, s 53(4)*].

> *Example 1*
>
> Jules, who is married to Linda (his second wife), dies on 12 January 2020 having made gifts on 21 May 2018 of £350,000 utilising his available annual exemptions and nil rate band. By his will, he leaves his assets to his second wife Linda in trust for life and then on her death on trusts to his son Stephen now aged 30. See extract below. His estate is valued at £760,000 including the value of the house in which they live of £340,000. Jules had made no gifts in the year to 5 April 2018 but had used his annual exemptions prior to 2017/18.
>
> Linda dies on 8 January 2022 when the trust assets are valued at £800,000. Linda has no assets in her own personal estate. The terms of the continuing trust are as follows:

TRUST INCOME

Subject to the Overriding Powers below I leave my residuary estate on trust:

(1) My Trustees shall pay the income of the Trust Fund to my widow during her life and my Trustees shall have power to pay or apply capital for her benefit.

(2) Subject thereto, my Trustees shall pay the income of the Trust Fund to Stephen during his lifetime and my Trustees shall have power to pay or apply capital for his benefit.

(3) Subject to that the Trust Fund shall be held for all the children of Stephen in equal shares absolutely, or if none survive him for the Red Cross.

Calculation on death of Jules

	£	£
Value transferred on 21 May 2008		350,000
Deduct annual exemption 2018/19	3,000	
annual exemption 2017/18	3,000	6,000
		£344,000

IHT on chargeable gift of £344,000 is charged in the nil rate band up to £325,000 and balance at 40%.

£0–300,000 at Nil%	Nil
£19,000 at 40%	£7600
The estate on death is exempt under *IHTA 1984, s 18*	Nil

Calculation on death of Linda

Value of Linda's estate at 8 January 2022 by reason of *IHTA 1984, s 49(1)(1A)*. See above.	£800,000
See table at **37.1** 2010.A1 RATES OF TAX.	
£0–325,000	Nil
£325,001–£800,000 at 40%	£190,000
IHT payable	£190,000
See Note (B).	

Notes to the example

(A) Most married couples and those in civil partnerships would want to defer the IHT burden until the last death especially where there is a property of substantial value in the estate which may have to be sold. In this particular case, it is a second marriage and Jules wishes to benefit his spouse with a life interest but that his son Stephen ultimately benefits on the death of his stepmother. Under *IHTA 1984, s 49A* Linda has an IPDI which arises under the will of Jules and so she is treated as beneficially entitled to an interest in possession in settled property in which the interest subsists, i.e. see (1) in extract above where Linda is treated as owning it absolutely and certain disposals of interests in possession by individuals (e.g. renouncing by Linda of her life interest or the Trustees terminating her interest) may be potentially exempt transfers. However, as Linda did not survive seven years but dies within three years of her husband's death, and as part of her estate is an IIP, that interest is potentially chargeable at 40% after the deduction of her nil rate band. Note that an IPDI does not necessarily have to be in favour of a surviving spouse/civil partner and could be an alternative source of providing funds for the next generation or younger individuals.

(B) The settlement of the trust assets in favour of the son would have been treated as an IIP settlement but following *FA 2006, Sch 20 para 4* it will not now be treated as such. See SETTLEMENTS: DISCRETIONARY TRUSTS AND OTHER TRUSTS OF RELEVANT PROPERTY (40). Therefore, as this IIP in favour of the son is created out of an existing IIP on or after 6 October 2008 it cannot be either a transitional serial interest (TSI see below) or an IPDI. An immediate charge of 40% has been levied as above and there will be further charges incurred under the relevant property taxing rules for discretionary trusts to the extent that the assets are held on continuing trusts. See SETTLEMENTS: DISCRETIONARY TRUSTS AND OTHER TRUSTS OF RELEVANT PROPERTY (40) for a continuation of this example.

Example 2

Frank wishes to leave his estate on trust for his son Robert for life, then to Robert's wife Sylvia if she survives him for life, and then to his grandchildren absolutely. Before the changes made by *FA 2006 Sch 20*, the IHT position would be a chargeable transfer on the death of Frank, an exempt transfer on the death of Robert if Sylvia survives, and a further chargeable transfer on the death of Sylvia. However, the position is now that there is no spouse exemption on the death of Robert, assuming Sylvia survives him because Sylvia's interest is not an IPDI; it does not arise on the death of the testator whose will created the settlement (Frank).

To resolve this problem Frank's will could give Robert a power to appoint the settled funds by his own will on trust to Sylvia for life, following which the trusts for the grandchildren will take effect. If Robert exercises this power, the trusts for Sylvia will then be effected by Robert's will, not Frank's, and the trusts for Sylvia will arise on the death of Robert, thus satisfying the requirements for an IPDI. The spouse exemption will then be available on the death of Robert.

Transitional serial interest (TSI)

1. On or after 22 March 2006 and before 6 October 2008 (Category 1)

[39.3] Where a person (stipulated as being 'B' in the legislation) is beneficially entitled on or after 22 March 2006 but before 6 October 2008 to an interest in possession in settled property then for the purposes of *IHTA 1984, Pt III, Ch II* that interest is a transitional serial interest only if a number of conditions are satisfied:

- the settlement must have commenced before 22 March 2006 and the property comprised in the settlement was property to which 'B' (the beneficiary of the current interest), or some other person, was beneficially entitled an interest in possession which for these purposes is designated 'the prior interest';
- the prior interest came to an end on or after 22 March 2006 but before 6 October 2008;
- 'B' becomes beneficially entitled to the current interest on or after 22 March 2006 and before 6 October 2008;
- neither *IHTA 1984, s 71A* (bereaved minor's trust) applies to the property in which the interest subsists nor is the interest a disabled person's interest.

2. On death of spouse or civil partner on or after 6 October 2008 (Category 2)

[39.4] Alternatively, a TSI arises where a person (stipulated as being 'E' in the legislation) is beneficially entitled to an interest in possession in settled property then for the purposes of *IHTA 1984, Pt III, Ch II* that interest is a transitional serial interest only if a number of conditions are satisfied:

- the settlement must have commenced before 22 March 2006 and the property comprised in the settlement was property to which a person other than 'E' was beneficially entitled an interest in possession which for these purposes is designated 'the previous interest';
- the previous interest came to an end on or after 6 October 2008 on the death of the other person who for these purposes is designated as 'F';
- immediately before 'F' died, F was the spouse or civil partner of 'E';
- E became beneficially entitled to the successor interest on F's death;
- neither *IHTA 1984, s 71A* (bereaved minor's trust) nor a disabled person's interest applies to the property in which the successor interest subsists.

[*IHTA 1984, ss 49B–D, 51(1A), 52(2A), 54A(1A); FA 2006, Sch 20 paras 5, 12, 13, 16; FA 2008, s 141; FA 2010, s 53(4)*].

In circumstances where there is a settled life insurance contract under *IHTA 1984, s 49E* that is to be treated as a TSI see **28.1** LIFE ASSURANCE POLICIES AND ANNUITIES.

Example 3

A transferred £260,000 on 1 October 2004 into an interest in possession trust of which his brother C is the life tenant. On 31 August 2008, C released his life interest i.e. 'the prior interest' in the first condition above, then valued at £320,000, to an IIP settlement in favour of his child 'B'. A's cumulative chargeable transfers in the last seven years amounted to £230,000. A was still alive on 31 August 2008, at which date C's cumulative chargeable transfers in the last seven years amounted to £130,000 and he (C) had not used his annual exemptions for 2008/09 and 2007/08. See table at **37.1** 2010.A1 RATES OF TAX.

The transfer by A on 1 October 2004 is a potentially exempt transfer which will not become chargeable unless A dies before 1 October 2011.

The transfer by C meets the four conditions at 1. above and B's interest is therefore a TSI. The transfer is therefore a potentially exempt transfer and is not charged at lifetime rates, i.e. one-half of death rates 20%, after taking into account cumulative transfers of £130,000.

If, however, C released his life interest i.e. 'the prior interest' on 5 May 2010 when valued at £350,000 then the second condition above would not be met and the IHT relevant property regime would apply going forward with the following results.

Normal calculation

	£	£
Value transferred by C on 5 May 2010		350,000
Deduct annual exemption 2010/11	3,000	
Annual exemption 2009/10	3,000	6,000
		£344,000

IHT on £344,000 is charged in the band £130,001 to £474,000.

See table at **37.1** 2010.A1 RATES OF TAX.	£
£130,001–325,000	Nil
£325,001–474,000 at 20%	29,800
IHT payable	£29,800

Notes to the example

(A) C's cumulative chargeable transfers following the gift on 5 May 2010 will incur an immediate 20% IHT charge due to his having made other chargeable transfers prior to that date but within seven years of the gift. In addition, if C dies within seven years of the gift then his estate will be subject to a further 20% charge. A report of the transfer on 5 May 2010 should be made to HMRC on Form IHT100 and 100a with C paying the tax due. See ACCOUNTS AND RETURNS (**2**).

(B) The funds of £350,000 in the trust for B will be held under the discretionary trust taxing regime so that a charge on the trust fund assets will occur every 10th anniversary of up to 6%. See SETTLEMENTS: DISCRETIONARY TRUSTS AND OTHER TRUSTS OF RELEVANT PROPERTY (**40**) for a continuation of this example including exit charges. [*IHTA 1984, ss 51, 51A; FA 2006, Sch 20 para 12*].

(C) Had C died on or after 6 October 2008 and chosen to leave his interest in possession to his wife so that she succeeded his interest and the five Category 2 conditions mentioned above are met then a succeeding interest will arise to the wife. This is potentially very useful in the context of a trust that is an IIP for one spouse with a succeeding IIP for the survivor which under normal rules applying under *IHTA 1984, s 49C* would not have applied after 5 April 2008.

Close company entitled to IIP

Where a *close company* is entitled to an interest in possession, this is treated for IHT purposes as being owned by the participators. From 22 March 2006 where a close company is entitled to an interest in possession in settled property, that interest in possession will also include an immediate post-death interest (IPDI) and a transitional serial interest (TSI). See below and **11.12** CLOSE COMPANIES.

Value of property in which interest subsists

Entitlement to all income or property

[39.5] If the interest is in all the income arising from the settled property, the beneficiary is treated as owning the whole property. The position is the same where there is no income but the beneficiary is entitled to the use or enjoyment of the property.

Subject to the application of the *Ramsay* principle or the associated operations provisions, HMRC accept that, where an interest in possession comes to an end during the lifetime of the person entitled to it, the settled property in which the interest subsisted should be valued in isolation without reference to any similar property in the estate of the beneficiary. Previously, HMRC's view was that the value should be determined as a rateable proportion of the aggregate value of that settled property and other property of a similar kind in the person's estate (letter from Capital and Valuation Division reproduced at [1990] STI 446). The value of settled property continues to be determined in this latter manner, where the interest in possession is terminated through the death of the person entitled to it. The construction of the legislation supports this view.

Example 4

A has a life interest in a trust set up under the will of her late husband. The settlement contains a 24% interest in the family property investment company and no other assets. A also has a personal holding of shares in the company amounting to 52% of the share capital.

The total value of the company is £10 million. Accordingly, the value of A's personal holding of shares plus the holding in the trust will be 76% of £10 million less a small discount of say 5%. On the death of A, that will be the value charged to IHT.

If, however, A's life interest in the trust is terminated during her lifetime and the 24% interest is distributed out to A's children, the transfer of value by A at that time will be 'the value of the property in which [her] interest subsisted' (see *IHTA 1984, s 52(1)*). That value will be 24% of £10 million less a substantial discount for a minority interest, which discount might be 60% or 70%. For this purpose, the fact that A also has a holding of shares in the company is irrelevant. Subsequently, on A's death, her holding of 52% of the share capital will have greater discount than 5% due to her holding being a substantial interest under 75%.

Entitlement to part of the income only

Entitlement to part of the income only (if any) of the property is treated as giving an interest in possession in the same proportion of the property as his income entitlement bears to the whole income. Where a person is entitled to a specified amount of income i.e. an annuity (or the whole income less a specified amount) in any period, his interest in the settled property is such part (or the whole less such part) of the property as produces that amount in that period. Where there is a chargeable transfer of such an interest, the Treasury prescribe higher and lower income yields (to prevent manipulation of the value transferred by altering the income). Where it is the property supporting an annuity which is to be charged, the minimum value is the 'actual' dividend yield compiled for the FT Actuaries Share Indices in place of the previous method which took the 'gross' yield. Where the remainder of the settled property is to be charged, the maximum value of the property supporting the annuity is the annuity grossed up at the gross dividend yield for British Government Stocks ('Irredeemables') at the date the property has to be valued (the balance of the settled property being the value of the property to be charged). The Treasury has power to alter the higher and lower values by statutory instrument and the most recent change was on 28 January 2000. [*IHTA 1984, s 50(1)–(4); SI 1980/1000; SI 2000/174*].

Cessation of annuity

[39.6] Where an annuitant dies or disposes of his interest in possession, and the annuity is charged wholly or in part on real or leasehold property and the Board is satisfied that a capital valuation of the property at the relevant date restricted to its existing use reflects an anticipated increase in rents obtainable for that use after that date, appropriate relief will be given in calculating the 'slice', i.e. proportion of the property on which tax is payable.

Entitlement to shared use of property

[39.7] Where a person entitled to an interest in possession is not entitled to any income of the property but is entitled, jointly or in common with one or more other persons, to its use and enjoyment, his interest is taken to subsist in such part of the property as the proportion which the annual value of his interest bears to the aggregate annual value of his and the other interest(s). See *Woodhall (Woodhall's Personal Representatives) v CIR* [2000] STC (SCD) 558 regarding the right to occupy a house jointly. [*IHTA 1984, s 50(5)*].

Leases

[39.8] Where a lease is treated as a settlement (see point (b) at **38.7** SETTLEMENTS — GENERAL), the lessee's interest in the property is in the whole of the property less the value of the lessor's interest, see **53.14** VALUATION. [*IHTA 1984, s 50(6)*].

Termination of an interest in possession

[39.9] Inheritance tax is chargeable (but see exceptions below) when a beneficial interest in possession in settled property comes to an end because of (i) the death of the person entitled to the interest or (ii) the actual or deemed termination of that person's interest during his life (including disposal to a third party). That person is treated as if he had made a transfer of value and the value chargeable is the value of the property in which his interest subsisted, as if he were the transferor of that property, so that tax is charged at his personal cumulative rate of tax (but see also **39.11** below). References to property or to an interest in property include references to part of any property or interest. [*IHTA 1984, ss 51(1)(3), 52(1)*]. In *Mrs Patch's Executors v HMRC* [2007] STC SCD 453 Sp C 600 a deed of partition had resulted in a transfer of value under *IHTA 1984, s 52(1)*. See *Miller and Others v CIR* CS 1986, [1987] STC 108 where, on the death of the life tenant, it was held that the trustees' powers regarding disposition of the trust fund were administrative and not dispositive and CTT on the whole fund was chargeable. From 22 March 2006 where the interest disposed of is IPDI or a TSI (see **39.1** above) and is not an interest to which *IHTA 1984, s 71A* (bereaved minor's trust) applies then that person is treated as if he had made a transfer of value and the value chargeable is the value of the property in which his interest subsisted, as if he were the transferor of that property. In such circumstances tax is charged at his personal cumulative rate of tax. References to property or to an interest in property include references to part of any property or interest. [*IHTA 1984, ss 51(1), 52(1) as amended by FA 2006, Sch 20 paras 12, 13*].

Example 5

John has a life interest in a family settlement set up many years ago (i.e. prior to 22 March 2006). In 2010, the trustees decided to terminate his life interest in favour of a life interest for his son, Percy. On this event, John will make a chargeable transfer of the value of the settled property and the interest that now subsists for Percy comes within the relevant property regime **40** SETTLEMENTS: DISCRETIONARY TRUSTS AND OTHER TRUSTS OF RELEVANT PROPERTY. In 2014, John died and the trustees then terminated Percy's life interest in order to assist John's wife, Janet, by giving her an interest in the settlement income. The termination of Percy's interest has no relevance for IHT purposes and the settlement remains within the relevant property regime. Had the trustees not made the appointment in favour of Percy, but instead had arranged for Janet's interest to arise on John's death, Janet's interest would have been a TSI and would not at that stage come within the relevant property regime. At some stage in the future, Janet's life interest will be terminated and, at that stage, the settlement will enter the relevant property regime.

Close company entitlement

From 22 March 2006 where a close company is entitled to an interest in possession in settled property, that interest in possession will also include an immediate post-death interest (IPDI) and a transitional serial interest (TSI) as an interest in possession to which a company is beneficially entitled. Where there is a disposal of rights and interests in the close company to 'a later participator' then for these purposes the later participator will be entitled to that interest in possession according to their respective rights and interests in the company. See **11** CLOSE COMPANIES for full details. [*IHTA 1984, s 101 as amended by FA 2006, Sch 20 para 26*].

Annual and marriage gifts exemption set-off

Although termination of an interest in possession during a person's life is generally treated as if he were the transferor, the exemption for small gifts and for normal expenditure out of income (see **21** EXEMPT TRANSFERS) do not apply. The annual exemption and the exemption for gifts in consideration of marriage apply subject to the transferor giving notice in such form as the Board may prescribe (currently Form 222) to the trustees, within six months of the transfer, informing them of the availability and extent of the exemption. For the purposes of gifts in consideration of marriage (see **21.13** EXEMPT TRANSFERS) references to outright gifts and settled gifts include cases where property respectively ceases or remains settled property after the termination of the interest in possession.

SETTLED PROPERTY—ANNUAL AND MARRIAGE GIFTS EXEMPTION

Notice under Inheritance Tax Act 1984, sections 57(3) to . . . . [Trustees full names]. . . . . the Trustees of the . . . . [Name and title of settlement]. . . . .

I . . . . [Full name]. . . . . in the knowledge that my beneficial interest in possession in property in the sum of £. . . . . comprised in the above Trust was terminated on . . . . [Date]. . . . . hereby give notice that the amounts of

(a) £. . . . . of the annual exemption*

(b) £. . . . . of the exemption for gifts in consideration of marriage*

was/were then available to me and is/are to be applied against the transfer value deemed to be made by the termination.

Signed. . . . . Dated. . . . .

* Delete as appropriate

Notes to the Claim

(A) The Trustees should retain the completed form in case it is subsequently required for presentation to HMRC.

(B) If the person signing the form later becomes aware that any correction is required he/she should inform the Trustees immediately.

(C) Notice has to be given within six months of the release.

It is also possible to incorporate the notice into the deed of release so that the releasor signs the notice at one and the same time. This may be worded as below:

DEED OF RELEASE

The Releasor . . . . [Name]. . . . . gives notice to the Trustees of . . . . [Name]. . . . . Settlement that pursuant to Inheritance Tax Act 1984, sections 57(2) and/or (3)* that the £3,000 annual exemption and/or the [£1,000/£2,500/£5,000*] gift in consideration of marriage exemption for 2010/11 are available to him/her and are to be applied against the transfer of value deemed to be made by this deed. The Releasor undertakes to notify the Trustees if he/she becomes aware that a correction is necessary to the notice contained in this clause.

Signed. . . . . Dated. . . . .

Releasor [Name]

Notes to the Release

(A) The annual exemption for the previous year may also be used by the Releasor if it is available.

(B) *Asterisks denote where deletion of non-applicable exemptions should be made by the Releasor.

If the interest is disposed of for a consideration in money or money's worth, the amount of the value transferred is reduced by that consideration (but excluding from the consideration the value of any reversionary interest in the property or any interest in other property in the same settlement). Where the property consists of an interest in a pre-owned asset which is disposed of by an individual in an arm's length transaction to a person not connected with him then that property will be treated as excluded for the purposes of *FA 2004, Sch 15*. [*IHTA 1984, s 52(2); FA 2004, Sch 15 para 10(1)*]. A reduction also applies where a close company disposes of the interest (see HMRC Statement of Practice E5). See **39.10** part (b) below for position of person acquiring the interest.

Tax not chargeable on disposal of IIP

Tax is not chargeable in the following circumstances.

(a) Where, after 16 March 1987, the disposal of a beneficial interest in possession by a beneficiary is a POTENTIALLY EXEMPT TRANSFER (**35**) which is made seven years or more before death (and is consequently an exempt transfer). [*IHTA 1984, s 3A(2)(4); FA 1986, s 101(3), Sch 19 para 1; F(No 2)A 1987, s 96(1)(2), Sch 9 Pt III*].

(b) On a *disposal* of an interest in possession for maintenance of family, see **21.14** EXEMPT TRANSFERS. [*IHTA 1984, s 51(2)*].

(c) Where the settled property is EXCLUDED PROPERTY (**20**). [*IHTA 1984, s 53(1)*]. For consideration of the position where settled property is excluded property in relation to a person who holds similar property in his free estate (e.g. shares in a company) in the light of the Board's statement mentioned above regarding principles of valuation, see Taxation, 9 July 1992, p 371.

(d) Where the person whose interest comes to an end becomes on the same occasion beneficially entitled to the property or, prior to 12 March 2008, to another interest in possession in the property (but if the value of the new interest is less than the old, tax is chargeable on the difference); from 12 March 2008 it is a requirement that the replacement interest qualifies as a disabled person's interest or a transitional serial interest. [*IHTA 1984, ss 52(4)(b), 53(2)*]. This also applies where a close company becomes entitled to an absolute interest, etc. (see HMRC Statement of Practice E5).

(e) Where the interest comes to an end and reverts to the settlor in his lifetime, unless the settlor (or his spouse after 11 April 1978) had purchased the reversion for money or money's worth but see **5** ANTI-AVOIDANCE. This relief does not apply where its application depends on a reversionary interest having been transferred into a settlement after 9 March 1981. [*IHTA 1984, ss 53(3)(5)(7), 54(1)(3)*]. (See Notes (i) and (ii) below, **5.5** ANTI-AVOIDANCE and also **49.2** TRANSFERS ON DEATH.)

(f) Where the interest comes to an end and the settlor's spouse or civil partner becomes beneficially entitled to the settled property either absolutely or on qualifying interest in possession trusts, provided the settlor's spouse or civil partner is then domiciled in the UK and neither the settlor nor the spouse or civil partner had acquired a reversionary interest in the property for money or money's worth. This exemption also applies where the property reverts to the settlor's widow or widower or surviving civil partner if the settlor died less than two years before the interest comes to an end. This relief does not apply where its application depends on a reversionary interest having been transferred into a settlement after 9 March 1981. [*IHTA 1984, ss 53(4)(5), 54(2)(3)*]. (See Notes (i) and (ii) below, **5.5** ANTI-AVOIDANCE and also **49.2** TRANSFERS ON DEATH.)

(g) On the coming to an end of an interest held by a surviving spouse (or surviving former spouse) of a person who died before 13 November 1974 where estate duty was paid on that death on the property in which the interest subsists (or would have been paid but for any exemption). [*IHTA 1984, Sch 6 para 2*]. (See also **49.2** TRANSFERS ON DEATH.)

(h) Where the principal beneficiary's interest in a protective trust is determined, see **42** SETTLEMENTS: INTERESTS HELD ON PROTECTIVE TRUSTS.

(i) Where a trustee is remunerated for his services as a trustee by an interest in possession in settlement property (e.g. an annuity) except to the extent that it represents more than reasonable remuneration. [*IHTA 1984, s 90*].

(j) Where a person disclaims an interest in settled property to which he has become entitled. This does not apply if the disclaimer is made for a consideration in money or money's worth. [*IHTA 1984, s 93*].

(k) Where property comprised in a settlement (but not a reversionary interest in settled property, see **40.13**) is a holding in an authorised unit trust or a share in an open-ended investment company unless the settlor was domiciled in the UK at the time the settlement was made. [*IHTA 1984, s 48(3A)(a) as inserted by FA 2003, s 186*].

(l) Where a person's beneficial interest entitlement before 22 March 2006 comes to an end on or after that date but the interest was one to which *IHTA 1984, s 71A* (bereaved minor's trust) applies. See **43.1** SETTLEMENTS: TRUSTS FOR BEREAVED MINORS. [*IHTA 1984, s 53(1A) inserted by FA 2006, Sch 20 para 14*].

(m) Where an immediate post-death interest comes to an end in the lifetime of the beneficiary and on that occasion the settled property becomes held on a bereaved minor's trust, in which case the transfer of value is potentially exempt. [*IHTA 1984, s 3A (1A)*].

Notes

(i) For the purposes of (e) and (f) above, a person is treated as acquiring an interest for a consideration in money or money's worth if he becomes entitled to it as a result of transactions which include a disposition for such consideration (whether to him or another) of that interest or of other property. [*IHTA 1984, s 53(6)(8)*].

(ii) For the purposes of (e) and (f) above as they apply on the termination by death of an interest in possession, where it cannot be known which of two or more persons died first, they are assumed to have died at the same instant. [*IHTA 1984, s 54(4)*]. See also **49.13** TRANSFERS ON DEATH.

(iii) For relief for successive charges on an interest in possession, see **36.1** QUICK SUCCESSION RELIEF.

Example 6

A had an interest in possession in a settlement valued at £265,000. On 1 July 2008, A released his life interest to S in consideration of S's marriage on 2 July 2008. A had made no gifts since 5 April 2008 but had used his annual exemptions prior to that date. His cumulative total of chargeable transfers at 5 April 2008 was £88,000, and these had all been made since 1 July 2001. A died on 30 June 2010.

The release of A's life interest is a potentially exempt transfer which becomes chargeable by reason of A's death within seven years. The charge is at full rates with no tapering relief as the transfer took place within three years before death. See table at **37.1** 2010.A2 RATES OF TAX.

	£	£
Value of property		265,000
Exemptions		
Annual 2008–9	3,000	
In consideration of marriage	5,000	
		8,000
Chargeable transfer		£257,000

	Gross	Tax	Net
	£	£	£
Cumulative total b/f	88,000	—	88,000
Chargeable transfer	265,000	8,000.00	257,000
See table at **37.1** 2010.A2	£353,000	£8,000.00	£345,000
Tax payable by trustees as a consequence of A's death			£8,000

Notes to the example

(A) The annual gifts exemption and the exemption of gifts in consideration of marriage apply if notice is given to the trustees by the donor within six months of the gift — see Deed of Release form earlier. This requirement seems to apply even though the gift is potentially exempt when made.

(B) The tax payable is computed by reference to the transferor's cumulative total of chargeable transfers within the previous seven years, and the chargeable transfer forms part of his cumulative total carried forward.

(C) The release of A's life interest to S in consideration of S's marriage is a PET because S's interest becomes a transitional serial interest (TSI) because a new settlement is created on or after 22 March 2006 but out of an old IIP which commenced before 22 March 2006 and the original interest came to an end prior to 6 October 2008 i.e. 1 July 2008 when S (stipulated as being 'B' in the legislation) became beneficially entitled to the interest in possession on 1 July 2008. S will benefit from the transitional rules as detailed in Example 7 below.

Example 7

A typical case to which both category 1 and category 2 TSIs will apply is where property is settled before 22 March 2006 upon trust for S for life, with remainder to S's spouse (or civil partner) for life. Say S died before 6 October 2008 leaving a widow, her successor life interest will be a category 1 TSI within **39.1** above. But if S died on or after 6 October 2008, that life interest will be a spouse/civil partner category 2 TSI within **39.1** above. It should be noted that had S surrendered his life interest before 6 October 2008 so that his wife's life interest then fell into possession, her life interest would have been a category 1 TSI, whereas if S surrenders his life interest on or after 6 October 2008, his wife's successor life interest would not be a TSI since an interest in possession will only be a category 1 TSI when it falls into possession before 6 October 2008, and will only be a spouse/civil partner category 2 TSI when it falls into possession on the death of the holder of the previous interest.

Notes to the example

(A) It is not a requirement of a category 2 spouse/civil partner TSI at **39.1** above (or indeed a category 1 TSI) that the trust of the successor (or current) interest is declared or appointed before 22 March 2006. Therefore, where property is settled before 22 March 2006 upon trust for S for life remainder to S's children, and on or after 22 March 2006 but during S's lifetime and in exercise of a special power of appointment in the settlement deed, a life interest is appointed to S's widow, S's widow's life interest should be a category 1 or 2 TSI if and when it falls into possession following S's death.

(B) One important consequence of a surviving spouse's or civil partner's interest in possession being a TSI is that the spouse/civil partner exemption from inheritance tax should apply on the death of the first spouse/civil partner to die to the extent of the settled property in which both interests in possession subsist.

Anti-avoidance

[39.10] Anti-avoidance provisions apply as follows.

(a) Where there is a transaction between the trustees of a settlement and a person who is, or is connected with:
   (i) the person beneficially entitled to an interest in the property, or
   (ii) a person beneficially entitled to any other interest in that property or to any interest in any other property comprised in the settlement, or
   (iii) a person for whose benefit any of the settled property may be applied,

   and, as a result of the transaction, the value of the first-mentioned property is reduced, a corresponding part of the interest is deemed to come to an end (with consequent tax liability). An exception to this provision is where there would be no TRANSFER OF VALUE (**48**) if the trustees themselves were beneficially entitled to the property (e.g. an arm's length transaction with no gratuitous benefit intended). [*IHTA 1984, s 52(3)*].

(b) Where the person acquires an interest in possession in settled property as a result of a disposition for a consideration in money or money's worth, the actuarial value of the interest acquired and not the value of the underlying assets supporting the interest, must be looked at to determine whether the consideration given equals the market value of the interest. [*IHTA 1984, s 49(2)*]. The difference between the consideration given and the actuarial value of the interest acquired is a transfer of value. In relation to transfers of value made, and other events occurring, before 17 March 1987, no transfer of value resulting from the giving of consideration so mentioned could be a POTENTIALLY EXEMPT TRANSFER (35). [*IHTA 1984, s 49(3); FA 1986, Sch 19 para 14; F(No 2)A 1987, s 96(4)*].

(c) New wide-ranging anti-avoidance provisions of *FA 2010, s 53* ensure that the pre-22 March 2006 IHT regime for settled property subject to an interest in possession now applies to settled property subject to an interest in possession to which a person domiciled in the UK became beneficially entitled (on or after 9 December 2009) which is within *IHTA 1984, s 10* (not conferring gratuitous benefit) is not to be treated as a PET. See 5 ANTI-AVOIDANCE.

Chargeable transfer on termination of interest in possession where funds settled by a potentially exempt transfer

[39.11] Where the circumstances below apply, special anti-avoidance provisions apply to a chargeable transfer of a '*relevant interest*' i.e. a chargeable transfer made on the coming to an end of an interest in possession in settled property during the lifetime of a person beneficially entitled to it or on the death of a person beneficially entitled to an interest in possession in settled property. From 22 March 2006, in this latter case where special anti-avoidance provisions apply to a chargeable transfer of a '*relevant interest*' on the death of a person beneficially entitled to an interest in possession in settled property that interest is either a disabled person's interest or a transitional serial interest. See above and SETTLEMENTS: TRUSTS FOR DISABLED PERSONS (**44**).

Special anti-avoidance provisions

The circumstances are as follows.

(a) The whole or part of the value transferred by the chargeable transfer is attributable to property in which the relevant interest subsisted and which became settled property in which there subsisted an interest in possession (whether the relevant interest or an earlier one) on the making by the settlor of a potentially exempt transfer after 16 March 1987 and within seven years of the chargeable transfer.

(b) The settlor is alive at the time when the relevant interest comes to an end.

(c) On the coming to an end of the relevant interest, any of the property in which the interest subsisted becomes settled property in which no 'qualifying interest in possession' subsists other than property to which *IHTA 1984, s 71* applies (accumulation and maintenance trusts). From 22 March 2006 references to *IHTA 1984, s 71* (accumulation and maintenance settlements) are omitted. For '*qualifying interests in possession*' see **40.1** SETTLEMENTS: DISCRETIONARY TRUSTS AND OTHER TRUSTS OF RELEVANT PROPERTY.

(d) Within six months of the coming to the end of the relevant interest any of the property in which that interest subsisted has neither become settled property in which a qualifying interest in possession subsists nor the subject of an accumulation and maintenance trust, but only in this latter case up until 21 March 2006, nor become property to which an individual is beneficially entitled.

The IHT chargeable in such circumstances is the greater of the tax calculated under the *special rate of charge* below and the tax calculated under the normal rules (i.e. as if the person entitled to the interest in possession has made a transfer of the trust property).

Special rate of charge

The special rate of charge is the aggregate of:

(i) IHT at lifetime rates on an *assumed chargeable transfer* equal to the value transferred by the relevant transfer (or where only part of the value is attributable to 'special rate property' that part of the value) and which is made at the time of the relevant transfer by an *assumed transferor* who has made aggregate chargeable transfers in the preceding seven years equal to the aggregate of the values of chargeable transfers made by the settlor in the seven years ending with the date of the settlor's potentially exempt transfer; and

(ii) IHT, if any, that would otherwise have been chargeable on the value transferred by the relevant transfer and which is attributable to the value of the property other than the special rate property.

The tax under (i) above is treated as tax attributable to the value of the settled property in which the relevant interest subsisted.

'*Special rate property*' means the property in which the relevant interest subsisted or, where any part of that property does not fall within (a) above or does not become settled property of the kind mentioned in (c) above, so much of that property as appears to the Board (or, on appeal, the Special Commissioners) to be just and reasonable.

The death of the settlor after the chargeable transfer cannot increase the tax chargeable unless, at the time of the transfer, the tax under the special rule is greater than the tax under the normal rules.

The death of the person beneficially entitled to the relevant interest in possession after the chargeable transfer cannot increase the tax chargeable unless, at the time of the transfer, the tax under the normal rules is greater than the tax under the special rules.

Where two or more previous chargeable transfers within these provisions have been made during the period of seven years ending on the date of the current transfer and the settlor is the same in each case, on calculating the tax on the current transfer, the value relating to the previous transfer or transfers attributable to the value of property which was special rate property in relation to those transfers is deemed to be the value of a chargeable transfer of equivalent value made by the settlor immediately before the potentially exempt transfer. This applies whether or not the transfers relate to the same settlement. [*IHTA 1984, ss 54A, 54B; F(No 2)A 1987, s 96, Sch 7 para 1; FA 2006, Sch 20 para 16, Sch 26 Pt 6*].

Example 8

B transferred £100,000 on 1 October 2005 into an interest in possession trust of which his brother C is the life tenant. On 31 August 2010, C released his life interest, then valued at £182,000, to a discretionary settlement in favour of his children. B's cumulative chargeable transfers in the last seven years amounted to £230,000. B was still alive on 31 August 2010, at which date C's cumulative chargeable transfers in the last seven years amounted to £155,000 and he (C) had not used his annual exemptions for 2010/11 and 2009/10. See table at **37.1** 2010.A1 RATES OF TAX.

The transfer by B on 1 October 2005 is a potentially exempt transfer which will not become chargeable unless B dies before 1 October 2012.

The transfer by C is a chargeable lifetime transfer, which is charged at lifetime rates, i.e. one half of death rates, taking into account cumulative transfers of £155,000. If, however, a higher tax liability would be produced by substituting B's cumulative transfers at the time of his PET for those of C at the time of his transfer, this takes precedence over the normal calculation.

Normal calculation

	£	£
Value transferred by C on 31 August 2010		182,000
Deduct annual exemption 2010/11	3,000	
annual exemption 2009/10	3,000	6,000
		£176,000

IHT on £176,000 is charged in the band £155,001 to £331,000.

	£
£155,001–325,000	Nil
£325,001–331,000 at 20%	1,200
	£1,200

Calculation under Section 54A

Value transferred by C on 31 August 2010, after exemptions as above	£163,000

IHT on £176,000 is charged in the band £230,001 to £406,000.

£230,001–325,000	Nil
£325,001–406,000 at 20%	£16,200

IHT payable is therefore £16,200.

Notes to the example

(A) C's cumulative chargeable transfers following the gift in August 2010 will be £331,000 (*not* £406,000).

(B) If B dies after 31 August 2010 and before 1 October 2012, the IHT liability of £16,200 may increase. For example, B's cumulative chargeable transfers at 1 October 2005 may increase due to his having made other PETs prior to that date but within seven years of death. If the IHT liability had been determined under normal rules because this produced a liability greater than that produced by a calculation under *IHTA 1984, s 54A*, such liability could not be affected by the death of B. [*IHTA 1984, s 54B(1)*].

Key points concerning settlements with interests in possession

[39.12] Points to consider are as follows.

- For the purposes of establishing if there has been a transfer on death, where it cannot be known which of two or more persons died first they are assumed to have died at the same instant (i.e. the rule in the *Law of Property Act 1925, s 184* that the elder is deemed to have died first does not apply for these purposes). [*IHTA 1984, s 4(2)*]. In the case of married couples (and now civil partnerships) this may require a survivorship condition to be imposed in their respective wills but that the survivorship condition should not apply in the will of the elder in the situation where there are simultaneous deaths. The survivor condition inserted into the will of the elder, would be worded along the lines of:

  > '. . . if . . . [spouse/civil partner] survives me by 30 days, or he/she is deemed to survive me under *section 184* under the *Law of Property Act 1925*, I give the residue of my estate to him/her absolutely.'

  However, where a testator ensures, there is an IPDI for the first beneficiary which is then followed by a successive life interest for another beneficiary then the latter successive interest would not be an IPDI because the second beneficiary's life interest does not arise on the testator's death but that of the life tenant. In these cases, a survivorship such as that above in the testator's will regarding the first beneficiary's survivorship would ensure that the interest for the second beneficiary would qualify as an IPDI under *IHTA 1984, s 92*. See also IHTM16110.
- The commencement date of a settlement is important for a number of reasons e.g. in the case of a discretionary settlement the ten-yearly anniversary charge, but the date will vary depending on a number of factors as follows:
  (i) the settlement of the *initial capital* notwithstanding later larger additions of capital sets the commencement date so if the settlement is within the relevant property regime the periodic ten-year anniversary charge will be by reference to the date the initial capital was introduced to the settlement;

(ii) a settlement created by will commences at the date of death under *IHTA 1984, s 83* but if a small pilot trust was set up before death and the will merely adds capital to that trust then the date of the pilot trust will apply.

(iii) where a settlement is created by deed of variation the date of commencement will be the date of death and not the date of the variation which may be up to two years later. However, for income tax and CGT purposes the date will not necessarily be the same as IHT i.e. date of death, because income will have already been paid out for that interim period and a CGT election may not actually be made under *TCGA 1992, s 62*.

(iv) Where the settlor or settlor's spouse has an initial qualifying interest in possession in a settlement, for the purposes of the charges on relevant property the settlement is deemed to commence on the date the settlor's or their spouse/civil partner's beneficial interest in possession comes to an end. However, the date of the ten-yearly anniversary charge is not affected as this is related to the original settlement commencement date under *IHTA 1984, s 61(2)*. See **40.1**.

40

Settlements — Discretionary Trusts and other Trusts of Relevant Property

Cross-references. See **10** CHARITIES; **24** INTEREST IN POSSESSION for meaning of interest in possession; **30.16** NATIONAL HERITAGE for settlements of such property and **30.23** for maintenance funds for historic buildings; **38** SETTLEMENTS — GENERAL for definitions of settlement and settlor; **41** SETTLEMENTS — ACCUMULATION AND MAINTENANCE TRUSTS; **42** PROTECTIVE TRUSTS; **43** SETTLEMENTS — TRUSTS FOR BEREAVED MINORS; **44** SETTLEMENTS — TRUSTS FOR DISABLED PERSONS and **52** TRUSTS FOR EMPLOYEES.

Simon's Taxes. See I5.3.

Other Sources. HMRC Customer Guide to Inheritance Tax; Foster, Part E3–4.

Introduction to discretionary trusts and other trusts of relevant property

[40.1] Separate charging rules apply to settlements containing 'relevant property'. Before 22 March 2006, these were primarily discretionary trusts, being those where no beneficiary had interests in possession. From 22 March 2006, the scope of the provisions was widened considerably.

A settlement commences when property first becomes comprised in it [*IHTA 1984, s 48A*].

For transfers and events occurring after 17 March 1986, amendments are made to the rules governing the calculation of tax to incorporate the reduction in the cumulation period for the settlor's chargeable transfers before the commencement of the settlement to seven from ten years.

Note that charges under these provisions are not affected in any way by gift with reservation of benefit charges on the settlor where he or she retains an interest in the trust. Therefore, a settlor-interested trust may be within the ten yearly charging regime described in this chapter and the settlor will potentially be liable to IHT in respect of the trust funds in the event of death whilst still having an interest in the settlement, or having had such an interest within seven years prior to death. This is subject to very limited exceptions.

A consultative document entitled 'Inheritance Tax: A fairer way of calculating trust charges' was published on 6 June 2014 and this contained a number of proposals for changes to the IHT relevant property regime, said to have negligible tax impact. Some of the proposals were enacted in *F(No 2)A 2015, ss 11* and 13 and *Sch 1 para 3(2)* with effect from 18 November 2015 and these are:

(a) that non-relevant property in the trust will not be brought into the IHT calculations;
(b) that where there are additions on the same day to two or more settlements which have the same settlor, ten-year charges on each settlement will take into account the initial value and the same-day additions in the other settlement or settlements. This will commonly impact on the use of multiple lifetime pilot trusts to which funds are added by will. There are equivalent changes to the calculation of exit charges between anniversaries; and
(c) that the special IHT provision for settlements with an initial interest in possession to settlor or spouse (*IHTA 1984, s 80*) is amended to correct a defect in the changes made in 2006. Those changes applied to settlements made on or after 22 March 2006, but earlier settlements were unaffected with the result that if the initial interest to one spouse was followed by an interest to the other, the settlement continued to be outside the relevant property regime.

Post 21 March 2006 rules

From 22 March 2006 any new trusts that are set up *inter vivos* will be trusts of relevant property, subject to limited exceptions (see **40.3** below). In broad terms relevant property trusts are subject to an IHT charge of up to 6% on the value of the assets in the trust every tenth anniversary. In addition, there will also be an exit charge of up to 6% on the value of capital distributions to beneficiaries in line with **40.3** and **40.9–40.12** below.

Similarly relevant property trusts which arise on death are subject to this charging regime. These are trusts other than:

- trusts created by will or intestacy under which a beneficiary became entitled to an interest in possession on the death of the testator i.e. IPDI (see **39.1** SETTLEMENTS WITH INTERESTS IN POSSESSION);
- trusts set up for a bereaved minor whose full entitlement vests at the age of 18 years, similar trusts set up for a child upon attaining the age of 25 or earlier and certain existing A & M trusts up until 6 April 2008 (see **41.4** SETTLEMENTS — ACCUMULATION AND MAINTENANCE TRUSTS); or
- trusts set up for disabled persons (see **44** SETTLEMENTS — TRUSTS FOR DISABLED PERSONS)

Charitable trusts and certain other special purpose trusts

There is a charge to IHT (under the ordinary rules, see INTRODUCTION AND BASIC PRINCIPLES (**1**)) when property enters a settlement without an interest in possession with the exception of certain lifetime transfers into accumulation and maintenance trusts prior to 22 March 2006 and trusts for the disabled which are POTENTIALLY EXEMPT TRANSFERS (**35**). There is also a ten-yearly charge on property remaining in the settlement and a proportionate charge to tax, based on the time that has elapsed since the date of settlement or the last full ten-year charge, on property leaving the settlement. For this treatment of existing trusts without interest in possession existing before 22 March 2006 and those created after that date see below.

The legislation refers to a 'principal charge to tax at the ten-year anniversary' and a 'principal charge to tax at other times'. In this chapter, the terms 'ten-year anniversary charge' and 'proportionate charge' have been adopted.

Certain special trusts are singled out for favourable treatment, principally charitable trusts, maintenance funds for historic buildings, employee trusts, protective trusts, trusts for bereaved minors and trusts for the disabled. This is achieved by excluding property held on such trusts from the definition of 'relevant property'. (See **40.3** below.) These trusts are dealt with in other chapters. See the cross-references at the beginning of this Chapter.

Qualifying interest in possession

[40.2] The special charging rules apply to relevant property which is settled property in which there is no qualifying interest in possession. 'Interest in possession' is not defined in the IHT legislation and its interpretation is a matter of general law as applicable in the context of IHT. See **24** INTEREST IN POSSESSION. A '*qualifying interest in possession*', for the purposes of the special charging rules, means an interest in possession to which:

(a) an *individual* is beneficially entitled; or
(b) a *company* is beneficially entitled provided:
  (i) that the business of the company consists wholly or mainly in the acquisition of interests in settled property; and
  (ii) that the company has acquired the interest for full consideration in money or money's worth from an individual who was beneficially entitled to the interest.

'*Individual*' includes participators of a close company which is entitled to an interest in possession. See **11.12** CLOSE COMPANIES for full details.

Where the acquisition under (b)(ii) was before 14 March 1975, the condition in (b)(i) above is satisfied if the business of the company was as described at the time of the acquisition or the company has permission to carry on contracts of long-term insurance under the *Financial Services and Markets Act 2000, Pt 4*. 'Contracts of long-term' means contracts which fall within *Financial Services and Markets Act 2000 (Regulated Activities) Order 2001, SI 2001/544, Sch 1, Pt II*. Also, if it carries on, through a branch or agency in the United Kingdom, the whole or any part of any long-term business which it is authorised to carry on by an authorisation granted outside the UK for the purposes of the first long-term insurance Directive. [*IHTA 1984, s 59; FA 1995, s 52(4)(5)*].

Key concepts of discretionary trusts and other trusts of relevant property

Relevant property

[40.3] The provisions impose a charge to tax on relevant property i.e. settled property in which there is no qualifying interest in possession, other than:

(a) property held for charitable purposes only, whether for a limited time or otherwise (see **10** CHARITIES);
(b) property held in TRUSTS FOR BEREAVED MINORS (**43**) 'age 18–25 trusts' and up to 6 April 2008 at the latest accumulation and maintenance trusts;
(c) property held on discretionary trusts arising on the forfeiture of a protective life interest before 12 April 1978 (see **42** SETTLEMENTS — INTERESTS HELD ON PROTECTIVE TRUSTS);
(d) property held on TRUSTS FOR DISABLED PERSONS (**44**) including such trusts settled before 10 March 1981 in which there is no interest in possession;
(e) property held in TRUSTS FOR EMPLOYEES (**52**), including employee trusts in which there is an INTEREST IN POSSESSION (**39**) to which the employee became entitled on or after 22 March 2006 which is not an IPDI, a TSI or a disabled person's interest;
(f) property held in approved maintenance funds for historic buildings (see **30.23** NATIONAL HERITAGE);
(g) property held in PENSION SCHEMES (**34**) (but not benefits which, having become payable under a fund or scheme, become comprised in a settlement);
(h) property comprised in a trade or professional compensation fund i.e. any fund, maintained or administered by a representative association of persons carrying on a trade or profession, the only or main objects of

which are compensation for, or relief of, losses or hardship that, through the default (or alleged default) of persons carrying on the trade or profession or their agents or servants, are incurred or likely to be incurred by others;

(i) EXCLUDED PROPERTY (**20**);

(j) a sum received in respect of and assets representing (but not income or gains arising from them) a payment made in lieu of pool betting duty for football ground improvements or to support games etc. and;

(k) property forming part of a premiums trust fund or ancillary trust fund of a corporate member of Lloyd's;

(l) property held on SETTLEMENTS WITH INTERESTS IN POSSESSION (**39**) which are settled on or after 22 March 2006 which are an IPDI or a TSI;

(m) property held on SETTLEMENTS WITH INTERESTS IN POSSESSION (**39**) which are settled on or after 22 March 2006 whereby CLOSE COMPANIES (**11**) acquired the interest for full consideration in money or money's worth from and individual who was beneficially entitled to it and that acquired entitlement was not an IPDI or a TSI;

(n) property applied to pay a lump sum death benefit within *FA 2004, s 168(1)* (registered pension scheme lump sum death benefits) from the date of death of the scheme member to the date when the payment is made by the pension scheme;

(o) property held in an *ICTA 1988, s 615(3)* scheme or a qualifying non-UK pension scheme where the lump sum benefit is paid out within two years beginning with the earlier of the:
  (a) date of notification to the scheme trustees, or persons having control of the scheme, of the scheme member's death; or
  (b) day on which the trustees, or persons having control of the scheme, could reasonably be expected to know of the scheme member's death.

(p) property held in an oil and gas decommissioning trust. This is effective from 20 March 1993.

(q) Works of art held in trust and situated in the United Kingdom for one or more of the purposes of public display (but not with a view to sale), cleaning and restoration (and for no other purpose) where the settlor of the trust was non domiciled in the UK at the time when the settlement was made. This applies in relation to the charge on ten year anniversaries only. [*IHTA 1984, s 64(2)* inserted by *Enactment of Extra-Statutory Concessions Order 2009, Article 13*].

[*IHTA 1984, s 58(1)(1A)(1B)(1C),(2),(2A); FA 1990, s 126(1)(5); FA 1991, s 121(1)(4); FA 1994, s 248; FA 2006, Sch 20 para 19; FA 2007, Sch 20 paras 20, 24(9); FA 2008, Sch 29 para 18*].

See the appropriate chapters for events giving rise to a charge to tax.

Treatment of income

[40.4] HMRC take the view that:

(a) *undistributed* and *unaccumulated* income should not be treated as a taxable trust asset; and

(b) for the purposes of determining the rate of charge on *accumulated income*, the income should be treated as becoming a taxable asset of the trust on the date when the accumulation is made.

See HMRC Statement of Practice SP 8/86.

Where income is left undistributed without any specific decision to accumulate it, HMRC have in the past argued that there has been de facto accumulation after a period of a few years, but there is no such presumption under trust law except where *Trustee Act 1925, s 31* applies. For ten year charges arising on or after 6 April 2014 the position is governed by legislation. Where the income arose more than five years before that date of charge from relevant property in which there was no interest in possession (of any type) it is to be treated as relevant property within the settlement, and as having been such throughout the ten year period. Exceptions from this rule are:

(a) where the settlor was non-UK domiciled at the time property became comprised in a settlement, and is not a formerly domiciled resident for the tax year in which the ten-year anniversary falls, any income arising directly or indirectly from that property which is held outside the UK or is invested at the date of charge in an authorised unit trust or open-ended investment company is not to be regarded as relevant property caught by the five-year rule as set out above. For this purpose, any income accumulations arising from settled property are treated as becoming comprised in the settlement at the same time as that settled property first became comprised in it (and not therefore at the time the income was accumulated); or
(b) where the income is invested at the date of charge in FOTRA securities and the securities qualify for the settled property FOTRA exemption (see **20.5**(c)).

HMRC have stated that it is not necessary for trustees to keep highly detailed records of movements on income account. Unless a specific part of income has been distributed, HMRC will allow allocation of distributions to income received on a 'first in, first out' basis, so that to arrive at any balance to be treated as relevant property, trustees may take the balance on income account at the ten year anniversary date and deduct from it income that has arisen in the five preceding years (Trusts and Estates Newsletter August 2014).

Note that the above provisions effective from 6 April 2014 have no application to income which has been accumulated by trustees before the anniversary date. In that case the income becomes relevant property from the date of accumulation and there is no deeming it to have been such throughout the whole of the ten year period up to the next anniversary date.

In *Gilchrist v HMRC* [2014] UKUT 169 (TCC) it was held that the proceeds of scrip dividend shares, treated as income for purposes of trust taxation due to the particular legislation now at *ITTOIA 2005, s 410(3)*, is trust capital for the purposes of IHT charges.

[*FA 2014, Sch 25 para 4; IHTA 1984, s 64(1A), (1B), (1C); IHTA 1984, s 66(2A)*].

Related settlements

[40.5] These are brought into account when considering the rate at which tax is charged. Two settlements are related only if they have the same settlor and they commenced on the same day. If, however, the property in either settlement is held for charitable purposes only without a limit of time (defined by date or otherwise), the settlements will not be related. [*IHTA 1984, s 62*]. The concept of related settlements is only applicable to settlements commencing after 26 March 1974.

Commencement of a settlement is the time when property first becomes comprised in the settlement. [*IHTA 1984, s 60*]. See Key Points in **38** SETTLEMENTS — GENERAL.

Property becoming comprised in a settlement in pursuance of a will or intestacy is treated for the purposes of the rules on settlements without interests in possession, *IHTA 1984, Pt III, Ch III*, as having become so comprised on the death of the testator or intestate. [*IHTA 1984, s 83*].

Ten-year anniversary charge

[40.6] **A charge to tax arises** if, immediately before the ten-year anniversary of a settlement, all or any part of the settled property is relevant property (see **40.3** above). Tax is calculated on the value of the relevant property at that time. See *Henderson & Henderson (Black's Trustees) v CIR*, Sp C November 2000, STC (SCD) 572 Sp C 263. Multiple settlements in identical terms created by the same settlor on different days are not to be treated as a single settlement: *Rysaffe Trustee Co (CI) Ltd v IRC* [2003] EWCA Civ 356, but HMRC appear to consider that a disclosure under DOTAS is required when they are created under the current disclosure requirements. See **40.3** above for the treatment of income. All Trustees must sign Form IHT 101 'Account of a Chargeable Event' relating to the ten-year anniversary charge: note 10 of IHT 111. [*IHTA 1984, s 64*].

Definition — 'Ten-year anniversary'

The ten-year anniversary is the tenth anniversary of the commencement of the settlement (see **40.3** above) and subsequent anniversaries at ten-yearly intervals. Where a settlor or his or her spouse or civil partner, widow or widower or surviving civil partner is beneficially entitled to a qualifying interest in possession in property immediately after it becomes comprised in a settlement, and as a result of *IHTA 1984, s 80* (see **40.19** below) the property or part is treated as becoming comprised in a separate settlement at the time when neither of those persons are so entitled, this does not affect the date of the ten-year anniversaries, which are the dates that are (or would be apart from that section) the anniversaries of the original settlement. No date falling before 1 April 1983 could be a ten-year anniversary. The date when a settlement is made is in most cases when property first becomes comprised in it under *IHTA 1984, s 60*. This date of commencement is particularly important under the relevant property regime as this determines the when the ten year periodic charge is applied. See Key Points in **38** SETTLEMENTS — GENERAL. [*IHTA 1984, s 61*].

Rate of ten-year anniversary charge

[40.7] The rate at which the charge is levied depends upon whether a settlement commenced before, or on or after, 27 March 1974.

Where a settlement commenced before 27 March 1974, the rate is determined by reference to the settlement's cumulative transfers in the ten years preceding the anniversary.

Where a settlement commenced on or after 27 March 1974, the rate is determined by reference to the settlor's cumulative transfers in the seven years preceding the date on which the settlement commenced, as well as the settlement's cumulative amounts on which charges have arisen under *IHTA 1984, s 65* in the ten years preceding the anniversary.

Tax is calculated using lifetime Tables at the following rates:

(a) where the whole of the relevant property has been comprised in the settlement throughout the ten-year period ending immediately before the ten-year anniversary, at 30% of the effective rate (see **40.8** and **40.10** below);
(b) and where the whole or part of the relevant property was not relevant property or was not comprised in the settlement throughout the ten years ending immediately before the ten-year anniversary, at 30% of the effective rate reduced by one-fortieth for each successive 'quarter' in the ten-year period which expired before the property became, or last became, relevant property.

The '*effective rate*' is the rate found by expressing the tax chargeable as a percentage of the amount on which tax is charged on an assumed chargeable transfer by an assumed transferor. See **40.8** below. [*IHTA 1984, s 66(1)(2)*].

'*Quarter*' means a period of three months. [*IHTA 1984, s 63*].

Post-26 March 1974 settlements

[40.8] For ten-year charges arising on or after 18 November 2015, in broad terms, only relevant property in the settlement or a related settlement is brought into the calculations. This is the culmination of the consultation on simplification of the rules and it should be noted that other proposals which were under consideration have not been continued with. Thus, for example, the settlor's cumulative total of chargeable transfers at commencement of the settlement remains part of the calculations. A further amendment ties in with the rules relating to same-day additions (see **40.11**).

Thus with these changes the effective rate for post-26 March 1974 settlements is calculated as follows for ten-year charges arising on or after 18 November 2015:

(a) an *assumed chargeable transfer* equal to the aggregate of:
   (i) the value of the relevant property immediately before the ten-year anniversary (see **40.3** above for the treatment of income);
   (ii) the value immediately after a related settlement (see **40.3** above) commenced of any relevant property then comprised in it; and

   - (iii) the value of any same-day addition to another settlement (see **40.11**) and where that other settlement is not a related settlement, the value of any relevant property in it at commencement,
- (b) made immediately before the ten-year anniversary by an *assumed transferor* who, subject to the adjustment for added property and same-day additions etc. in **40.11** below, has made chargeable transfers in the preceding seven years equal to the aggregate of:
   - (i) the values of chargeable transfers made by the settlor in the seven years ending with the day on which the settlement commenced (but disregarding transfers made on that day or before 27 March 1974); and
   - (ii) the amounts on which any proportionate charges (see **40.12** below) have been imposed in the ten years before the anniversary concerned.

For ten-year charges arising up to 17 November 2015, the effective rate for post-26 March 1974 settlements is defined as the rate at which tax would be charged on:

- (a) an *assumed chargeable transfer* equal to the aggregate of:
   - (i) the value of the relevant property immediately before the ten-year anniversary (see **40.3** above for the treatment of income); and
   - (ii) the value immediately after it became comprised in the settlement of any property which was not then relevant property and has not subsequently become relevant property while remaining in the settlement; and
   - (iii) the value immediately after a related settlement (see **40.3** above) commenced of any property comprised in it,
- (b) made immediately before the ten-year anniversary by an *assumed transferor* who, subject to the adjustment for added property and same-day additions etc. in **40.11** below, has made chargeable transfers in the preceding seven years equal to the aggregate of:
   - (i) the values of chargeable transfers made by the settlor in the seven years ending with the day on which the settlement commenced (but disregarding transfers made on that day or before 27 March 1974); and
   - (ii) the amounts on which any proportionate charges (see **40.12** below) have been imposed in the ten years before the anniversary concerned; and
   - (iii) in relation to the first ten-year anniversary of a settlement which commenced after 26 March 1974 and before 9 March 1982, the amounts of any distribution payments made in that period (or in some circumstances later) and within ten years before that anniversary.

[*IHTA 1984, s 66(3)–(6); FA 1986, Sch 19 para 16; F(No 2)A 2015, s 11 and Sch 1 para 3(2)*].

Post-26 March 1974 settlements — Examples

Example 1

[40.9]

X, who is married to L (his second wife), dies on 12 January 2008 having already made gifts on 21 May 2005 of £281,000 utilising his available annual exemptions and nil rate band. By his will he left his assets valued at £500,000 to his second wife L in trust for life and then on her death on discretionary trusts for his son S, now aged 30, and X's grandchildren.

L dies on 8 January 2015 leaving her estate of £400,000 on life interest trusts for her son by her first marriage. The assets in X's will trust, now valued at £600,000, are to be held on relevant property trusts with overriding powers to apply capital and accumulated income to the beneficiary S. In consequence therefore the settlor of the discretionary trusts for S is L, by virtue of *IHTA 1984, s 80* and X's cumulative total of chargeable transfers on death is not relevant. The funds in L's will trust are a related property settlement as regards the funds in the settlement held for S. Notwithstanding this treatment, the first ten-year anniversary charge for X's settlement is on 12 January 2018.

The trustees made a capital advance of £200,000 (gross) to beneficiary S on 8 September 2015.

Assumed chargeable transfer	£
Value of settled property at commencement	600,000
Value of property in related settlements	400,000
	1,000,000
IHT at lifetime rates	£135,000
Effective rate	13.50%
Appropriate fraction:	
$^3/_{10}$ × 13.50% × 3/40ths = 0.3037%	£546.66
IHT charge on appointment: £180,000 × 0.3037%	

Notes to the example

(A) The first ten-year anniversary arises on the tenth anniversary when the settlement commenced, this being the date on which property first became comprised in the settlement. [*IHTA 1984, s 60*]. When property is left on trusts set up by a will, the date of death is the commencement of the settlement i.e. 12 January 2008. Even though the property is held on IIP settlement for the wife, the actual date of the commencement is still taken as 12 January 2008 when calculating any subsequent ten-yearly charges appropriately apportioned for the number of quarters that have elapsed since X's death on 12 January 2008 to the ten-year anniversary on 12 January 2018, but not counting any quarter which expired before the settled property became relevant property. It became relevant property on 8 January 2015 and so the last quarter which is not counted is the quarter to 12 October 2014. That leaves three full quarters before the distribution on 8 September 2015.

(B) Under *IHTA 1984, s 80*, the settlor of the discretionary trusts for X is L and thus the settlement made by her will is a related settlement. The funds in that settlement are therefore taken into account in calculating the charge on the appointment in favour of S on 8 September 2015. However, under *F(No 2)A 2015*, this will cease to be the case for appointments made after 18 November 2015.

(C) The exit charge before the first ten-year anniversary takes the effective rate payable on the value of the settled property when the settlement was made, treated for this purpose as being the death of L, plus the value of funds in a related settlement. From 18 November 2015, only relevant property in a related settlement is now taken into account, and in this case, there would under this new rule be no relevant property in L's will trust.

Example 2

On 22 May 2000, M, who had already used all available exemptions, settled property worth £56,000 on each of two settlements. One settlement is discretionary and the other is subject to a life interest. By 22 May 2010, the discretionary settlement is valued at £277,000, ignoring assets representing undistributed income.

Assuming no prior proportionate charge to tax or distribution payment, the first ten-year anniversary charge will be

Assumed chargeable transfer	£
Value of relevant property on 22.5.2010	277,000
Value of property in related settlement on 22.5.2000	56,000
	333,000
Assumed cumulative total	—
	£333,000
IHT at lifetime rates	£1,600

Effective rate $\frac{1,600}{333,000} = 0.48048\%$

Rate of ten-year anniversary charge:
$\frac{3}{10} \times 0.48048\% = 0.144144\%$

Ten-year anniversary charge: 0.144144% × £277,000	£399

Example 3

Assume the facts in Example 2 above except that the settlement subject to a life interest was made on 21 May 2000.

	£
Assumed chargeable transfer (as (2) above)	277,000
Assumed cumulative total	—
	277,000
IHT at lifetime rates	Nil
Ten-year anniversary charge	Nil

Example 4

On 22 May 2000, N, who had already used all available exemptions, settled £167,000. One half of the settlement was discretionary and the other half was subject to a life interest. On 22 May 2004, the life tenant dies and all the property of the trust becomes held on discretionary trusts. By 22 May 2010, the settlement is valued as follows.

Original discretionary fund, ignoring net assets representing undistributed income	£97,000
Funds previously subject to a life interest, ignoring net assets representing subsequent undistributed income	£238,000
The first ten-year anniversary charge will be:	
Assumed chargeable transfer	
Value of relevant property on 22.5.2010	335,000
Assumed cumulative total	—
	£335,000
IHT at lifetime rates	£2,000
Effective rate $\frac{2{,}000}{335{,}000} = 0.59701\%$	

Rate of ten-year anniversary charge: $^{3}/_{10} \times 0.59701\% = 0.179103\%$

Ten-year anniversary charge:	
$0.179103\% \times £97{,}000$	174
$^{24}/_{40} \times 0.179103\% \times £238{,}000$	256
	£430

Notes to the examples

(A) In Example 2, the value of the property in the related settlement when it was made is taken into account on the first ten-year anniversary. On the second ten-year anniversary, which would have been on 22 May 2020, the initial value of funds in the related settlement would no longer be taken into account due to the amendment to the relevant provisions effective from 18 November 2015.

(B) In Example 3, there is no related settlement and the gift into trust on 21 May 2000 was a potentially exempt transfer. It is not therefore relevant for the purposes of the ten-year charges on the settlement created on the following day. However, if M had not survived the gift into the first trust by seven years, that transfer would then become a chargeable transfer and the ten-year charges on the relevant property settlement would be recalculated to include the chargeable transfer of £56,000 made the previous day.

Pre-27 March 1974 settlements

[40.10] The effective rate for **pre-27 March 1974 settlements** is defined as the rate at which tax would be charged:

(a) on an *assumed chargeable transfer* equal to the value of the relevant property immediately before the ten-year anniversary;

(b) made immediately before that anniversary by an *assumed transferor* who, subject to the adjustments for added property etc. in **40.11** below, has made chargeable transfers in the preceding seven years equal to the aggregate of:
   (i) the amounts on which any proportionate charges (see **40.12** below) have been imposed in the ten years before the anniversary concerned; and
   (ii) in relation to the first ten-year anniversary, the amount of any distribution payment made out of the settled property before 9 March 1982 (or in some circumstances later) and within ten years before that anniversary.

[*IHTA 1984, s 66(3)–(6); FA 1986, Sch 19 para 16*].

See **40.3** above for the treatment of undistributed or unaccumulated income.

Example 5

On 1 June 1971 T settled property on discretionary trusts. The trustees made the following advances (gross) to beneficiaries:

1.1.74	H	£10,000
1.1.77	B	£20,000
1.1.82	C	£60,000
1.1.88	D	£40,000
1.1.94	E	£80,000

On 1 June 1991 the settled property was valued at £175,000 and on 1 June 2001 £180,000.

1 June 1991 Ten-year anniversary charge

Assumed chargeable transfer	£	£
Value of relevant property		£175,000
Assumed transferor's cumulative total		
(i) Aggregate of distribution payments made between 1 June 1981 and 8 March 1982	60,000	
(ii) Aggregate of amounts on which proportionate charge arises between 9 March 1982 and 1 June 1991	40,000	£100,000
	Gross	Tax
	£	£
Assumed cumulative total	100,000	—
Assumed chargeable transfer	175,000	27,000
	£275,000	£27,000

$$\text{Effective rate of tax} = \frac{27,000}{175,000} \times 100 = 15.429\%$$

Ten-year anniversary charge

The IHT payable is at 30% of the effective rate on the relevant property.

IHT payable = 30% × 15.429% × £175,000 = £8,100

1 June 2001 Ten-year anniversary charge

Assumed chargeable transfer		£180,000
Value of relevant property		
Assumed transferor's cumulative total		£80,000
Aggregate of amount on which proportionate charge arises between 1 June 1991 and 1 June 2001		
	Gross	Tax
	£	£
Assumed cumulative total	80,000	—
Assumed chargeable transfer	180,000	3,600
	£260,000	£3,600

Effective rate of tax =

$$\frac{3,600}{180,000} \times 100 = 2\%$$

Ten-year anniversary charge

The IHT payable is at 30% of the effective rate on the relevant property.
IHT payable = 30% × 2% × £180,000 = £1,080

Adjustments for added property, etc.

[40.11] The previous chargeable transfers of the assumed transferor in **40.8**(b) and **40.10**(b) above are adjusted in the following circumstances.

(a) Where after the settlement commenced and after 8 March 1982, but before the ten-year anniversary concerned, the settlor makes a chargeable transfer which increases the *value* of the property in the settlement, the aggregate of the values of chargeable transfers made by the settlor in the seven years before the chargeable transfer in question is:
 - (i) if the settlement commenced after 26 March 1974, substituted for **40.8**(b)(i) above if greater than that figure; and
 - (ii) if the settlement commenced before 27 March 1974, added to the aggregate at **40.10**(b) above.

 For the purposes of both (i) and (ii) above, transfers made on the same day as the chargeable transfer in question are disregarded, but not transfers caught by the same-day additions rules (see **40.11**) and any values attributable to property brought into account under **40.8**(a) or **40.10**(a) above, and any amounts on which proportionate charges have been imposed and which are already taken into account in **40.8**(b)(ii) or **40.10**(b)(i) above are excluded. Where the settlor makes two or more such chargeable transfers in the period, the transfer which gives rise to the highest aggregate is used.

 At one time the scope of these provisions was open to doubt given the definition of settlement in *IHTA 1984, s 43(2)*, which includes 'any disposition'; thus arguably, an addition to an existing settlement is 'any disposition' and therefore forms a new and separate settlement. However, in *Barclays Wealth Trustees (Jersey) Ltd and Dreelan v HMRC* [2017] STC 2465, it was held that additions to existing settlements do not fall to be treated as new settlements. Accordingly, the provisions set out above apply.

It is immaterial whether the *amount* as well as the *value* of the property in the settlement is increased as a result of the chargeable transfer. Where, however, the *amount* of the property is not increased, these provisions will not apply if the transfer was not primarily intended to increase the value of the settled property and it did not increase that value immediately after the transfer by more than 5% of its value immediately before the transfer.

[*IHTA 1984, s 67(1)–(5); FA 1986, Sch 19 para 17*].

(b) Where property subject to the ten-year anniversary charge has previously, on ceasing to be relevant property within the preceding ten years, been subject to a proportionate charge (see **40.12** below), the aggregate of items at **40.8**(b) and **40.10**(b) above is reduced by the lesser of the amount subject to the proportionate charge *and* the value of the relevant property at the ten-year anniversary. Where only a part of the settled property was previously subject to the proportionate charge, the reduction is based on so much of the amounts mentioned above as is attributable to the part in question. If there were two or more occasions in the preceding ten years when the property was subject to a proportionate charge, the reduction above applies to each occasion. [*IHTA 1984, s 67(6)(7)*].

(c) *Same-day additions*. Up to 18 November 2015, it was possible to reduce IHT charges on relevant property trusts by forming two or more pilot trusts with minimal capital on separate days and then subsequently transferring more substantial funds to each on the same day, or by will. By virtue of the charging structure on the trusts (see **40.8**), the settlements would not be related settlements and the additions would not be taken into account as a prior cumulative total of the settlor.

This planning is now obsolete for IHT charges arising on or after 18 November 2015, subject to the exceptions detailed below. The planning is blocked by legislation for 'same-day additions' to two or more settlements. Any such additions to other settlements are taken into account as part of the assumed chargeable transfer on the occasion of ten-year charge to IHT on a settlement (see **40.8**(a)). They are also brought into account in relation to (a) interim charges before the first anniversary by treating the same-day addition as part of the assumed chargeable transfer (see **40.15**(a)), (b) interim charges between ten-year anniversaries by treating the same-day addition as having been made immediately before that anniversary, and (c) and in relation to the charges on age 18–25 trusts (see **43.4**).

A *same-day addition* applies where there are transfers into two or more settlements on the same day, thereby increasing the value of the settlements and the same person is the settlor of each settlement. Note that such transfers can be exempt transfers as it is not stated that they must be chargeable transfers. Each settlement must contain relevant property in the 'relevant period' which, for each settlement, is the period from its commencement to the time of the same-day addition. The provisions can apply to the initial transfer into the settlement concerned but not if they are related settlements. These provisions do not however apply in the following cases:

(a) where the settlements concerned are related settlements (see 40.5);
(b) where the funds in the settlement concerned are held for charitable purposes only without any time limit;
(c) where the settlement concerned is a 'protected settlement', broadly defined as those which commenced before 10 December 2014 and to which no additions have been after that date apart from certain additions by will before 6 April 2016 (see further below);
(d) where the additions concerned are the payment of life insurance premiums on a policy or policies with premiums due regularly at one year or less throughout the term; and
(e) where a *de minimis* exception for additions of £5,000 or less applies, as detailed below.

A *protected settlement* is one which commenced before 10 December 2014 and where either condition A or condition B is met. Condition A is that there have been no transfers of value after that date by which the value of the settled property was increased. Condition B applies where property is added by will on a death before 6 April 2017 where the will is in substance the same as it was before 10 December 2014.

The *de minimis* exception referred to at (e) above is for lifetime settlements where additions are not made on death. If the additions to each settlement on the same day are £5,000 or less, then the new provisions do not apply. If there is more than one same-day addition to the settlements, then the value of the property in each settlement before the first such addition must be £5,000 or less than the value of the property in each settlement after the last such addition. [*F(No 2)A 2015, Sch 1*].

Example 6

Arthur creates two discretionary trusts with capital of £100 each for his two adult children, one dated 30 December 2013 and the other dated 31 December 2013. He dies on 5 May 2017 and by his will dated 1 January 2014 he leaves £500,000 to each trust.

£100,000 is released from the first trust to the beneficiary on 29 December 2018. The IHT charge on this is calculated as follows:

Assumed chargeable transfer	
Value of settlement at commencement	£100
Value of relevant property added after settlement commenced	£500,000
Value of 'same-day addition' to settlement dated 31 December 2013	£500,000
Initial value of settlement dated 31 December 2013	£100
Total assumed chargeable transfer	£1,000,200
IHT thereon at lifetime rate (20% × (£1,000,200 – £325,000)	£135,040

Assumed chargeable transfer

Effective rate $\frac{135,040}{1,000,200} \times 100$

$= 13.501\%$

Appropriate fraction: 3/10ths × 19/40ths = 57/400ths

Charge on funds released: £100,000 × 13.501% × 57/400 = £1,923.89

Note: if Arthur had died on 5 April 2017, the settlements would be protected settlements and no amounts would then be included above in relation to the settlement dated 31 December 2013.

Charge at other times (the proportionate charge)

[40.12] A charge to tax arises:

(a) where property comprised in a settlement, or any part, ceases to be relevant property (see **40.3** above) whether because it ceases to be comprised in the settlement or otherwise; and

(b) where (a) does not apply, where the trustees of the settlement make a disposition which reduces the value of the relevant property. '*Disposition*' includes an omission to exercise a right (unless not deliberate) which is treated as made at the latest time that the right could be exercised.

See **11.5** CLOSE COMPANIES for details of when a charge arises on a close company's transfer of value being apportioned to trustees.

Tax is charged on the amount by which the value of the relevant property is reduced as a result of the chargeable event (i.e. the loss to donor principle) grossed-up where the settlement pays the tax.

[*IHTA 1984, s 65(1)(2)(9)*].

Exceptions from charge

[40.13] No charge arises:

(i) if, under **40.12**(b) above, the trustees do not intend to confer gratuitous benefit and either the transaction is at arm's length between persons not connected with each other (see **12** CONNECTED PERSONS) or is such as might be expected in such a transaction (see **48.2**(a) TRANSFER OF VALUE); or

(ii) if, under **40.12**(b) above, the disposition is a grant of tenancy of agricultural property in the UK, Channel Islands or Isle of Man for use for agricultural purposes made for full consideration in money or money's worth; or

(iii) on the payment of costs or expenses so far as they are fairly attributable to relevant property; or

(iv) where any payment is, or will be, income for income tax purposes of any person (or, in the case of a person not resident in the UK, would be if he were so resident); or

(v) in respect of a liability to make a payment under (iii) or (iv) above; or

(vi) if the chargeable event occurs in the three month period beginning with either the day on which the settlement commenced or a ten-year anniversary (see **40.6** above); or

(vii) if the settlor was domiciled outside the UK, and not deemed domiciled in the UK, at the time when property became comprised in it, and by virtue of *IHTA 1984, s 48(3)(a)*, the property becomes excluded property by ceasing to be situated in the UK (see more detailed analysis at **20.2**). At one time this relief did not expressly extend to circumstances where settled property becomes excluded property within *IHTA 1984, s 48(3)* — the purchase of units in an authorised unit trust or OEIC. However this omission is rectified by the *FA 2013, s 175* with full retrospective effect to 16 October 2002. See also **40.19** below where the settlor or his spouse or civil partner retains an interest in the settlement and **40.22** below where property moves between settlements; or

(viii) if the settlor was domiciled outside the UK at the time when property became comprised in it and that property is invested in exempt Government securities and thereby becomes excluded property by virtue of *IHTA 1984, s 48(4)(b)* because all known beneficiaries are of a description specified in the condition in question. The 'condition in question' is usually that referred to in *FA (No 2) 1931, s 22* and modified by *FA 1940, s 60* relating to questions of domicile and ordinary residence but is now in most cases to residence abroad. [*IHTA 1984, s 48(4); FA 1996, s 154, Sch 28 para 8*]. See **20.5** EXCLUDED PROPERTY. The special provisions relating to domicile in *IHTA 1984, s 267* (see **16.5** DOMICILE) are disregarded. But see **40.19** below where the settlor or his spouse or civil partner retain an interest in the settlement and **40.22** below where property moves between settlements; or

(ix) if the property becomes held for charitable purposes only without limit of time *or* the property of a qualifying political party *or* national body mentioned in *IHTA 1984, Sch 3; or* the subject of a gift for public benefit (see **21.4, 21.6–21.8** EXEMPT TRANSFERS);

(x) where shares or securities of a company cease to be relevant property on becoming held on employee ownership trusts within *IHTA 1984, s 86(1)*, if the company concerned meets the trading requirement of *TCGA 1992, s 236I*, the trusts are of a settlement which meets the all-employee benefit requirement of *TCGA 1992, s 236J*, and the settlement does not meet the controlling interest requirement of *TCGA 1992, s 236M* immediately before the beginning of the tax year in which the shares or securities cease to be relevant property but does meet it at the end of that year. [*IHTA 1984, s 75A* applicable from 6 April 2014].

[*IHTA 1984, ss 65(4)–(8), 76*].

Pre-ten-year anniversary charge

[40.14] Rate of proportionate charge before the first ten-year anniversary. On an occasion of charge before the first ten-year anniversary (see **40.6** above) the rate depends upon whether the settlement commenced before, or on or after, 27 March 1974.

Where a settlement commenced before 27 March 1974, the rate is calculated by reference to the settlement's own cumulative transfers in the preceding ten years.

Where a settlement commenced after 26 March 1974, the rate is determined by reference to the settlor's chargeable transfers in the seven years preceding the commencement of the settlement. [*IHTA 1984, ss 65(3), 68*].

Post-26 March 1974 settlements tax calculation

[40.15] **The rate of tax for post-26 March 1974 settlements** is the 'appropriate fraction' of the 'effective rate' at which tax would be charged using lifetime rates,

(a) on an *assumed chargeable transfer* equal to the aggregate of:
  (i) the value of property comprised in the settlement immediately after it commenced (see **40.5** above); and
  (ii) the value of any property comprised in a related settlement (see **40.3** above) immediately after its commencement; and
  (iii) the value, immediately after it became comprised in a settlement, of any property which became so comprised after the settlement commenced and before the occasion of charge (whether or not it has remained so comprised);
(b) made at the time the proportionate charge arises by an *assumed transferor* who in the seven years ending with the day of the occasion to charge had aggregate chargeable transfers equal to those made by the settlor in the seven years ending with the day on which the settlement commenced (but, subject to the provisions relating to same-day additions (see **40.11**) excluding any transfers made on that day).

For ten-year charges arising on or after 18 November 2015, the rules are modified so that in broad terms, only relevant property in the settlement or a related settlement is brought into the calculations. Amendments are also made to tie in with the provisions relating to same-day additions (see **40.11**). Thus the assumed chargeable transfer will be:

(i) the value of relevant property comprised in the settlement immediately after it commenced (see **40.3** above);
(ii) the value of any relevant property comprised in a related settlement (see **40.3** above) immediately after its commencement;
(iii) the value, immediately after it became comprised in a settlement, of any relevant property which became so comprised after the settlement commenced and before the occasion of charge (whether or not it has remained so comprised);
(iv) the value at the time it became relevant property, of any property which became so comprised on or after the time the settlement commenced and before the occasion of charge and which was not relevant property at the outset. For this purpose it does not matter whether or not it has remained comprised in the settlement; and
(v) the value of any same-day addition to another settlement (see **40.11**) and where that other settlement is not a related settlement, the value of any relevant property in it at commencement.

Definitions

The '*effective rate*' is the rate found by expressing the tax chargeable as a percentage of the amount on which it is charged.

The '*appropriate fraction*' is three-tenths multiplied by so many fortieths as there are complete successive quarters in the period beginning with the day on which the settlement commenced and ending with the day before the occasion of charge. However, where the whole or part of the amount on which tax is charged was not relevant property or was not comprised in the settlement throughout that period, no quarter which expires before the day on which the property became, or last became, relevant property comprised in the settlement is counted except that if that day fell in the same quarter as that in which the period ends, that quarter is counted whether complete or not.

'*Quarter*' is a period of three months. [*IHTA 1984, ss 63, 68*].

See **40.3** above for the treatment of undistributed or unaccumulated income.

Example 7

On 19 May 1999, R settled £169,000 on discretionary trusts. He had previously made cumulative chargeable transfers of £167,000 in the previous seven years and had already used all available exemptions. On 18 July 2008, the trustees appoint £180,000 to beneficiaries absolutely (with the beneficiaries paying the IHT), and on 31 December 2008 appoint the remaining funds, then valued at £60,000 (ignoring assets representing undistributed income), to beneficiary C absolutely (who again pays the tax). The proportionate charges will be:

(a) 18 July 2008

	£
Assumed chargeable transfer	
Value of property in settlement at 19.5.99	169,000
Assumed cumulative total	
Aggregate chargeable transfers by settlor in seven years to 19.5.99	154,000
	£323,000
IHT at lifetime rates on £323,000	2,200
Deduct IHT at lifetime rates on £154,000	—
IHT on assumed chargeable transfer	£2,200

Effective rate $\frac{2,200}{169,000} = 1.30177\%$

No. of complete successive quarters between 19.5.99 and 17.7.08 = 36

Proportionate charge:

1.30177% × $^{3}/_{10}$ × $^{36}/_{40}$ × £180,000 — £633

(b) 31 December 2008

Effective rate (as above) = 1.30177%

No. of complete successive quarters between 19.5.99 and 30.12.08 = 38

Proportionate charge:

1.30177% × $^{3}/_{10}$ × $^{38}/_{40}$ × £60,000 — £223

See 40.17 below for occasion of charge arising following one or more ten-year anniversaries.

[40.16] **The rate of tax for pre-27 March 1974 settlements** is 30% of the 'effective rate' at which tax would be charged, using lifetime rates:

(a) on an *assumed chargeable transfer* equal to the amount on which the proportionate charge is calculated (see **40.12** above);

(b) which is made at the time of the proportionate charge by an *assumed transferor* who in the seven years ending with the day of the occasion of charge has made aggregate chargeable transfers equal to the aggregate of:

   (i) any amounts on which any proportionate charges have previously been imposed in the period of ten years ending with that day; and

   (ii) any distribution payments made out of the settled property after 26 March 1974 and before 9 March 1982 (or in some circumstances later), and within that ten-year period.

The '*effective rate*' is the rate found by expressing the tax chargeable as a percentage of the amount on which it is charged.

[*IHTA 1984, s 68; FA 1986, Sch 19 para 18*].

See **40.3** above for the treatment of undistributed or unaccumulated income.

Rate of the proportionate charge between ten-year anniversaries

[40.17] Where an occasion of charge arises following one or more ten-year anniversaries, tax is calculated as follows.

(a) The rate of tax is, subject to (b) below, the 'appropriate fraction' of the rate charged at the most recent ten-year anniversary ignoring any reduction made under **40.7**(b) above.

(b) If, at any time before the occasion of charge and on or after the most recent ten-year anniversary:

   (i) property becomes comprised in the settlement; or

   (ii) property which was comprised in the settlement immediately before that anniversary, but was not then relevant property (see **40.3** above) has become relevant property,

   then, whether or not the property has remained comprised in the settlement or has remained relevant property, the rate of tax is the appropriate fraction of the rate at which tax would have been charged at the most recent ten-year anniversary (see **40.7–40.11** above) if the property under (i) or (ii) above had then been relevant property comprised in the settlement. For these purposes, any property under (i) above which was relevant property immediately after it became comprised in the settlement or was not then, and has not subsequently become, relevant property while remaining comprised in the settlement, is included at its value immediately after becoming comprised in the settlement. All other property is included at its value when it became, or last became, relevant property.

For charges arising on or after 18 November 2015, the rules are modified so that in broad terms, only relevant property in the settlement or a related settlement is brought into the calculations. Amendments are also made to tie in with the provisions relating to same-day additions (see **40.11**).

The tax will be calculated as follows.

(a) The rate of tax is, subject to (b) below, the 'appropriate fraction' of the rate charged at the most recent ten-year anniversary ignoring any reduction made under **40.7**(b) above.

(b) If, at any time before the occasion of charge and on or after the most recent ten-year anniversary:
   (i) relevant property becomes comprised in the settlement; or
   (ii) property has become comprised in the settlement which was not relevant property at the outset but has since become relevant property, but was not then relevant property (see **40.3** above) has become relevant property; or
   (iii) property was comprised in the settlement on the last anniversary date which was not relevant property at that time but has since become relevant property then, whether or not the property has remained comprised in the settlement or has remained relevant property, the rate of tax is the appropriate fraction of the rate at which tax would have been charged at the most recent ten-year anniversary (see **40.7–40.11** above) if the property under (i), (ii) or (iii) above had then been relevant property comprised in the settlement. For these purposes, any property under (i) is included at its value immediately after becoming comprised in the settlement. All other property is included at its value when it became, or last became, relevant property. To tie in with the rules relating to same-day additions, any such addition made on or after the most recent ten-year anniversary is to be treated as made immediately before that anniversary.

The '*appropriate fraction*' is so many fortieths as there are complete successive quarters in the period beginning with the most recent ten-year anniversary and ending with the day before the occasion to charge. Where the whole or part of the property on which tax is charged was not relevant property, or was not comprised in the settlement, throughout that period, no quarter which expired before the day on which the property became or last became relevant property comprised in the settlement is counted except that if that day fell in the same quarter as that in which the period ends, that quarter is counted whether or not complete.

[*IHTA 1984, ss 68(3), 69*].

See **40.3** above for the treatment of undistributed or unaccumulated income.

Reduction of rates

[40.18] For the purposes of (a) and (b) above, where there have been one or more substitutions of new Tables of rates between the most recent ten-year anniversary and the occasion of charge, the latest Table of rates is to be used in calculating the rate at which tax would have been charged at that most recent ten-year anniversary (and not the Table in force at the ten-year anniversary). [*IHTA 1984, Sch 2 para 3; FA 1986, Sch 19 para 37*].

Initial interest of settlor or spouse or civil partner

General

[40.19] Where a settlor, or his spouse or civil partner (including widow or widower or surviving civil partner), is beneficially entitled to an interest in possession in property immediately after it becomes comprised in a settlement (the 'first' settlement), then, if that event occurs after 27 March 1974, the property is treated as not having become comprised in the settlement on that occasion for the purposes of the rules on settlements without interests in possession in *IHTA 1984, Pt III, Ch III*. Instead, when the property or any part of it becomes held on trusts under which neither the settlor nor spouse (or civil partner) is beneficially entitled to an interest in possession, such property is treated as becoming comprised at that time in a separate settlement (the 'second' settlement) made by whichever of them last ceased to be so entitled. But the dates of the ten-year anniversaries of the deemed second settlement are those of the actual first settlement (see **40.6** above).

For a settlement made on or after 22 March 2006, this rule applies only where the interests in possession referred to are either IPDI, transitional serial interests or a disabled person's interest. If the initial interest in possession arose prior to that date and the spouse's interest arises after that date other than on the death of the first (so that it is not a transitional serial interest), the position was not adequately covered by the legislation. The second interest will be within the relevant property regime but no settlement is treated as subsisting for IHT until the death of that beneficiary and so no charge to IHT arises during the life of the second beneficiary or on his or her death. This anomaly has now been recognised by HMRC and with effect from 19 November 2015, inheritance tax charges will apply. When a qualifying interest in possession (see **40.2**) in the settled property comes to an end, and is followed by a non-qualifying interest to the spouse or civil partner, the settled property will become relevant property at that time. Where there is a subsisting interest in possession in place at 18 November 2015, the settled property will not become relevant property until that subsisting interest terminates. This therefore prevents the legislation having immediate effect from 18 November 2015, being the date of Assent to *F(No 2)A 2015* in such cases. A *subsisting interest in possession* is an interest in possession of the settlor, or spouse or civil partner of the settlor (including in each case widows and widowers of such individuals), where either of such interests has been in place throughout the period from the commencement of the settlement up to 18 November 2015.

Excluded property

[40.20] Property will only qualify as excluded property within an *IHTA 1984, s 80* trust for the purposes of the rules on settlements without interests in possession in *IHTA 1984, Pt III, Ch III* if it is situated outside the UK and the settlors of both the 'first' and 'second' settlements were domiciled outside the UK when their respective transfers of property into the trust were made. A further condition introduced with effect from 6 April 2017 is that neither are formerly domiciled residents for the tax year in which a chargeable event arises. [*IHTA 1984, ss 48(3), 81B*]. Legislation at *IHTA 1984, s 81B* to have effect for settlements within *IHTA 1984, s 80* on or after the date on which *FA 2020* is passed, rewrites these provisions so that conditions A and B must be met if any of the settled property is to be excluded property within *s 48(3)(a)* (property with foreign situs) or *s 48(3A)(a)* (authorised unit trusts) (see further detail at **20.2**) for the purposes of the charges on relevant property other than conditionally exempt property:

(a) Condition A is that the actual settlor of the settlement, that is the person who created it, was not domiciled in the UK when property first became comprised in the settlement subject to an immediate interest in possession for the settlor or spouse or civil partner;
(b) Condition B is that the actual settlor is not a formerly domiciled resident for the tax year (see **16.5**).

On the termination of the initial interest in possession, a new settlement is treated as made at that time by the life tenant. It follows therefore that the rules for excluded property in *s 48* apply so that the domicile of the life tenant at that time is relevant in deciding whether property in the settlement can qualify as excluded property. Similarly, the life tenant as deemed settlor must not thereafter become a formerly domiciled resident.

Condition A also applies to *IHTA 1984, s 65(8)* in so far as a domicile test still applies to Government securities held in the settlement; see **40.13**(viii).

Because, owing to a drafting defect, *s 82* did not include a reference to *s 48(3A)(a)* (authorised unit trusts) that omission continues to apply to settlements created before the date on which *FA 2020* is passed (*IHTA 1984, s 81B(7)*). For such investments, therefore there is no testing, as above, of the domicile status of the actual settlor when the settlement was created; only the domicile status of the life tenant when that interest comes to an end is relevant.

Application

[40.21] The above applies to provisions on settlements without interests in possession in *IHTA 1984, Pt III, Ch III* except that the provisions on excluded property above do not apply to the rules relating to NATIONAL HERITAGE (**30**) property in *IHTA 1984, ss 78, 79, Ch III* includes both the general rules for settlements without interests in possession and also the provisions for various special trusts. See CHARITIES (**10**), NATIONAL HERITAGE (**30**) for settlements for heritage property and maintenance funds for historic buildings, SETTLEMENTS — ACCUMULATION AND MAINTENANCE TRUSTS (**41**), PROTECTIVE TRUSTS (**42**), TRUSTS FOR DISABLED PERSONS (**44**) and TRUSTS FOR EMPLOYEES (**52**).

Property moving between settlements

General

[40.22] For the purposes of the rules on settlements without interests in possession in *IHTA 1984, Pt III Ch III* where after 9 December 1981 property ceases to be comprised in one settlement (the 'first settlement') and becomes comprised in another (the 'second settlement'), then, unless in the meantime any person becomes beneficially entitled to the property (and not merely to an interest in possession in it), it is treated as remaining comprised in the first settlement. However, property which ceased to be comprised in the first settlement after 26 March 1974 and became comprised in the second settlement by the same disposition is to be treated as remaining comprised in the first settlement for the purposes of charges under the relevant property regime. For events *after 14 March 1983*, this does not apply where a reversionary interest in the property expectant on the termination of a qualifying interest in possession under the first settlement was settled in the second settlement before 10 December 1981. [*IHTA 1984, s 81*].

This rule is intended to ensure that all the originally settled property can only have the benefit of one IHT threshold. However, it gives rise to considerable practical difficulties where the assets of one trust are distributed to another trust on the winding up of the first trust, and particularly if the second trust is overseas. The transfer of funds to the second trust will give rise to no exit charge and the funds will continue to be treated as remaining in the first settlement, even after it is wound up.

Excluded property

[40.23] Where property in the second settlement is treated as remaining in the first settlement, it qualified as excluded property for the purposes of the rules on settlements without interests in possession in *IHTA 1984, Pt III Ch III* (but see application below) only if it is situated outside the UK and the settlors of both the first and second settlements were domiciled outside the UK when their respective settlements were made. [*IHTA 1984, ss 48(3), 82(1)(3)*]. This rule was examined in *Barclays Wealth Trustees (Jersey) Ltd and Dreelan v HMRC* [2017] EWHC Civ 1512 where funds offshore were transferred from a settlement made by a non-domiciled settlor to a second settlement made by the same individual but at a time when he was deemed domiciled in the UK. Subsequently, the funds were appointed back to the first settlement and it was claimed that they became excluded property again after that second transfer. It was held that a settlement is made when it is first established and therefore, it was irrelevant that the settlor had become deemed domiciled in the UK when the transfers were made. The settled property continued to be excluded property. This decision is reversed for transfers between settlements made after 22 July 2020 by *IHTA 1984, s 82A*. There is also an amendment applying to transfers before that date.

For transfers between settlements after 22 July 2020, the excluded property provisions will continue to apply to the transferred property only if a non-domicile condition is satisfied in relation to all past qualifying transfers and also the latest (post-*FA 2020*) transfer. In addition, the existing rule that the settlor must not be a formerly domiciled resident continues to apply. The non-domicile condition is:

(a) where the qualifying transfer occurs as a result of a beneficiary assigning an interest in the settlement, or as a result of a person exercising a general power of appointment, such beneficiary or person must not be domiciled in the UK at that time, nor be a formerly domiciled resident for the year concerned (see **16.5**). The latter condition, as to not being a formerly domiciled resident, does not apply in relation to FOTRA securities;
(b) where property is transferred from a settlement as referred to in *IHTA 1984, s 81*, otherwise as in (a) above, the settlor of the settlement from which the property is transferred must, if still alive, not be domiciled in the UK at the time of the transfer;
(c) in any other case where the property is transferred the settlor of the first settlement, if still alive, must continue to be non-domiciled in the UK.

A *qualifying transfer* is defined as the occasion on which *s 81* applies to the property, and any subsequent occasion when that property is transferred to a relevant property settlement. However, a transfer on an assignment of an interest in the settlement by a beneficiary which took place before 22 July 2020 is not a qualifying transfer, nor is an exercise of a general power of appointment before that day. *Inheritance Tax Act 1984, s 48(3)* requires that the settlor of the transferee settlement must be non-UK domiciled and not a formerly domiciled resident at the time the property is added to that settlement.

For transfers made before 22 July 2020, the existing provisions of *IHTA 1984, s 82* still apply for relevant property charges going forward but with one amendment. This is that the settlor of the settlement from which property is transferred must have been non-UK domiciled at the time when the property concerned was added to the settlement; this applies by virtue of the amendments to *IHTA 1984, s 48*. In addition, the existing rule that the settlor must not be a formerly domiciled resident continues to apply. As regards the settlement to which the property is transferred, it remains the case that the settlor of the settlement must have been non-UK domiciled at the time the settlement was made and also not a formerly domiciled resident.

Where the property in the second settlement is relevant property which becomes excluded property on being invested in Government securities subject to a non-domicile condition (see **20.5**) or and AUT or OEIC within *IHTA 1984, s 48(3A), (4)(b)* (see **20.5**(c) EXCLUDED PROPERTY and **40.13**(viii) above), it will be exempt from the proportionate charge on that occasion if both settlors were domiciled outside the UK at the respective dates on which the property became comprised in the settlements. For this purpose, where the property became comprised in the settlement before 10 December 1974, the special provisions relating to domicile in *IHTA 1984, s 267* (see **16.5** DOMICILE) are disregarded. This provision now has very limited application in relation to Government securities as the non-domicile condition does not apply to securities acquired after 6 April 2013 nor to certain acquisitions before that date [*IHTA 1984, ss 65(8), 82(2)(3), 267(3)*].

Application

[40.24] The above applies to the provisions on settlements without interests in possession in *IHTA 1984, Pt III Ch III* except that the provisions on excluded property above do not apply to the rules relating to NATIONAL HERITAGE (30) property in *IHTA 1984, ss 78, 79. Chapter III* includes both the general rules for settlements without interests in possession and also the provisions for various special trusts. See CHARITIES (10), NATIONAL HERITAGE (30) for settlements of heritage property and maintenance funds for historic buildings, SETTLEMENTS — ACCUMULATION AND MAINTENANCE TRUSTS (41), SETTLEMENTS — INTERESTS HELD ON PROTECTIVE TRUSTS (42), SETTLEMENTS — TRUSTS FOR DISABLED PERSONS (44) and TRUSTS FOR EMPLOYEES (52).

Offshore trusts

Non-resident trusts may be within the charging provisions on relevant property. If the settlor was not domiciled or deemed domiciled in the UK when property was transferred into the settlement, that property will be excluded property and therefore outside the scope of charge if its situs is outside the UK, or if it is reinvested into property the situs of which is outside the UK. This is always provided that, at any relevant time, the settlor is not a formerly domiciled resident.

Although there is no charge on the value of excluded property, up to 17 November 2015 such property had to be taken into account in the calculation of ten yearly charges under *IHTA 1984, s 66(4)(b)*, as being property which was not relevant property when it became comprised in the settlement and has not subsequently become relevant property. This no longer applies for charges after that date (see 40.8).

Credit for tax paid under the FA 1975 provisions

[40.25] Any tax charged on a foreign settlement under *FA 1975, Sch 5 para 12(2)* (annual charge of 3% under the periodic charge provisions was allowable as a credit against subsequent capital distributions made (but not later annual charges). Any excess could be carried forward against capital transfer tax chargeable on the settlement under the 1982 provisions. Any further excess is allowed as a credit against the tax chargeable under *IHTA 1984, Pt III, Ch III* (other than tax on NATIONAL HERITAGE (30) property under *IHTA 1984, s 79*) in respect of the settled property or part. [*IHTA 1984, s 85*].

Key points concerning discretionary trusts and other trusts of relevant property

[40.26] Points to consider are as follows.

- All trusts in existence now and set up in the future, with the exception of those listed below, will come within the relevant property regime. The exceptions are:

(i) a qualifying IIP already in existence at 22 March 2006;
(ii) an immediate post-death interest (IPDI);
(iii) a transitional serial interest (TSI); or
(iv) a disabled trust and certain other tax-favoured trusts (e.g. Charitable trusts – see more detailed list at **40.3**).

Following the changes in 2006, the only lifetime settlement created by a settlor that is a PET is a transfer into a disabled trust, which may be more common than one expects as the definition of disabled beneficiary includes a person in receipt of attendance allowance. With that exception, a transfer into a lifetime trust will be an immediately chargeable transfer at the lifetime rate subject to any available nil rate band of the settlor which will be deducted. Once a relevant property regime settlement is set up, then the income beneficiaries of the settlement can be altered as many times as the trustees think fit without any additional IHT consequences other than the ten-year anniversary charge and exit charges. An IHT charge arises when the outright capital distribution is made, other than within the first three months after the settlement is made or after a ten-year anniversary, and also on ten-year anniversaries.

There are likely to be less IIP trusts as time progresses as more and more interests fall within the relevant property regime. Once the trust falls into that regime the trustees have the option, where this is within the trust deed, to revoke interests in favour of other beneficiaries and incur no IHT charge. See further below. Note in particular that the absence of an IHT charge within the three-month periods mentioned above also means that CGT hold over relief is not available on such occasions.

- Different rules can apply for tax purposes as to who is treated as the settlor of a trust where there has been a deed of variation (DoV). For example where H dies and leaves everything absolutely to W, W may decide to make a DoV putting assets into a discretionary trust, of which she is a beneficiary. She is treated as the settlor for income tax and capital gains tax purposes and the trust will be a '*settlor interested settlement*' for IT and CGT purposes. However, for IHT purposes, H is treated as the settlor (at the date of death) and all IHT charges will be calculated on this basis. Consider also the effect of the related property rules where other Will Trusts are created by H.
- Where a trust has more than one settlor, this is treated as two (or more) separate trusts for IHT purposes, which can make relevant property calculations quite complex. By the same token it can offer a worthwhile reduction in IHT charges. In practice, the two funds of the settlement should be kept separate wherever possible, in order to ease the administrative burden. It may, in some cases, not be possible to determine which assets were initially provided by which settlor, particularly in cases where there have been a large number of transactions, such as where the trust fund consists only of a managed investment portfolio. In such cases, a practical

approach would be to pro rata the current value of the trust fund (at the date of the IHT charge) in relation to the initial amounts settled by each settlor.

- Relevant property trusts can be set up by will to contain any business or agricultural property qualifying for 100% relief. There will then be no IHT liability on the death and the trust assets will remain outside the estates of any of the beneficiaries. Where the spouse survives, consider whether to arrange that he or she purchases the trust assets so that they will qualify for relief a second time on his or her death. The purchase could be made by swap of other assets inherited on the death, where these did not benefit from any IHT reliefs, or by IOU given to the trustees by the spouse.
- Where an estate on death will in any event bear full IHT liability, for example where the spouse does not survive and no other reliefs are in point, consider whether it would be more appropriate for the assets to be left on discretionary trusts rather than to be given to legatees absolutely. This will prevent their falling into the estate of any legatee and the prospective charges under the relevant property regime may lower than a full 40% charge on the death of a legatee.
- Trusts set up by non-domiciled settlors should take steps to ensure that only excluded property is held on ten-year anniversary dates. Moveable property, such as works of art, may be taken out of the country before the anniversary date, thereby securing treatment as excluded property on the anniversary date. Note, however, that it would not be acceptable tax planning for the items to be brought back to the UK soon afterwards. Immoveable UK assets could be sheltered by new borrowings secured on them with the borrowed money being distributed out of the trust. However, the GAAR guidance examples indicate that if the distribution is subsequently resettled into the trust by the settlor, this will be regarded as an abusive arrangement subject to counteraction under the GAAR provisions. Following 17 July 2013, it is no longer possible to reduce IHT liability by depositing the borrowed funds overseas as the liability will not be deductible from the UK asset.
- The rule set out at **40.22** above as regards property moving between settlements means that any appointment of funds across to a new settlement does not alter the anniversary date in relation to the appointed funds. Nor is there an exit charge in relation to the appointment, unless the funds become subject to a disabled person's trust with interest in possession. If there is no exit charge there will be no capital gains tax hold over relief under *TCGA 1992, s 260*. Transfers of excluded property between settlements are now inadvisable in view of the provisions of *IHTA 1984, s 82A* as set out at **40.23**.
- A chargeable transfer arises when assets are settled on relevant property trusts and equally when there is an exit charge on the distribution of assets. This has the effect of bringing any IHT paid on any such occasion within the provision for relief of IHT against CGT on subsequent disposal of the asset by the transferee: see

TCGA 1992, s 260(7) and **8.3** CAPITAL GAINS TAX.

41

Settlements — Accumulation and Maintenance Trusts

Cross-references. 40 SETTLEMENTS — DISCRETIONARY TRUSTS AND OTHER TRUSTS OF RELEVANT PROPERTY; 43 SETTLEMENTS — TRUSTS FOR BEREAVED MINORS.

Other Sources. Foster's Inheritance Tax, Parts E5 and M8.04; IHTM16000.

Simon's Taxes. See I5.5.

Introduction to accumulation and maintenance trusts

The accumulation and maintenance trust regime

[41.1] Following the 2006 changes to the settled property provisions for IHT, the favourable regime for children's trusts, known as accumulation and maintenance trusts, was brought to an end and although in theory, trusts of this type can still be formed, there is no further point in doing so, since a widely drafted discretionary trust will have identical tax treatment and will give more flexibility than the erstwhile accumulation and maintenance trust.

Transfers into accumulation and maintenance trusts

[41.2] After 17 March 1986 but before 22 March 2006, a gift by an individual into an accumulation and maintenance trust, by virtue of which property becomes comprised in the trust, was a potentially exempt transfer. After 21 March 2006, a gift by an individual into an accumulation and maintenance trust, is no longer treated as a PET. See 35 POTENTIALLY EXEMPT TRANSFERS for further details. Accumulation and maintenance settlements that were reviewed before 6 April 2008 to ensure that the beneficiaries become absolutely entitled on or before the age of 18 remained settlements to which *IHTA 1984, s 71* applied otherwise they now come within the charging provisions of 'age 18–25 trusts' (see 43.3 SETTLEMENTS — TRUSTS FOR BEREAVED MINORS AND 'AGE 18–25 TRUSTS') or within the relevant property taxing regime. [*IHTA 1984, ss 58, 71, 71E–F*].

[*IHTA 1984, s 3A; FA 1986, Sch 19 para 1; F(No 2)A 1987, s 96; FA 2006, Sch 20 para 9*].

Transfers out of accumulation and maintenance trusts

[41.3] Until property settled on accumulation and maintenance trusts vested, there was no interest in possession so that, in the absence of special provisions, such settlements would have been liable to tax under the provisions relating to **40** SETTLEMENTS — DISCRETIONARY TRUSTS AND OTHER TRUSTS OF RELEVANT PROPERTY. Where, however, a settlement qualified as an accumulation and maintenance trust, its liability to tax was limited to circumstances similar to those now applying to trusts for bereaved minors: see **43.2** SETTLEMENTS — TRUSTS FOR BEREAVED MINORS AND 'AGE 18–25 TRUSTS'.

Qualification as accumulation and maintenance trust

Settlements created before 22 March 2006

[41.4] To qualify as an accumulation and maintenance settlement prior to 22 March 2006, the detailed conditions had to be satisfied, one of the primary ones being that one or more 'persons' (beneficiaries) would, on or before attaining a specified age, not exceeding 25, become beneficially entitled to, or to an interest in possession in, the settled property, prior to which income was to be paid out or accumulated at the discretion of the trustees (see Example 4 below).

Accumulation and maintenance settlements created prior to 22 March 2006 continued to be treated under the old regime but only until 6 April 2008. From that date onwards any existing accumulation and maintenance settlement have to conform to the new rules so that the beneficiary or beneficiaries must obtain a right to *capital* on or before the age of 18 and not as in (a) above at age 25 to continue to attract the taxing benefits of the old regime of *IHTA 1984, s 71*. This may be achieved by the existing terms of the settlement which already allow the beneficiary or beneficiaries to obtain a right to capital at 18 or the terms of trust powers of appointment providing for such entitlement. See example in **41.6** below. All such existing accumulation and maintenance settlements will have ceased to exist by 22 March 2024. All other existing accumulation and maintenance settlements formed prior to 22 March 2006 will otherwise from 6 April 2008 become subject to the '18–25 trusts' taxing regime or they may, in other circumstances, become subject to the relevant property trust regime. See Example 1 below, **40** SETTLEMENTS — DISCRETIONARY TRUSTS AND OTHER TRUSTS OF RELEVANT PROPERTY and **43.3** SETTLEMENTS — TRUSTS FOR BEREAVED MINORS AND 'AGE 18–25 TRUSTS'. [*IHTA 1984, ss 71, 71D; FA 2006, Sch 20 paras 1, 2, 3; Sch 26 Pt 6*].

Settlements created after 21 March 2006

[41.5] New trusts from 22 March 2006 will not qualify as an accumulation and maintenance settlement under the old *IHTA 1984, s 71* regime but alternative trusts designated 'bereaved minors' (see **43** SETTLEMENTS — TRUSTS FOR BEREAVED MINORS AND 'AGE 18–25 TRUSTS') may attract similar taxing benefits, although these cannot apply to lifetime settlements.

[*FA 2006, Sch 20 paras 1, 2, 3*].

Taxation of settlements from 22 March 2006

[41.6] From 22 March 2006, new taxing rules apply with regard to accumulation and maintenance trusts in existence such that where one or more 'persons' (the beneficiaries) fail to, on or before attaining a specified age not exceeding 18, become beneficially entitled to the settled property that trust will come within the '18–25 trusts' or relevant property trust regime and be subject to an initial proportionate ten-yearly charge and charges on exit of funds from the trust. The *maximum* charge within the '18–25 trusts' will be 4.2% on, broadly, the value of the trusts fund over the period of the life of the trust if the beneficiary takes capital, income and accumulated income at the age of 25. If this event is deferred until the beneficiary is beyond that age before they take the capital, then charges under the relevant property regime will apply (see **40** SETTLEMENTS — DISCRETIONARY TRUSTS AND OTHER TRUSTS OF RELEVANT PROPERTY). Otherwise, where a trust ceases to comply with the provisions of either *s 71A* or *s 71D*, a charge will apply under *IHTA 1984, s 70* as detailed at **43.2** SETTLEMENTS — TRUSTS FOR BEREAVED MINORS AND 'AGE **18–25** TRUSTS'. [*IHTA 1984, ss 71, 71D–G; FA 2006, Sch 20 paras 1, 2, 3*].

Example 1

On 6 April 1983, G settled £50,000 on trust equally for his grandchildren. The beneficiaries were to take absolute entitlements at age 25, income being accumulated for minor beneficiaries as detailed within the accumulation and maintenance trust deed below. By 2007, G had three grandchildren; Alex, who becomes 25 on 28 February 2008, and Stephanie, born 27 September 1994, and Roger, born 25 July 1996.

On 28 February 2008 Alex became entitled to an interest in possession in one-third on reaching age 25. There was no charge on the distribution of capital entitlement under the old rules on Alex attaining the age of 25. The remaining two-thirds continues to be held equally for Stephanie and Roger but is not subject to an interest in possession. On 6 April 2008, 25 years had elapsed since the date of the settlement but the settlement would not have ceased to qualify as an accumulation and maintenance trust as a result since all of the remaining beneficiaries have a common grandparent. The settlement does, however, cease to be an accumulation and maintenance settlement from that date because the remaining beneficiaries do not become entitled to settled property on or before attaining age 18 as required from that date by *IHTA 1984, s 71* as amended by *FA 2006, Sch 20 paras 2, 3*.

As this was an existing accumulation and maintenance settlement, the existing pre-22 March 2006 rules for accumulation and maintenance trusts continued until 5 April 2008 so that if the beneficiaries will become absolutely entitled no later than age 18, the settlement will remain within *IHTA 1984, s 71*. Otherwise, the settlement will fall within the '18–25 trust' regime from 6 April 2008 within *IHTA 1984, s 71D(3)(4)*, but in this case, applying from each of their 18th birthdays. [*IHTA 1984, s 71F(1)(2)(a)*]. Consequently, there would have been no 'exit' tax charge on 6 April 2008 when the accumulation and maintenance settlement failed to qualify under the new rules under *IHTA 1984, s 71(1)(a)*. Also, there will have been no entry charge when it failed and became a '18–25 trust' with effect from 6 April 2008 but a charge will commence from the date of each of their birthdays at 18. From that point onwards, the exit charges will apply to distributions of capital entitlement on or before Stephanie and Roger become aged 25. The value of the remaining settlement is £600,000 and on 26 September 2019, Stephanie's birthday at 25 years, when the Trustees decide to distribute the respective capital entitlements to Stephanie of £325,000 and Roger of £275,000.

27 September 2019 distribution charge within *IHTA 1984, s 71F*	
Assumed chargeable transfer (as above)	600,000
Assumed cumulative total	—
Deduct Nil rate band, say,	(325,000)
	£275,000
IHT at lifetime rates	£55,000
Effective rate $\frac{55,000}{600,000} = 9.16\%$	
Stephanie's exit charge: 27 September 2012 to 27 September 2019 = 7 years i.e. 28 complete quarters	
Rate of Stephanie's exit charge:	
$^{28}/_{40} \times 9.16\% = 6.412\%$	
Exit charge: $^{3}/_{10} \times 6.412\% \times £325,000$	£6,252
Roger's exit charge: 25 July 2014 to 27 September 2019 = 5 years i.e. 20 complete quarters	
Rate of Roger's exit charge:	
$^{20}/_{40} \times 6.412\% = 3.206\%$	
Exit charge: $^{3}/_{10} \times 3.206\% \times £275,000$	£2,645

Notes to the example

(A) There was no charge to IHT on Alex becoming entitled to his one-third absolute interest on his 25th birthday in February 2008 but his brother and sister who are beneficiaries of the remainder of the trust will effectively suffer an exit charge when they take their benefit at the appropriate time but see (C) below.

(B) As Stephanie and Roger are minors, they may not be regarded as mature enough to receive distributions from the settlement at the age of 18. Therefore, from 6 April 2008, the settlement can come within an '18–25 trust' within *IHTA 1984, s 71D(3)(4)* but the exit charge under *IHTA 1984, s 71F(5)* does not commence until each of them attain their 18th birthdays and ending on the day before the occasion of charge, e.g. their attaining age 25 or receiving capital entitlement or advance.

(C) In order to ensure that this existing pre-22 March 2006 accumulation and maintenance settlement continues to benefit from IHT exemption after 6 April 2008, the assets in the trust must go to the beneficiaries absolutely on or before their attainment of the age of 18 years. Therefore, trustees must have modified the terms of the settlement prior to 6 April 2008 under a suitable power of appointment so that the beneficiaries will be fully entitled to the assets and accumulations on or before the age of 18. HMRC have confirmed that the inclusion of the statutory power of advancement, or a wider power of similar effect, in the trust deed does not cause the trust to fail the requirements of *IHTA 1984, s 71A* or *s 71D*, even though such powers can be used to create continuing trusts for the beneficiary. Also, it was queried with HMRC whether the legislation should be interpreted as no longer permitting the pooling of the trust funds after 6 April 2008 so that separate trusts must exist for the beneficiaries who then become the sole beneficiary of that fund. HMRC, in published replies to submissions jointly by the CIOT and STEP, confirmed that pooling remains permissible for bereaved minors trusts and age 18–25 trusts.

Example 2

On 31 December 2000 G, who had made no cumulative chargeable transfers within the previous 7 years, settled £150,000 on accumulation and maintenance settlement for his son GS born on that date. The trust is contingent on GS attaining the age of 25 years subject thereto to G's nephew N, aged 21 at 22 March 2006, attaining the age of 26, subject thereto for H absolutely with *Trustee Act 1925, s 31* being applicable. GS died on 6 April 2009 at the age of 9 years.

The settlement is valued at £640,000 on 30 December 2010. The property in the settlement is valued at £700,000 at 21 March 2012, the day before N attains his 26th birthday when the funds are released to him.

As the settlement was an accumulation and maintenance settlement prior to 22 March 2006, it continued to be so until 6 April 2008 when it ceased to be subject to *IHTA 1984, s 71* when there was no charge. *IHTA 1984, s 71D(3)(4)* '18–25 trust' subsequently applied by reason particularly of *s 71D(3)(a)*. On the death of GS on 6 April 2009, *s 71D* ceased to apply by reason of *s 71D(6)(c)* which, at that point, does not give rise to a charge. N, although entitled to income, does not yet have an interest in possession within *IHTA 1984, s 49(1A)* and therefore the relevant property trust regime will commence resulting in a ten-year anniversary charge on 31 December 2010 and an exit charge on 22 March 2012 when N reaches his birthday at 26 within the terms of the settlement.

	£
Ten-year anniversary charge 31 December 2010	
Value of relevant property on 31.12.2010	640,000
Less nil rate band £325,000	325,000
IHT at lifetime rates on £315,000 @ 20%	£63,000

Effective rate $\dfrac{63{,}000}{640{,}000} = 9.84375\%$

Rate of charge for period 6.4.2009 to 31.12.2010:	
$^{3}/_{10}$ × 9.84375% = 2.953125% × $^{6}/_{40}$ × £640,000	
Ten-year anniversary charge:	£1,019
Exit charge on N becoming absolutely entitled at 22 March 2012	
Effective rate (as above) = 9.84375%	
No. of complete successive quarters between 31.12.2010 to 22.3.2012 = 4	
Proportionate charge:	
9.84375% × $^{3}/_{10}$ × $^{4}/_{40}$ × £700,000	£2,067

In cases where an accumulation and maintenance settlement is replaced with a life interest in favour of a beneficiary prior to 22 March 2006 that beneficiary is treated as beneficially entitled to the property in which the interest subsists, i.e. the settled property is in his or her estate for IHT purposes. There is an IHT charge based on the value of the settled property in which his interest subsists when a beneficiary disposes of his interest or it otherwise comes to an end, i.e. either as a transfer on death or as a PET where the termination of the interest occurs during the lifetime of the tenant, for example where there is an exercise of a power of appointment. [*IHTA 1984, ss 49(1), 51(1), 51A, 52(1); FA 2006, Sch 20 paras 11–13*]. From 22 March 2006 newly created IIP settlements will be treated under the relevant property taxing regime unless the interest is an immediate post-death interest (IPDI) or a transitional serial interest (TSI) or a disabled person's interest. See **39** SETTLEMENTS WITH INTERESTS IN POSSESSION.

Example 3

On 6 June 1989 G settled shares on trust equally for his three grandchildren on an accumulation and maintenance settlement. He had made no cumulative chargeable transfers within the previous seven years. He settled shares in a property investment company that he had set up many years before on an accumulation and maintenance settlement for his grandchildren. The trust is contingent on the grandchildren attaining 25 years when they would receive life interests. The first born grandchild, Graham, attained the age of 25 years on 28 February 2006, while Stephanie, who was born 27 September 1994, and Roger, born 25 July 1996, are 14 and 12 years old respectively.

The settlement is comprised of 1,000 shares in the company which were valued at £100 per share when the settlement was made but are valued at £6,000 per share on 6 June 2009. The property in the settlement is valued at £7,000 per share at 6 June 2019.

As the settlement is an accumulation and maintenance settlement prior to 22 March 2006, it continued to be so until 6 April 2008 when it ceased to be subject to *IHTA 1984, s 71*, at which point there is no charge. From 6 April 2008, it becomes a relevant property trust and, from that point, becomes subject to ten-yearly charges because the settlement is within *IHTA 1984, s 58*. The settlement will also suffer exit charges. The first charge arising after 6 April 2008 will be on 6 June 2009 and this is the first ten-yearly charge which will be appropriately apportioned. The next charge will be either a ten-yearly charge on 6 June 2019 or an exit charge prior to that date depending on the trustees' decisions.

	£
Ten-year anniversary charge 6 June 2009	
Value of relevant property on 6 June 2009 (see note A)	4,002,000
Value of other property (see note B)	33,333
Less nil rate band £325,000	325,000
IHT at lifetime rates on £3,710,333 @ 20%	£742,067

Effective rate $\dfrac{742{,}067}{4{,}002{,}000} = 18.5424\%$

Rate of charge for period 6.4.2008 to 6.6.2009:

$\frac{3}{10}$ × 18.5424% = 5.56272% × $\frac{4}{40}$ × £4,002,000	
First ten-year anniversary charge	£22,262
Ten-year anniversary charge 6 June 2019	
Value of relevant property on 6 June 2019 (see note A)	4,669,000
Less nil rate band, say, £325,000	325,000
IHT at lifetime rates on £4,344,000 @ 20%	£868,800

Effective rate $\frac{868,800}{4,669,000} = 18.6078\%$

Rate of charge for period 7.6.2009 to 6.6.2019:	
$\frac{3}{10}$ × 18.6078% = 5.5823% × $\frac{40}{40}$ × £4,669,000	
Second ten-year anniversary charge	£260,638

Notes to the example

(A) The value of the remaining 667 shares after deducting Graham's share which he had an interest in possession at 22 March 2006 is £6,000 per share. The ten-yearly charge then applies from 6 April 2008 when the new relevant property rules apply up to the date of the first ten-yearly anniversary date of the setting up of the settlement. This conveniently turns out to be only four quarters after the new rules come into force and the charge is a comparatively small £22,340. However, the Trustees will find it difficult to meet this liability if the company does not pay a dividend. It may be possible to pay the tax in ten annual instalments (see **32.5** PAYMENT OF TAX)

(B) For exit charges and ten-year charges up to 17 November 2015, Graham's one-third portion must still be brought into account at its value when the settlement commenced, being other property in the trust which was never relevant property and which has not subsequently become relevant property: see *IHTA 1984, s 66(4)(b)*. This does not apply on or after 18 November 2015.

Key points concerning accumulation and maintenance trusts

[41.7] Points to consider are as follows.

- It is no longer possible to set up an A&M settlement as from 22 March 2006 by which date there were three options:
  - (a) to wind up the trust on or before 5 April 2008 or the date on which the beneficiaries attain the age of 18 years if sooner;
  - (b) to have changed the terms of the trust on or before 5 April 2008 to ensure that income and capital vest absolutely at or before the beneficiary's eighteenth birthday; or,
  - (c) to leave the trust unaltered so that it falls within the relevant property regime.

See 40 SETTLEMENTS — DISCRETIONARY TRUSTS AND OTHER TRUSTS OF RELEVANT PROPERTY. The attractions of the third option above are that it gave the trustees control and flexibility especially over shares which the options at (a) and (b) would not.

- Another alternative to the A&M settlement is the setting up of a bare trust which is not a settlement for IHT purposes within *IHTA 1984, s 43(2)(a)* and is a potentially exempt transfer. Such trusts may be ideal for grandparents or other relatives but if a parent sets up a bare trust for their child any income arising from that trust in excess of £100 is assessed on the parent/settlor under *ITTOIA 2005, ss 629–632*. The difficulty is that under a bare trust the beneficiary has an immediate and absolute entitlement to the income and capital. The inclusion of *Trustee Act 1925, s 31*, which allows trustees to withhold income, accumulate it or distribute it at their discretion, is not thought to bring the bare trust within the definition of a settlement at *IHTA 1984, s 43(2)(b)* because the accumulations belong to the beneficiary (see also CIOT/STEP questions and answers on IHT Schedule 20, question 33). The provisions of *Trustee Act 1925, s 32* may be included so as to enable trustees to make a settled advance of the trust fund before the beneficiary attains the age of 18, thereby deferring his or her entitlement to a later time. It is not considered that an IHT charge arises by the exercise of the *s 32* power. Further advantages arise with a bare trust in relation to CGT where the minor would be entitled to the annual CGT allowance and there is no disposal for CGT purposes when the trustees pass the assets on to the beneficiary at 18 years old.
- In relation to any trusts that were created as A&M trusts and which are still in existence, it should be noted that the beneficiaries may be treated differently for inheritance tax purposes. For example, take the case of two beneficiaries of an A&M trust that was created to give an interest in possession at age 25 and absolute entitlement to capital at age 50. The first beneficiary turned 25 in 2005 and has a qualifying interest in possession — that is to say, the assets effectively form part of his estate for inheritance tax purposes. The second beneficiary turned 25 in 2007 (i.e. after 22 March 2006) and so his interest in possession falls within the relevant property regime and will suffer ten yearly charges and exit charges whenever capital leaves the trust, including on his absolute entitlement.

42

Settlements — Interests held on Protective Trusts

Cross-reference. See also **40** SETTLEMENTS — DISCRETIONARY TRUSTS AND OTHER TRUSTS OF RELEVANT PROPERTY.

Simon's Taxes. See **I5.6**.

Other Sources. HMRC Customer Guide to Inheritance Tax; Foster, Part E6.

Introduction to interests held on protective trusts

[42.1] 'Protective trust' is defined by the *Trustee Act 1925, s 33* and, broadly, is a trust under which a person ('the principal beneficiary') is entitled to an interest in possession in the settled property for the trust period unless he forfeits his interest e.g. by attempting to assign his interest or by becoming bankrupt. Usually, if the interest of the principal beneficiary is forfeited, the trust property is held on discretionary trusts for a class of beneficiaries. The class includes the principal beneficiary and his spouse and his children or more remoter issue or, in the absence of spouse and issue, the principal beneficiary and the persons who would be entitled to the trust fund or the income thereof on his death. Where property is held on trusts to the like effect as those specified in *Trustee Act 1925, s 33(1)*, special provisions apply. Trusts of 'like effect' to those defined in the *Trustee Act* are those that are not materially different in their tax consequences i.e. where there are only minor variations or additional administrative powers or duties. A 'minor variation' does not include the extension *ab initio* of the class of beneficiaries to brothers and sisters (although it is appreciated that so long as the principal beneficiary has no spouse or issue the statutory trusts extend to the next of kin for the time being who might well be brothers and sisters) (see HMRC Statement of Practice E7 with additions derived from the original source which was a former Inland Revenue letter published in the Law Society's Gazette of 3 March 1976 and reprinted in British Tax Review 1976, p 421). A protective trust of income for the benefit of the settlor is a trust of 'like effect' (*Thomas & Thomas v CIR* Ch D 1981, [1981] STC 382).

Forfeiture after 11 April 1978

[42.2] Where the principal beneficiary's interest in possession comes to an end after 11 April 1978, the 'failure or determination' of such trusts before the end of the trust period will be disregarded for the purposes of inheritance tax and the principal beneficiary will continue to be treated as beneficially entitled to an interest in possession while discretionary trusts similar to those in *Trustee Act 1925, s 33(1)(ii)* (see **42.1** above) continue to apply under the *Trustee Act*. The effect is that any distribution to the principal beneficiary is not chargeable (because he is treated as having an interest in possession) but distributions to any other beneficiary will have the same treatment as with interest in possession trusts generally: see **39** SETTLEMENTS WITH INTERESTS IN POSSESSION. Also, the value of the principal beneficiary's deemed interest will form part of his estate on his death. [*IHTA 1984, s 88*]. For a consideration of the meaning of '*failure or determination*', see *Cholmondeley v CIR* Ch D, [1986] STC 384.

Forfeiture on or after 22 March 2006

[42.3] Where protective trusts are created by the forfeiting of a beneficiary's interest, as for example, where the beneficiary attempts to sell the interest on or after 22 March 2006, then *IHTA 1984, s 88(3)* treats forfeiture out of a protective trust interest in possession created on or before that date as if it had happened on or before that date. The effect is that the deemed interest in possession arising on forfeiture is treated as created before 22 March 2006 and therefore the position is as in **42.2** above.

In circumstances where a protective trust is created under *Trustee Act 1925, s 33(1)(i)* after 21 March 2006, the trust will be a relevant property trust unless the interest in possession of the beneficiary is an immediate post-death interest, a disabled person's interest or a transitional serial interest. Any change of beneficial interest in a relevant property trust has no effect on the IHT position of the trust. If the trust is not a relevant property trust, then forfeiture of the interest in possession under the protective trusts will have the same treatment as in **42.2** above. [*IHTA 1984, s 88(3)–(6) as inserted by FA 2006, Sch 20 para 24*].

Forfeiture before 12 April 1978

[42.4] The following provisions apply where the principal beneficiary's interest in possession came to an end before 12 April 1978. Note that this could have been at any time before this date and not just in the era of capital transfer tax.

There is a charge to tax:

(a) where the settled property ceases to be held on discretionary trusts similar to those specified in *Trustee Act 1925, s 33(1)(ii)* (see **42.1** above) otherwise than by being applied for the principal beneficiary (but see also **21.4** EXEMPT TRANSFERS for certain situations where there is no charge when property becomes held for charitable purposes only without limit of time or that of a qualifying political party *or* a national body mentioned in *IHTA 1984, Sch 3* or, under certain conditions, a body not established or conducted for profit), or

(b) if the trustees make a 'disposition' otherwise than by way of payment for the benefit of the principal beneficiary which reduces the value of the settled property. '*Disposition*' includes an omission to exercise a right, unless not deliberate, which is treated as made at the latest time that the right could have been exercised.

Thus, in cases where the forfeiture of the interest in the trust arose before 12 April 1978, charges may still currently arise at special rates of tax as set out below when funds are paid out of the protective trusts. [*IHTA 1984, ss 70(10), 73(1)(2), 76*].

No charge arises:

(i) if, under (b) above, the trustees do not intend to confer a gratuitous benefit and either the transaction is at arm's length between persons not connected with each other (see **12** CONNECTED PERSONS) or is such as might be expected in such a transaction; or
(ii) if, under (b) above, the disposition is a grant of a tenancy of agricultural property in the UK, Channel Islands or Isle of Man, for use for agricultural purposes and is made for full consideration in money or money's worth; or
(iii) on the 'payment' of costs or expenses attributable to the property; or
(iv) where any payment is, or will be, income for income tax purposes of any person (or, in the case of a non-resident, would be if he were so resident), or
(v) in respect of a liability to make a payment under (iii) or (iv) above.

'*Payment*' includes the transfer of assets other than money. [*IHTA 1984, ss 63, 70(3)(4), 73(3)*].

Tax is charged on the amount by which the trust property is less immediately after the event giving rise to the charge that it would have been but for the event (i.e. the loss to the donor principle), grossed-up where the settlement pays the tax.

The rate at which tax is charged is the aggregate of the following percentages for each complete successive 'quarter' in 'the relevant period':

	Cumulative Total
0.25% for each of the first 40 quarters	10%
0.20% for each of the next 40 quarters	8%
0.15% for each of the next 40 quarters	6%
0.10% for each of the next 40 quarters	4%
0.05% for each of the next 40 quarters	2%
Maximum rate chargeable after 50 years	30%

'*Relevant period*' is the period beginning with the day on which the property became (or last became) held on the discretionary trusts, or 13 March 1975 if later, and ending on the day before the chargeable event.

'*Quarter*' means any period of three months. [*IHTA 1984, ss 63, 70(5)(6)(8), 73(3)*].

Excluded property

[42.5] Where the whole or part of the amount on which tax is charged as in **42.4** above is attributable to property which was **20** EXCLUDED PROPERTY at any time during the relevant period, then, in determining the rate at which tax is charged in respect of that amount or part, no quarter throughout which the property was excluded property is to be counted. [*IHTA 1984, ss 70(7), 73(3)*].

See also the provisions under **40.19** and **40.22** SETTLEMENTS — DISCRETIONARY TRUSTS AND OTHER TRUSTS OF RELEVANT PROPERTY which also apply to property settled or appointed on protective trusts.

Example

In 1951 X left his estate on protective trusts for his son Z. On 1 January 1978 Z attempted to assign his interest and the protective trusts were accordingly determined. On 1 May 1983 the trustees advanced £25,000 to Z to enable him to purchase a flat. At the same time, they also advanced £10,000 (net) to his granddaughter D. On 1 May 2010 Z died and the trust fund, valued at £200,000, passed equally to his grandchildren absolutely.

1 May 1983

There is no charge to IHT on the payment to Z, but a charge arises on the payment to D.

The relevant period is the period from the determination of the protective trusts (1 January 1978) to 1 May 1983, i.e. 21 complete quarters.

The rate of tax is 0.25% for each of 21 quarters 5.25%.

IHT payable is:

$$\frac{5.25}{100 - 5.25} \times £10,000 = £554$$

The gross payment is £10,554.

1 May 2010

There is a charge to IHT when the trust vests on the death of Z. 129 complete quarters have elapsed since the protective trusts determined.

The rate of tax is:

	%
0.25% for each of the first 40 quarters	10.00
0.20% for each of the next 40 quarters	8.00
0.15% for the next 40 quarters	6.00
0.10% for the next 9 quarter	0.90
	24.90%

IHT payable is 24.90% × £200,000 = £49,800

Key points concerning interests held on protective trusts

[42.6] Points to consider are as follows.

- Where a protective trust is created after 22 March 2006 during the lifetime of a settlor, it does not receive any special treatment for IHT unless it qualifies as a disabled person's trust. With that exception, it will be subject to the relevant property regime with an appropriate chargeable disposal by the settlor on creation and then subsequent ten-yearly charges and exit charges.
- A protective trust set up by a will to commence on the death secures treatment as an immediate post-death interest for the principal beneficiary. The result of this is that on termination of the principal beneficiary's interest e.g. due to bankruptcy, the interest in possession is deemed to continue as an immediate post-death interest. Hence no ten-yearly, proportionate or exit charges will arise thereafter as with relevant property trusts. However, on the principal beneficiary's death as an immediate post-death interest, the value of the trust at that time is treated as part of the principal beneficiary's estate for IHT purposes. There are, however, no special income tax or CGT advantages of such trusts other than the automatic uplift for CGT purposes on the creation of the immediate post-death interest by the testator.
- Protective trusts must follow the wording in *Trustee Act 1925, s 33*. In the case of *Dennis's Settlement Trusts Re* [1942] 1 All ER 520, a deed varying the terms of the protective trust resulted in a protective discretionary trust arising. *Section 33(1)(i)* permits advances of capital to be made to the principal beneficiary under a statutory or express power without triggering a discretionary trust.

43

Settlements — Trusts for Bereaved Minors and 'Age 18–25 trusts'

Cross-references. 41 SETTLEMENTS — ACCUMULATION AND MAINTENANCE TRUSTS; 40 SETTLEMENTS — DISCRETIONARY TRUSTS AND OTHER TRUSTS OF RELEVANT PROPERTY.

Other Sources. HMRC Customer Guide to Inheritance Tax; Tolley's UK Taxation of Trusts; Foster, Part E1.02.

Introduction — transfers into trusts for bereaved minors

[43.1] A trust created under the terms of a person's will or intestacy will not come within the relevant property trust regime if it is a trust for a bereaved minor. Subject to the conditions detailed below, a 'trust for a bereaved minor' is a trust for the benefit of a person under the age of 18, at least one of whose parents, or as the case may be step-parent or person having parental responsibility e.g. legal guardian, has died and the trust arises in any one of the following circumstances:

(a) statutory trusts arising under *Administration of Estates Act 1925, ss 46, 47(1)* in relation to the estate of a person dying intestate with infant issue surviving; or

(b) settled property held on trusts established under the will of a deceased parent or, as the case may be, step-parent; or

(c) settled property held on trust for the benefit of a 'bereaved minor' as a result of payments from:

  (i) a scheme established by arrangements under the *Criminal Injuries Compensation Act 1995*;

  (ii) arrangements made by the Secretary of State for compensation for criminal injuries which were in operation before commencement of such Criminal Injuries Compensation schemes;

  (iii) a scheme being established by arrangements under the *Criminal Injuries Compensation (Northern Ireland) Order 2002*;

  (iv) with effect from 8 April 2010, the Victims of Overseas Terrorism Compensation Scheme.

[*IHTA 1984, ss 71, 71A, 71B, 71C, 71H; FA 2006, Sch 20 paras 1, 2, 3*].

In relation to (b) and (c), the bereaved minor must, prior to or upon the attainment of the age of 18 years, become absolutely entitled to the settled property and also absolutely entitled to any income arising therefrom and any income that has been accumulated. Whilst the beneficiary is under the age of 18 if any of the capital of the settled property is applied, it must be applied for the benefit of the bereaved minor only, subject to a relaxation for small payments for trusts set up on or after 8 April 2013, as detailed below. In relation to income whilst the beneficiary is under the age of 18, he or she must either be entitled to such income or alternatively none of the income may be applied for the benefit of any other person. There is a relaxation for small payments to other parties of either capital or income for trusts set up on or after 8 April 2013, as detailed below. The trust may be for a class of beneficiaries, i.e. all the children of the testator who are under the age of 18, but the trust must 'secure' that each beneficiary becomes entitled on attaining the age of 18 to his or her share of the fund. This prohibits altering the shares of the beneficiaries, as was possible with accumulation and maintenance trusts.

Trusts are not treated as failing the above conditions by virtue of trustee powers of advancement, whether under the *Trustee Act 1925, s 32* or *Trustee Act (Northern Ireland) 1958, s 33* or where trustees have similar powers but unrestricted. [*IHTA 1984, s 71A(4); FA 2006, Sch 20 para 1*]. For bereaved minors trusts set up on or after 8 April 2013, including those set up under a Will executed before that date, the trustees may have powers to apply sums, whether capital or income, for the benefit of someone other than the bereaved minor, but only up to an annual limit. This limit is the lower of either £3,000 or 3% of the amount that is the maximum value of the settled property in the period in question. The limit applies for each tax year. Where an amount is paid out in excess of the annual limit otherwise than for the benefit of the bereaved minor, and other exemptions do not apply, there is a tax charge under *IHTA 1984, s 71B* on that excess: *IHTA 1984, ss 71A (4)(za), 4A, 4B, and 4C.*

For these purposes 'parent' includes step-parent or 'guardian' who has parental responsibility for the minor as defined within the *Children Act 1989, s 3* or where applicable the *Children Act (Scotland) Act 1995, s 1(3)* or the *Children (Northern Ireland) Order 1995*. [*IHTA 1984, s 71H; FA 2006, Sch 20 para 1*].

Example 1

Mr and Mrs A both die in a boating accident on 12 July 2010 whilst on holiday and it is not known who survived the other and neither has made a will but Mr A is the elder of the two. They have two children who are aged four years and are twins and both the deceased have parents still living. Their estates are valued at £325,000 and £335,000 for Mr and Mrs A respectively. As there is no will or survivorship provision made by either there is the possibility that the parents of either Mr A or Mrs A may wish to prove their son/daughter survived the spouse and thereby share in both estates, however, under the *Law Reform (Succession) Act 1995, s 1* in the case of intestate spouses each estate passes as though the other had predeceased i.e. the estates pass as though each died as widow and widower. Note that there is a different treatment for IHT purposes where there is intestacy and deaths have occurred in *commorientes* circumstances. See Example 2 below.

The *Administration of Estates Act 1925, s 46(2A)* has the effect in Mr A's and Mrs A's case of their assets passing to their issue (applicable in this case to be held on statutory trusts as they are minors) so that no class of beneficiaries can participate unless all those in a prior class have predeceased. The parents of Mr and Mrs A will not therefore benefit from their children's intestate estates. The parents of Mrs A have agreed to act as guardians to the two children as the parents of Mr A are living abroad. Statutory trusts for the children due to their minority therefore arise on an intestacy and come within (a) above. However, see Example 2 below regarding the situation where settled property on bereaved minors trusts ceases to be property which satisfies the necessary conditions of *IHTA 1984, s 71B(2)(3) as inserted by FA 2006, Sch 20 para 1*.

Notes to the example

(A) Trustees for an infant may pay funds to a guardian since a minor cannot give good receipt for trust income unless he/she is married and that is not the case in this situation. [*Law of Property Act 1925, s 21*].

> 'Where the Trustees may apply the income for the benefit of a minor, they may do so by paying the income to the minor's guardian on behalf of the minor, or to minor if he has attained the age of 16. The Trustees are under no duty to enquire into the use of the income unless they have knowledge of circumstances which call for enquiry.'

(B) In many cases where the bereaved minor's trust has been set up the funds pertaining to that trust will have been subject to death rates of IHT where the estate is in excess of the appropriate nil rate band.

(C) Provided the grandparents secure parental responsibility for the minors within the meaning of the *Children Act 1989, s 3* then provided the requirements within (a)–(c) are met above on the death of one of the grandparents any trust set up in favour of the children under 18 will also become a trust for a bereaved minor thereby enabling capital to skip a generation. [*IHTA 1984, 71H; FA 2006, Sch 20 para 1*].

Definitions

'*Bereaved Minor*' means a person who has not yet attained the age of 18 years and at least one of whose parents, or, as the case may be, step-parent has died. For these purposes '*bereaved minor*' includes all beneficiaries within a relevant class provided they are alive and are under the specified age of 18. See CIOT/STEP clarification dated 29 June 2007. [*IHTA 1984, s 71C inserted by FA 2006, Sch 20 para 1*].

'*Parent*' for these purposes also means step-parent or person with 'parental responsibility' within the *Children Act 1989, s 3*. [*IHTA 1984, s 71H inserted by FA 2006, Sch 20 para 1*].

Note that unlike accumulation and maintenance settlements where no interest in possession subsists in the settled property and the income from that settled property is to be accumulated so far as not applied for the maintenance, education or benefit of a beneficiary the new '*bereaved minor*' can be given an interest in possession at the outset. The provisions for trusts for *bereaved minors* have priority over the immediate post-death interest regime. Therefore, there are varying possibilities in the drafting of the trust deed for the 'bereaved minor' which will need to address the fact whether a discretionary or interest in possession subsists. For income tax purposes it might be preferable to ensure that an interest in possession trust is formed. See 39 SETTLEMENTS WITH INTERESTS IN POSSESSION.

A bereaved minors trust may take effect after an immediate post-death interest for another beneficiary. On the termination of that other beneficiary's interest during his or her lifetime, a potentially exempt transfer arises (see **35.1**).

Treatment of payments out of trusts for bereaved minors

[43.2] A charge to tax arises:

(a) where settled property on bereaved minors trusts ceases to be property which satisfies the necessary conditions of *IHTA 1984, s 71A* as detailed in **43.1** at (a)–(c) above; or

(b) if the trustees make a 'disposition' which reduces the value of the settled property. '*Disposition*' includes an omission to exercise a right, unless not deliberate, which is treated as made at the latest time the right could have been exercised. [*IHTA 1984, ss 70(10), 71B(1)(3)*].

The rate is determined by reference to the settlor's cumulative transfers in the seven years preceding the date on which the settlement commenced, as well as the settlement's cumulative transfers in the ten years preceding the anniversary.

Tax calculation

Tax is calculated using lifetime Tables (see **37** RATES OF TAX) at the following rates:

(1) where the whole of the relevant property has been comprised in the settlement throughout the ten-year period ending immediately before the ten-year anniversary, at 30% of the effective rate;

(2) and where the whole or part of the relevant property was not relevant property or was not comprised in the settlement throughout the ten years ending immediately before the ten-year anniversary, at 30% of the effective rate reduced by one-fortieth for each successive 'quarter' in the ten-year period which expired before the property became, or last became, relevant property.

The '*effective rate*' is the rate found by expressing the tax chargeable as a percentage of the amount on which tax is charged on an assumed chargeable transfer by an assumed transferor. [*IHTA 1984, s 66(1)(2)*].

Circumstances of no charge

No charge arises:

(i) on a beneficiary's becoming absolutely entitled to the settled property (not necessarily in fixed shares) on or before attaining the specified age of 18 years; or

(ii) on the death of a beneficiary before attaining the specified age of 18 years (but see temporary charitable exit rules below); or

(iii) on being paid or applied for the advancement or benefit of the bereaved minor(s); or

(iv) on the '*payment*' of costs or expenses attributable to the property; or

(v) where any payment is, or will be, income for income tax purposes of any person (or, in the case of a non-resident, would be if he were so resident).

[*IHTA 1984, ss 70(3)(8)(10), 71B(2)(3); FA 2006, Sch 20 para 1*].

'*Payment*' includes the transfer of assets other than money. [*IHTA 1984, ss 63, 70(3)(4), 71(4)(5)*].

Tax charging provisions

Tax is charged on the amount by which the trust property is less immediately after the event giving rise to the charge than it would have been but for the event (i.e. the loss to donor principle), grossed-up where the settlement pays the tax. [*IHTA 1984, s 71B(3); FA 2006, Sch 20 para 1*].

The rate at which tax is charged is the aggregate of the following percentages for each complete successive 'quarter' in the 'relevant period'. [*IHTA 1984, ss 70(7); 71B(3); FA 2006, Sch 20 para 1*].

'*Quarter*' is a period of three months. [*IHTA 1984, ss 63, 70(5)(6)(8), 71(5)*].

'*Relevant period*' is the period beginning with the day on which the property became (or last became) held on bereaved minors trusts, or which immediately before it became property held on bereaved minors trusts was property held on accumulation and maintenance trusts but which had ceased to be so held on or after 22 March 2006, and ending on the day before the chargeable event. [*IHTA 1984, ss 70(3)–(8)(10), 71B(3); FA 2006, Sch 20 paras 1, 2*].

Where *s 71A* ceases to apply as in (a) above then the rate of charge will be that given at *IHTA 1984, s 70(6)* i.e., the temporary charitable exit rules. Potential circumstances are a trust for a bereaved minor is established but the minor dies, for instance, before the age 18 and the trust continues after the death of the minor. See also Example 2 below. In such circumstances the temporary charitable trust rules would apply with a maximum rate of 30% after 50 years have elapsed. See table below. A charge does not arise where settled property held on trusts for bereaved minors ceases to be so because the bereaved minor becomes absolutely entitled on or before the age of 18 or dies under the age of 18 or the property is applied or advanced to the bereaved minor before the age of 18. [*IHTA 1984, ss 70(6); 71B(2)(3); FA 2006, Sch 20 paras 1, 2*].

	Cumulative Total
0.25% for each of the first 40 quarters	10%
0.20% for each of the next 40 quarters	8%
0.15% for each of the next 40 quarters	6%
0.10% for each of the next 40 quarters	4%
0.05% for each of the next 40 quarters	2%
Maximum rate chargeable after 50 years	30%

The rate charged may be reduced if any of the property is, or was, EXCLUDED PROPERTY (20).

Example 2

Following on from the example above, assume that both the twin children fail to attain the age of 18 as a result of which funds held in trust for them as bereaved minors now pass to the parents. The effective date for this is 31 July 2021.

On 31 July 2021, the settlement fails to qualify as a bereaved minors trust and the clawback provisions apply. The settlement was valued at £594,000 on 12 July 2010 (see Note A) and at £750,000 on 31 July 2021. There will be a charge to IHT on the whole of the value of the settlement on 31 July 2021. The period from 12 July 2010 to 31 July 2021 is 44 complete quarters charged at the *IHTA 1984, s 70(6)* rate:

0.25% for each of the first	40	quarters	10%
0.20% for each of the next	4	quarters	0.8%
	44		10.8%

The IHT charge is 10.8% × £750,000 = £81,000

Notes to the example

(A) In the circumstances above or if trust for a bereaved minor continues after the death of that minor before his or her attaining the age of 18 years then the temporary charitable trust exit rules apply with a potential maximum rate of 30%. [*IHTA 1984, ss 70(6), 71B(3); FA 2006, Sch 20 paras 1, 2*].

Age 18–25 trusts

[43.3] Existing accumulation and maintenance settlements that satisfied the requirements detailed below by 6 April 2008 and newly created 'age 18–25 trusts' under the terms of a will or established under the Criminal Injuries Compensation Scheme will not come within the relevant property trust regime. [*IHTA 1984, s 71D(1)–(4) as inserted by FA 2006, Sch 20 para 1*].

'Age 18–25 trust' requirements

In order for the trusts to qualify as an 'age 18–25 trust', the following requirements and conditions must apply to it:

(a) the person for whom the trusts are held must, at some time prior to or upon the attainment of the age of 25 years, become absolutely entitled to the settled property, and also absolutely entitled to any income arising therefrom together with any income that has arisen from the property which has been accumulated; and

(b) whilst the beneficiary 'B' is living and under the age of 25, any settled property must be applied solely for 'B's benefit, but see relaxation of this rule under *FA 2013*, as detailed below. Although the legislation is drafted in terms of a single beneficiary 'B', HMRC accept that these provisions can equally apply to a trust with multiple beneficiaries under the age of 25 (see IHTM428126); and

(c) whilst the beneficiary 'B' is living and under the age of 25 any income arising from the settled property is applied solely for 'B's benefit or, if not applied, it is not applied for anyone else's benefit, but also subject to the relaxation of this rule under *FA 2013*, as detailed below.

The trust will be established by the will of a deceased parent for the benefit of a beneficiary or beneficiaries not having yet attained the age of 25, or as a result payments from the Criminal Injuries Compensation schemes within **43.1**(c) above. Note, however, that if the will gives the beneficiary an immediate interest in possession, the interest will not fall under the provisions for age 18–25 trusts but instead it will be treated as an immediate post-death interest (see further analysis under **43.5** below and **39.2** SETTLEMENTS WITH INTEREST IN POSSESSION). [*IHTA 1984, s 71D(1)–(2)*].

Alternatively, it must be settled property to which *IHTA 1984, s 71* ceases to have effect in the period 22 March 2006 to 6 April 2008 but that settled property may then be treated as an 'age 18–25 trust' if it continues to be held on trusts for a person who has not yet attained the age of 25 years and the trusts satisfy the conditions in (a)–(c) above. [*IHTA 1984, s 71D(3)–(4)*]. See Example 2 at **41.6** SETTLEMENTS — ACCUMULATION AND MAINTENANCE SETTLEMENTS.

In relation to (a) to (c) above, whilst the beneficiary is living and under the age of 25 if any of the capital of the settled property is applied it must be applied for the benefit of the beneficiary only. If the trust property is not so applied then whilst the beneficiary is under the age of 25 years the income arising therefrom, if any, must be a full entitlement or the income must not be applied for the benefit of any other person. [*IHTA 1984, s 71D(6)*].

Trusts are not treated as failing the above conditions by virtue of trustee powers of advancement, whether under the *Trustee Act 1925, s 32* or the *Trustee Act (Northern Ireland) 1958, s 33* or where trustees have similar powers but unrestricted [*IHTA 1984, s 71D(7)*].

[*IHTA 1984, s 71D as inserted by FA 2006, Sch 20 para 1*].

For trusts set up on or after 8 April 2013, including those set up under a Will executed before that date, the trustees may have powers to apply sums, whether capital or income, for the benefit of someone other than the bereaved minor, but only up to an annual limit. This limit is the lower of either £3,000 or 3% of the amount that is the maximum value of the settled property in the period in question. The limit applies for each tax year. Where an amount is paid out in excess of the annual limit otherwise than for the benefit of the bereaved minor, and other exemptions do not apply, there is a tax charge under *IHTA 1984, s 71E* on that excess: *IHTA 1984, s 71D(7A), (7B) and (7C)*. With effect from the same date, it is also provided that protective trusts within *Trustee Act 1925, s 33* may fall within the age 18–25 provisions where the other conditions set out above are satisfied. [*IHTA 1984, s 71D(6A)*].

Treatment of payments out of age 18–25 trusts

[43.4] A charge to tax arises:

(a) where 'B' becomes absolutely entitled the settled property, any income arising from it and any income that has arisen and been accumulated; on the death of 'B'; when the property settled is paid or applied for the advancement or benefit of 'B'; or

(b) if the trustees make a 'disposition' which reduces the value of the settled property. '*Disposition*' includes an omission to exercise a right, unless not deliberate, which is treated as made at the latest time the right could have been exercised.

[*IHTA 1984, ss 71E(1)(5), 71F(2) as inserted by FA 2006, Sch 20 para 1*].

Circumstances of no charge

No charge to tax arises:

(i) on a beneficiary at or under the age of 18 becoming absolutely entitled to, or to an interest in possession in, settled property on or before attaining the specified age of 25 years, or
(ii) on the death of a beneficiary before attaining the specified age of 18 years (but see temporary charitable exit rules below), or
(iii) on settled property becoming whilst the beneficiary is living and under the age of 18 property held under trust for a bereaved minor, or
(iv) on settled property being paid or applied for the advancement or benefit of the beneficiary before attaining the age of 18 but whilst still living or on attaining the age of 18, or
(v) on the 'payment' of costs or expenses attributable to the property, or
(vi) where any payment is, or will be, income for income tax purposes of any person (or, in the case of a non-resident, would be if he were so resident).

[*IHTA 1984, s 71E(2)(3); FA 2006, Sch 20 para 1*].

'*Payment*' includes the transfer of assets other than money. [*IHTA 1984, ss 63, 70(3)(4), 71(4)(5)*].

Tax calculation

Where tax is charged in accordance with an event arising under (a) or (b) above and it occurs after the beneficiary has attained the age of 18 years then the amount of the tax is calculated as follows:

Chargeable amount × Relevant fraction × Settlement rate = Tax due

- *Chargeable amount* is the amount by which the value of the property in the settlement has been decreased by following the event that gave rise to the charge or where the amount by which the value of the property in the settlement is reduced as a result of the chargeable event (i.e. the loss to donor principle) grossed-up where the settlement pays the tax;
- *Relevant fraction* is three-tenths multiplied by so many fortieths in the period beginning with the day on which the beneficiary attained 18 years or, if later, on the day when the property became subject to an '18–25 trust' and ending on the day prior to the occasion of the charge. For these purposes one fortieth is a complete three-month period;
- *Settlement rate* is the effective rate at which tax would be charged on the value transferred by a chargeable transfer where the value transferred is equal to the aggregate of the value of:
  - the settlement immediately after commencement; and
  - any related settlement on creation; and
  - any other property which became comprised in the settlement but before the charge arising under (a) or (b) above.

With effect for charges on or after 18 November 2015, only the value of property to which *IHTA 1984, s 71D* applies is counted in a related settlement.

[*IHTA 1984, s 71F; FA 2006, Sch 20 para 1*].

Example 3

X, a widower, dies on 29 August 2010 and by his will leaves all his assets in trust for his daughter Emily, aged 20 on 20 September 2010. The initial capital in the trust amounts to £640,000 after IHT deductions. Emily will become absolutely entitled to capital and income by the age of 25 and whilst she is living before that date the trustees will only apply the settled property for her benefit within the terms of the trust. On her birthday on 20 September 2015 at age 25, she becomes entitled to the capital and any accumulated income. The capital and remainder of accumulated income amounts to £640,000 on that date. X had made no previous transfers in the seven years prior to his death.

Assumed chargeable transfer 20 September 2015:	£
Value of relevant property on 20.9.2010	640,000
Less nil rate band, £325,000	325,000
	£315,000
IHT at lifetime rates on £315,000 @ 20%	£63,000

Effective rate $\frac{63,000}{640,000} = 9.843\%$

Rate of charge for period 29.8.2010 to 20.9.2015 (i.e. 20 complete quarters):

$\frac{3}{10} \times 9.843\% = 2.953\% \times \frac{20}{40} \times £640,000$

Exit charge on Emily becoming 25 payable by Emily:	£9,450

Notes to the example

(A) If between the ages of 18 and 25, the beneficiary becomes absolutely entitled or property is paid or applied out of the trust fund by the trustees for the beneficiary, or, the beneficiary dies, there will be a charge to IHT similar to that in this example and based on the number of complete quarters that have elapsed since the beneficiary attained the age of 18, or if later, the time when the settlement was created. See SETTLEMENTS — DISCRETIONARY TRUSTS AND OTHER TRUSTS OF RELEVANT PROPERTY (40).

(B) A clawback charge, a rare situation in the circumstances, similar to that shown in Example 2 above will apply where assets leave an 18–25 trust where *s 71D* above ceases to apply. In those unusual circumstances above then the rate of charge will be that given at *IHTA 1984, s 70(6)* i.e., the temporary charitable exit rules. [*IHTA 1984, ss 70(6)–(8), 71G; FA 2006, Sch 20 para 1*].

Key points concerning trusts for bereaved minors and 'age 18–25 trusts'

[43.5] Points to consider are:

- Under a bereaved minor's trust, the income arising may subject to either trusts for accumulation or alternatively may be payable for the benefit of the minor on interest in possession trusts. The trust may be for more than one child if the deceased had two or more children under the age of 18 but it is not permissible to alter the shares of the beneficiaries under trust before they attain the age of 18. When the child attains the age of 18, the funds become payable to him or her absolutely, with no IHT exit charge applying. Capital gains tax hold over relief is also available. The trusts may contain a power of advancement, and this may give the opportunity, if the trustees think fit, to resettle the funds on new trusts for the bereaved minor, for example to delay absolute entitlement until a later age than age 18. Any such continuing trusts will be within the relevant property trust regime with ten yearly charges applying, notwithstanding any interest in possession given to the beneficiary. In this respect therefore, bereaved minors trusts have an advantage over an absolute gift on bare trusts, payable at the age of 18.
- Under an Age 18-25 trust, an IHT exit charge applies where absolute entitlement is conferred after the beneficiary attains the age of 18, although often the amounts involved will not be substantial and the tax liability will be justified by enabling the trustees to have continuing control of the trust fund until the beneficiary is more mature. Capital gains tax hold over relief is also available.
- Where funds are left by will on age 18-25 trusts for the children of the deceased, it may be preferable to have trusts for accumulation of income up to the age of entitlement so as to ensure that the same tax treatment applies to all beneficiaries. Without such a provision, where *Trustee Act 1925, s 31* applies, beneficiaries over the age of 18 at the date of death, and those who will attain the age of 18 within two years of the death, will have immediate post death interests and, although there will as a result be no IHT exit charge on their becoming absolutely entitled capital gains tax hold over relief will not be available at that time. Note that the *Perpetuities and Accumulations Act 2009* came into force on 6th April 2010 and all new trusts created on, or after, that date have a trust period of 125 years from the date of creation, regardless of what the trust document states. In addition, all such trusts can accumulate income for the entire trust period unless the trust document states otherwise. However the provisions of that Act apply only to wills executed on or after 6 April 2010 and hence older wills must be re-executed in order to benefit from the newly extended accumulation period.

44

Settlements — Trusts for Disabled Persons

Cross-reference. 40 SETTLEMENTS — DISCRETIONARY TRUSTS AND OTHER TRUSTS OF RELEVANT PROPERTY.

Simon's Taxes. See I5.207.

Other Sources. HMRC Customer Guide to Inheritance Tax; Foster, Part E6.26–6.28; IHTM04102.

Introduction to trusts for disabled persons

[44.1] Special provisions in the IHT legislation apply to trusts for disabled persons. The purpose of these is to enable trusts to be set up in lifetime for the benefit of those within various categories of disability without a charge to IHT arising. The transfer into the trust will be either potentially exempt or in some cases may be within *IHTA 1984, s 11* as a transfer for the care and maintenance of a dependent relative. The trust assets will be in the estate of the beneficiary for IHT purposes.

Unfortunately, the relevant provisions are not easy to follow, there being four sub-categories which are poorly set out, each with their own detailed conditions. Coupled with the equally complex and entirely separate capital gains tax and income tax provisions, this must be regarded as a specialist area.

Definitions

'Disabled person's interest'

For IHT purposes there are four categories of disabled person's interests. In broad terms they cover a discretionary settlement made for the benefit of a disabled person (as defined), a settlement made by a person ahead of impending disabilities, and an interest in possession trust made after 22 March 2006 for a disabled person, whether by a third party or by the disabled person as settlor. In more detail, a disabled person's interest for IHT purposes means:

(i) a deemed interest in possession to which a person is beneficially entitled under *IHTA 1984, s 89(2)* (discretionary trusts for disabled persons); or
(ii) an interest in possession to which a person is beneficially entitled under *IHTA 1984, s 89A(4)* (self-settlement by person expected to become disabled); or
(iii) any other interest in possession to which the disabled person is beneficially entitled where the property of the settlement was transferred into settlement on or after 22 March 2006 (see also note below concerning impact of *FA 2013*); or
(iv) an interest in possession in settled property, other than in (i) and (ii) above, to which 'A' is beneficially entitled where A is the settlor and was entitled to the property immediately before its settlement on or after 22 March 2006 and satisfies HMRC that he had a condition at the time which it was reasonable to expect that it would lead to him becoming a disabled person within any of the categories (i), (ii) or (iii) listed under the definition of disabled person below.

[*IHTA 1984, s 89B*].

For property transferred into trust on or after 17 July 2013 the definition at (iii) above is amended so that if any settled property is applied during the beneficiary's life for the benefit of a beneficiary, the amount must be applied for the benefit of the disabled person, save for an amount of £3,000 or 3% of the maximum value of the settled property in the tax year concerned, whichever is the lower. Unrestricted powers of advancement are also permissible. [*FA 2013, Sch 44 para 10*].

An interest in any of the above four categories is a disabled person's interest for the purposes of the *IHTA 1984*. Accordingly by virtue of *IHTA 1984, s 49(1A)(b)*, the beneficiary is treated as being beneficially entitled to the trust property such that a transfer into the trust by a third party may have potentially exempt treatment for IHT. A self-settlement has no IHT consequence.

Definition of a 'disabled person'

A '*disabled person*' is one who, when property was transferred into settlement, was:

(i) incapable by reason of mental disorder within the meaning of the *Mental Health Act 1983* (but amended by the *Mental Health Act 2007* from 19 July 2007 and reference is made to any disorder or disability of the mind) of administering his property or managing his affairs, or
(ii) in receipt of an attendance allowance under *Social Security Contributions and Benefits Act 1992, s 64* or *Social Security Contributions and Benefits (Northern Ireland) Act 1992, s 64*, or
(iii) in receipt of a disability living allowance under *Social Security Contributions and Benefits Act 1992, s 71* or *Social Security Contributions and Benefits (Northern Ireland) Act 1992, s 71* by virtue of entitlement to the care component at the highest or middle rate.

With effect on or after 8 April 2013, a uniform definition of 'disabled person' applies across various taxes including inheritance tax. The definition is in *FA 2005, Sch 1A* and this includes the circumstances at (i), (ii) and (iii) set out above, and in addition:

(iv) a person in receipt of personal independence payment by virtue of entitlement to the daily living component;
(v) a person in receipt of constant attendance allowance;
(vi) a person in receipt of Armed Forces independence payment; or
(vii) a person in receipt of increased disablement pension.

The reference to disabled persons in *IHTA 1984, s 89(1)* from 22 March 2006 ignores the disallowance provisions relating to (ii) and (iii) above where the disabled person is in paid-for accommodation e.g. hospitalisation due to renal failure, or where the person is living outside the UK and would fail (ii) and (iii) above. [*IHTA 1984, s 89* as amended by *FA 2006, Sch 20, para 6(2)*].

Discretionary trusts for a disabled person

[44.2] Where property is transferred prior to 8 April 2013 into settlement under which, during the life of a 'disabled person', no interest in possession subsists, and which secures that not less than half of the settled property which is applied during his life is applied for his benefit, then the disabled person is treated as beneficially entitled to an interest in possession in the property. [*IHTA 1984, s 89*]. With effect for trusts created on and after 8 April 2013, this 50 per cent rule no longer applies and it is required that all income must be applicable for the disabled person, subject powers to apply sums, whether capital or income, for the benefit of someone other than the disabled person up to an annual limit, which is the lower of £3,000 and 3% of the maximum value of the settled property in the period in question. This is an annual limit applicable for each tax year.

A settlement will not fall outside these provisions by reason only of the trustees' power of advancement contained in *Trustee Act 1925, s 32* or *Trustee Act (Northern Ireland) 1958, s 33*. With effect for trusts created on or after 8 April 2013, it will be permissible to extend the *Trustee Act 1925, s 32* power of advancement beyond 50 per cent of the fund without infringing the rules for disabled persons trusts. [*FA 2013, Sch 42 para 6*].

Example 1

On 1 July 2002 Q settled £50,000 in trust mainly for his disabled son P, but with power to apply property to his daughter S as follows:

1.1 I give to my Trustees on the trusts set out hereinafter the sum of £50,000.
1.1.1 'the Trust Fund' means the assets at a particular time held by my Trustees on the trusts set out in . . . .
1.1.2 'my other Beneficiaries' means: my children other than. . . . . [P's name]. . . . .
1.2 My Trustees shall hold the Trust Fund on the following trusts:
1.2.1 During the lifetime of . . . . [P's name]. . . . .
(a) to apply the capital of the Trust Fund for the benefit of . . . . [P's name]. . . . . and my other Beneficiaries as my Trustees think fit so long as not less than half of any capital applied is for the benefit of . . . . [P's name]. . . . .;
(b) to have the power to accumulate the whole of any part of the income arising from the Trust Fund and to apply any income not accumulated solely for the benefit of . . . . [P's name]. . . . .

1.2.2 After the death of . . . . [P's name]. . . . .

(a) to apply the capital of the Trust Fund for the benefit of such of my other Beneficiaries as my Trustees think fit;

(b) to apply the income of the Trust Fund for the benefit of such of my other Beneficiaries as my Trustees think fit or to accumulate the whole or any part of it;

(c) within . . . . [Year(s)]. . . . . of . . . . [P's name]. . . . . death to end these trusts by distributing the Trust Fund among such Beneficiaries as my Trustees think fit.

1.3 My Trustees shall have the following powers: . . . ' *Details of Trustees' powers continue*

On 1 January 2011 the trustees advanced £5,000 gross to S on her marriage.

IIP treatment

If the trust secures that not less than half the settled property which is applied during P's life is applied for his benefit, then P is treated as beneficially entitled to an interest in possession in the settled property. The transfer to S is a potentially exempt transfer which may become chargeable in the event of P's death within seven years of the transfer. The gift in consideration of marriage exemption applies (£1,000 on a gift from brother to sister) subject to the required notice. See 39.9 SETTLEMENTS WITH INTERESTS IN POSSESSION for an example of a notice under *IHTA 1984, s 57(3)* and the deed of release.

Property settled after 21 March 2006

[44.3] From 22 March 2006 where a person (designated 'A' in the legislation) transfers property into a settlement and:

(a) that person was beneficially entitled to the property immediately before transferring it;

(b) HMRC are satisfied that he/she had a condition at the time which it was reasonable to expect that it would lead to becoming a disabled person as defined for the purposes of *IHTA 1984, s 89* (see above);

(c) the property is held on trusts that do not give 'A' during his lifetime an interest in possession,

then 'A' is treated as beneficially entitled to an interest in possession. Assumptions as to entitlement to state benefits may be made as detailed in *IHTA 1984, s 89A(5)*. Certain protective trusts may also qualify.

In addition, two conditions must apply:

- the requirement that if any of the settled property is applied during A's lifetime for the benefit of a beneficiary, it is applied for the benefit of A; and
- any power to terminate the trusts during the lifetime of A or another person is such that A or another person will have an absolute entitlement to, or a *disabled person's interest* subsisting in, the settled property. See also Fosters Inheritance Tax, para E6.29.

With effect for trusts created on and after 8 April 2013, it is required that all income must be applicable for the disabled person, subject powers to apply sums, whether capital or income, for the benefit of someone other than the disabled person up to an annual limit, which is the lower of £3,000 and 3% of the maximum value of the settled property in the period in question. This is an annual limit applicable for each tax year.

A settlement will not fall outside these provisions by reason only of the trustees' power of advancement contained in the *Trustee Act 1925, s 32* or *Trustee Act (Northern Ireland) 1958, s 33*. With effect for trusts created on or after 8 April 2013, it will be permissible to extend the *Trustee Act 1925, s 32* power of advancement beyond 50% of the fund without infringing the rules for disabled persons trusts: [*FA 2013, Sch 44, para 6; IHTA 1984, s 89A*].

Example 2

On 31 July 2010, X who is domiciled in England and is physically disabled but currently resides in Ireland settles £360,000 from liability insurance payments into a disabled trust for his benefit in the future. X who intends to return to the UK would have qualified for receipt of a disability living allowance under *Social Security Contributions and Benefits Act 1992, s 71* by virtue of entitlement to the care component at the highest rate (see Note D below) due to severe disability. Despite not qualifying for disability benefit because of not being resident for the relevant period X is still able to set up a trust and benefit from both the CGT and IHT advantages attaching to such settlements of property so that after seven years the £360,000 will effectively drop out of account for cumulation purposes. See (C) below.

Notes to the example

(A) Prior to 22 March 2006 the transfer into trust would not have qualified as a trust for disabled persons within *IHTA 1984, s 89* but following the amendments in *FA 2006, Sch 20 para 6(2)* the residence conditions of *Social Security Contributions and Benefits Act 1992, s 71(6)* are treated as if they were fulfilled.

(B) Similarly, if a disabled person's entitlement to attendance allowance is restricted because of *Social Security Contributions and Benefits Act 1992, s 64(1)* requirements of residence but the person would have qualified for attendance allowance then from 22 March 2006 the settlement may notwithstanding this be allowed as a trust for disabled person.

(C) The IHT advantages are that the funds in the disabled trust are treated as remaining in the beneficial ownership of X so that on death of X, trust funds will be amalgamated with his free estate for IHT purposes.

(D) The highest rate applies where the individual is so physically or mentally disabled that he/she requires:

   (1) frequent attention throughout the day in connection with bodily functions, or continual supervision throughout the day to avoid substantial danger to them or others; and

   (2) prolonged or repeated attention at night in connection with bodily functions, or in order to avoid substantial danger to themselves or others he/she requires another person to be awake at night for a prolonged period or at frequent intervals to watch them; or

   (3) he/she is terminally ill.

Example 3

On 31 July 2010 X, who is in the early stages of dementia and currently resides in a care home, settles £300,000 into discretionary trust for his benefit in the future. X has been assessed by the care home at which he is registered to attend as Elderly Mentally Incapable (EMI). The trust qualifies as a settlement under *s 89A* because X's present condition advancing from dementia to Alzheimer's satisfies the criteria of the definition of a disabled person within *IHTA 1984, s 89(4)* that is required. The trust has been set up by X in conjunction with MENCAP. See *Mental Health Act 2007*, and also Note (A) below. See also *Masterman-Lister v Brutton & Co*, CA [2003] WTLR 259; CA [2003] All ER (D) 59 (Jan).

X is treated as beneficially entitled to an interest in possession in the settled property. As it is X himself who is making the transfer, there is no transfer of value for IHT purposes. See (A) below and **39.9** SETTLEMENTS WITH INTERESTS IN POSSESSION for an example of a notice.

Notes to the example

(A) In certain cases, such as the example above, it is often difficult to ensure that relatives or acquaintances have sufficient knowledge or time to act as trustees to the disabled trust. In these cases, it is often possible to obtain independent trusteeship from a commercial organisation and one such as the Mencap Trust Company Ltd may be chosen. See www.mencap.org.uk.

(B) Where the disabled person's disability may fluctuate so that entitlement to the disability living allowance changes between the lower and middle care component entitlement above then provided the beneficiary qualifies at the time at which the funds are given into trust then a subsequent reduced entitlement to the disability living allowance will not change the status of the trust.

Capital gains implications

In respect of the counter measures within *TCGA 1992, s 226A* to prevent exploitation of the interaction between private residence relief and gifts relief for CGT these measures do not apply in the case of beneficiaries of trusts for disabled persons as *IHTA 1984, s 89* provides that a beneficiary of such a settlement has an interest in possession in the settled property. As a consequence of this, any transfer to such a trust is a potentially exempt transfer for IHT purposes and does not fall within *TCGA 1992, s 260* gifts holdover relief. [*TCGA 1992, s 226A inserted by FA 2004, Sch 22 para 6*].

Transfers into trusts for disabled persons

[44.4] In relation to transfers of value made, and other events occurring, after 17 March 1986, a gift by an individual into a trust for a disabled person, is a potentially exempt transfer subject to the transfer not being primarily exempt under *IHTA 1984, s 11* i.e. dispositions for family maintenance: see 44.7. In addition, in relation to transfers of value made, and other events occurring, after 16 March 1987, a potentially exempt transfer occurs where an individual disposes of or terminates his beneficial interest in settled property by gift and on that event the property is settled on disabled trusts. Provided the transferor survives seven years or more from the date of the original gift, the gift is exempt for inheritance tax purposes. See **35** POTENTIALLY EXEMPT TRANSFERS for further details. [*IHTA 1984, ss 3A, 3B; FA 1986, Sch 19 para 1; F(No 2)A 1987, s 96; FA 2006, Sch 20 para 9*].

Property settled before 10 March 1981

[44.5] Where property was transferred into a settlement before 10 March 1981 and is held on trusts under which there is no interest in possession but the property is to be applied only or mainly for the benefit of a disabled person within **44.1**(i)–(iii) above during his life, then there is a charge to tax

(a) where it ceases to be settled property otherwise than by being applied for the benefit of the disabled person (but see also **21.4**, **21.6–21.8** EXEMPT TRANSFERS for certain situations where there is no charge when property becomes held for charitable purposes only without limit of time or the property of a qualifying political party or a national body mentioned in *IHTA 1984, Sch 3* or, under certain conditions, a body not established or conducted for profit), or
(b) if the trustees make a 'disposition' otherwise than for the benefit of the disabled person which reduces the value of the settled property. *Disposition* includes an omission to exercise a right (unless not deliberate), which is treated as made at the latest time that the right could be exercised.

Where no charge arises

No charge arises:

(i) if, under (b) above, the trustees do not intend to confer gratuitous benefit and either the transaction is at arm's length between persons not connected with each other (see **12** CONNECTED PERSONS) or is such as might be expected in such a transaction; or
(ii) if, under (b) above, the disposition is a grant of tenancy of agricultural property in the UK, Channel Islands or Isle of Man, for use for agricultural purposes and is made for full consideration in money or money's worth; or
(iii) on the payment of costs or expenses attributable to the property; or
(iv) where any payment is, or will be, income for income tax purposes of any person (or, in the case of a person not resident in the UK, would be if he were so resident); or
(v) in respect of a liability to make a payment under (iii) or (iv) above.

'*Payment*' includes the transfer of assets other than money.

[*IHTA 1984, ss 63, 70(3)(4), 74(3)*].

Amount on which tax is charged

Tax is charged on the amount by which the trust property is less immediately after the event giving rise to the charge than it would have been but for the event (i.e. the loss to the donor principle), grossed-up where the settlement pays the tax.

The rate at which tax is charged is the aggregate of the following percentages for each complete successive quarter in 'the relevant period':

	Cumulative Total
0.25% for each of the first 40 quarters	10%
0.20% for each of the next 40 quarters	8%
0.15% for each of the next 40 quarters	6%
0.10% for each of the next 40 quarters	4%
0.05% for each of the next 40 quarters	2%
Maximum rate chargeable after 50 years	30%

The rate charged may be reduced if any of the property is, or was, EXCLUDED PROPERTY (20), see 44.5 below.

Definitions

'*Relevant period*' is the period beginning with the day on which the property became (or last became) held on trusts for disabled persons or 13 March 1975 if later, and ending on the day before the chargeable event.

'*Quarter*' means any period of three months.

[*IHTA 1984, ss 63, 70(5)(6)(8), 74(3)*].

Excluded property

[44.6] Where the whole or part of the amount on which tax is charged as in 44.5 above is attributable to property which was EXCLUDED PROPERTY (20) at any time during the relevant period, then, in determining the rate at which tax is charged in respect of that amount or part, no quarter throughout which the property was excluded property is to be counted. [*IHTA 1984, ss 70(7), 74(3)*].

[*IHTA 1984, ss 74(1)(2)(4), 76*].

Example 4

In 1968 Q settled £50,000 in trust mainly for his disabled son P, but with power to apply property to his daughter S. On 1 January 2011 the trustees advanced £5,000 gross to S on her marriage.

There will be a charge to IHT on the payment to S

The relevant period is the period from settlement of the funds or, if later, 13 March 1975, to 1 January 2010, i.e. 139 complete quarters.

The rate of IHT is the aggregate of:

0.25% for each of the first	40	quarters	10.00%
0.20% for each of the next	40	quarters	8.00%
0.15% for each of the next	40	quarters	6.00%

0.10% for each of the next	23	quarters	2.30%
	143		26.30%

IHT payable is £5,000 × 26.30% = £1,315

Key points concerning trusts for disabled persons

[44.7] Points to consider are as follows.

- Unfortunately, the relevant provisions for disabled persons trusts are not easy to follow, there being four sub-categories each with their own detailed conditions. Coupled with the equally complex and entirely separate capital gains tax and income tax provisions, this must be regarded as a specialist area, which is regrettable given the circumstances for which they are designed to give assistance.
- Disabled trusts are not simply for those who one might commonly regard as disabled, for example, those with mobility difficulties. The trusts apply equally to anyone in receipt of attendance allowance, a Social Security benefit available to persons who are usually elderly but not necessarily having apparent disabled status.
- Where a family member transfers property into a disabled persons trust, it may be that no potentially exempt transfer arises because the gift is in any event exempt under *IHTA 1984, s 11* 'dispositions for maintenance of family'. By virtue of *s 11(3)*, a disposition is not a transfer of value if it is made in favour of a dependent relative of the person and is reasonable provision for his care or maintenance. In *McKelvey v HMRC* [2008] STC (SCD) 944, a widow who was 85 and in poor health was cared for by her daughter who lived with her. The daughter gave two houses to her mother valued at £169,000. These were rented properties and it was successfully argued that the gift was largely exempt under *s 11*. Where a gift is greater than can be regarded as reasonable care and maintenance, only the excess falls outside the exemption, and that might qualify as a potentially exempt transfer. *IHTA 1984, s 11* can apply to gifts into trust although there could be difficulty with any significant amounts of capital where the likelihood is that the trust funds will pass to other beneficiaries on the death of the disabled person.

45

Shares and Securities

Cross-reference. See **11** CLOSE COMPANIES.

Simon's Taxes. See **D6.617, I7.102, I7.103.**

Other Sources. HMRC Customer Guide to Inheritance Tax; SVD 1 'Shares Valuation Division'; Foster, Part H3; IHTM18000.

Definitions related to shares and securities

[45.1] In relation to transfers of value made, and other events occurring, after 16 March 1987, '*quoted*' in relation to any shares or securities, means quoted on a recognised stock exchange. Up to 1996 it also included shares quoted on the erstwhile Unlisted Securities Market. '*Unquoted*', in relation to any shares or securities, means neither so quoted nor so dealt in. Shares on the London Alternative Investment Market (AIM) are unquoted for this purpose but if shares dealt in on AIM are also listed on a recognised stock exchange overseas, they will not be 'unquoted' and will not qualify for business property relief. Therefore a check should be made that AIM-listed shares are not listed elsewhere but also see **45.5** below. [*IHTA 1984, s 272; FA 1987, s 58(2), Sch 8 para 17*]. As from 1 April 1996 the word '*quoted*' on a recognised stock exchange is substituted by the word '*listed*'. [*FA 1996, Sch 38 para* 2]. In IHT 110 the definition of '*quoted*' and '*unquoted*' respectively are as follows:

> 'This means a company that is listed on a recognised stock exchange. This includes shares traded on the American NASDAQ and European EASDAQ for chargeable events after 9 March 1992.'

and

> 'This means a company that is not listed on a recognised stock exchange. Some companies although they are listed in the Stock Exchange Daily Official List are still "unquoted" for business relief.

This includes shares

- shares listed on the Alternative Investment Market (AIM)
- shares listed on the Unlisted Securities Market (USM), there are some compli-cated rules that apply to chargeable events before 10 March 1992. You should telephone our Helpline if the transferor owned shares listed on the USM and the date of the chargeable event, is before 10 March 1992.'

The above definition applies for all IHT purposes except that, in relation to transfers of value made, and other events occurring, after 9 March 1992, an alternative definition, whereby Unlisted Securities Market shares and securities are treated as unquoted, applies for the purposes of defining relevant business property (see **6.4** BUSINESS PROPERTY) and payment by instalments (see **32.5** PAYMENT OF TAX).

In relation to transfers of value made, and other events occurring, before 17 March 1987, shares and securities in companies dealt in on the Unlisted Securities Market were not treated as 'quoted on a recognised stock exchange' for all IHT purposes (Inland Revenue Statement of Practice SP 18/80, 23 December 1980). For amendment to the term 'recognised stock exchange' see **6.4** BUSINESS PROPERTY. Whilst *FA 2007* inserted new definitions of 'recognised stock exchange' for the purposes of income tax and capital gains tax the change did not include inheritance tax. However, it may be that in the future the inheritance tax definition will fall into line with the *FA 2007* changes. [*ITA 2007, s 1005; FA 2007, s 109, Sch 26 paras 1, 3, 4*].

See also **53.24** VALUATION.

Agricultural and business property reliefs

[45.2] Controlling shares in agricultural companies may attract AGRICULTURAL PROPERTY (4) relief.

Shares and securities in companies carrying on a business may attract BUSINESS PROPERTY (6) relief.

Payment of tax by instalments

[45.3] Under certain conditions, inheritance tax on shares and securities transferred may be paid by annual instalments over ten years, see **32.5–32.9** PAYMENT OF TAX for details.

Related property

[45.4] See **53.21** VALUATION.

Sales within one year after death

[45.5] Special provisions apply, see **53.26** VALUATION. Also, investments on the stock exchanges described in the list at IHTM34140 as qualifying investments for the purposes of loss on sale of shares relief.

Transfers within seven years before death

[45.6] See 50 TRANSFERS WITHIN SEVEN YEARS BEFORE DEATH for special provisions.

Trading companies

[45.7] Controlling shares or securities or a minority holding of unquoted shares may attract BUSINESS PROPERTY (6) relief.

Valuation

[45.8] See 53.24 VALUATION for valuation of quoted and unquoted shares and securities. See also www.voa.go.uk.

American depositary receipts

[45.9] American depositary receipts (ADRs) are securities which represent shares of non-US companies. They may be listed on major US exchanges in the form of American depositary shares, in which case the ADRs fall to be regarded as quoted shares for IHT purposes. Where an ADR represents shares in an unquoted company, business property relief for it will be available, subject to the conditions applying to that relief, if the holder is the beneficial owner of the underlying shares under the law of the territory or state where the ADRs are issued. In cases where the holder is not regarded as the beneficial owner, no business relief will be allowed: see IHTM25193.

Purchase by company of own shares

[45.10] A payment by an *unquoted trading* company (or *holding company* of a trading group) on the purchase, redemption or repayment of its own shares is not treated as a distribution if the price received from the company is used to meet the recipient's inheritance tax liability on a death. Substantially the whole of the payment (apart from any sum applied in paying capital gains tax on the purchase etc.) must be used for this purpose within two years of the death. The IHT liability must be one which could not be met without undue hardship otherwise than by means of such purchase etc. [*CTA 2010, s 1033(3) and (4)*].

An *unquoted company* is one which has none of its shares listed in the official list of a stock exchange and which is not a 51% subsidiary of a company so listed.

A *trading company* is one whose business consists wholly or mainly of the carrying on of a trade or trades, excluding dealing in shares, securities, land or futures.

A *holding company* is one whose business, disregarding any trade carried on by it, consists wholly or mainly in the holding of shares or securities of one or more companies which are its 75% subsidiaries. [*ICTA 1988, s 229*].

Certain changes in company law have enabled listed companies to acquire their own shares as well as hold or dispose of them. *FA 2003, s 195* treats own shares held without cancellation as if they were cancelled for tax purposes.

46

Situs

Cross-reference. See **20** EXCLUDED PROPERTY.

Simon's Taxes. See I9.329, I9.4.

Introduction to situs

[46.1] As the inheritance tax legislation contains no specific rules for determining whether property is or is not situated in the UK, the general law situs rules apply. The situs of property has particular relevance for the purposes of determining whether or not it qualifies as excluded property for IHT purposes: see **20.2** EXCLUDED PROPERTY ABROAD.

Assets	Location/situs
Registered shares and securities.	Situated where the title of ownership at which they must be registered, i.e. the share register, is located. If more than one register is maintained, one being an overseas branch register, shares on the overseas register will be situated where that register is located. Apart from these rules, shares which are transferable in more than one country are situated in the one in which they would be likely to be dealt with in the ordinary course of affairs. (*Standard Chartered Bank Ltd v CIR* Ch D, [1978] STC 272; *Treasurer for Ontario v Aberdein* PC 1946, [1947] AC 24; *R v Williams and Another* PC, [1942] 22 All ER 95).

Renounceable letters of allotment.	Shares in UK private companies have been held to be situated in the UK. (*Young and Another v Phillips* Ch D 1984, 58 TC 232).
Bearer shares and securities.	Situated in the country in which the certificate of title is kept. (*Winans and Another v A-G (No 2)* HL 1909, [1910] AC 27).

Interests in land and chattels

[46.2] Situs depends upon actual physical situation. However, *ships* are situated where registered unless within UK territorial or national waters when this is displaced by the actual situs. (*The Trustees Executors and Agency Co Ltd v CIR* Ch D 1972, [1973] 1 All ER 563). Agricultural land and woodland situated within the European Economic Area (EEA) from 22 April 2009 onwards qualifies now for existing reliefs. [*FA 2009, s 122(4); Interpretation Act 1978, Sch 1*].

For IHT purposes the application of extra-statutory concession F7 'Foreign owned works of art' ensures that even though a work of art is in the UK temporarily for cleaning or restoration or for a loan to a public exhibition by a non-UK domicile and a chargeable event arises then no charge to tax arises. This concession on the usual situs rules is perhaps designed to ensure that those owners of art works that are domiciled abroad do not remove valuable works of art from this country in fear of a tax charge arising out of the temporary situs in the UK of the work of art at a time of a chargeable event.

Debts and bank accounts

[46.3] Generally, a simple contract debt is situated where the debtor resides (*Kwok Chi Leung Karl v Commissioner of Estate Duty* PC, [1988] STC 728). However, if there is more than one country of residence the terms of the contract may serve to localise the debt. (*New York Life Insurance Co Ltd v Public Trustee* CA, [1924] 2 Ch 101). A specialty debt has been regarded as situated where the bond or specialty is kept. (*Royal Trust Co v A-G for Alberta* PC 1929, [1930] AC 144), but on 21 September 2018, HMRC published an amendment to para 27079 of its IHT Manual to state that they now regard a specialty debt as situate in the UK where the debt is secured on land or other tangible property in the UK, but that unsecured specialty debts are usually situate where the relevant document is kept. But if the document is temporarily removed from the UK to avoid a charge to IHT, it may be possible to argue that it remains situate in the UK for IHT purposes.

A debt owed by a bank (e.g. bank account) is situated at the branch where it is primarily recoverable. (*R v Lovitt*, [1912] AC 212). However, a building society account is an interest in the society, and not a debt due, so the situs of the account is where the society is based, and not, if otherwise, the territory (e.g. the Channel Islands) in which the branch is located where the account is held.

Life policies under deed or under seal are specialty debts and HMRC regard the principles set out above for unsecured specialty debts as being applicable to them. Lloyd's policies are not regarded by HMRC as specialty debts unless bearing the witnessed personal signature of the general manager of Lloyd's Policy Signing Office (IHT Manual, para 27104).

Other assets

[46.4] See also 20.6 EXCLUDED PROPERTY for foreign pensions and 32.24 PAYMENT OF TAX for foreign-owned works of art temporarily in the UK.

Double taxation agreements

[46.5] A double taxation agreement may determine where property is to be treated as situated for IHT purposes. [*IHTA 1984, s 158(1)*].

Inter-American development bank

[46.6] Securities issued by this bank are treated as situated outside the UK notwithstanding the UK having become a member and shareholder of the bank. [*FA 1976, s 131*].

International organisations

[46.7] Securities issued by certain international organisations may be designated by the Treasury as being situated outside the UK for IHT purposes. The Asian Development Bank, the African Development Bank, the three European Communities and the European Investment Bank have been so designated. [*ICTA 1988, s 324 now repealed and replaced by ITTOIA 2005, s 774; FA 1985, s 96; SI 1984/1215; SI 1984/1634; SI 1985/1172*].

Key points concerning situs

[46.8] Points to consider are as follows.

- The situs or location of assets is an important matter for individuals neither domiciled nor deemed domiciled in either England, Scotland or Northern Ireland. Only UK situated assets held by such individuals come within chargeability (and overseas assets are excluded). A short summary of asset locations is set out below:

Asset	Location/situs
Land, buildings and leases including any share in land or a building.	Where the land is physically situated.
Registered shares and securities (but see Government stocks above).	Where the shares or securities are registered or traded.
An interest in an unincorporated business or an interest in a partnership.	Where the business is carried out.
Chattels and personal possessions.	Where the item is situated at the time of the transfer or at the date of death.
Debts owed to the deceased.	Where the debtor lives at the time of transfer or on death.
Bank accounts.	Where the bank or branch holding the account is situated.

- As stated above situs depends upon actual physical situation. However, *ships* are situated where registered unless within UK territorial or national waters when this is displaced by the actual situs. In this latter case ownership and therefore as a consequence situs may change due to a declaration of trust which may be created orally as well as by deed. Because of an express declaration of trust a boat's situs may change due to the fact that actual situs i.e. in UK, is displaced by a declaration of trust to whereby a non-domiciled individual obtains ownership and the boat is re-registered abroad thereby effecting a change in situs and chargeability to IHT. See also *Rowe v Prance* [1999] 2 FLR 787.

47

Time Limits

In some cases the periods can be extended at the discretion of HMRC. See HMRC Customer Guide to Inheritance Tax; IHTM30151–30159.

Simon's Taxes. See **I11.2, I11.3, I11.4**.

Time limits of one year or less

[47.1] Time limits of one year or less are treated as follows:

(a) **30 days**
- (i) Appeal against a notice of determination. See **14.3** DETERMINATIONS AND APPEALS. From 1 April 2009 onwards where HMRC offer a review under the rules of the new Tax Chamber of the First-tier Tribunal, the taxpayer has 30 days in which to accept the offer. See **14.11** DETERMINATIONS AND APPEALS.
- (ii) Stated case from Special Commissioners, request. See **14** DETERMINATIONS AND APPEALS. For the position from 1 April 2009 regarding Tax Chamber First-tier Tribunal rules see **14.11** DETERMINATIONS AND APPEALS.
- (iii) Information must be furnished if requested by the Board. See **2.19** ACCOUNTS AND RETURNS.
- (iv) Appeal against an information notice issued by HMRC. See **2.19** ACCOUNTS AND RETURNS.

(b) **Three months**
- (i) Return to be made, in certain circumstances, by professional advisers acting for settlors. See **2.18** ACCOUNTS AND RETURNS.

(c) **Six months**
- (i) With effect from 6 April 2014, accounts to be delivered for charges in relation to relevant property trusts. Also, accounts to be delivered after ending of conditional exemption for works of art, historic buildings etc. and disposal of woodlands. See **2.15** ACCOUNTS AND RETURNS.
- (ii) Board may call for an account following an 'excepted termination'. See **2.12** ACCOUNTS AND RETURNS.

(iii) Corrective and supplementary accounts to be delivered after discovery of defect. See **2.16** ACCOUNTS AND RETURNS. This limit applies also in cases of innocent reporting errors where the CTO do not seek a penalty.

(iv) Payment of tax. Normal due date after end of month in which chargeable transfer occurs. See **32.1** PAYMENT OF TAX.

(v) A scheme administrator of an Alternatively Secured Pension (ASP) has six months from the end of the month in which he becomes aware or discovers the scheme member's death to pay IHT due. See **34.2** PENSION SCHEMES.

(d) **Twelve months**

(i) Delivery of accounts after lifetime transfers, transfers on death and transfers by trustees of settlements. See **2.15** ACCOUNTS AND RETURNS. A consultation document issued by HMRC on 6 June 2014 contains proposals to introduce new time limits with effect from 5 April 2015 in relation to relevant property trusts.

(ii) Valuation reduced for certain quoted shares if sold for less within twelve months after death. See **53.26** VALUATION.

(iii) Waiver of dividends within previous twelve months before any right accrues is not a transfer of value. See **48.1** TRANSFER OF VALUE.

(iv) Unused portion of annual exemption can be utilised against transfers during following twelve months. See **21.12** EXEMPT TRANSFERS.

(v) A scheme administrator of an ASP has twelve months from the end of the month in which he becomes aware or discovers the scheme member's death to file a return. See **34.2** PENSION SCHEMES.

Two-year time limits

[47.2] Two-year time limits are treated as follows:

(a) Variations and disclaimers of dispositions on death are valid if made within two years after death. See **13** DEEDS OF VARIATION AND DISCLAIMERS.

(b) Woodlands. Election after a death to defer tax on trees and underwood. However, woodlands relief from 22 April 2009 onwards applying to property in the European Economic Area (EEA) and any IHT due from 23 April 2003 will become eligible for relief by claim from 21 April 2010. See **54.1** WOODLANDS.

(c) Scottish executors may elect to pay tax, ignoring legitim. See **49.21** TRANSFERS ON DEATH.

(d) Heritage property. A claim for conditional exemption on or after 17 March 1998 relating to death or other transfers and heritage property held in a discretionary trust. See **30.3** NATIONAL HERITAGE.

(e) Heritage property. A claim for exemption for transfers into maintenance funds for historic buildings, etc. See **30.3** NATIONAL HERITAGE and **8.2** CAPITAL GAINS TAX.

(f) Claims for the transfer of the nil rate band from the end of the month in which the survivor dies or (if it ends later) three months beginning with the date on which the personal representatives begin to act. See **21.9** EXEMPT TRANSFERS.

Three-year time limits

[47.3] Three-year time limits are treated as follows:

(a) Penalties. No proceedings by Board after notification of tax payable. See **33.11** PENALTIES.
(b) Valuation reduced for land or 'related property' sold for less within three years (four years in certain cases) after death. See **53.9** and **53.22** VALUATION.
(c) Woodlands. Expenses of replanting trees and underwood within three years after disposal are deductible. See **54.5** WOODLANDS.
(d) In relation to transfers of value made, and other events occurring, after 29 November 1993, property which is the subject of a lifetime transfer for which agricultural or business property relief is claimed but which is subsequently disposed of by the transferee, must be replaced by similar property within three years of the disposal. See **4.11** AGRICULTURAL PROPERTY and **6.11** BUSINESS PROPERTY.

Four-year time limit

[47.4] A four-year time limit for IHT applies in the following circumstances:

(a) Any claim for repayment of tax overpaid. See **32.20** PAYMENT OF TAX.
(b) Subject to any clearance certificate which may have been issued by HMRC (see **32.15** PAYMENT OF TAX), any underpayment of IHT where tax attributable to the property concerned has been paid in accordance with an account duly delivered to the Board and the payment has been accepted in full satisfaction. In such cases HMRC cannot revise the liability more than four years after the later of:
    (i) the date on which the payment (or in the case of tax paid by instalments, the last payment) was made and accepted; and
    (ii) the date on which the tax or the last instalment became due. [*IHTA 1984, s 240(2)*].

Six and twelve-year time limits

[47.5] A six-year time limit applies, in place of the four-year time limit detailed at **47.4**, where loss of tax was brought about by careless behaviour. [*IHTA 1984, s 240(4)*].

For underpayment of tax in relation to a chargeable transfer where an offshore matter is involved, or where there has been an offshore transfer which makes the lost tax significantly harder to identify, a twelve-year time limit applies in place of the four-year time limit at **47.4**.

Twenty-year time limit and no time limit situations

[47.6] A twenty-year time limit applies, in place of the four-year time limit detailed at **47.4**, where loss of tax was brought about by deliberate behaviour. This would be, for example, where an account disclosed an asset but there was an incorrect statement deliberately made in relation to it. [*IHTA 1984, s 240(5)*].

The twenty-year time limit also applies where no account has been delivered and the loss of tax was not brought about deliberately by the person liable for the tax, or a person acting for them. This is therefore the normal time limit for recovery of IHT where past liabilities come to light and no account has been delivered. [*IHTA 1984, s 240(7)*]. Equally if an account has been delivered, but it omitted an asset which was transferred, either in the estate on death or in a lifetime transfer, the four-year time limit cannot apply, nor does the six-year time limit in the view of HMRC, so a twenty-year time limit remains.

If the omission of an asset was deliberate, there is no time limit at all (IHTM30462).

48

Transfer of Value

Cross-references. See **9** CHARGEABLE TRANSFER; **19** ESTATE; **21** EXEMPT TRANSFERS.

Simon's Taxes. See **I3.1, I3.342, I4.151**.

Other Sources. HMRC Customer Guide to Inheritance Tax; Foster, Part C1; IHTM04000.

Introduction to transfer of value

[48.1] **A transfer of value** is any disposition (see **48.2** below) made by a *person* ('the transferor') as a result of which the value of his estate immediately after the disposition is less than it would be but for the disposition; and the amount by which it is less is the value transferred by the transfer. No account is taken of the value of EXCLUDED PROPERTY (**20**), which ceases to form part of a person's estate as a result of a disposition. References in *IHTA 1984* to a transfer of value made include references to events on the happening of which tax is chargeable *as if* a transfer of value had been made. [*IHTA 1984, s 3(1)(2)(4)*].

In *CIR v Eversden* [2003] STC 822 the Court of Appeal held that 'rightly or wrongly . . . . the draftsmen clearly did find it possible to equate a disposal by way of gift with a transfer of value'. This suggests that the two terms have a similar meaning.

The reduction in the transferor's estate will include any inheritance tax (but no other tax or duty or expenses of sale) borne by him on the value transferred. [*IHTA 1984, s 5(4)*]. For individuals, the 'net' value transferred, i.e. after taking account of any EXEMPT TRANSFERS (**21**), is grossed-up at the appropriate tax rate (see **7** CALCULATION OF TAX and **37** RATES OF TAX) when the transferor bears the tax (but not when the transferee pays it) in order to obtain the CHARGEABLE TRANSFER (**9**). If the transferee bears any related capital gains tax or incidental expenses (e.g. professional fees, stamp duties etc.) relating to the transfer, the value transferred is reduced by those charges. The reduction for capital gains tax applies to settled property only if the tax on the gain accruing to the trustees is borne by a person who becomes absolutely entitled to the settled property concerned. [*IHTA 1984, ss 164, 165*].

No transfer of value in the following circumstances

The following circumstances result in no transfer of value for IHT purposes:

(a) **Grant of agricultural tenancies.** See **4.15** AGRICULTURAL PROPERTY. See also **4.17** for the transfer of Scottish agricultural leases.

(b) **Waiver of remuneration** (including the repayment of remuneration already received) if such remuneration would otherwise have been subject to income tax as employment income [formerly Schedule E] and is not allowable as a deduction to the employer for purposes of income tax and corporation tax. [*IHTA 1984, s 14; ITEPA 2003, s 7*]. The employment income assessment must not have become final, the remuneration must be formally waived (usually by deed) and the employer's profits or allowable losses must be adjusted accordingly. (Inland Revenue Press Release 11 November 1975).

(c) **Waiver of dividends** by any person provided the waiver is within twelve months *before* any right to the dividend has accrued does not by itself make a transfer of value. [*IHTA 1984, s 15*]. See IHTM04052 regarding the use of the word 'person'.

Disposition

[48.2] Disposition is not defined in absolute terms but is thought to include payments of money, transfers of assets wholly or partly by way of gift, and any disposals of assets generally. It includes the following.

(i) A disposition effected by associated operations. See **5.5** ANTI-AVOIDANCE. [*IHTA 1984, s 272*].

(ii) An omission to exercise a right (unless shown not to be deliberate) by a person which diminishes his estate and increases the estate of another person or the value of a discretionary trust. The time of the disposition is the time or latest time when the right could be exercised. [*IHTA 1984, s 3(3)*]. In *HMRC v Parry as Personal Representatives of Staveley deceased* [2017] UKUT 4 (TCC) the Upper Tax Tribunal rejected an argument for the taxpayer that the reduction of the person's estate and the increase in another person's estate must take place at the same time; what is relevant is that one brings about the other.

(iii) Certain arrangements involving life insurance in conjunction with an annuity (a 'back to back' arrangement). [*IHTA 1984, s 263*]. See **28** LIFE ASSURANCE POLICIES AND ANNUITIES.

(iv) Certain loans of money or property for a fixed or minimum period granted for inadequate consideration. See **48.3** below.

(v) A disposition effected on the death of a registered scheme member on or after the age of 75 where funds are held in an alternatively secured pension (ASP) within *FA 2004, s 165*. The disposition on which a tax charge is imposed is the relevant amount of the ASP within *IHTA 1984, s 151A(2)(3)*. See **34.2** PENSION SCHEMES.

Dispositions not a transfer of value

Certain dispositions are not transfers of value as follows:

(a) it is shown that it was not intended, and was not made in a transaction (or series of transactions or by associated transactions) intended, to confer any gratuitous benefit on any person and either:

(i) it was made in a transaction at arm's length between persons not connected with each other; or

(ii) it was such as might be expected to be made in a transaction at arm's length between persons not connected with each other.

The above exception does not apply to a disposition whereby a person entitled to an interest (whether in possession or not) in any settled property acquires a reversionary interest expectant (whether immediately or not) on the interest. It also does not apply to a sale of unquoted shares or debentures (in relation to transfers of value made, and other events occurring, before 17 March 1987, shares or debentures not quoted on a recognised stock exchange) unless it is shown that it was at a price freely negotiated at the time of the sale or at a price such as might be expected to have been freely negotiated at that time. [*IHTA 1984, ss 10, 55; FA 1986, Sch 19 para 15; FA 1987, s 58, Sch 8 para 1*]. See also **5** ANTI-AVOIDANCE.

It is not sufficient, for example, that the shares were sold at a price which had been fixed under a provision of the company's articles of association (Originally in former Inland Revenue Booklet IHT 1 (1991) para 8.10).

The question of whether a disposition is excepted from being a transfer of value in the circumstances of (ii) above is one of fact although the burden of proof is on the taxpayer (*CIR v Spencer-Nairn* CS 1990, [1991] STC 60). (The facts were special in that a seller of land did not realise, at the time of sale, he was connected with the purchaser, and it was later found the advice he had received in connection with the sale, to the effect that he was liable under statute to incur expenditure to improve the land, was erroneous, with the effect that the sale was carried out at an apparent undervalue.)

The relevance of associated operations was considered in *CIR v Macpherson and Another* HL, [1988] STC 362. See **5.5** ANTI-AVOIDANCE.

(b) It is a disposition for family maintenance etc. see **21.14** EXEMPT TRANSFERS.

(c) It is allowable for income tax or corporation tax. [*IHTA 1984, s 12(1)*].

(d) It is a contribution to an approved retirement benefit scheme (occupational pension scheme) or is to provide retirement benefit for employees and their dependants or is a contribution under approved pension arrangements or, from 6 April 2006, a registered pension scheme (or *ICTA 1988, s 615(3)* scheme) entered into by an employee of the person making the disposition. [*IHTA 1984, s 12(2)–(5); F(No 2)A 1987, s 98(2)(3); FA 2004, s 203(2); FA 2006, Sch 22 para 2*]. See **21.18** EXEMPT TRANSFERS and **34.2** PENSIONS SCHEMES.

(e) It is by a close company to trustees for benefit of employees. [*IHTA 1984, ss 13, 13A*]. See **52** TRUSTS FOR EMPLOYEES.

(f) It is a capital gains tax liability of a close relative paid by an individual which has previously been postponed under *FA 1984, Sch 14*. [*IHTA 1984, s 163(5)*]. See **53.18** VALUATION.

(g) The disposition falls within the provisions relating to GIFTS WITH RESERVATION (**22**).

Loans, etc.

[48.3] A loan for a fixed or minimum period granted for inadequate consideration may be a transfer of value under the rules in *IHTA 1984, ss 3, 10*, see **48.1** and **48.2**(a) above. The value transferred is the difference between the amount or value of the property lent and the value of:

(a) the right to receive repayment or the return of the property when the loan has expired, plus
(b) the right to receive any interest or other consideration agreed between the parties.

See IHTM19010.

Example 1

David lends Albert £100,000 to buy a house but is unsure of the potential IHT implications. He might lend the money (a) interest free and repayable after a set period of time, say ten years time, or (b) repayable on demand with no interest.

The IHT treatment of the situation in (a) is that the repayment of the capital in ten years time is worth less than the current value of £100,000. If the value in ten years time is, say, £80,000 then David has made a PET of £20,000 at the time of the loan to Albert.

The IHT treatment in (b) is that David is entitled to receive repayment of the £100,000 loan on demand and so long as Albert is solvent, has not given anything away and his estate includes the amount of the loan. If David releases the loan by way of deed then his estate is diminished by that amount for IHT purposes and it is a PET.

In addition, HMRC consider that the foregone interest by David is treated as 'a clear intention to confer bounty' and 'the property disposed of is the interest foregone'. See IHTM14317. However, this view is not generally agreed; nothing is foregone with a cash loan since cash itself produces no income.

In the case of a lease, it is the difference between the value of the lessor's interest before the lease was granted and the value of his interest subject to the lease. The values are those at the time the loan is made. See **19.1** ESTATE for a deed of loan waiver.

Modification of exemptions for loans

[48.4] The exemptions that apply to outright gifts (see **21** EXEMPT TRANSFERS) apply, with appropriate modifications, to loans as follows.

(i) In the case of loans etc. to political parties (see **21.7**) the exemption limit in respect of transfer of value made within a year of death (which applied for transfers before 15 March 1988) does not apply.
(ii) For the purposes of loans etc. to charities (**21.2**), registered housing associations (to which only loans of land made after 13 March 1989 can be exempt) (**21.5**), political parties (**21.7**) or used for national purposes (see **21.6**) or public benefit (see **21.8**) the funds or property lent must be used solely for charitable purposes or the purposes of the appropriate political party or body. The value transferred is then treated as attribut-

able to the property the borrower is allowed to use and the property is treated as having been given to, or having become the property of, the borrower. In addition, the exceptions to the exemptions in each of those paragraphs do not apply.

(iii) For the purposes of loans etc. between spouses or civil partners (see **21.9**) the borrower's estate is treated as increased by the amount of the value transferred but see *Phizackerley* below.

(iv) For the purposes of the small gifts exemption (see **21.12**(b)) and gifts in consideration of marriage (see **21.13**) the transfer of value is treated as made by outright gift.

(v) The normal expenditure out of income exemption (see **21.15**) applies if the transfer is a normal one on the part of the transferor and, after allowing for all transfers of value forming part of his normal expenditure, he is left with sufficient income to maintain his usual standard of living.

[*IHTA 1984, ss 29, 56(6); FA 1988, Sch 14*].

Repayment of certain debts during lifetime

[48.5] Under *FA 1986, s 103* certain debts may not be deducted from the value of a deceased's estate if owed to a person who has received property from the deceased, see **49.9** TRANSFERS ON DEATH. Where a debt incurred after 17 March 1986 which would have been disallowed under those provisions is repaid by the donor in whole or in part during lifetime, he is treated as having made a transfer of value at the time of the payment equal to the money or money's worth paid or applied by him and such transfer is treated as a POTENTIALLY EXEMPT TRANSFERS (35). [*FA 1986, s 103(5)(6)*]. The effect of this is that the repayment (or part repayment) of a gift loaned back to the donor, although reducing the amount disallowed on death, is treated as a potentially exempt transfer and may be subject to tax if the donor dies within seven years of the repayment.

Example 2

Bernard gives his son Andrew shares worth £200,000. Some time thereafter Andrew, who is wealthy, lends his father £250,000 at a time when the shares have dropped in value to £170,000. Bernard dies and a deduction is claimed of the £250,000 owing by the Executors to Andrew.

In such a situation it is open to the parties to claim that the whole of the loan is to be allowed on the grounds that the gift was not made to facilitate the loan (see *IHTA 1984, s 103(2)(b)*). If the parties cannot establish this to the satisfaction of HMRC then the 'realisable value' at the time the debt was created will be in point and not £250,000, that is to say £80,000 (i.e. £250,000 – £170,000 shares). *IHTA 1984, s 103(2)* permits the deduction to the extent that the value of the consideration for the debt is shown by the parties to have exceeded the amount available by the application of all the property derived by the creditor from the deceased.

49

Transfers on Death

Cross-references. See **2.9** ACCOUNTS AND RETURNS; **7** CALCULATION OF TAX; **13** DEEDS OF VARIATION AND DISCLAIMERS; **19** ESTATE; **21.24** EXEMPT TRANSFERS; **32** PAYMENT OF TAX; **36** QUICK SUCCESSION RELIEF; **50** TRANSFERS WITHIN SEVEN YEARS BEFORE DEATH; **51** TRANSITIONAL PROVISIONS; **53** VALUATION.

Simon's Taxes. See **Part I4**.

Other Sources. Mellows, Chapter 5; Foster, Part D; HMRC Customer Guide to Inheritance Tax; IHTM05000.

Introduction to transfers on death

[49.1] On the death of any person after 17 March 1986, inheritance tax is chargeable as if he had made a transfer of value of his 'estate' immediately before his death. [*IHTA 1984, s 4(1)*]. The rate of tax applicable to the chargeable estate on death and to gifts which are chargeable transfers made within the seven years previously is 40%, but see **49.14** below for the 36% rate applicable where there are charitable gifts amounting to more than 10% or more of any component of the estate.

Where the chargeable estate on death includes the free estate and a pre-22 March 2006 life interest in settled property, the tax payable is calculated by aggregating all chargeable amounts including the settled property, after deduction from each of any reliefs due. The available nil rate band is then deducted from the total and the tax calculated on the net figure. The tax is then divided between the free estate and the settled fund by reference to the chargeable amounts of each.

Definition — 'Estate'

'*Estate*' of a deceased person is the aggregate of all the property to which he was beneficially entitled immediately before death, but not including EXCLUDED PROPERTY (20). [*IHTA 1984, s 5(1) as amended by FA 2006, Sch 20 para 10*]. See **19** ESTATE for details, and in particular for the extended IHT meaning of 'beneficially entitled'.

For a summary of the rules applying on intestacy see **49.24** below.

Valuation of estate on death

[49.2] The value transferred on death is the total value of all the property in the deceased's estate (see above) at a price which the property might reasonably be expected to fetch if sold in the open market at that time, less liabilities (see **49.10** below). [*IHTA 1984, ss 5(3), 160*]. See **53** VALUATION.

For the treatment of joint bank accounts, see **19.1** ESTATE.

Tangible property

Prior to August 2018, HMRC guidance stated that valuations should be obtained for individual items over £500. This figure is now revised to £1 500, so that professional valuations need only be obtained where it is thought that an item is worth more than that amount, or where the value cannot be reasonably estimated (HMRC Trusts and Estates Newsletter, August 2018).

Accrued income scheme (AIS)

Since 6 April 1996, a person's death has not been an occasion of charge under the accrued income scheme (AIS) and valuations of holdings of AIS stocks have included gross interest and IHT has been charged on that gross interest. However, this has led to a double charge to tax: that is, IHT is charged on the gross interest to the date of death and when the next interest payment is made, a further charge arises on the personal representatives on the whole payment of interest including that accruing up to the date of death. The personal representatives have had no recourse to a deduction of the deceased's element of the accrued interest. HMRC have confirmed that interest on AIS securities quoted 'cum-dividend' should be included net of tax at basic rate in the valuation (see IHTM18098). Similarly, where the securities are 'ex-dividend' at the date of death, the allowance for interest accruing after death should be net of tax to the personal representatives.

(VOA IHT manual, section 7, para 7.13).

As regards accrued income in trusts, the *Trusts (Capital and Income) Act 2013* provides that no apportionments should be made for any entitlement to income under a trust in England and Wales created or arising on or after 1 October 2013, unless the trust provides otherwise.

Building work in progress

Where a deceased had entered into a contract for property development or improvement work to be carried out which was in progress at the date of valuation, HMRC will require the VOA to value the property at the relevant date as if the work had been completed. From this value will then be deducted the cost of remaining work to completion as a charge payable against the deceased's estate. The same approach will apply in share valuation cases where the company has construction work in progress (VOA IHT manual, section 7, para 7.13).

Changes in the value of the estate

Any change in the value of the estate by reason of the death (e.g. life assurance monies receivable or loss of goodwill) are included as if occurring before death except:

(a) the termination on the death of any interest; or
(b) the passing of any interest by survivorship; or
(c) a decrease in value resulting from an alteration of a close company's unquoted share or loan capital or any rights attached thereto, see **11.8** CLOSE COMPANIES.

See IHTM04046 for further examples of changes in value deemed to occur before death.

[*IHTA 1984, s 171*].

Claims for reduction in value

Claims for a reduction in value of the estate may be made where:

(A) quoted shares are sold at a loss within one year of death (Form IHT35), see example below and **53.26** VALUATION;
(B) land is sold at a loss within three years (four years in certain cases) of death (Form IHT38), see **53.9** VALUATION; or
(C) 'related property' is sold at less value within three years of death, see **53.22** VALUATION.

[*IHTA 1984, ss 176, 179, 191; FA 2009, Sch 51 para 10*].

Example 1

When Bill Blogs died on 15 December 2020, his estate included a portfolio of quoted and unquoted investments. The PRs are considering selling certain investments within twelve months of death. The realisations likely to be made are as follows.

	Probate Value	Gross Sales
	£	£
Share A plc	66,000	57,[illegible]00
Share B plc	104,000	80,[illegible]00
Share C plc	57,000	60,[illegible]00
Share D Ltd (unquoted)	25,000	£10,[illegible]00
Net proceeds of sale	£252,000	£207,[illegible]00

Loss on D Ltd unquoted shares not allowed.

The PRs have therefore potential losses on sale of qualifying investments of £30,000 making a total reduction in IHT of £12,000 (i.e. £30,000 × 40%) available to be claimed by Bill's personal representatives on his death.

Notes to the example

(A) No costs of selling investments may be deducted from the sale proceeds. Note 5 on IHT35.

(B) The probate value of each of the investments sold will be adjusted, both for CGT and IHT purposes.

(C) Although excluded from computation of the loss on sale for inheritance tax purposes, incidental costs of sale and deductible from proceeds in calculating CGT. For deaths after 5 April 2004 see Inland Revenue Statement of Practice SP2/04.

Settled property

[49.3] Where the deceased was entitled to a qualifying interest in possession (see **24.1** INTEREST IN POSSESSION) which terminated on his death, the value of the settled property is included in that individual's estate. See **19** ESTATE and Form IHT418. However, where such settled property:

(I) reverts to the settlor who is still living and neither the settlor (nor his spouse after 11 April 1978) had acquired the reversionary interest for money or money's worth, or

(II) reverts to the settlor's spouse or civil partner who is domiciled in the UK at the time of death and neither the settlor nor his spouse (or civil partner as the case may be) had acquired a reversionary interest for money or money's worth,

the value of the settled property is left out of account in determining the deceased's estate. The exemption also applies as under (II) where the reversion is to the widow or widower or surviving civil partner of the settlor where the settlor died less than two years before the deceased. Relief under these provisions does not apply to a reversionary interest transferred into a settlement after 9 March 1981. Where more than one person is the settlor in relation to such a settlement and the circumstances so require these provisions apply as if the settled property were comprised in separate settlements.

Post-21 March 2006 IIPs

From 22 March 2006 where a person becomes beneficially entitled to an interest in possession, it is not included as part of his estate unless it is an immediate post-death interest, a transitional serial interest, or a disabled person's interest. The exclusion also applies as under (II) in **49.3** above where the reversion is an IPDI to the widow or widower or surviving civil partner of the beneficiary where the settlor has died less than two years before the deceased beneficiary. In such a case, the value of the settled property is left out of account in determining the deceased's estate. See **39** SETTLEMENTS WITH INTERESTS IN POSSESSION. [*IHTA 1984, ss 44(2), 54; FA 2006, Sch 20 para 15*].

Interests in unadministered estates

See **53.6** for the valuation of an interest in an estate still in the course of administration at the time of the death of a residuary legatee.

Surviving spouse exemption

[49.4] Where a surviving spouse has received a life interest in property under the will of the deceased spouse who died before 13 November 1974, no inheritance tax will arise on that interest when the surviving spouse dies (because estate duty was or would have been payable on the first death). [*IHTA 1984, Sch 6 para 2*]. See **51.2** TRANSITIONAL PROVISIONS.

Survivorship clauses

[49.5] Where under the terms of a will, or otherwise, property is held for a person if he survives another for a specified period of six months or less, the subsequent dispositions at the end of that period (or on the person's earlier death) are treated as having had effect from the beginning of the period. In effect therefore, the person who takes a gift under a will on surviving for a period of six months or less (commonly 28 days is specified) is treated as inheriting as from the date of death. This does not affect any distributions or applications of property occurring before those dispositions take effect. [*IHTA 1984, s 92*].

The *Law Reform (Succession) Act 1995, s 1* inserting a new *subs 2A* to *s 46* in the *Administration of Estates Act 1925* applying to all deaths after 1 January 1996 states that where a husband or wife of a person dying intestate survives the intestate but then dies before the end of the 28-day period beginning on the date on which the first death occurred, that husband or wife is to be deemed not to have survived the intestate. This will prevent problems where the intestate's assets are inherited by the spouse or civil partner where in most circumstances either, or both, would not wish this to occur on such deaths in quick succession.

Example 2

Mr and Mrs A both die in a boating accident on 12 July 2020 whilst on holiday but neither has made a will. They do not have any children but both have parents still living. The estates are valued at £325,000 and £335,000 for Mr and Mrs A respectively. As there is no will made by either the parents of either Mr A or Mrs

A might wish to prove their son/daughter survived the spouse and thereby share in both estates as well as the claiming of the transferability of the nil rate band under *IHTA 1984, s 8A*. See also HMRC Inheritance Tax manual IHTM43040. However, the *Administration of Estates Act 1925, s 46(2A)* has the effect of ensuring that where such deaths occur, the survivorship of the one spouse over the other must be for at least 28 days.

Notes to the example

(1) On intestacy where the estate comprises little more than an interest in the family home, the survivor may not see the need to take any formal steps to deal with the estate. For such a situation, see *Daffodil (Daffodil's Administrator) v CIR* [2002] STC (SCD) 224 Sp C 311 summarised at **55.1** TAX CASES.

(2) The *Law of Property Act 1925, s 184* provides for the younger to have survived the elder in cases of disaster and where it is not known which of them died first. The consequences of this will be overridden where a survivorship clause is included in the will. Hence if, in this example, Mr and Mrs A had mutual wills with survivorship clauses, their estates would both pass as if the other had predeceased, and *IHTA 1984, s 92* would ensure that the beneficiaries entitled in default of the spouse surviving for the stated period would be treated as being entitled as from the date of death.

(3) If the example were a case of mutual wills without survivorship clauses the deaths of Mr and Mrs A would be within what is known as the *commorientes* rule. See **49.14** below for the unusual effect of this for IHT purposes. With the transferability of the nil rate band afforded by *IHTA 1984, s 8A* the personal representatives of the younger spouse/civil partner will be able to claim the full nil rate band of £325,000 notwithstanding the elder spouse's estate is not subject to IHT at all under *IHTA 1984, s 4(2)*. See also HMRC Inheritance Tax manual IHTM43040. See also **49.24** below.

Non-residents' bank accounts

[49.6] On the death prior to 6 April 2013 of a person not domiciled, resident or ordinarily resident in the UK immediately before his death, the balance on any 'qualifying foreign currency account' is not included in the value of his estate immediately before his death. This also applies to such an account held by trustees of settled property in which the deceased held a beneficial interest in possession unless the settlor was domiciled in the UK at the time he made the settlement or the trustees are domiciled, resident and ordinarily resident there at the time of the beneficiary's death. Residence and ordinary residence are determined as for income tax purposes. The trustees of a settlement, however, were for these purposes regarded as not resident or ordinarily resident in the UK unless the general administration was ordinarily carried on there and the trustees or a majority of them (and where there is more than one class of trustees, a majority of each class) were resident and ordinarily resident in the UK. '*Qualifying foreign currency account*' means any foreign currency account with a bank or the Post Office. [*IHTA 1984, s 157; FA 1996, Sch 37 para 12(1), Sch 41 Pt VIII*].

For these purposes 'bank' has the same meaning as that given by *ITA 2007, s 991* (formerly *ICTA 1988, s 840A*). [*FA 1996, Sch 37 para 12(2)*].

With effect for deaths on or after 6 April 2013, this exemption continues to apply but is modified to delete the requirements relating to ordinary residence outside the UK. The conditions for exemption of a foreign currency bank account held by a person at the time of death are therefore that he is not domiciled and not resident in the UK immediately before his death. In relation to the trustee exemption, the requirement for the trustees is that a majority of them are not resident in the UK and that they are not domiciled in the UK. As to residence for tax purposes see the Statutory Residence Test in *FA 2013, Sch 45*.

Works of art temporarily in the UK

[49.7] Where the person beneficially entitled to foreign-owned work of art is not domiciled in the United Kingdom and on his or her death the work of art is situated in the United Kingdom for one or more of the purposes of public display (but not with a view to sale), cleaning and restoration (and for no other purpose), the item concerned is not to be included in that person's chargeable estate for IHT purposes. [*Enactment of Extra-Statutory Concessions Order 2009, Art 13*].

Compensation and other claims

[49.8] The right to pursue a claim for compensation is an item of property and therefore an asset of the estate. The open market value of the right at the date of death depends on several factors, but is fundamentally down to what was known, or capable of being known, at the date of death about:

(a) the amount of compensation that might be reasonably anticipated based on the information available;
(b) the likelihood of the claim being successful;
(c) the likely costs that would be expected to be incurred in obtaining a successful outcome; and
(d) the time delay between the date of death and the date when the compensation might reasonably be expected to be made.

The right to pursue a claim can be valuable whether or not the individual entitled to make the claim was aware of this right, provided that the information was capable of being known at the relevant date.

The open market value of the right to pursue the claim becomes more valuable as the outcome becomes more certain, so particular events can trigger a substantial increase in value.

Where personal representatives are aware of a potential claim at the date of death, they should record the existence of the claim on form IHT400 and provide as much information about the claim as they can. They should include a reasoned estimate of the open market value of the right to pursue the compensation where they are able to do so. (Source: HMRC Trust and Estates Newsletter August 2013.)

Certain tax claims may become available after a death but in relation to income or gains arising before the death. Examples are the carry back of CGT losses and terminal loss relief on cessation of trading. There is a view that tax recovered under such claims is not part of the estate on death, since at the time of death, no such claim was in progress or possible.

For various reliefs available for certain statutory compensation schemes, see 21.22 EXEMPT TRANSFERS AND OTHER RELIEFS.

NHS Continuing Care Scheme payments

[49.9] Where NHS care for a deceased up to the date of death has been provided outside a hospital, often by at a residential care home, a claim for reimbursement of the costs of the care may be made on the NHS. This is known as the NHS Health Care Scheme. Any payment received is an asset of the estate of the deceased and is liable to IHT as such. However, at the date of death, a claim may be in progress but without any firm indication as to whether it will be accepted or how much will be received; or a claim may not be made until after the death. In such cases, HMRC allow a valuation discount of 10% from the sum received. If the claim has been finalised by the date of death, the discount will not be applied. See IHTM10270. There were larger discounts for deaths before 17 December 2004.

The discount reflects the potential uncertainty of success in a claim for reimbursement and arises from the *Coughlan* case and subsequent reports by the Health Service Ombudsman. See also *R v North East Devon Health Authority, ex p Coughlan (Secretary of State for Health and another intervening* [2000] 3 All ER 850.

Liabilities deductible

[49.10] In determining the value of a person's estate, his liabilities at that time must be taken into account except as otherwise provided by *IHTA 1984*. Except in the case of a liability imposed by the law, a liability incurred by the transferor may be taken into account only to the extent that it was incurred for a consideration in money or money's worth. [*IHTA 1984, s 5(3), (5)*]. By concession, income tax in Canada charged on deemed gains immediately before death will be allowed as a deductible liability. A deceased's worldwide estate of which the Canadian tax on deemed gains comprises a liability may be set-off against the value of UK assets where it exceeds assets (liable or not to IHT) held outside the UK. (ESC F18) *IHTA 1984, s 5(3)* provides that 'in determining the value of a person's estate at any time his liabilities at that time shall be taken into account, except as otherwise provided by this Act . . . ' and in *Robertson v HMRC* [2005] STC (SCD) 723 Sp C 494 lump sum maintenance payments made to an ex-wife, which were not sanctioned under the maintenance agreement or by the court, were not to be treated as a liability to be returned to him and should be treated as part of the deceased ex-wife's estate for IHT purposes on her death.

A liability which is an encumbrance on any property shall, so far as possible, be taken to reduce the value of that property (*IHTA 1984, s 162(4)*) but see the provisions of *IHTA 1984, s 162A* which override this rule with effect for transfers of value made on or after 17 July 2013 in the case of liabilities incurred at any time which are attributable to financing excluded property, or if incurred after 5 April 2013 and which are attributable to property qualifying for business or agricultural reliefs or, in respect of woodlands, deferral of charge.

These disallowances are extended to any liabilities attributable to financing non-residents' foreign currency accounts, with effect for transfers of value made on or after 17 July 2014. These provisions are explained at **53.19**.

Liabilities not discharged after death

The position of liabilities owing at the date of death, but which were not paid thereafter has historically been rather unclear. If the liability is released without payment during the executorship period, it will be appropriate to notify HMRC by way of a corrective IHT account. If however the liability is left unpaid and is not released during the administration period, the view might be taken that it remains deductible as a debt due at the time of death. It may however be released at some later time. Such circumstances might in particular arise in relation to loans made by employee benefit trusts.

With effect from 17 July 2013, it is now provided that a liability due from a person's estate on death may only be taken into account to the extent that it is discharged on or after the death out of the estate, or from excluded property owned by the person immediately before death, in money or monies worth, subject always to any other specific provision in the IHT legislation preventing the liability from being taken into account (for example, *FA 1986, s 103*, see below). For this purpose, the estate refers to the person's estate for IHT purposes immediately before death, and therefore includes IPDI property, pre-22 March 2006 life interest property and gift with reservation property.

Where the liability is not discharged out of the estate, it may be taken into account only if there is a real commercial reason for it not being discharged, wholly or in part, and the non-payment is not part of arrangements having a main purpose of securing a tax advantage. This is once again subject to any overriding provisions in the IHT legislation preventing deductibility. For these purposes, there is a real commercial reason for liability not being discharged, wholly or partly, where it is shown that either it is to a person dealing at arm's length, or if it were to such a person, that person would not require the liability to be discharged. If the debt is secured on an asset passing to the surviving spouse, and the debt is disallowed, the spouse exemption nevertheless applies to the full unencumbered value of the asset. In *Pride as trustee of the estate of the late Geraldine Pride v HMRC* [2023] UKFTT 316 (TC), it was held that loan notes with long repayment dates held by a children's trust were not a deductible liability in the estate of the debtor since they were released after her death and a commercial creditor would have required repayment. See **55.1** TAX CASES.

Example 3

David had a mortgage of £300,000 on a property in his name. He leaves the property to his son Edward, subject to the debt, and also takes out a life policy written in trust for Edward to provide a sum of £300,000 payable on David's death. If following David's death Edward uses to policy proceeds to pay off the mortgage, the debt will not be deductible for IHT purposes in David's estate because the liability is not discharged out of the estate after the death. If on the other hand Edward lends the policy proceeds to the executors so that they then pay off the mortgage, the debt will be deductible even though Edward may subsequently waive repayment of the debt due to him.

See also *Taxation* 31 October 2013 pp 15–16: where executors take out a new mortgage to repay one owing at death and then convey the property to a beneficiary subject to the new borrowing, a charge to stamp duty land tax arises. There is no such charge where the property is conveyed subject to a liability incurred by the deceased, but non-payment of that liability out of the estate could cause it to be disallowed as a deduction on the death, unless the commercial reason test is satisfied. See example in HMRC's inheritance tax manual at IHTM28029 where the test is considered to be satisfied in the case of a commercial mortgage.

These provisions are tied in with the rules relating to liabilities to finance excluded property or relievable property detailed at **53.19**. Where a liability is only partly paid off after the date of death, and it partly relates to a loan to finance excluded property, then that part is taken to be discharged first. After that, any part which was incurred to finance property qualifying for business property relief, agricultural property relief or woodlands is then to be taken as discharged and any remainder after the foregoing is to be treated as a general liability of the estate. [*IHTA 1984, s 175A*].

Specific liabilities deductible

Liabilities deductible (apart from normal debts) include the following.

(i) Reasonable funeral expenses, including a reasonable amount for mourning and the cost of a tombstone or gravestone (see IHTM10375 and IHTM10373). The word 'reasonable' depends upon the standard of living of the deceased so that in a case similar to the funeral of the Duke of Athol in 1996, where the expense of his private army acting as an honour guard would have been allowed, any expenses that are reasonable for the attendance of family and servants will be allowed as a funeral expense. For deaths abroad embalming and transport costs will be allowed as an expense (see also Foster Inheritance Tax, para D1.42).

(ii) Inheritance tax or capital transfer tax liabilities outstanding from a previous transfer, but if the tax is not eventually paid out of the estate, an adjustment must be made.

(iii) Expenses in administering or realising property situated outside the UK, up to 5% of the property's value where the expenses are shown to be attributable to the situation of the property. The allowance is intended to cover the costs (in excess of the normal costs) of resealing a grant of probate etc. and obtaining the relevant tax clearance and not substantive expenses e.g. tax liabilities. A separate note of charges should be kept to justify the claim. [*IHTA 1984, s 173*].

(iv) Liabilities for future payments or transfer of assets taxable under *IHTA 1984, s 262*, see **7.11** CALCULATION OF TAX. Such liabilities are to be valued by reducing the amount of the further payments or assets by the chargeable portion.

(v) Income tax liabilities arising on deemed disposals on death in respect of offshore income gains under the provisions in *ICTA 1988, ss 757–764, 27, Sch 28* as amended by *FA 2004, Sch 26* and deep discount securities under the provisions in the former *ICTA 1988, s 57* as amended by *FA 1996, Sch 15*.

[*IHTA 1984, ss 172–175; FA 1996, Sch 13 para 4, Sch 14 para 2*].

Treatment of certain debts and encumbrances

[49.11] Certain liabilities may not be deducted if owed to a person who has received property from the deceased. Specifically, subject to below, where a debt incurred or encumbrance created by the deceased after 18 March 1986 would otherwise be taken into account in valuing his estate immediately before death, that liability is subject to abatement proportionate to the value of any consideration given for the debt etc. which consisted of:

(a) 'property derived from the deceased'; or
(b) consideration (not within (a) above) given by any person who was at any time entitled to, or amongst whose resources there was at any time included, any property derived from the deceased.

The abatement under (b) above does not apply to the extent it can be shown that the donee's loan etc. to the deceased was greater than the gifts received from the donor or that the deceased's gift was not made to facilitate the loan.

'*Property derived from the deceased*' means any property which was the subject matter of a disposition by the deceased (alone or with any other person) or which represented any of the subject matter of such a disposition (directly or indirectly) by one or more intermediate dispositions. If, therefore, a gift of cash is made and thereafter the donee lends money back to the donor, the loan will not be deductible to the extent of the amount of cash previously given; any excess of loan over the amount of cash gift will be deductible.

More commonly, cases fall within (b) above which deals with the situation where a gift is made, and a loan back is made from the donee's own resources. HMRC's view is that this provision has wide scope so as to cover the donee's resources 'at any time', thus including gifts made to him by the borrower before the legislation was introduced with effect from 18 March 1986. Where the original gift was an asset such as shares or a property, any disallowance of a loan back by the donee will be by reference to the value of the asset gifted at the time the loan is made. Changes in value of the asset after that time will not be relevant.

If, however, the disposition by the deceased was neither:

(A) a transfer of value (for example it was a gift of excluded property, or was a sale for full value); nor
(B) part of associated operations which included a disposition *by the deceased* (with or without another person) otherwise than for full consideration in money or money's worth to the deceased for his own use or benefit or a disposition *by any other person* which reduced the value of the deceased's property,

it is left out of account. For the purposes of the above, an exempt transfer, e.g. to a spouse, is nevertheless a transfer of value and so these provisions apply to gifts and debts between married persons as they do to transactions between other family members or unrelated individuals.

In *Pride as trustee of the estate of the late Geraldine Pride v HMRC* [2023] UKFTT 316 (TC), certain properties were acquired in 2002 by a trust from the settlor by a number of steps which resulted in the purchase price being satisfied by loan notes issued to the settlor. She had an interest in possession in the trust. The settlor then gave the loan notes away to a trust for her children. These arrangements were being widely marketed at the time and have been challenged by HMRC on a number of grounds, one of them being that the debt is not deductible from the funds in the trust for the settlor as it is owed by trustees who have property derived from the deceased. The exception for dispositions which are not transfers of value does not assist because of the associated operations which involve a gift of the debt by the settlor. It was argued for the trustees that the debt was not incurred by the settlor, as required by *IHTA 1984, s 103*, but the First-tier Tribunal rejected this on the basis that the trust fund was part of the settlor's estate, and so it could be regarded as a debt incurred by her. For other technical arguments raised, see **55.1** TAX CASES.

The repayment in lifetime of a debt caught by these provisions is treated as a potentially exempt transfer. In theory, multiple loans and multiple part repayments between the same persons can give rise to a series of potentially exempt transfers by reference to the repayments.

The disallowed debt in the estate of the borrower is treated as a specific gift from the estate and grossing up may be applicable (IHTM28365).

[*FA 1986, s 103(1)–(4), (6)*].

Case law

A married woman died in 2000 and by her will she left an amount equal to the IHT nil rate band to a discretionary trust for her husband (P) and their children, and the residue to P. P agreed to pay £150,000 plus indexation to the discretionary trust in return for his wife's half-share in the matrimonial home, this purchase price being left outstanding as a loan. P had previously provided all the finance to purchase the property. He died in 2002, and HMRC issued a notice of determination charging IHT on his estate. His personal representative appealed, contending that the £153,222 which P owed to the discretionary trust should be deducted from the value of his estate. The Special Commissioner rejected this contention and dismissed his appeal, holding that the effect of *FA 1986, s 103* was that the debt was not deductible. The estate of his late wife included property derived from P and so the debt due to her estate was not deductible. It was argued that the section was prevented from applying because P's transfer of the property to his wife was not a transfer of value by virtue of *IHTA 1984, s 11* (providing that a 'disposition for maintenance' is not a 'transfer of value') but it was held that *s 11* did not apply to a situation 'when a husband puts a house in joint names of himself and his wife during their marriage'. It is thought that the position would have been different if the executors had charged the property with the sum due to the discretionary trust before transferring it to P. See also **5** ANTI-AVOIDANCE; **39.1** SETTLEMENTS WITH INTERESTS IN POSSESSION; *Phizackerley (Personal Representative of Dr PJR Phizackerley) v HMRC* [2007] STC (SCD) 328 Sp C 591.

Double charges relief

Double charges — liabilities subject to abatement and death. Relief from double charge to tax is given where, after 17 March 1986, a transfer of value which is or proves to be a chargeable transfer ('the transfer') is made by an individual ('the deceased') by virtue of which the estate of the transferee is increased or by virtue of which property becomes comprised in a settlement of which the transferee is a trustee *and* at any time before his death the deceased incurs a liability to the transferee ('the liability') which is subject to abatement under the provisions above.

Two separate calculations of tax payable as a result of death are made. In the first, the amount of the transfer of value is reduced by the amount of the debt which is disallowed or abated and, in the second, the amount of the transfer of value and of the debt are both taken into account. The higher amount of total tax is payable and, subject to below, relief is given, as the case may be, by either reducing the value of the transfer of value or by allowing the debt and charging the transfer of value in full.

Where the first calculation gives the higher amount:

(1) credit is available for any tax which became payable before the death of the deceased as is attributable to the amount of the reduction in that calculation (but not exceeding the difference between the amount of tax under the first calculation and the amount of tax which would have been paid under the second calculation if the liability had been taken into account); and
(2) the reduction applies for all IHT purposes other than a ten-year anniversary charge or a proportionate charge to tax on a discretionary settlement arising before the death of the deceased if the transfer of value was a chargeable transfer when it was made.

Where the total tax chargeable under the first and second calculations is the same, the first calculation is treated as producing the higher amount of tax.

Where there are a number of transfers by the deceased before his death which are relevant to the abated liability on death, the above provisions are applied to those transfers in reverse order i.e. latest first. [*FA 1986, s 104(1)(c); SI 1987/1130, Regs 6, 8*]. See also **22.15** GIFTS WITH RESERVATION regarding double charges relief in connection with pre-owned assets.

Example 4

A makes a potentially exempt transfer to B of £203,000 on 1 May 2013 and a further such transfer to him of £40,000 on 1 January 2014. On 1 July 2014, A makes a gift into a discretionary trust of £160,000 on which the trustees pay tax of £Nil. He makes a further potentially exempt transfer to B of £30,000 on 1 January 2015 but on 1 July 2015, B makes a loan to A of £100,000. No annual exemptions are available.

A dies on 1 December 2017 with a death estate of £200,000 against which a deduction is claimed for the debt of £100,000 due to B.

First calculation: disallow the debt and ignore corresponding amounts of potentially exempt transfers from A to B, starting with the latest

	IHT payable
	£
1 May 2013	
Potentially exempt transfer now reduced to £173,000*	—
1 January 2014	
Potentially exempt transfer now reduced to nil	—
1 July 2014	
Gift into trust £160,000 as top slice of £333,000	
Tax £3,200 less Nil already paid	3,200
1 January 2005	
Potentially exempt transfer now reduced to nil	—
1 December 2007	
Death estate £200,000 as top slice of £533,000	80,000
Total tax due as result of A's death	£83,200

* See note (C) below.

Second calculation: allow the debt and charge the potentially exempt transfers in full

	IHT payable
	£
1 May 2013	
Potentially exempt transfer £203,000	—
1 January 2014	
Potentially exempt transfer £40,000 as top slice of £243,000	—
1 July 2014	
Gift into trust £160,000 as top slice of £403,000	
Tax £41,200 less Nil already paid	31,200
1 January 2015	
Potentially exempt transfer £30,000 as top slice of £433,000	12,000
1 December 2017	
Death estate £100,000 as top slice of £533,000	40,000
Total tax due as a result of A's death	£83,200

Notes to the example

(A) If the two calculations above result in the same tax chargeable, as in this case, the first of the calculations is taken by reason of *Inheritance Tax (Double Charges Relief) Regulations 1987, SI 1987/1130, Reg 8* but no such provision applies in respect of *Inheritance Tax (Double Charges Relief) Regulations 2005, SI 2005/3441.*

(B) In the first calculation, the debt of £100,000 is disallowed from B to A less the corresponding amounts of potentially exempt transfers from A to B which are ignored, starting with the latest i.e. (£30,000 + £40,000 + £203,000) = £173,000 balance.

Life insurance policies

[49.12] In determining the value of a person's estate immediately before death, no account is to be taken of any liability arising under or in connection with life insurance made after 30 June 1986 unless the whole of the sums assured under the policy form part of that person's estate immediately before his death. [*FA 1986, s 103(7)*]. See also April/May 2002, p 2 IHT Newsletter.

Reduced rate for certain estates with 10% gifts to charities

[49.13] For deaths on or after 6 April 2012 inheritance tax will be charged on the net chargeable value of any component of the estate at a rate of 36% where 10% or more of that component has been left to charity.

Where the estate comprises only the deceased's 'free estate' without any joint property passing by survivorship, the value of the estate on which the 10% threshold will be based (the 'baseline amount') will be the value of the net estate charged to IHT after deducting all available reliefs, exemptions and available nil rate band, but adding back the charitable legacy itself. So for example the amount of exempt gifts to the spouse and the value of assets qualifying for 100% business property relief are deducted from the total value of the estate to find the baseline amount, but charitable gifts are not. If the gifts to charities total 10% or more of the baseline amount, then the rate of tax applicable to the chargeable estate will be 36%.

In cases in which the estate for IHT purposes includes assets additional to those in the 'free estate', the 10% test will be applied to each category of assets, described as a 'component', that makes up the aggregate estate. The components are:

(a) the 'general component' being the free estate passing under the terms of the will. This excludes other components listed below and also gifts with reservation of benefit chargeable on the death;

(b) the 'survivorship component' being jointly owned assets passing by survivorship (in England, Wales and Northern Ireland), or under a special destination in Scotland, or under corresponding provisions of any applicable foreign law;

(c) the 'settled property component', being settled property comprised in the estate by virtue of an interest in possession to which the deceased was beneficially entitled.

If the assets passing to charity from one component exceed 10% of its baseline amount, other components may be merged with it to give an aggregate baseline amount for all of them. This merging of components will require an election to be made by all those who are 'appropriate persons' for each of the components involved; the appropriate persons are the personal representatives in relation to the general component, the settlement trustees in relation to the settled component and the surviving joint owner or owners in relation to the survivorship component. It should be noted that because gifts with reservation of benefit which form part of the chargeable estate on the death do not themselves comprise any component of the estate, they can only be brought within the scope of the reduced rate charge by election to merge them with one of the three components at (a), (b) or (c) above. If survivorship component relates an asset held jointly with the spouse, that component will not usually be relevant for the purposes of this relief because it is exempt, except where the limitation on the exemption applies owing to the deceased being UK domiciled and the spouse non-domiciled for IHT purposes.

The value of the assets passing to charity from a particular component will be compared to the baseline amount for that component. The baseline amount is calculated after deducting from that component all available reliefs, exemptions and the appropriate proportion of the available nil rate band, as increased by the transfer of nil rate band provisions. To find the appropriate proportion of the available nil band, deduct first the amounts of any chargeable transfers in the seven years ending with the date of death, as the nil band is allocated primarily to these, then find the percentage of the total chargeable transfers on the death which is represented by the value of component concerned. That percentage of the available nil band is the appropriate proportion of it to be deducted from the component. If the 10% test for a component is passed, IHT will be charged on that particular component at 36%.

Where the grossing up rules apply to gifts under a will (see 7.7 CALCULATION OF TAX), for the purpose of calculating the baseline amount the rate to be used for grossing up is 36%.

The reduced rate of IHT will apply automatically if the estate or component passes the 10% test. If it does not, IHT will be charged at the full rate. However, personal representatives and other relevant persons may elect for the reduced rate not to apply if, for example, the benefit obtained from applying the reduced rate is likely to be minimal and they do not wish to incur additional costs of valuing items left to charity. Elections must be made in writing to HMRC and no later than two years and one month after the date of death of the deceased. HMRC have discretion to extend this deadline.

The new provisions will apply equally to charitable legacies made by will or by an Instrument of Variation. The conditions for an Instrument of Variation to be taken into account for these purposes require that the charity has been notified that the devolution of the estate has been varied in its favour.

Example 5

The estate of Percival who died on 30 April 2022 is valued at £425,000, comprising quoted investments and cash. He leaves a legacy of £10,000 to the National Trust and the residue of £415,000 less IHT passes to his children. The

IHT payable will be £90,000 at 36% – £32,400 because 10% of the estate after deduction of the nil-band is left to charity. So the gift to the charity reduces the residue by only £2,400 (£10,000 gift less IHT reduction £40,000 – £32,400).

Example 6

The estate of Albert, a widower, who died on 30 April 2022 is valued at £1,630,000, including a trust fund in which he has had an interest in possession since 2000 worth £500,000. He inherited the whole of his late wife's estate some years previously and neither had ever made any lifetime gifts within seven years of death. He leaves a legacy of £100,000 to the NSPCC and the residue of £1,030,000 along with the trust fund pass to his children after payment of IHT. The IHT payable by the free estate at the rate of 36% because 10% of the estate after deduction of the appropriate fraction of the nil-band is left to charity. The appropriate fraction is:

$£650,000 \times 1,030,000/1,530,000 = 437,581$

The chargeable estate is therefore £1030,000 – £437,581 = £592,419. To test whether the 10% threshold is satisfied, add back the amount of the charitable gifts (£100,000), The baseline amount is therefore £692,419 and the estate therefore qualifies for the 36% rate of IHT.

The trustees of the late wife's trust fund may elect to merge the settled property component with the general component (that is, the residue of the free estate) as the baseline amount for the merged components will be:

General component		£692,419
Settled component	£500,000	
less balance of nil band	£212,419	£287,581
Baseline amount of merged components		£980,000

The charitable gift under the will exceeds 10% of the merged components and so an election will enable both the free estate and the trust fund to bear IHT at the rate of 36%.

Quick successive relief: Where assets in the estate qualify for quick succession relief (see **36** QUICK SUCCESSION RELIEF), and it is necessary to apportion that relief between assets in different components of the estate, the apportionment is to be made by reference to the tax payable by each component and not the capital value of each component.

Conditionally exempt property: where a chargeable event arises in respect of heritage property which was allowed conditional exemption on the death of the owner (see **30.10** NATIONAL HERITAGE), the lower 36% rate of IHT cannot be claimed on that event even if the remaining estate had satisfied the conditions for that rate.

Woodlands: equally deferred charges in respect of woodlands (see **54.4** WOODLANDS) cannot benefit from the lower 36% rate of IHT even if the estate had satisfied the conditions for that rate.

[*FA 2012, s 207, Sch 32*].

Commorientes

[49.14] For the purposes of establishing if there has been a transfer on death, where it cannot be known which of two or more persons died first they are assumed to have died at the same instant (i.e. the rule in the *Law of Property Act 1925, s 184* that the elder is deemed to have died first does not apply for IHT purposes). [*IHTA 1984, s 4(2)*].

> *Example 7*
>
> If father and son die in the same accident, any property bequeathed by the father to the son passes to the son's estate (since the father is deemed under the rule quoted above to have died first) and then to the beneficiaries under the son's will, but inheritance tax is chargeable only on the transfer of the property to the son's estate and not again on the transfer of it to the beneficiaries of the son's estate.

In the case of spouses or civil partners who die in *commorientes* circumstances (that is, so that it is not possible to say whether one survived the other), the situation is complicated further by the inter-spouse/civil partner exemption under *IHTA 1984, s 18*. If their estates are bequeathed to each other if he or she survives, without any requirement that such survival be for a specified period, there is a transfer of the estate of the elder of the two to the estate of the younger spouse or civil partner by virtue of the *Law of Property Act 1925, s 184*. The spouse exemption applies to this transfer. However, for the purposes of inheritance tax, *IHTA 1984, s 4(2)* treats the deaths as simultaneous for IHT purposes. Hence the transfer of the estate of the elder to the younger is disregarded in relation to the IHT position of the estate of the younger spouse/civil partner. The result is therefore that, on this interpretation, the elder's estate escapes inheritance tax completely. Therefore a survivorship condition, which is normally desirable, should be deliberately excluded in the event of the spouses/civil partners dying simultaneously (see Taxation magazine 24 September 1992 p 649 and 6 July 1995 p 362). This view is not universally accepted (see British Tax Review 1995 p 390). See also **49.5** above. See IHTM12197 for text and a useful example, which supports the view above that the elder spouse's estate is not subject to IHT at all.

With the transferability of the nil rate band afforded by *IHTA 1984, s 8A*, the personal representatives of the younger spouse/civil partner will be able to claim the full unused nil rate band of the elder spouse/civil partner notwithstanding that the elder spouse's estate is not subject to IHT at all under *IHTA 1984, s 4(2)*. See also HMRC Inheritance Tax manual IHTM43040 and **49.25** below.

As noted at **49.5** above, the situation described here cannot apply where both spouses die intestate, nor where they have mutual wills with survivorship clauses.

See also **49.2** above regarding survivorship clauses, **49.25** below and **36** QUICK SUCCESSION RELIEF.

Transferability of nil rate bands

[49.15] From 9 October 2007 on the death of the survivor of a married couple or civil partnership a claim may be made for the nil rate band to be increased by reference to any unused proportion of the nil rate band which there was on the death of the spouse or civil partner who pre-deceased. This provision described as the 'transfer of unused nil rate band between spouses and civil partners' is available to the widow, widower or surviving civil partner irrespective of when the original spouse or civil partner died. [*IHTA 1984, s 8A as inserted by FA 2008, s 10, Sch 4 para 2*]. Note that it is not available for chargeable transfers made in the lifetime of the survivor, except those within seven years of death in which case HMRC will apply the total nil bands primarily to the lifetime gifts (although there is an argument that this is incorrect in that the tax on the gifts is not part of the charge to tax on the death as required by *IHTA 1984, s 8A(3)*). The size of the estate of the first to die is not relevant as such, and so for example, if he or she had no assets at all, a full additional nil rate band will be available on the death of the survivor. Also the domicile status of either spouses or civil partners is not relevant, except that where after 9 March 1982 the spouse or civil partner who predeceased was UK domiciled but at that time the survivor was not, bequests to a value in excess of £55,000 to the survivor will have been within the nil rate band. Prior to 9 March 1982, lower limits applied from the introduction of capital transfer tax. Gifts of excluded property do not impact on the nil rate band.

The parties must have been spouses or civil partners at the time of the death of the one who predeceased, and divorce prior to that time will prevent any claim. Equally, the relief will not apply in cases of couples living together. See *Burden & Burden v United Kingdom* [2006] ECHR Case 13378/05; [2007] STC 252, in which two elderly sisters lived together in a jointly-owned house on land which they had inherited from their parents. They lodged a complaint with the ECHR, contending that the provisions of *IHTA 1984, s 18* (as amended by the Tax and Civil Partnership Regulations 2005) were a breach of Article 14 of the European Convention on Human Rights, because when one of them died, the survivor would be required to pay IHT on her sister's share of their home, whereas no IHT would have been charged if they had lived together as a registered lesbian civil partnership. The ECHR rejected their application holding that 'the inheritance tax exemption for married and civil partnership couples . . . pursues a legitimate aim, namely to promote stable, committed heterosexual and homosexual relationships by providing the survivor with a measure of financial security after the death of the spouse or partner'. See also *Courten v United Kingdom* [2008] ECHR 1546.

Those in gay or lesbian relationships living together who do not have a civil partnership document within *CPA 2004, s 2(1)* but have a relationship was recognised under overseas law before the UK Act came into force are to be treated as having formed a civil partnership recognised in the UK on the date the Act came into force. In such cases the survivor's personal representatives will be able to claim the unused nil rate band of the predeceased but only in cases where the first death was after CPA 2004 coming into force, i.e. 5 December 2005. See HMRC Inheritance Tax manual IHTM43001.

See also Example 7 for the transferability of the unused nil rate band in cases of alternatively secured pensions in PENSION SCHEMES (34). See also HMRC Inheritance Tax manual IHTM43001–IHTM43035.

To calculate the increased amount available on the death of the survivor, it is first necessary to find the nil rate band maximum at the time of the death of the spouse or civil partner who predeceased. For deaths after the introduction of capital transfer tax on 13 March 1975 the current nil band provisions and spouse exemption (although with certain alterations to the limited amount available between spouses of mixed domicile) have been in operation; a table of nil bands from 26 March 1974 is set out below. It is then necessary to establish what amount of that nil rate maximum was not utilised on the death of the first to die. The unutilised amount is then converted to a percentage of nil rate band maximum. That percentage of the nil rate band in force on the death of the survivor can then be claimed as an additional nil rate band on that death.

CAPITAL TRANSFER TAX AND INHERITANCE TAX NIL RATE BANDS

From	To	Nil rate band
13 March 1975	26 October 1977	£15,000
27 October 1977	25 March 1980	£25,000
26 March 1980	08 March 1982	£50,000
09 March 1982	14 March 1983	£55,000
15 March 1983	12 March 1984	£60,000
13 March 1984	05 April 1985	£64,000
06 April 1985	17 March 1986	£67,000
18 March 1986	16 March 1987	£71,000
17 March 1987	14 March 1988	£90,000
15 March 1988	05 April 1989	£110,000
06 April 1989	05 April 1990	£118,000
06 April 1990	05 April 1991	£128,000
06 April 1991	09 March 1992	£140,000
10 March 1992	05 April 1995	£150,000
06 April 1995	05 April 1996	£154,000
06 April 1996	05 April 1997	£200,000
06 April 1997	05 April 1998	£215,000
06 April 1998	05 April 1999	£223,000
06 April 1999	05 April 2000	£231,000
06 April 2000	05 April 2001	£234,000
06 April 2001	05 April 2002	£242,000
06 April 2002	05 April 2003	£250,000
06 April 2003	05 April 2004	£255,000
06 April 2004	05 April 2005	£263,000
06 April 2005	05 April 2006	£275,000
06 April 2006	05 April 2007	£285,000
06 April 2007	05 April 2008	£300,000
06 April 2008	05 April 2009	£312,000
06 April 2009	onwards	£325,000

When estate duty applied, there was no spouse exemption prior to 21 March 1972 and therefore any amounts transferred to a spouse were deducted from the tax-free band that existed at that time – any balance of that tax free band will comprise the proportion of the unused nil rate band to be transferred. See Example 9 below.

Where a surviving spouse or civil partner was married to, or was in a civil partnership with, someone who (a) had survived an earlier marriage or civil partnership and (b) was entitled to transfer an unused nil rate band from that earlier death, the amount of any nil rate band available for transfer on the death of the survivor is first calculated by reference to the actual nil rate band that was appropriate on the intervening death, including the transferred element of nil rate band. Any chargeable transfers and bequests on taken into account on the intervening death are then primarily treated as deducted from that transferred element and only the excess is deducted from ordinary nil band available on that death. See example at IHTM43032.

A claim for transferability of the nil rate band must be made on form IHT402 on the death of the surviving spouse or civil partner by their personal representatives or accountable persons to obtain the use of the unused nil rate band of the predeceased spouse or civil partner. [*IHTA 1984, s 8B as inserted by FA 2008, Sch 4 para 2*]. A claim must be made in the permitted period, which is two years from the end of the month in which the survivor dies, or if later, three months beginning with the date on which the personal representatives act as such. HMRC have discretion to allow late claims — see IHTM43009 for circumstances in which late claims may be accepted. Claims can be withdrawn within one month after the end of the permitted period. Form IHT402 asks for the gifting history of the predeceased spouse or civil partner and once completed it is sent to HMRC with documentation such as the death certificate, marriage certificate and the will.

Where a person survives more than one spouse or civil partner who predeceased, claims can be made in relation to the unused nil bands of either or both of them, but the maximum claim on the death of the survivor is capped at the maximum nil rate band available on the survivor's death; thus at the present time the maximum claim under these provisions is £325,000. Accordingly, on the death of the second spouse, it may be appropriate to ensure that his or her nil rate band is used at that time by suitable legacies, so that on the death of the survivor the nil rate band of the first spouse who predeceased can be claimed for carry forward. See Example 3 at **13.4** DEEDS OF VARIATION AND DISCLAIMERS. [*IHTA 1984, s 8A(5) as inserted by FA 2008, Sch 4 para 2*]. In the case of deferred charges regarding heritage property and woodlands which affect the calculation of the transferable nil rate band, see **30.10** NATIONAL HERITAGE and **54.7** WOODLANDS. [*IHTA 1984, s 8C as inserted by FA 2008, Sch 4 para 2*].

Where a widow or widower has been previously married on more than one occasion, then on their death, the availability of unused nil rate bands of their previous spouses may be aggregated with their own by their personal representatives but the aggregate of the predeceased spouses' unused nil rate bands should not exceed the nil rate band pertaining at the date of death of the widow or widower. See IHTM 43030. A similar situation will also apply in cases of civil partnerships for civil marriages that took place from 5 December 2005. [*IHTA 1984, s 8A(5)(6) as inserted by FA 2008, Sch 4 para 2*].

Example 8

John dies on 25 August 2007 with an estate of £300,000 and he leaves by his will £50,000 to each of his two grandchildren on discretionary trusts and the balance is left to his widow, Jean. Jean dies in October 2020 when the nil rate band at that time is £325,000. John's balance of nil rate band available to pass on to his wife is 66.66666% (i.e. (£300,000 – £100,000) ÷ £300,000 × 100%) and therefore when Jean dies her personal representatives can claim an unused nil rate band applicable to John of £216,667 (i.e. 66.66666% × £325,000). This is added to Jean's unused nil rate band at her date of death also of £325,000 to make a total of £541,667 which is within the maximum of £650,000 (i.e. £325,000 × 2).

Notes to the example

(A) The up rating of the pre-deceased's nil rate band on the death of the survivor spouse's or civil partner's death is calculated by applying the unused nil rate band (i.e. M > VT) under *IHTA 1984, s 8A(2)(4)* as follows:

$$\text{Percentage} = \frac{E}{NRBMD} \times 100$$

where:

M = maximum amount that could be transferred on the predeceased person's death where it is chargeable at the nil rate band at that time;
VT = value actually transferred by the chargeable transfer or nil if applicable;
E = the amount by which M above is greater than VT above;
NRBMD = the nil rate band maximum applying at the time of the deceased spouse's or civil partner's death.

(B) The claim for the unused nil rate band by Jean's personal representatives must be made within two years from the end of the month in which the survivor spouse or civil partner dies or, if later, the period three months after the personal representatives first begin to act. HMRC may specify a longer period in certain circumstances. [*IHTA 1984, s 8B*].

(C) Under Scottish law, children (or remoter issue) have the right to share in the movable estate of a deceased parent. This is called legitim. In Scotland, a claim for legitim (see also **49.21** below) may result in a delay in claim due to the child's age which then has a knock on effect with regard to the transferability of the nil rate band to the survivor spouse or civil partner who will have predeceased the minor. If a claim is made then the nil rate band claimed by the personal representatives of the survivor spouse or civil partner will have to be amended to take into account the legitim. The child may renounce his claim to legitim by his twentieth birthday (or longer if the Board permit). [*IHTA 1984, s 147(10) as inserted by FA 2008, Sch 4 para 3*]. See also HMRC Inheritance Tax manual IHTM43041.

Example 9

Betty has been married and widowed twice before. Her first husband died in October 1974 soon after they were married when estate duty applied and 5 TRANSITIONAL PROVISIONS applied. He left all his assets in his will to Betty and this was within the £15,000 spouse's exemption applying at that time so that none of his tax free band was utilised in 1974. Betty's second husband Jack died on 18 June

2005 and left his assets to Betty excepting a £165,000 gift he made to his daughter in 2003. Jack therefore had used 60% of his £275,000 nil rate band at his death and a further 40% is available to transfer on to Betty on her death.

Betty died in December 2019. Her personal representatives would be entitled to claim 100% of her first husband's nil rate band (i.e. £325,000 × 100%) and also 40% of Jack's nil rate band (i.e. £325,000 × 40% = £130,000) as well as her own unused nil rate band of up to £325,000. This makes a total of £780,000 but is restricted to £650,000 (i.e. £325,000 × 2).

Notes to the example

(A) In such similar situations where the aggregate unused nil rate bands of previous deceased spouses or civil partners add up to more than the current amount pertaining at the date of death of the survivor a proportion will be wasted. It is, in this case, too late to effect a deed of variation within *IHTA 1984, s 142* as more than two years have elapsed since Jack's death. See Example 3 at **13.4** DEEDS OF VARIATION AND DISCLAIMERS.

(B) It may be appropriate in such circumstances to effect a deed of variation on the death of the second spouse, Jack in this example, to ensure that assets are passed on to the children to utilise the wasted portion of the nil rate band.

Example 10

Jeffrey, who is married to Margaret, dies on 2 January 2008 and leaves an estate of £450,000. A sum of £100,000 is left on trust for life for his ex-wife Pat and £50,000 legacies to each of his two sons by his first marriage with the balance of his estate going to his second wife, Margaret. Margaret dies on 6 April 2020 and leaves to her four children her estate valued at that date including the assets derived from Jeffrey's estate which are valued at £480,000.

Jeffrey's available nil rate band at death was £300,000 but £200,000 has been utilised in respect of the trusts in favour of his ex-wife and legacies to his two sons. Therefore, on Margaret's death her estate will benefit from 33.3333% of the nil rate band unutilised by Jeffrey. This amount of £108,333 is added to her available nil rate band of £325,000 making a total of £433,333 and gives a taxable estate of £46,667.

Notes to the example

(A) This is a second marriage and the children of Jeffrey's first marriage, it could be said, are disadvantaged by the rules that give Margaret's estate the benefit of his unused nil rate band. Jeffrey could have amended his will to ensure that on his death some or all of his assets are left on trust to Margaret with the remainder going to his sons. This would constitute an immediate post death interest and as such there would be no IHT payable on Jeffrey's death but on the death of Margaret the trust assets would form part of her estate and be covered by a proportion of aggregate nil rate band and ensure that Jeffrey's sons inherit his relevant proportion. See Note A in Example 1 at **39.1** SETTLEMENTS WITH INTERESTS IN POSSESSION.

(B) A deed of variation may be appropriate but all the beneficiaries must agree to the variation. It should also be remembered that where any potential beneficiaries are minors, it will be necessary for any variation to be approved on their behalf by the courts. This could include unborn children if the wording of the will is wide-ranging. Even though HMRC will normally accept that a woman who is aged over 55 is past childbearing age this is not necessarily true in practice. [*Variation of Trusts Act 1958; Trusts (Scotland) Act 1961*].

Relief for closely inherited main residence

[49.16] With effect for deaths on or after 6 April 2017 a *residence nil rate amount* is available for transfers on death where the deceased's interest in a qualifying residential interest, which has been their residence at some point, is included in their estate. This can be by virtue of owning outright an interest in the residence; by virtue of having a qualifying interest in possession in the residence (see **24.1** INTEREST IN POSSESSION); by virtue of having a pre-22 March 2006 interest in possession in settled property which includes the residence; or by virtue of the reservation of benefit provisions. The residential interest must be 'closely inherited', meaning inherited by one or more direct descendants on death (see further details below). The property interest may be inherited by survivorship. To be 'inherited' under the terms of a will or on intestacy, there must be a disposition of the property to an individual in any of the following ways:

(a) a specific gift of the property;
(b) a gift of an interest in residue where the property forms part of the residue;
(c) a gift on trust where the trust gives an immediate post-death interest in possession to a direct descendant, or alternatively, the trust is a bereaved minor's trust or age 18–25 trusts for a direct descendant;
(d) an immediate entitlement on termination of a life interest in possession in a property on the death of the life tenant;
(e) a gift in lifetime to an individual which remains within the donor's estate until death as being within the gift with reservation provisions.

HMRC guidance indicates that, where a property forms part of residue, it is to be regarded as closely inherited to the extent that the residuary estate is closely inherited. However, a cash legacy to descendants which is satisfied by appropriation of an interest in a residence does not satisfy the requirement that there must be a disposition of the property to the legatee under the will. Equally, if a residence forms part of residue which is bequeathed to descendants but the property is in fact appropriated to a legatee who is not a descendant, the relief will be due. There is no guidance to determine which assets in an estate form part of residue but HMRC guidance indicates that they will accept that if there is a qualifying residence in the estate and there is a residuary gift to descendants, then the relief is available in respect of the residuary gift. It is not, on the other hand, required that the residuary legatees actually receive the property, or the sale proceeds of it. If the executors choose to sell the property and use the proceeds to pay pecuniary legacies, with other assets being transferred to the residuary legatees in satisfaction of their entitlement, this will not affect the amount of the relief.

The nil rate amount will not be available where the property is left on trust except as set out at (c) above. Since trusts for infant grandchildren are not in any of the categories stated (save in very exceptional circumstances), it follows that for a gift to such grandchildren to qualify, it must be outright and not subject to any contingency; alternatively, it could be on immediate post-death interest trusts so long as *Trustee Act, s 31* is excluded.

The relief is given, in respect of the estate on death, in priority to the nil rate band of £325,000 and any transferred nil rate band, although it is not available against lifetime gifts so such nil rate bands continue to apply primarily to gifts in the seven years prior to death. The relief is given against the total chargeable transfer on the death in the same way that the nil band is given. It does not require a claim, except in relation to any brought forward allowance (see further below), so no time limit applies to notifying HMRC of the availability of a residence nil rate amount although Form IHT435 should be completed to enable the relief to be processed.

To be '*closely inherited*', the qualifying residential interest must be inherited by one or more direct descendants. These are defined as a child of the deceased, including a step-child, adopted child, foster child, and an infant subject to guardianship arrangement or a special guardianship order under the *Children Act 1989* or corresponding laws. Also included are the lineal descendants of any of these and a person who was the spouse or civil partner of a lineal descendant at the time of the death of the testator or where the descendant predeceased the testator, at the time of the descendant's death so long as such spouse or civil partner has not since remarried or become the civil partner of another.

This additional nil amount will be available only against transfers on death, and not against lifetime transfers that are chargeable on death. To prevent the relief applying in cases where the donee was given the interest as trustee rather than beneficially, with effect for deaths after 29 October 2018 it is provided that the donee does not inherit the property for the purposes of these provisions unless it became comprised in the donee's estate on the making of the disposal. It should be noted that the relief operates as a reduction in the inheritance tax payable by the estate, and therefore the individual who benefits from this reduction will be determined by the terms of the will, or the rules of intestacy. Therefore, if there is a specific gift of the residence to a descendant free of tax and the residuary estate is given to an unrelated person, the latter gets the benefit of the reduction in tax.

Any unused excess of the nil rate amount on the death of one spouse or civil partner is available to transfer to a surviving spouse or civil partner as a *brought forward allowance*. The provisions relating to this are detailed at **49.17** below. It does not matter if the spouse who predeceased did not have any interest in a property in his or her estate. The *default allowance* comprises the total of the main residence nil amount for the year in which the death occurs, as set out below, plus any brought forward amount. The table of reliefs to commence with effect from 6 April 2017 is as follows.

- £100,000 for 2017/2018
- £125,000 for 2018/2019
- £150,000 for 2019/2020
- £175,000 for 2020/2021

The relief is subject to tapering in larger estates. For this purpose, property forming part of the estate by virtue of the reservation of benefit provisions, or the provisions relating to interests in possession, must be included. The taper will apply to give an *adjusted allowance* where the net value of the estate, before reliefs and exemptions but after deduction of liabilities, exceeds £2 million. In such cases, the default allowance will be reduced by £1 for every £2 of the excess over £2 million. Where the value of the residence inherited by direct descendants exceeds or is equal to the adjusted allowance, none of the nil rate amount is available for transfer to a surviving spouse or civil partner, but if that value is below the adjusted allowance, the unused excess may be transferred. In cases where any part of the allowance is transferred to a surviving spouse's estate, tapering may operate twice over: if the estate of the first to die exceeds the taper threshold, the brought forward allowance will be subject to the tapering provisions; in the survivor's estate, the tapered brought forward allowance will form part of his or her default allowance which once again is subject to tapering if the survivor's estate exceeds the taper threshold.

The main residence nil band and the applicable taper threshold was to increase in line with the Consumer Price Index for years after 2020/2021 but this has been overridden by *Finance Act 2021, s 86*. As a result, the current rates will remain in place up to 2025/2026.

The value of the main residence nil rate amount for an estate will be the lower of the net value of the interest in the residential property inherited by direct descendants (after deducting any liabilities secured on it and any agricultural or business property reliefs) or the default allowance, as reduced where applicable to the amount of the adjusted allowance.

A *qualifying residential interest* is a dwelling house which has been the person's residence at any time whilst it formed part of his or her estate. No minimum period for use as a residence is specified but it is thought likely that the interpretation adopted for capital gains tax main residence relief will apply, so that the usage must have been with some degree of permanence. The property need not be in the UK, but if it is excluded property at the time of death it will not qualify for relief. The reference to dwelling house includes its garden or grounds (and not limited as with capital gains tax main residence relief), but not woodlands left out of account on the death under *IHTA 1984, s 125*. It may be a holiday home if that qualifies as a residence. The relief is limited to one residential property but personal representatives will be able to nominate which residential property should qualify if there is more than one in the estate. A property which was never a residence of the deceased, because for example it was always let, will not qualify, but if the non-occupation of a home was due to the person residing in job-related accommodation (within *TCGA 1992, s 222(8A–8D)*), that home may be treated as occupied as a residence during the time that the deceased lived at the job-related accommodation.

Transferring the residence nil rate amount

[49.17] On the death of a person's surviving spouse or civil partner after 5 April 2017, it will be possible to make a claim to transfer the residence nil rate amount of the spouse or civil partner who predeceased, in the same way that the existing nil rate amount can be transferred. This applies irrespective of when the first of the couple died and the transferred amount is described as a brought forward allowance. Where the first death was on or after 6 April 2017, any proportion of the residence nil rate amount which was unused by the spouse or civil partner who predeceased is the brought forward amount, subject to tapering where the net value of that estate before reliefs and exemptions was in excess of £2 million. In such cases, the additional nil amount will be reduced by £1 for every £2 of the excess over £2 million.

If the first death was before 6 April 2017, a full allowance as at the death of the survivor is brought forward but again subject to tapering where the net value of the estate before reliefs and exemptions was in excess of £2 million. The tapering is against a deemed allowance of £100,000, so that if the estate was in excess of £2,200,000 there will be no brought forward allowance because the taper will eliminate it. The actual devolution of the estate is irrelevant in such cases.

Example 11

Mavis died on 1 January 2014 leaving an estate of £2,100,000, including a half share in the home worth £450,000. She left her estate to her husband Jack.

Jack dies on 5 May 2017 leaving an estate of £2,200,000 after liabilities. He leaves gifts to charities of £100,000 and the residue to their two children.

The IHT on Jack's death will be calculated as follows:

Estate			£2,200,000
Nil band			(£325,000)
Transferred nil band			(£325,000)
Main residence nil amount: default allowance:			
		£100,000	
Brought forward amount:	$\frac{£2.1m - £2m}{2}$	£50,000	
		£150,000	
Adjusted allowance:			
Default allowance		£150,000	
Less	$\frac{£2.2m - £2m}{2}$	(£100,000)	
Net amount available for claim		£50,000	(£50,000)
Charitable exemption			(£100,000)
IHT payable on			£1,400,000
IHT payable at 40%			£560,000

Note: the main residence nil amount cannot exceed the value of the interest inherited by direct descendants but this restriction does not apply in this example.

If the first death is on or after 6 April 2017, and that person's estate is below the £2 million threshold, the carry forward amount is the unused nil rate amount on the first death, expressed as a percentage of the full nil rate amount applicable at the time. That percentage of the nil rate amount applying on the death of the survivor will be added to the amount available on the survivor's death.

If the first death is on or after 6 April 2017, and that person's estate is above the £2 million threshold, the carry forward amount is the unused adjusted nil rate amount on that death (see above), expressed as a percentage of the full nil rate amount applicable at the time. That percentage of the nil rate amount applying on the death of the survivor will be added to the amount available on the survivor's death.

Claims for a brought forward allowance must be made either by the person's personal representatives within the permitted period, or by any other person liable to the tax chargeable on the person's death within such later period as HMRC may in the particular case allow. The *permitted period* is either (*a*) the period of two years from the end of the month in which the person dies or (if it ends later) the period of three months beginning with the date on which the personal representatives first act as such, or (*b*) such longer period as HMRC may in the particular case allow. Claims may be withdrawn no later than one month after the end of the permitted period. A further provision allows a late claim in situations where there is a series of deaths and on one of the earlier deaths no claim was made for a transfer of unused allowance. If this affects the IHT liability in the latest estate, a claim may be made for a brought forward allowance within the same period detailed above for that estate.

Where there is a series of deaths and a claim for a brought-forward allowance was not made on one of the earlier deaths, the personal representatives acting in relation to the latest death may make a claim for the brought-forward allowance in relation to that earlier death (*IHTA 1984, s 8L(4)*). This claim must be made in the same time limit as applies to brought-forward claims on the latest death, and equally may be withdrawn in the same time limit as applies to the withdrawal of claims on that death. Provision is made for cases where a residence left to direct descendants qualifies for conditional exemption. To the extent that a residence is conditionally exempt, it is treated as not closely inherited so that the appropriate proportion of the residence nil rate band is available to carry forward. The residence nil band may apply to charges which arise when conditional exemption ceases to apply (that is, if the undertakings to secure the conditional exemption are not kept, the owner dies, or the property is sold, given away or disposed of). Where the deceased's surviving spouse or civil partner dies before the charge arises and the residence nil rate band, or part of it, is transferred to that surviving spouse or partner, the residence nil rate band available against the charge is reduced by the amount so transferred. Similarly where the charge arises before death of the surviving spouse or partner, the amount of residence nil rate band available for transfer is recalculated to take account of the amount (if any) of the residence nil rate band that was used by the charge when conditional exemption ceases to apply.

Downsizing relief

[49.18] Complex provisions permit a claim for additional relief where a person has sold a home in lifetime which they lived in at some stage, thus losing to any extent the possibility of claiming the main residence nil rate amount. The legislation envisages two different circumstances, first that where the deceased downsized from a more valuable residence and there is a less valuable residence left in the estate on death, and second where a residence was previously sold and no other residence purchased. The personal representatives can nominate which former residence is to be used for this relief. The downsizing must have taken place on or after 8 July 2015; there is no relief for any downsizing before that date.

In a distinction from the main residence nil rate band provisions, the relief is available for any assets in an estate which are closely inherited (as defined), and this may be in the form of a cash legacy, a specific bequest, a gift of residue or an entitlement on intestacy. All that is required is that some form of bequest equal in value to the relief is made in favour of a direct descendant of the deceased. Note however that the relief may not benefit the person receiving the bequest, since the relief is given as an additional nil rate band deducted from the chargeable estate. A further distinction is that, unlike the residence nil rate amount, downsizing relief must be claimed and the same time limit applies as to claims for a brought forward allowance (see above).

Downsizing to a less valuable residence

Conditions A–E must be satisfied under this heading:

Condition A is that either:

(a) there is a residence in the estate on death which qualifies for the residence nil rate band (a qualifying residential interest) but the full amount is not due because the value of the residence, or the proportion inherited by direct descendants (i.e. closely inherited) is below the maximum residence nil rate band available for that person; or
(b) there is a residence in the estate on death but none of it is closely inherited and, for deaths on or before 29 October 2018, the value of the residence in the chargeable estate on the death is less than the maximum residence nil rate band available for that person. For deaths after that date, in place of chargeable estate on death, this is amended to the value transferred by the transfer of value under *IHTA 1984, s 4* on the death, so that exempt gifts are no longer left out of account.

Condition B is that the value transferred by the chargeable transfer on death is more than the value of the residence (the person's qualifying residential interest).

Condition C is that the person previously had a residence which could have qualified for the residence nil rate band (the qualifying former residential interest).

For deaths on or before 29 October 2018, condition D is that the value of the former residence has a value greater than the value of the residence in the chargeable estate at death (that is the total estate less exempt gifts). After 29 October 2018, in place of chargeable estate on death, this is amended to the value transferred by the transfer of value under *IHTA 1984, s 4* on the death, so that exempt gifts are no longer left out of account.

Condition E is that at least some of the other assets in the estate must be inherited by direct descendants (closely inherited).

Where these conditions are satisfied the downsizing addition is *the lost relievable amount* – see below. However, the amount is limited to the value of other assets, or proportion of that value, which is closely inherited.

Sale of residence without purchase of another

Conditions H–J must be satisfied under this heading:

Condition H is that the value transferred by the chargeable transfer on death must be greater than nil.

Condition I is that the person previously had a residence which could have qualified for the residence nil rate band (the qualifying former residential interest).

Condition J is that at least some of the other assets in the estate are inherited by direct descendants (closely inherited).

Where these conditions are satisfied the downsizing addition is *the lost relievable amount* – see below. However, the amount is limited to the value of other assets, or proportion of that value, which is closely inherited.

If there is an entitlement to the downsizing addition because a person has downsized but no residence has been inherited by direct descendants, or if the person has disposed of a residence so that it cannot be inherited by direct descendants, the downsizing addition will still apply. In these cases the residence nil rate band will be equal to the downsizing addition.

Carry forward amounts to surviving spouse

Where the value of the estate is equal to or below the taper threshold and the downsizing addition is less than the residence nil rate band plus any transferred residence nil rate band (the default allowance), the difference between the downsizing addition and the default allowance is available for transfer to a spouse or civil partner's estate.

Where the value of the estate is above the taper threshold and the downsizing addition is less than the residence nil rate band plus any transferred residence nil rate band (the adjusted allowance), the difference between the downsizing addition and the adjusted allowance is available for transfer to a spouse or civil partner's estate.

Upper limit on relief for pre-April 2017 disposals

If the residence was disposed of before 6 April 2017, the residence nil rate band is treated as £100,000 and the brought-forward allowance is the amount of that allowance available on the survivor's death.

The lost relievable amount

The calculation of *the lost relievable amount* as a result of downsizing to a less valuable residence is calculated by four steps. Step 1 is to express the market value of the former residence as a percentage of *the former allowance* – see definition below (but not exceeding 100%). Step 2 calculates the percentage of the residence nil rate band at death that is used up by a residence: (*i*) up to 29 October 2018 in the chargeable estate at death, and (*ii*) after that date in the whole estate at death and not just the chargeable estate. Step 3 is to subtract the percentage given by Step 2 from that given by Step 1 (but not less than 0%). Step 4 multiplies the person's allowance on death by this percentage to determine the lost relievable amount.

The calculation of *the lost relievable amount* as a result of the disposal of the residence with no purchase of a residence is calculated by two Steps. Step 1 is express the market value of the former residence as a percentage of *the former allowance* (but not exceeding 100%). Step 2 multiplies the person's allowance on death by this percentage to determine the lost relievable amount.

A person's *former allowance* is the total of:

(a) the maximum residence nil rate band available at the time of the disposal (defined as date of completion);

(b) any transferred residence nil rate band (brought-forward allowance) that would have been due if the person had died at the time of the disposal; and

(c) any difference between the brought-forward allowance which would have been due at the time of disposal and the actual brought-forward allowance at the time of the person's death. The brought-forward allowance is the amount of that allowance that would have been due had the person died at the time of disposal of the former residence, but uplifted to the brought-forward allowance on death if that is greater. For this purpose where the estate on death exceeds the taper threshold, the taper reduction must be applied proportionally to the residential enhancement and the brought-forward allowance.

Example 12

Steve owned a residence known as First Gables, which he sold in July 2016 for £800,000. He downsized to Final Gables which cost £400,000. On his death in June 2019 he still has Final Gables worth £400,000 and his remaining assets are valued at £1 million.

He leaves one-quarter of his estate to his children and three-quarters of his estate to other more distant relatives. HMRC have said that they will regard this as a gift of one-quarter of the assets to direct descendants. The children are therefore treated as inheriting a one-quarter interest in Final Gables worth £100,000 and other assets worth £250,000.

The residence nil-rate amount is limited to the value of the residence inherited by lineal descendants, so in this case it is £100,000 and £50,000 goes to waste. Downsizing relief is due because the conditions above are satisfied, and in particular that under the first subheading under condition A. The lost relievable amount must now be calculated. On the sale of First Gables in 2016, the residence nil-rate amount is treated at that time as being £100,000. Therefore under step 1, the value of First Gables far exceeded this allowance so the percentage under this step is 100. Under step 2 the percentage of the main residence nil band used up at death is £100,000 out of £150,000 this being 66.66% of the full relief which would otherwise be available. Under step 3 subtract 66.66% from 100% to arrive at 33.33%. Step 4 therefore allows one-third of the allowance of £150,000 on death to be given relief, this being £50,000. Thus the full relief is restored by the downsizing relief claim.

Example 13

Assume the facts are as in Example 12 except First Gables was owned jointly by Steve and his wife Julie and they sold it in July 2016. Julie dies in June 2018 and Steve dies in June 2019 leaving one-quarter of his estate to his children as in the example above. Steve has an allowance on death of £150,000 plus the full brought forward allowance of £150,000. The allowance which he might have had when First Gables was sold is the limited amount of £100,000 plus the brought forward allowance on death of £150,000, total £250,000 (see above *Upper limit on relief for pre-April 2017 disposals*). It will be seen that on these figures the percentage figure in step 1 remains at 100%, his one-half of the sale proceeds of First Gables being far in excess of £250,000. The fraction at step 2 is 33.33% being £100,000 divided by £300,000. Under step 3 subtract 33.33% from 100% to arrive at 66.66%. So the downsizing relief is 66.66% of £300,000, which is £200,000. This is the relief to be given in relation to the other assets which are closely inherited and so will always be limited to whatever the value of them is. Once again the relief has restored the full residence nil-rate amount on Steve's death.

Example 14

If in Example 13 First Gables had been sold for only £400,000, then Steve's one-half share would be £200,000 at the time of sale. This value would not have used all of Steve's potential residence nil-rate amount at that time (deemed to be £250,000 as above) and so the figure at step 1 becomes 80%. Under step 3 deduct 33.33% from 80% to give 46.67% and so the downsizing relief on death is that percentage of £300,000, to give an amount of £140,010.

Where a residential interest is held on any of the types of interest in possession trust where the settled property forms part of the beneficiary's estate (eg IPDI trusts), the downsizing relief can apply where the trustees sell the interest, other than a sale to the life tenant, during the time that the interest in possession subsists. Equally, where the beneficiary's life interest terminates, or is disposed of, at a time when the trustees hold the residential interest this is treated as a disposal of that residential interest by the beneficiary. But the downsizing relief applies to only one property interest, so if the claim is made in relation to an interest held in trust, this cannot be supplemented by further interest held outside the trust.

Further provisions deal with residences to which conditional exemption applies.

[*IHTA 1984, ss 8D–M*; *FA 2019, s 66*].

Alterations of dispositions on death

[49.19] Dispositions under a will or on an intestacy may be varied or disclaimed by an instrument in writing made by the persons who benefit or would benefit under the dispositions. Such variation or disclaimer may not be a transfer of value and may be treated as if effected by the deceased. For full details, see **13** DEEDS OF VARIATION AND DISCLAIMERS.

Two-year discretionary will trusts

Where property is settled by a person's will and, within two years after his death and before any IPDI or disabled person's interest has subsisted in the property, an event occurs (for example an appointment in favour of a beneficiary) on which tax would otherwise be chargeable under the provisions for SETTLEMENTS: DISCRETIONARY TRUSTS AND OTHER TRUSTS OF RELEVANT PROPERTY (40) (except in relation to a ten-year anniversary charge), no tax is chargeable and for IHT purposes the will is to be deemed to have provided that the assets concerned should be held as they are held as a result of the event. Equally, where the event within two years of death is one on which tax would be chargeable but for *IHTA 1984, ss 75, 76, Sch 4 para 16(1)* (property becoming subject to employee trusts or held for charitable purposes, national purposes, public benefit or a qualifying political party or comprised in a maintenance fund for historic buildings) then the will is deemed to have provided that the property should be held on the testator's death as it is after the event (i.e. the subsequent distribution to the employee trust etc.).

This provision applies to all appointments, including those which are outright or on trust, except those on IPDI, bereaved minors or age 18–25 trusts; these are subject to a separate but very similar provision (see below). [*IHTA 1984, s 144(1), (1A) and (2)*]. HMRC accept that, where the executors are also the trustees, an appointment can be made at any time during the administration period and the trust is validly constituted as from the date of death so that it is not necessary to fund the trust before making an appointment.

Because a proportionate charge (as in **40.12** SETTLEMENTS: DISCRETIONARY TRUSTS AND OTHER TRUSTS OF RELEVANT PROPERTY) would not arise on a distribution from a discretionary settlement where made within three months of the settlement's creation, in the past it was important not to make a distribution under the above provisions within three months of the death (see *Frankland v CIR* CA [1997] STC 1450 and *Harding and Leigh v CIR* [1997] STC (SCD) 321 Sp C 140). However, this anomaly was removed by *F(No 2)A 2015* in relation to appointments to the surviving spouse or civil partner where the death occurs on or after 10 December 2014 so that for such cases it is not necessary to wait until the three-month period has elapsed. The Capital Taxes Sub-Committee asked HMRC's views on the interaction between *s 142* and *s 144* in relation to intestacy; HMRC replied that in their view an event under *s 144(1)* could follow a variation satisfying *s 142(1)*. Accordingly, it would be inconsistent to distinguish between testate and intestate estates when, all other things being equal, the ability to vary the disposition is the same. This is subject to the caveat that the tax position will depend on the facts as they are at the relevant time. See Taxation Practitioner, June 1999 p 9.

If an appointment out of a two-year discretionary will trust is in favour of new ongoing trusts, such trusts are treated as commencing on the date of death, not the date of the appointment. [*IHTA 1984, s 83*].

As a separate provision, albeit one with similar effect, where a testator dies after 21 March 2006 and his estate is held on discretionary trusts, if within two years after the death an appointment is made on trusts which would have qualified as IPDI or under *IHTA 1984, ss 71A, 71D* (i.e. bereaved minor's trusts and 18–25 trusts) then providing no IPDI or disabled person's interest has previously subsisted in the property concerned, no tax is chargeable and the event is treated as if the will had provided for it. In this case, it has never been necessary to ensure that the appointment is made more than three months from the death. [*IHTA 1984, s 144(3), (4)*]. A further provision was made to ensure that trusts for a bereaved minor, an 18–25 trusts and an IPDI created under *s 144* write back into the will of a deceased within two years of death will be treated as if established by the will regardless of whether before or after 22 March 2006. HMRC accept that an appointment under these provisions to existing pilot trusts in which the spouse has an interest in possession can qualify as an appointment on IPDI trusts. [*IHTA 1984, s 144; FA 2006, Sch 20 para 27*]. See also 5 ANTI-AVOIDANCE.

Where a person disclaims his entitlement to an interest in settled property, then providing the disclaimer is not made for a consideration in money or money's worth, he is treated as not having become entitled to the interest. [*IHTA 1984, s 93*].

See **49.20** below for orders made under *Inheritance (Provision for Family and Dependants) Act 1975* and **49.22** below for legitim. See also **30.26** NATIONAL HERITAGE where, for deaths after 16 March 1987, settled property is exempt from IHT on the death of a person who has an interest in possession in the property if the terms on which the property is held are altered after his death so that it goes into a heritage maintenance fund within two years particularly with regard to the position after 21 March 2006. [*IHTA 1984, s 57A; FA 1987, s 59, Sch 9 paras 1, 4; FA 2006, Sch 20 para 17*].

Inheritance (Provision for Family and Dependants) Act 1975

[49.20] Under the above Act, as amended by the *Law Reform (Successors) Act 1995* and *Civil Partnership Act 2004, Sch 4 paras 15–27,* a court may order financial provision for family, civil partners and dependants of a deceased person out of his net estate. If the deceased died on or after 1 January 1996 a new category of applicant is defined as a person who 'during the whole of the period of two years ending immediately before the date when the deceased died' was living (a) in the same household as the deceased, and (b) as the husband or wife of the deceased. However, in (a) above 'living in the same household as the deceased' could also mean a period of temporary separation due to prevailing circumstances at the time. See *Gully v Dix; In re Dix deceased* CA [2004] TLR 28 January 2004. See TAX CASES (55).

Where an order is made under these provisions in relation to any property forming part of the estate of a deceased person, the estate is treated as devolving on death in accordance with the terms of the order. [*IHTA 1984, s146(1)*]. From 26 July 1989, it is not possible to circumvent this treatment where the surviving spouse settles a claim out of her own resources as a transfer without gratuitous intent, leaving the IHT exemption for the estate unaffected; see *IHTA 1984, s 29A* and further details at **21.24** EXEMPT TRANSFERS.

Case law on claims for financial provision

[49.21] In the case of *Goodchild v Goodchild* [1997] 3 All ER 63, mutual wills were drawn up by Mr Goodchild and his wife as follows:

'1. I REVOKE all former Wills and Codicils made by me. 2. IF my wife [. . . . .] survives me for the space of twenty-eight days then I DEVISE

> AND BEQUEATH all my real and personal estate to her absolutely and appoint her to be the sole Executrix of this my Will. 3. IF my said wife does not survive me for the period aforesaid then I APPOINT my son [. . . . .] and my daughter [. . . . .] to be the Executors and Trustees of this my Will and I DECLARE that the following clauses shall take effect . . . CLAUSE 5. UPON TRUST for my said son [. . . . .] if he survives me for the space of twenty-eight days and if he does not so survive me then UPON TRUST for . . . '

The Goodchilds' wills did not contain the legal words 'mutually agreed' and the husband subsequently altered his will after Mrs Goodchild's death in favour of his new wife. It was held that in the circumstances, the husband had a moral obligation to provide for his son and not a legal obligation. In consequence, a sum was awarded to the son under *s 2* for reasonable financial provision.

Where during his lifetime, the deceased made a disposition of property, without full consideration, with the object of defeating an application under the Act, the court may order (under *s 10* of the Act) the donee to refund any money or property required for the deceased's family or dependants. In addition, if a subsequent windfall arises to the estate and a hearing decides that provision, whether or not a moral obligation, is required then the windfall may be deemed to make any previous provision unreasonable: *Snapes v Aram* [1998] 20 LS Gaz R 35, (1998) Times, 8 May, [1998] Lexis Citation 2423. If the disposition was a chargeable transfer, the personal representatives may claim the inheritance tax paid on that transfer be repaid to them (whether or not they paid the tax in the first instance) with interest from the date of claim. A reduction in the total of lifetime chargeable transfers by the deceased is made equal to the value of the transfer refunded. Any claim under *s 146(2)(a)* must be made not more than four years after the date on which the order (see above) is made. (*Note*. This reduction will affect the tax rate applicable to the deceased's estate but not the rate on the other chargeable lifetime transfers). [*IHTA 1984, ss 146(2)(3), 236(3); FA 1989, s 179(1); FA 2009, Sch 53 para 8*].

The court may make orders for financial provision out of the net estate which is deemed to include property held by persons as a result of:

(i) *donatio mortis causa*;
(ii) any sums nominated by the deceased under any statute; and
(iii) the deceased's severable share of property held in joint tenancy.

Any such property on which inheritance tax is payable is treated as part of the net estate after deduction of the tax and for this purpose the amount of tax deducted is not affected by any court order. Any repayment of that tax is made to the personal representatives and not to the person holding the property. [*IHTA 1984, s 146(4)*].

Treatment of tax refunds

Any tax refund (including any interest thereon) to the personal representatives or property recovered is treated as part of the deceased's estate for the purposes of transfer of value made by him on his death. In the case of an amount which is repayable on a claim under *s 146(2)*, the repayment interest start date is from the date the order is made and not before. [*IHTA 1984, s 146(2)(5)(7); FA 2009, Sch 54 para 11*].

The court may also order financial provision out of settled property, or for property to be settled on variation of a settlement. In this case there is no charge to tax under *IHTA 1984, s 52(1)* (deemed transfer of value on termination of a life interest in settled property). Anything done in compliance with such a court order is not an occasion for charge under the provisions relating to SETTLEMENTS: DISCRETIONARY TRUSTS AND OTHER TRUSTS OF RELEVANT PROPERTY (**40**). [*IHTA 1984, s 146(6)*].

Northern Ireland. Corresponding provisions are applied by *SI 1979/924* and *927*.

Legitim

[49.22] Under Scottish law children (or remoter issue) have the right to share in one-third of the movable estate of a deceased parent but also see 52.24 below. This is called legitim. Where a testator dies after 12 November 1974 bequeathing property to the surviving spouse/civil partner and leaving insufficient property in the estate to satisfy entitlement to legitim of a minor by their eighteenth birthday, inheritance tax is charged as if legitim had been satisfied (i.e. the spouse/civil partner exemption will not apply to that much of the property) but this may be varied as follows.

(a) The executors or judicial factor of the testator may elect in writing (within two years of the death or longer if the Board permit) that tax be charged as if the gift to the surviving spouse/civil partner took effect in full (so obtaining benefit of the spouse/civil partner exemption and the transferability of the nil rate band within *IHTA 1984, s 8A*). If the minor subsequently claims his legal rights by their eighteenth birthday or has not renounced his rights by his twentieth birthday (or longer if the Board permit), the spouse/civil partner exemption is lost to that extent and tax becomes payable (by the child) on the scale applicable at the date of death with interest from the original due date (i.e. six months after the end of the month in which death occurred). In the case of an amount which is payable under *IHTA 1984, s 147(4)*, the late payment interest start date is the day after the end of the period of six months beginning with the date of the testator's death. In the case of a renouncement of a claim to legitim an amount which is repayable under *IHTA 1984, s 147(2)*, the repayment interest start date is the date on which the tax was paid. If the child claiming legitim does not pay the tax, see points (b)–(d) at **27.5** LIABILITY FOR TAX for persons with secondary liability.

(b) The child may renounce his claim to legitim by his twentieth birthday (or longer if the Board permit) and tax will be repayable (because of the spouse/civil partner exemption or transferability of the nil rate band between spouses) with interest (which shall not constitute income for any tax purposes) from the date on which the tax was originally paid. Such a renunciation is not a transfer of value. See also HMRC Inheritance Tax manual IHTM43041.

(c) Where a child dies before renouncing his claim under (b) above, his executors may renounce his claim within two years of his death, and his legal rights to legitim will not form part of his estate on his death.

[*IHTA 1984, ss 17(d), 147, 209(2)(3), 236(4); FA 1989, s 179(1)(3); The Tax and Civil Partnership Regulations 2005, SI 2005/3229, Regs 6, 32; FA 2008, Sch 4 para 3; FA 2009, Sch 53 para 9, Sch 54 para 12*].

Scottish agricultural leases

[49.23] See **4.17** AGRICULTURAL PROPERTY for special rules regarding such leases passing on death.

Intestacy

The Distribution of Intestate Estates

[49.24] Under the rules of intestacy applying up to 30 September 2014, where the deceased was survived by both the spouse and children, the spouse received a fixed sum and a life interest in one-half of the remainder of the estate. He or she could elect under the *Administration of Estates Act 1925, s 47A* that his or her life interest in the residuary estate be redeemed by the personal representatives by payment of its capital value. Where such an election was made, the redemption was not a transfer of value and the surviving spouse/civil partner was treated as having been entitled to that capital value instead of the life interest. [*IHTA 1984, ss 17(c), 145 as amended by The Tax and Civil Partnership Regulations 2005, SI 2005/3229, Regs 6, 31*].

The *Inheritance and Trustees Powers Act 2014* received Royal Assent on 14 May 2014 and came into force on 1 October 2014. It made significant changes to the rules on intestacy in relation to the entitlements of the surviving spouse on a death occurring on or after that date. Under this Act, the statutory legacy remains the same as before, that is £250,000 but a provision is introduced for it to be regularly increased in line with the consumer prices index. Interest on this legacy is to be paid at the Bank of England rate applying at the end of the month in which the death occurred.

Spouse and issue survive

Note. For these purposes, spouse should also mean '*civil partner*'.

Spouse receives	*Issue receive*
All personal chattels; £270,000 absolutely for deaths on or after 6 February 2020, or the entire estate where this is less (£250,000 prior to that date); for deaths up to 30 September 2014, a life interest in one half of residue (if any). For deaths on or after 1 October 2014, a one half of residue absolutely.	One half of residue (if any) on statutory trusts *plus*, for deaths up to 30 September 2014, the other half of residue on statutory trusts upon the death of the spouse.

Spouse survives without issue

Spouse receives	*For deaths up to 30 September 2014, remainder distributable to*
All personal chattels; plus, for deaths up to 30 September 2014 £450,000 absolutely (or the entire estate where this is less); plus one half share of residue (if any) absolutely. For deaths on or after 1 October 2014, the residue is held for the surviving spouse absolutely.	(a) The deceased's parents. If no parent survives: (b) on trust for the deceased's brother and sisters of the whole blood and the issue of any such deceased brother or sister.

Spouse survives but no issue, parents, brothers or sisters or their issue

Whole estate to surviving spouse.

No spouse survives

Estate held for the following in the order given with no class of beneficiaries participating unless all those in a prior class have predeceased. Statutory trusts may apply except under (b) and (e).

(a) Issue of the deceased.
(b) Parents.
(c) Brothers and sisters and the issue of a deceased brother or sister.
(d) Half-brothers and half-sisters and the issue of any deceased half-brother or half-sister.
(e) Grandparents.
(f) Uncles and aunts and the issue of any deceased uncle or aunt.
(g) Half-brothers and half-sisters of the deceased's parents and the issue of any deceased half-uncle or half-aunt.
(h) The Crown, the Duchy of Lancaster or the Duchy or Cornwall.

Notes

(A) See IHTM12177, IHTM35161 and IHTM35165 for disclaimers including disclaimers of absolute benefits under intestacy.

(B) In this context 'Spouse' means a person to whom the deceased was married at the date of death even where there is a separation or estrangement applicable. 'Spouse' does not mean cohabiter, who has no rights of benefit under the rules of intestacy or a divorced ex-spouse.

(C) 'Child' means an adopted child and an illegitimate child but excludes a stepchild or the child of a co-habitee.

(D) Note that the *Civil Partnership Act 2004, Sch 4 paras 7–12* amends the *Administration of Estates Act 1925* to ensure that the remaining surviving partner in a civil partnership will effectively acquire the same rights as a spouse in a case of intestacy.

(E) The above Table applies to England and Wales only. In Northern Ireland the statutory legacy rules are different and in Scotland the 'Prior rights' and *The Family Law (Scotland) Act 2006* limits vary markedly from the

England and Wales statutory legacy rules.

Key points concerning transfers on death

[49.25] Points to consider are as follows.

- The 36% rate for estates where more than 10% of any component is left to charity can be secured by deed of variation where necessary, and in certain circumstances can be achieved at no cost to the beneficiaries of the estate. For example if there is a gift of £25,000 to charity and apart from that the residue of £275,000 (all chargeable with nil rate band otherwise utilised) is left to children, the IHT payable will be £110,000. The children will therefore receive £165,000. If however they enter into a deed of variation to increase the charitable gift to £30,000, the IHT payable will be 36% of £270,000, amount due £97,200. The children then receive £172,800, an increase of £7,800, whilst the charity receives £5000 more.
- When drafting a will, consideration should be given to the situation where individuals die in commorientes circumstances, such as an accident in which both are killed instantaneously. If one spouse has assets in excess of the nil rate band and the other does not, a survivorship clause will give the result that the estate of the richer spouse passes to, say, the child of both and the estate of the poorer to which the survivorship provisions also apply passes independently to the child as well. The unutilised nil rate band of the poorer will not be able to be utilised whereas if the survivorship clause was not in place, the nil rate bands of both would be fully utilised (one by transfer to the other) and the estate of the elder would be free of IHT (see **49.14** above).
- Property owned jointly will pass to the surviving joint owner notwithstanding anything in the will of the deceased joint owner. In a case where there is a survivorship clause the jointly owned property is not affected by the survivorship clause and passes to the surviving joint owner. See page 5 of IHT404.
- In connection with the above if the property is jointly owned with someone who is not the deceased person's spouse or civil partner, the value of the deceased person's fractional share can be subject to discount of between 10 and 15%. This does apply to property jointly held by husband and wife or by civil partners because of the related property rules. See **53.6** VALUATION.
- In relation to the residence nil rate band, a common scenario for married couples is for the first to die to leave their estate to the survivor. However, this aggregation of the two estates may impact on the available relief for closely inherited residence in the estate of the survivor, due to the threshold of £2m above which the relief is tapered. For example if each spouse has an estate of £1.2m, the

survivor's estate will not benefit from any residence nil rate band. But if assets of £400,000 had been left to other legatees on the first death, with IHT duly paid as necessary, the survivor's estate will have the full relief available.

- Will drafting must take account of the requirement that the deceased's residence must be inherited by descendants if the residence nil rate band is to be available. A will leaving substantial pecuniary legacies to children and residue to siblings will not be considered by HMRC to satisfy the required test of inheritance by the children, even if residue is insignificant so that value of the residence in practical terms will be required to pay the legacies. Wills should therefore be drafted to ensure that sufficient of the value of the residence is in a gift to descendants, whether by specific devise or a residuary gift.
- In Scotland the spouse and/or children have certain prior rights which entitle them to benefit from the deceased's moveable estate (not land and buildings) and therefore benefit, unless there is no moveable property, unlike the situation in England where a spouse and/or minor can be disinherited.

50

Transfers Within Seven Years Before Death

Cross-references. See 7 CALCULATION OF TAX; 37 RATES OF TAX; 49 TRANSFERS ON DEATH.

Simon's Taxes. See I3.361–I3.364, I3.511.

Other Sources. HMRC Customer Guide to Inheritance Tax.

Introduction to transfers within seven years before death

[50.1] Personal representatives are expected to make reasonable enquiries in order to establish whether any gifts were made by the deceased in the seven-year period up to the date of death. A return which fails to include a gift which becomes chargeable on death will be an incorrect return and penalties will apply unless it can be shown that the inaccuracy was neither careless nor deliberate. Therefore, to avoid a penalty for inaccuracy, it must be shown that reasonable care was taken before the return was made, which will normally involve enquiries of family members and research through the bank statements of past years. IHT403 requires details name/relationship of the donee, description of assets (for their valuation purposes), value ascribed to the gifted assets and any exemptions available.

Taper relief

Where a chargeable lifetime transfer is made, tax on the value transferred is initially charged at one half of the death rates. Where a transferor then dies within seven years of the transfer, the tax is recomputed at the death rates but the tax rates (but not the value of the lifetime chargeable transfer) are subject to below, tapered as follows.

Years between transfer and death	Percentage of full tax rate
Not more than 3	100%
More than 3 but not more than 4	80%
More than 4 but not more than 5	60%
More than 5 but not more than 6	40%

Years between transfer and death	Percentage of full tax rate
More than 6 but not more than 7	20%

Where, between the chargeable transfer and the date of death, tax rates are reduced by the substitution of a new table of rates, the additional tax is charged as if the new table applicable on death had applied to the transfer.

The tapering provisions above do not apply where the tapered tax as calculated would be less than the tax which would have been chargeable using half death rates if the transferor had not died within seven years of the transfer i.e. the tax payable cannot be reduced below that originally chargeable at half death rates. [*IHTA 1984, s 7(2)(4)(5), Sch 2 para 2; FA 1986, Sch 19 paras 2, 37*].

Treatment of PETs

Where POTENTIALLY EXEMPT TRANSFERS (35) are made within seven years of death, no tax would have been payable at the time of the transfer. On death, tax is calculated at the full death rates applying at the time of death, subject to the tapering of tax rates (but not of values) above. (There is no lower limit on the tax, as no tax was chargeable when the transfer was made.) [*IHTA 1984, s 7(4)(5), Sch 2 para 1A; FA 1986, Sch 19 paras 2, 37*].

If no tax is actually due on a death in relation to a lifetime chargeable transfer or potentially exempt transfer which proves to be a chargeable transfer (e.g. because the value concerned falls within the nil rate band), the above relief can have no effect.

See 35.2 POTENTIALLY EXEMPT TRANSFERS for a calculation of the tax due on a failed PET where there was a chargeable transfer in the seven years prior to it.

See 27.7 LIABILITY FOR TAX for the persons liable for the additional tax. The primary liability falls on the transferee and for this reason, there is normally no grossing up of the tax on failed PETs. However, it appears that grossing up would apply in the unusual case of the transferor being obliged to pay the tax (IHTM14593).

Relief

[50.2] Where tax or additional tax becomes payable because of the transferor's death within seven years of a transfer, relief is available where all or part of the value transferred is attributable to the value of property which:

(a) at the date of death is the property of the transferee or his spouse or civil partner; or

(b) before that date has been sold by the transferee or his spouse or civil partner by a '*qualifying sale*'

unless the property is tangible movable property that is a wasting asset (i.e. if, immediately before the transfer, it had a predictable useful life not exceeding 50 years, having regard to the purposes for which it was held by the transferor; and always treating plant and machinery as wasting).

Definitions

A '*qualifying sale*' is a sale at arm's length for a price freely negotiated at the time of sale where no person concerned as vendor (or any person having an interest in the proceeds) is connected with the purchaser (or any person having an interest in the purchase). No provision must be made in connection with the sale for the vendor etc. to have any right to acquire any part of the property sold or any interest in or created out of it.

Where the above conditions are satisfied, then on a claim by a person liable to pay the whole or part of the tax or additional tax payable as a result of the transferor's death within seven years of the transfer, the tax is calculated on the market value of the property at the 'relevant date' if lower than at the time of the chargeable transfer. The claim for relief under this section must be made not more than four years after the death of the transferor. [*IHTA 1984, ss 131, 132; FA 1986, Sch 19 para 23; The Tax and Civil Partnership Regulations 2005, SI 2005/3229, Reg 25; FA 2009, Sch 51 para 6*].

The '*relevant date*' is the date of death under (a) above or qualifying sale under (b) above.

Example

A makes transfers on 21 September 2016 to B of properties valued at that date at £490,000 and to C of cash of £240,116 on the same day. A died on 28 April 2020 when the properties gifted to B were valued at £390,000.

		Gross	Tax
		£	£
Value of properties to B	£490,000		
Less annual exemption (apportioned) Note B	£4,027	485,973	107,143
Cash to C	£240,116		
Less annual exemption (apportioned) Note B	£1,973	238,143	52,503
		724,116	
Less nil rate band		325,000	
		£399,116	£159,646

Recalculate the tax on the gifts to take into account the 20% taper relief as gifts were made between three and four years before death and in the case of B there has also been a fall in value of £100,000 in the properties since the gift of them by A to B and the executors have completed form IHT 38. With regard to the completion of form IHT 38 by the executors or personal representatives see 53.6 VALUATION.

Tax payable on PETs that have become chargeable because of A's death within seven years.

Value of properties	£490,000
Less annual exemption	4,027
	485,973
Less fall in value	100,000

	385,973	
Value of cash	238,143	
	624,116	
Less nil rate band	325,000	
	£299,116	@ 40% = £119,646

Apportionment of tax:

Gift to B

$$£119{,}646 \times \frac{385{,}973}{624{,}116} \times 80\,\% = £59{,}194$$

Gift to C

$$£159{,}646 \times \frac{238{,}143}{724{,}116} \times 80\,\% = £42{,}003$$

Notes to the example

(A) *Section 131* relief only reduces the value of a transfer for the purpose of calculating the tax on that transfer (i.e. B's gift) and it does *not* affect its value for cumulation purposes (i.e. C's gift).

(B) A's gifts to B and C were made on the same day so the annual exemption for 2016/17 and the unutilised annual exemption for 2015/16 are apportioned between B and C's gifts respectively.

(C) Tapering relief applies as the gifts were made between three and four years before death of A therefore 80% applies.

(D) The claim should be signed by one or more of the persons liable and should:
- identify the transfer and transferred property;
- confirm the property is retained (or sold by a qualifying sale in which case provide details);
- confirm that the property is the same at the date of death (or sale) as it was at the date of transfer (or give details of any changes).

(See IHTM14627).

Market value

[50.3] For these purposes, market value is the price which the property might reasonably be expected to fetch if sold in the open market but that price must not be assumed to be reduced on the ground that the whole property is on the market at one and the same time. In determining the price of unquoted shares, it is assumed that there is available to any prospective purchaser all the information which such a person might reasonably require if he were proposing to purchase them from a willing vendor by private treaty and at arm's length.

Where the property transferred is subject to AGRICULTURAL PROPERTY (**4**) or BUSINESS PROPERTY (**6**) relief, the market value at any time is calculated as reduced by the appropriate percentage under those provisions. [*IHTA 1984, s 131(2A), 140(2); FA 1986, Sch 19 para 23*].

Special provisions

Special provisions apply to ascertaining the market value of specified property at the relevant date as follows:

(a) *Shares — capital receipts.* Any capital payment (i.e. any money or money's worth which is not income for the purposes of income tax), including the sale of a provisional allotment of shares, received by the transferee or his spouse or civil partner before the relevant date in respect of shares transferred is added to the market value of the shares unless already reflecting the right to the payment. See note 7 of form IHT 35.

(b) *Payments of calls* made by the transferee or his spouse or civil partner before the relevant date on the shares transferred reduce the market value unless already reflecting the liability.

(c) *Reorganisation of share capital etc.* A new holding received for the original shares transferred is treated as the same property, but where the transferee or his spouse or civil partner gives any consideration for the new holding before the relevant date, the market value is reduced accordingly unless already reflecting the liability.

Consideration for the new holding does not include any surrender, cancellation or other alteration of any of the original shares or rights attached thereto *or* any consideration consisting of the application, in paying up the new holding or any part of it, of assets of the company concerned or any dividend or other distribution declared out of those assets but not made.

(d) *Transactions of close companies.* Where the transferred property consists of shares in a close company and at any time after the chargeable transfer and before the relevant date, there is a '*relevant transaction*' in relation to the shares the market value of the property transferred on the relevant date is increased by the difference between:

(i) the market value of the transferred property at the time of the chargeable transfer; and

(ii) what that value would have been if the relevant transaction had occurred before rather than after that time.

Where the relevant transaction increases the estate of the transferor or his UK-domiciled spouse or civil partner, the increase to the market value of the property on the relevant date is reduced by that amount.

'*Relevant transactions*' is a transfer of value by the company or an alteration in the company's share or loan capital not consisting of quoted shares (in relation to transfers of value made, and other events occurring, before 17 March 1987, shares quoted on a recognised stock exchange) or in any rights attaching to unquoted shares or debentures in the company (in relation to transfers of value made, and other events occurring, before 17 March 1987, shares or debentures in the company not quoted on a recognised stock exchange). See Note below.

(e) *Interests in land.* Where there has been a change in the 'interest in land' or its state between the date of transfer and the relevant date, the difference between the market value at the date of transfer and what would have been the market value if the change had prevailed at that date is added to the market value at the relevant date. Any statutory compensation received is also added. '*Interest in land*' does not include any estate, interest or right by way of mortgage or other security. See Note below.

(f) *Leases.* Where the transferred property is a lease with less than fifty years to run at the time of the chargeable transfer, the market value on the relevant date is increased by the fraction:

$$\frac{P(1) - P(2)}{[P(1)]}$$

where

P(1) = the appropriate percentage from the table for depreciation of leases contained in *TCGA 1992, Sch 8 para 1* for the duration of the lease at the time of the chargeable transfer; and

P(2) = the appropriate percentage for the duration of the lease on the relevant date.

(g) *Other property.* Where the property at the relevant date is not the same in all respects as the property transferred, the difference between the value transferred and what that value would have been if the change in the property had prevailed at the time of the transfer, is added to the market value at the relevant date. Where, between the time of the chargeable transfer and the relevant date, any benefits in money or money's worth are derived from the property which exceed a reasonable return on its market value at the time of transfer, the excess is added to the market value at the relevant date. See Note below.

Note. In (d), (e) and (g) above, if the market value at the date of transfer is less than it would have been if a change had prevailed at that date, the market value at the relevant date is reduced to what it would have been if the change had not occurred. [*IHTA 1984, ss 133–140; FA 1987, s 58; Sch 8 paras 10, 11; The Tax and Civil Partnership Regulations 2005, SI 2005/3229, Regs 26–30*].

See **45.1** SHARES AND SECURITIES for the definition of 'quoted' or 'listed' and 'unquoted' in relation to shares and securities.

51

Transitional Provisions

Simon's Taxes. See **I1.118**, **I1.121**.

Estate and death duties

[51.1] Any reference (in whatever terms) to estate duty or death duties in any document (whenever executed) is to have effect as if it included a reference to IHT. [*IHTA 1984, Sch 6 para 1; FA 1986, s 100(1)(b)*].

Surviving spouse exemption

[51.2] Where a person's spouse (or former spouse) died before 13 November 1974 and left an interest in possession in property to the surviving spouse, estate duty would have been chargeable on that death. To avoid a double charge to tax, there is no charge to IHT on either the subsequent death of the surviving spouse, or on the lifetime termination of the interest provided that there would have been no charge on death. [*FA 1894, s 5(2); IHTA 1984, Sch 6 para 2; FA 1986, s 100(1)(b)*].

Sales and mortgages of reversionary interests

[51.3] The CTT or IHT payable by a purchaser or mortgagee when a reversionary interest purchased or mortgaged for full consideration before 27 March 1974 falls into possession is not to exceed the estate duty which would have been charged before the introduction of CTT. This limitation does not apply if the interest was sold or mortgaged to a close company of which the seller or mortgagor was a participator except to the extent that other persons had rights or interests in the company. [*IHTA 1984, Sch 6 para 3; FA 1986, s 100(1)(b)*].

National heritage objects

[51.4] Where there is a chargeable event in relation to objects of national etc. interest which were conditionally exempt for estate duty purposes, there may be a charge to estate duty rather than CTT or IHT in certain circumstances. [*IHTA 1984, Sch 6 para 4; FA 1986, s 100(1)(b)*].

Example 1

Lord Alan died in 1952 leaving Netherington Hall in Wiltshire together with all its contents to his son Bertie. In the past public access by members of the general public has been allowed to the Hall. The contents of the Hall include a paintings by Whistler of Netherington Hall and also a rare painting of Mary Queen of Scots alongside Lord Bothwell her second husband. The pictures were exempted from estate duty which, at the time Lord Alan died, was applied at a marginal rate of 80%. Unfortunately, the son, Lord Bertie, dies in a hunting accident on Boxing Day 2000 and the Hall together with contents passed to his son, now Lord Charles. The Board considered the painting by Whistler of the Hall to be pre-eminent as it has a special close association with its historical setting, i.e. Netherington Hall. The painting was accepted as pre-eminent and is re-exempted on the death of Lord Bertie, subject to a contingent liability to IHT on any breach of undertaking or subsequent disposal by sale when the rate of IHT would be 40%. The Board did *not* consider the painting of Mary Queen of Scots, now valued at £5 million, to be pre-eminent in this context.

As the Mary Queen of Scots painting fails the pre-eminence test, IHT of £2 million (£5 million × 40%) is due and paid by the estate. Lord Charles decides to sell the painting for £8 million (net of expenses and CGT) thereby breaking the estate duty undertaking.

In view of the Board's decision there will be a tax charge in respect of the Mary Queen of Scots painting calculated as follows:

Estate duty at 80% on £8 million	6,400,000
Less credit for IHT paid on Lord Bertie's death	2,000,000
Estate duty payable on sale	£4,400,000

Notes to the example

(A) Reference to 'estate duty exemption' means estate duty exemption obtained on a death on or after August 1930 (*Finance Act 1930, s 40*).

(B) The conferring of an exemption on death deferred the liability to estate duty, but with the possibility of triggering the charge later whether this was by way of sale (*FA 1930, s 40(2)*), breach of undertaking (*FA 1950, s 48(1)(3)* or otherwise *FA 1965, s 31(7)*).

Capital transfer tax

[51.5] Capital transfer tax was introduced by the *Finance Act 1975* and charged on lifetime transfers made after 26 March 1974 and on transfers on deaths occurring after 12 March 1975 when it replaced estate duty. Following the *Finance Act 1975* there were substantial alterations to the legislation including the reduction of the open-ended cumulation period to one of ten years and the introduction of a new regime for the taxation of discretionary trusts. The legislation was consolidated in *Capital Transfer Tax Act 1984* which came into force on 1 January 1985.

CTT was effectively replaced by the revised provisions relating to inheritance tax for events occurring after 17 March 1986.

The *Capital Transfer Act 1984* may be cited as the *Inheritance Tax Act 1984*. Any reference to CTT in the *1984 Act* or any other *Act* passed before or executed, made, served or issued on or before 25 July 1986 has effect as a reference to inheritance tax unless relating to a liability arising before that date. [*FA 1986, s 100*].

Transfers before 18 March 1986

[51.6] Although the provisions relating to IHT apply to events occurring on or after 18 March 1986, where a death or other event occurs on or after that date, the amendments to the CTT legislation in *FA 1986, Sch 19, Pt I* do not affect the tax chargeable on a transfer of value occurring before that date. [*FA 1986, Sch 19 para 40(1)*]. The effect of this provision is that any additional tax payable on a chargeable lifetime transfer made before 18 March 1986 as a result of the transferor's death after 17 March 1986 is calculated under the CTT rules. The tax is, however, calculated using the rates in force at the time of death. [*FA 1986, Sch 19 para 44*]. It should be noted that the rate of tax on a chargeable transfer (whether a lifetime chargeable transfer, a deemed transfer on death or a potentially exempt transfer proving to be a chargeable transfer) made after 17 March 1986 (i.e. when IHT rules apply) will depend on the cumulative value of previous chargeable transfers made within the seven-year period ending with the date of the transfer (including, where applicable, chargeable transfers made before 18 March 1986 when CTT rules applied). See **1.5** INTRODUCTION AND BASIC PRINCIPLES.

The above provision does not authorise the making of a claim under the rules relating to DOUBLE CHARGES RELIEF (**17**) where the donee's transfer occurs after 17 March 1986. [*FA 1986, Sch 19 para 40(2)*].

52

Trusts for Employees

Cross-reference. See also 40 SETTLEMENTS: DISCRETIONARY TRUSTS AND OTHER TRUSTS OF RELEVANT PROPERTY.

Simon's Taxes. See I3.156, I5.630, I5.631, I5.648.

Other Sources. HMRC Customer Guide to Inheritance Tax; Foster's Inheritance Tax, Part E6.31; IHTM04100.

Introduction to trusts for employees

[52.1] Subject to conditions, trusts for the benefit of employees of a company are exempt from inheritance tax liability on the ten-year anniversary charge (see 40 SETTLEMENTS: DISCRETIONARY TRUSTS AND OTHER TRUSTS OF RELEVANT PROPERTY). Also, transfers to such trusts may be made by individuals, close companies and settlements without interests in possession without liability to inheritance tax.

From 6 April 2014, the reliefs apply under two separate headings: (i) employee trusts within *IHTA 1984, s 86*, and (ii) employee ownership trusts for which wide-ranging reliefs were introduced by *FA 2014, Sch 37*.

Conditions for the trust

Employee trusts

[52.2] The conditions are that the settled property is held on trusts which, either indefinitely or until the end of a period (whether defined by a date or in some other way) do not permit that property to be applied otherwise than for the benefit of:

(a) persons employed in a particular trade or profession, or

(b) employees, or office holders, of a body carrying on a trade, profession or undertaking, or
(c) spouses, civil partners, relatives or dependants or partners of (a) or (b) above.

For the settled property to qualify under (b), either all or most of the employees or office holders must be included as beneficiaries or the trust must be an approved profit sharing scheme under formerly *ICTA 1988, Sch 9* (now repealed by *ITEPA 2003, s 722, Sch 6* but see *ITEPA 2003, s 723, Sch 7*) or an employee share ownership plan approved under *FA 2000, Sch 8*. Where there are beneficiaries falling within (a), (b) or (c) above, the trusts are not disqualified by reason only that they also permit settled property to be applied for charitable purposes. [*IHTA 1984, s 86(1)–(3) as amended by FA 2000, s 138(4); Sch 8; The Tax and Civil Partnership Regulations 2005, SI 2005/3229, Reg 12*]. See **52.10** below regarding newspaper trusts.

The settled property:

(i) is treated as comprised in one settlement;
(ii) may contain an interest in possession (e.g. a right by a beneficiary to an annuity) of less than 5% of the whole. Such interests are disregarded for IHT purposes, with the exception of those in *IHTA 1984, s 55* relating to the acquisition by a person of a reversionary interest expectant on an interest to which he is already entitled; and
(iii) may cease to be comprised in one settlement and, if within one month it becomes wholly comprised in another settlement satisfying the above conditions, it is treated as if it had remained comprised in the first settlement.

[*IHTA 1984, s 86(4)(5)*].

Employee ownership trusts

Under the reliefs for employee ownership trusts the following three tests must be satisfied:

(a) the company must meet 'the trading requirement';
(b) the trusts must meet 'the all-employee benefit requirement'; and
(c) the settlement must not meet 'the controlling interest requirement' immediately before the beginning of the tax year in which the disposition of property occurs but does meet it at the end of that year.

The definitions of these requirements are as follows:

The trading requirement

The company meets the trading requirement if it is:

(a) a trading company which is not a member of a group, or
(b) the principal company of a trading group.

'Trading company' means a company carrying on activities in the course of, or for the purposes of, a trade being carried on by it, and whose activities do not include to a substantial extent activities other than trading activities.

'Trading group' means a group one or more of whose members carry on trading group activities, and the activities of whose members, taken together, do not include to a substantial extent activities other than trading group activities.

'Trading group activities' means activities carried on by a member of the group in the course of, or for the purposes of, a trade being carried on by any member of the group. The activities of the members of a group are to be treated as one business (with the result that activities are disregarded to the extent that they are intra-group activities), but a business carried on by a company in partnership with one or more other persons is to be treated as not being a trading activity or a trading group activity.

The all-employee benefit requirement

A settlement meets the all-employee benefit requirement if the trusts of the settlement do not permit any of the settled property to be applied, at any time, otherwise than for the benefit of all the eligible employees on the same terms, and do not permit the trustees at any time to apply any of the settled property by creating a trust, or by transferring property to the trustees of any settlement other than by an authorised transfer. In addition, the settlement must not permit the trustees at any time to make loans to beneficiaries of the trust, and must not permit the trustees or any other person at any time to amend the trusts in a way such that the amended trusts would not comply with the foregoing requirements. Benefits may be provided to a surviving spouse or civil partner of a deceased employee for up to 12 months. There are other detailed rules relating to employees or office-holders who may be excluded as well as transitional provisions for certain existing settlements.

An 'eligible employee' is any individual who is employed by or is an officeholder of the company or, if appropriate, of a relevant group company, but does not include an 'excluded participator'. 'Excluded participator' means:

(a) a person who is a participator in the company, or, where appropriate, in any relevant group company;
(b) any other person who is a participator in any close company that has made a disposition by which property became comprised in the same settlement, being a disposition which but for *IHTA 1984, s 13 or 13A* would have been a transfer of value for the purposes of inheritance tax;
(c) any other person who has been a participator in any company mentioned in paragraph (a) or (b) at any time on or after the look-back date, this being 10 years ending with the later of 10 December 2013 or, if later, the date on which the settlement was first funded;
(d) any person who is connected with any person within paragraph (a), (b) or (c).

However, a participator entitled to, or holding rights to acquire, less than 5% of any class of the company's shares, and less than 5% of the assets on a winding up is not excluded.

An 'authorised transfer' means a transfer of property consisting of or including any ordinary share capital of a company where that company meets the trading requirement, and the transfer is made to the trustees of a settlement which (i) meets the controlling interest requirement with respect to that company immediately after the transfer, and (ii) meets the all-employee benefit requirement with respect to the company.

The controlling interest requirement

A settlement meets the controlling interest requirement if:

(a) the trustees hold more than 50% of the ordinary share capital of the relevant company and have powers of voting on all questions affecting it as a whole which, if exercised, would yield a majority of the votes capable of being exercised on them;
(b) the trustees are entitled to more than 50% of the profits available for distribution to the equity holders of the company;
(c) the trustees would be entitled, on a winding up of the company, to more than 50% of the assets of C available for distribution to equity holders; and
(d) there are no provisions in any agreement or instrument affecting the company's constitution or management or its shares or securities whereby the condition in paragraph (a), (b) or (c) can cease to be satisfied without the consent of the trustees.

[*FA 2014, Sch 37*].

Creation of the trust

[52.3] Separate provisions apply to the creation of employee trusts by individuals (see **52.4** below) and close companies (see **52.6** below) and to property transferred from discretionary trusts (see **52.7** below).

Individual transferor

[52.4] A transfer to a trust as described in **52.2** above, by an individual who is beneficially entitled to shares in a company, is an exempt transfer if the value transferred is attributable to shares in or securities of the company and the conditions below are satisfied.

For a transfer to *employee trusts* the conditions are:

(a) the beneficiaries of the trust include all or most of the persons employed by or holding office with the company;
(b) within one year of the transfer:
  (i) the trustees hold more than one half of the ordinary shares of the company, and have majority voting powers on all questions affecting the company as a whole (but ignoring powers of any class of shares or securities limited to questions of winding up the company or primarily affecting that class); *and*
  (ii) there are no provisions or agreements which can affect (i) above without the trustees' consent;
(c) the trust does not permit *any* of the settled property (i.e. not only the shares or securities) *at any time* to be applied (except payments which are income of the recipient for income tax purposes, or would be if he were resident in the UK) for the benefit of:
  (i) a participator in the company; or
  (ii) any other person who is a participator in any close company that has made a disposition under *IHTA 1984, s 13* whereby property became comprised in the same settlement, see **52.6** below; or

(iii) any other person who has been a participator as mentioned in (i) or (ii) above at any time after, or during the ten years before, the transfer now being made; or

(iv) any person connected with the persons in (i) to (iii) above.

For these purposes, a participator mentioned above does not include any participator in a company who is not beneficially entitled to, or to rights entitling him to acquire, 5% or more of, or of any class of shares comprised in, its issued share capital and would not, on a winding up of the company, be entitled to 5% or more of its assets. Also participator includes, in the case of a company which is not a close company, a person who would be a participator in the company if it were a close company.

In *Barker v Baxendale Walker Solicitors (a firm)* [2017] EWCA Civ 2056, the interpretation of the condition at (c)(iv) above was examined. It was submitted on behalf of the respondent that the connection test should be applied on a rolling basis from year to year, such that once the participators in a company have died, other family members cease to be connected with them. As a result, an employee trust may qualify under *IHTA 1984, s 28* if individuals can only benefit after the death of all participators with whom they are connected for IHT purposes. This interpretation was not accepted by the Court of Appeal, which held that it is 'very unlikely' to be correct. The connection test must be applied at the time when the trust is set up and the fact that on the death of the participators other individuals cease to be connected with them is not relevant. The respondent had relied on HMRC guidance applicable to the CGT legislation, where two individuals cease to be connected after the death of one of them, but the wording of *s 28(c)* makes it clear that those who have been participators at any time in the ten years before the transfer must be taken into account, and connection with such individuals means that the trust will not fall within *s 28*.

[*IHTA 1984, ss 13(5), 28*].

For a transfer to *employee ownership trusts* the relief applies where:

(a) the company meets 'the trading requirement'; and

(b) the trusts of the settlement meet 'the all-employee benefit requirement'; and

(c) the settlement does not meet 'the controlling interest requirement' immediately before the beginning of the tax year in which the shares leave the relevant property trust, but does meet it at the end of that year.

See **52.2** for the definitions of these three 'requirements'.

[*IHTA 1984, ss 28 and 28A*].

See **21.24** EXEMPT TRANSFERS for abatement of the exemption.

Application of general anti-avoidance rule

[52.5] In a decision of the GAAR panel issued on 2 March 2020, it was concluded that a scheme to avoid IHT by the use of an employee trust was an abusive arrangement to which HMRC could apply the GAAR. Shortly before her death, the taxpayer subscribed a sum of £720,000 for ordinary shares in a newly formed company. She gave the shares to an employee benefit trust which the panel accepted as falling within the conditions of *IHTA 1984, s 28*. The company used the cash funds to buy an investment property and some quoted investments. The company had no employees, other than its directors who were initially the taxpayer and one of her sons; following her death, the son's wife was appointed a director. It was argued that the case was a straightforward use of the statutory relief under *IHTA 1984, s 28*. However, the panel said that the company did not have and did not need employees and the arrangement was therefore contrived and abusive.

Close company transferor

[52.6] A close company may transfer property to a trust as described in 52.2 above without it being a transfer of value.

For *employee trusts* the relief applies where:

(a) the beneficiaries of the trust include all or most of either:
  (i) the persons employed by or holding office with the same company; or
  (ii) the persons employed by or holding office with the company or where it is a holding company, the company and its subsidiaries taken as a single class. Therefore, persons holding office or employment with the holding company may be excluded if they are in the minority. Where the participators outnumber the other employees, the exemption is not irretrievably lost. The requirement to exclude participators and those connected with them from benefit is modified by *IHTA 1984, s 13(3)* (formerly *FA 1976, s 90(4)*). This limits the meaning of 'a participator' for this purpose to those having a substantial stake in the assets being transferred and makes an exception in favour of income benefits. So even where most of the employees or their relatives are also major participators, an exempt transfer could be made if the trust provided only for income benefits and the eventual disposal of the capital away from the participators and their families (see HMRC Statement of Practice E11); and

(b) the trust does not permit *any* property at *any time* to be applied to any of the persons mentioned in **52.4**(c) above except as payments which are income of the recipient for the purposes of income tax (or would be if he were resident in the UK), or as an appropriation of shares from a profit sharing scheme under formerly *ICTA 1988, Sch 9* (now repealed by *ITEPA 2003, s 722, Sch 6* but see *ITEPA 2003, s 723, Sch 7*) or

(c) the trust is an employee ownership share plan approved under *FA 2000, Sch 8*.

[*IHTA 1984, s 13 as amended by FA 2000, s 138(2) and Sch 8*].

For *employee ownership trusts* the relief applies where:

(a) the company meets 'the trading requirement'; and
(b) the trusts of the settlement meet 'the all-employee benefit requirement'; and

(c) the settlement does not meet 'the controlling interest requirement' immediately before the beginning of the tax year in which the shares leave the relevant property trust, but does meet it at the end of that year.

See **52.2** for the definitions of these three 'requirements'.

[*IHTA 1984, ss 13A*].

A close company with five or fewer participators may become subject to an *ICTA 1988, s 419(1)* (loans to participators incurring an income tax charge of 25% of the loan into the trust). In order to avoid this charge the loan into the trust might be conditional on, say, distribution amongst the beneficiaries on exit or repayable on substitution by third party funding within nine months of the end of the accounting period in which the loan was made or it is an outright gift to the trust. Note that now the *Companies Act 2006, ss 197–200* requires approval by a resolution by the members for loans to directors as from October 2007. See Taxation magazine 18 June 2009, page 610.

Property transferred from a discretionary trust etc.

[52.7] SETTLEMENTS: DISCRETIONARY TRUSTS AND OTHER TRUSTS OF RELEVANT PROPERTY (**40**) may transfer shares or securities in a company to trusts as described in **52.2** above without a proportionate charge to tax, provided:

For *employee trusts*:

(a) the beneficiaries of the trust include all or most of the persons employed by or holding office with the company; and
(b) without taking account of shares etc. held on other trusts, both conditions in **52.4**(b) above are satisfied at the date when the shares etc. cease to be comprised in the original settlement or within one year of that time; and
(c) the trust does not permit *any* property at *any time* to be applied:
  (i) to any of the persons mentioned in **52.4**(c) above except as payments which are regarded as the income of the recipient for the purposes of income tax (or would be if he were resident in the UK); or
  (ii) for the benefit of the settlor; or
  (iii) for the benefit of any person connected with the settlor. [*IHTA 1984, s 75*].

For *employee ownership trusts*:

(a) the company meets 'the trading requirement'; and
(b) the trusts of the settlement meet 'the all-employee benefit requirement'; and
(c) the settlement does not meet 'the controlling interest requirement' immediately before the beginning of the tax year in which the shares leave the relevant property trust, but does meet it at the end of that year.

See **52.2** for the definitions of these three 'requirements'.

[*IHTA 1984, ss 75A*].

See also the provisions of **40.19** and **40.22** SETTLEMENTS: DISCRETIONARY TRUSTS AND OTHER TRUSTS OF RELEVANT PROPERTY which also apply to property settled or appointed on trust for employees.

Position of the trust

[52.8] Settled property held on the conditions in **52.2** above for either employee trusts or employee ownership trusts is not subject to the principal charge to tax at the ten-year anniversary or the proportionate charge to tax under *IHTA 1984, ss 64, 65* but where the property is held in a SETTLEMENTS: DISCRETIONARY TRUSTS AND OTHER TRUSTS OF RELEVANT PROPERTY (**40**), the trust is subject to a charge when:

(a) the property ceases to be held on qualifying employee trusts otherwise than by virtue of a payment out of the settled property (but see also **21.4**, **21.6–21.8** EXEMPT TRANSFERS for certain situations where there is no charge when property becomes held for charitable purposes only without limit of time or the property of a qualifying political party *or* a national body mentioned in *IHTA 1984, Sch 3* or, under certain conditions, a body not established or conducted for profit); or

(b) a payment is made for the benefit of a person who is, or is connected with:
   (i) a person who has directly or indirectly provided any of the settled property by amounts over £1,000 in any tax year; or
   (ii) where the employment in question is by a close company, a participator of that company who *either* is beneficially entitled to, or to rights entitling him to acquire, 5% or more of, or of any class of shares comprised in, its issued share capital, *or* would, on a winding up of the company be entitled to 5% or more of its assets (but this does not apply to any appropriation of shares under a profit sharing scheme approved under formerly *ICTA 1988, Sch 9* now repealed by *ITEPA 2003, s 722, Sch 6* but see *ITEPA 2003, s 723, Sch 7*); or
   (iii) a person who has acquired an interest in the employee trust for money or money's worth or as a result of transactions which include a disposition for such consideration (whether to him or another) of that interest or of other property, or

(c) the trustees make a 'disposition' (otherwise than by virtue of a payment out of the settled property) which reduces the value of the settled property.
   '*Disposition*' includes an omission to exercise a right, unless not deliberate, which is treated as made at the latest time that the right could be exercised.

[*IHTA 1984, ss 70(10), 72, 76*].

No charge arises:

(i) if, under (c) above, the trustees do not intend to confer gratuitous benefit and either the transaction is at arm's length between persons not connected with each other (see **12** CONNECTED PERSONS) or is such as might be expected in such a transaction; or

(ii) if, under (c) above, the disposition is a grant of tenancy of agricultural property in the UK, Channel Islands, Isle of Man or EEA state for use for agricultural purposes and is made for full consideration in money or money's worth; or

(iii) on the payment of costs or expenses attributable to the property; or

(iv) where any payment is, or will be, income for income tax purposes of any person (or, in the case of a person not resident in the UK, would be if he was so resident); or

(v) in respect of a liability to make a payment under (iii) and (iv) above; or

(vi) on an appropriation of shares to an individual under an employee share ownership plan if the trusts are approved under *TA 1988, Sch 9* or *ITEPA 2003, Sch 2*; or

(vii) where a trust ceases to meet the requirements for employee ownership plans (see **52.2**) because either or both of the trading requirement or the controlling interest requirement is no longer met with respect to the company concerned.

'*Payment*' includes the transfer of assets other than money.

[*IHTA 1984, ss 63, 70(3)(4), 72(5); FA 2000, s 138(3)(b), Sch 8*].

Tax is charged on the amount by which the trust property is less immediately after the event giving rise to the charge than it would have been but for the event (i.e. the loss to the donor principle), grossed-up where the settlement pays the tax.

The rate at which tax is charged is the aggregate of the following percentages for each complete successive quarter in 'the relevant period'.

	Cumulative Total
0.25% for each of the first 40 quarters	10%
0.20% for each of the next 40 quarters	8%
0.15% for each of the next 40 quarters	6%
0.10% for each of the next 40 quarters	4%
0.05% for each of the next 40 quarters	2%
Maximum rate chargeable after 50 years	30%

The rate charged may be reduced if any of the property is, or was, EXCLUDED PROPERTY (**20**), see **52.9** below.

'*Relevant period*' is the period beginning with the day on which the property became (or last became) held on employee trusts, or 13 March 1975 if later, and ending on the day before the chargeable event. Where property in respect of which tax is chargeable was relevant property (see **40.3** SETTLEMENTS: DISCRETIONARY TRUSTS AND OTHER TRUSTS OF RELEVANT PROPERTY) immediately before 10 December 1981 (e.g. in a discretionary trust) and became (or last became) comprised in an employee trust after 9 December 1981 and before 9 March 1982, the relevant period begins with the day on which the property became (or last became) relevant property before 10 December 1981, or 13 March 1975 if later.

'*Quarter*' means a period of three months.

[*IHTA 1984, ss 63, 70(5)(6)(8)(9), 72(5)*].

Example

A qualifying trust for employees of a close company was created on 1 July 1993. On 4 May 2003, £15,000 is paid to a beneficiary who is a participator in the close company and holds 15% of the issued ordinary shares. On 4 August 2020, the whole of the remaining fund of £200,000 ceases to be held on qualifying trusts.

4 May 1993

There is a charge to IHT. The relevant period is the period from 1 July 1993 to 4 May 2003, i.e. 39 complete quarters.

The rate of tax is

0.25% for 39 quarters = 9.75%

IHT payable is

$$\frac{9.75}{100 - 9.75} \times £15{,}000 = £1{,}620$$

1 July 2003 and 1 July 2013

There is no liability at the ten-year anniversaries.

4 August 2020

The relevant period is the period from 1 July 1993 to 4 August 2020, i.e. 108 complete quarters.

The rate of tax is:

0.25% for 40 quarters =	10.00
0.20% for 40 quarters =	8.00
0.15% for 28 quarters =	4.20
	22.20%

IHT payable is £200,000 × 22.2% = £44,400

Excluded property

[52.9] Where the whole or part of the amount on which tax is charged as in 52.8 above is attributable to property which was EXCLUDED PROPERTY (20) at any time during the relevant period, then, in determining the rate at which tax is charged in respect of that amount or part, no quarter throughout which the property was excluded property is to be counted. [*IHTA 1984, s 70(7)*].

Newspaper trusts

[52.10] Newspaper publishing companies (i.e. companies whose businesses consist wholly or mainly in the publication of newspapers in the UK) are included among the persons within **52.2**(a) to (c) above as permissible beneficiaries. The only or principal property comprised in a newspaper trust must be shares in a newspaper publishing company or a newspaper holding company (i.e. a company which has as its only or principal asset shares in a newspaper publishing company and has majority voting powers on all or most questions affecting the publishing company as a whole). Shares are treated as the principal property in a settlement or the principal asset of a company if the remaining property in the settlement or assets of the company are such as may be reasonably required to enable the trustees or the company to secure the operation of the newspaper publishing company concerned. [*IHTA 1984, s 87*].

Key points concerning trusts for employees

[52.11] Points to consider are as follows.

- The transfer of the shares into an EBT is an exempt transfer if the value transferred is attributable to shares or securities in the company provided:
  (i) the beneficiaries of the trust include all *or most* of the person's employed by holding office with the company;
  (ii) within one year the trustees hold more than half of the ordinary shares of the company having majority voting powers (there being no provision or agreement affecting this without the trustees consent);
  (iii) the trust does not permit any of the settled property to be applied for the benefit of a participator in the company or a participator in another close company that has benefited the same trust or any person connected with the previously mentioned.
- In order to qualify for favoured treatment an employee trust must satisfy the conditions set out in *IHTA 1984, s 86* and the necessity that all or most of the employees must be within a class of potential beneficiaries (see below). If the trust falls outside *IHTA 1984, s 28 (or ss 13, 86)* then contributions to the trust may be a transfer of value. If *IHTA 1984, s 86* does not apply then the trust will be subject to a ten-year anniversary charge and an exit charge when capital is distributed. An exit charge will in certain circumstances arise under *IHTA 1984, s 72*.
- There are a number of important uses of an employee trust; the trust offers a non-quoted company the opportunity of creating a market for the sale and purchase of shares. These trusts can also be used to build up large shareholdings under sympathetic control so that the company will be protected against unwanted takeover offers and outside interference. The employee trust should also build up good relations between staff and the employer. The trust provides for protection of workers and ex-workers in times of

hardship or ill health.

53

Valuation

Cross-references. See **5.5** ANTI-AVOIDANCE; **30.14** NATIONAL HERITAGE; **39.5** and **39.9** SETTLEMENTS WITH INTERESTS IN POSSESSION; **50** TRANSFERS WITHIN SEVEN YEARS BEFORE DEATH.

Simon's Taxes. See C2.121, I3.252, I3.611, I4.301–I4.309, I4.312–I4.319, Part I8.

Other Sources. VOA IHT manual; HMRC Customer Guide to Inheritance Tax; Foster, Part H; IHTM09000.

Introduction to valuation

[53.1] The general valuation rule is that the value at any time of any property for the purposes of inheritance tax is the price which the property might reasonably be expected to fetch if sold in the open market at that time; but that price shall not be assumed to be reduced on the ground that the whole property is to be placed on the market at one and the same time. [*IHTA 1984, s 160*]. The valuation of particular property or in particular circumstances is dealt with below and under appropriate headings elsewhere in this book. See also the Valuation Office Agency website on www.voa.gov.uk.

Case law

In particular see *CIR v Clay* CA 1914, [1914–15] All ER 882 for position where special circumstances would affect the market price, and *Duke of Buccleuch and Another v CIR* HL 1966, [1967] 1 AC 506 for the need to assume property would be sold in 'natural units'. The decision in this last case was applied in *Gray (Executor of Lady Fox) v CIR* CA, [1994] STC 360, where the deceased was a freeholder of farm land and one of three partners in a partnership which farmed the land under an agricultural tenancy. It was held that a unit of property for the purposes of *IHTA 1984, s 160* above could comprise two or more component parts where at least one of those parts was 'land' and at least one of those parts was not 'land', and in this respect, although the question did not arise, the interest in the partnership included 'land'. See IR Tax Bulletin, August 1996, p 337. The freehold reversionary interest in the land and the 92.5% interest in the partnership held by the deceased at the time of death did, on the facts, form a unit of property to which the *Buccleuch* principle, as a matter of law, applied. The decision in the Lands Tribunal case of *Walton (Executor of Walton deceased) v CIR*, [1996] STC 68 diverged from the Capital Taxes Office [now HMRC] approach to a farm tenancy valuation. In this case the actual circumstances and intentions of co-owners of a tenancy were properly brought into account in assessing the value of the share in the tenancy of the outgoing interest. This case shows that the facts as to whether the landlord was in the market to buy in a tenant and, if the landlord was not, the only value is likely to be the capitalisation of the difference between the rent actually charged and the full market rental. See Taxation Vol 134, No 3492 pp 486–487 and Taxation Practitioner February 1995 pp 7–10).

Interests in land

For the valuation of an interest in land taking into account the liability to repay a discount allowed to a purchaser under the 'right to buy' provisions of *Housing Act 1980*, see *Alexander v CIR* CA, [1991] STC 112. The appeal concerned the valuation of a flat for Capital Transfer Tax purposes which had recently been acquired from the Local Authority under the right to buy. The difficulty was that the lease, and the *Housing Act 1980*, required the discount to be repaid on a sliding scale if it was resold within five years.

The death of the deceased did not trigger this clause but if the flat was sold at the date of death, as this was within one year of the original purchase, the full amount of the discount would have been repayable.

The Lands Tribunal had determined the value, without deduction for this obligation at £63,000. The parties successfully argued at an earlier hearing before the Special Commissioners that this value should be reduced by the discount of £24,600. HMRC contended for the DV's valuation of £50,000, being what someone would pay on the footing that if they then resold within the relevant period the discount (or part of it) would be payable, but not otherwise, and no further deduction.

Ralph Gibson LJ said:

> 'The essential question may be described thus: is the value of the lease to be taken as the value which the lease would have, if transferred, on the basis that the transferee must pay the relevant percentage of repayable premium, or is the lease to be valued as in the hands of the deceased immediately before her death when nothing had happened to cause any proportion of premium to be repayable?'

Gibson LJ concluded that the principles stated in *Inland Revenue Commissioners v Crossman and Others* HL, [1936] 1 All ER 762 are applicable.

The DV is reminded that the use of 'hindsight' is to be avoided whenever possible when considering evidence and the valuation should be based upon such knowledge as would be available on the particular date of the valuation. (VOA IHT manual, section 7, para 7.15). Also, in this connection, see *Tapp (Atkinson's Administratix) v Ryder* [2008] Lands Tribunal 5 September 2008 unreported at **55** TAX CASES.

District Valuer's considerations

The DV should have regard to the following when considering the effect on value of a restriction:

(a) the amount of the potential liability;
(b) the effective duration of the restriction;
(c) how onerous it is to comply with any restriction;
(d) the type of property;
(e) the state of the property market at the valuation date.

(VOA IHT manual, section 17, para 17.23).

The Royal Institute of Chartered Surveyors (RICS) published a new Guidance Note, GN 21, effective from 1 August 2003, which gives advice to members of RICS on the meaning of 'market value' for CGT and Inheritance Tax purposes. Further guidance on property valuations for CGT, IHT and other taxes, together with a full explanation of the 'market value' basis of valuation can be found in the VOA's CGT and IHT Manuals which can be viewed on their website www.voa.gov.uk/ under 'Publications'.

For the purposes of the pre-owned assets anti-avoidance legislation the valuation of any property is the price which the property might reasonably be expected to fetch if sold in the open market at that time, but with the price not being reduced because the whole of the property is being placed on the market at one and the same time. See **53.24** below. [*FA 2004, Sch 15 para 15*].

Where there is a disagreement with a land valuation by the Valuation Office, the matter may be negotiated with HMRC or, if that is not possible, then it can be referred to the Lands Tribunal.

Inspection of property

[53.2] The powers within *FA 2008, Sch 36* are extended so that a HM Revenue & Customs officer or person accompanying the HMRC officer in assistance can enter and inspect premises and any other property on those premises in connection with checking a person's position with regard to inheritance tax. The valuation, measurement or determination of the premises or property must be *reasonably* required by HM Revenue & Customs. There are a number of inspection procedures that must be met before the Tribunal approves the inspection of the property or premises and these are set out at *Sch 36, para 12B*. [*FA 2008, Sch 36 paras 12A, 12B as inserted by FA 2009, Sch 48 para 5*]. Previously, if the Board authorised any person to inspect any property to ascertain its value for IHT purposes, the person having custody or possession of that property had to permit him to inspect it at such reasonable time as the Board considered necessary. Any person who wilfully delaying or obstructing a person acting under those powers was liable on summary conviction to a fine not exceeding level 1 on the standard scale within the meaning of *Criminal Justice Act 1982, s 75*. [*IHTA 1984, s 220 now repealed*].

Agricultural property

[53.3] See **4.4, 4.15** and **4.17** AGRICULTURAL PROPERTY for agricultural value, etc. See *Willett and Another v CIR Lands Tribunal*, [1982] 264 EG 257 and *Gray (Executor of Lady Fox) v CIR* (see **53.1** above) for valuation of a freehold interest in tenanted agricultural property. See *Baird's Exors v CIR Lands Tribunal for Scotland 1990*, [1991] 09 EG, 10 EG 153 for valuation of the tenant's interest in an agricultural lease containing a standard prohibition on assignation. Where there is an agricultural tie to a property it has been assumed that there should be a discount in the market value of that property, Traditionally this has been taken to be a one-third reduction, however, *IHTA 1984, s 115(3)* does not require the exclusive occupation of the property and this is a factor that should be borne in mind when assuming such discounts. In addition, in some cases, there has been a breach of the agricultural tie for more than ten years and the legal protection for the tenant has expired so negating any perceived depression in the market value because of the agricultural tie.

The Lands Tribunal in *Lloyds TSB plc (Antrobus' Personal Representative) v Twiddy* [2004] DET/47/2004 reviewed and rejected the contention that the market value of a farmhouse represented the agricultural value, holding that the open market value of the farmhouse should be discounted by 30% to arrive at its 'agricultural value'. HMRC IHT Manual IHTM24051 sets down nine considerations as to 'character appropriateness' of a farmhouse which should be reviewed when considering a claim for relief under *IHTA 1984, s 115(2)*. See also IHT Manual IHTM24036.

Valuation based on local knowledge

Where land is situated in the United Kingdom, HMRC rely on professional advice from the Valuation Office Agency (VOA), or the Valuation and Lands Agency (VLA) in Northern Ireland, in arriving at a valuation unless specifically stated otherwise. Although most land in the UK which is chargeable to tax on the death is referred to the VOA there are some exceptions such as land subject to a binding contract for sale at the date of death. The role of the District Valuer (DV) is to agree the agricultural value and in cases where, the property has value for development or value for other non-agricultural uses or there is an imposing farmhouse in a location that would appeal to non-farming purchasers e.g. 'lifestyle farmers' the DV will also agree an open market value for the property. The DV bases his valuation at inspection on local knowledge, or on the basis of information provided by the parties and the inspection itself. If the DV has doubts as to whether or not part, or the whole, of the property was occupied for the purposes of agriculture he will let HMRC know and await further instructions from HMRC. This often occurs in the context of barns and other farm buildings, where the information provided by the parties suggests that there has been an agricultural element to the occupation but inspection suggests no recent such use.

Development, amenity or mineral value

The open market value of agricultural property may exceed its agricultural value where the land has planning permission or there is development or amenity value, or mineral value (such as gravel or sand extraction potential). A difference between the open market value and the agricultural value often occurs on farms where there are ranges of traditional buildings suitable for conversion into residential or commercial use; in many areas these can have significant excess value. Agricultural relief will not be available in respect of the excess value but business relief may be available as an alternative. Care should be taken to confirm that the parts of the farm with excess value for non-agricultural use are actually used as an asset of a qualifying business if business relief is to be claimed. Problems frequently arise with traditional buildings suitable for development that are obsolete for modern farming methods and have not been used for the business for some considerable time and do not qualify for 100% BPR or APR.

Example

Victor Acre died on 30 June 2020. He has been working as a full-time farmer of Lower Meadow farm for the last 40 years after inheriting the farm from his father. The farm is a working farm and comprises of 1,000 acres of land, a farmhouse and barns. He has by his will left his whole farm to his son Bert who has worked with him on the farm since he was a boy. The farm had previously been the subject of planning order on 25 acres in conjunction with a local mineral extraction company and was subject of planning consent at the time of the death valuation. At the time of the District Valuer's visit a public enquiry was under review by the Secretary of State. The District Valuer had valued the 25 acres at £1,250 an acre and a premium of £50,750 per acre due to the hope value of the potential mineral extractions over the next 20 years by the company. Since Victor Acre's death local objections have been raised and in the appeal to the Secretary of State the rights to mine the minerals at Lower Meadow have been upheld after a hearing and the rights of the gravel extraction company should be dismissed hence resulting in the lower market valuation of £1,250 compared the hope value at the time of the inspection by the District Valuer. For special valuation matters concerning minerals see IHTM23197.

Valuations for IHT purposes		£
1,000 acres at £1,250 per acre		1,250,000
Farmhouse (see above)		234,000
Development value		1,268,750
Total value		2,752,750
The transfers subject to tax on D's death:		
(i) Agricultural value of land		
1,000 acres × £1,250	1,250,000	
Less agricultural property relief at 100%	(1,250,000)	—
(ii) Farmhouse	234,000	
	(234,000)	—
(iii) Hope value of mineral workings not attracting BPR		2,752,750
		2,752,750
Deduct Nil rate band 2020/21		325,000
Chargeable at 40% on death of D		£2,427,750
IHT payable		971,100
Payable by ten-yearly instalments (*IHTA 1984, s 227*) of		147,800

Notes to the example

(A) Where qualifying agricultural property has an open market value in excess of its agricultural value under *IHTA 1984, s 115(3)* where for example the whole or part of it has hope value arising out of development potential or change of use then such excess value will not attract agricultural relief. As the excess value may attract business relief but a claim for business relief on the value of agricultural property on the excess over its agricultural value – e.g. farmland with planning permission, development value or mineral value (such as gravel and sand) is dependent on it being 'relevant business property'.

(B) The hope value by reference to the potential development is liable to tax and will include quarries, sand and gravel pits and the extraction of the stone, sand and gravel, etc. which is or is likely to be carried on by a company or business in which the deceased was interested.

(C) It would be advantageous for the son to receive the development land at a high value for CGT purposes for any future disposal but this is only of benefit where the land is covered by the APR or BPR 100% exemptions. The drop in the value of the 25 acres where the planning permission has been rescinded post death on appeal may in certain circumstances require a third-party sale or transfer into a settlement to ensure that the correct value is substituted within the four-year period.

(D) In *Tapp v HMRC* [2008] EW Lands TMA/284/2008 a Lands Tribunal case shows the necessity of documentation, including photographs, regarding the state of repair of property at the time of death but a subsequent visit by the District Valuer at a later date may indicate a higher value which was not reflected at the time of death. See IHTM23203. Where property is damaged or defective, commonly from subsidence or damage from fire or storms, the personal representatives should assume the deceased's role and may be able to make a claim under an insurance policy or against a third party, for example a neighbour or negligent surveyor. If no insurance policy or right of action exists the Valuation Officer is instructed by HMRC to value the property in its defective or damaged state.

Creditors' rights

[53.4] In determining the value of a right to receive a sum it must be assumed that amounts receivable under any obligation will be received in full unless recovery of the sum is impossible or not reasonably practicable and has not become so by any act or omission of the person to whom the sum is due. [*IHTA 1984, s 166*].

See Form IHT416.

Death

Capital gains tax

[53.5] Where, on the death of any person, inheritance tax (or, when extant, capital transfer tax or estate duty) is chargeable on the value of his estate immediately before his death and the value of an asset forming part of his estate has been ascertained for those purposes, that value is to be taken as the market value at the date of death for capital gains tax purposes. However, in calculating the amount of nil rate band available for transfer under *IHTA 1984, s 8A* the value ascertained for that purpose shall not be adopted as the value for capital gains tax purposes. [*TCGA 1992, s 274, Sch 11 para 9; FA 2008, Sch 4 para 8*]. Because of the existence for inheritance tax of such factors as the spouse/civil partner exemption and 100% business and agricultural property relief, it is unclear whether in an appropriate case inheritance tax is 'chargeable' and a value has been 'ascertained'. In such cases, and where no IHT is payable on the deceased's estate, the value of an asset is not ascertained for IHT purposes and therefore no IHT value is available, then the normal rules of *TCGA 1992, s 272* are applied to determine the capital gains tax acquisition of the beneficiary (see HMRC Capital Gains Tax Manual paras 32222 and 32230).

A danger lies in cases where agricultural property comprises part of an estate and is expected to attract the 100% relief under *IHTA 1984, s 116* and a nominal or ill-considered valuation is made rather than a professional valuation. Subsequently, if relief is not due for any reason then the value of the asset will not have been 'ascertained' for the purposes of *TCGA 1992, s 274*. In such a case where there is an uplift in the value to the open market value then a penalty may be applicable.

See **53.24** below in the case of quoted shares and securities.

Joint property

[53.6] The value of a half share of land owned by joint tenants or tenants in common is half vacant possession value less a discount to reflect the restricted demand for this type of interest. An appropriate discount has been held to be 15%. (*Wight and Moss v CIR Lands Tribunal*, [1982] 264 EG 935; *Barrett (Barrett's Personal Representatives) v HMRC Lands Tribunal*, 23 November 2005 unreported). It should be borne in mind that interests of joint owners will be 'related property' if they are spouses or civil partners, and in that event the valuation discount does not apply; see **53.21** below and **55** TAX CASES.

Where at the valuation date a co-owner remains in occupation the normal approach is for the DV to take half the freehold vacant possession value and deduct 15%. In cases where the co-owner has rights to occupy but does not and the purpose behind the trust for sale still exists then the discount would normally be 15% and 10% in other cases. A half share without rights of occupation will obtain a 10% deduction from the value. See paras 18.5 and 18.6 of section 18 in VOA IHT manual at www.voa.gov.uk/. The example in the VOA manual shows circumstances where the 10% and 15% discounts are appropriate as follows:

Example

Mr and Mrs A bought a house as tenants in common for their joint occupation. When Mr A died he left his one-half share to his son Mr B who lives elsewhere. Mrs A has now died and it is therefore necessary to value her one half-share.

When Mrs A dies the other co-owner is Mr B. Mr B is not in occupation and the house was not purchased for his occupation. When valuing Mrs A's one-half share a 10% discount should be applied.

If Mr B had died before Mrs A then, at the date of Mr B's death, the other co-owner, Mrs A, would still have been in occupation and the purpose behind the trust would still have existed. When valuing Mr B's one-half share a 15% discount should be applied.

Notes to the example

(A) The example in the VOA IHT manual shows in the first two paragraphs that a 10% discount would be due because the original purpose behind the trust for sale (be it a 'financial' trust for sale or an 'occupation' trust for sale) still exists on the death of the wife in occupation or the son not in occupation. However, in the third paragraph where Mr B dies first his estate would be entitled to the higher 15% discount because Mrs A is still in occupation of the property.

(B) Where an 'interest in land' in a deceased person's estate is sold within three years after the death by the '*appropriate person*', a claim (on Form IHT38) may be made by that person for the 'sale value' to be substituted for the value on death of *every* interest in land owned by the deceased and sold within three years of death by the same 'appropriate person' for which such a claim would be available. See **53.9** below. However, in cases where a discount of 10% has been claimed and then the interest is sold and a claim is made under *IHTA 1984, s 191* the 10% discount for joint ownership is not allowed as a further deduction from the sale proceeds. This may have the effect of HMRC assessing a higher than expected figure than was the case intended by the appropriate person.

(C) This (point B above) of course places the estate in a disadvantageous position and, as in many cases of HMRC elections which, once made, cannot be withdrawn, HMRC are instructed to ensure that they consider any disadvantageous elections under Form IHT38, see IHT manual extract at IHTM33182 where the claim is reviewed to 'help prevent the taxpayer making a disadvantageous claim'. See also Fosters at D3.12. However, HMRC confirm that such an instruction will not be binding where the IHT38 has been made on a commercially supplied copy of the form and submitted unsolicited to HMRC under *IHTA 1984, s 191*.

See also *St Clair-Ford (Youlden's Executor) v Ryder*, [2006] Lands Tribunal 22 June 2006 unreported. When dealing with minority shares in property which is vacant, or commercially let, it is necessary to consider the purpose behind the trust for sale and if it exists and can be fulfilled then the discount may be increased. (VOA IHT manual, section 18, paras 18.3–18.7). In *HSBC Trusts Co (UK) Ltd (Farmbrough's Executor) v Twiddy*, [2006] Lands Tribunal 24 August 2006 unreported, a woman had held a 16.25% interest in two large buildings comprising 28 flats and 9 shops. The Lands Tribunal held that since this was a minority interest, it should be valued on an income basis, declining to follow the earlier decision in *Charkham v CIR*, Lands Tribunal 1996, [2000] RVR 7.

HMRC do not automatically allow a discount for jointly held chattels and household goods. In many cases, these will be held by married persons or civil partners, in which case a discount is not in any event applicable. But in other situations, HMRC will need details of the 'nature and purpose of the joint ownership, together with details of any trust on which it is held. Ask the taxpayer or agent to state how the property was acquired and, if purchased, what proportion of the purchase price was provided by the deceased.' (IHTM21043)

Scottish law

Under Scots Law, the 'survivorship destination' does not by itself pass the ownership of the funds in a joint account to the survivor. An account with a bank or building society is not a document of title as it is not a Deed of Trust in terms of the *Bank Bonds and Trusts Act 1696*. Instead, it is a contract between the bank and the customer which regulates the conditions on which the account is to be operated and is for administrative convenience only. See *Cairns v Davidson* [1913] SC 1054. If under the terms of the Will/Intestacy, the funds in the account do not pass wholly to the surviving spouse, then inheritance tax will be payable as appropriate. If under the terms of the Will/Intestacy, the funds in the joint account pass to the spouse, then the spouse exemption should be claimed on page 4 of the IHT400 under the head 'Exemptions and Reliefs' on page 9. This applies to all bank/building society accounts governed by Scots Law so this is a point which practitioners should bear in mind when administering an estate subject to Scots Law.

Partnership interests

[53.7] The partners are collectively entitled to each and every asset of the partnership, in which each of them therefore has an undivided share. Consequently, the valuation of an interest in a business carried on as a partnership should be by reference to the appropriate share of each asset, including any goodwill (except for farming where goodwill does not apply), less a deduction for a corresponding share of partnership liabilities. Reference must be made to the partnership deed to ascertain what that share is. If there is no deed or agreement, the provisions of the *Partnership Act 1890* will govern the position.

Partnership agreements may contain provisions to the effect that in the event of the death or retirement of a partner any interest in partnership property is taken over by the other partners with specific terms as to what consideration, if any, is to be payable. If the consideration is not to be full market value, the agreement will fall to be treated as a restriction on the freedom to dispose of property. Any such restriction is taken into account only to the extent that consideration was given for it in money or money's worth when it was created [*IHTA 1984, s 163*]. Often such terms can be construed as being for the mutual benefit of all the partners with no intended gratuitous transfers. However HMRC will review the full facts in the case of family partnerships to establish whether and to what extent *IHTA 1984, s 163* applies.

The VOA accept that it will normally be necessary to make some discount from the appropriate arithmetical share of the full partnership value in order to reflect the fact that the hypothetical purchaser of the partner's share will have to take steps to dissolve the partnership or negotiate a sale to the other partners. The discount will not normally exceed 10%. Following *Walton v CIR* [1996] STC 68, [1996] 1 EGLR 159, CA no discount is applied to the value of agricultural tenancies valued by capitalising profit rent. See VOA IHT manual, para 19.8 and 19.9.

Interest in unadministered estate

[53.8] HMRC do not accept that an absolute interest in another estate in the course of administration can be valued as future receivable with discount applied. Instead, a similar approach is applied as with interests in possession in unadministered estates (see **24.9**) so that the assets of the unadministered estate must be valued on the relevant date and a deduction made for liabilities outstanding on that date, including costs of administration. A deceased residuary beneficiary of that estate is then treated as being entitled to the net value produced by this calculation, or if the interest is in part only of the residue, then the entitlement is to the deceased's fractional share of this valuation. There is in strictness no authority for this treatment, as there is with interests in possession in unadministered estates (see *IHTA 1984, s 91*), save that *FA 1984, Sch 21, para 13* amended the Capital Transfer Tax legislation so as to apply to all interests in other estates, but this was not carried into *IHTA 1984* on consolidation. The practice has the result that the related property rules can apply between the two estates, and in the case of a property held partly in one estate and partly in the other there can be no discount for joint ownership.

Land sold within three years (four years in some cases) of death

Claim

[53.9] Where an 'interest in land' in a deceased person's estate is sold within three years after the death by the '*appropriate person*', a claim (on Form IHT38) may be made by that person for the 'sale value' to be substituted for the value on death of *every* interest in land owned by the deceased and sold within three years of death by the same 'appropriate person' for which such a claim would be available. In the case of a death after 15 March 1990, a sale in the fourth year after death is treated as having occurred within three years of death unless *either* **53.13** below applies *or* the 'sale value' would exceed the value on death. The claim for relief under *IHTA 1984, s 191* must be made not more than four years from the date of death of the person where the interest in land was comprised in that deceased person's estate. [*IHTA 1984, s 191(1A); FA 2009, s 99, Sch 51 para 10*].

Definitions

'*Interest in land*' does not include any estate, interest or right by way of mortgage or other security.

'*Appropriate person*' is the person liable for the tax or, if there is more than one such person and one of them is paying the tax, that person. For instance, if personal representatives pay the tax on the estate and then assent shares or land to a beneficiary who sells them at a loss, within the respective time limits, then no relief will be due as the beneficiary is not an 'appropriate person' under *IHTA 1984, ss 179(1), 191(1)*. In cases where 100% business or agricultural property relief is available then a substitution claim under *IHTA 1984, s 191* would not apply because there would not be an '*appropriate person*' who could make a claim. This may have a knock-on effect with regard to the capital gains tax position. See *Stoner and Another (Executors of Dickinson deceased) v CIR* [2001] STC (SCD) 199 Sp C 288 which underlines the fact that a claim can only be made where an IHT issue (not a CGT saving issue) is at stake. This would also exclude cases where the value was covered by business property relief, the spouse/civil partner exemption and the nil-rate. See **55** TAX CASES.

'*Sale value*' is the 'sale price' as adjusted by the provisions in **53.11** to **53.16** below. Note that an abortive contract is not a sale and the sale price cannot be the said to be the price stated in the contract. (*Jones and Another (Balls' Administrators) v CIR*, Ch D [1997] STC 359).

'*Sale price*' is the price for which the land is sold or, if greater, the best consideration that could reasonably have been obtained at the time of sale, ignoring incidental expenses of commission, stamp duty or otherwise. [*IHTA 1984, ss 190, 191(1), 197A(1)(2); FA 1993, s 199*].

No claim is available if in respect of the interest in land giving rise to the claim:

(a) the sale value differs from the value on death by less than the lower of £1,000 and 5% of the value on death (see note 7 on IHT38); or

(b) the sale is by a personal representative or trustee to:
   (i) a person who, at any time between death and the sale, has been beneficially entitled to, or to an interest in possession in, property comprising the interest sold; or
   (ii) the spouse, civil partner, child or remoter descendant of a person within (i) above; or
   (iii) a trustee of a settlement under which a person within (i) or (ii) above has an interest in possession in property comprising the interest sold, or

(c) the vendor or any person within (b) above obtains a right in connection with the sale to acquire the interest sold or any other interest in the same land.

For the above purposes, a person shall be treated as having the same rights in the property in an unadministered estate as he would have if the administration of the estate had been completed. In the case of (b)(ii) and (iii) above the restriction will not apply to a parent or sibling of the beneficiary or to the trustees of a discretionary settlement in which he is a potential object.

[*IHTA 1984, s 191(2)(3)*].

Further purchases of land

Because of the possibility of further purchases (see **53.15** below), the above loss on sale relief cannot be formally granted until four months have elapsed from the date of the last sale of an interest in land (see note 4 on IHT38). In many estates there is one interest in land and it has to be sold to give effect to the terms of the deceased's will so that there is no prospect of further purchases. In such circumstances, HMRC will accept a loss on sale relief claim in advance of the statutory time limit and make a provisional repayment of tax accordingly. However, formal clearance by way of certificate of discharge (see **32.15** PAYMENT OF TAX) must await the personal representatives' confirmation (subsequent to the expiry of the four-month statutory time limit) that no changes have taken place since the claim was made (CTO Practice Note published in Taxation Practitioner August 1994 p 6).

Date applicable

[53.10] Date of sale or purchase of land by the 'appropriate person' is the date of the contract. If the transaction results from the exercise (by him or any other person) of an option granted not more than six months earlier, then the date of the transaction is the date on which the option is granted.

Where an interest in land is acquired in pursuance of a notice to treat served by an authority possessing powers of compulsory purchase, the date of sale is whichever is the earlier of:

(a) the date when the compensation is agreed or otherwise determined (any variation on appeal being disregarded), and

(b) the date when the authority enters on the land in pursuance of their powers.

If an interest in land is acquired from the 'appropriate person' by a general vesting declaration under the *Compulsory Purchase (Vesting Declarations) Act 1981* or, in Scotland, the *Town and Country Planning (Scotland) Act 1972, Sch 24* or, in NI, by a vesting order, the date of sale is the last day of the period specified in the declaration (in NI, the date on which the vesting order becomes operative). [*IHTA 1984, s 198*].

Adjustments

[53.11] **Sales to beneficiaries etc. and exchanges** require adjustment where the person making the claim, acting in the same capacity as that in which he makes the claim:

(a) sells land (or an interest in land) within three years after the death (a sale within four years after death which is treated as within three years under **53.9** above being ignored for this purpose) to any person within **53.9**(b) or (c) above; or
(b) within three years after the death exchanges (with or without payment) any interest in land which was comprised in the deceased's estate,

and the sale price (or market value in the case of an exchange) exceeds its value on death. In such a case an addition is made to the sale price of any interest to which the claim relates. If the claim relates to one interest only, the addition is the amount of the excess. If there is more than one interest, the addition is that part of the excess given by the fraction:

$$\frac{A}{B}$$

where:

A = the difference between the value on death of that interest and its sale price (as adjusted under **53.12** to **53.14** below); and
B = the aggregate of that difference and the corresponding differences for all other interests to which the claim relates, calculated without regard to which is the greater, in the case of any particular interest, of its value on death and its sale price. [*IHTA 1984, ss 196, 197A(4); FA 1993, s 199*].

Example

A (a bachelor) died on 1 May 2017 owning four areas of land, as follows.

(a) 10 acres valued at death £20,000
(b) 15 acres valued at death £30,000
(c) 20 acres valued at death £30,000
(d) 30 acres valued at death £40,000

He also owned a freehold house valued at death at £50,000.

In the four years following A's death, his executors made the following sales.

(i) Freehold house sold 15.11.17, proceeds £53,000, expenses £2,000
(ii) Land area (c) sold 1.6.19, proceeds £29,500, expenses £1,500
(iii) Land area (b) sold 8.8.20, proceeds £27,000, expenses £1,000

(iv) Land area (d) sold 19.9.20, proceeds £42,000, expenses £3,000

The disposals in the three years following the death produce the following profits and losses.

	£	
Gross sale proceeds of house	53,000	
Deduct probate value	50,000	£3,000
Gross sale proceeds of land area (b)	27,000	
Deduct probate value	30,000	£(3,000)
Gross sale proceeds of land area (c) (see Note (A))	29,500	
Deduct probate value	30,000	£(500)

Notes to the example

(A) The sale of area (c) is disregarded as the loss on sale (before allowing for expenses) is less than 5% of £30,000 (£1,500) and is also lower than £1,000. [*IHTA 1984, s 191*]. Note 7 on IHT38.

(B) The overall allowable reduction on all sales is therefore nil even though there is a loss after expenses.

(C) For deaths after 15 March 1990, a sale *for less than the value at death* which is made in the fourth year after death is treated as having been made in the three years after death. [*IHTA 1984, s 197A; FA 1993, s 199*]. The sale of land area (d) is not therefore brought into account.

Changes between death and sale

[53.12] Where there has been a change between the date of death and the date of sale so that the interest is not the same in all respects and with the same incidents and the land in which the interest subsists is not in the same state and with the same incidents, the sale price is adjusted by the difference between the value on death and what that value would have been if the changed circumstances had prevailed at the time of death. The difference is added to the sale price if the original value on death was more than the new valuation and deducted if less. See also example at 53.9 above.

If compensation under any Act has been received by the 'appropriate person' (or any other person liable to tax on the interest in the land) between the death and the sale because of a restriction on the use or development of the land or because its value has been reduced for any other reason, such restriction or reduction is ignored for the adjustment of the sale price mentioned above but the sale price is increased by the amount of the compensation. [*IHTA 1984, s 19*[illegible]]. See question 7 on form IHT38.

Compulsory acquisition more than three years after death

[53.13] Where an authority possessing powers of compulsory acquisition has served notice to treat before the death or within the following three years and has acquired the land *after* those three years from the 'appropriate person', the acquisition is treated in the same way as a sale during the three years. This provision is ignored if the sale value exceeds the value on death. [*IHTA 1984, s 197(1)(2)*].

Other interests in same or other land

[53.14] If in determining the value at death of any interest to which the claim relates, any other interests, whether in the same or other land, were taken into account, an addition must be made to the sale price of the interest equal to the difference between the value on death of the interest and the value which would have been the value on death if no other interests had been taken into account. [*IHTA 1984, s 195*].

Subsequent purchases

[53.15] Further purchases of any interests in land by the person making the claim as above in the same capacity during the period beginning with the death and ending four months after the date of the last sale may reduce the relief claimable on the sales. For this purpose any sale in the fourth year after death and taken into account under **53.9** above and any compulsory acquisition more than three years after death and taken into account under **53.13** above are ignored, and if the claim relates only to such sales, the following provisions are ignored.

The relief is lost if the aggregate of the purchase prices of all the interests purchased equals or exceeds the aggregate of the sale prices (as adjusted by **53.12** and **53.14** above and **53.16** below). Otherwise an addition is made to the sale price of every interest to which the claim relates given by the formula:

$$(V - S) \times \frac{A}{B}$$

where:

V = value on death of the interest;
S = sales price (as adjusted by **53.11**, **53.12** and **53.14** above and **53.16** below as appropriate);
A = aggregate of the purchase prices; and
B = aggregate of the sales prices.

Where the value on death of an interest is less than its sale price as adjusted above, the sale price is reduced by the amount calculated from the above formula. [*IHTA 1984, ss 192, 197(3), 197A(3); FA 1993, s 199*].

Example

B died on 30 June 2020 owning a house and a seaside flat.

At death the valuations were

	£
House	150,000
Flat	130,000
	£280,000
Sales by the executors realised (gross)	
House proceeds 1.7.2021	142,000
Flat proceeds 1.12.2011	133,000
	£275,000

On 1 May 2021, the executors bought a townhouse for the deceased's daughter for £140,000 (excluding costs).

Initially relief is due of £(280,000 – 275,000) = £5,000

Recomputation of relief

$$\text{Appropriate fraction} = \frac{\text{Purchase price}}{\text{Selling price}} = \frac{140,000}{275,000} = \frac{28}{55}$$

		House		Seaside Flat
	£	£	£	£
Value on death		150,000		130,000
Sale price	142,000			
Add (£150,000 – £142,000) × $^{28}/_{55}$	4,072			
Revised value for IHT		146,072		
Sale price			133,000	
Deduct (£133,000 – £130,000) × $^{28}/_{55}$			1,527	
Revised value for IHT				131,473
Revised relief		£3,928		£(1,473)
Total			£2,455	

Note to the example

(A) The purchase is taken into account because it is made within the period 30 June 2020 (date of death) and 1 April 2022 (four months after the last of the sales affected by the claim). [*IHTA 1984, s 192(1)*]. If a sale made in the fourth year after death was affected by the claim (under *IHTA 1984, s 197A*), it would *not* be taken into account in determining the above-mentioned period. [*IHTA 1984, s 197A(3); FA 1993, s 199*].

Leases

[53.16] Where a claim relates to an interest in a lease of under 50 years duration at the date of death, the sale price is increased by the proportion of the amount of the value on death given by the fraction:

$$\frac{P(1) - P(2)}{P(2)}$$

where:

P(1) = the appropriate percentage from the table for depreciation of leases contained in *TCGA 1992, Sch 8 para 1* (see 8 CAPITAL GAINS TAX) for the duration of the lease at the date of death; and
P(2) = the appropriate percentage for the duration of the lease at the date of sale.

Note that on form IHT38 the unexpired term of the lease at the date of death must be entered on the form under the heading 'Tenure'.

[*IHTA 1984, s 194*].

Leased property

[53.17] If full consideration originally passed for the lease then the market value of the lease is taken when it is later transferred. Where a lessee's interest is for life or otherwise determinable by reference to a death, it may be treated as a settlement (see 38.7 SETTLEMENTS — GENERAL) and the value is calculated as the full value of the property less the value of the lessor's interest. The value of the lessor's interest is the proportion of the value of the property given by the fraction:

$$\frac{A}{B}$$

where:

A = the value of the consideration given by the lessee at the time the lease was granted; and B
B = the value of a full consideration in money or money's worth of the lease at that time.

[*IHTA 1984, ss 50(6), 170*].

Liabilities

[53.18] In determining the value of a person's estate at any time his liabilities at that time must be taken into account, except as otherwise provided by *IHTA 1984*. Except in the case of a liability imposed by the law, a liability incurred by the transferor may be taken into account only to the extent that it was incurred for a consideration in money or money's worth. [*IHTA 1984, s 5(3)(5)*].

The following rules apply for determining the amount or value of the liability.

(a) A liability in respect of which there is a right to reimbursement is taken into account only to the extent that reimbursement cannot reasonably be expected to be obtained.

(b) Subject to (c) below, where a liability falls to be discharged after the time at which it is to be taken into account, it must be valued at the time of being taken into account (i.e. at its discounted value).

(c) In determining the value of the transferor's estate immediately after the transfer, his liability for inheritance tax is computed:
  - (i) without making any allowance for the fact that the tax will not be due immediately; and
  - (ii) as if any tax recovered otherwise than from the transferor (or, under certain circumstances, the transferor's spouse or civil partner, see **27.2** LIABILITY FOR TAX) were paid in discharge of a liability in respect of which the transferor had a right to reimbursement.

(d) A liability which is an encumbrance on any property must, as far as possible, be taken to reduce the value of that property. However with effect from 17 July 2013 (the date of Royal Assent to the *Finance Act 2013*), any liability incurred on or after 6 April 2013 which financed excluded property or 'relievable property' is primarily deducted from the value of that property, notwithstanding the fact that it may be secured on other property. See details at **53.19** below.

(e) A liability due to a person resident outside the UK which neither falls to be discharged in the UK nor is an encumbrance on UK property must, as far as possible, be taken to reduce the value of non-UK property. [*IHTA 1984, s 162*]. See *Whittaker v CIR*, [2001] STC (SCD) 61 Sp C 272.

Where an individual receives a capital payment from a non-UK resident trust and, under the provisions in *FA 1984, Sch 14* that payment crystallises a previously deferred capital gains tax liability of a close relative of his, the payment by the individual of the capital gains tax is treated for inheritance tax purposes as made in satisfaction of a liability of his. [*IHTA 1984, s 165(3)*].

See also **49** TRANSFERS ON DEATH.

The value transferred is also reduced by:

(i) any capital gains tax (or income tax on a development gain) borne by the donee. In the case of settled property the reduction applies only if the tax on the gain accruing to the trustees is borne by a person who becomes absolutely entitled to the settled property concerned;

(ii) any incidental expenses incurred by the transferor in making the transfer but borne by the transferee. If borne by the transferor they are left out of account i.e. they do not have to be added to the amount of the gift.

[*IHTA 1984, ss 164, 165*].

See now form IHT419 and **53.4** VALUATION.

Liabilities to finance excluded property or relievable property

[53.19] For transfers of value made or treated as made on or after 17 July 2013, it is no longer possible to reduce the value of an asset for IHT purposes by securing a loan on it where the loan is used to acquire or maintain (directly or indirectly) another asset which qualifies for certain IHT reliefs. Instead the loan will be primarily deductible from the asset qualifying for relief. These rules have equal effect for charges on settlements holding relevant property within *IHTA 1984, s 58*.

In the case of (ii) and (iii) below, this rule applies to any liability incurred on or after 6 April 2013. In the case of (i) and (v) below the rule applies to liabilities whenever incurred, but (i) has effect for transfers of value made or treated as made on or after 17 July 2013, whereas (v) effect for transfers of value made or treated as made on or after 17 July 2014. The provisions apply to liabilities incurred to acquire, finance, maintain or enhance the value of:

(i) excluded property (see **20** EXCLUDED PROPERTY);
(ii) property qualifying for business property relief (see **6** BUSINESS PROPERTY);
(iii) property qualifying for agricultural property relief (see **4** AGRICULTURAL PROPERTY);
(iv) woodlands where the value of them is to be left out of account on a person's death (see **54.1**(c)).
(v) a balance on any foreign currency account which is to be left out of account of a person's estate on death under the relief in *IHTA 1984, s 157* (NON-RESIDENTS' BANK ACCOUNTS) (see **21.23**).

In the case of a liability incurred in respect of excluded property, as above, the loan is not to be taken into account for IHT purposes. However, if the excluded property is subsequently disposed of for full consideration, the liability may then be deductible for IHT purposes to the extent that the proceeds of the disposal are not used to acquire or maintain other excluded property, or to pay off another loan which cannot not to be taken into account by virtue of this provision. A liability may be taken into account to the extent that it exceeds the value of any of the excluded property not disposed of, but not where this excess is attributable to arrangements to secure a tax advantage, an increase in the amount of the liability, or a disposal of any of the excluded property. For example, if a loan is taken out to buy shares in a foreign incorporated company, and arrangements are then made for tax reasons to reduce the value of those shares, the loan will remain non-deductible.

In the case of a liability which was incurred wholly or partly to finance the balance on a foreign currency account within (v) above, the loan may be deducted from the estate of the borrower to the extent that it exceeds the balance on the account so long as this excess does not arise either as a result of arrangements to secure a tax advantage or to increase the amount of the liability (e.g. by accruing interest on the loan).

In the case of a liability incurred in respect of business or agricultural property, or woodlands, as detailed above, the loan is to be primarily deducted from the value of that property before the any applicable reliefs for such property are given. If the business or agricultural property is gifted during lifetime, the loan is to be deducted only from the value of that property if the lifetime gift is or becomes a chargeable transfer, so that the liability cannot also be deducted from the estate on death. But if the lifetime gift is a PET and the donor survives for seven years, retaining liability for the loan, it may then be deducted from the estate on death.

A loan is considered by HMRC to indirectly finance an asset where it is initially used to buy asset 1 which is later sold and the proceeds reinvested in asset 2. The loan then indirectly finances asset 2 (see HMRC IHT Manual IHTM28018). On this view it is not possible to circumvent the disallowance by first acquiring UK property with a loan, subsequently selling that property and then acquiring excluded property with the proceeds. Equally where a loan is taken out to buy a UK asset, say a painting, and that asset becomes excluded property, for example by being removed from the UK, the loan is deductible only to the extent that it exceeds the value of that asset and subject also to there being no arrangements to secure a tax advantage.

Where a liability is incurred partly for relievable property, as described above, and partly for other assets not qualifying for the reliefs, any part repayments of a liability are to be attributed first to the proportion of it incurred for the non-relievable property. If a loan is incurred partly in relation to assets within any of (ii), (iii) or (iv) above and partly in relation to assets within (i) above, part repayments are to be attributed primarily to the part relating to the assets within (ii), (iii) or (iv). For HMRC's view on apportionments of liabilities between relievable and non-relievable property, see IHT Manual para 28021. [*IHTA 1984, ss 162A and 162B*].

Life assurance policies and annuities

[53.20] See 28 LIFE ASSURANCE POLICIES AND ANNUITIES for the valuation of policies and contracts and 39.5 SETTLEMENTS WITH INTERESTS IN POSSESSION for annuities which are interests in possession.

HMRC have stated:

> 'Life insurance policies taken out on one person's life may be held in trust for the benefit of others. Parents and grandparents may often take out a life insurance policy but put it in trust for their children or grandchildren. Business partners or the directors of a company also take out insurance on their lives but for the benefit of their partners and co–directors. So, if the deceased died whilst still working, or they died before their parent(s), there is a possibility that they may have a right to benefit under a policy held in trust. If the deceased had a right to benefit under a life insurance policy held in trust, that right may be settled property.'

See Form IHT410. Note that reserved rights to a life annuity where there is a projected life expectancy can result in a discount in the valuation of the policy at death. In *CJ Bower & DN Chesterfield (Mrs ME Bower's Executors) v HMRC* [2008] STC (SCD) 582 Sp C 665; Ch D [2009] STC 510 there was a deduction of £4,200 allowed representing the deceased's reserved rights to the life annuity. HMRC appealed to the Ch D against this decision. The appeal in Chancery Division was allowed. For HMRC's practice, see HMRC Brief 23/08, issued on 11 April 2008. New cases regarding the discounted gift will continue to be dealt with in accordance with the May 2007 Technical Note www.hmrc.gov.uk/cto/dgs-tech-note.pdf.

Related property

[53.21] The value of any property in a person's estate is found by taking related property into account if by so doing a higher value for all or part of the property in his estate would be obtained. Property is related to the property in a person's estate if:

(a) it is in the estate of his spouse/civil partner, or
(b) it is, or was during the preceding five years, the property of a charity, charitable trust, qualifying political party (see **21.7** EXEMPT TRANSFERS), specified national body (see **30.29** NATIONAL HERITAGE), non-profit making body (see **21.8** EXEMPT TRANSFERS) or registered housing association (see **21.5** EXEMPT TRANSFERS), and became so as the result of a transfer of value made by him or his spouse or civil partner after 15 April 1976 and was exempt to the extent that the value transferred was attributable to the property.

The value of the estate property and the related property taken together is then apportioned to the estate property in the proportion that its value on its own bears to the sum of the separate values. See *Arkwright and Another (Williams' Personal Representatives) v CIR* Ch D [2004] STC 1323, Sp C 392. [*IHTA 1984, s 161(1)–(3); FA 1989, s 171(4)*].

Example 1

Husband owns a property worth £150,000 and his wife owns adjoining land worth £250,000. The combined value is £800,000.

The proportioned value of the husband's land is:

$$\frac{150{,}000}{150{,}000 + 250{,}000} \times £800{,}000 = £300{,}000$$

In the above example if the properties were each owned in equal shares and, say, the house was encumbered by mortgage of £60,000 in the husband's name sole then the value of the house is divisible in equal shares after the deduction of the mortgage even though this is in the husband's sole name in the sum of £45,000 (i.e. £150,000 – £60,000 ÷ 2).

In the case of shares etc. of the same class or similar units of property, the proportion is that which the number of shares in the estate bears to the total number of those and the related shares. Shares are of the same class if they are, or would be, so treated by the practice of a recognised stock exchange. [*IHTA 1984, s 161(4)(5)*].

The DV should value both interests together and make no reduction in the aggregate value because the related property is owned by the spouse/civil partner and not by the transferor. If vacant possession would become available on the merging of the interests the property should be valued with vacant possession. The aggregate value should reflect the full enhancement attributable to the merging of the transferor's property with the related property and no deduction should be made because more than one ownership is involved. (VOA IHT manual, section 15, para 15.5).

Example 2

On the death of a husband on 31 October 2020, the share capital of a private company was held as follows

	Shares	
Issued capital	10,000	
Husband	4,000	40%
Wife	4,000	40%
Others (employees)	2,000	20%
	10,000	100%

The value of an 80% holding is £80,000, while the value of a 40% holding is £24,000. In his will, the husband left his 4,000 shares to his daughter.

The related property rules apply to aggregate the shares of:

Husband	4,000	
Wife	4,000	
Related property	8,000	shares
Chargeable transfer on legacy to daughter		
IHT value of 8,000 shares (80%)		£80,000
IHT value attributed to legacy of husband's shares (4,000)		£40,000

(Subject to 100% business property relief if conditions satisfied.)

Sale within three years after death

[53.22] If property was valued on a death by reference to related property as in 53.21 above and is sold within the following three years at less than that valuation (allowing for any difference in circumstances between the times of death and sale), a claim may be made to revert to the value of that property at death without reference to the related property. The sale must qualify under the following conditions, namely that:

(a) the vendors are the persons in whom the property vested immediately after death or are the deceased's personal representatives; and

(b) the sale is at arm's length for a price freely negotiated at the time of the sale and is not made in conjunction with a sale of any of the related property; and

(c) no vendor (or any person having an interest in the sale proceeds) is or is connected with, any purchaser (or any person having an interest in the purchase); and

(d) neither the vendors nor any other person having an interest in the sale proceeds obtain in connection with the sale a right to acquire the property sold or any interest in or created out of it.

Where the property is shares or securities of a close company, the above relief does not apply if between the death and sale the value is reduced by more than 5% as a result of an alteration in the company's share or loan capital or rights attaching thereto.

The above rules also apply where the property was valued at death in conjunction with other property which did not devolve on the vendors e.g. property in a trust of which the deceased was life tenant. [*IHTA 1984, s 176*].

Restriction on freedom to dispose

[53.23] If the right to dispose of any property has been excluded or restricted by a contract made at any time, then, on the next chargeable transfer of the property, the exclusion or restriction will be taken into account only to the extent that consideration in money or money's worth was given for it. If the contract was before 27 March 1974, this provision applies only if the next chargeable transfer is a transfer made on death.

If the contract was itself a chargeable transfer (including part of an associated operation), an allowance is made for so much of the value transferred thereby (ignoring tax) as is attributable to the exclusion or restriction. [*IHTA 1984, s 163*].

In *Shelford (as trustee of the Herbert Life Interest Settlement) v HMRC* [2020] UKFTT 0053 (TC), [2020] SFTD 437, [2020] SWTI 322 it was held that *IHTA 1984, s 163* would have applied to an arrangement under which the taxpayer contracted to sell his home to a trust for himself as life tenant (see **23.6** for further details of this type of planning). In fact, the documentation was held to be void but had this not been the case, the sale would have been treated as a restriction on freedom to dispose without any consideration given for it.

Shares and securities

[53.24] Unquoted shares and securities are valued at what they might reasonably be expected to fetch if sold in the open market on the assumption that there is available to any prospective purchaser all the information which a prudent prospective purchaser might reasonably require if he were proposing to purchase them from a willing vendor by private treaty and at arm's length. [*IHTA 1984, s 168; FA 1987, s 58, Sch 8 para 12*]. See also *CIR v Crossman and Others* HL, [1936] 1 All ER 762; *In re Lynall (decd.)* HL 1971, 47 TC 375; *Battle and Another v CIR* Ch D 1979, [1980] STC 86.

In a capital transfer tax case, both earlier arm's length transactions in the shares in question and previous agreements with HMRC were held to be admissible evidence for valuation purposes (*CIR v Stenhouse's Trustees* CS 1991, [1992] STC 103).

Shares quoted on the Alternative Investment Market, the Specialist Fund Market and the High Growth Segment of the main market of the London Stock Exchange are all within the category of unquoted shares for IHT purposes. In

Netley v HMRC [2017] UKFTT 442 (TC), TC05904, the First-tier Tribunal held that the price of shares quoted on the Alternative Investment Market was not necessarily the relevant value for tax purposes, although the background to the valuation in this case was unusual and it involved the listing of the shares on AIM and a gift of some of them to charity on the same date. Being unquoted shares, the size of the holding and the information which would be made available to a hypothetical investor was taken into account. In the case of a small uninfluential holding, only publicly available information would be required for a valuation.

In order to ensure uniformity of approach, the DV should, unless otherwise instructed by Shares and Assets Valuation (SAV), value the underlying company property or assets on the basis of the statutory definition in *IHTA 1984 s 160* of 'open market value' disregarding any 'flooding of the market' effect and apply any relevant legal principles which have evolved over the years when the courts have ruled on the meaning of the similar definition for ED purposes contained in *FA 1894, s 7(5)* (VOA IHT manual, section 16, para 16.3). For these purposes the costs of sale are ignored.

The address of Shares and Assets Valuation is Shares and Assets Valuation, HMRC, BX9 1BJ.

Where it is evident that any possible variation in the value of shares in an unquoted company shown in the HMRC Account will still leave the total value of an estate below the IHT threshold, it is not necessary to ascertain the value of those shares. Where the total value of an estate is close to the IHT threshold, values may be considered but not necessarily 'ascertained'. For example where SAV regard the value of such shares to be too high it is unlikely to negotiate an ascertained value for IHT when no tax is at stake. However, if the value of the shares seems too low, SAV may negotiate an ascertained value if the likely amount of IHT at stake warrants this (HMRC Tax Bulletin April 1995, pp 209, 210). See also *IC Mc Arthur's Executors v HMRC* [2008] STC (SCD) 1100 Sp C 700 and 55 TAX CASES.

Quoted shares and securities are those listed on a recognised stock exchange which, for UK quotation, means being included in the official UK list maintained by the Financial Services Authority. Shares with a UK quotation are in practice, unless there are special circumstances, valued (as for capital gains tax) at the lower of:

(a) the lower of the two prices quoted in the Stock Exchange Daily Official List for the relevant date, plus a quarter of the difference between those prices ('*the quarter-up rule*'), and
(b) the average of the highest and lowest prices for normal bargains recorded on that date, if any.

If there was no trading on the relevant date, the prices are to be taken by reference to the latest previous date or to the earliest subsequent date, whichever produces the lower figure.

The London Stock Exchange offers an historical price service for which there is a charge which is currently £5 plus VAT. To access this service go to www.londonstockexchange.com/personal-investing/tools/historical-price-service.

Shares in unit trusts, subject as above, are valued at the lower of the two prices published by the managers on the relevant date or, if no price is published at that time, on the latest date before the relevant date. [*TCGA 1992, s 272(3)(4)*].

Note that in the case of sales of shares there is no *de minimis* amount applicable as applies to land and there is no restriction with regard to whom the sale is made.

Definitions

[53.25] In relation to transfers of value made, and other events occurring, after 16 March 1987, '*quoted*', in relation to any shares or securities, means quoted on a recognised stock exchange or dealt in on the Unlisted Securities Market (see Alternative Investment Market under **32.8**), and '*unquoted*', in relation to any shares or securities, means neither so quoted nor so dealt in. [*IHTA 1984, s 272; FA 1987, s 58(2), Sch 8 para 17*]. This applies for all IHT purposes except that, in relation to transfers of value made, and other events occurring, after 9 March 1992, an alternative definition whereby Unlisted Securities Market (and AIM) shares and securities are treated as unquoted, applies for the purposes of defining relevant business property (see **6.4** BUSINESS PROPERTY) and payment by instalments (see **32.5** PAYMENT OF TAX). As from 1 April 1996 the word '*quoted*' is substituted by the word '*listed*'. [*FA 1996, Sch 38 para 2*]. In relation to transfers of value made, and other events occurring, before 17 March 1987, shares and securities in companies dealt in on the Unlisted Securities Market were not treated as 'quoted' or 'listed' on a recognised stock exchange for all IHT purposes where those terms were used in tax provisions. The shares or securities did, however, satisfy the tests of being 'authorised to be dealt in' and 'dealt in (regularly or from time to time)' on a recognised stock exchange (HMRC Statement of Practice SP 18/80, 23 December 1980).

Quoted shares sold within twelve months after death

[53.26] Where 'qualifying investments' comprised in a deceased person's estate are sold within twelve months for less than their value on death the 'appropriate person' may claim (specifying the capacity in which he makes the claim and using form IHT35) a reduction in the estate values equal to the amount by which the aggregate of the value of *all* the qualifying investments included in the estate which are sold in the twelve-month period exceeds the aggregate of the 'sale values' of those investments (i.e. the loss on sale). See *Lee & Lee (Lee's Executors) v CIR* [2003] STC (SCD) 41 Sp C 349 for strict adherence to the twelve-month time limit. For this purpose, if death occurred after 15 March 1992:

(a) qualifying investments which are 'cancelled' (this term is not defined but may cover the final act of a company liquidation; if so, any 'capital payments' received during the liquidation will presumably be dealt with as below) within the twelve-month period without being replaced by other shares etc. are treated as having been sold immediately before cancellation for a nominal sum of £1, and
(b) qualifying investments of which the listing is suspended at the end of the twelve-month period are treated as having been sold immediately before the end of that period at their value at that time (if this is lower than their value at death).

Where an individual died in the period 22 February 2007 to 21 February 2008 (inclusive) owning shares in Northern Rock, and the shares were subsequently taken into temporary public ownership before they were either sold by the personal representatives or transferred to the person(s) entitled under the deceased's will or intestacy, then for the purposes only of *IHTA 1984, s 186A* the shares will be treated as if they had been cancelled as at 22 February 2008. Provided the other conditions of *s 186A* are met, a claim to relief under those provisions may be made by the appropriate person. See IHT and Trusts Newsletter dated August 2008. [*IHTA 1984, ss 178(1), 179, 186A(1), 186B(1)(2); FA 1993, s 198; FA 1996, Sch 38 para 4(1)(2)*].

Definitions

'*Qualifying investments*' are shares or securities which at the date of the death in question are quoted (in relation to transfers of value made, and other events occurring, before 17 March 1987, quoted on a recognised stock exchange), holdings in an authorised unit trust and shares in any common investment fund established under the *Administration of Justice Act 1965, s 1* (i.e. certain funds managed by the Public Trustee and held in court on behalf of the persons entitled). Note that this relief is limited to the investments just described and does not extend to crypto-assets such as bitcoin despite the real possibility of loss on them due to their inherent volatility. Where a listing on a recognised stock exchange or, in relation to transfers of value made, and other events occurring, after 16 March 1987, dealing on the Unlisted Securities Market (see Alternative Investment Market under **32.8** PAYMENT OF TAX) is suspended at the date of death, the investments are qualifying investments if they are again so listed or dealt in at the time of sale or exchange under **53.29** below. Where an individual died in the period 29 September 2007 to 28 September 2008 (inclusive) owning shares in Bradford & Bingley, and the shares were subsequently taken into public ownership before they were either sold by the personal representatives or transferred to the person(s) entitled under the deceased's will or intestacy, then for the purposes only of *IHTA 1984, s 186A*, the shares will be treated as if they had been cancelled as at 29 September 2008. Providing the other conditions of *s 186A* are met, a claim to relief under those provisions may be made by the appropriate person i.e. personal representatives or executor on Form IHT35. [*IHTA 1984, s 178(1)(2); FA 1987, s 58, Sch 8 para 13; FA 1996, Sch 38 para 4(1)(3)*].

The '*appropriate person*' is the person liable for the tax attributable to the value of the investment concerned or, if there is more than one such person and one of them is paying the tax, that person. Note 2 of Form IHT35 states that the 'capacity' of the claimant (i.e. executor, administrator, trustee or donor) must be indicated but this must not include an agent. See **53.9** above.

'*Sale value*' of qualifying investments means the price for which they were sold or (except in the case of (a) or (b) above), if greater, the best consideration which could reasonably have been obtained for them at the time of the sale (ignoring incidental expenses of commission, stamp duty or otherwise). Any 'capital payment' (whether during or after the twelve months following the death) as is attributable to the investments comprised in the estate and sold by the appropriate person is added to the sale value. '*Capital payment*' includes consideration received for the disposal of a provisional allotment of shares or debentures and any money or money's worth which does not constitute income for income tax purposes. It does not include the price paid on the sale of the investment. [*IHTA 1984, ss 178(1)(5), 179(1), 181, 186A(2), 186B(3); FA 1993, s 198*].

Date of sale or purchase of investments by the 'appropriate person' is the date of the contract. If the transaction results from the exercise (by him or any other person) of an option, then the date of the transaction is the date on which the option was granted. [*IHTA 1984, s 189*].

Value at death of qualifying investments includes any calls on them paid by the 'appropriate person' during or after the twelve months following the death. [*IHTA 1984, s 182*]. Where part only of a holding of qualifying investments is comprised in a person's estate (e.g. if he is a joint tenant of settled property) and a claim is made as above, the whole of the holding is included in the calculation and the loss on sale is reduced by the proportion which the value of that part of the investments included in the estate bears to the entire value of those investments. [*IHTA 1984, s 186*].

Further qualifying investments

[53.27] **Further purchases** of qualifying investments by the 'appropriate person', in the same capacity in which he made the claim above, during the period beginning with the death and ending two months after the date of the last sale will reduce the 'loss on sale' by the proportion which the total of the purchase prices (ignoring incidental expenses) bears to the total of the sales values in the claim. If the aggregate purchase prices equals or exceeds the sales values, the loss is extinguished. [*IHTA 1984, s 180(1)*]. See form IHT35, p 3.

If a person makes a claim other than as personal representative or trustee, any purchase as above is ignored unless it is of qualifying investments of *the same description* (i.e. they are not separately listed on a recognised stock exchange nor, in relation to transfers of value made, and other events occurring, after 16 March 1987, separately dealt in on the Unlisted Securities Market (or AIM) nor in a different unit trust or common investment fund) as included in the claim and the purchase is made otherwise than in the capacity of personal representative or trustee. [*IHTA 1984, s 180(2)(3); FA 1987, s 58, Sch 8 para 14; FA 1996, Sch 38 para 3*].

Changes in holdings

[53.28] On any change within the period of twelve months following death due to a reorganisation, conversion, exchange, amalgamation or reconstruction to which *TCGA 1992, s 127* applies (or such a change in unit trust holding to which *TCGA 1992, s 127* is applied by virtue of *TCGA 1992, s 99*), the new holding is treated as the same as the original holding.

If within the twelve-month period the appropriate person sells any investment comprised in the new holding, the value on death of those investments are determined by the formula:

$$\frac{Vs}{Vs + Vr} \times (H - S)$$

where:

Vs = sales value of the investment;
Vr = market value at the time of sale of any investment remaining in the new holding after the sale;
H = value on death of the new holding; and
S = value on death of any investments which were originally comprised in the new holding but have been sold on a previous occasion or occasions.

The value on death of the new holding is the same as the value on death of the original holding increased by any consideration which the appropriate person gives, or becomes liable to give, as part of or in connection with the transaction by which he acquires the new holding. For this purpose, 'consideration' excludes any surrender, cancellation or other alteration of the investments comprised in the original holding or rights attached thereto. It also excludes any application, in paying up the new holding or part of it, of assets of the company concerned or any dividend or other distribution declared out of those assets but not made. [*IHTA 1984, s 183*].

Exchange of qualifying investments

[53.29] If, apart from 53.28 above, an 'appropriate person' exchanges qualifying investments within twelve months of the death for other property of any kind (with or without any payment by way of equality of exchange) and the market value of the investments at the date of exchange is *greater* than their value at the date of death, they are treated as having been sold at their market value at the date of exchange. [*IHTA 1984, s 184*].

Identification

[53.30] Where an 'appropriate person' has, in the same capacity, (i) investments comprised in the deceased's estate at death and (ii) investments of the same description subsequently acquired in some other way (but not under 53.28 above), any part of such investments sold within the twelve months after death is apportioned between (i) and (ii) in the same proportions as they bore to each other immediately before the sale. [*IHTA 1984, s 185*].

Attribution of specific values

[53.31] It is necessary (for the purposes of both inheritance tax and capital gains tax) to attribute values to specific investments included in a claim as under 53.26 above. Generally, the value of a specific investment is its sale value. Where the loss on sale is reduced by further purchases (see 53.27 above), that reduction is apportioned over all the investments sold in proportion to the differences between their sale values and their values at death.

Where a call has been paid, the sale value of that investment is reduced by the amount of the call.

Where under a reorganisation etc. under 53.28 above, consideration has been paid for the new holding, the sale value of any specific investment comprised in the new holding is reduced by an amount which bears to that consideration the like proportion as the value on death of the specific investment sold bears to the value on death of the whole of the new holding.

In no case can the value of an investment be reduced to a minus quantity. [*IHTA 1984, ss 187, 188*].

Example

An individual died on 30 June 2020 and included in his estate was a portfolio of quoted investments. The executors sold certain investments within 12 months of death. The realisations were as follows.

	Probate Value	Gross Sales
	£	£
Share A	7,700	7,200
Share B	400	600
Share C	2,800	2,900
Share D	13,600	11,600
Share E	2,300	2,300
Share F	5,700	5,100
Share G	19,400	17,450
Share H	8,500	8,600
	£60,400	55,750
Incidental costs of sale		2,750
Net proceeds of sale		£53,000

On 1 September 2020, share J, having a probate value of £200 and still held by the executors was cancelled.

On 1 December 2020, share K, having a probate value of £1,000 has its stock exchange quotation suspended. On 30 June 2011, the investment is still held by the executors, its estimated value is £49 and the quotation remains suspended.

On 30 April 2021, the executors purchased a new holding for £1,750.

The executors would initially be able to claim a reduction of

(£60,400 – £55,750) + (£200 – £1) + (£1,000 – £49) = £5,800

After the purchase, the reduction is restricted as follows:

$$\text{Relevant proportion} = \frac{\text{Reinvestment}}{\text{Total sales}} = \frac{1{,}750}{£55{,}750 + £1 + £49} = \frac{1{,}750}{55{,}800}$$

Original relief restricted by:

$$\frac{1{,}750}{55{,}800} \times £5{,}800 = £182$$

Total relief £5,800 less £182 = £5,618

Notes to the example

(A) No costs of selling investments may be deducted from the sale proceeds. Note 5 on IHT35.

(B) The cancelled shares are treated as sold for £1 immediately before cancellation. The suspended shares are treated as sold on the first anniversary of death at their value at that time (provided that value is less than their value on death). [*IHTA 1984, ss 186A, 186B; FA 1993, s 198*].

(C) The purchase is taken into account as it is made during the period beginning on date of death and ending two months after the end of the last sale taken into account (including deemed sales as in (B) above).

(D) The probate value of each of the investments sold will be adjusted, both for CGT and IHT purposes, to the gross sale proceeds plus the relevant proportion of the fall in value. Thus the probate value of share A will be revised from £7,700 to:

$$£7{,}200 + \left(\frac{1{,}750}{55{,}800} \times (7{,}700 - 7{,}200)\right) = £7{,}216$$

and in the case of share B where the sales price exceeds the probate value (i.e. profit on sale) the revised value will be:

$$£600 - \left(\frac{1{,}750}{55{,}800} \times £200\right) = £594$$

(i.e. £600 – £6) = £594

(E) Although excluded from computation of the loss on sale for inheritance tax purposes, incidental costs of sale and deductible from proceeds in calculating CGT. For deaths after 5 April 2004 see Inland Revenue Statement of Practice SP2/04.

Unincorporated business

[53.32] See 6.4 BUSINESS PROPERTY.

Demutualisations

Valuing the estate

[53.33] The valuation of the deceased's share, or other interest, in a building society or mutual insurance company is not directly concerned with the actual amount of cash received or the value of free shares received by their successors on or after vesting day. Rather, it is a matter of determining the value by reference only to the information that was available at the date of death. This is generally the information provided for the qualifying members in the Transfer Document or Prospectus.

Each Transfer Document or Prospectus provides:

- an anticipated price per share of the free share, or
- details of the proposed cash bonuses,

calculated by reference to the amounts involved.

These anticipated prices, or proposed amounts, are the starting point for determining the gross value of the qualifying member's share or other interest at the relevant time. A discount is then applied to reflect any uncertainty or delay.

For example, if a qualifying member died after the issue of the Transfer Document but before the extraordinary general meeting at which the demutualisation was formally approved by the voting members, the discount would be greater than if the member died after the extraordinary general meeting but before vesting day.

Example

An individual who is a UK policy holder of AMP, the Australian insurer which undertook demutualisation, died on 1 May 1998 a few days before the prospectus was published on 6 May 1998. The estimated share price was between A$12.50–16.00 per share when trading commenced on the Australian and New Zealand stock exchange on 15 June 1998.

As the individual died before the issue of the transfer document/prospectus, the value of the individual's qualifying member's share has increased but a discount is given of approximately 25–30%. However, if the individual had died after the prospectus issue then the discount may have been between 0–10%. The personal representative's valuation of the right to the shares owned by the deceased at the date of death can be valued as:

Value of shares at vesting day, say,	£3,700
Less: 25%, discount prior to vesting	(925)
Executor's value for estate	£2,775

If the shares are disposed of within twelve months of the death for, say, £4,200 then where this comprises part of the aggregate sale values under *IHTA 1984, s 179(1)* the increase of £1,425 (i.e. £4,200 – £2,775) will serve to reduce any overall loss on sale.

Note to the example

(A) In view of the effective loss of 'discount' where shares are sold within twelve months of the death and comprise part of a claim under *IHTA 1984, s 179* it is perhaps better to defer the disposal until a later date.

54

Woodlands

Cross-references. See also **4** AGRICULTURAL PROPERTY; **6** BUSINESS PROPERTY.

Simon's Taxes. See **I7.302, I7.4.**

Other Sources. Foster, Parts G3 and 4; HMRC Customer Guide to Inheritance Tax; HMRC IHT manual IHTM24000.

Introduction to woodlands

[54.1] For IHT purposes, three main reliefs can be available in respect of woodlands:

(a) woodlands managed as a commercial business with a view to realisation of profits, and not held wholly or mainly as an investment, will qualify for 100% business property relief so long as the other requirements for that relief are satisfied (e.g. the two-year period of ownership requirement): see **6** BUSINESS PROPERTY. Note that this relief can apply to woodlands outside the UK.

(b) woodlands occupied with agricultural land or pasture, and the occupation being ancillary to that of the agricultural land or pasture, will qualify for agricultural property relief: see **4** AGRICULTURAL PROPERTY;

(c) **On a person's death**, an election may be made within two years (or such longer time as the Board allow *IHTA 1984, s 125(3)*) for the value of any trees or underwood on any land in the UK or, from 22 April 2009 to 5 April 2024 in another state which is an EEA state, and not being AGRICULTURAL PROPERTY (**4**) for the purposes of agricultural property relief, to be left out of account in determining the value transferred on death. The value of the land cannot be excluded so the claim relates only to the value of the trees. The claim must be made by a person liable for the whole or part of the tax. This is a deferral relief and the tax becomes chargeable on a later disposal. [*IHTA 1984, ss 125, 125(1A)* as inserted by *FA 2009, s 122(5)(6); Interpretation Act 1978, Sch 1*].

Deferral relief

[54.2] For the purposes of deferral relief, woodlands are considered to be any land on which trees or underwood are growing. Woodlands may, therefore, include wooded parkland, strips of land with trees lining roads, tree belts, etc. (VOA IHT Manual 10.3). The District Valuer (DV) will advise HMRC if woodlands should be excluded from deferral relief because they are agricultural property as defined in *IHTA 1984, s 115(2)*. Land dedicated under the *Forestry Act 1967* is unlikely to be agricultural property. In woodlands deferral relief cases, the DV should value the underlying land leaving out the trees or underwood growing on it. (VOA IHT manual, section 10, paras 10.7 and 10.9).

Pro-forma woodlands election

HMRC Inheritance Tax

IHT reference

Date of death:. . . . .

<u>A B deceased</u>

1. Attached to this election are:

   1.1 Schedule 1 being details of the land on which the trees and underwood are growing and to which the election is to apply.

   1.2 Ordnance survey map of the area of trees and underwood to which the election is to apply with relevant areas boundaried in red. [*Note 1:10,000 or in Scotland 1:50,000 will normally suffice*].

   1.3 Copy of the deceased's will pertaining to the land to which this election is to apply.

2. The deceased AB was:

   2.1 beneficially entitled to the land on which the trees and underwood grow [for the five years immediately preceding AB's death]* [by entitlement otherwise than for money or money's worth].*

* *Delete as appropriate*

3. We, being the parties making the election, elect pursuant to section 125, Inheritance Tax Act 1984 shall apply to such woods and underwood referred to at 1 above.

Signed:. . . . . Capacity. . . . .

Address:. . . . .

Date:. . . . .

Signed:. . . . . Capacity. . . . .

Address:. . . . .

Date:. . . . .

Schedule 1

[*Full description including the precise location of the land to be included at Schedule 1*].

Notes to the election

(A) Normally it will be appropriate to pay the tax at the date of death where the trees are very young and in such a case the election would not be appropriate.

(B) This relief is also available where the deceased had an interest in possession in woodlands under a trust: *IHTA 1984, ss 5(1), 49(1), 125(1).*

Condition for election

[54.3] A condition for the election is that the deceased either was beneficially entitled to the land for the five years immediately preceding his death or became beneficially entitled to it otherwise than for money or money's worth. [*IHTA 1984, s 125(1)*]. A life tenant in possession under a settlement is treated as beneficially entitled but not a shareholder in a company owning woodlands. If a retrospective claim for relief is being made in respect of woodlands relief under the new EEA arrangements then a claim under *IHTA 1984, s 125* is to be made in writing quoting the Inheritance Tax file reference, name and date of death of the deceased and headed 'Retrospective claim for APR and/or WR for land in EEA'.

Tax charge

[54.4] Tax becomes chargeable on any disposal (other than between spouses or civil partners) of the trees or underwood (whether with or apart from the land on which they grow) before another death (which would be either another chargeable occasion itself or another occasion for an election). The liability for the tax is on the person who is entitled to the proceeds of sale or would be so entitled if the disposal were a sale. Where tax has been charged on a disposal under these provisions, it cannot be charged in relation to the same death on a further disposal of the same trees or underwood. [*IHTA 1984, ss 126, 208; The Tax and Civil Partnership Regulations 2005, SI 2005/3229, Reg 24*]. An account (Form C–5 (Timber)) must be delivered by the person liable within six months of the end of the month in which the disposal occurs. [*IHTA 1984, s 216(7)*]. Where the disposal is a chargeable transfer (e.g. by gift into a discretionary trust), tax will become chargeable both in respect of the previous death and on the later transfer, in which case the later value transferred is that value less the tax charged by reference to the previous death under **54.5** below. [*IHTA 1984, s 129*]. The deferred tax is payable in one sum but the tax on the lifetime transfer may be paid by instalments over ten years at the option of either the transferor or the transferee (see **32.5** PAYMENT OF TAX) and payment by instalments does not cease if the timber is later sold.

Woodlands in the European Economic Area (EEA)

The *Finance Act 2009* introduced legislation to extend inheritance tax deferral relief for woodlands with effect from 22 April 2009 to woodlands in the European Economic Area (EEA) and there were certain retrospective provisions allowing repayment claims for tax paid after 21 April 2003. This extended relief is, however, withdrawn with effect from 6 April 2024, so that deferral relief is once again be restricted to woodlands in the UK. [*IHTA 1984, ss 125, 229; FA 2009, s 122(6)(7), Sch 51 para 13, Sch 53 paras 7(2); F(No 2)A 2024, s 11*].

IHT 100 completion

A new account on Form IHT 100 (old forms IHT 100 and IHT 101 have been replaced as from April 2003) is required when there is a chargeable event described below:

- Assets ceasing to benefit from conditional exemption and being subject to a recapture charge (supplementary event form IHT 100f) e.g. sale of trees, timber or underwood.

Form D36, part of IHT 100, should be filled in to give details of land, buildings, timber and underwood included in the chargeable event. In box F4 of IHT 100 the value of any timber and woodland included in the chargeable event valued at the date of the chargeable event should be inserted which is not part of a farm. Most farms have coppices, small woods and belts of trees that shelter the land and these are to be valued separately and included in a separate box (F2) on the IHT 100. See LIFETIME TRANSFERS (29).

Tax rate

[54.5] The tax rate is what would have applied to the value of the deceased's (i.e. the last person to die) estate if the trees or underwood had been included at the highest part and is charged:

(a) if the disposal is a sale for full consideration in money or money's worth, on the 'net proceeds' of the sale; and
(b) in any other case, on the 'net value', at the time of disposal, of the trees or underwood.

The availability of the 36% rate of tax where 10% or more of the relevant component of the estate was given to charity is disregarded for this purpose. For deaths on or after 6 April 2012 therefore the tax rate must be calculated assuming that the chargeable estate was liable at 40%, even though in fact all or part may have been liable at 36%.

Definitions

'*Net proceeds*' or '*net value*' mean the proceeds of sale or value after any deduction of any of the following expenses so far as not allowed for income tax.

(a) if the disposal is a sale for full consideration in money or money's worth, on the '*net proceeds*' of the sale; and
(b) in any other case, on the '*net value*', at the time of disposal, of the trees or underwood.

'*Net proceeds*' or '*net value*' mean the proceeds of sale or value after any deduction of any of the following expenses so far as not allowed for income tax.

(i) The expenses incurred in disposing of the trees or underwood.
(ii) The expenses incurred in replanting, within three years of a disposal (or such longer time as the Board may allow), to replace the trees or underwood disposed of.
(iii) The expenses incurred in replanting to replace trees or underwood previously disposed of, so far as not allowed on the previous disposal.

Where, if the value of the trees or underwood had not been left out of account in determining the value of the deceased person's estate, BUSINESS PROPERTY (**6**) relief would have been available at a rate less than the current 100% rate the amount on which tax is charged is reduced by 50%. This relief relates to cases where the death was before 10 March 1992; from that date the rate of business property relief was increased to 100% and thus in such cases deferral relief would not be appropriate.

Deferred tax which becomes chargeable after tax has been reduced by the substitution of a new table of rates will be calculated on the new scale, even though the death occurred when the old scale applied. [*IHTA 1984, ss 9, 127, 128, 130, Sch 2 para 4; FA 1986, Sch 19 para 45*]. See also **54.7**(b) below.

'Net value'

In arriving at the 'net value' the DV's valuation should ignore any allowable expenses as well as any obligations to replant. The value will be the higher of (i) the value of the trees for sale for felling including any underwood, or (ii) the value of the standing trees or underwood as part of the transferor's estate. The DV's valuation will always exclude the value of the underlying land. The valuation on basis (ii) will probably only apply when immature woodland or growing timber of high amenity value is involved. (VOA IHT manual, section 10, para 10.16).

Example 1

A died owning woodlands valued at £275,000 being land valued at £200,000 and trees growing on the land valued at £75,000. The woodlands passed to his son D. The marginal IHT rate applicable was 40% but the executors elected to exclude the value of the trees from the taxable estate on A's death. D died six years later leaving the woodlands to trustees for his grandchildren. They were then valued at £400,000 being land at £250,000 and trees at £150,000. The rate of tax which would have applied to the value of trees on D's death was 40%, but once again the executors elected to exclude the value of the trees from his estate.

The trustees sold the woodlands for £500,000, including trees valued at £180,000, four years later.

The IHT on the trees is payable when the trees are sold. The trustees of the settlement pay IHT at what would have been the marginal rate on D's death had the tax scale at the time of the sale applied on D's death, e.g. 40% on £180,000 (the proceeds of sale) = £72,000.

Note to the example

(A) If D had gifted the land (with the trees) just before his death, the IHT would have become payable on the trees at what would have been the marginal rate on A's death had the scale at the time of the gift applied on A's death, on the value of the trees at the date of the gift. IHT would also have been payable on D's lifetime transfer (this being a PET but becoming chargeable by virtue of D's death shortly afterwards) but the value transferred by this transfer would have been reduced by the deferred IHT charge. See Example 2 below.

Example 2

B died in 1984 leaving woodlands, including growing timber valued at £100,000, to his daughter C. The executors elected to exclude the value of the timber from the taxable estate on B's death. B had made prior transfers of £50,000 and his taxable estate (excluding the growing timber) was valued at £210,000.

On 1 February 2005 C gave the woodlands to her nephew N, when the land was valued at £355,000 and the growing timber at £125,000. N agreed to pay any IHT on the gift. C died in January 2011, and had made no prior transfers other than to use her annual exemptions each year.

IHT on B's death

No IHT is payable on the growing timber until C's disposal when tax is charged on the net value at that time. The rates are those which would have applied (using the death scale applying on 1 February 2005) if that value had formed the highest part of B's estate on death. The tax was payable on 1 September 2004.

Deferred IHT payable £125,000 at 40% =	£50,000

IHT on C's lifetime transfer

IHT is payable on C's gift to N as C died within seven years of the gift. The deferred IHT is deducted from the value transferred.

			£
Value of land and timber			480,000
Deduct deferred IHT			50,000
Chargeable transfer			£430,000
IHT at death rates			
On first	£325,000		Nil
On next	£105,000	at 40%	42,000
	£430,000		£42,000
IHT payable at 40% of full rates (death between 5 and 6 years after gift)			£16,800
Total IHT payable			
Deferred IHT			50,000
Lifetime transfer			16,800
			£66,800

Note to the example

(A) In the above calculations it has been assumed that the woodlands were not run as a business either at the time of B's death or at the time of C's gift. If B had been running the woodlands as a business, such that business property relief would have been available on his death, the amount chargeable on C's disposal would have been reduced by 50%, i.e. to £62,500, on which IHT payable would have been £25,000. [*IHTA 1984, s 127(2)*]. If C ran the woodlands as a business (whether or not B had done so), business property relief would be available on her gift to N provided N also ran the woodlands as a business, but would be given after the credit for the deferred IHT. (With business property relief now usually at 100%, the order of set-off is not so relevant.)

	£
Value of land and timber	480,000
Deduct deferred IHT say	25,000
	455,000
Deduct business property relief at, say, 100%	455,000
Chargeable transfer	Nil

Liabilities to acquire woodlands

[54.6] For transfers of value made or treated as made on or after 17 July 2013, it is no longer possible to reduce the value of an asset for IHT purposes by securing a loan on it where the loan is used to acquire or maintain (directly or indirectly) another asset which qualifies for certain IHT reliefs, including woodlands where the value of them is to be left out of account on a person's death (see **54.1**(c)). Instead the loan will be primarily deductible from the value of the woodlands. These rules have equal effect for charges on settlements holding relevant property within *IHTA 1984, s 58*, and apply to loans incurred on or after 6 April 2013. See further commentary at **53.19**.

Estate duty

[54.7] *F(1909–10)A 1910, s 61(5)* is an estate duty provision and still applicable for deaths before 13 March 1975. It provides for the value of timber etc. to be left out of account on the deceased's death but with estate duty charged at the estate rate on subsequent net moneys (less outgoings since death) received from time to time in respect of cut or felled timber etc. sales in the period from the death until the underlying land, on the death of some other person, again became or would, but for the provision itself, have become liable to estate duty. However, if at any time the timber etc. is sold, with or without the underlying land, the amount of estate duty on its principal value which, apart from the provision itself, would have been payable on the death of the deceased, after deducting any amount of estate duty already paid as above on previous timber sales since death, becomes payable. For the purposes of inheritance tax it is provided that where estate duty is payable under *F(1909–10)A 1910, s 61(5)* on the net moneys received from the sale of timber etc. when felled or cut during the period referred to in that provision, that period ends immediately after the first transfer of value made in which the value transferred is, or is determined by reference to, the value of the land concerned, other than an exempt transfer between spouses or civil partners. [*FA 1975, s 49(4)*].

Where a transfer of value is made the value of which is partly attributable to woodlands subject to a deferred estate duty charge in respect of timber and that transfer brings to an end the period during which estate duty is payable on the net sale proceeds of the timber, that transfer is not a potentially exempt transfer (35) for inheritance tax purposes to the extent that the value transferred is attributable to those woodlands. [*FA 1986, Sch 19 para 46* as amended] Up to 5 April 2017, this result was achieved by virtue of HMRC Concession F15, but the legislation is amended by *SI 2017/495* with effect from 6 April 2017.

Other reliefs for woodlands

[54.8] Other reliefs are as follows:

(a) AGRICULTURAL PROPERTY (4) relief applies instead of the above if the woodlands are occupied and the occupation is ancillary to that of agricultural land or pasture. [*IHTA 1984, ss 115(2), 125(1)*].

(b) NATIONAL HERITAGE (30) property. Conditional exemption on a transfer may apply in certain circumstances.

(c) EXEMPT TRANSFERS **21.9** and the transferable nil rate band. In cases where there has been a deferred charge under *IHTA 1984, s 126* before the death of the surviving spouse and there is unused nil rate band available in the estate of the surviving spouse, the charge under *s 126* must be taken into account in calculating the unused nil rate band of the surviving spouse or civil partner. See Example 3 below. Note that the deferred charge is taken into account even though the woodlands may not have been inherited by the spouse. If there is more than one deferred charge before the transfer of the nil rate band to the spouse or civil partner, these deferred charges similarly reduce the nil rate band that may be claimed. See Example 4. Further, if there is a deferred charge after the nil rate band of the deceased has been claimed by the surviving spouse's personal representatives, then any available nil rate band will be reduced by the amount claimed by the survivor's personal representatives. See Example 3 below. [*IHTA 1984, ss 8A, 8C* as inserted by *FA 2008, Sch 4 para 2*]. See HMRC Inheritance Tax manual IHTM04121, IHTM43044–IHTM43046.

Example 3

Chargeable event during lifetime of 'survivor' spouse or civil partner

C, who died in August 2002, had made previous lifetime chargeable transfers of £62,500, leaves his long-term ownership of woodlands to his brother, B. An election under *IHTA 1984, s 125* was made. His wife, D, received his remaining assets. In October 2008, the woodland trees are sold by B for £176,000 with deductible expenses of regarding sale and replanting £20,000. D dies in February 2011.

The claim for C's unused nil rate band by D's personal representatives must be calculated after taking into account the proportion of the current transferable nil rate band on D's death, i.e. £325,000 that has been reduced by the chargeable event under *IHTA 1984, s 126* by reference to the proportion of the nil rate band used at the time of the chargeable event, i.e. £312,000. C had used ¼ of his nil rate band on his death and therefore ¾ was unused (i.e. (£250,000 – £62,500) ÷

£250,000 × 100%) so at the time of the chargeable event when B sold the woodlands in October 2008 the nil rate band at that time is £312,000. As the amount on which tax is chargeable is £156,000 (see below) this is the amount referred to as TA below and NRBME is the nil rate band at the date of sale of the woodlands (i.e. (£156,000 ÷ £312,000 × 100% = $^1/_2$). Therefore, the remaining available nil rate band on C's death, i.e. $^3/_4 - ^1/_2 = ^1/_4$, i.e. 25%. At the time of D's death the nil rate band has increased to £325,000 and the remaining portion of C's nil rate band available to D's personal representatives at that time is £81,250 (i.e. £325,000 × $^1/_4$). [*IHTA 1984, s 8C(2)* as inserted by *FA 2008, Sch 4 para 2*].

Notes to the example

(A) The transferable amount of the unused nil rate band of the predeceased C to D in this example is calculated by applying the unused nil rate band under *IHTA 1984, s 8A(2)(4)* as follows:

$$\text{Percentage} = \left(\frac{\text{E}}{\text{NRBMD}} - \frac{\text{TA}}{\text{NRBME}}\right) \times 100$$

where

M = maximum amount that could be transferred on the predeceased person's death where it is chargeable at the nil rate band at that time, i.e. £250,000;

VT = value actually transferred by the chargeable transfer or nil if applicable, i.e £62,500;

E = the amount by which M above is greater than VT above, i.e. £187,500;

NRBMD = the nil rate band maximum applying at the time of the deceased spouse's or civil partner's death, i.e. £250,000;

TA = the amount on which tax is charged, i.e. £156,000;

NRBME = the nil rate band maximum at the time of the event giving rise to the deferred charge, i.e. £312,000.

(B) The expenses of sale and replanting of the trees would be allowed as a deduction. C's estate at death will be increased to take account of the chargeable event to determine the rates applicable to any later chargeable event as in Example 4 below. [*IHTA 1984, s 126; FA 1985, Sch 26 para 5*].

		£
Cumulative total of previous chargeable transfers of relevant person, i.e. VT above		62,500
Sale proceeds of woodlands	176,000	
Deduct allowable costs	(20,000)	
Balance, i.e. TA above		156,000
Revised cumulative total for relevant person, i.e. C above		£218,500

Example 4

Two or more chargeable events during lifetime of surviving spouse or civil partner

C, who died in August 2002, had made previous chargeable transfers of £125,000, left by will two separate woodlands to his brother, B. An election under *IHTA 1984, s 125* was made. His wife, D, received his remaining assets. In October 2008 and December 2008, the two areas of woodlands are sold for £63,415 each with expenses of sale of £11,415. D dies in February 2011.

The claim for the unused nil rate band by D's personal representatives must be calculated after taking into account the proportion of the current transferable nil rate band on D's death, i.e. £325,000 that has been reduced by the two chargeable events under *IHTA 1984, s 126* by reference to the proportion of the nil rate band used at the time of the chargeable events, i.e. £312,000. C had used ½ of his nil rate band on his death (i.e. (£250,000 – £125,000) ÷ £250,000 × 100%) so at the time of the chargeable events in October and December 2008 one half of the nil rate band at that time is £312,000 which is available. As the amount on which tax is chargeable after expenses is £52,000 on each chargeable event (see below) these are the amounts referred to as TA below and NRBME is the nil rate band at the date of sale of each of the woodlands (£52,000 ÷ £312,000 × 100% = 1/6). Therefore, the remaining available nil rate band on C's death is 1/2 – (1/6 + 1/6) = 16.66667%. At the time of D's death, when the nil rate band has increased to £325,000, the portion of C's nil rate band available to the personal representatives at that time is therefore £54,167 (i.e. £325,000 × 16.66667%), which together with her unused nil rate band of up to £325,000 makes a total of £379,167. [*IHTA 1984, s 8C(2)(3)* as inserted by *FA 2008, Sch 4 para 2*].

Note to the example

(A) The transferable amount of the unused nil rate band of the predeceased C to D in this example is calculated by applying the unused nil rate band under *IHTA 1984, s 8A(2)(4)* as follows:

$$\text{Percentage} = \frac{\text{E}}{\text{NRBMD}} - \left(\frac{\text{TA}}{\text{NRBME}} + \frac{\text{TA}}{\text{NRBME}}\right) \times 100$$

where:

M = maximum amount that could be transferred on the predeceased person's death where it is chargeable at the nil rate band at that time, i.e. £250,000;

VT = value actually transferred by the chargeable transfer or nil if applicable, i.e. £125,000;

E = the amount by which M above is greater than VT above, i.e. £125,000;

NRBMD = the nil rate band maximum applying at the time of the deceased spouse's or civil partner's death, i.e. £250,000;

TA = the amount on which tax is charged i.e. the sales in October and December 2008, i.e. £104,000;

NRBME = the nil rate band maximum at the time of the event giving rise to the deferred charge, i.e. £312,000, but if the second sale had been in December 2010 this figure would have been £325,000 not £312,000.

		£
Cumulative total of previous chargeable transfers of relevant person C		125,000
Net sale proceeds of woodlands in October 2008	63,415	
Deduct allowable expenses	(11,415)	52,000

Sale proceeds of conditionally exempt property December 2008	63,415	
Deduct allowable expenses	(11,415)	
Chargeable transfer		52,000
Revised cumulative total for relevant person of C		£229,000

Example 5

Chargeable event after the death of the surviving spouse or civil partner

C, who died in August 2002, had made previous chargeable transfers of £125,000, left by will woodlands to his brother, B. An election under *IHTA 1984, s 125* was made. His wife, D, received his remaining assets. D dies in February 2011 with an estate of £350,000. In October 2012, the woodland is sold by B for £300,000 and allowable expenses of £54,000 are paid.

The claim for the unused nil rate band by D's personal representatives on form IHT 402 (previously IHT 216) has already been made by the time the woodland is sold and becomes chargeable. C had used half of his 50% nil rate band on his death (i.e. (£250,000 – £125,000) ÷ £250,000 × 100%) so D's personal representatives are entitled to claim ½ × £325,000, i.e. the rate applicable at D's death. D's nil rate band of £325,000 added to the predeceased C's available nil rate band of £162,500 (i.e. (£250,000 – £125,000) = ½ × £325,000) makes a total of £487,500 of which £350,000 is used to cover the estate of D. Of this amount £25,000 is part of C's original nil rate band. In October 2012 the woodland is sold for £300,000, less expenses of £52,000, making net proceeds of £248,000 chargeable. Therefore the unused proportion of C's nil rate band of £200,000 (i.e. (£125,000 + £25,000) – £350,000), which is available to set against the net sale proceeds of the woodland to compute the tax payable by B. [*IHTA 1984, s 8C(4)(5)* as inserted by *FA 2008, Sch 4 para 2*].

Notes to the example

(A) In a case of breach of undertaking or death the person who is liable to pay the tax is the person who, if the property were sold at that time, would be entitled to receive (whether for his benefit or not) the proceeds of sale or any income arising from them, i.e. B. [*IHTA 1984, s 208*]. The tax is due six months after the end of the month in which the disposal took place. [*IHTA 1984, s 226(4)*].

(B) The personal nil rate band used is the one that is in force at the date of the breach which is October 2012, i.e. £325,000. This figure is 'appropriately reduced' by the amount of C's unused nil rate band used on the death of the survivor, D, i.e. £25,000. From this revised figure is deducted the chargeable transfers of the deceased (C) added to the net sale proceeds of the woodland and IHT charged accordingly. See below.

		£
Cumulative total of previous chargeable transfers of relevant person C		125,000
Value of woodland at date of breach in October 2012	300,000	
Deduct allowable expenses	(52,000)	
Chargeable transfer		248,000

Revised cumulative total for relevant person <u>£37[illegible],000</u>

Inheritance tax payable after deducting the available nil rate band (by reference to death rates in February 2011), i.e. £325,000 – £150,000 (£125,000 + £25,000) = £175,000 – £248,000

£73,000 at 40% = <u>£29,200 payable by B</u>

55

Tax Cases

[55.1] This chapter includes summaries of IHT/CTT cases and also a number of estate duty cases and other decisions with relevance to IHT. Cases relating to other taxes, but which have general relevance to all areas of taxation are not included. Some of the legislation interpreted in the earlier cases has been amended, repealed or replaced. Nevertheless, the cumulative nature of IHT means that knowledge of the law in earlier years will continue to be necessary for some time to come. Where the CIR (or, in Scotland, the Lord Advocate) are a party, the case is listed under the name of the other party only. Judicial review cases are listed under the name of the applicant and the person who is the subject of the review but again excluding the CIR etc.

Legislative references marked with an asterisk (*) are to legislation which has replaced, or is substantially similar to, that involved in the case summarised.

Allen v HMRC

Land let on conacre arrangement; decision in McCall case considered but not followed.

The taxpayer let land in Northern Ireland on a conacre licence agreement. Under this agreement, his obligations were minimal but included supply of water, maintenance of hedges and control of poisonous weeds, and maintenance of field drains. He also controlled the fertiliser to be used and occasionally supplied it to the tenant. It was held that he was occupying the land for the purposes of agriculture. [2016] UKFTT 342 (TC).

Arkwright (Williams' Personal Representatives) v CIR

Related property under IHTA 1984, s 161.

A married couple owned a freehold property as tenants in common. The husband (W) died in 2001. By his will, he gave his widow a life interest in his 50% share of the property, with the remainder to his daughters. In January 2002 his widow and the daughters executed a deed of variation so that W's interest in the property vested in his daughters. The Inland Revenue issued a notice of determination that IHT was due on £275,000 (being 50% of the agreed open market value of the property). W's daughters (as his personal representatives) appealed to the Special Commissioners, contending that W's interest should be valued at less than 50% of the vacant possession value, because his widow had the right to occupy the property and not have it sold without her consent. The Commissioner accepted this contention and allowed the appeal in principle, holding that the value of W's interest should be determined in accordance with *IHTA 1984, s 161(3)*, and making various observations concerning the effect of *s 161(3)*. The Inland Revenue appealed to the Ch D, contending that the Commissioner had exceeded her jurisdiction and that the case should be referred to the Lands Tribunal. The Ch D accepted this contention. Gloster J held that 'the Special Commissioner was clearly entitled to conclude that, because *s 161(4)* did not apply, the value of the deceased's interest in the property was not inevitably a mathematical one-half of the vacant possession value'. However, she had exceeded her authority in purporting to determine 'that, as matter of fact, the value of his interest was indeed less than a mathematical one-half of the vacant possession value. That was properly an issue that should have been referred to the Lands Tribunal for determination by it.' Ch D [2004] STC 1323.

Arnander, Lloyd & Villiers (McKenna's Executors) v HMRC

Farmhouse and adjoining buildings – whether qualified for agricultural property relief – not main dwelling from which the agricultural operations over the land were conducted and managed.

A married couple had owned a small country estate comprising a large house with six acres of gardens and some domestic outbuildings, and 187 acres of land, most of which was farmland. They both died in 2003. HMRC issued notices of determination charging IHT on the house (while accepting that 110 acres of land and a farm outbuilding qualified for agricultural property relief). The executors appealed, contending that the house was a farmhouse which also qualified for agricultural property relief, as did 11 more outbuildings on the estate. The Special Commissioner reviewed the evidence in detail and held that three of the outbuildings qualified for relief but that the main house and eight of the outbuildings did not. The Commissioner observed that the farming activities were carried on by contractors who were managed by a land agent in a nearby town. The house which the couple lived in was not 'the main dwelling from which the agricultural operations over the land were conducted and managed'. [2006] STC SCD 800 Sp C 565.

Ashcroft v Barnsdale & Others

Rectification of deeds

A married woman's will left £10,000 plus some farmland to her husband, with the residue passing to her children. The executors of the will varied it by a deed of family arrangement giving £410,000 to the children and treating the husband as the residuary beneficiary. This deed had the unintended effect that the husband (as residuary beneficiary) became liable to additional inheritance tax. He applied to the Ch D for a deed of rectification. Judge Hodge granted the application, holding that there was an established distinction 'between a mistake as to the meaning or effect of a document (which may be amenable to rectification) and one as to its consequences (which is not)' and that 'the fact that the parties intended to use a particular form of words in the mistaken belief that it was achieving their common intention does not prevent the court from giving effect to their true intention'. On the evidence, he held that 'this is not a case where the parties merely proceeded under a misapprehension as to the true fiscal consequences of the deed of variation as actually drafted. Rather, the claimant has demonstrated a specific common intention as to how the parties' fiscal objectives were to be achieved; and he has established that, owing to a mistake in the way in which that intention was expressed in the deed of variation, effect has not been given to that intention. Underlying the parties' adoption of the deed of variation was the common intention, unarticulated and unexpressed, that the claimant should receive his entitlement under his late wife's will, as varied, free from all liability for inheritance tax, thereby replicating the position under the will as executed. There was never any intention to vary the burden of, or the incidence of the parties' liability for, inheritance tax. To the extent that the deed of variation had this effect, then it was executed under a relevant mistake, because it failed to give effect to the parties' true intention.' [2010] STC 2544.

Atkinson & Smith (WM Atkinson's Executors) v HMRC

IHTA 1984, s 117 – whether property occupied for agricultural purposes.

In 1957 a farmer (W) purchased some farmland. Initially he farmed it himself, but in 1980 he let it to a family farming partnership of which he was a member. W lived in a bungalow on the farm from 1966 until 2002, when he became ill. After leaving hospital he moved to a care home where he died in 2006. His bungalow remained unoccupied during his illness, although he occasionally visited it. His executors claimed that the bungalow qualified for agricultural property relief. HMRC rejected the claim on the basis that the bungalow had not been occupied for the purposes of agriculture throughout the seven years ending with W's death. The executors appealed. The First-tier Tribunal allowed their appeal, on the basis that 'occupation by the partnership continued until (W's) death, and it was occupation for the purposes of agriculture in the relevant sense because the bungalow was still used to accommodate the diminishing needs of the senior partner. However, this decision was reversed on appeal by HMRC. The Upper Tribunal held that because there was little or no actual use of the property up to the date of death it was not possible to regard the property as continuing to be occupied for the purposes of agriculture. No relief was therefore available. [2010] UKFTT 108 (TC), TC00420 (Upper Tax Tribunal decision [2012] STC 289).

A-G v Boden and Another

Valuation – partnership goodwill – whether transfer for full consideration.

A father in partnership with his two sons was not required to devote as much time to the business as his sons. On his death his share accrued equally to his sons, subject to their paying his estate the value of his share exclusive of any amount of goodwill. The obligations of the sons under the partnership deed were held to constitute full consideration for the deceased's share of the goodwill. KB 1911, [1912] 1 KB 539; 105 LT 247.

A-G v Ralli

Valuation – partnership reserves – whether transfer for full consideration.

The deceased was a partner in a partnership of bankers which held large reserves for the partnership business. The partnership deed provided that each partner's share in the reserves accrued on his death or retirement to the remaining partners. The court held that ED was not payable on the deceased's interest in the reserves. There was no gift but merely an ordinary commercial transaction for full consideration. KB 1936, 15 ATC 523.

Bailhache Labesse Trustees Ltd & Others v HMRC

Charitable donation – whether IHTA 1984, s 23 applicable.

In 1985 an individual (K), who was domiciled in the UK, established a Jersey settlement, of which he was the life tenant. He died in 2001. Within twelve months of his death, the trustees of the settlement appointed 25% of the trust property to each of two charities. They appealed against a determination charging IHT on K's death, contending that the appointments should be treated as exempt transfers under *IHTA 1984, s 23* with effect from the date of K's death. The Special Commissioner rejected this contention and dismissed the appeals, holding that the settled property had to be treated as passing from K to the trustees on his death. The subsequent appointment to the charities could not 'turn what would otherwise be chargeable transfers of value into exempt transfers'. [2008] STC SCD 869 Sp C 688.

Banks v HMRC

Donations to the UK Independence Party – whether exemption for gifts to political party should be available despite the conditions in IHTA 1894, s 24 not being satisfied.

The taxpayer made gifts to the UK Independence Party which were assessed as chargeable transfers. On appeal, the taxpayer challenged the restrictions in *IHTA 1894, s 24* (gifts to political parties) on the grounds that they were in breach of the European Convention of Human Rights, amounting to discrimination by reference to political views, and also they were in breach of the UK's obligations under the Treaty on European Union. The challenge under the latter failed on the basis that the Treaty does not give any directly enforceable rights. As regards the possible breach of human rights, the Tribunal accepted that the provisions for exemption are inappropriately drafted, in that they required either two elected members of Parliament or one elected member and not less than 150,000 votes for the party at the last election; and s 24 failed to give proper recognition in the present case to the level of support for UKIP. Thus, the lack of exemption for gifts to UKIP could not be objectively justified. However, the appeal failed because the Tribunal could not rewrite the statutory provision and was not able to make a declaration of incompatibility with the Human Rights legislation. [2018] UKFTT 617 (TC).

Barclays Bank Trust Co Ltd v IRC

Business property relief regarding whether cash held by a company an excepted asset. IHTA 1984, s 112.

A married woman (W) died in 1990. Her estate included a 50% shareholding in a family company, which held cash of about £450,000 at her death. The Revenue issued a notice of determination, accepting in principle that the shares qualified for business property relief, but computed on the basis that the company only required cash of some £150,000 for the purposes of its business, and that the balance of £300,000 was an 'excepted asset', within *IHTA, s 112(2)*, and did not qualify for relief. W's executor appealed, contending that the company had held the cash 'as a contingency measure' in case 'an appropriate business opportunity should arise', so that the cash was 'required . . . for future use', within *IHTA, s 112(2)(b)*. The Special Commissioner rejected this contention and dismissed the appeal, holding on the evidence that the £300,000 was not 'required'. The Commissioner held that, for the purposes of *s 112*, 'required' did not include 'the possibility that the money might be required should an opportunity arise to make use of the money in two, three or seven years' time . . .
The word "required" implies some imperative that the money will fall to be used upon a given project or for some palpable business purpose'. [1998] STC SCD 125 Sp C 22.

Barclays Wealth Trustees (Jersey) Ltd and Dreelan v HMRC

Foreign assets transferred from excluded property trust to another trust made when settlor was deemed – domiciled in UK and later transferred back to first trust – whether the assets continued to be excluded property. IHTA 1984, ss 48(3) and 81.

An individual (D) created a jersey trust in 2001 when he was not domiciled in the UK. In due course the trust came to hold shares in a Jersey company Q. In 2008 D created with his three brothers a second trust but by this time he was deemed domiciled in the UK. The shares Q were appointed across to D's fund in the 2008 settlement and later sold. On 2011, the cash proceeds were then appointed back to the 2001 settlement and held offshore. It was claimed that these funds were excluded property by virtue of *IHTA 1984, s 81* which provides that, for the purposes of the IHT charge on relevant property trusts, assets moving between settlements are to be treated as remaining in the first settlement, unless in the meantime any person becomes beneficially entitled to them. For HMRC, it was argued that the 2011 appointment was a separate disposition or settlement made when the settlor was UK domiciled so that the funds concerned ceased to be excluded property. In the Court of Appeal, it was held that the 2011 appointment was not a new disposition or settlement. Hence, the funds were held under the 2001 settlement created when the settlor was non-domiciled and were excluded property. [2017] STC 2465.

Barrett (Barrett's Personal Representatives) v HMRC

Lands Tribunal decision – 15% discount for joint ownership

An individual (B) was joint owner of a semi-detached house built in the 1930s. He died in 2002. HMRC determined the value of his interest in the property as £144,500. His personal representative (who was the other joint-owner) appealed, contending that the house should be valued at £288,000, and that with a 15% discount for the joint ownership, the value of B's interest should be taken as £122,400. The Lands Tribunal reviewed the evidence in detail and held that the house should be valued at £315,000, so that with a 15% discount for joint ownership, the value of B's interest was £133,875. Lands Tribunal 23 November 2005 unreported.

Beckman v IRC

Relevant business property – IHTA, s 105(1).

A woman (H) and her daughter (B) had carried on business in partnership for many years until H retired in 1993. B then continued the business as sole proprietor. H died in 1997, having retained an interest in the business through her capital account. The Revenue issued a notice of determination charging IHT on the amounts owed by B to H at H's death. B appealed, contending that the amounts in question were 'relevant business property' within *IHTA, s 105(1)*. The Special Commissioner rejected this contention and dismissed the appeal. For the purposes of *IHTA, s 105*, H's interest in the business 'ceased when she retired from the partnership'. Following H's retirement from the business, her rights 'were simply those of a creditor of the business'. [2000] STC SCD 59 Sp C 226.

Benham's Will Trusts re (Lockhart v Harker & Others)

IHTA 1984, s 41 – allocation of exemptions.

A testatrix bequeathed her residuary estate between some charitable beneficiaries and some non-charitable beneficiaries. The executor issued an originating summons seeking the opinion of the court as to whether the non-charitable beneficiaries should receive their shares subject to IHT (as the charitable beneficiaries contended) or whether their shares should be grossed up (as the non-charitable beneficiaries themselves contended). The Ch D upheld the contention of the non-charitable beneficiaries, holding that the plain intention of the executrix was that each beneficiary in the list should receive the same amount, that this was not inconsistent with the provisions of *IHTA 1984, s 41*, and accordingly that the non-charitable beneficiaries should receive grossed-up shares. Ch D 1994, [1995] STC 210.

Bennett & Others v CIR

Gifts to sons – whether exempt from IHT as 'normal expenditure of the transferor' – IHTA 1984, s 21.

Under a will, the shares in a family company were held on trust, with the income from the shares and the residuary estate being paid to the testator's widow for her life and thereafter to the testator's three sons. The testator's widow authorised the trustees to distribute equally between her three sons such of the trust income for each accounting year as was surplus to her financial requirements. In February 1989 the trustees paid £9,300 to each of the sons, and on 5 February 1990 they paid £60,000 to each of the sons. The widow died suddenly on 20 February 1990. The Revenue issued determinations that the payments to the sons were chargeable to IHT. The sons appealed, contending that the gifts were exempt from IHT under *IHTA 1984, s 21(1)* as 'part of the normal expenditure of the transferor'. The QB accepted this contention and allowed the appeals. Lightman J held that ' "normal expenditure" connotes expenditure which at the time it took place accorded with the settled pattern of expenditure adopted by the transferor . . . For an expenditure to be "normal" there is no fixed minimum period during which the expenditure shall have occurred. All that is necessary is that on the totality of evidence the pattern of actual or intended payments shall have been established and that the item in question conforms with that pattern . . . The pattern need not be immutable; it must however be established that the pattern was intended to remain in place for more than a nominal period and indeed for a sufficient period (barring unforeseen circumstances) fairly to be regarded as a regular feature of the transferor's annual expenditure. Thus a "death bed" resolution to make periodic payments "for life" and a payment made in accordance with such a determination will not suffice . . . The fact that the objective behind the expenditure is tax planning, e.g.

to prevent an accumulation of income in the hands of the transferor liable to inheritance tax on his death, is no impediment.' On the evidence, the widow had adopted 'a pattern of expenditure in respect of the surplus, and the payments to the sons were made in accordance with this pattern'. Ch D 1994, [1995] STC 54.

Best (Exor of Buller deceased) v HMRC

Company holding business park – whether business property relief to be allowed – whether a business of mainly holding investments

A company held and managed a business centre comprising approximately 10% offices, and the balance being two thirds warehousing used by retailers or wholesalers and one third light industrial use. In total there were approximately 400 people in or around the Centre on a typical working day. The deceased spent considerable time each week at the Business Centre dealing with the everyday matters that might arise with occupiers. On his death the company employed a full time replacement as a site administrator. Units were occupied under licence agreements not conferring exclusive possession of a unit. Twenty-four hour security was provided along with a receptionist, forklift driver, maintenance person, office facilities, meeting rooms, central telephone switchboard and various other business facilities. Nevertheless it was held that the investment activity of letting the units was the predominant activity and the company was therefore mainly an investment company. The claim to business property relief on the shares was therefore refused. [2014] UKFTT 77 (TC).

Brander (Earl of Balfour's Personal Representative) v HMRC

Application of IHTA 1984, s 107 regarding replacement property vis BPR.

In 1968 the Earl of Balfour inherited a liferent interest in a family estate, much of which was used for farming. In November 2002 he entered into a farming partnership with his nephew (who was his heir and intended successor). In June 2003 he died. HMRC issued a ruling that business property relief (BPR) was not due. The Earl's personal representative appealed, contending that the effect of the 'replacement property' provisions in *IHTA 1984, s 107* was that the estate qualified for BPR. The First-tier Tribunal accepted this contention and allowed the appeal, finding that the Earl had 'appeared to manage the estate in a way that was characteristic of his generation' and 'dominated and in practice controlled the running of the estate'. On the evidence, the Earl's interest in the partnership which subsisted immediately before his death replaced the business which he had previously carried on. The tribunal also held that *IHTA 1984, s 105(3)* did not apply, since the management of the estate comprised far more than simply 'the making or holding of investment', and had been 'mainly a trading activity' in which 'the letting side was ancillary to the farming, forestry, woodland and sporting activities. The farming activities, albeit they included agricultural tenancies, occupied by far the greater area of the estate.' Accordingly, the Earl's interest in the partnership was 'relevant business property' which qualified for relief. The Upper Tribunal upheld this decision as one of fact, holding inter alia that the fact that the Earl 'as liferenter did not have a direct interest in the capital realisations of timber from the woodlands' did not prevent the woodlands from constituting 'business property' which qualified for relief. HMRC v AM Brander (Earl of Balfour's Personal Representative), CA 1991, 64 TC 59; FTT [2009] UKFTT 101 (TC), TC00069; FTT [2009] UKFTT 101 (TC), TC00069; UT [2010] UKUT 300 (TC).

Brown's Executors v CIR

IHTA 1984, s 105 – Proceeds of sale of a nightclub held on deposit to be reinvested – allowed.

An individual (B), who owned a 99% shareholding in an unquoted UK company, died in 1986. The company had operated a nightclub, but had sold this in 1985. The proceeds of the sale were held on short-term deposit pending re-investment in similar premises, but no such premises had been acquired at the time of B's death. The executors claimed that B's shareholding qualified for business property relief. The Revenue rejected the claim on the basis that the company's business consisted 'wholly or mainly . . . of making or holding investments'. The executors appealed, contending that until B's death, the company had been actively seeking alternative sites to open a new nightclub, and accordingly should not be treated as an investment-holding company. The Special Commissioner accepted the executors' evidence and allowed the appeal. [1996] STC SCD 277 Sp C 83.

Buccleuch (Duke of) & Another v CIR

Valuation – division of estate into units.

In an ED case the Revenue valued a substantial estate by dividing it into 532 'natural units' for valuation purposes. The trustees appealed, accepting that 46 of the units could be sold individually but contending that the remaining 486 could only be sold within a reasonable time if they were sold as a whole to an investor or speculator, and that the price payable by such a buyer would be some 20% less than the total valuation of the individual units. Their appeal was dismissed by the Land Tribunal, the CA and the HL. The HL held that the open market value was to be determined by reference to the aggregate of the proceeds of sale in a hypothetical market of each individual unit. The fact that it would have taken a long time to sell individual units separately, and that delay would have been caused by the need to avoid flooding the market, were held to be irrelevant. HL 1966, [1967] 1 All ER 129; [1967] 1 AC 506.

Bullock, CIR v

Domicile.

A Canadian married a woman of English parentage in 1946 and came to live in the UK. By 1966, he had given up any idea of returning to Canada during his wife's lifetime. He was held not to have acquired an English domicile of choice for the relevant years (1971–72 and 1972–73). CA 1976, 51 TC 522; [1976] STC 409; [1976] 1 WLR 1178; [1976] 3 All ER 353.

Burden & Burden v United Kingdom

IHTA 1984, s 18 – whether any breach of European Convention on Human Rights.

Two elderly sisters lived together in a jointly-owned house on land which they had inherited from their parents. They lodged a complaint with the ECHR, contending that the provisions of *IHTA 1984, s 18* (as amended by the *Tax and Civil Partnership Regulations 2005*) were a breach of *Article 14* of the *European Convention on Human Rights*, because when one of them died, the survivor would be required to pay IHT on her sister's share of their home, whereas no IHT would have been charged if they had lived together as a registered lesbian civil partnership. The case was referred to the Fourth Section of the ECHR, which rejected their application (by a 4-3 majority), holding that 'the inheritance tax exemption for married and civil partnership couples . . . pursues a legitimate aim, namely to promote stable, committed heterosexual and homosexual relationships by providing the survivor with a measure of financial security after the death of the spouse or partner'. The United Kingdom's decision 'to treat differently for tax purposes those who were married or who were parties to a civil partnership from other persons living together, even in a long-term settled relationship' was within the 'margin of appreciation' available to national authorities. The Grand Chamber upheld this decision (by a 15-2 majority), holding that 'the relationship between siblings is qualitatively of a different nature to that between married couples and homosexual civil partners . . . The fact that the applicants have chosen to live together all their adult lives, as do many married and *Civil Partnership Act* couples, does not alter this essential difference between the two types of relationship.' The absence of 'a legally binding agreement between the applicants' rendered 'their relationship of co-habitation, despite its long duration, fundamentally different to that of a married or civil partnership couple'. Accordingly, 'the applicants, as co-habiting sisters, cannot be compared for the purposes of *Article 14* to a married or *Civil Partnership Act* couple. It follows that there has been no discrimination and, therefore, no violation of *Article 14*'. [2008] ECHR Case 13378/05 unreported.

Burkinyoung (Burkinyoung's Executor) v CIR

Business property relief – deeds of variation.

Martin & Horsfall v CIR was applied in a similar case where the deceased had let four flats on shorthold tenancies. The Commissioner held that the letting of the flats was a business which was 'wholly one of making or holding investments', so that the effect of *IHTA 1984, s 105(3)* was that business property relief was not due. [1995] STC SCD 29 Sp C 3.

Butler and others v HMRC

Business property relief for barn let for weddings

The deceased was partner in a limited liability partnership which conducted various business activities but the main activity was the letting of a barn for wedding events. The Tribunal compared this business to two other common situations: first, the letting of a village hall, normally an investment activity and second, a fully serviced conference venue, which normally be a trading business. In this case, all the required marketing and catering was exclusively undertaken by a third-party catering business so that the LLP's involvement with booked events was principally meetings with customers prior to the event to help plan the event; the provision of an event pack of checklists and summaries for customers; use the venue and outside garden suitably decorated with tables and chairs, music system, lights and a dance floor; provision of traffic marshalls and availability of a team of people on the day to deal with set up, cleaning and maintenance. The First-tier Tax Tribunal found that the business activities were predominantly the provision of the premises, suitably cleaned and other security arrangements such that it was an investment business not eligible for business property relief. [2023] UKFTT 872 (TC).

Buzzoni and others v IRC

Mrs K held a lease for 100 years less one day commencing on 25 March 1994 in respect of a residential property. On 21 November 1997 she granted an underlease commencing on 24 November 1997 to a nominee company. The underlease was then transferred to a trust for her sons. The superior landland consented to the grant of the underlease on condition that the underlease contained the usual covenants on the part of the underlessee. The covenants which were contained in the underlease mirrored many of those contained in the headlease, e.g. payment of the service charges and an undertaking to keep the property in good repair, these all taking effect on the date when the underlease fell into possession. Although rent was payable under the headlease, there was however no rent payable under the terms of the underlease. Mrs K died on 2 May 2008 and HMRC contended that the covenants in the underlease fell to be treated as benefits reserved by her from the gift of it to the trust. For the executors it was argued that there was no benefit, but simply reimbursement of equivalent sums payable to the superior landlord. Both the First-tier Tax Tribunal and the Upper Tribunal held that the covenants were a clear benefit reserved to the headlessee out of the gift of the underlease. Accordingly on the death of Mrs K the value of underlease formed part of her estate by virtue of *FA 1986, s 102*. These decisions were reversed by the Court of Appeal in December 2013. The central point is whether or not the donee's enjoyment of the property gifted is to the exclusion of any benefit to the donor. The focus is not primarily on the question whether the donor has obtained a benefit from the gifted property but whether the donee's enjoyment of that property remains exclusive. In this case any benefit to the donor did not have any impact on the donee's enjoyment of the property and therefore the reservation of benefit rules were not in point. [2013] EWCA Civ 1684.

Cairns (VDE Webb's Personal Representative) v HMRC

IHTA 1984, s 249 HMRC seeking to impose penalty.

A former Inland Revenue employee died in October 2004. He owned a house in Midlothian, which was in poor condition. The solicitor who acted as his personal representative submitted a form IHT200 in which he valued the house at £400,000. HMRC subsequently formed the opinion that this valuation was too low. They laid an information before the Special Commissioners with a summons seeking to impose a penalty of more than £33,000 on the solicitor. The Special Commissioner signed the summons in accordance with *IHTA 1984, s 249(4)*, and the solicitor appealed. The appeal was heard by a different Special Commissioner (Mr Reid, who is now a Tribunal judge but was a Special Commissioner at the time of the hearing), who dismissed the summons, holding that it was 'wholly lacking specification'. Mr Reid held that 'the initiating document, be it summons, summary complaint or indictment must set out the parameters of the enquiry, and the essential facts and basis in law upon which the public authority relies. If it does not do so, there is bound to be significant prejudice or the risk of such prejudice'. The solicitor was 'entitled to fair notice of the allegations being made against him and a reasonable opportunity to respond to them. Something more than bare words of the relevant statute are required to ensure that fair notice is given.' Mr Reid observed that when the previous Commissioner had issued the summons, that was 'a purely administrative act by which the summons reflects the material contained in the information'. It was not the responsibility of the Commissioner who signed the summons 'to make substantial revisions to the material produced and by a process of drafting create a relevant and specific summons. It might have been better in this case if the Special Commissioners had simply refused to issue a summons in terms of the draft presented to them on the grounds that the information which was reflected in the draft presented to them was a wholly inadequate basis upon which to commence proceedings, particularly as those proceedings appeared to involve bare allegations of fraud or negligence'. With regard to the merits of the case, Mr Reid held that the form IHT200 should have specifically declared that the valuation of the house was 'a provisional estimate.' Accordingly 'there had been a narrow, technical failure to comply with the provisions' of *s 247(1)*. However, the penalty should have been reduced to 'a nominal amount'. FTT May 2009 (TC00008).

Cancer Research Campaign and others v Ernest Brown & Co

Duty to exercise reasonable care in advising a deceased's beneficiary of the possibility of executing a deed of variation – IHTA 1984, s 142.

N died on 11 December 1986 leaving a will dated 21 December 1985 giving his residuary estate to his sister who then died on 28 May 1988. Seven charities named as residuary beneficiaries under the testatrix's will dated 14 September 1987, brought an action for damages for negligence against the defendant firm of solicitors. The plaintiffs claimed that by reason of the solicitors' negligence they were unable to take advantage of a deed of variation under *IHTA 1984, s 142* at a cost to them of some £200,000 of unnecessarily paid IHT on N's estate because the statutory election period had expired on 10 December 1988. The plaintiffs contended that the solicitors were in breach of their duty of care during the testatrix's lifetime in failing to advise her of the possibility of executing a deed of variation of N's bequests. In addition, a breach of duty of their care had arisen, following the testatrix's death, in the administration of the estate in failing to notify them of their prospective legacies.

The court could not accept that there was a duty to advise an intended testator/testatrix about the tax avoidance schemes of another estate. The executor's duty was to collect the assets and he was under no obligation to inform the beneficiaries of the contents of the will as well as owing no duty to inform a legatee that there was a prospective legacy. The action was dismissed. [1997] STC 1425.

Charkham v IRC

Valuation of a joint owner's minority interest in undivided shares in property secured varying discounts of 15%, 20% and 22.5%-LPA 1925, s 30 and TLATA 1996, s 14.

A joint owner's interest in *investment* properties are routinely discounted by between 10%–15% but in this case the taxpayer's valuer chose to adopt an income approach in arguing that a minority owner could not obtain an order for sale. A multiple was calculated by the valuer derived from the investment market. In its considerations the Tribunal chose to exercise its discretion on the basis of the likelihood of a holder of the percentage obtaining an order for sale from the court. In this connection the holder as a purchaser would be aware of the uncertainty of a *LPA 1925, s 30* application and therefore discount the open market value. Also, there should be a single discount notwithstanding the difference in the IHT values of 24.04% to 6.04%. In applying this the Tribunal held for discounts of 15% on certain properties (Tottenham Court Road) and 20% and 22.5% on other properties (Alderney Street). *Charkham v IRC* Lands Tribunal 1997.

Charnley and Hodgkinson (as Gill's executors) v HMRC

A grazing agreement was held to be sufficient to allow both agricultural relief on both the land and the farmhouse, and business relief on the farm machinery. The farm owner, Mr Gill, had entered into an agreement with a third party B under which the latter's animals would be allowed onto Mr Gill's land, who would provide full care for them and only inform B if there was a problem. The evidence was that Mr Gill worked every day around the farm and was said therefore to be farming his own land but using B's stock. Apart from taking full care of the animals, he also carried out all maintenance work, including fencing and hedges, harrowing and rolling the land, reseeding it, and generally operating as a full-time farmer whilst not actually owning any animals. HMRC took the view that agricultural relief was not due because he was simply dealing with general property maintenance and did not rear any animals. Business relief was not due because the land was held as an investment. Both these arguments were roundly rejected by the First-tier Tax Tribunal which held that Mr Gill's activities were clearly that of an active farmer. [2019] UKFTT 650 (TC).

Civil Engineer v CIR

Taxpayer setting up trusts in Guernsey and Jersey – Guernsey trust was discretionary in form and the Jersey trust was established under Jersey law to pay income and capital for such charitable objects as trustees thought fit – Trustees of the Jersey trust resident outside the UK. Whether chargeable transfers for IHT purposes – Whether Jersey trust charitable under UK law – Whether Guernsey trust discretionary.

The taxpayer was born in England and he was English domicile. He worked in England as a consulting civil engineer in 1949. In 1960 he moved to Hong Kong and took up a permanent and pensionable post with the Hong Kong government. In 1967 he also became a partner in a London firm of consulting engineers. He and his wife were also shareholders of a Dutch company, HBV. He left Hong Kong in September 1989. Whilst in Hong Kong he rented accommodation but from 1960 to 1976 he owned property in the United Kingdom. Following changes in the Finance Act 1974 he closed his London office and ceased to own any property. His visits to the United Kingdom varied between zero and 36 days in a tax year between 1980 and 1988. He left Hong Kong in September 1989 severing his business and social connections with Hong Kong in November 1990. His P86 recorded that he had left for Jersey on 31 January 1990 and returned to the UK permanently on 23 April 1990. On 22 March 1990 he created the S

Foundation, a charity, under Jersey law (£75,000) and A Trust in Guernsey on 27 March 1990 (£375,000). All the Trustees were resident in Jersey and A Trust was discretionary naming only the Red Cross of Geneva as beneficiary but with the power to add other beneficiaries.

The Inland Revenue took the view that the transfers on 23 April 1990 were chargeable transfers and IHT was payable. The taxpayer appealed stating that he had acquired a domicile of choice of Hong Kong and that A Trust and S Foundation were not properly constituted or alternatively that A Trust was a life interest Trust and S Foundation a charity. Leaving Hong Kong with the intention of not returning revived the UK domicile of origin and therefore at the time of the transfers to the Trust and Foundation he was within the UK for IHT purposes. A Trust and S Foundation were valid trusts and A was a discretionary trust. S Foundation was not governed by the law of part of the UK and not subject to the jurisdiction of the UK courts. See *Camille and Henry Dreyfus Foundation Inc v CIR* [1955] All ER 97.

The appeal was dismissed. [2002] STC (SCD) 72.

Clark & Southern (Clark's Executors) v HMRC

Company's business consisted 'mainly of holding investments'.

A woman owned a number of shares in a company which owned more than 100 different properties from which it received rents, and also managed 141 dwellings owned by members of the family for which it charged 7.5% of the rent. The company had its own workforce for carrying out building work, maintenance and refurbishment of all properties. More than half the income was from the company's own properties. Her executors claimed business property relief. The Revenue rejected the claim on the basis that the shares were not 'relevant business property', because the company's business consisted mainly of 'making or holding investments', within *IHTA 1984, s 105(3)*. The executors appealed, contending that because the company carried out maintenance work on the properties itself, it should not be treated as falling within *s 105(3)*. The Special Commissioner rejected this contention and dismissed the executors' appeal, holding that 'the company's maintenance activity is not the separate provision of services; it is inherent in property ownership'. On the evidence, the company's business consisted 'mainly of holding investments'. [2005] STC SCD 823 Sp C 502.

Clore (deceased) (No 2), Re (Official Solicitor v Clore and Others)

Domicile.

Sir Charles Clore died in London on 26 July 1979, an immensely wealthy man. The Revenue claim to CTT on his free estate outside the UK, and on the assets of a Jersey settlement he had made on 20 February 1979, depended on whether, as considered by the Revenue, he was domiciled in England when he made the settlement and at his death. Towards the end of his life he spent part of each year abroad for tax reasons, and had been provisionally accepted by the Revenue as not resident or ordinarily resident in the UK since February 1977. He had taken steps to be associated with Monaco, as an acceptable 'tax haven', but there was no convincing evidence that he had formed a settled intention to reside permanently in Monaco. The Ch D held that, on the evidence, his father was domiciled in England when Sir Charles was born. His domicile of origin was therefore England and he had not abandoned this domicile at his death. Ch D, [1984] STC 609.

Clore (deceased) (No 3), Re (CIR v Stype Trustees (Jersey) Ltd and Others)

Delivery of accounts.

Foreign trustees contended that their admitted liability to pay CTT did not mean that they were liable to deliver accounts of the trust property under *IHTA 1984, s 216**. The Ch D rejected the trustees' argument that there was a territorial limitation to the section and held that their liability to pay tax meant that they were liable to comply with the administrative machinery of delivering accounts which normally precedes payment of tax. On a separate point, a former trustee was required to deliver an account giving details of settlement property 'to the best of his knowledge and belief'. 'Knowledge' was held to extend to the contents of documents in his possession, custody or power, but no further. He was not required to act as an information gatherer. Ch D, [1985] STC 394; [1985] 1 WLR 1290; [1985] 2 All ER 819.

Cox (Executors of) v HMRC

Business of holiday lettings – whether business property relief applied.

The deceased held three flats used for a business of holiday letting. There were gardens outside available for the use of guests and leisure items such as tennis rackets and beach balls were also supplied. Flats were let fully furnished with bedding and towels and including a wide range of consumables and basic self-catering food items. The First-tier Tax Tribunal held that the business was mainly an investment business and business property relief was therefore denied. [2020] UKFTT 442 (TC).

Crossman and Others, CIR v

Valuation – value of unquoted shares subject to restrictions on transfers.

The open market value of unquoted shares had to be established for ED purposes. The articles of association imposed restrictions on transfer including a right of pre-emption in favour of existing shareholders. The value was not limited to that fixed by the pre-emption clause, but was estimated at the price obtainable in a hypothetical open market on the terms that the purchaser was registered as holder of the shares and held them subject to the same restrictions as his predecessor. HL 1936, 15 ATC 94; [1936] 1 All ER 762; [1937] AC 26.

Curnock (Curnock's Personal Representatives) v CIR

Cheque clearance after date of death but gift made before treated as part of deceased's estate.

A pensioner (P) had granted a power of attorney to his father (C). On 21 December 2001 C issued a cheque for £6,000 on behalf of P. On 22 December 2001 P died. The cheque was not cleared until 27 December. The Revenue issued a Notice of Determination on the basis that the £6,000 was part of P's estate. C (who was P's personal representative) appealed, contending that the £6,000 did not form part of P's estate, since he had disposed of the money on the day before he died. The Special Commissioner rejected this contention and dismissed C's appeal. Applying *dicta* of Pollock MR in *Re Swinburne*, CA [1926] Ch 38, a cheque was 'nothing more than an order to obtain a certain sum of money . . . and if the order is not acted upon in the lifetime of the person who gives it, it is worth nothing'. Accordingly, the £6,000 was part of P's estate when he died. [2003] STC SCD 283 Sp C 365.

Delamere's Settlement Trusts, Re (Kenny and Others v Cunningham-Reid and Others)

Interest in possession – effect of Trustee Act 1925, s 31.

An appointment in 1980 by trustees of a settlement which partly revoked the trusts of a 1971 appointment of income was expressed to have effect only if no interest in possession already subsisted in the relevant property for CTT purposes. The question before the CA was to what extent the *Trustee Act 1925, s 31* applied to the 1971 appointment. If it applied, a minor beneficiary's share of the accumulated income would fall back into the general capital of the trust in the event of his death before attaining 18 or marrying, and his interest in the accumulations would although vested, be defeasible. If *s 31(2)* did not apply, the accumulated income vested in the minor beneficiary as it accrued and was held by the trustees for him indefeasibly. The CA held that *s 31(2)* did not apply. The use of the word 'absolutely' and the fact that no time limit was placed on the duration of the income interests appointed, indicated the intention that the interests should not be defeasible in any circumstances during the subsistence of the 1971 appointment. CA 1983, [1984] 1 WLR 813; [1984] 1 All ER 584.

Dixon v CIR

Garden and orchard – whether 'agricultural property' for the purposes of Agricultural Property Relief under IHTA 1984, ss 115(2), 117(a).

A woman (B) died in 1998, owning 60% interest in a property consisting of a cottage, garden and orchard, with a total area of 0.6 acres. B had sometimes allowed a neighbouring farmer to graze sheep on the land, and had sometimes sold damsons from the orchard. The Inland Revenue issued a notice of determination charging IHT. B's executor appealed, contending that the property qualified for agricultural property relief. The Special Commissioner rejected this contention and dismissed the appeal, finding on the evidence that the property was not 'agricultural land or pasture' but was occupied as a private residence. [2002] STC SCD 53 Sp C 297.

Dreyfus (Camille & Henry) Foundation Inc v CIR

Charities – overseas trusts.

A foundation for the advancement of chemistry, etc. incorporated in the USA claimed exemption under *ICTA 1988, s 505(1)(c)** in respect of royalties. The claim was refused. The relief is limited to bodies and trusts subject to the jurisdiction of the courts of the UK. (The question of whether the foundation was established for charitable purposes was not considered.) HL 1955, 36 TC 126; [1956] AC 39; [1955] 3 All ER 97.

DWC Piercy's Executors v HMRC

IHTA 1984, s 105(3) – business of 'making or holding investments'.

A property development company (T) owned some land in Islington, on which it had erected some workshops which it let out. T's major shareholder died in 1999. His executors claimed business property relief. HMRC rejected the claim on the grounds that because T received significant rental income, its business consisted mainly of 'making or holding investments', within *IHTA 1984, s 105(3)*. The executors appealed, contending that it still wished to develop the land in Islington for residential purposes but had been unable to do so because of uncertainty about proposals for a new railway line. The Special Commissioner accepted this evidence and allowed the appeal, finding that the company continued to hold its land as trading stock, and holding that it was not an 'investment company' for the purposes of *IHTA 1984, s 105*. The Commissioner also held that 'the only type of land-dealing company whose shares fail to qualify for the relief is . . . some sort of dealing or speculative trader that does not actively develop or actually build on land'. [2008] STC SCD 858 Sp C 687.

Essex & another (executors of Somerset deceased) v CIR

Relevant date for the purposes of FA 1986, s 102(5).

In 1988 a married woman (S) settled a 95% interest in a house on trust, to pay the income to her husband for life, and after his death to hold the capital and income on discretionary trusts for a class of beneficiaries that included herself and her children. S's husband died in 1992 and she died in 1998. The Inland Revenue issued a notice of determination on the basis that, at her death, the property held by the settlement fell to be treated as her property by reason of *FA 1986, s 102*. Her executors appealed, contending that the effect of *FA 1986, s 102(5)* was that no IHT was due, since the settlement had taken advantage of the exemption under *IHTA 1984, s 18* for transfers between spouses. The Special Commissioners accepted this contention and allowed the appeal, holding that the creation of the settlement involved a single gift to S's husband. This was an exempt transfer between spouses to which *s 102(5)* applied. For the purposes of *s 102(5)*, the relevant date was the date of the settlement, rather than the date of S's death. [2002] STC SCD 39 Sp C 296.

Eversden and Another, CIR v

Relevant date for the purposes of FA 1986, s 102(5).

In 1988 a married woman (S) settled a 95% interest in a house on trust, to pay the income to her husband for life, and after his death to hold the capital and income on discretionary trusts for a class of beneficiaries which included herself and her children. S's husband died in 1992 and she died in 1998. The Revenue issued a notice of determination on the basis that, at her death, the property held by the settlement fell to be treated as her property by virtue of *FA 1986, s 102*. Her executors appealed, contending that the effect of *FA 1986, s 102(5)* was that no IHT was due, since the settlement had taken advantage of the exemption under *IHTA 1984, s 18* for transfers between spouses. The Special Commissioner accepted this contention and allowed the appeal, holding that, for the purposes of *FA 1986, s 102(5)*, the relevant date was the date of the settlement, rather than the date of S's death. The Ch D and CA upheld this decision. Carnwath LJ held that 'the "disposal of the property by way of gift" was the transfer of the property in 1988'. This was accepted as an exempt transfer under *IHTA 1984, s 18*. It was, therefore, outside the scope of *FA 1986, s 102*. He also observed that the effect of *IHTA 1984, s 49* was that 'in the present case, the estate of the settlor's husband is taxed on the property, but that of the settlor is not. There is nothing in *s 102* to modify that . . . If that is of concern to the Revenue, they must look for correction to Parliament, not to the Courts.' (*aka Essex & Essex (Somerset's Executors) v CIR*), CA [2003] STC 822; [2003] EWCA Civ 668. (*Note*. On 20 June 2003 the Government tabled an amendment to the 2003 Finance Bill (resulting in *FA 2003, s 185*) to amend *FA 1986, s 102* to reverse the effect of this decision. See the Inland Revenue Press Release issued on 20 June 2003.)

Farmer and another (Executors of Farmer deceased) v CIR

Relevant business property – deceased carrying on business of farming and letting some buildings and land on the farm – whether BPR excluded as consisting mainly of making or holding investments.

An individual (F), who owned a farm comprising 449 acres, died in 1997. Several of the properties at the farm were surplus to the requirements of the farm, and he had let these to tenants. The farm had an agreed probate value of £3,500,000. It was accepted that £2,250,000 of this related to the farmhouse, farm buildings and farmland, and qualified for 100% agricultural property relief. The balance of £1,250,000 related to the properties that had been let. F's executors claimed business property relief on the basis that there was a single business which qualified for relief (accepting that, by virtue of *IHTA 1984, s 114(1)*, the business property relief was restricted to the £1,250,000 which did not qualify for agricultural property relief). The Revenue rejected the claim and issued a notice of determination that the farm business consisted mainly of making or holding investments, within *IHTA 1984, s 105(3)*, and therefore was not 'relevant business property'. The executors appealed, accepting that the letting of property was 'making or holding investments' but contending that F's business had consisted mainly of farming. The Special Commissioner accepted this contention and allowed the appeal, holding on the evidence that 'the overall context of the business, the capital employed, the time spent by the employees and consultants, and the levels of turnover, all support the conclusion that the business consisted mainly of farming'. The fact that the lettings were more profitable than the rest of the business was not conclusive. See [1999] STC SCD 321 Sp C 216.

Faulkner (Adams' Trustee) v CIR

Licence to occupy property given to third party – whether interest in possession within IHTA 1984, s 49(1) – present right to present enjoyment of the property even though not occupied by the deceased.

In 1980 a widower (R), with no children, made a will allowing a friend (H) and his wife 'or the survivor of them for the time being still living' to live in his house 'and have the use of the furniture as long as he she or they so wish'. R died in 1981 and the couple duly moved into the house. H died in 1998 (having outlived his wife) and the house was sold later that year. The Revenue issued a notice of determination to R's surviving trustee, on the basis that H's right of occupation had been an interest in possession in settled property, within *IHTA 1984, s 49(1)*. The trustee appealed, contending firstly that R's will had given H a licence to use the house but had not conferred an interest in possession, and alternatively that if H had had an interest in possession, he should be deemed to have shared it with the three residuary beneficiaries under R's will. The Special Commissioner rejected these contentions and dismissed the appeal, holding that H had had a 'present right to the present enjoyment of the house'. This was an interest in possession in the whole of the house. [2001] STC SCD 112 Sp C 278.

Fetherstonaugh & Others v CIR

Business property relief – death of life tenant using settled property for business purposes.

In 1977 the life tenant of settled land, who had used that land in his farming and forestry business, died. The trustees claimed that the value of the settled land qualified for business property relief. The Revenue rejected the claim but the CA allowed the trustees' appeal. Although the land itself was not relevant business property, the life interest in the land was an asset used in the business. For CTT purposes the asset had to be valued as if the deceased was beneficially entitled to the land itself. 50% business property relief was therefore due. (*Note*. The relief would now be 100%—see *IHTA 1984, s 104* as amended by *F(No 2)A 1992, 13 Sch 1*.) CA 1984, CTTL 21; [1984] STC 261; [1984] 3 WLR 212.

Fitzwilliam (Countess) & Others v CIR

Discretionary trust – mutual transfers of value – whether Ramsay principle applicable.

Trustees, appointed under a will, had discretion to appoint the residue among a class of beneficiaries during a period of 23 months from the testator's death. The main beneficiaries were the testator's widow (F), who was aged 81 and in poor health, and her daughter (H). There was a potentially heavy liability to CTT and the trustees undertook a number of transactions to mitigate the tax liability. On 20 December 1979, they declared that £4m should be held in trust as to both capital and income for F absolutely. On 9 January 1980 F made a gift to H of £2m net of CTT. On 14 January 1980 the trustees appointed £3.8m to be held on trust, subject to the income being paid to F until 15 February 1980 or her death, one half for H absolutely (the vested half) and the other half for a contingent interest. On 31 January 1980 F assigned to H, for £2m, her beneficial interest in the income of the contingent half. On 5 February 1980 H settled £1,000 on trust to pay the income to F until 15 March 1980 or her death, whichever was the earlier, and subject thereto in trust absolutely for herself. On 7 February 1980 H assigned to the trustees of her settlement her beneficial interest in the vested half of the trust established on 14 January 1980, to be accrued to the £1,000 as one fund. The Revenue served a notice of determination on the trustees, charging CTT on the basis that £4m and £3.8m had been appointed absolutely to F and H respectively. The trustees appealed, contending that the £4m was within what is now *IHTA 1984, s 144** and that the gift of £2m was exempt under *FA 1976, ss 86, 87*. The Ch D allowed the trustees' appeals and the HL upheld this decision (Lord Templeman dissenting). The Revenue's contention that the steps amounted to a single composite transaction within the *Ramsay* principle and that the original testator, rather than H, should be deemed to be the settlor of the settlement of the vested half made on 5 February were rejected. The steps taken in January and February 1980 could not be treated as a 'single and indivisible whole in which one or more of the steps was simply an element without independent effect'. The fact that they formed part of a 'pre-planned tax avoidance scheme' was not sufficient in itself 'to negative the application of an exemption from liability to tax which the series of transactions (was) intended to create', unless the series was 'capable of being construed in a manner inconsistent with the application of the exemption'. The series of transactions here could not be construed in such a way. *Craven v White* applied; *Furniss v Dawson* distinguished. With regard to the Revenue's alternative contention, the fact that the settled funds were historically derived from the original testator did not mean that he could reasonably be regarded as having provided property for the settlement made on 5 February 1980. HL, [1993] STC 502; 1 WLR 1189; [1993] 3 All ER 184.

Fox (Lady), Gray (Executor of) v CIR

Valuation of related property.

Duke of Buccleuch was applied in a case where the freeholder of a large estate had, at the time of her death, held a 92.5% interest in a partnership which farmed the land. The Revenue issued a Notice of Determination claiming IHT on the combined value of the deceased's freehold reversion and her interest in the partnership. The CA upheld the Notice of Determination (reversing the decision of the Lands Tribunal). Hoffman LJ held that the hypothetical sale had to be supposed to have taken the course which would get the largest price provided that it did not entail 'undue expenditure of time and effort'. The freehold reversion and the partnership should be valued as one unit of property. CA [1994] STC 360.

Frankland v CIR

Distribution from property settled by will – whether IHTA 1984, s 144 applicable.

A married woman died on 26 September 1987, leaving property on discretionary trusts for the benefit of her husband and children. On 22 December 1987 the property was transferred to a trust, the income from which was to be paid to the deceased's husband for the duration of his life. The object of the transfer was to secure the benefit of the spouse exemption of *IHTA 1984, s 18(1)* in respect of the charge to tax otherwise payable in respect of the death. The Revenue issued a notice of determination on the basis that the spouse exemption did not apply since the transfer had not been made by the deceased. The trustee appealed, contending that the effect of *IHTA 1984, s 144* was that the husband's interest in possession should be treated as having arisen under the deceased's will. The Ch D rejected this contention and dismissed the appeal, holding that *IHTA 1984, s 144* did not apply. The effect of *IHTA 1984, s 65(4)* was that, since the December transfer had taken place within three months of the death, that transfer itself was not an event giving rise to a charge to tax. *IHTA 1984, s 144* only applied where there was an event on which tax would otherwise be chargeable. The wording of *IHTA 1984, s 144* was unambiguous. Accordingly the transfer could not be treated as having been made by the deceased, and the spouse exemption did not apply. The Court of Appeal reaffirmed the decision. CA [1997] STC 1450. See now the amendment to *IHTA 1984, s 144(1)(b)* by *F (No2) 2015* to correct the anomalous result of this decision, so that the spouse exemption will apply in such circumstances where the death was on or after 10 December 2014.

Fryer, DM & Others (Personal Representatives of Ms P Arnold) v HMRC

Deferment of pension benefits – whether IHTA 1984, s 10 applicable.

A woman was born in 1942. In 1995 she set up a discretionary trust. Later that year she took out a pension plan. It was agreed that if she died before taking her retirement benefits, then the value of those benefits would pass to her discretionary trust. In 2002, shortly before her 60th birthday, she was diagnosed as suffering with terminal cancer. She died in 2003 without having taken the available benefits. HMRC issued a determination charging IHT on the basis that, by failing to take her retirement benefits when she reached the age of 60 in 2002, she had made a disposition of value for the purposes of *IHTA 1984, s 3(3)*. Her personal representatives appealed, contending firstly that she should not be treated as having made any such disposition, and alternatively that if she had made such a disposition, it was not 'intended to confer a gratuitous benefit', so that *IHTA 1984, s 10(3)* applied. The First-Tier Tribunal rejected these contentions and dismissed the appeal in principle, subject to a reduction in HMRC's valuation of the disposition. Clark J upheld HMRC's contention that 'the concept of a "disposition" was widened by *s 3(3)* to include passive dispositions, meaning omissions which resulted in the enhancement of another person's estate or of settled property in which no interest in possession subsisted'. He rejected HMRC's contention that the deemed disposition should be treated as having taken place on her 60th birthday (which was her normal retirement date under her pension policy), holding that the disposition should be treated as having taken place on the date of her death. Her omission to exercise her rights had increased the value of the settled property, and the evidence showed that this had been intentional. Accordingly *IHTA 1984, s 10* did not apply. With regard to the appropriate valuation, Clark J reviewed the evidence in detail and found that the total benefits amounted to £119,800. He directed that this should be discounted by 25%, resulting in a chargeable consideration of £89,950. FTT [2010] UKFTT 87 (TC), TC00398.

(Notes. (1) The determinations had been made in the name of the Commissioners of Her Majesty's Revenue & Customs. Clark J observed that the Commissioners' statutory title was 'the Commissioners *for* Her Majesty's Revenue & Customs' (see *CRCA 2005, s 1*), and commented that 'to avoid any possible suggestion that Notices of Determination (or any other documents issued by HMRC) are invalid, it is strongly desirable for the correct title to be used'. (2) The appellants were represented by an 'independent financial adviser', rather than by a lawyer. Clark J observed that it would have been better for the appellants 'to be represented by counsel, or by someone else equally experienced in representing parties before the Tribunal'.)

Furse (deceased), In re, Furse v CIR

Domicile.

A US citizen came to England as a boy in 1887. After completing his education in England he took up employment in America, where he married an American. In 1923, originally on medical advice, he came with his family to England, where his wife purchased a farm which remained the matrimonial home until he died in 1963, aged 80. From 1950 onwards he said that he would remain at the farm so long as he was able to do physical work there; he remained so able until his death. In an application by his executor for a declaration of his domicile for estate duty purposes, he was held to have acquired an English domicile of choice, distinguishing *CIR v Bullock*. Ch D, [1980] STC 597; [1980] 3 All ER 838.

Gaines-Cooper v IRC

Domicile.

Mr G-C, who was born in England, had a house and 27 acres in Henley-on-Thames,

Oxfordshire, where he kept a collection of paintings, classic cars and guns, but claimed that his chief residence since 1976 had been on the Seychelles where he expressed the wish to spend his last days and have his ashes scattered there. His second wife had however taken up residence at the UK home together with his son who went to an English school. In 2002 Mr G-C had his will drawn up under English law. HMRC had rejected his claim that he was not domiciled in the UK and he therefore appealed. A succession of eminent witnesses had told the Special Commissioners that he had 'fallen in love' with the Seychelles and wished to 'stay there forever' but it was nevertheless held that he remained domiciled in the UK. The High Court confirmed this decision, holding that the taxpayer, because the taxpayer had maintained a presence in England, the Commissioners simply did not accept his plea that he made his home on the Seychelles his chief residence in 1976. [2008] STC 1665.

George and Another, CIR v

Business Property Relief claim regarding caravans – provision of services not the holding of investments.

A widow (S) had owned 85% of the shares in a company which operated a residential caravan park, comprising 167 mobile homes, and a country club with a licensed bar. The Revenue issued a notice of determination on the basis that her shares in the company were not 'relevant business property', because the company's business consisted mainly of 'making or holding investments'. S's executors appealed. The Special Commissioner reviewed the evidence in detail and allowed the appeal, observing that the company had several full-time employees and was classed as a trading company for corporation tax purposes, and finding that '72% of the site fees goes in overheads (*sic*) . . . most of which relate to the provision of upkeep of the common parts'. On the evidence, the Commissioner held that the company's business was 'the provision of services and not the business of holding investments'. The Ch D upheld the notice. Laddie J held that the business of receiving site fees from the owners of the mobile homes in return for the right to use the company's land, and the receipt of fees for the storage of caravans, constituted the exploitation of the proprietary rights in the land and amounted to the holding of an investment. Accordingly the shares in the company failed to qualify for business property relief. [2002] STC SCD 358 Sp C 32[illegible]; Ch D [2003] All ER (D) 376 (Feb); Ch D 2003, TL 3683; [2003] STC 468; [2003] EWHC 318.

George & Loochin (Stedman's Executors) v CIR

The holding of property as an investment was only one component of the business, and did not prevent the company from qualifying for business property relief.

A woman (S) had owned 85% of the shares in a company which operated a residential caravan park, comprising 167 mobile homes, and a country club with a licensed bar. The Revenue issued a notice of determination on the basis that her shares in the company were not 'relevant business property', because the company's business consisted mainly of 'making or holding investments'. S's executors appealed. The Special Commissioner reviewed the evidence in detail and allowed the appeal, observing that the company had several full-time employees and was classed as a trading company for corporation tax purposes, and finding that '72% of the site fees goes in overheads . . . most of which relate to the provision of upkeep of the common parts'. On the evidence, the Commissioner held that the company's business was 'the provision of services and not the business of holding investments'. The Ch D reversed this decision but the CA restored it. Carnwath LJ held that, on the evidence, the holding of property as an investment was only one component of the business, and did not prevent the company from qualifying for business property relief. CA [2003] EWCA Civ 1763; [2004] STC 147.

Gilchrist (as trustee of the J P Gilchrist 1993 Settlement) v HMRC

Proceeds of scrip dividend shares – whether trust capital for the purposes of the IHT 10 yearly charge on a discretionary trust.

Trustees of a relevant property had entered into a scrip dividend scheme to reduce the tax liability on a sale of the shareholdings in the company concerned. They contended that the proceeds of the scrip shares were income for the purposes of trust law and not therefore part of the capital of the settlement, liable to IHT under *IHTA 1984, s 64* on the next 10 yearly charge date. Certain aspects of the income tax treatment of scrip dividend schemes had been considered by the Court of Appeal, in *Howell v Trippier* [2004] STC 1245. The Tribunal noted that at no point in that appeal was there any suggestion that scrip dividends were income for purposes of trust law although the point would have been relevant. In the subsequent case of *Pierce v Wood* [2009] EWHC 3225 (Ch) the High Court, Chancery Division, did however expressly state that the decision in *Howell v Trippier* meant that a scrip dividend received by trustees was income in their hands for all purposes. The trustees relied on that decision. However the Upper Tribunal held that it was not bound by a decision of the High Court if it was satisfied that the decision in question was wrong. The Tribunal was satisfied that the decision in *Pierce v Wood* was wrong and so declined to follow it. Therefore the scrip dividend shares and their proceeds of sale were trust capital, both for general trust purposes and for the purposes of IHT, the trustees' appeal was accordingly dismissed. [2014] UKUT 169 (TCC).

Gladstone v Bower

Agricultural holding – agreement to let land for a fixed period.

A landlord let a farm to a tenant for a fixed term of 18 months. He gave no notice to quit but at the end of the term brought an action for possession of the farm. The tenant contended that the letting took effect as a tenancy from year to year and could only be terminated by notice to quit. The CA held that, since the letting for 18 months created an interest greater than a tenancy from year to year at common law which could be terminated at the end of the first year, the landlord was entitled to possession. CA [1960] 3 All ER 353.

Glowacki's Personal Representatives v HMRC

IHTA 1984, s 142 – whether deed of variation effective.

A woman (G) died in 2004. Under her will, she left most of her estate to her husband. He died three months later. G's personal representatives purported to execute a deed of variation giving most of her estate (including her house) to her sister and the remainder to her nieces and nephew. HMRC issued a notice of determination, accepting that the deed was effective but holding that its effect was that the benefit of the nil rate of IHT was to be set first against G's house rather than against the pecuniary legacies. The personal representatives appealed, contending that the deed should be construed as meaning that the house was excluded from IHT and that the nil rate band was available to be set against the pecuniary legacies. The Special Commissioner reviewed the evidence in detail and rejected this contention, holding that the first part of the deed of variation was ineffective. The Commissioner held that *IHTA 1984, s 142* 'cannot operate to remove property from a person's estate so that it is no longer part of the estate subject to the deemed transfer of value on death under *s 4*. What *s 142* must vary is the destination of the estate on its deemed transfer under *s 4*.' In this case, the deed had purported 'to negate any disposition of the house as part of (G's) estate immediately before her death by pretending that she had transferred it immediately before the deemed *s 4* transfer of value'. However, 'nothing in *s 142* suggests that the variation that it permits should be other than a variation of the disposition on death effected by the deceased as part of the deemed transfer under *s 4* immediately before the death'.

The Commissioner also held that HMRC's notice of determination had been issued on an incorrect basis, observing that HMRC appeared 'to have put the cart before the horse in terms of claiming to give effect to the deed and then considering its tax consequences'. The Commissioner concluded that 'the "variation" purported to be made by Clause 1 of the deed was not a variation capable of taking effect under *s 142* and, as a result of the proviso, did not therefore take effect at all'. [2007] STC SCD 188 Sp C 631.

G J Graham deceased (Personal representatives of) v HMRC

Whether a holiday letting business was of an investment nature or non-investment nature – IHTA 1984, s 105(3).

Four flats were let by the deceased as self-catering holiday accommodation and in addition two guest bedrooms within the house occupied by her were used occasionally for the provision of bed and breakfast accommodation. There was a sauna, barbecue area, games room and laundry plus a swimming pool and covered areas housed a golf buggy and bicycles which were made available to guests for payment. Inside the house was a separate guest lounge with a collection of books and open fire (in season). At the start of each visit, each flat was supplied with flowers, home-made marmalade, either a bottle of wine or on special occasions a bottle of champagne, home-made bread, milk, tea, coffee, sugar, toilet rolls, soaps and shampoos, washing-up liquid and bathroom bleach. Running the business in season required in total about 200 hours work per 35 week.

The Tribunal concluded that this was an exceptional case and the business was not one which consisted wholly or mainly of holding investments. The services provided in the package more than balanced the mere provision of a place to stay. An intelligent businessman would regard it as more like a family run hotel than a second home let out in the holidays. Accordingly, business property relief was allowed. [2018] UKFTT 306 (TC).

Green v HMRC

Furnished holiday letting business – whether eligible for business property relief.

The taxpayer held a number of units at a house and in its grounds which were let as self-catering holiday accommodation, producing income of around £87,000 per annum. The business was liable to business rates and VAT registered. All normal facilities for a holiday let were supplied, including furniture, household goods, linen and towels, plus wi-fi and a caretaker. Guests did their own laundry and had to leave the premises clean and tidy. Evidence was given that the properties would generate income of around £35,000 if let on assured shorthold tenancies, so that it was argued that the services element of the business therefore commanded the additional annual sum of £52,000. HMRC rejected this contention, saying that the additional rent was due to the scenic location of the properties. The Tribunal rejected the claim for relief on the basis that the services element of the business was insufficient to make the business one which was not mainly the holding of investments. [2015] UKFTT 236 (TC).

Grimwood-Taylor & Mallender (Mallender's Executors) v CIR

IHTA 1984, s 103 (3) – business 'carried on otherwise than for gain'.

An individual (M) died in 1986, owning substantial shareholdings in two companies. Each of the companies had purchased property, which was occupied by shareholders. The Revenue issued notices of determination charging IHT on the value of shares in the companies. M's executors appealed, contending that the shares qualified for business property relief. The Special Commissioner rejected this contention and dismissed the appeal, holding that the effect of *IHTA, s 103(3)* was that the shares did not qualify for relief, because the companies had used their funds to purchase land for occupation by their shareholders, so that their businesses had been carried on 'otherwise than for gain'. [2000] STC SCD 39 Sp C 223.

Guild v CIR

Bequest for sporting purposes – whether within IHTA 1984, s 23.

A testator left the residue of his estate to the town council of North Berwick for use in connection with the North Berwick sports centre or for 'some purpose in connection with sport'. The Revenue issued a determination to capital transfer tax, against which the executor appealed, contending that the bequest was charitable under the *Recreational Charities Act 1958, s 1*, and was therefore exempt from CTT by virtue of what is now *IHTA 1984, s 23(1)*. The HL allowed the executor's appeal (reversing the decision of the CS). The facilities at the sports centre were provided with the object of improving the conditions of life of the community generally. The phrase 'some similar purpose in connection with sport' implied a bequest which would display the leading characteristics of the sports centre, which lay in the nature of the facilities provided there and the fact that they were available to the public at large. *Dicta* of Bridge LJ in *CIR v McMullen & Others* approved and applied; *dicta* of Walton J in the same case disapproved. HL, [1992] STC 162; [1992] 2 WLR 397; [1992] 2 All ER 10.

Hall v Hall (Hall's Executors) v CIR

Making or holding investments – BPR

A widow (H) had owned a caravan park. The caravans were let from March to October each year. The park also contained 11 chalets which were let on 45-year leases. H's executors appealed against a notice of determination, contending that the park qualified for business property relief. The Special Commissioners rejected this contention and dismissed the appeal. On the evidence, almost 84% of H's income from the park consisted of rent and standing charges. It followed that H's business consisted 'mainly of making or holding investments' within *IHTA 1984, s 105(3)*. [1997] STC SCD 126 Sp C 114.

Hanson v HMRC

A farmhouse was owned by a settlement in which the deceased had an interest in possession. The house had been jointly occupied by him and his son up to the date of his death. The son ran his own farming business from the property on land which he owned personally. Originally the business was conducted in partnership with the deceased but on dissolution of the partnership the son continued the business as a sole trader. The trustee of the settlement claimed agricultural property relief in respect of the farmhouse as it was occupied for agricultural purposes. HMRC refused the claim, citing the decision in *Rosser v CIR* [2003] STC SCD 311 Sp C 368 as authority for the proposition that the house and applicable farmland must be in both common occupation and common ownership. The First Tier Tax Tribunal allowed the trustee's appeal on the basis that a test of common occupation of farmhouse and farmland, without any additional requirement of common ownership, fits the scheme of the IHT legislation best. The trustee's appeal was therefore allowed.

A subsidiary point concerned improvements to the property at a cost of approximately £175,000 which had been carried out by the trustee in a personal capacity as he also lived at the property. The trustee claimed that he had acquired an equitable interest in the property as a result of this expenditure, under a constructive trust in his favour, and thus the full value of the property should not be attributed to the life interest trust. This contention failed at the Tribunal on the reasoning that a constructive trust arises only where there is a common intention between two parties which has formed the basis of their mutual expectations and dealings. It could not be shown that there is any such mutual understanding in the present case. [2012] UKFTT 95.

Hardcastle & Hardcastle (Vernede's Executors) v CIR

Lloyd's Underwriter owing money on accounts open at date of death – whether 'liabilities incurred for the purpose of the business' – IHTA 1984, s 110(b).

A Lloyd's underwriter (V) died in 1994. It was accepted that his underwriting activities constituted a business, within *IHTA 1984, s 105(1)(a)*, qualifying for business property relief. The Revenue issued a determination charging IHT on the basis that, when computing the net value of V's business for the purposes of business property relief, the amounts owing on accounts open at the date of his death constituted 'liabilities incurred for the purposes of the business', and should be deducted from the value of the assets used in V's business. His executors appealed, contending that the amounts owing were not 'liabilities incurred for the purposes of the business', and should therefore be deducted from the value of his other estate. The Special Commissioner accepted this contention and allowed the appeal. Applying the principles in *Van den Berghs v Clark*, the insurance contracts in question were 'ordinary commercial contracts made in the course of carrying on the trade' and were not 'assets used in the business' for the purposes of *IHTA 1984, s 110*. Accordingly, the money owing on open accounts 'was not a liability incurred for the purposes within the meaning of *s 110(b)*'. [2000] STC SCD 532 Sp C 259.

Harding & Leigh v CIR

Appointment by Trustees in favour of testator's widow – whether IHTA 1984, s 143 applicable.

A married man died on 14 November 1993, leaving property on discretionary trust for the benefit of his wife and children. On 25 January 1994 the executors executed a deed of appointment, giving the deceased's widow a life interest in residue. The Revenue issued a notice of determination on the basis that the spouse exemption in *IHTA 1984, s 18* did not apply, since the appointment had not been made by the deceased, and that *IHTA 1984, s 144* did not apply for the reasons set out in *Frankland v CIR*. The executors appealed, contending that the appointment should be treated as a transfer made by the deceased by virtue of *IHTA 1984, s 143*. The Special Commissioner rejected this contention and dismissed the appeal, holding that *s 143* did not apply. Firstly, while 'in some contexts a legatee may include a trustee', the trustees here could not be treated as legatees for the purposes of *s 143*. Secondly, an appointment of property was not the same as a transfer of property. Thirdly, the Commissioner found that 'the evidence falls short of showing that the appointment was made in accordance with the deceased's wishes'. [1997] STC SCD 321 Sp C 140.

Hatton v CIR (and related appeals)

Two settlements executed on successive days – whether a preordained series of transactions – whether Ramsay principle applicable.

In August 1978 C, who was terminally ill, granted a power of attorney to her daughter (H) and her solicitor. The solicitor executed a settlement which provided that a fund was to be held on trust and that the income from the fund should be paid to C until midnight on the following day or until her death, whichever was the shorter period, and that subsequently the fund was to be held for the absolute benefit of H. On the following day a settlement was executed whereby H assigned her interest under the previous settlement to trustees to pay the income to C until midnight on the following day or until C's death, whichever occurred first, and subsequently to hold the fund for the absolute benefit of H. C died nine days later. The Revenue issued notices of determination on the basis that C had effected a chargeable transfer. H appealed, contending that what is now *IHTA 1984, s 53(3)** applied, and that no CTT was due since the property in question had reverted to her as settlor. The Special Commissioners upheld the notices of determination, holding that the creation of the two settlements was a 'preordained series of transactions' within the principle laid down in *W T Ramsay Ltd v CIR*. Accordingly C was to be treated as the settlor of both settlements and *IHTA 1984, s 53(3)** did not apply. The Ch D upheld the Commissioners' decision. The conditions laid down by Lord Oliver in *Craven v White* were satisfied. The transactions constituted a single composite transaction whereby C had created a settlement under which she was entitled to a beneficial interest in possession in the settled property at midnight two days after the creation of the settlement. As she was then living, tax was chargeable as if she had effected a chargeable transfer at that time. (Chadwick J commented that, even if the *Ramsay* principle had not applied, C would still fall to be treated as a joint settlor of the second settlement.) Ch D, [1992] STC 140.

Higginson's Executors v CIR

IHTA 1984, s 115(2) re large hunting lodge in 134 acres not a farmhouse.

In 1954 H purchased an estate comprising 134 acres and including a large hunting lodge, built in the early nineteenth century. He farmed the estate until 1985, from when he let the farmland but continued to live in the lodge. He died in 2000, and the property was sold in 2001 for £1,150,000. The Inland Revenue accepted that the land and agricultural outbuildings qualified for agricultural property relief, but issued a ruling that the lodge was not 'of a character appropriate to the property' for the purposes of *IHTA 1984, s 115(2)*, and thus did not qualify for agricultural property relief. H's executors appealed. The Special Commissioner dismissed the appeal, holding that 'for the purposes of *s 115(2)* the unit must be an agricultural unit: that is to say that within the unit, the land must predominate . . . (and) any qualifying cottages, farm buildings or farmhouses must be ancillary to the land'. However, in view of the price paid for the property, it was clear that 'within this particular unit it is the house which predominates, and that what we have here is a house with farmland going with it (and not vice versa)'. Accordingly, the lodge was not a 'farmhouse' for the purposes of *s 115(2)*. [2002] STC SCD 483 Sp C 337.

Holmes & Another v McMullen & Others (re Ratcliffe (deceased))

IHTA 1984, s 41 – allocation of exemption.

The decision in *Lockhart v Harker & Others (re Benham's Will Trusts)*, see above, was not followed (and was implicitly disapproved) in this subsequent case in which the testatrix had left half her estate to two relatives and the other half to be held on trust for four charities. The executors issued a summons seeking the court's declaration as to the correct method of administering the net residuary estate. The Chancery Division held that the half shares were to be calculated before the payment of inheritance tax due in respect of the relatives' shares (so that the net amount received by the relatives would be less than the net amount received by the charities). Blackburne J held that an equal division of disposable residue between the relatives and charities inevitably meant that the inheritance tax attributable to the relatives' share had to be borne by that share, since to subject the charities' share to any part of that burden was prohibited by *IHTA 1984, s 41(b)*. [1999] STC (SCD) 262.

Hood (Viscount) v HMRC

IHTA 1984, s 102 – gift of reversionary sub-lease – whether benefit reserved.

In June 1997 Lady Diana Hood gave a reversionary sub-lease over a property in London to her three sons, retaining the head lease. The term of the sub-lease was from 25 March 2012 to 22 December 2076. Lady Hood died on 15 March 2008, appointing Viscount Hood as her executor. It was contended by HMRC that she had reserved a benefit in the sub-lease due to the covenants in her favour which were contained in it, these identical to the covenants contained in the head lease in favour of the freeholder. For HMRC it was noted that the case was different in one important respect from that of *Buzzoni v HMRC* [2013] EWCA Civ 1684 because in that case (where the taxpayer succeeded) the covenants were given by the sub-lessees directly to the freeholder and were not therefore in favour of the donor, the head lessee. HMRC also rejected the argument that what the sub-lessees received was an asset with obligations embedded in it, such that they could not be regarded as benefits reserved by the donor, and HMRC also argued that the case was not economically the same as that in *Buzzoni*. The First-tier Tax Tribunal accepted these arguments and dismissed the executor's appeal against the determination of HMRC. [2016] UKFTT 59 (TC).

Ingram and Another v CIR

Transfer of freehold interest in property to family trust – equitable leasehold interest retained by transferor – whether a gift with reservation.

In 1987 a widow transferred a property which she owned to her solicitor, who executed declarations that he held the property as her nominee. The solicitor executed two leases purporting to give the widow a rent-free leasehold interest on the estate for 20 years, and the land subject to the leases was transferred to a family trust. The widow continued to live at the property until her death in 1989. The Revenue treated the transfer as a gift with reservation, within *FA 1986, s 102*, and issued a notice of determination accordingly. The House of Lords allowed the executors' appeal. Lord Hoffman held that 'although (*s 102*) does not allow a donor to have his cake and eat it, there is nothing to stop him from carefully dividing up the cake, eating part and having the rest. If the benefits which the donor continues to enjoy are by virtue of property which was never comprised in the gift, he has not reserved any benefit out of the property of which he disposed.' For these purposes, 'property' was 'not something which has physical existence like a house but a specific interest in that property, a legal construct, which can co-exist with other interests in the same physical object. *Section 102* does not therefore prevent people from deriving benefit from the object in which they have given away an interest. It applies only when they derive the benefit from that interest.' The policy of *s 102* was to require people to 'define precisely the interests which they are giving away and the interests, if any, which they are retaining'. The interest, which the widow retained, was 'a proprietary interest, defined with the necessary precision'. The gift was 'a gift of the capital value in the land after deduction of her leasehold interest in the same way as a gift of the capital value of the fund after deduction of an annuity'. *Munro v Commrs of Stamp Duties of New South Wales*, and *dicta* of Lord Simonds in *St Aubyn v Attorney-General*, HL 1951, [1952] AC 15; [1951] 2 All ER 473 applied. Furthermore, the leases were valid in law. Applying *Rye v Rye*, HL [1962] AC 496; [1962] 1 All ER 146, an owner of freehold property could not grant a lease to himself. However, a 'trustee in English law is not an agent for his beneficiary'. (The House of Lords declined to follow the Scottish stamp duty case of *Kildrummy (Jersey) Ltd v CIR*, CS [1990] STC 657, where the Court of Sessions held that the lease granted by a landowner to a nominee acting on his behalf was equivalent to the grant of a lease to himself.) *Dicta* of Goff J in *Nichols v CIR*, see below, disapproved. HL [1999] STC 37; [1999] 1 All ER 297.

Jones & Another (Ball's Administrators) v CIR

Uncompleted contract for sale of land – whether relief under IHTA 1984, s 191 available.

A farmer (B) died on 26 June 1988. On 25 June 1991 his administrators entered into a contract to sell the farm for £300,150. However, the contract was not completed and the farm was eventually sold for £400,000 under another contract in 1992. The probate value of the farm was agreed at £447,000, but the administrators claimed relief under *IHTA 1984, s 191*, contending that for IHT purposes the farm should be valued at £300,150 (the price payable under the 1991 contract). The Revenue rejected the claim and the Ch D dismissed the administrators' appeal. An abortive contract was not a sale, and the farm had not been sold within three years of B's death. Accordingly *IHTA 1984, s 191* was not applicable and the farm had to be valued at its probate value of £447,000. Ch D 14 February 1997, [1997] STC 358.

Judge & Judge (Walden's Personal Representatives) v HMRC

Testator's widow continuing to occupy property at trustees' discretion – whether testator's will conferred interest in possession.

A woman (W) was widowed in 2000. Her husband's will gave his house to trustees, with a declaration that they should allow W to occupy the house 'for such period or periods as they shall in their absolute discretion think fit'. W continued to occupy the house until her death in 2003. The Revenue issued a notice of determination on the basis that her husband's will had given her an interest in possession in the house. Her personal representatives appealed. The Special Commissioner allowed their appeal, holding that the effect of W's husband's will was that she 'had no right to occupy the property but the trustees were given a discretion (but not a duty) to allow her to occupy'. Accordingly W did not have an interest in possession in the property. [2005] STC SCD 863 Sp C 506.

Kempe and Roberts (personal representatives of Lyon, deceased) v CIR

Life policy designation – whether deceased beneficially entitled to sum assured by reason of having a general power to dispose as he thought fit under IHTA 1984, s 5(2).

A company insured the life of one of its employees (L). Under the policy, L was allowed to designate the beneficiaries who would benefit on his demise and he nominated his two sisters as the beneficiaries in the event of his death. L died in 2001. The Inland Revenue issued a notice of determination charging IHT on the basis that the death benefits payable under the policy formed part of L's estate. His sisters (who were his personal representatives) appealed contending that the policy was not part of the estate of the deceased as it was for the benefit of the next of kin and to treat it as part of the estate of the deceased was to defeat the primary purpose of the policy. The Special Commissioner dismissed their appeal, holding that 'the deceased had a general power under (*IHTA 1984, s 5(2)*) which enabled him to dispose of the sum assured under the policy as he thought fit. That means that he was beneficially entitled to the sum assured and so it formed part of his estate and accordingly is chargeable to tax.' [2004] STC SCD 467 Sp C 424.

Lake v Lake & Others

Rectification of deeds.

A testator died in November 1986, and a Deed of Variation was executed three months later by his widow and the trustees. However, the solicitors drew up the Deed incorrectly, resulting in an increased inheritance tax liability. A second Deed was subsequently executed to correct the error, but following the decision in *Russell & Another v CIR*, the liability was nevertheless determined in accordance with the original Deed. The widow sought an Order for the rectification of the original Deed in accordance with the intentions, which the Ch D granted. On the facts, there was no doubt that the original Deed did not carry out the intentions of the parties, and the fact that there was no issue before the court did not present an obstacle to rectification. Ch D [1989] STC 865.

Lau (W Lau's Executor) v HMRC

IHTA 1984, s 142 – Whether deed of variation effective.

An individual (L) died in October 2004. His widow (M) acted as his executrix. L left specific legacies of £665,000 to each of his two daughters and to his stepson (H), who was M's only child from a previous marriage. M was the residuary beneficiary. In July

2005 L's two daughters and H executed deeds of variation renouncing their legacies. In October 2005 M paid each of them £1,000,000. HMRC formed the opinion that this payment represented consideration for the recipients having renounced their legacies under L's will, so that the effect of *IHTA 1984, s 142(3)* was that the deed of variation was ineffective. They issued a notice of determination accordingly. M appealed, accepting that the deed was ineffective with regard to L's two daughters, but contending that she had given H the £1,000,000 so that he could start a business, and that her gift to H was not connected with his renunciation of his legacy. The Special Commissioner reviewed the evidence in detail, rejected this contention and dismissed M's appeal, finding that H 'was entirely dependent upon the appellant for financial support. He had been out of work for most of his adult life, and at the time of his renunciation owned no assets of significant value.' On the evidence, 'the correspondence from the Appellant's solicitors and the circumstances of the payment demonstrated a direct connection between the £1,000,000 payment and (H's) renunciation of the bequest of £665,000. The appellant's evidence denying the existence of a connection was unconvincing and utterly unpersuasive.' Accordingly, the renunciation did not meet the requirements of *IHTA 1984, s 142(1)*, and 'was of no legal effect'. [2009] STC SCD 352 Sp C 740.

Lloyds Private Banking Ltd v CIR

Life interest in matrimonial home given to husband, daughter absolutely entitled on death of her father – whether an interest in possession conferred by the wife on husband. IHTA 1984, s 43(2).

A married couple lived together as tenants in common. The wife died in 1989. By her will, she appointed a trustee and bequeathed her 50% share in the matrimonial home to the trustee, directing that her husband should be permitted to continue to live there until his death, and that her share should then pass to her daughter. The husband continued to live in the property until his death in 1993. The Revenue issued a notice of determination, charging IHT on the basis that the deemed transfer of value on the husband's death included the entire interest in the property, on the basis that his wife's will had given him an interest in possession in her 50% share of the property. The trustee appealed, contending that the will did not confer an interest in possession, and that the will had conferred no new rights on the husband, who was entitled to the use and enjoyment of the property as a co-owner. The Special Commissioner accepted this contention and allowed the appeal. On the wife's death, the husband had continued to enjoy the right to reside in the property and that right could only have been terminated by the husband's volition or by a court order under Law of Property Act 1925 s 30. The effect of the wife's will was that there had been an absolute gift of her 50% share in the property to her daughter, subject to a direction to the trustee to postpone sale. The case was taken on appeal to the Chancery Division and in a reserved judgment Lightman J allowed the appeal brought by originating summons by the Inland Revenue. Lightman J stated that the critical issue was whether clause 3 was dispositive or merely laid down administrative directions to the Trustee. Clause 3 was dispositive and conferred on Mr Evans a determinable life interest in the half share although it was dressed up as a set of administrative instructions. See also dicta of Wood VC in *Maddison v Chapman*, 1859, 4 K & J 709, and Farwell J in *Re Shuckburgh's Settlement*, Ch D [1901] 2 Ch 794, applied. [1997] STC SCD 259 Sp C 133; [1998] STC 559.

Lloyds TSB plc (Antrobus' Personal Representatives) v CIR

Farmhouse set in 132 acres was 'a farmhouse with a farm and definitely not a house with land'.

A deceased estate included a six-bedroom house, part of which had been built in the sixteenth century, and a number of agricultural buildings, set in about 132 acres of agricultural land. The site had been used as a farm by the same family for more than 90 years. The Revenue issued a notice of determination that the house was not 'of a character appropriate to the property' for the purposes of *IHTA 1984, s 115(2)*, and thus did not qualify for agricultural property relief. The company which acted as the deceased's personal representative appealed. The Special Commissioner allowed the appeal, finding that the property 'was in a poor state of repair and maintenance. The result was that, even if the dwelling-house had at one time been a family home of some distinction, it had, both in appearance and in use, become a farmhouse on a working farm.' On the evidence, the house was 'a farmhouse with a farm and definitely not a house with land'. It was 'of a character appropriate to the property' for the purposes of *s 115(2)*. [2002] STC SCD 468 Sp C 336.

Lloyds TSB plc (Antrobus' Personal Representative) v Twiddy

Lands Tribunal decision – 30% discount for farmhouse to reflect agricultural value.

HMRC issued a notice of determination that the farmhouse (see case report above) in question had a market value in excess of its value as agricultural property, so that IHT was payable on the amount by which the market value exceeded the agricultural value. The personal representatives appealed, contending that the agricultural value was the same as the market value. The Lands Tribunal reviewed the evidence in detail, rejected this contention and dismissed the appeal, holding that the open market value of the farmhouse should be discounted by 30% to arrive at its 'agricultural value'. [2004] DET/47/2004.

Lynall (deceased), In re

The amount or value of the consideration for an asset – value of unquoted shares while public flotation under consideration.

In an estate duty case the question at issue was the price which certain unquoted shares 'would fetch if sold in the open market at the time of the death of the deceased'. At the time of the death, the directors were considering public flotation and favourable confidential reports had been made to them for that purpose by a firm of accountants and a firm of stockbrokers. The HL held, *inter alia*, that although no general rule could be laid down as to the information a hypothetical purchaser in an open market may be deemed to have, the board could not be deemed to disclose confidential information. HL 1971, 47 TC 375; [1972] AC 680; [1971] 3 All ER 904. (*Note*. See now *TCGA 1992, s 273*, deriving from *FA 1973*. The substantive decision here is therefore no longer applicable, but the judgments include a useful review of estate duty cases dealing with the valuation of unquoted shares. See also *Battle v CIR* and *CIR v Crossman*, *Caton's Administrators v Couch* and *Clark (Clark's Executor) v CIR*.)

Lyon's Personal Representatives v HMRC; Trustees of the Alloro Trust v HMRC

FA 1986, s 102(1) – settlor retaining powers of revocation over discretionary trust – whether a gift with reservation.

In 1999 a settlor (L) gave £2,700,000 to the trustees of a discretionary trust. Under the trust deed, L retained the power of revocation, and was also a potential beneficiary of the trust. During his lifetime, L received distributions totalling £15,965 from the trust. L died in 2004. Following his death, HMRC issued a notice of determination on the basis that his transfer of the £2,700,000 to the trust was a 'gift with reservation', within *FA 1986, s 102*. The trustees, and L's personal representatives, appealed. The Special Commissioner dismissed the appeals, holding that there had been a 'reservation of benefit', within *s 102(1)(b)*. Furthermore, the manner in which the trust had been operated meant that the 'possession and enjoyment of the property' had not been 'bona fide assumed by the donee at the beginning of the relevant period', within *s 102(1)(a)* [2007] Sp C 616.

MacArthur's Executors v HMRC

Value of unquoted shares including loans with conversion rights.

A solicitor (M) died in 1994. He held shares in three family investment companies, and had made loans to two of the companies. HMRC issued notices of determination on the basis that these loans had given M options to acquire further shares in the companies, and were of the nature of convertible unsecured loan stock. HMRC's determination valued the shareholdings on an assets basis. For two of the companies, where M had a majority shareholding, HMRC allowed a discount of 12.5% to take account of lack of marketability. For the third company, where the shareholding was a minority one, HMRC allowed a discount of 45%. M's executors appealed, contending that the conversion rights had little or no value. The Special Commissioner reviewed the evidence in detail, rejected this contention, and upheld HMRC's determinations. The Commissioner observed that there was 'more than sufficient evidence in the form of writs of the debtor to prove the existence of the loans and conversion rights . . . the unit of valuation is the shares in each company plus the relevant conversion rights or options which must be regarded as valid, subsisting and enforceable'. [2008] STC SCD 1100 Sp C 700.

McCall & Keenan (Personal Representatives of Mrs E McClean) v HMRC

IHTA 1984, s 105(3) – business of 'making or holding investments'.

In 1983 a widow (M) inherited 33 acres of farmland on the death of her husband. She did not farm the land herself, but let it to local farmers under conacre or agistment agreements. She died in 1999. The Revenue issued a notice of determination charging IHT on her estate. Her personal representatives appealed, contending that the farmland qualified for business property relief. The Special Commissioner rejected this contention and dismissed the appeal, holding that although M was carrying on a business on the land, that business consisted mainly of making or holding investments, within *IHTA 1984, s 105(3)*, so that the land was not 'relevant business property'. The Commissioner observed that 'the activities of the business consisted of the making available of its major asset to other persons for payment without the separate provision of any substantial other goods or services'. The Court of Appeal (Northern Ireland) unanimously upheld this decision. Girvan LJ held that 'the use by the graziers was sufficiently exclusive for the land to be shown to be used as an investment. The agisting farmer had exclusive rights of grazing; he was entitled to exclude other graziers including the deceased; the deceased could not use the land for any purpose that interfered with the grazing and the letting for grazing was the way in which the deceased decided that the grasslands could be used and exploited as uncultivated grassland short of the creation of a lease. The deceased's business consisted of earning a return from grassland whose real and effective value lay in its grazing potential.' [2008] STC SCD 757 Sp C 678; CA(NI) [2009] NICA 12.

McDowall & Others (McDowall's Executors) v CIR (and related appeal)

Power of attorney – gifts out of deceased estate – whether valid.

In 1993, an elderly man (M) granted a deed conferring a power of attorney on his wife, and providing that if she predeceased him, the power should pass to his son-in-law. M's wife died in 1996. M's son-in-law used the power of attorney to make substantial gifts out of M's estate. M died in April 1998. His solicitors submitted an inventory to HMRC, accepting that gifts of £604,645 were chargeable transfers on which IHT was due, but treating gifts of £12,000 to each of the five children of the deceased as exempt transfers within the normal expenditure out of income exemption. The Revenue issued notices of determination to M's executors, determining that these gifts were not validly made nor within the exemption for gifts out of income. The executors appealed. The Special Commissioners reviewed the evidence in detail and dismissed the appeals, holding that on a proper construction of the power of attorney, M's son-in-law had no authority to make the gifts. Applying *dicta* of Russell J in *Re Reckitt*, CA [1928] 2 KB 244, 'the primary object of a power of attorney is to enable the attorney to act in the management of his principal's affairs. An attorney cannot, in the absence of a clear power to do so, make presents to himself or to others of his principal's property.' The gifts which M's son-in-law had purported to make were *ultra vires*, and M's executors were entitled to recover them. Therefore the amounts in question formed part of M's estate at the time of his death, and were chargeable to IHT accordingly. However, had this not been the case, the Special Commissioners said that there was a clear intention to make further gifts each year to the children and therefore the sums of £12,000 given to each of them would otherwise have been within the exemption for normal expenditure out of income. [2004] STC SCD 22 Sp C 382.

McKelvey (personal representative of DV McKelvey) v HMRC

Dispositions for maintenance of family within IHTA 1984, s 11.

A spinster (D) lived with her widowed mother (M), who was 85-years-old, blind and in poor health. D, who owned two houses, was told that she was suffering from terminal cancer. In early 2003, D gave the houses to M. D died in 2005 and M died in 2007. HMRC issued a notice of determination, charging IHT on D's gift of the houses to M (the combined value of the houses being agreed as £169,000). D's executor appealed, contending that D had given the houses to M so that they could be sold in order to pay for nursing care, so that they were exempt transfers within *IHTA 1984, s 11(3)*. The Special Commissioner reviewed the evidence in detail and allowed the appeal in part, finding that it had been reasonable for D to have assumed that M 'would require nursing care in a residential setting'. The Commissioner held that, in order to determine what amount had been 'reasonably required' for M's care, 'the approach adopted in personal injury cases is appropriate'. On the evidence, he held that it would be reasonable to have assumed that M would have required paid nursing care for five and a half years, and that this care would have cost £21,000 pa, leading to a basic sum of £115,500. He also held that a further £25,000 should be made added 'to cover the contingency of (M's) admission to a home', so that 'reasonable provision at the time the transfers were made amounted in all to £140,500'. The Commissioner concluded that £140,500 of the transfers qualified as exempt within *IHTA 1984, s 11*, while the balance of £28,500 was a chargeable transfer within *IHTA 1984, s 3A(4)*. [2008] STC SCD Sp C 694.

Macpherson & Another v CIR

Associated operations.

On 29 March 1977, trustees of a discretionary settlement entered into an agreement with D which meant, in effect, that D would have custody of some valuable trust paintings for 14 years. Although the agreement was on commercial terms, it reduced the value of the trustees' interest in the paintings. On the following day, the trustees appointed a protected life interest in the paintings, subject to the agreement, to D's son. The Revenue charged CTT on the reduction in value, and the trustees appealed, contending that *IHTA 1984, s 10** applied since the transactions had not been intended to confer gratuitous benefit. The HL rejected this contention and upheld the charge to CTT. The agreement and appointment were associated operations, and together constituted a transaction intended to confer gratuitous benefit on D's son. HL [1988] STC 362; [1988] 2 WLR 1261; [1988] 2 All ER 753.

Mallender & Others (Drury-Lowe's Executors) v CIR

IHTA 1984, s 110(b) – Lloyd's underwriter – commercial property charged to bank – whether 'assets used in the business'.

A Lloyd's underwriter (D) died in 1993. His underwriting business was supported by several bank guarantees. In consideration for the guarantees, D had indemnified the bank against all liabilities and had secured this liability by a charge over some commercial property which D owned. The Revenue issued notices of determination on the basis that the commercial property did not qualify for business property relief. D's executors appealed, contending that the effect of the charge over the commercial property was that it was within the definition of 'assets used in the business' within *IHTA 1984, s 110(b)*. The Ch D rejected this contention and upheld the notices (reversing the decision of the Special Commissioner). Jacob J held that an asset used as a security for a guarantee was not 'relevant business property' within *IHTA 1984, s 105(1)(a)*. The property was not itself used in the business, and did not qualify for relief. STC SCD 574 Sp C 264; Ch D [2001] STC 514.

Martin & Horsfall (Moore's Executors) v CIR

Business property relief – relevant business property – IHTA 1984, s 105(3)

A widow owned a number of industrial units. On her death, the Revenue issued a notice of determination. Her executors appealed, contending that the industrial units qualified for business property relief. The Special Commissioner dismissed the appeal, holding that the effect of *IHTA, s 105(3)* was that the property was not relevant business property', since the widow's business consisted 'wholly or mainly . . . of making or holding investments'. The Commissioner noted that *s 105(3)* derived from *FA 1976*, and that, during the relevant Finance Bill Debates, the Chief Secretary of the Treasury had stated that the letting of land did not qualify for business property relief. [1995] STC SCD 5 Sp C 2.

Melville and Others v CIR

IHTA, s 272 – definition of 'property'.

In 1993 a settlor (M) made a discretionary settlement under terms which conferred on him a general power to direct the trustees to exercise a power of apportionment, and included the power to direct the trustees to transfer the whole of the trust fund to him absolutely. In 1999 the Revenue issued a notice of determination on the trustees. They appealed, contending that M's right to require them to revest all or part of the settled property on him was part of the 'rights and interests of any description' which by virtue of *IHTA, s 272*, formed part of M's estate immediately after the settlement. The Ch D accepted this contention and allowed the appeal. Lightman J noted that the settlement had been intended 'to create a situation in which the settlor is able to make a substantial transfer of assets into a settlement which gives rise to a charge to inheritance tax in respect of the entire disposal, while at the same time ensuring that the amount of inheritance tax actually payable is negligible'. However, he held that not to treat the general power of appointment as 'property' within *s 272* would open the way 'to the artificial diminution of settlors' estates by the purchase of valuable consideration of enduring general powers of appointment under unconnected settlements'. A general power of appointment was 'something of very real value vested in the appointor'. [2000] STC 628; Ch D [2000] All ER(D) 832; CA [2001] STC 1271. The Court of Appeal upheld this decision. (*Note*. See now *FA 2002, s 119*. This is intended to ensure that, with effect from 17 April 2002, 'powers over trust property are to be disregarded for IHT purposes . . . except where doing so would create new scope for tax avoidance'.).

Miller & Others v CIR

Interest in possession – power to appropriate revenue to meet depreciation of capital value of assets – whether administrative or dispositive.

Property was held in trust to pay the whole of the free annual income to the wife for life but with the trustees having power, before striking the free income from any year, to appropriate such portion of the revenue as they thought proper to meet depreciation of the capital value of any asset or for any other reason they deemed advisable in their sole discretion. On the death of the wife, survived by her husband and children, the husband was entitled to one-third of the free income and the remainder was held for the maintenance and education of the children, also subject to the trustees' power to appropriate revenue to meet depreciation of assets etc. Following *Pearson and Others v CIR*, the CS held that, on the facts, the powers given to the trustees were administrative and not dispositive and that the wife had an interest in possession in the whole fund. On her death, therefore, a liability to CTT arose, subject to the exemption to the extent of the one-third interest passing to the husband, under the provisions of *CGTA 1984, ss 4(1), 5(1), 49(1)**. CS 1986, [1987] STC 108.

Millington v Secretary of State for the Environment

Wine making can be agriculture. Section 55, Town and Country Planning Act 1990.

Land was used for the creation of a new product from produce grown on that land, the land was still capable of being used for the purpose of agriculture and therefore was exempt from planning control. Mr Millington owned a site of nine hectares which included part of an old Roman city and this was turned over to vine growing, wine making and visits to the Roman site. The planning authority served Mr Millington with an enforcement notice relating to that part of the site on which a building stood which stored wine, wine making equipment and retail area. Mr Millington appealed to the Secretary of State who dismissed the appeal but granted planning permission for an existing building to provide facilities for the making of wine but selling the wine from the premises was disallowed. The Millingtons appealed and Judge Rich, QC, after due consideration remitted the case back to the Secretary of State. The Court of Appeal held that the making and selling of wine made from grapes grown on the land was capable of being an agricultural use. [1999] TLR 29 June 1999.

Montagu Trust Co (Jersey) Ltd and Others v CIR

Excluded property – trust fund invested in government securities – beneficiaries domiciled abroad.

The trust fund of a settlement made by K in 1970 was invested in a single holding of 1976 Treasury Loan Stock. This stock was exempt from taxation so long as it was in the beneficial ownership of persons neither domiciled nor ordinarily resident in the UK. K's daughter, W, made a similar settlement in 1976. The settlor, trustees and beneficiaries were all domiciled outside the UK but the trust was to be governed by English law. The trustees of the two settlements transferred the 1970 settlement trust fund to themselves as trustees of the 1976 settlement, to be held on trusts for the exclusive benefit of W's four children and their issue. On the following day the trustees executed a deed of appointment whereby each child became entitled to an interest in possession of one quarter of the trust fund. The Revenue raised assessments on the ground that the making of the appointment constituted a deemed capital distribution. The trustees' appeals were dismissed by the Ch D. There was a possibility that the fund might benefit people domiciled in the UK. On the facts, the trusts of the 1976 settlement were not exclusively for the benefit of W's four children, but might also benefit W's grandchildren. Accordingly, there were resulting trusts to persons who might be resident in the UK and thus the trust fund was not excluded property. Ch D, [1989] STC 477.

Munro v Commrs of Stamp Duties of New South Wales

Gifts with reservation – exclusion of the donor from any benefit.

Arrangements between the donee and a third party to give the donor benefit is within the provisions but retention of rights under a contract made prior to the gift and quite separate from it is not. The gift of land already subject to a lease to the donor is not a gift with reservation as the lease is not part of the gift. PC [1934] AC 61; [1933] All ER 185.

Nader v HMRC

Death-bed avoidance scheme involving purchase of income interest in a trust.

Shortly before her death, an individual entered into an IHT avoidance scheme under which she borrowed £1 million from a company to buy an income interest in a settlement. That loan was repaid out of and replaced by a £1 million loan to her from the settlement itself. On her death, the beneficiaries under her will were then appointed as beneficiaries under the settlement. After probate was granted, the trustee of the settlement distributed the benefit of the loan amongst the beneficiaries of the will.

Expert evidence was given to the effect that the income interest under the trust was not saleable on the open market and the appellants were unable to produce any evidence to the contrary. Accordingly, it was held that the purchase of the income interest resulted in a reduction in the value of the individual's estate equal to the purchase price paid. That reduction was a chargeable transfer with gratuitous intent in that it was intended to benefit the beneficiaries of her estate. [2018] UKFTT 294 (TC).

Nadin v CIR

Irregular payments to close relatives – whether exempt from IHT as 'normal expenditure of the transferor' – IHTA 1984, s 21.

An elderly spinster (P) died in 1995. During the years before her death, she had made a number of irregular payments to close relatives. The Revenue issued a notice of determination charging IHT on the basis that the gifts made in the seven years before P's death were transfers of value. Her executor appealed, contending that the gifts were exempt from IHT under *IHTA 1984, s 21* as 'part of the normal expenditure of the transferor'. The Special Commissioner rejected this contention and dismissed the appeal. On the evidence, the payments in question were abnormal expenditure rather than normal expenditure, and thus failed to qualify for exemption. Dicta of Lightman J in *Bennett & Others* applied. [1997] STC SCD 107 Sp C 112.

Nelson Dance Family Settlement Trustees v HMRC

Transfer of farmland with development value.

In 2002 a farmer transferred some farmland, which had development value, to the trustees of a family settlement. HMRC issued a ruling that 'none of the value transferred was attributable to the value of relevant business property'. The trustees appealed. The Special Commissioner allowed the appeal, specifically disapproving passages in Dymond's Capital Taxes and Foster's Inheritance Tax which suggested that the transfer of business assets (as distinct from the transfer of a business itself) would not qualify for relief. The Commissioner (Dr. Avery Jones) held that 'everything turns on the loss in value to the donor's estate, rather than what is given or how the loss to the estate arises, except where the identity of the recipient is crucial to a particular exemption' He held that business property relief was 'much more concerned with values than property. Although the attribution is to the net value of the business as a whole, this does not imply that the value transferred must relate to the whole business. Indeed the exclusion for value attributed to excepted assets in *s 112* shows that the value transferred may need to be attributed to the value of particular business assets (although that would equally be the case if the relief were restricted to transfers of the whole business). Presumably the attribution to the net value of the business is to put a ceiling on the relief to prevent a transferor giving away the total assets of the business, claiming business relief for them, while retaining the liabilities and paying them out of other assets (although that seems to be possible for agricultural relief as the relief is given in terms of attribution to the agricultural value of agricultural property).' *IHTA 1984, s 104* should be construed as meaning that 'all that is required is that the value transferred by the transfer of value is attributable to the net value of the business'. Accordingly, the transfer of the farmland qualified for 100% business property relief. The Ch D upheld this decision. Sales J held that 'the general principle governing the operation of the *IHTA* is the loss to donor principle, which directs attention to changes in the value of the transferor's estate rather than in that of the transferee', and that 'any charge to tax does not turn upon what happens to property transferred when it is in the hands of the transferee'. [2008] STC SCD 792 Sp C 682; Ch D [2009] EWHC 71 (Ch).

New South Wales Commrs of Stamp Duties v Permanent Trustee Co of New South Wales Ltd

Gifts with reservation – exclusion of donor from enjoyment.

The PC held that this condition is not fulfilled if at some later date after the gift the property or income therefrom is voluntarily applied by the donee to the donor, even if the latter is under an obligation to repay sums used by him. PC [1956] AC 512; [1956] 2 All ER 512; [1956] 3 WLR 152.

New South Wales Commrs of Stamp Duties v Perpetual Trustee Co Ltd

Gifts with reservation – settlements.

A settlement of shares in favour of an infant child with absolute gift provided he reached the age of 21 but with a resulting trust to the donor if the child failed to reach that age was not a gift with reservation as the property comprised in the gift was the equitable interest which the donor had created in the shares. PC, [1943] AC 425; [1943] 1 All ER 525.

Nichols v CIR

Gifts with reservation – exclusion of the donor from any benefit.

A gift of land subject to an agreement to a lease-back created at the same or a later time is the grant of the whole with something reserved out of it and not a gift of a partial interest leaving something in the hands of the grantor which he has not given away. CA, [1975] STC 278; [1975] 2 All ER 120; [1975] 1 WLR 534.

Ninth Marquess of Hertford and others (Executors of Eighth Marquess of Hertford deceased) v CIR

IHTA, s 110(b) – historic house used for business purposes and as private residence – whether 'assets used in the business'.

Part of a historic house was open to the public, while part was used as a private residence and not open to the public. The freeholder died in 1997. The Inland Revenue issued a notice of determination charging IHT on 22% of the value of the house, on the basis that only 78% of the house was open to the public and thus only 78% of the house qualified for business property relief. The freeholder's executors appealed, contending that the house was a single asset and that the effect of *IHTA 1984, s 110(b)* was that the whole of the house qualified for business property relief even though 22% of the house was not open to the public. The Special Commissioner accepted this contention and allowed the appeal, observing that *s 110* made no provision for apportionment, and holding that 'it is natural to consider a single building as a single asset where the unencumbered freehold is in single ownership'. The house was 'plainly important as a single structure and the whole building is a vital backdrop to the business carried on.

The whole of the exterior is essential to the business.' [2005] STC SCD 177 Sp C –4.

Oakes v Commrs of Stamp Duties of New South Wales

Gifts with reservation – exclusion of the donor from any benefit.

Remuneration paid to the settlor as trustee, but not money spent on the maintenance and education of the donor's children, is a benefit. PC [1954] AC 57; [1953] 2 All ER 1563; [1953] 3 WLR 1127.

Oakley & Hutson (Jossaume's Personal Representatives) v CIR

Testator's will giving company right to occupy property – whether testator's widow had interest in possession.

A company director (J) died in 1993. Under his will, as modified by a deed of family arrangement, he gave his shares in the company to his son, and two freehold properties to trustees, with directions to pay the trust income to his widow for her lifetime and thereafter to his three children in equal shares. One of the freehold properties was occupied by the company, and J directed that the trustees of his will should not require the company to pay any rent. J's executors treated the property as having been transferred to his widow, and as qualifying for the exemption for transfers between spouses. J's widow died in 2000, and the Inland Revenue issued a notice of determination that IHT was chargeable on her interest in possession in the premises which were occupied by the company. Her personal representatives appealed, contending that the executors had made an error in treating the interest in the premises as having been transferred to J's widow, that J's will had conferred an interest in possession on the company, and that his widow did not have an interest in possession. The Special Commissioner accepted this contention and allowed the appeal, holding that J had intended that his will should 'protect the position of the company and . . preserve its use and occupancy' of the premises. The will gave the company a right to occupy the premises, and that right arose 'solely under the will'. The right in question was 'a present right to present enjoyment of property' and was an 'interest in possession' within *IHTA 1984, s 49(1)*. (The Commissioner observed that the effect of this decision was that IHT 'will have become due in respect of the transfer of the yard at his death . . . (but) that a lower amount of inheritance tax will be payable than would have been the case' if IHT had been charged on the death of J's widow.) [2005] STC SCD 343 Sp C 460.

Ogden & Hutchinson (Griffiths' Executors) v Trustees of the RHS Griffiths 2003 Settlement & Others

Application for transfers of assets into settlements to be set aside.

In April 2003 an individual (G) granted a deferred lease of his property to a settlement, and transferred his shares in a company to a short-term discretionary trust. In February 2004 he transferred his reversionary interest in the shares to a third settlement. Later that year he was diagnosed as suffering from cancer. He died in April 2005, so that the transfers became chargeable to IHT. His executors applied to the Chancery Division (Ch D) for the transfers to be set aside. The Ch D granted the application in part. Lewison J declined to set aside the April 2003 transfers, as medical evidence indicated that it was 'extremely unlikely' that G had been suffering from cancer at that time. Applying the principles laid down in *Ogilvie v Allen*, HL 1899, 15 TLR 294, 'a donor can only obtain back property which he has given away by showing that he was under some mistake of so serious a character as to render it unjust on the part of the donee to retain the property given to him'. However, the evidence suggested that G had already been suffering from cancer in February 2004, so that his chances of surviving for three years were very remote. If G had been aware of this, he would not have transferred his reversionary interest in the shares. It would be 'unjust for the donees to retain the gift in circumstances which impose upon the donor an unintended liability to a very substantial amount of inheritance tax'. Accordingly, the Ch D exercised its discretion to set aside the February 2004 transfer. Ch D [2008] EWHC 118 (Ch); STC 776.

O'Neill and others v IRC

Deposit account in joint names of deceased and daughter – whether general power to dispose of the whole account. IHTA 1984, s 5.

An individual (O) died in 1992. In 1980 and 1984 he had opened deposit accounts in an Isle of Man bank, in the joint names of O and his daughter. He had deposited substantial sums in the accounts. The Revenue issued a notice of determination charging IHT on the basis that the whole of the amounts in the deposit accounts formed part of O's estate. O's daughter and executors appealed, contending that only 50% of the sums in the accounts should be treated as part of O's estate. The Special Commissioner rejected this contention and dismissed the appeals, holding on the evidence that O 'enjoyed the entire beneficial interest in the accounts during his lifetime'. O's daughter had not known that the accounts existed until after her father's death. The fact that O's daughter was never informed of the accounts in her father's lifetime rebutted the presumption of advancement except to the extent that it applied to the right of survivorship. While she had a beneficial right of survivorship, she did not have 'a present beneficial interest in the accounts during her father's lifetime'. Only O had been able to operate the accounts, and this *de facto* control of the accounts was 'a clear pointer to the conclusion' that he had not made a lifetime gift of an immediate interest in the accounts to his daughter. [1998] STC SCD 110 Sp C 154.

Owen, Re, Owen v CIR

Time of disposition – time of gift by cheque.

More than three years before his death O gave a cheque to each of three relatives. However the cheques were not presented for payment until within the three-year period before O's death. The gifts were held to have been made when the cheques cleared into each donee's own account and were therefore liable to ED as being gifts made within three years of the donor's death. Ch D, [1949] 1 All ER 901.

Parry and others as Personal representatives of R F Staveley deceased v HMRC

Transfer of value for IHT purposes – whether transfer made without gratuitous intent – IHTA 1984, s 10 – omission to exercise rights.

Mrs R F Staveley had been diagnosed with terminal cancer early in 2006. Subsequent to that, she transferred the funds in a section 32 pension plan into a personal pension plan, the terms of which would allow the entire fund to be paid to her estate or to other beneficiaries. The purpose of the transfer was to ensure that her ex-husband could not benefit from the fund. She took no benefits from the policy prior to her death in December 2006 and nominated her two sons as the beneficiaries to receive the death benefits from the fund.

HMRC considered that the transfer of funds from the section 32 policy was a transfer of value for IHT purposes but her executors argued that it was exempt as being made without gratuitous intent – the purpose was to ensure the fund could not benefit the ex-husband. The Supreme Court held that the exemption did not apply in the circumstances and the transfer was not made with intention of providing a benefit to the sons.

HMRC also considered that the failure to take pension benefits after the transfer was an omission to exercise a right which caused an increase in the sons' estates. The Upper Tribunal rejected this argument because it could not be said that the sons' estates were necessarily increased; the pension trustees might have exercised their discretion to pay the funds to other potential beneficiaries. However, the Court of Appeal reversed this decision on the basis that the pension trustees would inevitably follow the wishes of the deceased and distribute the funds to the sons. The Supreme Court agreed this decision and upheld the charge to IHT by virtue of the omission to take benefits from the scheme whilst in ill health. See now *IHTA 1984, s 12(2Z)* which removes tax charges where a person omits to take pension rights. [2020] UKSC 35.

Pawson deceased (personal representatives of) v HMRC

Business property relief – bungalow used for holiday lettings

A seaside bungalow was let on a weekly basis as holiday accommodation. It was a standard holiday let business, in that the property was fully furnished and equipped, and it was cleaned between lets and freshly laundered bedding provided on each occasion, but no supplementary services were provided. The appellant claimed that the property qualified for IHT business property relief, but the claim was refused by HMRC on the grounds that the business was mainly one of holding the property as an investment for rental income. The appeal was allowed on the basis that significant services were provided, such that 'an intelligent businessman would not regard the ownership of a holiday letting property as an investment and would regard it as involving far too active an operation for it to come under that heading'. On the appeal by HMRC to the Upper Tax Tribunal, the decision was reversed. The Upper Tribunal held that the only conclusion which it was reasonably open to draw from the facts was that the property was held as an investment. It was a typical example of a property letting business and the services did not preponderate to such an extent that the investment nature of the business was not the main element. *Pawson deceased v HMRC* [2013] UKUT 50 (TCC).

Pearson and Others v CIR

Meaning of interest in possession.

Subject to the trustees' overriding power of appointment, to their power to accumulate income and to the possibility of partial defeasance on the birth of further children to the settlor, property in a 1964 settlement was held upon trust in equal shares absolutely for the three daughters of the settlor upon their attaining the age of 21. They were all 21 by the end of February 1974. On 20 March 1976 the trustees appointed the income of £16,000 to one of the daughters, F. The Revenue determined that F had become entitled to an interest in possession in the £16,000 at a time when no such interest subsisted in that part of the trust fund and that accordingly CTT became payable by virtue of *FA 1975, 5 Sch 6(2)*. By a three to two majority, and reversing the unanimous decision of the CA in favour of the trustees, the HL upheld the Revenue's determination. The trustees' power of accumulation prevented the interests the daughters obtained upon reaching 21 from being interests in possession. For there to be an interest in possession there must be a present right to the present enjoyment of something and the power of accumulation prevented the daughters from having an immediate right to anything. A distinction was drawn by Viscount Dilhorne between trustees' administrative powers, such as those to pay duties, taxes etc., and their dispositive power to dispose of the net income of the trust fund. A mere administrative power will not prevent an interest from being in possession. HL 1980, CTTL 5; [1980] STC 318; [1980] 2 All ER 479; [1980] 2 WLR 872.

Perry v CIR

IHTA 1984, s 200(1) – transfer on death – person liable.

A property dealer (K) had a joint bank account with a young woman (P), who lived in a property which K owned. K died in 1989, at which time there was more than £1,000,000 in the account. K's executors (a solicitor and an accountant) provided the Revenue with details of his estate, but made no reference to this bank account. In 1991

P replaced the accountant as K's personal representative. In 1995 the personal representatives (P and the solicitor) presented a bankruptcy petition, declaring that the estate was insolvent. The Revenue subsequently ascertained details of the bank account, and in 1997 they issued a notice of determination that P was liable to IHT in respect of half of the money in the account at K's death. The Special Commissioner upheld the determination and dismissed P's appeal, holding on the evidence that 'the joint account constituted a gift from (K) to the appellant of the balance for the time being in the account'. The effect of *IHTA 1984, s 200(1)(c)* was that P was liable to account for tax on the money in question. (The Commissioner also upheld a further notice of determination, holding that in 1984 K had given P 'an irrevocable licence to occupy rent-free . . . for life' the property in which she lived.) [2005] STC SCD 474 Sp C 474.

Phillips and Others (Phillips' Executor) v HMRC

Business property relief – activities of a money-lender who lent money to family companies qualified for business property relief.

A widow held a majority shareholding in a company (P) which lent money to related family companies. Her executors claimed business property relief. The Revenue rejected the claim on the basis that the shares were not 'relevant business property', because P's business consisted mainly of 'making or holding investments', within *IHTA 1984, s 105(3)*. The Special Commissioner allowed the executors' appeal, finding that P was 'a banking arm for in-house transactions' and holding that 'few would regard the activities of a money-lender as investment'. On the evidence, P 'was in the business of making loans and not in the business of investing in loans . . . the loans were not investments for their own sake but the provision of a finance facility to the other companies'. Accordingly, the shares in P qualified for business property relief. [2006] STC SCD 639 Sp C 555.

Phizackerley (Personal Representative of Dr PJR Phizackerley) v HMRC

FA 1986, s 103 – treatment of certain debts.

A married woman died in 2000. Her will left an amount equal to the IHT nil rate band to a discretionary trust for her husband (P) and their children, and the residue to P. He agreed to pay £150,000 plus indexation to the discretionary trust in return for his wife's half-share in the matrimonial home. P died in 2002, and HMRC issued a notice of determination charging IHT on his estate. His personal representative appealed, contending that the £153,222 which P owed to the discretionary trust should be deducted from the value of his estate. The Special Commissioner rejected this contention and dismissed his appeal, holding that the effect of *FA 1986, s 103* was that the debt was not deductible. The Commissioner also held that *IHTA 1984, s 11* (providing that a 'disposition for maintenance' is not a 'transfer of value') did not apply to a situation 'when a husband puts a house in joint names of himself and his wife during their marriage'. [2007] STC SCD 328 Sp C 591.

Plummer v CIR

Domicile – whether foreign domicile of choice acquired.

A taxpayer aged 18 at the beginning of the relevant years, whose domicile of origin was English, claimed that she was domiciled in Guernsey for the purpose of a claim under *ICTA 1988, s 65(4)**. She was born in London of English parents. When she was aged 15, her mother and a sister went to take up residence in Guernsey with her grandmother. From then the taxpayer divided her residence between England and Guernsey, generally continuing her education and training in England (where she was reading for a degree at London University in the relevant years) and living with her father there during the week, and going with him to Guernsey for the weekend. She gave evidence before the Special Commissioners of her attachment to Guernsey and her intention to live and work there. The Commissioners held that she had not become an 'inhabitant' of Guernsey in the years of claim and therefore could not be said to have acquired a domicile of choice in Guernsey. Hoffmann J upheld their decision. A person who kept a residence in his domicile of origin could only acquire a domicile of choice in another country if the residence established there was his chief residence. On the facts the Commissioners were entitled to conclude that the taxpayer had not yet settled in Guernsey and therefore had not acquired a domicile of choice there. Ch D 1987, 60 TC 452; [1987] STC 698; [1988] 1 WLR 292; [1988] 1 All ER 97.

Portland, Duchess of v CIR

Domicile – domicile acquired on marriage – effect of Matrimonial Proceedings Act 1973.

The taxpayer's domicile of origin was Canada. She acquired her husband's English domicile by dependence on her marriage. She lived in England with her husband but had a house in Canada which she visited annually and where she intended to live on her husband's retirement or death. The Ch D, reversing the decision of the Special Commissioners, held that by virtue of the *Matrimonial Proceedings Act 1973, s 1(2)* she retained her English domicile as a deemed domicile of choice, and her visits to Canada did not amount to an abandonment of that domicile. Ch D 1981, 54 TC 648; [1982] STC 149; [1982] 2 WLR 367; [1982] 1 All ER 784.

Postlethwaite's Executors v HMRC

Payment by close company to FURBS for controlling shareholder – whether IHTA 1984, s 10 applicable.*

A motor racing engineer (P) incorporated a Jersey company (L) in 1990. In 1991 L agreed to provide P's services to an Italian company (G) for £600,000 pa, and also agreed to employ P at a salary of £75,000 pa. In 1993 L paid £700,000 to a funded unapproved retirement benefits scheme for P. P died in 1999, aged 55. Subsequently the Inland Revenue issued a notice of determination that the payment of £700,000 was a transfer of value within *IHTA 1984, s 94*. P's executors appealed, contending that the payment was a disposition not intended to confer gratuitous benefit, within *IHTA 1984, s 10*. The Special Commissioners reviewed the evidence in detail, accepted this contention and allowed the appeal. The Commissioners observed that the fees paid by G to L were 'in line with the cost of the services of comparable motor racing engineers'. By contrast, 'the basic salary paid by (L) to (P) was very low for a person of his standing'. The payment of £700,000 was not unreasonable or gratuitous, since 'if (P) had contributed at the maximum allowable level to an approved UK scheme until he was 60 and his salary of £75,000 had increased with inflation, the pension which he would have obtained was about the same as that which the £700,000 would secure'. Furthermore, 'the fact that on legal analysis the payment was for past consideration does not mean that it was made with the intention of conferring a gratuitous benefit'. [2007] STC SCD 83 Sp C 571.

Powell & Halfhide, executor of G E Pearce v CIR

IHTA 1984, s 105(3). Business of managing a caravan park – making or holding investments.

The deceased and her daughter ran a caravan park where 23 of the 33 caravans were privately owned. The deceased or her representative needed to be in attendance at the site at all times. The profits of the business were assessed to tax under Schedule D, Case I. On death the personal representatives claimed relief under *s 105(3)* and this was refused by the Inspector who argued the 'making or holding investments' applied in this instance. The activities undertaken in the caravan park were either required under the terms of the lettings or the terms of the site licence which governed the lettings, or consisted of activities such as the social visits and organised medical visits, for which no charge was made, and so accordingly fell to be in the ambit of 'making and holding investments'. On the facts of the case it was determined that there was little difference in principle between, say, the owner of a portfolio of long leases receiving ground rents and the instant case where the main source of income was derived from pitch fees from long-term residents who owned their own caravans. The case has been withdrawn from application to be heard in the High Court by the taxpayers. [1997] STC SCD 181 Sp C 120.

Powell-Cotton v CIR

Interest in possession – life interest in settlement sold in consideration for shares in close company – subsequent transfer of shares by way of gift – whether a disposal of interest in possession in settled property.

In 1941 the taxpayer sold to a close company his life interest under a settlement for £25,000, to be paid by 25,000 £1 shares in the company. In 1964 he reacquired from the company his life interest in part of the settled property. His interest in the remainder of the settled property continued to be vested in the company. In 1982 the taxpayer transferred 2,999 of his shares to a charity by way of gift. Immediately before the transfer, he had held 8,993 of the 46,000 shares in the company. Accordingly, by virtue of what is now *IHTA 1984, s 101(1)* he fell to be treated as having been entitled to a part (8,993/46,000) of the interest in possession in the part of the settled property retained by the company. Following the transfer, he fell to be treated as being entitled to 5,994/46,000 of the interest in possession in question. The Revenue issued a notice of determination on the basis that he had made a transfer of value equal to (2,999/8,993 × 8993/46,000) of the settled property vested in the company. The taxpayer appealed, contending firstly that no part of the interest in possession had come to an end within *s 52(1)*, so that he had not made a disposal within *s 51(1)*, and alternatively that any transfer of value was exempt since it was attributable to property given to a charity within the meaning of what is now *IHTA 1984, s 23(1)*. The Ch D dismissed his appeal. The provisions of what is now *IHTA 1984, s 101(1)* required the interest in possession held by the close company to be treated as vested in the participators in that company. Accordingly, on the disposal of the shares, part of the taxpayer's interest in possession had come to an end within *IHTA 1984, s 52(1)*. The corollary of *IHTA 1984, s 101(1)* was that the company could not be treated as having an interest in possession in the settled property, since that would be inconsistent with the beneficial ownership attributed to the participator, and the company's right to the income of the retained part therefore had to be disregarded. Additionally, the effect of *IHTA 1984, s 56(3)* was that the deemed transfer of part of the settled property was not exempted by *IHTA 1984, s 23(1)*; Ch D, [1992] STC 625.

Price AL (Executor of Mrs RHP Price) v HMRC

Related property – IHTA 1984 s 161.

A married couple owned a freehold property as tenants in common. The wife (P) died in 1999. By her will, she left her share of the property to her children. It was agreed that if the property were to be sold as a whole, it would be valued at £1,500,000. HMRC issued a notice of determination charging IHT on this basis. P's husband (who was also her executor) appealed, contending inter alia that the effect of *IHTA 1984, s 161(1)* was there should be a substantial reduction in the valuation of P's half share of the property, to take account of the fact that the property could not be sold with vacant possession. The First-Tier Tribunal rejected this contention and dismissed the appeal in principle, applying the principles laid down by the CA in *Gray & Others (Lady Fox's Executors) v CIR*, see above, and holding that for the purposes of *IHTA, s 161*, the 'value of the aggregate' should be taken to be 'the price which the two items of property would fetch in the open market if offered for sale at the same time'. The tribunal directed that, if the parties were unable to agree the valuation in the light of this decision, any further points of dispute should be heard by the Lands Chamber of the Upper Tribunal. [2010] UKFTT 474, TC00736.

Pride as trustee of the estate of the late Geraldine Jill Pride v HMRC

IHTA 1984, ss 103 and 175A – sale of properties to trustees – purchase consideration in the form of loan notes – whether the trustees' debt to the settlor was deductible for IHT purposes

This case concerns arrangements which were known as a double trust or home loan scheme. Certain properties were acquired in 2002 by a trust from the settlor by a number of steps which resulted in the purchase price being satisfied by loan notes with long repayment dates issued to the settlor. She had an interest in possession in the trust. The settlor then gave the loan notes away to a trust for her children. HMRC challenged the arrangements principally on three grounds that: (1) there was a reservation of benefit by the settlor in the loan notes, an argument rejected by the Tribunal because the children's trust had full enjoyment of them under their terms; (2) the debt was not deductible from the funds in the trust for the settlor as it was owed by trustees who have property derived from the deceased (see *IHTA 1984, s 103*). It was argued for the trustees that the debt was not incurred by the settlor, as required by *IHTA 1984, s 103*, but the First-tier Tribunal rejected this on the basis that the trust fund was part of the settlor's estate, and so it could be regarded as a debt incurred by her; (3) the liability under the loan notes trust was not a deductible liability in the estate of the debtor since they were released after her death and a commercial creditor would have required repayment (see *IHTA 1984, s 175A*). The First-tier Tribunal accepted HMRC's the contentions of HMRC under (2) and (3) above. The trustee's appeal therefore failed. [2023] UKFTT 316 (TC), [2023] SFTD 796.

R v Williams and Another

Situation of property – registered shares.

Per Lord Maugham, shares are situate where they can be effectively dealt with as between the shareholder and the company so that the transferee will become legally entitled to all the rights of a member. PC, [1942] 2 All ER 95; [1942] AC 541.

Reynaud & Others v CIR

Settlement of shares in company followed by purchase of shares by company – whether IHTA, s 268 applicable.

Four brothers were negotiating to sell their shares in a family company (C). Before the sale took place, they each transferred some of their shares to a discretionary trust. On the following day C purchased the shares from the trustees, and the remaining shares in C were sold to an unrelated purchaser (M). The Revenue issued notices of determination charging IHT on the transfer, on the basis that the settlement of the shares in C, and the subsequent purchase of those shares by C, were 'associated operations' (so that, by virtue of *IHTA 1984, s 268(3)*, business property relief was not available on the transfer of the shares). The brothers appealed, contending that C's purchase of the shares 'was not a relevant associated operation because it did not contribute anything to the transfer of value', so that the transfer of the shares to the trusts qualified for business property relief. The Special Commissioners accepted this contention and allowed the appeal, finding that 'when the discretionary trusts were made, there was a real possibility that the sale to (M) would not proceed' and that 'the discretionary trusts had more than just a tax purpose' since they also had the purpose of 'benefiting the families of the settlors and charity'. Although the transfer of shares to the trusts, and C's subsequent purchase of those shares, were 'associated operations' within *IHTA 1984, s 268*, an associated operation was relevant to a disposition 'only if it is part of the scheme contributing to the reduction of the estate'. The value of the brothers' estates 'were diminished as a result of the gift into settlement alone. The purchase of own shares contributed nothing to the diminution which had already occurred and was not therefore a relevant associated operation.' [1999] STC SCD 185 Sp C 196. (*Note*. The Commissioners also held that the principles in *WT Ramsay Ltd v CIR*, did not apply, finding that 'completion of the sale took place after a day of negotiations with the purchaser and there must have been a reasonable likelihood that the negotiations would fail. Accordingly . . . the two transactions were not part of a single composite transaction for the purpose of the doctrine.' Furthermore, there was no 'inserted step which could be cut out in such a way so as to transform the gift of shares into a gift of cash'.)

Robertson v CIR

IHTA 1984, s 216(3A) – whether personal representatives made 'the fullest enquiries that are reasonably practicable'.

A woman (S) died in October 1999. She owned a house and its contents in Scotland, and a cottage in England. Her executors, one of whom was a solicitor, wished to sell the properties as soon as possible. In November, the solicitor (R) submitted an inventory of S's estate to HMRC, showing the Scottish house at a value of £60,000; its contents at £5,000; and the English cottage at £50,000. Although R had instructed valuers to carry out valuations of the two properties, he had not received these valuations at the time of submitting the inventory. Later that month the contents of the Scottish house were valued at £24,845, and in December the house was sold for £82,000. In January 2000 the English cottage and its grounds were valued at £315,000. R submitted a corrective inventory to the Capital Taxes Office, and paid the additional IHT due. The CTO informed him that they considered that the executors had not made 'the fullest enquiries that are reasonably practicable', as required by *IHTA 1984, s 216(3A)*, and they proposed to charge a penalty of £9,000, under *IHTA, s 247*. The Special Commissioner reviewed the evidence and held that R was not liable to any penalty, since he had made the fullest enquiries that were reasonably practicable in the circumstances. On the evidence, R had made a thorough examination of S's home shortly after her death, had appreciated that a valuation of the contents would be required, and had instructed a valuation promptly. In the meantime, he had, in accordance with accepted practice, inserted estimated valuations in the inventory and had disclosed that they were estimates. He had followed what was acceptable practice in the legal profession, and had fulfilled his duties as an executor and as a solicitor. The Revenue were not justified in seeking to impose a penalty. [2002] STC SCD 182 Sp C 309.

Rose, Re, Rose and Others v CIR

Time of disposition – registered shares.

A transfer under seal in the form appropriate to the company's regulations, together with delivery of the transfer and share certificate to the transferee, was held sufficient to constitute the transferee the beneficial owner of the shares at that time, although the transferee did not register the shares until a later date. So far as lay in his power the transferor had done all that he could to divest himself of his interest in the shares. CA, [1952] 1 All ER 1217; [1952] Ch 499.

Ross (Executors of the Estate of Marjorie) (Dec'd):

Business property relief claim for holiday lettings – IHTA 1984, s 105(3).

The deceased was a partner in a partnership which ran a business of letting eight cottages in Cornwall for self-catering holidays. In addition to the cottages two staff flats were held one of which was occupied by a handyman on site who not only dealt with maintenance issues but also arranged transport and other holiday trips for the guests. Other staff included a cleaner and a housekeeper. Receptionist services were provided at a hotel nearby. Guests had the opportunity to take meals at the hotel, some at preferential rates, or to have bar meals delivered to them. Most guests used the hotel facilities to some extent during their stay. There were other delivery services (milk and newspapers) and a wide range of equipment was available. Notwithstanding these additional services, the Tribunal held that essentially the business was the letting of land and therefore IHT business property relief was not available. TC05959 [2017] UKFTT 507 (TC).

Rosser v CIR

'Farmhouse' for the purpose of IHTA 1984, s 115(2).

P and his wife owned a farm with 41 acres of land. In 1989 they gave 39 acres to their daughter (R), who was carrying on a farming business with her husband seven miles away. P and his wife retained the farmhouse and two acres of land. Following the transfer, R and her husband farmed all 41 acres of land, including the two acres which P and his wife continued to own. P died in April 2001, and his wife died seven weeks later. The Revenue issued a notice of determination charging IHT on the farmhouse and a barn. (The Revenue accepted that the two acres of land were 'agricultural property' within *IHTA 1984, s 115(2)*.) R appealed, contending that she was entitled to agricultural property relief. The Special Commissioner allowed the appeal in part, holding that by 2001 the house was not a 'farmhouse' for the purpose of *IHTA 1984, s 115(2)*, since its 'prime function' was 'as a retirement home'. However, the barn was 'a working farm building' and qualified for relief. [2003] STC SCD 311 Sp C 368.

Routier and Venables (as executors of the late Beryl Coulter) v HMRC

The deceased was domiciled in Jersey but held assets of £1.8m in the UK. She died in 2007 and left her estate to a Jersey charitable trust. It was accepted that the trusts qualified as charitable under English law but HMRC denied relief on the basis that the trust must be governed by the law of the United Kingdom and subject to the jurisdiction of the United Kingdom courts. The High Court Chancery Division held in favour of HMRC on this point and the Court of Appeal upheld that decision. This was in accordance with the House of Lords' judgment in *Camille and Henry Dreyfus Foundation Inc v IRC* [1956] AC 39 and the Court of Appeal said that this has equal application to IHT. A further argument for the executors was that the denial of relief was an unlawful restriction on the movement of capital under European law was considered in a further hearing in June 2017 but it was held that there was adequate justification for the limitation to charities in the EEA due to the need for HMRC to be able to check the charitable status of the organisation concerned. [2016] EWCA Civ 938 and [2017] EWCA Civ 1584.

Russell & Another v CIR

Business property relief – deeds of variation.

A testator's residuary estate included a reserve fund at Lloyd's which qualified for business property relief. His executors entered into a Deed of Variation in 1983 and executed a further variation in 1985. The Revenue made a determination to the effect that business property relief was not available on the first variation. The Revenue also refused to accept that the second variation was within the scope of the relieving provisions in *FA 1978, s 68* (subsequently *IHTA 1984, s 142*). It was held that the second variation was not effective for capital transfer tax, as *FA 1978, s 68* did not apply to variations of dispositions previously varied under *FA 1978, s 68*. However, business property relief was held to be due in respect of the first variation because on the facts of the case the legacies in question could only be satisfied out of qualifying assets. (The rules on which the case was decided have been altered by *IHTA 1984, s 39A* with effect from 18 March 1986.) Ch D, [1988] STC 195; [1988] 1 WLR 834; [1988] 2 All ER 405.

Rysaffe Trustee Co (CI) Ltd v CIR

Valuation of settled property which comprised five discretionary settlements comprising trust funds of £10 each by way of a cheque for £50 with property to be added at a later date – deferred shares in a private company of which the settlors were members and directors were subsequently transferred to the five settlements. Was each settlement for the purposes of the ten yearly tax charge to be taken as property comprised in one settlement – whether creation of five settlements and transfer of shares to trustee associated operations – whether five settlements comprised five dispositions of property resulting in one settlement. IHTA 1984, ss 43(2), 64, 268(1)(b) and 272.

A settlor executed five settlements within a period of 35 days, and transferred shares of equal value to each settlement. The Inland Revenue issued a notice of determination that the five holdings should be treated as a single settlement for the purposes of the charge to tax under *IHTA 1984, s 64*. The company which acted as the trustee of the settlements appealed. The Ch D allowed the appeal, holding that there were five separate settlements for the purposes of *s 64*. Park J held that 'it is up to the settlor who places property in trust to determine whether he wishes to create one trust or several trusts, or for that matter merely to add more property to a settlement which had already been created in the past'. Each settlement was created by a 'disposition' within *IHTA 1984, s 43*. The 'associated operations' provisions of *IHTA 1984, s 268* did not apply, since *s 268* was 'not an operative provision which of itself imposes inheritance tax liabilities. It is a definition of an expression (associated operations) which is used elsewhere. The definition only comes into effect in so far as the expression "associated operations" is used elsewhere, and then only if the expression in another provision is relevant to the way in which that other provision applies to the facts of the particular case.' The CA unanimously upheld this decision. Mummery LJ held that 'the inclusion of "associated operations" in the statutory description of "disposition" is not intended for cases, such as this, where there is no dispute that there was a "disposition" of property falling within *s 43(2)*. They are intended for cases where there is a dispute as to whether there was a relevant "disposition" at all.' CA [2003] EWCA Civ 356; CA [2003] STC 536.

Salinger and Kirby

Avoidance scheme – purchase of interest in excluded property settlement.

Interests in an Isle of Man trust containing cash overseas and settled by a company domiciled outside the UK were purchased in 2009 by a UK domiciled beneficiary who died thereafter in 2011. The main trust interest purchased was as the sole income and capital beneficiary for the trust period of 150 years, but subject to a trustees' power to accumulate, hence the anti-avoidance legislation at *IHTA 1984, ss 3B, 3C* relating to purchased life interests did not apply. The First-tier Tax Tribunal accepted that the acquisition of this interest was a commercial bargain and so did not give rise to a chargeable transfer. [2016] UKFTT 0677 (TC).

Scott v HMRC

Gift of paintings during the lifetime of the deceased – whether effective delivery had taken place.

The appellant claimed that his mother had given certain paintings to him during her lifetime. At the time of the gifts the family home where the paintings were displayed was also the appellant's home. On the advice of their solicitor the paintings were removed in turn from the walls, handed to the appellant and then on his instruction re-hung where they had previously been. HMRC contended that there had been no effective delivery of the paintings to the appellant. The Tribunal noted that to effect a gift there has to be intention and (in the absence of a Deed of Gift) delivery. The procedure followed was sufficient for an effective gift to have been made. Similar issues arose in relation to a gift of paintings by the appellant's great aunt and the same principles were applied. [2015] UKFTT 266 (TC).

Seddon (Trustees of Mrs M Seddon's Second Discretionary Trust) v HMRC

Scrip dividend received by discretionary trustees and subsequently sold – whether the scrip dividend was capital to be taken into account under IHTA 1984, s 68(5)(c) in the calculation of a later IHT exit charge.

The trustees of a discretionary trust received a scrip dividend in January 2000 which was partly realised for cash two days later. In March 2009, shortly before the trust ten-year anniversary, the trustees made certain capital distributions. The trustees contended that the scrip dividend was income in their hands on the authority of the Court of Appeal decision in *Howell v Trippier* [2004] EWCA Civ 885, a case which related to the income tax treatment of the scrip shares. However that decision was held not to apply as regards trust law generally in *Gilchrist v HMRC* [2014] UKUT 169 (TCC). The First-tier Tax Tribunal held that in case of conflict it was bound to follow the later authority where it had fully considered earlier authorities. On this basis the scrip dividend was received as capital in the settlement and was therefore to be taken into account in the calculation of IHT exit charges. [2015] UKFTT 140 (TC).

Shelford (as trustee of the Herbert Life Interest Settlement) v HMRC

Home Loan Scheme – sale of property to trust in exchange for debt which was given away – validity of contract.

The taxpayer had entered into an inheritance tax saving arrangement commonly known as a home loan scheme (see **23.6**). A contract for the sale of a property to a trust was entered into, the terms of the trust being interest in possession to the taxpayer as settlor. The contract was never completed in order to avoid stamp duty. At the same time, a document was completed by which an interest-free loan repayable on demand was given to the trustees by the taxpayer for the purchase price of the property and the benefit of this debt, as an asset of the taxpayer was assigned by him to his children. The nature of the scheme was that it enabled the home to be continuously occupied by the taxpayer until his death in 2013 by virtue of his interest under the trust but the value in his estate would be reduced by the debt given away. Initially, HMRC challenged the arrangements with the arguments set out at **23.6** but in further submissions made after the Tribunal hearing they challenged the validity of the sale agreement on the basis that it did not set out all the terms of the sale as required by property law and so was void. The Tribunal agreed with this point with the result that the property remained in the taxpayer's estate. Had the scheme succeeded the Tribunal held that the position would be worse in that the house remained in his estate without deduction for the trustees rights (due to *IHTA 1984, s 163*), and in addition the trustees' contractual rights to acquire the property were part of his estate. [2020] UKFTT 53 (TC), [2020] SFTD 437, [2020] SWTI 322.

Sillars and Another v CIR

The effect of IHTA 1984, s 5(2) was that the whole of a joint building society account formed part of the deceased's estate.

In 1995 a woman (S) transferred her building society account into the names of herself and her two daughters. On her death her personal representatives treated her as having owned only one-third of the balance in the account. The Revenue issued a notice of determination that IHT was due on the whole balance in the account. The personal representatives appealed. The Special Commissioner dismissed the appeal, holding on the evidence that S retained power over the account. She was able to dispose of the balance as she thought fit, and withdrawals were made for her benefit. The effect of *IHTA 1984, s 5(2)* was that the whole of the account formed part of her estate. [2004] STC SCD 180 Sp C 401.

Smith v HMRC (and related appeals)

IHTA 1984, s 200(1)—transfer on death—person liable.

A woman (J) died in March 2003. She appointed one of her two sons (M) and his wife (S) as her executors and trustees. However, the IHT return which they submitted failed to include a building society account in the joint names of J and M. HMRC issued Notices of Determination to M, K and S, charging IHT on the amount held in the building society account. All three appealed. The Special Commissioner reviewed the evidence in detail and partly allowed the appeals by S and K, but dismissed the appeal by M. The Commissioner observed that the executors had not divided the amount held in the building society account between M and K as if it had formed part of J's residuary estate. Instead, M had retained the whole of the amount in question. On the evidence, it appeared that both J and M had 'considered that the interest earned in respect of the account belonged without question to the deceased whilst she was alive', and that the capital would pass to M on her death. It followed that the account had been 'settled property', within *IHTA 1984, s 200(1)(d)*. Since the amount was settled property, 'the person liable for the tax attributable to it' was M 'in his capacity both as trustee and recipient of it'. However, 'the existence of the account will make the executors in their capacity as such to be liable for additional tax because the tax attributable to the property that was not settled increases as a result of including the value of the account in the deceased's estate for inheritance tax purposes but they do not have a liability for the tax attributable to the value of the settled property in their capacity as such'. With regard to K, the Commissioner observed that the fact that the value of the account had formed part of J's estate for IHT purposes 'will have given rise to a tax liability attributable to the property received by (K) that was not wholly discharged by the executors and he remains liable for tax to that extent'. [2009] Sp C 742.

Smith v HMRC (and related appeals)

IHTA 1984, s 263 – annuity purchased in conjunction with life policy.

In October 1996 a married couple took out three life assurance policies coupled with three annuities, and executed three 'declarations of trust' in favour of their children. The wife died in 2000 and the husband died in February 2003. HMRC issued notices of determination that the vesting of the life assurance policies under the terms of the 'declarations of trust' was a transfer of value under *IHTA 1984, s 263*. The executors and the beneficiaries appealed, contending that the purchase of the annuities and the making of the life assurance policies should not be treated as 'associated operations' by virtue of Revenue Statement of Practice E4. The Special Commissioner rejected this contention and dismissed the appeals, and the Ch D upheld this decision. Lightman J observed that the purpose of Statement of Practice E4 was to provide 'an effective means of protecting the Revenue from efforts made to avoid payment of inheritance tax by means of associated transactions in the form of life assurance policies and annuities. This is achieved by requiring that the life policy must be issued on the basis of the provision to the insurer of full medical evidence of the assured's health.' The information which the husband had given to the life assurance company did not constitute the 'full medical evidence' required by Statement of Practice E4. Ch D [2007] EWHC 2304; STC 1649 Sp C 605.

Soutter's Executry v CIR

IHTA 1984, s 142 – whether deed of variation effective.

A woman (S) died in November 1999. The value of her estate was less than the IHT threshold. She owned a house, in which she lived with a friend (G). Under her will she gave G the right to live in the house, rent-free. G died in November 2000. In an attempt to reduce the IHT due on G's death, S's executors and G's executors purported to execute a deed of variation of S's estate, under *IHTA 1984, s 142*, removing the provision whereby G could live in the house rent-free. The Revenue issued a notice of determination that the purported deed of variation was ineffective. S's executors appealed. The Special Commissioner dismissed the appeal, observing that 'the executors of a liferentrix have nothing they can vary'. G's executors 'had neither right, title or interest to any liferent'. They 'could not have continued to receive the liferent so they had nothing to give up or vary. The liferent was not and could not be assigned to them . . . a purported assignation of an expired liferent has no reality'. [2002] STC SCD 385 Sp C 325.

Spencer-Nairn v CIR

Sale of property at undervalue – whether any gratuitous benefit.

In 1976 a landowner sold a farm, several buildings on which were in need of repair and replacement, to a Jersey company for £101,350. His son was a major shareholder in the company, which was, therefore, connected with him for the purposes of both CGT and IHT. The Revenue took the view that the sale had been at undervalue, and the Lands Tribunal subsequently valued the property (for CGT purposes) at £199,000. The Revenue issued a determination on the basis that the disposition of the farm was within *IHTA 1984, s 3(1)**, and constituted a chargeable transfer of value. The landowner appealed, contending that he had not known that the purchasing company was connected with him for IHT purposes, and that he had had no intention of conferring a gratuitous benefit on the company. The Special Commissioner allowed his appeal and the CS upheld this decision. On the evidence, the tenant of the farm had not wished to purchase it and the farm was unlikely to have been of interest to institutional investors. Accordingly it was reasonable to conclude that the sale had not been intended to confer a gratuitous benefit on the Jersey company, and was a disposition which 'might be expected to be made in a transaction at arm's length'. The transaction was within *IHTA 1984, s 10(1)(b)** and there was no chargeable transfer of value. CS 1990, [1991] STC 60.

Starke & Another (Brown's Executors) v CIR

Agricultural property relief – definition of 'agricultural property'.

A deceased's estate included a 2.5 acre site containing a substantial six-bedroomed farmhouse and a number of outbuildings. The site was used as part of a moderately-sized farm. The Revenue issued a notice of determination under *IHTA 1984, s 221* that the transfer of the site was not a transfer of 'agricultural property' within *IHTA 1984, s 115(2)*, and thus did not qualify for agricultural property relief. The executors applied by way of an originating summons for leave to appeal and for a declaration that the determination was wrong. The Ch D dismissed the appeal and refused the declaration, holding that the site was not 'agricultural property', since it was not 'agricultural land or pasture'. The CA upheld this decision and dismissed the executor's appeal. CA [1995] STC 689; [1995] 1 WLR 1439; [1996] 1 All ER 622.

St Clair-Ford (Youlden's Executor) v Ryder

Joint owner of a retail shop – discount should be 15% rather than 10%. Lands Tribunal held that the discount should be 10%.

An individual (Y) was joint owner of a retail shop. He died in 2003. The Revenue determined the value of his interest in the shop as £175,000 (applying a 10% discount for joint ownership). Y's executor appealed, contending *inter alia* that the discount should be 15% rather than 10%. The Lands Tribunal rejected this contention and upheld the Revenue's determination, applying the decision in *Cust v CIR*, KB 1917, 91

EG 11 and holding that the discount should be 10%. *Lands Tribunal 22 June 2006 unreported.*

St Dunstan's v Major

Variation of will by sole legatee – tax repaid to charity, IHT on estate reduced. Whether 'qualifying donation' within FA 1990, s 25.

The sole legatee under a will entered into a Deed of Variation, whereby £20,000 was bequeathed to a charity. The legatee claimed relief under *FA 1990, s 25* and signed a form R190(SD) certifying that he had paid £26,666 (i.e. £20,000 grossed-up at 25%) to the charity. The charity claimed a repayment of £6,666, which the Revenue made. Subsequently the Revenue formed the opinion that the donation of £20,000 did not satisfy the requirements of *FA 1990, s 25(2)(e)* and thus was not a 'qualifying donation', since the legatee had saved inheritance tax of £8,000, and had therefore received a benefit in consequence of making it, so that the charity should not have received any repayment. They issued an assessment to recover £6,666. The charity appealed, contending that the inheritance tax saving should not be treated as a benefit within *s 25(2)(e)*. The Special Commissioner rejected this contention and dismissed the appeal, holding that since the legatee was the 'sole or residuary beneficiary of the estate, he ultimately benefited from the inheritance tax saving'. Accordingly, the donation was not a qualifying donation within FA 1990, s 25. [1997] STC SCD 212 Sp C 127.

A Jew, born in Czechoslovakia, who acquired a domicile of origin in Germany but came to England in 1939 to escape Nazi persecution and obtained British naturalisation, was held to have acquired an English domicile of choice. CA 1973, 49 TC 13; [1973] STC 547.

Stenhouse's Trustees v Lord Advocate

Time of capital distribution – trustees in breach of trust.

On 8 April 1975, trustees of a discretionary trust appointed shares in the trust fund to the three daughters of the settlor. As the trustees only had power to make such an appointment to each daughter on her attaining the age of 22, and as the youngest was not yet 22, the trustees were in breach of trust. They therefore resolved that payment would not be made until all three had signed an indemnity. The question before the court was whether the three became entitled to interests in possession on 8 April 1975 (as opposed to the date the indemnities were signed or the date the youngest became 22). The CS held that the interests of the daughters were severable, and that the two who were already 22 became entitled to interests in possession on 8 April 1975. However, the youngest daughter did not, as it would have been *ultra vires* the trustees to confer an absolute entitlement on her on that date. CS 1983, [1984] STC 195.

Stoner and another (executors of Dickinson deceased) v CIR

Valuation – sale of land from deceased's estate – residuary estate to charity included freehold property which was sold by executors at prices exceeding probate values – executors made claim that sale prices values for IHT purposes – whether appropriate persons for IHTA 1984, ss 190, 191.

The deceased's will left the residue of her estate exceeding the nil rate band to charities. There was therefore no IHT payable. Freehold properties in the estate were valued at £582,000. Some of these properties were sold and the CTO was informed of the amount of £918,457. The executors were informed that confirmation by the CTO was not necessary as charity relief was applicable. In 1998 the executors made a formal claim under *IHTA 1984, s 191*. Reference in that section to 'appropriate person' making the claim was important to the executors as they wished the uplift in the values of the properties for CGT purposes. The IR issued a notice of determination in April 2001 that in relation to the deemed disposal for the purposes of *s 190(1)* there was no appropriate person to make the claim. The executors appealed contending that they were the appropriate person because they would have been liable for the tax if the residuary beneficiaries had not all been charities or if the value of the part estate not passing to the residuary beneficiaries had exceeded the nil rate band. The Special Commissioner noted that *s 191* was to grant relief where there was a fall in the value of the land after death. The section did not state that it should not apply to increases in values but did refer to 'appropriate person' who was defined as the person liable to IHT. Gifts to charities were exempt transfers and so no tax was chargeable. It followed that *s 190(1)* 'the person liable for inheritance tax' meant the person who either had paid the tax or had obligation to pay it. There was no person liable to pay IHT if there was no tax to pay. Therefore as there was no appropriate person under *s 191* the executors' appeal would be dismissed. [2001] STC SCD 199 Sp C 288.

Swales and Others v CIR

Interest in possession – effect of Trustee Act 1925, s 31.

In 1970 trustees appointed income from a trust fund to R absolutely, although the (complex) provisions of the trust prevented R's right to the income from vesting until one of her children became 21 in 1976 (the vesting date). The trustees disagreed with the Revenue as to whether an interest in possession was created in 1970 or in 1976. The interest in possession was held to have arisen in 1970. The 1970 appointment was a contingent appointment of income which was intended to carry the intermediate income of the fund before the vesting date, and *Trustee Act 1925, s 31(1)(ii)* applied so that R had a present right to that income as it arose and as such to an interest in possession in the trust fund. Ch D 1984, CTTL 24; [1984] STC 413; [1984] 1 All ER 16.

Taylor (Executrix Mrs K Boland) v HMRC

Beneficial ownership of bank accounts.

In 1996 a widow (B) inherited two building society accounts from her husband. She subsequently put the accounts into the joint names of herself and her brother-in-law (P). B died in 2004. HMRC issued a notice of determination that B had been beneficially entitled to the whole of the money in these accounts. B's Executrix appealed, contending that the money in the accounts should be treated as having belonged to P, and that B had simply held the accounts as a trustee. The Special Commissioner rejected this contention and dismissed the appeal, holding that B had not held the accounts as a trustee and that B had 'a general power which enabled her to dispose of the whole of the accounts'. Accordingly, she had to be treated as beneficially entitled to the whole of the money in the accounts at the date of her death. [2008] STC SCD 1159 Sp C 704.

Thomson (Thomson's Executor) v CIR

Determination under IHTA 1984, s 221 charging value on house bequeathed to daughter but non-evidence of transfer documents.

A widow died in 1971 and bequeathed her house to her daughter (J). J died in 2002. The Inland Revenue issued a Notice of Determination under *IHTA 1984, s 221*, charging IHT on the value of the house. J's executor appealed, contending that despite the terms of her mother's will, J should not be treated as having been the sole owner of the house, because she had never 'signed any document accepting the title to the house'. The Special Commissioner reviewed the evidence and dismissed the appeal, finding that J was the sole owner of the house, which accordingly formed part of her estate for IHT purposes. [2004] STC SCD 520 Sp C 429.

Trustees Executors and Agency Co Ltd and Others v CIR

Situation of property – ships.

The artificial situs abroad of a ship registered abroad was displaced by the actual situs when within English territorial or national waters. Ch D 1972, [1973] 1 All ER 563; [1973] Ch 254.

Trustees of the Douglas Trust (for Mrs I Fairbairn) v HMRC

Whether 'inter vivos' trust conferred interest in possession.

In a Scottish case, an individual (D) transferred certain securities and investments to trustees in 1962. The income arising from the trust was treated for tax purposes as income of the settlor under *FA 1958, s 22* (now *ITTOIA 2005, ss 624–628*). D died in 1981 and then his wife died in 2002. HMRC issued a notice of determination on the basis that she had enjoyed an interest in possession in the settled property. The trustees appealed. The Special Commissioner dismissed the appeal, finding that D's widow had effectively enjoyed 'a power of veto: the whole of the free annual income of the trust fund had to be paid or applied to her or for her benefit from year to year unless or until she should concur with a consideration by the trustees that it was proper and expedient for a lesser amount to be so paid or applied'. Accordingly the trust deed had conferred an interest in possession. [2007] STC SCD 338 Sp C 593.

Trustees of the David Zetland Settlement v HMRC

Business property relief claim in respect of tenanted building and associated shareholding.

Trustees held a commercial building divided into small office units let to tenants for periods normally ranging between one and five years, although these terms were operated on a flexible basis so that they might be terminated earlier. The senior trustee was engaged for much of his time on strategy and management in relation to the premises. There was also a team of staff, including a receptionist, cleaner, handyman and porters, each employed by the trustees. On the premises were a café, operated with the trustees' support, and other facilities such as bicycle park and meeting rooms available for hire on a daily or hourly basis. The trustees also carried out conversion work to suit the tenants and dilapidations work on termination of each tenancy, some of which produced profits for the trust. Although it was accepted that most of the trust income was in the form of the rents receivable, it was contended that the business was eligible for business property relief in view of the fact that most of the daily work of the trustee and the staff involved providing their services to the tenants. HMRC denied the claim on the basis that the business was wholly or mainly one of holding an investment. The trustees also held 50% of the shares in a company which owned the freehold for the office building. It was held by the First-tier Tribunal that the business in the round was not eligible for business property relief. Although it was actively managed the services provided which were not investment related were not sufficient to tip the balance in favour of obtaining business property relief. [2013] UKFTT 284 (TC) TC02690.

Vaughan-Jones and Griffiths v Vaughan-Jones

Deed of variation – statement of intent required by IHTA 1984, s 142(2) omitted – whether deed should be rectified to insert this statement.

A deed of variation of a will erroneously omitted to state that the parties intended that the provisions of *IHTA 1984, s 142* should apply to it. HMRC therefore said that it was ineffective to alter the IHT treatment of the estate under the terms of the will. The parties applied to the High Court, Chancery Division, for rectification of the document. The Court was satisfied that the necessary clause had been omitted by mistake and that the omission gave rise to an issue between the parties to the document. It therefore granted the request for rectification but only in relation to the statement for IHT purposes. The court said there was insufficient evidence to allow rectification in relation to the similar clause applying for capital gains tax purposes. [2015] EWHC 1086 (Ch).

Vigne deceased (Personal Representatives of) v HMRC

A claim for business property relief was successful in relation to a livery business operated by the deceased on approximately 30 acres of land. The services provided included worming of the horses, provision of hay feed, removal of manure and daily check of the health of the horses. Some of the owners of the horses did not attend the premises regularly enough to ensure the proper care of the animal concerned and thus Mrs Vigne and her staff were on hand each day to ensure that an acceptable level of care was provided in the absence of the owner. The First-tier Tax Tribunal held that 'no properly informed observer could or would have said that the deceased was in the business of holding investments'. [2017] UKFTT 632 (TC).

Vincent v HMRC

A property was jointly owned by a married couple with another family member, Mr Thom, who had a five-eighths share. After the deaths of both of the married couple in 2001, their three-eighths share in the property was to be held 'upon trust to permit Mr Thom to reside therein for so long as he shall desire free from rent but he being responsible for general rates, water rates, insurance and maintenance repairs of an income nature'. It was held that this gave Mr Thom an interest in possession in that share so that the whole of the property formed part of his estate on his death. He had a right to reside at the property by virtue of being a co-owner and the provision allowing rent-free occupation was designed to give him additional protection, amounting to an interest in possession. [2019] UKFTT 657 (TC).

Vinton & Green (Mrs M Dugan-Chapman's Executors) v HMRC

IHTA 1984, s 107(4) – identification of shares.

In December 2002 a widow (D), who was in poor health, was allotted one million shares in a family company (W). She died two days later. HMRC issued a determination charging IHT. D's executors appealed, contending that she had been allotted the shares as part of a reorganisation of W's share capital, within *TCGA 1992, s 126*, so that the effect of *IHTA 1984, s 107(4)* was that the shares should be identified with shares which she already held and qualified for business property relief. The Special Commissioner rejected this contention and dismissed the appeal, holding that there had not been a reorganisation of W's share capital within *TCGA 1992, s 126*. Accordingly the provisions of *s 107(4)* did not apply and the shares did not qualify for business property relief. [2008] STC SCD 592 Sp C 666.

Von Ernst & Cie SA and Others v CIR

Discretionary settlement – whether capital distribution – whether excluded property – jurisdiction of High Court.

On 25 March 1976 the trustees of a discretionary settlement appointed property consisting of exempt government securities to the two children of the settlor. Neither was resident nor domiciled in the UK. On the failure of the trusts to the children the property would have been held on constructive discretionary trusts for two UK charities. The Board determined that the appointment was to be treated as giving rise to a capital distribution under *FA 1975, 5 Sch 6(2)*. The trustees appealed direct to the High Court, contending that para 6(2) did not apply because the property was excluded property as soon as there were interests in possession in it. After losing in the Ch D, the trustees adduced two new arguments before the CA. The CA held that (i) the question of whether settled property was excluded property for the purposes of *para 6(2)* depended on the state of affairs which existed immediately before the appointment; (ii) exemption from CTT depends on CTT legislation, not on *F(No 2)A 1931*; (iii) the exempt securities were excluded property before the appointment by virtue of *IHTA 1984, s 48(4)(b)** since the charities were not 'known persons' who might 'benefit' or become 'beneficially entitled' within the meaning of that provision. The appeal was therefore allowed. The Ch D had held that where a CTT appeal is taken direct to the High Court, the latter has the same power to quash etc. a determination of the Board as the Special Commissioners would have had if the appeal had gone first to them. (This was not contested in the CA.) CA 1979, CTTL 6; [1980] STC 111; [1980] 1 WLR 468; [1980] 1 All ER 677.

Walding & Others (Walding's Executors) v CIR

IHTA 1984, s 269(1) – whether deceased had control of company.

A woman held 45 of the 100 shares in a company at the time of her death. Of the remaining 55 shares, 24 were in the name of her four-year-old grandson. Her executors claimed that, since the grandson was not in a position to exercise the voting rights attached to his 24 shares, the deceased had had control of the company so that her shareholding qualified for business property relief. The Revenue rejected the claim and the Ch D dismissed the executors' appeal. *IHTA 1984, s 269(1)* dealt with the ambit of the powers of voting, not the capabilities of the shareholders in whose names the shares were registered. Ch D 1995 [1996] STC 13. (*Note.* See also *Hepworth v Smith* Ch D 1981, 54 TC 396; [1981] STC 354, a capital gains tax case, in which shares were taken into account for the purposes of *TCGA, s 163** although the relevant voting rights had never been exercised.)

Walker's Executors v CIR

Business property relief – casting vote gave control over the company IHTA 1984, s 269(1) – entitlement to BPR on land from which the company traded.

A married couple had formed a company to operate a road haulage business and petrol station. The husband died in 1983 and the wife died in 1996. At the time of her death, she was chairman of the company and held 50% of the shares in it, with a casting vote at general meetings. She also owned the land from which the company traded. The Revenue issued a determination charging IHT on the land. Her executors appealed, contending that she had control of the company by virtue of her casting vote, so that the land qualified for business property relief under *IHTA, s 105(1)(d)*. The Special Commissioner accepted this contention and allowed the appeal, holding that the casting vote had given her control of the company, within *IHTA 1984, s 269(1)*. *Dicta* of Rowlatt J in *CIR v BW Noble Ltd* applied. [2001] STC SCD 86 Sp C 275.

A widow had acquired her late husband's domicile on marriage. It was held, in an intestacy case, that she retained this until her death, not having changed it; her domicile of origin had not revived on her husband's death. HC 1949, 28 ATC 486; [1950] 1 All ER 199.

Walton (Walton's Executor) v CIR

Valuation of partnership interest in non-assignable agricultural tenancy.

The freehold of a farm was held by a father and his two sons as tenants in common in equal shares. The farm was let to a partnership comprising the father and one of the sons. In August 1984 the father died. It was agreed that the vacant possession premium (i.e. the difference between the open market value of the freehold interest in the farm with vacant possession and that when subject to the tenancy) was £200,000. The value of tenant-right and tenants' improvements, less dilapidations, was £40,000. The Revenue issued a notice of determination to CTT, valuing the tenancy at half the vacant possession premium with a 10% discount to reflect the part interest (i.e. at £90,000), plus the net value of tenant-right and tenants' improvements, thereby arriving at a value of £130,000. The father's half-share was, therefore, valued at £65,000. The executor appealed against the valuation, contending that it was excessive, since it assumed an immediate purchase by the freeholders, whereas in fact the freeholders would not have been interested in securing the surrender of the tenancy and did not have the financial resources for such a purchase. The Lands Tribunal accepted this evidence and allowed the appeal, holding on the evidence that the realisation of the vacant possession premium was 'so far from any market expectation as to make a valuation by reference to an apportionment of the vacant possession premium wholly inappropriate'. The property which was required to be valued in accordance with what is now *IHTA 1984, s 94* was an undivided beneficial interest in the joint tenancy as a partnership asset. The tenancy could only be sold and its value realised if the terms of the partnership agreement permitted it, which they did not. The sole value of the tenancy, as a partnership asset, rested upon the extent to which its terms enhanced the partnership profits by enabling the partners to exploit the partnership assets without paying a full market rent for the farm. The tribunal reviewed the evidence in detail and held that the value of the entire tenancy, on the basis of a valuation of profit rental and on the assumption that the landlords could not be regarded as a hypothetical purchaser, was approximately £12,600, so that the value of the deceased's share was £6,300. The Revenue appealed to the CA, which upheld the Tribunal decision as one of fact. The Tribunal had been entitled to conclude that the landlords were not to be regarded as a hypothetical purchaser, and it was for the tribunal to consider what premium (if any) any special purchaser would be prepared to pay. CA 1995, [1996] STC 68.

Westminster's (4th Duke of) Executors v Ministry of Defence (aka Barty-King v Ministry of Defence)

Death on active service – cause of death.

The Duke of Westminster, who was wounded in action in 1944, died of cancer in 1967. The septicaemia caused by his war wound was noted on the death certificate as a significant condition contributing to the death 'but not related to the disease or condition causing it'. Exemption from estate duty was provided by *FA 1952, s 71* for the estate of any person who was certified by the Defence Council to have 'died from a wound inflicted . . . when . . . the deceased was a member of the armed forces of the Crown . . . on active service against an enemy'. The Defence Council turned down the executors' application for a certificate. The QB held that the executors were entitled to a declaration that they ought to have been granted a certificate. Although a wound had to be a cause of death, it did not have to be the direct or only cause. QB 1978, CTTL 2; [1979] STC 218; [1979] 2 All ER 80. (*Note.* The equivalent IHT exemption is provided by *IHTA 1984, s 154.*)

Weston (Weston's Executor) v CIR

Inheritance tax – exempt transfers and reliefs – business property – relevant business property – business of managing caravan park – whether business excluded from business property relief as consisting wholly or mainly of making or holding investments – IHTA 1984, s 105(3).

At the deceased's death in 1993 her estate included shares in a company. The business of the company, which was a single business, included the purchase and sale of caravans, the sale of caravans for commission on behalf of owners, and the grant of the right to pitch caravans on the caravan park run by the company for a consideration consisting of the pitch fees. The business also included the maintenance and administration of the park and the provision of facilities, and the supply for a consideration of electricity and bottled gas used by the pitch holders at the park. The park was situated near the M25 motorway, and was not a holiday park. It was entirely residential, and residents had to be over 50. It did not accommodate touring caravans or caravan rallies. The appearance of the park was that of a suburban residential development in miniature and the appearance of the caravans was that of small neat bungalows. The park had no shop or social club, but each caravan owner had the use of a brick-built laundry and storeroom. The caravans were owned by their occupiers. Residents were obliged to purchase a caravan from the company or another resident, usually through the company, which took a commission on sales between residents. The number of sales of caravans was not large. The company's three employees spent a total of 111 hours per week on park maintenance and 37 hours per week on sales activities. The company's accounts showed that pitch fees exceeded in amount the sums realised by caravan sales in four out of the six years from 1989 to 1994. Also, the profits from pitch fees exceeded the profits from caravan sales in every year from 1988 to 1994, with the exception of 1989, and that from 1988 to 1994, there was a substantial excess of pitch fees, and bank interest produced by a considerable cash reserve, over caravan sales. Following the deceased's death, HMRC issued a determination that that holding was not relevant business property for IHT purposes, on the ground the business consisted wholly or mainly in the making or holding of investments. The executor appealed.

The Commissioner concluded that, standing back and looking at the matter in the round, the pitch fees were not ancillary to caravan sales; the caravan sales were ancillary to pitch fees at the park. The company operated a caravan park, and was not a dealer selling caravans. Accordingly, the business of the company consisted mainly in making or holding investments. The notice of determination would therefore be upheld. [2000] STC SCD 30 Sp C 222.

Subsequently, W's executor appealed. The Ch D upheld this decision as one of fact. [2000] STC 1064; Ch D [2000] All ER (D) 1870.

Wheatley and another (Executors of Wheatley deceased) v CIR

Grazing of horses on pasture – whether meadow qualified for APR within provisions of IHTA 1984, s 117.

An individual (W) owned a meadow, which he let to a woman who owned some horses. She used the meadow for grazing her horses, paying rent to W. W died in 1997 and the Revenue issued notices of determination charging inheritance tax. W's executors appealed, contending that the meadow qualified for agricultural property relief. The Special Commissioner rejected this contention and dismissed the appeal, holding that, although the meadow constituted 'pasture' within *IHTA 1984, s 115 (2)*, it was not 'occupied for the purposes of agriculture', as required by *IHTA 1984, s 117*. On the evidence, the horses which grazed the meadow 'were not connected with agriculture' but were used by their owner for 'leisure pursuits'. Horses were not 'livestock' and grazing by horses would only fall within the provisions of *s 117* if the horses were connected with agriculture, which was not the case here. [1998] STC SCD 60 Sp C 149.

Wight and Moss v CIR

Valuation – joint property – value of half share.

Two women lived in a house which they owned as tenants in common in equal shares. When one of them died the value of her half share in the house had to be ascertained for CTT purposes. It was agreed that the other co-owner would be the most likely purchaser and that this was a relevant factor in the valuation. The Lands Tribunal held that the value was half vacant possession value less a discount to reflect the restricted demand for this type of interest. It was held that it was not likely that an outside purchaser would be able to obtain an order for sale under *Law of Property Act 1925, s 30* and, reflecting this, that the discount should be 15% rather than the 10% which had become customary following the earlier decision in *Cust v CIR* (1917) 91 EG 11. Lands Tribunal, [1982] 264 EG 935.

Williams and another (as executors of D S Campbell deceased) v HMRC

The executors claimed a deduction from the deceased's general estate for outstanding liabilities under a lease of business premises from which the deceased had operated a fine art business. The value of the business qualified for business property relief, but it was claimed that the liabilities were not deductible from the value of the business assets having regard to statements to that effect by the Special Commissioner in *Hardcastle v HMRC* [2000] STC (SCD) 532. The Tax Tribunal concluded that the statements in the *Hardcastle* case were not binding and were illustrative only. In the present case, the liabilities related to a business asset and should therefore be deducted from the value of it. [2018] UKFTT 136 (TC).

Williams (Williams' Personal Representative) v HMRC

'Broiler houses' used for intensive rearing of poultry – whether 'agricultural property' within IHTA 1984, s 115(2).

A farm occupied 7.41 acres of land. Part of the land was used for three 'broiler houses', which were used for the intensive rearing of poultry. In April 2000 the owner of the farm (W) let the broiler houses, and 2.59 acres of the land, to a company (S). W died in 2001. The Inland Revenue issued a ruling that the broiler houses, and the 2.59 acres of land which had been let to S, did not qualify as 'agricultural property' within *IHTA 1984, s 115(2)*. W's personal representative appealed. The Special Commissioner reviewed the evidence in detail and allowed the appeal in part, holding that the effect of *s 115(2)* was that the broiler houses could only qualify for relief if they had been 'a subsidiary part of the purpose of an overall agricultural activity carried out on the land'. Since they had been let to a separate company, this was not the case. Accordingly, the broiler houses had not been 'ancillary' to the farm, within *s 115(2)*, and did not qualify for relief. However, on the evidence, the broiler houses only occupied 0.68 acres of land. The Commissioner held that the remaining 1.91 acres of land which had been let to S was within the definition of 'agricultural property' and did qualify for relief. [2005] STC SCD 782 Sp C 500.

Willett and another (Mrs Benson's Executors) v CIR

Valuation – value of freehold interest in tenanted agricultural property.

The owner of a freehold interest in tenanted agricultural land died in 1977. The Revenue valued the interest for CTT purposes at £45,000. The executors appealed, contending that the valuation should be £28,000. The Lands Tribunal reviewed the evidence in detail and held that the valuation should be £39,000. The Tribunal reaffirmed the principle that a valuation must assume property is suitably lotted if it would fetch a better price if sold in that way, applying *Earl of Ellesmere v CIR* [1918] 2 KB 735. Although the length of time the tenant would continue in occupation was a relevant factor in the executors' valuation, the Tribunal rejected a strict life expectancy approach in favour of the Revenue's method of using the number of years before his probable retirement at the age of 75. In one of the two methods of valuation used by the Revenue, the vacant possession value had been taken at £70,000, and an allowance of £25,000 had been deducted from this, being an estimate of the amount a prospective purchaser would consider appropriate to cover deferment and obtain possession. The Tribunal held that the estimate was too low in view of the fact that the purchaser would be taking a considerable risk as to whether the tenant would vacate for £25,000, and bearing in mind a purchaser's requirement for profit. The Revenue's alternative method was to divide the vacant possession value between the 'pure investment value' (taking the reversion in perpetuity) and the 'vacant possession element' and to add 40% of the latter to the former, 40% being assumed to be what the tenant would pay to obtain the freehold interest. The Land Tribunal upheld this method in principle but held that the addition should be 33% rather than 40%. *Lands Tribunal 1982, 264 EG 257.*

Wills v Gibbs and Others

Rectification of deed of variation.

A farmer died in 2005, leaving most of his interest in the farm to his cousin (W). W wished to redirect some of his entitlement to his son by way of a deed of variation under

IHTA 1984, s 142(1). The farmer's solicitors prepared a deed of variation, but failed to include the statutory statement required to bring the deed within *s 142*. The solicitors subsequently noticed the omission, and W's son applied to the Ch D for rectification of the deed. The Ch D granted the application, applying the principles laid down in *Racal Group Services Ltd v Ashmore & Others*. Ch D [2008] STC 808.

Woodhall (Woodhall's Personal Representatives) v CIR

IHTA 1984, s 50(5) – interest in part of property.

An individual (GW) died in 1957, leaving three children. Under his will, he left his house to his two sons as trustees, and directed that it should not be sold as long as any of his three children was living in it. One of his sons (EW) had already moved out when GW died, and his daughter moved out the following year. However, his other son (AW) continued to live in the house until he died in 1997. The Revenue issued a notice of determination on the basis that, when AW died, he had a beneficial interest in the whole of the house. His personal representative appealed, accepting that the house was settled property but contending firstly that AW was not beneficially entitled to an interest in possession, and alternatively that he only had such an interest in one half of the house, as his brother (EW) had a beneficial entitlement to the other half. (Their sister had died in 1971.) The Special Commissioner accepted this contention and allowed the appeal in part, holding that the effect of GW's will was that, in 1997, both AW and EW 'had the right to claim to occupy the house jointly with the other'. Accordingly, when AW died, he was beneficially entitled to an interest in possession in the house within the meaning of *IHTA 1984, s 49(1)*, but that his interest subsisted in only half of the house, within *IHTA 1984, s 50(5)*. [2000] STC SCD 558 Sp C 261.

56 Table of Statutes

G

H

L

M

57 Table of Statutory Instruments

Table of Cases

A

B

C

D

E

F

G

H

I

J

K

L

M

N

O

P

R

T

V

W

Y

Z

59 Index

This index is referenced to chapter and paragraph number.

B

C

G

J

L

Q

R

S

U